Forties Film Talk

Forties Film Talk

Oral Histories of Hollywood, with 120 Lobby Posters

by

DOUG McCLELLAND

McFarland & Company, Inc., Publishers
Jefferson, North Carolina, and London

Frontispiece: Lobby poster for Universal's *The Wolf Man.*

British Library Cataloguing-in-Publication data are available

Library of Congress Cataloguing-in-Publication Data

McClelland, Doug.
Forties film talk : oral histories of Hollywood, with 120 lobby posters / by Doug McClelland.
p. cm.
Includes bibliographical references and index.
ISBN 0-89950-672-0 (lib. bdg. : 50# acid-free natural and 70# sterling gloss alk. papers)
1. Motion pictures—United States—Interviews. 2. Motion pictures—United States—Quotation, maxims, etc. 3. Film posters, American. I. Title.
PN1993.5.U6M217 1992
791.43'0973'09044—dc20 92-54087
CIP

Manufactured in the United States of America

McFarland & Company, Inc., Publishers
Box 611, Jefferson, North Carolina 28640

CONTENTS

PREFACE

To start, a word or two thousand about Evelyn Keyes.

In late April, 1991, Miss Keyes, who has appeared in some of Hollywood's biggest films from *Gone with the Wind* to *The Jolson Story* to *Around the World in 80 Days,* came to New York City to promote the second volume of her memoirs titled *I'll Think About That Tomorrow.* Since she was one of the most active and talented stars of the 1940s, the screen's great golden decade and the subject of this book, I decided to venture forth from my home on the New Jersey seashore and interview her.

Jennifer Romanello, the publicity woman from Miss Keyes' publisher, E. P. Dutton, arranged our meeting for what turned out to be a warm, sunny spring afternoon at Manhattan's Regency Hotel, where the Los Angeles–based Miss Keyes was staying during this stop on her hectic, multicity book tour. So far so good.

When I arrived at the Regency at the appointed hour, three o'clock, a message was waiting for me to call another publicity person at Dutton. Oh-oh, I thought, Miss Keyes has been detained at some other interview and is cancelling our session—after I've come all the way into New York expressly for this purpose. Just off the lobby I found a pay phone over which my latest Dutton contact explained, "Miss Keyes has had an accident. At first we thought we'd have to cancel the interview, but she has just informed us that she still wants to see you." I was given the number of her room and went up.

Miss Keyes, holding a hand towel with ice in it to her forehead, opened the door while publicity woman Romanello tended to business on the phone. "What happened?" I asked immediately. Smiling, the thin but still vivacious septuagenarian explained, "I'm such a klutz. I fell!" It seems that only an hour and a half before, the Misses Keyes and Romanello were leaving the building where the star had just done a television interview when suddenly, for whatever reason, Miss Keyes tripped and fell on the sidewalk, hitting her forehead above the right eye. She was taken to the emergency room of a local hospital, but cut that short to return to the Regency. She was now waiting for the hotel doctor to arrive. She was in excellent spirits, though, bouncing in and out of her chair and moving quickly and energetically around the small accommodations.

I said, "I can't possibly add to your stress by asking you to do an interview now, Miss Keyes."

"Sit right down," she quickly instructed, adjusting her impromptu icepack. "Of course we'll do the interview. I'm all right. It's Jennifer over there I've been worried about. She was hysterical when the accident occurred. Weren't you?" A much paler Jennifer, still on the phone, smiled sickly.

So we began the interview, my admiration for this cheerful, chatting, wounded actress soon to know no bounds. About half-way through, the doctor arrived. By then, Miss Keyes had a welt the size of an egg above her temple. Furthermore, it was rapidly turning a shiny black that was spreading down to the area around her right eye. The doctor asked her some questions, said it didn't appear to be a fracture and put a small dressing on the slight skin laceration. He told her what to watch for in case of complications. When he realized he was treating a Hollywood actress, however, he became so grinningly effusive, almost giggly, that I thought he was going to ask her to autograph a prescription pad.

He left and the interview continued. Whenever I looked up from my notebook scribblings, I could literally see the skin around Miss Keyes' eye darkening. Conscience-stricken at my imposition, I ended the interview somewhat earlier than I'd planned. Departing, I advised the ever-smiling and congenial patient to rest.

"Oh, I'm going to the theater tonight," she chirped.

A couple of days later, as scheduled, she was off to Boston, the next stop on her book tour.

Evelyn Keyes, with her courage and spirit and dedication to the job at hand, was the living embodiment of the old adage "The show must go on" that was prominent in many vintage Hollywood films. In fact, the incident related here makes her seem the perfect representative of the screen's most lustrous epoch, the 1940s. Films then had warmth and vitality, were adventurous and accomplished, moved well and entertained—all qualities shared with the peripatetic, irrepressible Evelyn Keyes.

As *New York Post* columnist Cindy Adams commented when she reported on Miss Keyes' accident and subsequent stalwart behavior during our interview, "They don't make 'em like that anymore."

For those who might still ask, "What made the forties so special?" there were several factors. Film techniques had become more fluid and skillful. During the early days of sound, ushered in by the great success of 1927's *The Jazz Singer,* starring Al Jolson, microphones were sometimes hidden in flower arrangements. Actors supposed to whisper sweet nothings into the ears of their leading ladies instead had to direct their terms of endearment to the inevitable floral spreads on nearby tables. And rolling cameras, so noisy in the beginning, had to be wrapped in large, soundproof cases to prevent them

A surprise debut on Broadway starts the Jolson era of song!

from being heard on the soundtracks. By 1939, the kinks had been ironed out to such an extent that we often hear that year—which produced such films as *Gone with the Wind, The Wizard of Oz, Ninotchka* and *Stagecoach*—called the screen's greatest. (And 1946 was often called the screen's *last* great year.) In the wake of 1939 came Hollywood's most prosperous, productive and creative decade: the forties.

The moguls, or studio bosses, were at the peak of their might. Erstwhile junk dealers, glove salesmen, furriers and song-pluggers, who in some cases had become the nation's highest salaried men, ruled the dozen or so Hollywood studios then, and did so with a sometimes crude but always genuine love for movies. They sought out and hired the best talent in the world to work behind and in front of the cameras. As World War II loomed, many of the great European stars, directors, writers, cinematographers and craftsmen fled the Holocaust for Hollywood. All of this provided a rare amalgam of talent that helped to enrich the American film as never before or since.

For instance, the German filmmakers' predilection for chiaroscuro played a major role in the creation of a new and popular Hollywood genre, the "film noir" (usually urban melodrama enacted on dark, dank streets). Also standing out among the Westerns, dramas, musicals, comedies, costume sagas, biographies and swashbuckling epics were the social commentaries. For the first time,

Hollywood seriously tackled the problems of racial prejudice, mental illness and alcoholism. Hungry for escapism, wartime audiences, especially, flocked to the films of that time in greater number than at any other time in motion picture history. And the star system, eventually to wilt during the breakdown of the nurturing old studio contract system, was still in full flower.

In the latter half of the decade, storm warnings went up. Washington's House Committee on Un-American Activities began its reinvestigation of alleged Communist infiltration and subversion of the American film industry. In the ensuing hysteria that reached a climax in the fifties, a number of film people were jailed and or blacklisted. Some deaths were even attributed to the pernicious aftermath of committee investigation. Meanwhile, the government, claiming antitrust violations, forced the Hollywood studios to divest themselves of their film theater chains. The biggest blow of all, though, was the new entertainment medium called television, first gawked at in shop windows but soon attracting the moviegoing audience in alarming proportions. Hollywood and the quality of films were never the same again.

Forties films weren't made to appeal to just one segment of the prospective audience, but were created with an eye toward the broadest possible attendance. Abbott and Costello, Bing Crosby and Betty Grable fans were satisfied, but so were fans of William Powell and Myrna Loy, Laurence Olivier and Bette Davis. The high level of literacy to be found in the films of the 1940s is indicated not only by the many fine writers who wrote the screenplays (original and or adapted from other sources), but by the notable literary lights whose novels and stories were translated to the screen then (sometimes by their own hand). The latter include Ernest Hemingway, Raymond Chandler, William Faulkner, James M. Cain, Laura Z. Hobson, Rachel Field, Thorne Smith, Feodor Dostoevski, Erich Maria Remarque, Joseph Conrad, Charles Dickens, Marjorie Kinnan Rawlings, Guy de Maupassant, Daphne du Maurier, Jane Austen, John Hersey, John Steinbeck, Edna Ferber, Gustave Flaubert, Ring Lardner, Fannie Hurst, J. D. Salinger, Eric Knight, Rumer Godden, Ayn Rand, Marcia Davenport, Charlotte Brontë, Nathaniel Hawthorne, W. Somerset Maugham, A. J. Cronin, Stefan Zweig, Pearl S. Buck, Henry James, Robert Nathan, Franz Werfel, Louisa May Alcott, John Galsworthy, Aldous Huxley, James Hilton, Eric Ambler, Graham Greene and Sally Benson.

Also, Dashiell Hammett, W. R. Burnett, B. Traven, John P. Marquand, Vicki Baum, Jack London, Oscar Wilde, Howard Fast, William Saroyan, Erskine Caldwell, Conrad Richter, James Thurber, Mary O'Hara, Damon Runyon, Rudyard Kipling, Robert Louis Stevenson, Thornton Wilder, Leo Tolstoy, Booth Tarkington, Theodore Dreiser, Rex Beach, Mark Twain, Sinclair Lewis, Alice Duer Miller, Edgar Allan Poe, Herman Wouk, Zane Grey, Cornell Woolrich, Agatha Christie, Louis Bromfield, Rafael Sabatini, Richard Llewellyn, Jerome Weidman, Stephen Longstreet, Margery Sharp, Marie Belloc Lowndes, Alexandre Dumas, F. Scott Fitzgerald and Ludwig Bemelmans.

Playwrights, too, were well represented by film versions of their celebrated works. Among them are Eugene O'Neill, Emlyn Williams, Lillian Hellman, George S. Kaufman, Moss Hart, Joseph Fields, Jerome Chodorov, Joseph Kesselring, Noel Coward, Philip Barry, Maurice Maeterlinck, F. Hugh Herbert, Maxwell Anderson, Sir Arthur Wing Pinero, Luigi Pirandello, George Kelly, Norman Krasna, Robert E. Sherwood, John van Druten, Anton Chekhov, Irwin Shaw, S. J. Perelman, Arthur Laurents, Samson Raphaelson, Rachel Crothers, S. N. Behrman, Ben Hecht, Charles MacArthur, George M. Cohan, Rose Franken, Ferenc Molnar, Arthur Miller, Sidney Howard, Elmer Rice, Howard Lindsay, Russel Crouse, George Bernard Shaw and William Shakespeare.

The films of the forties? Some titles at random: *The Grapes of Wrath, Pinocchio, His Girl Friday, Rebecca, Pride and Prejudice, The Philadelphia Story, Ziegfeld Girl, How Green Was My Valley, Buck Privates, The Maltese Falcon, Sergeant York, Citizen Kane, Sullivan's Travels, Kings Row, Now, Voyager, The Pride of the Yankees, Yankee Doodle Dandy, Holiday Inn, Mrs. Miniver, Wake Island, Casablanca, For Whom the Bell Tolls, Gaslight, Shadow of a Doubt, Phantom of the Opera, Heaven Can Wait, Cover Girl, The Miracle of Morgan's Creek, Since You Went Away, Meet Me in St. Louis, Double Indemnity, Going My Way, National Velvet, A Tree Grows in Brooklyn, Mildred Pierce, The Lost Weekend, State Fair, The Dolly Sisters, The Yearling, To Each His Own, The Big Sleep, The Postman Always Rings Twice, Gilda, Notorious, The Best Years of Our Lives, The Jolson Story, Anna and the King of Siam, The Razor's Edge, It's a Wonderful Life, The Killers, Gentleman's Agreement, Miracle on 34th Street, Monsieur Verdoux, Johnny Belinda, The Treasure of the Sierra Madre, Letter from an Unknown Woman, Red River, Sitting Pretty, The Snake Pit, Easter Parade, Out of the Past, Sorry, Wrong Number, Pinky, The Heiress, All the King's Men, A Letter to Three Wives, Champion, Samson and Delilah.*

Part I of this book is comprised of exclusive interviews I have done for this project with the gifted people who worked on many of the preceding productions as well as other celluloid offerings from the 1940s. They discuss their films of the period. So do participants in Part II, in which are collected hundreds of more succinct, standing comments from outstanding forties film folk. (The sources for most of the remarks in Part II are listed in the bibliography in the back of the book.) It is hoped that these two main sections jointly will provide a comprehensive record of the output of the screen's most glittering decade, in the words of those who made it sparkle.

Herewith, my deepest gratitude to the following 1940s film achievers who granted me interviews for this book:

Iris Adrian
June Allyson
Robert Arthur
Lew Ayres
John Beal
Ralph Bellamy
Joan Bennett
Eddie Bracken
Lucille Bremer
Vanessa Brown
Macdonald Carey
Marguerite Chapman
Nancy Coleman
Luther Davis
Laraine Day
Rosemary DeCamp
Myrna Dell
Julius J. Epstein
Joan Evans
Alice Faye
Geraldine Fitzgerald
Rhonda Fleming
Nina Foch
Susanna Foster
Farley Granger
Kathryn Grayson
Jane Greer
Signe Hasso
Celeste Holm
Victoria Horne
John Howard
Marsha Hunt
Ruth Hussey
Gloria Jean
Evelyn Keyes
Andrea King
Kurt Kreuger
Priscilla Lane
Janet Leigh
Joan Leslie
Viveca Lindfors
Dorothy McGuire
Catherine McLeod
Irene Manning
Victor Mature
Virginia Mayo
Constance Moore

Dick Moore
Dennis Morgan
Dorothy Morris
Janis Paige
David Raksin
Ann Richards
Lina Romay
Elizabeth Russell
Ellis St. Joseph
Richard Sale
Ann Savage
Risë Stevens
James Stewart
Barry Sullivan
Audrey Totter
William Travilla
Claire Trevor
Ruth Warrick
Barbara Whiting
Robert Wise
Alan Young

In addition, I want to thank Patrick Agan, Roger Blunck (Cinemax), Colin Briggs, John Cocchi, Maeve Druesne, Charlie Earle, George Eells, Film Favorites/Movie Poster Service, Michael Fitzgerald, Jeff Gordon (Jagarts), Lee Graham (*Hollywood Then & Now*), Seli Groves (King Features Syndicate), Boze Hadleigh, Thomas J. Harris, Jim Jeneji (MGM/UA Classics), Richard Lacey, Gregory Mank, Jim Meyer, Eduardo Moreno, the New York Public Library Performing Arts Research Center, Robert Osborne (*The Hollywood Reporter*), James Robert Parish, Lawrence J. Quirk (*Quirk's Reviews*), Karen Reynolds (ABC Television Publicity), Jennifer Romanello (E. P. Dutton Publicity), John Strauss, Wally Stroby (*The Asbury Park Press*), Gabe Taverney and Lou Valentino.

All of the lobby card film posters used to illustrate this book are from my personal collection. Originally used for display in movie theaters, the "lobbies" are 11 × 14 inches in actual size, usually tinted and found in sets of eight.

And now—back to the forties!

Doug McClelland
Spring, 1992

PART I

Iris Adrian——*ACTRESS*—

I made so many pictures I can't remember 'em all. Someone is always coming up to me and saying, "I loved you in such-and-such," and I say, "Jesus, was I in that?"

But I remember a couple I did for director "Wild Bill" Wellman, *Roxie Hart* and *Lady of Burlesque.* Ginger Rogers stars in *Roxie Hart* and I play Two-Gun Gertie, one of my best parts.

I have a photo of myself on Bill's lap which he inscribed, "To Gee Gee"—my name in *Lady of Burlesque*—"with love from Bill Wellman." He had been a hero in World War I, and people used to say that doing a picture with Wellman was like going off to war. On *Lady of Burlesque,* he got drunk and poked one of the producers in the nose. One thing I remember is that Gloria Dickson, who plays Dolly Baxter, died in a fire a few months later. Barbara Stanwyck is great as Dixie Daisy, the lead; people were surprised when she danced up a storm, but of course as Ruby Stevens she'd been a chorus girl in New York. Terrific broad, too.

I loved doing *Flamingo Road* because of Joan Crawford, who was another great broad. My part is really only a bit, but I have a line people still come up to me and quote. I tell Joan's character that the reason I'm in the hoosegow is that "my boyfriend stabbed himself with a knife I was holding at the time."

The director, Michael Curtiz, was another matter. Somehow, I was always landing in Curtiz pictures and the guy drove me nuts. But they were always big, important pictures, so I just said to myself, "Well, here I go again!" Anyway, I was used to being screamed at. I was in the chorus in New York, and dance directors like Bobby Connolly were always yelling at me—"Hey, you, third from the end, do it over again, you dumb sonofabitch!" Curtiz bawled me out all the time. He wouldn't dare bawl out the star, so he picked on me, a supporting player. I'd be starting on a Curtiz picture and an assistant would come over to me and say, "Mr. Curtiz hopes you're prepared and know your lines and are ready. We don't want to hold up production." You can imagine how that put me at ease.

Curtiz was just plain rude. And you couldn't understand his direction a lot of the time because he had a heavy Hungarian accent. To make matters worse on *Flamingo Road,* he also got laryngitis and I thought, "God, he might as well be talking Chinese to me!"

I remember saying to him, "Why do you always hire me? You hate me!"

And he replied, "No, I luff you. You have such a great personality and comedy timing"—all that bullshit.

Joan Crawford didn't like him any better than I did. She came over to me one day and said, "Take your mike off, Iris. I've got something to tell you." And she told me that, unbeknownst to Curtiz, she was in the next room listening when Curtiz told the producer of *Flamingo Road* that he didn't want Joan, "that big-eyed dame with the football shoulders," in the picture. She said, "I have a contract for five more years, so I've got to do this picture, but I wish I could've gotten out of it. It's not easy for me to be cute and darling for such a bastard."

At the end of one tough day, I said to Joan, "Well, home to mother."

"Home to *be* mother," she answered. "And if things don't get better there, too, I don't know *what* I'm going to do."

Those kids *and* Mike Curtiz. The poor dame had her hands full!

June Allyson—ACTRESS—

Little Women became my favorite picture, although while shooting it I was also finishing a number from a musical film and completing another dramatic movie. MGM bought me a bicycle to get from one set to another.

I wanted the role of Jo March, the tomboy, so badly, but so did every other actress on and off the lot. *Everyone* was tested. They asked me to test for it, too, but I refused. Not because I was such a big star, but because I knew I'd never be as good in the test as some of those others. Well, they wound up giving it to me after all.

Katharine Hepburn had had a great success in the story back in the thirties. Although the studio wanted me to run her version before we started, I was a great fan of Hepburn's and didn't want to look at it because I was afraid I might imitate something Miss Hepburn did. I still haven't seen her version.

While we were filming, we really thought we *were* the March family.

We giggled all the time, and I think we drove our producer-director, Mervyn LeRoy, a little crazy. For one thing, whenever he was ready for a scene one of us four "March" girls almost invariably would be missing, who-knew-where. Finally, Mervyn said, "I am not going to look for you anymore. One of *you* can be policeman from now on!"

Mr. LeRoy was such a fine director. Did he tell us what he wanted in a scene, or just let us go? It was a combination of both. If you brought what he wanted to a scene, he let you go. Otherwise, he'd tell you to do this or that.

They dyed my hair dark for *Little Women* because, I presume, Jo was a brunette in Louisa May Alcott's novel. Elizabeth Taylor, as Amy, wore a blonde wig, probably for the same reason. One time during the filming when we were all sitting in my dressing room, Liz looked over at me and said, "Gee, I wish I looked like you, Junie." Imagine, the most beautiful girl in the world saying that to *me!* It kept me alive for years! Liz was very funny in the film as the vain sister, She's funny in person, too. Has a delightful dry wit.

I loved the old-fashioned costumes designed by Walter Plunkett, although many of mine weighed more than I did! And those beautiful sets, in all seasons—*Little Women* won the Academy Award for Technicolor art direction. We shot the whole thing on sound stages and on the backlot. It took about three months; today, if anyone still wanted to do *Little Women,* it would have to be done in 18 days!

The "little women" were all great pals, and still are. I saw Liz Taylor a few months ago, and Margaret O'Brien and I live very close to each other in California. Last week, I ran into Janet Leigh while I was in New York promoting the MGM/UA home videos of my films. Happily, *Little Women* is among those videos available.

Little Women was, I think, the only time I got to do something really worthwhile on the screen. And it was a great success at the box office. Louis B. Mayer, our boss at Metro, loved it, too; family pictures were his "thing," and this was the family picture to end all family pictures. At the preview, I remember he sent us all flowers. A couple of years later he was forced out of MGM, which was never the same again.

Neither was the whole motion picture industry.

Robert Arthur——ACTOR—

In 1944, I received a medical discharge from the Navy. I didn't want to continue living in my hometown of Aberdeen, Washington, so I borrowed some money and went to Hollywood to become an actor.

The first night I stayed at the Hollywood Plaza Hotel for five dollars. I then found a room to rent in an apartment building owned by a character actress named Early whose husband was named Late. Years before, they had been Early & Late on the Pantages vaudeville circuit. I only had enough money left to last for three days so I had to find a job immediately. My landlady introduced me to her agent and I began making the rounds of the studios.

At Warner Bros., the famous Hungarian-born director Michael Curtiz agreed to hear me read for the film *Roughly Speaking,* the true saga of Louise Randall Pierson, a hapless entrepreneur who would be played by Rosalind Russell. Jack Carson was to co-star as her husband. The Piersons had several children, so there would be a number of young people at various stages of growth in the cast, too. For Mr. Curtiz, I worked up a scene between a boy and a girl and played both parts. Everybody laughed, except Mr. Curtiz.

"Vot is dot scene?" Curtiz asked.

"It's a comedy scene," I replied.

"But your character, Frankie, Mrs. Pierson's youngest son, is going avay to vor."

So, to get in the right mood, I thought about the time my dog died, doing the scene over again in a serious manner.

"Hire dot boy!" instructed Curtiz. "He'll break dair hearts."

The first day on the picture, Rosalind Russell gave me a lift home. So there I was, recently arrived in town, making my first movie and being driven home by the star.

I was signed for a week on *Roughly Speaking,* then it was extended to two weeks, then three. When we got to do the scene where I have to toast my mother on her birthday and say, "Ma, I think you're swell and I love you," Mr. Curtiz called out, "Keep the cameras on Bobby. Let's see vot he can do vit dis scene." So, I ad-libbed a lot of banter with Jack Carson about the wine we were all drinking, saying things like, "Ma, this is the first wine I've ever had—officially." And made something of the scene. Miss Russell was off-camera giving me wonderful support. On the strength of this scene, Warners gave me a seven-year contract.

I had little acting experience. At 14, I had won a radio announcer's contest and became an announcer for a while. I had done some school plays. But that was about it.

The first day I walked onto the set of *Roughly Speaking,* Louise Randall Pierson exclaimed, "My God, it's Frankie!" Mrs. Pierson and I hit it off right away. She sort of adopted me. I lived with her, her husband Harold and son Frank for two years. I'd go to their place at the beach and stay with them on weekends. Frank later became a very successful Hollywood producer, director and writer. And Mrs. Pierson bought a lot of acreage at Zuma Beach and became a multimillionaire. At the time of *Roughly Speaking,* which she wrote from her autobiography, she was under contract to Warners where she was also working [uncredited] on the screenplay of *Mildred Pierce.*

In *Nora Prentiss,* Wanda Hendrix and I play the children of Rosemary DeCamp and Kent Smith, who is having an affair with Ann Sheridan. My part was small, but I loved Ann, a warm, wonderful lady. In the early fifties, we did a TV pilot together that was set at a Las Vegas dude ranch. I was a bellboy, Ann a torch singer. Unfortunately, the series didn't get on the air.

I did a few films at Warners, but then got angry with them. They were getting ready to film the long-running Broadway hit, *Life with Father,* and Wanda Hendrix and I were told that we would play the juvenile and ingenue leads. Warners had me testing with all the leading ladies who wanted to play opposite William Powell, already set as Father. I remember testing with Dorothy Stickney, who had been Mother in the original stage production, Bette Davis, Claudette Colbert, Susan Hayward and Joan Fontaine. The tests went on for six months. Every day I would come to the studio and test with another actress who wanted the mother role.

One morning, I arrived and Michael Curtiz, who was to direct the film, too, told everybody, "Do your best today. And vatch your language. Ve vill haff a great lady of da silent screen vit us. Mary Pickford is coming to test for *Life with Father.*" I was thrilled to be doing the test with this legend, who was hoping to make a comeback. And she was the best of the lot, absolutely natural and totally believable. Eventually, though, Irene Dunne was chosen, probably because she was a bigger, more active screen name at the time.

The payoff came when they finally selected, not Wanda Hendrix and me for the teen-age leads, but James Lydon, who had been in the Henry Aldrich series, and Elizabeth Taylor, fresh from doing Lassie movies at MGM. Apparently, as with Miss Dunne, they felt Jimmy and Liz's names would mean more to ticket-buyers than Wanda's and my names. A while back, I ran into Jimmy somewhere and told him, "You know, I hated you for years." Poor Jimmy looked startled and asked why. I explained.

I was furious with the studio. I told Jack Warner to stick his contract in his ear and left the lot. I was sure I'd be blackballed. I went over to Monogram, which was usually the last stop in Hollywood, and did some turkeys, but at least I was getting a paycheck.

Eventually, 20th Century-Fox signed me. My first picture there was a hit, *Mother Wore Tights,* starring Betty Grable and Dan Dailey. Betty was pleasant, although she kept pretty much to herself. She was a tough, chorus-girl sort of dame but a terrific dancer. Dan Dailey was very talented, too, but he was a tortured transvestite. Once, he invited me to his house and there he was, in full female drag. Big, lanky Dan was quite a sight in an evening gown. I was speechless. I didn't know what to say. "You never looked lovelier?" Dan wasn't gay; he just liked to dress up in women's clothes. He was tormented by this and wound up at the Menninger Clinic.

This is how the Fox contract came about. One day Darryl Zanuck, the head of production there, called me. I thought he was phoning about the test I had done for *Mother Wore Tights* or about a contract, but he said he wanted me to take his daughter Susan to a dance. It seemed that

she had seen my test and thought I was cute. I wasn't crazy about the idea: I was an actor, not a gigolo. But this is how things often are done in Hollywood, so I said okay. When I picked Susan up, I also met Richard Zanuck, her brother and then about 15, who snapped orders about what time to bring her home. Anyway, I thought she was a stick-in-the-mud. She must have thought I was okay, however, because I got both *Mother Wore Tights* and a Fox contract. I was a friend of the Zanucks for years.

Later, when I learned that Susan was only 13 years old, I thought she was brilliant!

Again Zanuck called and asked me to take Susan horseback-riding. I told him I couldn't ride a horse, and he recoiled in horror: "How do you expect to have a movie career if you can't ride a horse?" I took her riding and had a dreadful time. I was sore for weeks. So of course Zanuck immediately put me into *Green Grass of Wyoming,* the third entry in the "Flicka" horse series. It was a starring part, though.

Green Grass was a tough picture to make. Louis King, the director, was a very nervous man, and the whole production seemed jumpy and tense, as I recall. Peggy Cummins is my leading lady. Only months before, she had come over from England with great fanfare to play the title role in *Forever Amber,* but she was soon removed from that picture and replaced by Linda Darnell. On *Green Grass of Wyoming* she was rude, flippant and generally unpleasant, one of only two actresses I have disliked working with in the movie business. (The other: Joan Fontaine, who was very rude to Joseph Cotten in the subsequent *September Affair,* in which I play his son.)

When I was first brought to Peggy on the set, someone said, "Miss Cummins, I'd like you to meet Robert Arthur, your leading man."

And she growled, "I look like his muthah!" No hello—nothing.

The chemistry between us couldn't have been worse. On top of this, she was having an affair during the shooting with Lloyd Nolan, the married, middle-aged actor who was playing my father in the film. None of this sat too well with the cast and crew. Charles Coburn was a wonderful old gentleman. We did our own sulky racing in the film. (A sulky is a two-wheel cart harnessed directly behind the horse.) One evening over dinner, I asked Mr. Coburn, "How do you like driving sulkies?"

"Fine," answered Mr. Coburn, "except when the horse breaks wind."

Burl Ives and I shared quarters. He was nice but drank too much. He had a big Great Dane with him and the two of them would burp and make strange noises all night long. I couldn't sleep. And to be a juvenile, I needed to look rested. I started wearing earplugs, something I still do.

Green Grass of Wyoming made a lot of money for Fox. However, I decided that if I never saw another horse again it would be too soon. And I was fed up with trying to please directors.

On the day I turned 21, Billy Gordon, the casting director at Fox, called me and said, "You're slated to do *Yellow Sky,* a Western. You have to go right over and see the director, William Wellman."

I protested. "I will not do another Western." It was quickly pointed out to me that I was under contract and could be suspended.

At the time, I was unaware that Wellman had done such great films as *A Star Is Born* and *The Ox-Bow Incident.* When I walked into Mr. Wellman's office at Fox, I saw all kinds of airplane knick-knacks around the room. He sat there with a leather brace on a bad arm puffing on a corncob pipe and looking like Popeye. I thought, "What am I getting into?" The first thing he said to me was, "Can you be tough?"

Out of the corner of my mouth, I said, "Sure."

He snapped, "Good, because this is going to be the goddamnedest, toughest Western ever made! We're shooting it in Death Valley. It's so goddamn hot there your piss dries up before it hits the ground!

"Can you grow a beard?"

"No problem."

I was in.

Wellman was a wild, tough Irishman. My relatives were Irish, and he brought back pleasant memories of them. He was my kind of guy. That afternoon, he screened *Ox-Bow Incident* for me. I'd already seen it when it came out a few years earlier, but this time I had the director commenting as it unwound.

That evening, Jane Powell and some other friends threw me a birthday party and showed *A Star Is Born* for me.

We filmed *Yellow Sky* in Death

Valley and at Lone Pine, California. Gregory Peck, Anne Baxter and Richard Widmark are the stars. Peck was one of the greatest professionals I ever worked with, but very introverted. You'd sit on the set with him for hours and then he'd finally say hello. We were shooting for quite a while and I kept referring to my "juice harp, my juice harp." At last, Peck boomed, "It's *jew's* harp!" I finally got a rise out of him. At the end, he gave me a beautiful Alsatian police dog. I did another picture with him, *Twelve O'Clock High.*

Anne Baxter and I became great friends. We worked together again on *You're My Everything.* She drank too much, you know. It wasn't the stroke that killed her; it was the drink.

Widmark was okay. Several years later, we did another picture called *Take the High Ground* at MGM and during a scene he accidentally knocked my tooth out. I was livid and belted him. It wasn't his fault, but it was my tooth.

Most of the time, I was pretty much typed as the all-American boy. I used to call myself "the poor man's Lon McCallister." Lon and I became friends and used to joke about this. In those days, the younger set was always doing layouts for *Modern Screen* and the other fan magazines cooking, swimming or opening another Will Wright's ice cream parlor. I remember one time I was at Lon's apartment when a magazine was doing a layout in the living room with Lon, Ann Blyth, Colleen Townsend and some others. I was in the kitchen helping Lon's mother when he came out. "Mother," he said, "I wish someone in that room would just say 'shit'!"

I had a drinking problem for a long time, but I just celebrated 20 years of continuous sobriety. Many of us Hollywood kids didn't make it. I've been pallbearer for some of my peers. I always say that the class of 1944 went to hell in a handbasket. I'm a survivor, but considering how rough things got at times, it sometimes seems like a miracle.

Lew Ayres — *ACTOR*

My first post-war films turned out to be three of my better ones, which somewhat surprised me. Actually, I really didn't think that Hollywood would want me anymore. I hadn't made a film in four years. I had been a medic during World War II and was overseas for two years. I was in three invasions in the South Pacific. Right after the war, I was thinking of becoming a minister when an offer came to co-star with Olivia de Havilland in *The Dark Mirror* at Universal.

I did it, and the picture turned out very well, but I never liked myself in it. I play a psychiatrist interrogating twin sisters (both played by Olivia), one of whom is a murderer. I thought I played it too

lightly; I should have been more serious and concerned. I felt that this was a most unusual case and my character should have struggled and sweated more over it. I did too much smiling.

If I had been Robert Siodmak, the director, I would have been on top of me. Olivia, on the other hand, carries off both of her roles subtly and very effectively. A couple of years later I was chatting with Olivia and told her my reservations about the job I did in *Dark Mirror* and she very kindly said, "Oh, no, no, you were fine." But I wasn't convinced. *The Dark Mirror* changed much of my attitude toward my work. I became determined that in the future I would throw myself more deeply into my roles.

Next, I went over to Warner Bros. to do *The Unfaithful,* with Ann Sheridan and Zachary Scott. This taught me something, too: to be more careful when selecting a part. When Warners spoke to me about doing the picture, they offered me either one of the two male leads: the husband or the lawyer.

I studied the script and saw that the attorney had these speeches to the jury, so I said, "I'd like to do the attorney." Zach Scott played the husband. Afterward, I discovered that it would have been better to have played Scott's role. As the husband, you're more involved in the drama, right in the thick of it, instead of the bystander that the attorney proved to be. Scott is fine, though. I don't know that I would have done as well. You learn as you go along.

Ann Sheridan? She was very cool to me. Maybe it was our different lifestyles. She seemed to take her role in *The Unfaithful* very lightly; her attention span was quite short. She'd be joking around on the set and I'd wonder, "How is she ever going to deal with this heavy dramatic role?" Somehow, she wound up doing a very good job. Still, I felt like a stranger on that film. Vincent Sherman, the director, and I have remained good friends, though. We chat on the phone from time to time and see each other for dinner.

My resolution to become more deeply involved in my characterizations served me well on my next picture, *Johnny Belinda,* which I stayed on at Warners to do. I play the doctor who teaches the deaf-mute farm drudge (Jane Wyman) how to communicate. Charles Bickford and Agnes Moorehead are also in it, and right from the start we all felt that the director, Jean Negulesco, wasn't giving us the help we needed. He was artistic and very extroverted, but none of us felt that he was on target with the characterizations.

So something happened which I've never had on any other film: we became our own directors. We knew each other and respected each other's opinions, becoming so close that we hardly listened to Negulesco. Jane, Charles, Agnes and I were on the set together all the time. When Jane and I would do a scene, we'd look at Charles and Agnes to see what they thought. If they nodded, things would proceed; if they shook their heads, we'd say, "I think we ought to do that again." And they would do the same. We did it discreetly, though, so we didn't offend our director.

We wanted to get everything out of the script, which we knew was special.

We filmed for about six weeks up the coast north of San Francisco, in the Fort Bragg–Mendocino area. The location provided a beautiful stand-in for Nova Scotia, the setting of the story.

Jane Wyman was remarkable. Audiences were stunned to see Jane, who for years had been playing bubble-headed second leads, enact this deep, silent, unglamorous star role. She won the Academy Award that year [1948] for *Johnny Belinda* and I won a Best Actor nomination.

In 1954, I took a year off and, with a technician, went around the world photographing religious leaders. I have been involved in comparative religions ever since. I've made films on all the world's religions, and some of them have won awards. I continue to show them at colleges and other places; films on religion never date. Although I don't belong to any religion myself, I am a deeply religious person.

I still act occasionally, but I'm in my eighties and have never had my face lifted. There aren't a lot of roles for people my age. Frankly, if I were young again, I don't think I would be an actor. I'm very grateful for the wonderful people I've met in the profession, and it's made many things possible for me, but I don't look at films anymore—old or new. A while back when I wrote my autobiography, the publisher refused it, saying that I didn't have enough in it about the Hollywood people. I think that if I had it all to do over again my field would be philosophy.

John Beal—ACTOR—

I have to confess mixed feelings about *Edge of Darkness.*

On one hand, I was delighted, after having done a string of "B" movies, to be asked to appear in an important "A" picture again boasting one of the finest casts of the day—Errol Flynn, Ann Sheridan, Walter Huston, Nancy Coleman, Helmut Dantine, Judith Anderson, Ruth Gordon, Morris Carnovsky, Charles Dingle, Roman Rohnen, Richard Fraser, Art Smith, Helene Thimig and Virginia Christine. But my part wasn't really that big. I'd have a short scene or two and then disappear from the film for a while. For one scene, I had to learn a whole Norwegian song phonetically. When the picture was put together, they only used a few bars; they opened the scene as I was finishing the song. And I wasn't happy about playing a Quisling, either, even though he somewhat redeems himself at the end with a spontaneous act of bravery. We were at war and I didn't think it would exactly enhance my popularity to portray a man who betrays his country [Nazi-occupied Norway].

The working conditions, however, were extremely pleasant—for the most part. Some of it was shot on the Warner Bros. lot and some of it on location near Monterey. The stars, Errol Flynn and Ann Sheridan, play underground fighters in a Norwegian fishing village captured by Nazis. They seemed very nice, although I never got to know them well. Flynn was elegant and much-admired, and Ann also was very well liked. I remember our director, Lewis Milestone, praising her, too—she was so warm, everybody loved her.

On the set, I did a number of portrait drawings, some of which were printed in the *Los Angeles Daily News* at the time. Roman Bohnen, a fine character actor who plays a village shopkeeper, was kind enough to pose patiently while I did a drawing of him that now sits in the Museum of the City of New York. Coincidentally, he mentioned that his father had been a portrait painter in, I think, Chicago. I also did a fast sketch of Walter Huston, one of Nancy Coleman and others.

The thing I remember best about *Edge of Darkness* is that when I began it my wife, the actress Helen Craig, was expecting our first child, Theadora Emily (named after my violinist sister, who died at age 25). Finally, Helen went to the hospital where I was up all night waiting for our daughter to be born. At last she came, and I went in to see my wife. Helen still seemed to be in such pain. Then I went to see my daughter, and she seemed to be in discomfort, too.

That morning, I was very worried and tired when I left for the studio to film on *Edge of Darkness.* And what did they give me to do that day? All the physical things! I had to carry Nancy Coleman up a flight of stairs, as well as jump off a balcony (onto a mattress, thank goodness). And there were many takes of both scenes. Later, I was called to the phone. It was Helen, obviously all aglow. She said, "I've just seen our baby. She's healthy and beautiful. I'm so happy!" I knew everything was all right. After that, I could have carried 10 Nancy Colemans and jumped off 20 balconies!

When I completed my role, I enlisted in the Army Air Force for three years. In a little while, Warner Bros. pulled some strings and brought me back to the studio for a couple of days of retakes on *Edge of Darkness.* That's how powerful the studios were then. They could even give orders to the Army!

Ralph Bellamy — ACTOR

I don't recall exactly how I got into *His Girl Friday.* I was under contract to Columbia, where we shot it. And I had played a similar role with Cary Grant a few years earlier in *The Awful Truth,* which was very successful. Maybe they were just looking for "a Ralph Bellamy type," which I heard they sometimes did during those years. You know, the reliable second lead foil.

And some genius probably said to them, "Hey! How about Ralph Bellamy?!"

Of course, I had already appeared on the stage in *The Front Page,* the Ben Hecht-Charles MacArthur play from which *His Girl Friday* was adapted. I did it several years earlier with George Cukor's stock company in Rochester, New York. I played one of the two leads then, Hildy Johnson, which director Howard Hawks and his writers re-wrote for a woman, Rosalind Russell, when they did *His Girl Friday.*

Stock was a grind but you learned professionalism. We did 10 performances a week. While you were doing one play at night, you might be rehearsing *Front Page* all day long, so that by the time you did that evening's show you would probably be hoarse. Most of those who went out to Hollywood when sound came in—people like Gable, Cagney, Davis, Bogart—came from a stock background, so they had that stage discipline which, I am sorry to say, is sadly lacking in films today. If you had to be at rehearsal at 10, you got there if you had to crawl, because everybody else would be there. We all aspired to Broadway. Some made it, some didn't. When sound came in, Hollywood needed people who could read lines, so they brought us out.

His Girl Friday was great fun. I was now playing Hildy's fiancé. I had not worked with Roz Russell before, although I knew her. And I didn't have a great deal to do with her in the picture; a lot of our dialogue was over the phone. But Cary Grant, whom I knew from *Awful Truth,* was great to work with. He had the unusual quality of listening, really listening, to the other actor, and reacting and responding. Our director, Howard Hawks, was terrific, too. He knew what he wanted in each scene, and more important, he knew when he got it. He was very good with actors—a great director.

Harry Cohn was my boss, the president of Columbia Pictures. What was he like? Have you got six months? He was one of the greatest characters this business ever saw. He was one of the tough, so-called moguls who had a finger on the pulse of the public; he knew what they would like. He went for the best, as in the cases of the directors Frank Capra and Leo McCarey. Then he'd wreck the relationships with them, they'd leave and never come back.

I'm one of the few who ever got along with Harry. If I had Saturdays off, I'd go to college football games with him.

Usually, I was working all the time. I remember that once I went to him and said, "I just can't go on at this pace. You've got to give me a stand-in." But Harry said, "We've never had a stand-in on the Columbia lot, and we never will have!" The early calls and working till someone fainted continued, and I went to him again and insisted, "I've got to have a six o'clock release!" That I got.

There is a famous story about Harry and his brother Jack, who ran the New York office. One day, the two of them were sitting at a table at a convention in Hollywood when Jack said, "Why don't we do a Bible story?" And Harry shrugged, "Why should we?" Jack pointed out, "They're kind of like Westerns. And you don't have to pay royalties."

"What do you know about the Bible?" Harry shot back. "You don't even know the Lord's Prayer."

Jack said he did, too, so Harry replied, "I've give you $50 if you can recite the Lord's Prayer."

Jack began, "Now I lay me down to sleep. . ."

"That's enough," interrupted Harry. "Christ, I didn't think you knew it." He gave Jack the $50.

Eventually, I found out that Harry was very rough in his language, and if you gave back as good as you got, he liked it. I learned that when I'd go to him for something, and wouldn't get it, I'd holler, "All right, tear up the goddamn contract, because I can't continue!" Then he'd say, "All right, all right, you've got it."

I recall that a few weeks before Christmas one year I wanted to get my wife a mink coat. I had a day off, so I had furriers deliver coats to the new dressing room Harry had given me after one of my squawks. Every half-hour, another coat would arrive. After a while, Harry phoned me. "What's going on down there with all those coats?" he screamed, leading me to believe he had my room bugged. I told him I hoped to buy my wife a mink and he answered, "Jesus, don't you know I used to be in that business? Come up to the office."

When I got there, he instructed

his secretary, "Get me Nate Spingold in the New York office." Harry told me, "Nate and I used to be in the fur business. In the beginning, I was plugging songs on stage before the picture began, and in our spare time Nate and I would sell coats. We'd dye rabbit skins and sell them for mink." To Nate he said, "I got a crazy actor here who wants a fur coat. Go to so-and-so and pick out a coat and have it here before Christmas." Evidently, they still kept their contacts in the fur trade. A few days before Christmas, I was shooting on the set when Harry called and said, "Get up here." When I arrived, he just looked at me, went out of the room and in a few seconds came back *wearing* the mink coat! I got it at a terrific price, too.

Dive Bomber was a big, splashy Warner Bros. production in Technicolor made on the eve of World War II. The old Enterprise ship, which was later sunk, was needed for a number of scenes, but the Navy said we couldn't use it. So Warners sent a "fixer" to Washington and we were soon at sea on the Enterprise. The first night out, all sorts of fireworks were set off on board by the Navy; it was so noisy that none of us in the film crew were able to sleep. It was a deliberate move, I'm sure—retaliation for our having commandeered the ship for a movie.

The director was Mike Curtiz, a Hungarian with a thick accent known throughout Hollywood for his strange utterances. We filmed for about a week at sea on the Enterprise. Mike saved all the close-ups to be shot against the superstructure as we were pulling into San Diego harbor. Suddenly, as we were docking there, great clouds of smoke happened to come billowing up around us, spoiling the shots. Mike rushed to the assistant director yelling, "Tell the captain to blow the smoke the other way!"

Errol Flynn stars in *Dive Bomber.* He became a good friend. We played tennis together (he was quite good), and I recall that we had dinner on his boat one evening. He had a lot of energy. He was a tongue-in-cheek fellow, always looking for a laugh. He liked to have fun with people, sometimes at their expense, but I liked him.

Just before *Dive Bomber,* Errol and I had acted in *Footsteps in the Dark,* a much less ambitious film shot very quickly on the Warner lot. On this, there was no time to do anything except go to sleep and get up again and go to work.

The Wolf Man and *The Ghost of Frankenstein,* two horror films I did at Universal in the early '40s, have wonderful casts. I think that's the main reason why they're so well remembered today. On *Ghost of Frankenstein,* for instance, one of the leads was my friend Sir Cedric Hardwicke. The director was Erle C. Kenton, a little man who really dressed the part: he wore a hunting jacket, riding britches and carried a swagger stick. One day, after Cedric and I had finished a scene, our director came over and said, "We're going down to do a silent shot with Evelyn Ankers on the old Notre Dame staircase"—which, by the way, was still standing at Universal right up until the recent fire there. "You can stay here and chat," he added. After about an hour and a half, I said to Cedric, "Let's go down there and see what's going on."

When we arrived on the staircase set, the director had exchanged his swagger stick for the biggest megaphone I have ever seen. His prim, skinny secretary was trying to keep out of its way as she followed him around. Finally, the assistant told him, "We're ready." The director said, "Get Miss Ankers on the stairway." When he was informed that she was there, he picked up the megaphone and boomed out, "All right, Evelyn. You're all alone in this dark, slimy, cold old castle. Your mother's been carried away by the Frankenstein monster. Your father's been killed by the Wolf Man. The servants have all run off and your boyfriend is being chased across the moors by wild dogs. As you come down the staircase, I want to get the feeling that you're fed up with it all!"

For years afterward, every time I'd run into Sir Cedric we'd try to beat each other asking, "Are you fed up with it all yet?"

Joan Bennett—*ACTRESS*—

Fritz Lang was my favorite director, and *Man Hunt,* the first of four films I did with him in the '40s, is one of my favorite pictures.

It's a melodrama in which I play this very sympathetic little Cockney streetwalker. The censors watched us very closely; in those days, you couldn't be too specific about this kind of thing. They wouldn't let me swing my purse from the handle as I walked, nor stand with my hands on my hips—they felt that such motions made her occupation too obvious, and that was a no-no.

The studio, 20th Century-Fox, had me study the Cockney dialect with a British character actress named Queenie Leonard. It was the first and last time I did a foreign accent on the screen, but I must have pulled it off because one of the critics of the day said he couldn't believe it was actually Joan Bennett speaking.

Most people hated Fritz, but I loved him and responded to his direction immediately. He had been a top director in Germany but fled Hitler—probably the only man who could intimidate Lang. He was very strict but painstaking; knew exactly what he wanted and would keep you doing a scene until you got it that way. I don't recall that I, personally, had any problems with him in this area, but when there were three or four of us working in a scene, he sometimes would make us do it again and again until whoever he felt wasn't up to the mark finally suited him. Sometimes he would lose his patience and shout.

Oh, I do remember one incident that was slightly humiliating. I am not a tall woman. I once had a complex about being too short for some of my leading men. Like my co-star in *Man Hunt,* Walter Pidgeon, who was about six-feet-three. Walter and I were doing a love scene and I was stretching with everything I had to

reach his shoulder when Fritz suddenly bellowed, "Get Joan an orange crate to stand on! Lovers should be on speaking terms, at least."

None of this fazed me, really, because I knew that Fritz was getting a good performance out of me. However, Walter Pidgeon didn't like Fritz at all because of his dictator methods on the set—"You will do this, you will do that!" I remember Walter saying, "Why does he insist on playing the German?" They were such opposites: Walter was so affable and easy to work with.

When I was signed for *Man Hunt,* I was thrilled to be playing a part that was both leading lady and a character role that would require real acting; I'd played so many "pretty heroines." But I had no idea that the film would be as successful as it turned out to be, or as enduring. No one did. Except maybe Fritz Lang!

Eddie Bracken——— *ACTOR*—

When Preston Sturges first wrote *The Miracle of Morgan's Creek,* he wanted Andy Devine for my part. But Betty Hutton and I had been doing well as something of a team in pictures then, so Buddy DeSylva, Paramount's head of production, decided to keep us together and had Sturges cast us in *Morgan's Creek.*

However, when I first read the script I didn't like it. Betty's role was much larger than mine. And I'd had the experience in the other films I'd done with Betty that musical numbers were always added during production to build up her parts. When this happened, I got peeved—not with Betty, whom I loved, but with those in charge.

So I had lunch with Preston (who also directed) and he swore to me, "There will be no numbers for Betty in this, except a quick comedy thing she will do in a low voice in her record shop. Your part is awfully good and very sympathetic." He talked me into it. I invented all the tics my character had, the sneezing, all the comic business. I'd be walking around Betty Hutton and teaching her a lesson, not because I wanted to upstage her but because I wanted to show her what you have to do in this business to survive.

But Betty knew how to handle herself. When we did the scene where we go to the justice of the peace to get married, rehearsals were so funny the crew was breaking up. When we did the take, she suddenly started to stutter, which she hadn't done before, and everyone *really* went bananas.

Another scene between Betty and Diana Lynn, who played her kid sister, was an incredible technical feat. They had to walk through the town of Morgan's Creek, past shop windows, talking all the time, but the problem was: the microphone was showing in the windows. So they decided to have the girls dub all their dialogue in later—about seven pages of script! They did it superbly.

William Demarest, cast as Betty and Diana's father, was the rock of Gibralter. He would not try to steal scenes, but he would have wonderful character touches. And those pratfalls! Years before, in vaudeville, the first thing he did was greet the audience and then fall into the drum in the pit.

Preston Sturges was an awfully good friend. He was like a father to me, sometimes a big brother, but always a friend. He was a cross between Jesus Christ and Satan: he could be brutal to actors. For *Morgan's Creek,* he hired many of the great Mack Sennett comedians, whom I'd grown up watching. He would be pretty rough on them, but he got great performances out of them. He didn't spare the leads, either. There was one scene with Betty and Diana where Betty shows Diana the curtain ring she got married with that Preston shot about 15 times. Finally, the girls were sobbing but they came back one more time and did the sensational take that's in the picture. He came up and hugged them. He could be mean but for a very short time and it always turned out all right.

Preston had a tremendous ego. He might talk over a scene with us, but what *he* wanted, that was the way it would be done. Most of his hits came while Jean La Vell was his secretary, and she was the only person he really listened to. There'd be a meeting about a project and if he was going overboard, or becoming excessive, which was his tendency, Jean

would tell him, "Why don't you do this or that instead?" and he might argue but he'd usually do it. Jean played a large part in the success of Sturges' great movies, though if I said this to her now she'd reply, "Oh, come on now. . . ." When he left Jean and Paramount and went over to Howard Hughes and Fox, his pictures didn't turn out so well.

Before it was released, *The Miracle of Morgan's Creek* ran into some problems with the Army and the censors. We were in the midst of World War II then. Everyone was very patriotic, and the Army didn't want the public to think our fighting men were a bunch of drunks, as Preston portrayed them in a couple of scenes. So he had character actor Frank Moran, as an M.P., say in that gruff voice of his, "If I drunk that much lemonade I'd be sour for a week." That placated the Army. Then there was the problem with the censors over Betty being an unwed mother. This was the early '40s, remember, and that just didn't happen on the screen then. So Preston had her hit her head, so she didn't really know what she was doing, then brought in the curtain ring which she was supposed to have worn during the marriage we never saw and she could no longer remember.

I went to the sneak preview and sat unnoticed in the balcony. The audience laughed hysterically, especially a middle-aged lady who literally fell into the aisle at one point. I said, "Are you OK? Did you hurt yourself?" but she just kept on laughing at us up there on the screen. At the end, she turned to her companion and said, "Wasn't that a funny movie? I had such a good time. Except for that jerk kid behind us!" Me!

A few years ago, I was going to be given an award for *Miracle of Morgan's Creek* and my other Preston Sturges picture, *Hail the Conquering Hero.* I told them I would appear only if Betty Hutton could be with me. She'd had terrible personal problems for years, but had come back and, in her sixties, put herself through college. Betty took some persuading, but I finally got her to come to the ceremony. I'm so proud of her.

Lucille Bremer—ACTRESS—

I was trained in ballet and was dancing at the Versailles Restaurant in New York when producer Arthur Freed and some others from MGM came in one evening. Evidently they liked what they saw because they asked me to come to Hollywood.

Just before that, I appeared in Gertrude Lawrence's Broadway hit, *Lady in the Dark.* I didn't open in the show but replaced someone later on. Actually, I played several different small parts in it. In one big musical number, Miss Lawrence had to go offstage and change her costume while the number continued. There wasn't time for her to change, though, so, wearing a replica of her outfit and a wig fashioned exactly like her hairdo, I filled in for her briefly and, since it was a big number with a lot of people, nobody in the audience was any the wiser (hopefully).

But one night there was a mishap. While I was playing in *Lady in the Dark,* I was also appearing in a nightclub. After a show at the club, I would rush to the theater late in the proceedings, put on my wig and dash on stage. This one evening the wrong wig was put out for me and I went on stage wearing it. Miss Lawrence had left the stage in an upsweep hairdo and, presto, there she (I) was with long straight hair. I wonder what the audience thought to see Miss Lawrence look one way one second and another the next?

I didn't know till I got to Hollywood that Arthur Freed and MGM were thinking of using me in *Meet Me in St. Louis.* For my movie debut, I was to play Judy Garland's slightly older sister in what was obviously going to be an important picture, so I was very excited, naturally. I didn't even have to test. I was just given the script on Friday and told to show up on Monday.

As I recall, Judy didn't want to make the picture. She had to be talked into it. At the time, she was very interested in doing heavier dramatic stories, and *Meet Me in St. Louis* seemed like a lighthearted vehicle for her. Ultimately, of course, it became one of the public's favorite Garland films and one of hers, too.

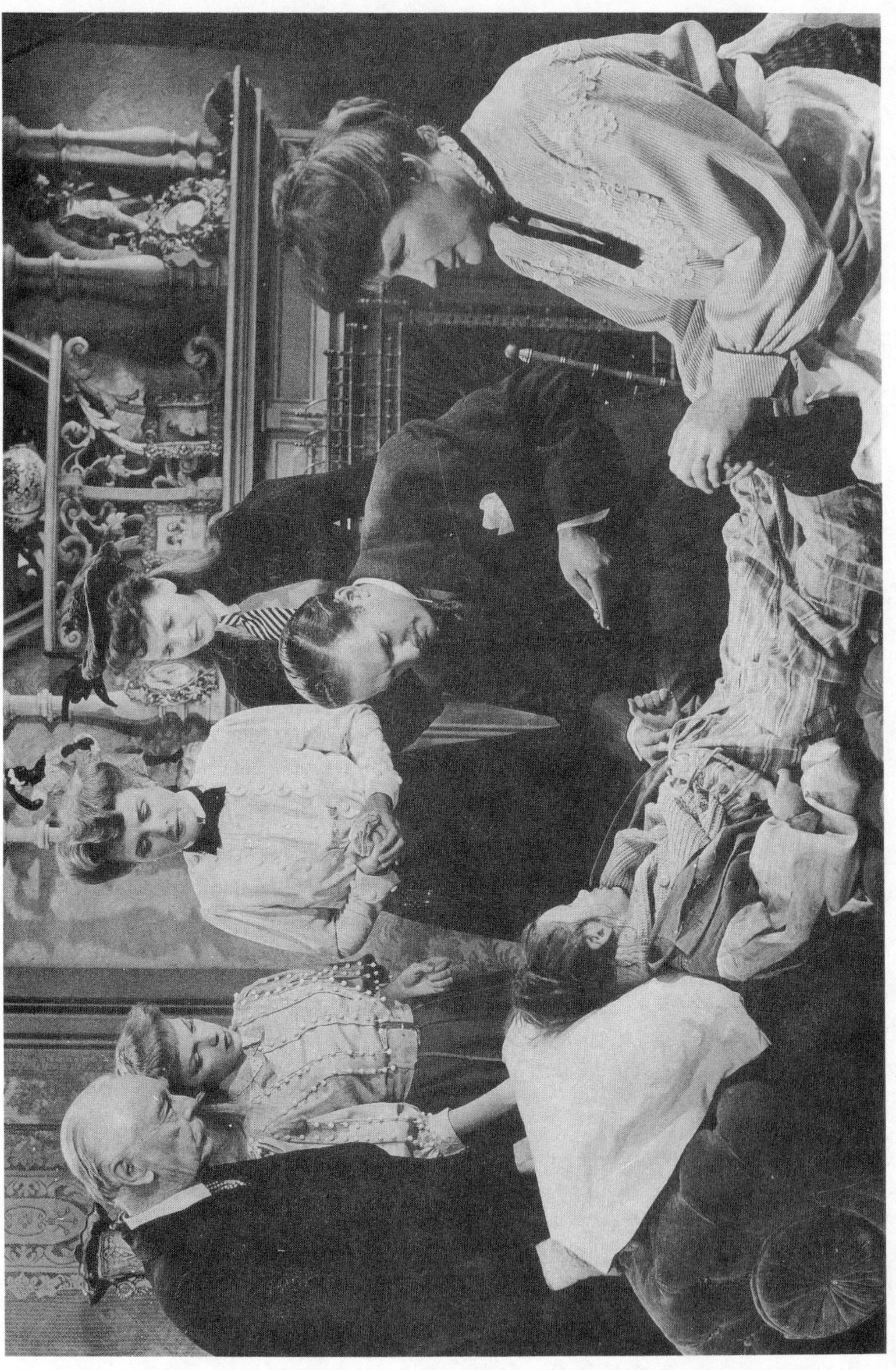

After we started filming, she had trouble getting to the set, although this was not unusual for her. The same thing happened on most of her pictures. But she was away a lot during *Meet Me in St. Louis* which caused the film to run way overtime and escalated the already sizeable budget. I'd arrive in the morning all ready to work, then wait around till someone would tell me, "Forget it. Judy's not coming." It's all been extensively written about over the years. Judy was a bit on the neurotic side; I don't think she slept well. Just as she would finally get to sleep in the morning it would be time to get up again and go to work. So she'd keep on sleeping. When she did show up, though, she was just great. We got along well. She could be very amusing.

It was a joy to work with Margaret O'Brien, Mary Astor, Tom Drake, Leon Ames and the other actors, too.

I didn't have much dialogue with Marjorie Main, who portrays the family cook, but it was obvious that she was quite a character. The first day on the set, I sneezed a couple of times. Although she was famous for playing the slovenly "Ma Kettle," I learned that she was a fanatic about germs. She became hysterical. "Who is that person sneezing?" she kept crying out. "Who is that person sneezing?" When she would talk on the phone, she would wear a little white surgical mask.

Everyone adored our director, Vincente Minnelli. He was very sensitive and creative. When we were doing our scenes, he would show us what he wanted by acting out all our roles, male and female, himself. I don't ever remember seeing MGM's boss, Louis B. Mayer, on the set. In my few dealings with him, he seemed like a kindly old gentleman. I know he loved to go dancing, frequently with Ann Miller.

Except for the delays, *Meet Me in St. Louis,* as memory and movie, is a delight.

Vanessa Brown—ACTRESS—

When I came to do my first film at 20th Century-Fox, *Margie,* I had three movies under my belt: Val Lewton's *Youth Runs Wild* plus *I've Always Loved You* and *Girl of the Limberlost.* I'd been at Warner Bros. for six months, Selznick for six months. I had done a play. I felt that my high school student role in *Margie* was a comedown. I always sort of seemed to be on the sidelines in it.

Paul Kohner was handling me, and he brought me to Fox. About two weeks after I was put under contract, Darryl F. Zanuck, the revered head of the studio, asked to see me. Everyone was saying, "People *never* see Zanuck! How did you manage it?" When I went in to his office, he was playing with his croquet mallet. I was very ambitious, had gotten rave notices and was very full of myself in

those days. I was not humbled in front of Darryl Zanuck. He said, "We're going to do big things for you, make you a star." Then he said, "That'll be all."

Right away I was given this role in *Margie,* which I considered a bit. I made four more movies at Fox: *The Late George Apley, The Ghost and Mrs. Muir, Mother Wore Tights* and *The Foxes of Harrow.* None were great parts, but the publicity department built me up and I became something you could sell. It became like a family there. Jean Peters, whom I met on the lot, is still my best friend. And shooting *Margie* was fun. They opened up the Sonja Henie ice stage for a scene in the picture, and we all ice-skated there and drank cocoa for about a month.

Much of the film was shot on location around the campus of the University of Nevada in winter. There was snow on the ground. We traveled there in a caravan of cars—colleagues, friends, mothers, everybody. When you go on location, people become very close.

The old-timer Henry King was the director. He never said much to me, but perhaps he worked more closely with our star, Jeanne Crain. You'd go in to see Mr. King and he'd talk about flying or your eyesight (I wore glasses)—he liked to give health tips, I guess. I was simply disgruntled at being reduced to such a minor role.

Lyle Wheeler, who ran the Fox art department, had to have been greatly responsible for the wonderful period look of the film; he was always one of the studio's greatest assets.

I was very close to the music department—I was born in Vienna. Kenny Williams was a Fox dance director with whom we studied. I remember one day we were practicing dancing when a young starlet named Marilyn Monroe came in and was staring at us. Nobody knew her.

"May I help you?" I said.

"Can I do that?" she asked.

I told her, "You can if you're under contract." She was, so I explained to her how to go about joining up. She seemed so shy.

I never got to know Jeanne Crain [Margie] very well, though she was wonderful in the picture. We didn't interact very much in the film. Most of her scenes were with Glenn Langan, Barbara Lawrence, Conrad Janis or Alan Young.

I have one Jeanne Crain story. Like all Hollywood studios then, Fox was very protective. For instance, if someone wanted you to do a layout for a magazine or newspaper, you told the publicity people and they cleared it, or not. Right after *Margie,* I remember being asked to go on a trip to a silver mine with Jeanne, her husband, Paul Brinkman, and some others, including my mother. Since Jeanne was one of the studio's top box office stars, I figured it must have been cleared with the publicity department. So we went. I forget where the silver mine was located, but it wasn't a long trip—just a weekend jaunt. We drove up in a Jeep or a van. We got up pretty high, and there were still two hours to go to get to the mine, when I finally said to Paul Brinkman, "Oh, let's go back. We've done the bit. It's getting dark and we'll have trouble going back down the cliffs." Some of the others continued on up to see the silver mine, but Jeanne, Paul, Mother and I went back down.

Not long afterward, I was in New York for something when the phone rang. A man said, "This is the district attorney's office. Do you, Jeanne Crain and Diana Lynn own a silver mine?" Now Diana Lynn wasn't even with us on the trip—she was off marrying someone. I told the man, "I don't own any silver stock. I wasn't given any stock. I wasn't told of any issue." And that was that.

Jeanne and her husband never said anything about getting involved in a silver mine, and I think they would have if there'd been anything to it. They had just said it would be a very exciting trip. If that was a prospectus meant to get investors, they never told us.

Margie was advertised as "the sweetheart of 1946," and for once they didn't exaggerate: it was a big hit. And I was pleasantly surprised to see that I was more in the thick of things on screen than I'd thought during the shooting.

In 1985, Conrad Janis, who plays the school heartthrob in *Margie,* and his girlfriend [Maria Grimm], thought it would be fun to have a reunion of the *Margie* company. I helped them get Howard Koch, who was a second assistant director on *Margie* and who went on to become a producer and head of Paramount Pictures, to give a *Margie* party in the Paramount commissary. The décor was 1928, the time of our film. The picture was screened, too, and among those attending were Jeanne Crain and Paul Brinkman, Glenn Langan, Alan Young, Barbara Lawrence, myself, Connie Janis, of course, and Jean Peters and her husband, Stanley Hough, who was third assistant director on the film. It was a wonderful chance for everyone to catch up on the last 40 years.

Macdonald Carey—ACTOR—

Nineteen forty-one was probably the greatest year of my life. I got my first big hit, the Broadway musical *Lady in the Dark,* with Gertrude Lawrence. I got married. And I was signed by Paramount Pictures. I only wish I could remember it all better, but I was well on my way to becoming an alcoholic. Finally, in 1982, when I felt I was near death, I joined Alcoholics Anonymous and got my life together at last. I haven't had a drink since and have never felt better.

My first film in Hollywood was a little quickie called *Dr. Broadway,* but my second, *Take a Letter, Darling,* was a major romantic comedy directed by Mitchell Leisen and co-starring Rosalind Russell and Fred MacMurray. Fred became a good friend, a sort of mentor who showed me the ropes. He was never a great actor but a very rudimentary guy who had done a remarkable job of surviving. Actors then not only had to please an audience but had to have the political sense to please people around them as well. Fred learned all this.

When we were completing *Take a Letter, Darling,* Fred advised me, "Never stay for the wrap party, Mac." I couldn't understand why he said this. Well, I found out. At the start of the party, some grips came up to tell me what a great guy I was. By the time they had had their second drinks, they were slapping me on the back. After the third round, I was "that stuck-up actor bastard."

As we talk, Fred is very ill, which makes me so sad. At the last presentation of the American Cinema Awards down in Orange County, I shared the limousine to the event with Jane Greer, Ann Rutherford and Fred's wife, June Haver. I could see that it was painful for her to talk about him, and by the time we dropped her at home afterwards, Fred's name had barely been mentioned.

Roz Russell was a lot of fun. After our first love scene in *Take a Letter, Darling,* she remarked to Mitch Leisen and the rest of the cast that I was a most able actor. She was distressed, though, that I ate garlicky salads for lunch. Some years later, we met again and I hoped she would remember our love scenes. Instead, she asked, "Are you still eating garlic?"

Mitch was another great booster of mine. He really took a shine to me and was grooming me. I was one of the few new actors who could do

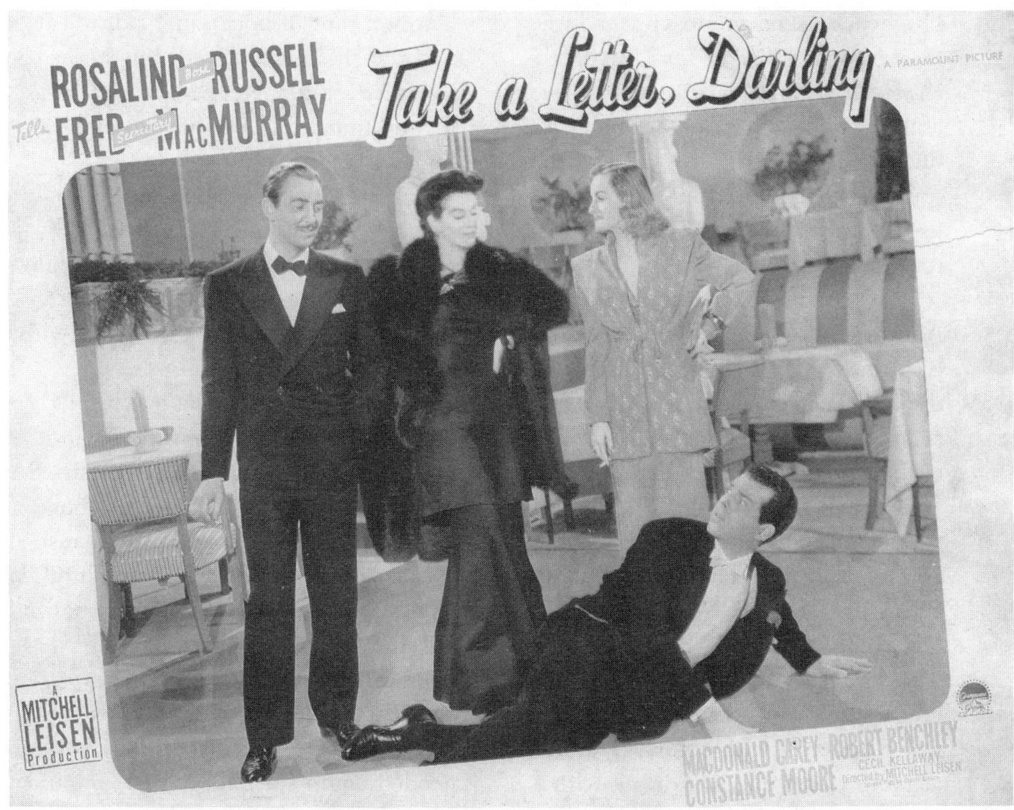

comedy as well as serious roles. If I hadn't gone off to war, which left a gap of several years in my career, I probably would have been brought along at Paramount like Fred MacMurray. Mitch would have pushed me into everything. He certainly used me whenever he could anyway.

We were all riddled by fear and booze when we did the war film *Wake Island* early in 1942. World War II had just begun, and none of us in the primarily male cast felt any restraints.

Most of *Wake Island* was shot at Salton Sea at the southern edge of California's Imperial Valley, near the Mexican border, though later we did some process shots and built some mock-up trenches back at Paramount. It was a murderous location, probably just as rough as anything they were experiencing overseas in the real war. The wind was high and the sand was blowing into our eyes, our ears, our mouths, our food. If it hadn't been for the camaraderie we all felt—Bob Preston, Walter Abel, Bill Bendix and Brian Donlevy, who was sort of a father figure to us—the ordeal would have been unendurable. It was a springboard for me to a lot of male bonding I would experience very shortly in the Marines. In fact, a large number of the company joined the Marine Corps after the picture was completed. It was a great recruiting film—even for *us!*

On the same day that I was accepted into the Marines, Alfred

Hitchcock asked me to appear in his new suspense thriller for Universal, *Shadow of a Doubt.* Fortunately, I was able to squeeze it in before being inducted. *Shadow* remains the best picture I ever appeared in—Hitchcock used to say that it was his favorite, too.

Hitch was a real family man. And to be part of his cast was to be part of his family—to be taken into the fold. You hear about this so-called "dark side" of Alfred Hitchcock. There have been books written about it. It's a lot of crap, something somebody picked up in some school. He loved people. He never treated actors like "cattle." Not long ago, I talked about this to Jimmy Stewart who was directed by Hitchcock several times. Jimmy agreed that Hitch was wonderful with actors. You ate at table with him, you drank with him, you visited his home. His daughter, Pat Hitchcock, is still a friend of mine. The Hitchcocks were Catholic and so am I. Everything conspired to make us friends.

Joseph Cotten plays a murderer of middle-aged women and I play the detective who is after him. Teresa Wright is Cotten's niece. Teresa and I also did another film together, *Count the Hours,* in the fifties, and is a friend to this day. This, despite the fact that I put her through a real test of friendship near the end of the picture. I never drank while working, but on this particular day I had a terrific hangover and the shakes. They couldn't get this scene between Teresa and me because I was shaking so much. Finally, Hitch, who also liked to drink (though hardly as much as I), instructed, "Get Mr. Carey a pint of bourbon!" I drank it and the shaking stopped, but I was so ashamed. The incident was a signpost for me that I had become an alcoholic.

After the war, I had my first starring role in an "A" picture, *Hazard,* directed by George Marshall who had worked with so many early comedy stars. Paulette Goddard, with whom I made several films and whom I adored, was the leading lady. She was then married—more than a little shakily—to Burgess Meredith. I remember her confiding to me that she didn't like him to drink "because it makes his face look like a potato." I wondered what mine reminded her of? She was a shrewd businesswoman. She told the studio she'd use her own seven-piece luggage set for an early scene, then when they were needed again she charged Paramount $50 a bag for each day they were used in a shot.

There are a number of delightful slapstick routines in *Hazard,* thanks to George Marshall, who really knew how to work these things out. I worked closely with George on several of the bits, including the one where I hit character actor Fred Clark, his toupée falls forward over his face and I lift it up to hit him again. I enjoy doing comedy more than anything. Sometimes, on my TV soap *Days of Our Lives,* which I have been doing for 25 years, the writers put in comedy bits for me because they know I like to do them.

I really thought *Dream Girl* was a plum, the big one that was going to put me over the top. Betty Hutton, the queen of the Paramount lot then, was going to play the title role, and I would be her co-star. It had been a hit Broadway play with Betty Field and Wendell Corey and my friend Mitch Leisen was going to direct. What could go wrong? Everything.

Most important, the concept was wrong. The appeal of the play was that it was about a poor girl who had nothing so she daydreamed herself into exciting situations. When he did the film, Mitch changed her to a Park Avenue heiress. Who cared about a spoiled Barbara Hutton? If given a chance, Betty could have played the hell out of the original character. She herself had been a poor little girl from Battle Creek, Michigan.

People at Paramount were always telling Betty what a big star she was. She had too many "yes" people around her. We'd all go to the rushes and in would come Betty with her vocal coach, her hairdresser and the cutter. They'd laugh only at her close-ups and stare at the screen when we other peasants came on. The first cut of the picture was one long close-up of Betty Hutton. The preview was a disaster. They put a little of me back in for the second preview (mostly two-shots with Betty), and it was slightly better received. Finally, they put all the other actors' close-ups back, too, and the picture was released. Nobody went. The sympathy for the character wasn't there. The concept, which had succeeded on the stage in Elmer Rice's play, had been altered too drastically.

Nothing we did on *Dream Girl* seemed to work out. For a phone conversation with Betty's character, I had to disguise my voice so I decided to talk through my nose. This gave the bit the humor it needed. After the picture was finished, the sound man said to me, "I know you had a cold the day you did that phone scene, but don't worry. When I mixed the sound, I fixed your voice up so you don't sound so nasal."

A few years ago, the Catholic Church gave Betty Hutton an award at our annual communion breakfast. I attended and Betty and I kissed and reminisced. A while later, she called and asked me to visit her in Rhode Island where she's teaching little children in school. She had incredible problems but turned her life around, too. Unfortunately, I've been too busy to get there to see her yet. Along with my continuing role as Dr. Tom Horton on *Days of Our Lives,* I've written three books of poetry and now an autobiography entitled—what else?—*The Days of My Life.*

Marguerite Chapman——ACTRESS—

Originally, I had no intention of becoming an actress. I was a top Powers model in New York, and when I began to think of what I would do in the future decided I might like to become fashion editor for *Vogue* or something like that.

I was going with Sherman Fairchild of Fairchild Aircraft and Cameras. He was a lovely, self-made man. I'd heard that Howard Hughes was looking for a leading lady for a film he was planning to produce and direct called *The Outlaw,* so simply as a matter of course I dropped off a picture at his New York office. I didn't know anything about the role, but models always did this when such things came up.

That week Sherman and I were having dinner at "21" when he suddenly asked, "What do you want to do in the future? Have you ever thought of becoming an actress?" He mentioned that Howard Hughes was looking for someone for *The Outlaw,* adding that he shortly would be seeing Hughes at a cocktail party.

"Would you like to go? I'll introduce you. But don't mention *The Outlaw,*" he advised.

We went. When Hughes saw Sherman, he walked across the room to us. "Let the men talk," I thought, and strolled off to say hello to some people. Instinctively, I also figured, "This way, Hughes can get a good look at me."

I continued modeling. My philosophy was, "If it happens, it happens." One day Sherman called to say that Hughes wanted me to do a screen test at his Long Island studio. It was a visual test, no dialogue. You sat on a chair and they kind of turned you around. Hughes liked the test and signed me to a contract with an option.

When I was boarding the plane to go to Hollywood, Sherman spied Olivia de Havilland who was returning from a promotional tour for *Gone with the Wind.* I was a real greenhorn at traveling, so he asked her to look after me. When I was ready to retire to my berth, Olivia explained how I should do it and gave me two sleeping pills. Nevertheless, all night long I heard a strange rat-a-tat-tat. It turned out that ice had formed on the wings; we were grounded in Kansas City. We had to railroad it to Albuquerque, and from there we flew to Los Angeles. On the train, Olivia and I dined together a couple of times. Once, there were some people who asked me if they could meet her, and she very sweetly came over, met them and went back to her friends. When I was getting off the plane in Los Angeles, I saw Olivia getting into her chauffeur-driven limousine with an expression on her face that seemed to say, "Thank God that's over!"

It was Christmas Eve afternoon, 1939. I was met by Lee Murin, who worked for Howard Hughes. Later, Lee and his wife Winnie would chaperone me around town. Hughes also had Pat di Cicco, Cubby Broccoli and Bruce Cabot squire me here and there. When I met Hoagy and Ruth Carmichael, they gave me advice appropriate for a young girl visiting Hollywood for the first time. They told me to keep away from my three escorts and to stay at the Beverly Hills Hotel. I did everything they told me not to. Pat, Cubby and Bruce were like big brothers to me. And I stayed at the Knickerbocker Hotel because I could walk to the stores from there.

On New Year's Eve, my three escorts took me to a party at Jack Warner's home. I met everybody! The stairs leading down to his playroom were covered by a treacherously deep shag rug, my heel got caught and I tripped! I was so embarrassed. When I looked up, there was Errol Flynn playing pool. His wife, Lily Damita, was standing nearby, but that didn't stop him from asking me, "Would you like to have dinner sometime?" I replied, "If your wife comes along."

I was introduced to Jack Warner's wife, Ann, a darling lady. She took me around and I met Charles Boyer, Ann Sheridan and so many others. Boyer was the only one who actually stood up and said, "How do you do?"—everybody was so wrapped up in their partying. Then Ann Warner introduced me to Forrest Tucker who took over her job of showing me around. I had a great time. Afterward, I made Bruce Cabot take me to six o'clock mass. He slept through it.

I finally met Howard Hughes. He took me to dinner. To prepare for my test for *The Outlaw,* he made an appointment for me to see a drama coach. We chose a scene from an Irene Dunne movie for me to do in the test. When I was being groomed to film it, the make-up people said, "Aren't you nervous?" And I answered, "Am I supposed to be?" I didn't know any better. Hughes, who was directing the test, told me the blocking—where to move. I said, "I'd rather do it this way," showing him what I meant. "I'll feel more comfortable." The crew was amazed that I spoke to him like that.

It was a very ladylike test. After all, it was a scene from an Irene Dunne picture. And the girl in *The Outlaw* was certainly no lady. Later, Hughes told me, "You're too much of a lady for me and too much of a lady for the film. I'm going to send your test to Joe Schenck," chairman of the board at 20th Century-Fox Pictures.

Fox signed me. Lew Schreiber, the studio's talent executive, called me to his office. He asked how much money I wanted. I had made 300 to 350 dollars a week as a model, which was top money then. But for some reason, I said, "A hundred dollars a week." This was a big mistake, one that plagued me throughout my career.

Schreiber went on to say that Mr. and Mrs. Darryl Zanuck [production chief at Fox] and Mr. and Mrs. Joe Schenck were dining at Ciro's the following evening and wanted me to join them. I stammered that my trunks hadn't all arrived yet, but he merely asked, "Do you have a dinner gown?"—meaning a long one. I did have a white gown, and a friend at the Studio Club, where I was now living, had a beautiful long red cape that she let me borrow for the occasion. Schenck arrived to pick me up with his whole entourage of chauffeur and footman and we went on to Ciro's. While we were having cocktails, Hedy Lamarr joined us in a white gown and long red cape, too. Cameras were popping like crazy. I thought, "I've arrived!" When the photos came out, they were all focused on Hedy. All you could see of me was my shoulder.

Joe Schenck, who was very short, asked me to dance. I towered over him, but I got through it. Then Zanuck, who was also short, asked me to dance. I said, "I'm sorry. I don't like to dance with men who are shorter than I am." Another mistake. In New York, though, a short man would never ask a taller girl to dance.

I made a couple of "B" pictures and went to drama school on the lot, but my option was dropped after six months. Then I went over to Warner Bros., where I stayed for a year and did a few small roles. Next, I joined Columbia Pictures where my career as an actress finally took off. I played leads in several "B"s until I got my first "A," the war drama *Destroyer,* with Edward G. Robinson and Glenn Ford. Robinson was a charming man, but I remember that he grew increasingly concerned because he was shorter than I, cast as his daughter. (Here we go again.) One day he asked the director, William A. Seiter, if I could wear low-heeled shoes for our close shots together. I said, "Okay. I always wear flats when my feet are not on camera anyway. But the high heels are already established in the long shots." If you look at the film, you'll notice that I am sitting down a lot.

I recall one of the first scenes I did with Glenn. By now, I had done many films and had gone to several drama coaches, including, then, the actress Josephine Hutchinson, from whom I learned more than I had from all of the others put together (although Sophie Rosenstein at Warners was very good). For this scene in *Destroyer,* Glenn and I were lining up a three-quarter shot together, almost a profile. As we did it, Glenn kept backing up and turning, which forced me to turn my face away from the camera—an old upstaging trick. I remarked to the director, "If he keeps doing this, we're going to have to move to the next stage." Mr. Seiter said, "Glenn—tsk-tsk. Naughty-naughty."

After another scene which had gone well, in my euphoria I went up to Glenn, who was with some friends, and kissed him lightly on the cheek. "Hey," he exclaimed loudly, "I'm engaged!" I certainly wasn't on the make.

Counter-Attack, opposite Paul Muni, was another important picture for me. I play "Comrade Lisa," a Russian guerrilla. A lot of gals had tested for the part, including Nina Foch. Max Arnow, who was talent head at Columbia and more or less my champion there, called to tell me, "Go and see Zoltan Korda. He's producing and directing *Counter-Attack.* I've already called Wardrobe. No make-up and straggly hair." I was on my way to see Zolie Korda, looking a wreck but right in character for the role I hoped to get, when I ran into Charles Vidor, one of the studio's top directors. He took one look at me and sighed, "You girls will do anything to get in movies."

When I saw Korda, he said, "You're just what I want. You look like a boy, but I know there's a woman underneath all that."

I didn't meet Paul Muni until we started the picture. My first scene had a group of us looking at a map. Later, we had to shoot it over again, partly because of my hair, which was swept up. Harry Cohn, the head of Columbia, had a real thing about hair. For some reason he wanted my hair down, so that's how it was when we re-did the scene.

Mr. Muni was one of the industry's most prestigious actors and a very intense man. We were never introduced. Actors rarely were, really. You just went in and did your job. However, I made a point of introducing myself to his wife, Bella. Then one time he just strolled over and talked. We got into a rather intellectual discussion. He seemed to take a fatherly interest in me and was trying to see whether I had any brains or not.

Eventually we got to rehearsing what was essentially his long soliloquy in *Counter-Attack.* His dialogue seemed endless. I was lying injured in the background rubble of the bombed-in cellar. Mr. Muni, as the one-time Russian sailor who now holds several German soldiers captive at gunpoint, hasn't slept in days. He can barely keep his eyes open. I give him a couple of short cues and, leaning on his rifle, he talks and talks and talks. He talks about the new ships that will sail the ocean after the war, ships without guns. "We'll shout to each other, 'Ahoy, brother!' Black man, white man, yellow man. . . ."

Mr. Muni's biggest concern was, "If *I'm* falling asleep, what is the audience going to do?" Observing him was a lesson in acting to me. The set was so tense. People stopped breathing as he continued on and on. I could feel him tensing up. I thought, "He's going to blow." Suddenly, I looked up and asked, "Have you read Freud, Mr. Muni?" He threw the gun down and said, "Don't you have anything else to do?" I replied, "Nope." The tension was broken, everyone breathed again and Mr. Muni got the scene in one take.

There were a lot of Germans in the cast of *Counter-Attack.* World War II was still on, and one of them was cited on Hollywood Boulevard for wearing his Nazi SS boots from the film.

Many of the others on the picture carried Commie cards, with the notable exceptions of Zolie Korda, Mr. Muni and myself. John Howard Lawson, who wrote it, went on to become one of the jailed "Hollywood 10." And Larry Parks, one of the actors, was later blacklisted when he admitted once having been a member of the Communist party.

Pardon My Past, which I did with Fred MacMurray, was more fun, a romantic comedy. On the first day of shooting, Fred said to me, "Which is your favorite side?" I replied, "My left." He had just done his umpteenth picture with Claudette Colbert, whom everyone knew always insisted that only the left side of her face be photographed, and he told me, "You're going to get your right. My neck is out of joint from having to keep playing to Claudette's left side!" Fred and Leslie Fenton, who directed, were also the producers, so I said, "Okay, boss."

I'm never late. *Almost* never. On a movie set, that's a strict no-no. But one day during the filming I forgot to set my alarm clock and showed up late. I was apologizing when I noticed that Fred wasn't there and thought, "My God, he's walked off because of me!" Later, they told me that he'd gone to the dentist, but I never knew whether or not he went because I wasn't there. We came in way under budget, though.

The night of the wrap party, Harry and Joan Cohn wanted me to come to dinner. It would have been

very rude of me, though, not to attend the festivities with my fellow workers, so I went to the party and then raced over to the Cohns. Late again. They were all seated and I apologized. Harry said, "If you'd been here earlier, I'd have given you nylons." Because of the war, nylon stockings were very hard to get then and he'd been giving them out. But I had plenty at home and told Harry so.

I was wearing this cute little dress that I'd bought at Lanz. Harry said, "Where did you get that dress?" I told him.

"How much did you pay for it? I'll pay for it."

I looked at Buddy Adler, later head of production at Fox and seated with his wife, Anita Louise. Buddy nodded as if to say, "Go ahead, tell him."

So I said, "I paid $75, my week's salary. Aren't you ashamed?"

I always talked like that to Harry. He was always calling me into his office. I think he enjoyed sparring with me.

Relentless is another favorite of mine. I was at Lakeside Country Club one afternoon, playing golf, when I ran into Don "Red" Barry, the cowboy actor. Over lunch, he told us that he'd found this book called *Three Were Thoroughbreds* which he'd brought to Gene Rodney and Robert Young. They were going to produce it as a major Technicolor Western for Columbia release, with Bob Young starring. Don said, "Marguerite, you're just right for the tomboyish leading lady. I'll mention it to them." Don was a hustler, which, when you had a family to support, you sometimes had to be in Hollywood. Still, I got hot. Afterward, I said to one of the gals at the club, "That's my studio. I'll push myself!"

I went to see Gene and Bob at Columbia. "If you don't give me this part," I said, "I'm going up and tell Uncle Harry." I had never done anything like that before, but I knew it was a good part. Gene said, "I think this little Irish lass can do it." He always called me the "little Irish lass." We filmed in Tucson, Arizona, under George Sherman's direction, and it turned out to be one of my best pictures. I enjoyed working with Bob Young. He was very warm, a real pro. Many years later, I appeared on his TV series *Marcus Welby, M.D.,* with him.

I acted in just about everything possible in movies in those years—"A"s, "B"s, serials, short subjects, even trailers ("Prevues of Coming Attractions"). And loved every minute of it.

Nancy Coleman—ACTRESS—

I was a New York actress who had done theater and a lot of radio. When Warner Bros. wanted to test me for pictures, I insisted that it be done in Hollywood. Two years before, Paramount had tested me in New York but it didn't turn out well. Naturally, it was important to look good, and I knew the cameramen were much better in California.

I had a very peculiar contract with Warners. I went out with a 13-week contract for a certain amount of money specifically for tests. I tested for several pictures, including *They Died with Their Boots On,* with Errol Flynn, and *Kings Row,* with Ronald Reagan. In five or six weeks, my option was picked up and I signed a long-term contract with Warners for more money. What's more, although several other actresses also had tested for the role (among them, Warners' Elizabeth Fraser), I was assigned to make my film debut in *Kings Row.* The part was a very dramatic one: "Louise Gordon," who, when she discovers that her doctor father (played by Charles Coburn) needlessly has amputated the legs of her boyfriend (Ronald Reagan), almost goes mad.

I'd read Henry Bellamann's best-seller and couldn't imagine how they were going to get around some of the sensational material in the novel, particularly the incest theme. I knew it would be tricky. When I read the script, I saw that screenwriter Casey Robinson had changed the incest problem to insanity; audiences seemed to accept this. But I thought this kind of censorship all wrong. In those days, you could show a shower

ANN SHERIDAN
as tempting 'RANDY'
ROBT. CUMMINGS
as handsome 'PARRIS'
RONALD REAGAN
as irresistible 'DRAKE'
BETTY FIELD
as stormy 'CASSIE'
Kings Row
RE-RELEASED BY DOMINANT PICTURES CO

and a sink but you couldn't show a toilet!

Our director, Sam Wood, was a very relaxed man who gave the actors very little direction. He'd tell me about hitting my mark, which for some reason I never had any problem doing, but not much else. I'm sure that if I were doing anything wrong, however, he would have told me. I was completely at ease under his direction.

Our cinematographer, James Wong Howe, did a great job. At the time he owned a Chinese restaurant on Ventura Boulevard. One evening after the picture came out, my mother and I were dining there and Jimmy came over to our table. He told my mother, "You know, I would have made your daughter prettier but they wouldn't let me." It seems that one of the stars [Betty Field], who was a fine actress but not a beauty, was always being told in the script that she was "the prettiest girl in town," and the studio didn't want to point up the discrepancy with too much competition. It was bad enough that "oomph girl" Ann Sheridan—a lovely, warm woman, by the way—was one of the other stars.

William Cameron Menzies, our distinguished production designer, was so funny. He told me about his family, a very important Scotch clan, having once owned this great ancestral castle. He went to Scotland to buy it back, stopping first at a local pub. He related his reason for being there to the bartender, who asked, "Have you seen the place?" Menzies said he hadn't. The bartender said, "It's just a pile of stone!" Which is what it turned out to be. Unlivable, really.

I could have had some of Menzies' exquisite sketches for *Kings Row,* if I had asked. But I didn't, I don't know why. One can be very silly when one is young.

Robert Cummings, another of our stars, was also a delight. He, too, had a wonderful sense of humor and was most helpful to the novice. He'd sit and listen to my lines in one of the portable dressing rooms. We *learned* our lines then. We didn't improvise all over the place like they do today. Improvisation is a good exercise if you're in a classroom, but not, I feel, when you're doing actual scenes. Today, it's gotten out of hand. There is too much improvisation in films now, and it's all too apparent.

What can I tell you? Everything seemed to go smoothly on Kings Row. I didn't observe anything very exciting on the set—*including* Ronald Reagan. He was just a very nice young man who happened to be playing my boyfriend. Although Ron and I would chat on the set, I don't remember much of what we said, except that he was wearing contact lenses, which I'd never seen then, and he showed me how to use them. Someone I know who talked to him when he was still our President told me that he had asked about me. I don't know why. I'd said some bad things about him—as a politician. Unlike many, I never criticized Reagan as an actor. I liked him in *Kings Row;* I always liked him as an actor. A little while after *Kings Row,* we did *Desperate Journey* together, with Errol Flynn, and I liked him in that, too. He stood right up to Errol. The reason he is sometimes called "a bland actor" is, I think, because he usually had bland parts. Except for *Kings Row,* in which he plays the small-town rake and which even he says was his best picture.

Judith Anderson and Charles Coburn, cast as my parents, couldn't have been nicer. Judith, known for her heavy dramatic roles, had a surprisingly wicked sense of humor. And Charles was a dear. He was just finishing up another picture at Universal and was, I think, terribly tired from doing the two films. The scene where he slaps me had to be done many times. He'd slap me, then have to say my name, but he always got it wrong. He remembered that it began with an "L," but instead of exclaiming "Louise" after the slap it always came out "Lucille" or "Lillian." I got slapped so many times my face was swollen. He was so upset. He sent me a Christmas card every year after that until his death. I knew Charles before we did *Kings Row,* incidentally. The summer before, I had done stock with him.

I first saw *Kings Row* in the balcony of a local theater. In general, I was pleased. I had seen some of the dailies but not all of them. I'm so critical of myself that they made me uncomfortable. I was such a perfectionist and could see little things in my performance that I didn't like; happily, no one mentioned them.

Kings Row is my favorite film. Then comes *Edge of Darkness,* which I did with Errol Flynn, Ann Sheridan and, it seemed, New York's whole Group Theater transplanted to Hollywood. I play a tragic Polish girl who services Nazis. One of the main reasons I enjoyed this one was the director, Lewis Milestone. He never overshot, did not do take after take like some directors. He had been an editor, so he knew what was right. He was very easy to work with—you didn't get exhausted.

Things were going well at Warner Bros. until I decided to marry Whitney Bolton of their publicity department. The studio didn't want me to, and Charlie Einfeld, the publicity director, sat me down for a long time and tried to talk me out of it. They were afraid of a conflict of interests: that Whitney would give me either too much publicity or too little. They told him that if we married, it would be the end of his contract. We did, and it was. But he went right over to Columbia, so that was all right.

But they began giving me terrible scripts with sometimes only one scene for me in them. And I'd go on suspension rather than do them. Then I was asked to star in a 13-week radio series based on the Ingrid Bergman film *Intermezzo.* Warners refused to allow me to do it. I had two unreleased films at the time, was pregnant and could not act in films but *could* act in radio and still they said no.

They were not nice to me. I loved the people I worked with, but not the front office. Warners had built me up in the beginning, but they never starred me. Although I was John Garfield's leading lady in *Dangerously They Live,* I was given only featured billing. I was permitted stardom briefly in *Devotion,* a somewhat glamorized biography of the Brontës with Ida Lupino, Olivia de Havilland, Arthur Kennedy and myself as Ann Brontë. But I married and for some reason they held up its release for so long that by the time *Devotion* finally came out, I not only had become the mother of two children but already had left the lot. I was reduced to featured billing in the picture.

I remember *Devotion* for another unpleasant reason. For one scene, I had to stand next to a lighted candelabra. I was wearing an extravagant period costume with puffy sleeves which suddenly caught fire. I didn't know what to do! Suddenly, the elderly character actress Ethel Griffies, who was playing the Brontës' aunt, flew to my side and put the blaze out with her hands! The crew was just standing around with their mouths open.

Luther Davis—SCREENWRITER—

The Hucksters was the first movie I wrote.

I had just come out of the Air Force. During my last months in the service, I had a three-week leave during which I wrote a Broadway play called *Kiss Them for Me.* It was based on the novel *Shore Leave,* by Frederic Wakeman. When I got to Hollywood as a junior writer at MGM, making $500 a week (after my Air Force pay, a fortune), I met producer Arthur Hornblow, Jr. He was planning to film another Wakeman novel, the best-seller *The Hucksters,* and already had an adaptation by Edward Chodorov and George Wells. The fact that I had just written a play from another Wakeman novel probably influenced him to sign me to write the screenplay of *The Hucksters.* I worked from the Chodorov-Wells adaptation and the novel and was given a very prominent sole screenplay credit.

I wrote the screenplay in eight weeks. After I had turned it in, I ran into Horace McCoy, author of the novel *They Shoot Horses, Don't They?,* in a corridor at the studio. He said, "You fink! I've been on an assignment for 108 weeks! You're going to ruin this business for us!"

Metro had been looking for a strong vehicle for Clark Gable. Clark had come back from the Army without a contract at MGM, and he and his agents were being very coy. His first post-war film was *Adventure,* with Greer Garson, which he did on a one-picture deal. When it flopped, he announced, "I won't re-sign until you get me a decent picture." *The Hucksters* seemed the right property—it was a satire of radio, which was very big at the time. And the Wakeman novel was a smash. But Gable still had qualms. "I don't want to play a man who sleeps with a woman whose serviceman husband is overseas," he informed everybody. We made her a widow.

Arthur Hornblow smuggled the first half of the screenplay to Gable, without going through the proper channels. If Gable had turned it down, Arthur would have gone with Ray Milland for the part. Frankly, Milland would have been better—more adept at handling all the words that this character, a radio ad executive called Vic Norman, had to say. Gable was never comfortable with a lot of words. But he liked the first half of the screenplay, so when it was completed Arthur submitted the manuscript to him with proper Metro protocol. Gable liked it enough not only to sign for the picture but to re-sign with MGM. So there was tremendous enthusiasm for me on the lot because my script had brought "The King" back to Mother Metro. There were no real problems with Gable after that, although he did want me to insert a joke at the end of every scene.

When he came over during lunch at the studio to tell Arthur and me that he had accepted the role, I walked back to the administration building with him. As I strolled along with Clark Gable, I thought, "Now everyone will know my screenplay has been accepted and I'll be the envy of all who see us." But no one even noticed me! They were all looking at Gable. That was the magic of those glamorous old stars.

The director was Jack Conway, who'd been a silents director and was strictly a Hollywood guy who knew nothing of New York City, the setting of our story. (Another reason why I'd gotten the job: I was a New Yorker.) One day Conway came to me and said, "Listen, Luther, Clark Gable don't put his hat on in scenes." I had devised a scene where Gable putting his hat on at the end of a scene led to another bit of business in the next scene. "Why don't Gable put on a hat in scenes?" I asked. And Conway told me, "Because he's got big ears and he's got to put his hat on in front of a mirror and it wouldn't look right for him to do that. Find another way to end the scene." And I did.

I liked Gable. We both had an interest in fast cars. So we talked about cars. He wasn't very interested in the artistic life.

Gable's leading lady, in her first American film, is Deborah Kerr. If she was presented a little stiffly, it's because MGM was overwhelmed by the idea that the character she was playing was such a lady. (My wife was in the Social Register, and this may be one more reason why they thought of me for the screenplay.) Anyway, they also were rather in awe of Deborah herself, treating her like this great legitimate actress who'd deigned to join MGM. She was a very talented *movie* actress. I knew her only from her British films, but when she was cast I was in New York and wrote her a note welcoming her to the project and wishing her good luck. Years later, I got to know Deborah and she told me that while she was very happy to receive Luther Davis' good wishes, at the time she didn't know who the hell I was!

It was because she had done so well in *The Killers* that we wanted Ava Gardner for *The Hucksters.* One night during the shooting Arthur Hornblow and I (neither of us lacking in ego) and our wives were dining at Chasen's Restaurant when Ava made a big entrance. Passing our table, she said "Hello, George" to

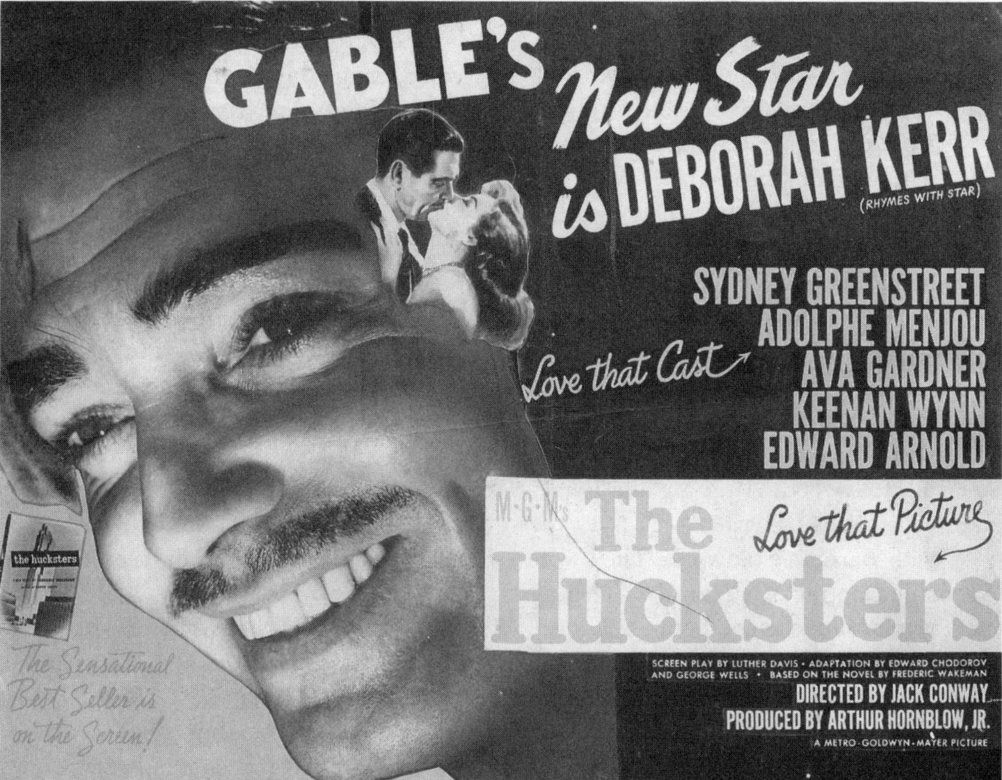

Arthur and "Hello, Everett" to me. Our wives thought we'd be annoyed that she didn't know us, but Arthur and I were too entranced by her loveliness. Aware of our normal egos, Leonora, Arthur's wife, remarked, "When you two fellows are not upset at being mistaken for someone else—*that's* beauty!"

Harold Rosson, who photographed *The Hucksters,* would spend a whole day on Ava's close-ups. Arthur wasn't overly concerned with budget, but at one point he did ask Rosson why he was taking all day. Sighed Hal, "Because it's such a pleasure!"

Sydney Greenstreet is wonderful in the picture as the eccentric soap advertiser Evan Llewellyn Evans. He was based on the man in charge of Lucky Strike cigarette advertising, George Washington Hill, for whom author Frederic Wakeman had worked. We purposely had Greenstreet wear a hat completely different from that worn by Hill, and we had him use pet phrases unlike Hill's, too, so there would be no legal problems with the real man. When the first draft of the script went to MGM's legal department, they (not knowing how we had purposely altered things) wanted everything changed to the way Hill *did* dress and talk. We kept it the way it was done originally, though.

I also met Joe Breen, who was the head censor then. I was in Arthur's office one day when in came this big, breezy Irishman who passed me by to go directly to Arthur and say, "Well, what kind of shit are you perpetrating now?" Replied Arthur, "Meet Luther Davis. He wrote the shit."

Later on, Breen said, "You can't have this upper class lady, a general's wife, sleeping around." So when it came time for Deborah to rendezvous with Gable, we made the setting a hotel that was so tacky she refused to go through with it.

After my work was done, my wife and I returned to New York. I thought of myself as a New York writer who had enjoyed an interlude in Hollywood. After a while I was called back to write *B.F.'s Daughter,* with Barbara Stanwyck. They were still shooting *The Hucksters.* They were doing a scene between Gable and Adolphe Menjou in a taxi. Arthur asked me to look at it, saying, "Those two men in a little taxi—that's not MGM."

"What do you want?" I asked. "Grand Central Station?"

In a day or two, there was Grand Central Station, reconstructed on the MGM lot for Gable and Menjou to act their scene in.

For its preview, we took *The Hucksters* to the Loyola Theater near the airport in Inglewood. There was the flashing sign, "Sneak Preview . . . Sneak Preview." All the studio brass was there. You could feel the excitement rising in the theater as the audience began to realize what it was going to see. When the title came on, here was an explosion of applause and cheers. It was a triumph for all of us.

However, Clark said to us, "I know I did it with no complaints, but now that I've seen it I just can't let the Jew scene go through." There was a scene where Gable's character said to Edward Arnold something like, "If you renege on this deal, people are going to say the Jew reneged on it." Gable went on, "I don't want to gamble on something that might be construed as anti-Semitic." So, before the film was released, we re-wrote the scene and it was re-filmed. Now the agent was involved in some society that was rehabilitating criminals and Gable says, "If you renege on this, people will say a former convict did it and you'll just prove they can't be rehabilitated."

I got a $50,000 bonus, which came in especially handy because my wife was pregnant at the time.

I was told that when MGM bought *The Hucksters,* it was over the objections of studio boss Louis B. Mayer. He was extremely conservative and felt that one industry shouldn't pick on another, especially a sister business like radio. But he was voted down by his executives.

Some time after *The Hucksters,* I had a contract dispute with MGM. I went to the studio's Benny Thau, then to Eddie Mannix, neither of whom could talk me out of my stand. When all else failed, you were sent to Mr. Mayer. He couldn't persuade me, either, but he sure tried. He said, "At MGM we're a family, and we want to see you grow. We don't want you to stay a writer. We want you to become a producer. We have a little ceremony when this happens where I break your pencil." But I stood my ground. I didn't want to be a producer.

Afterward, in the long hallway leading to Mayer's office, my agent asked, "What did he say?"

"He said I reminded him of Irving Thalberg."

"Let's get out of here," shuddered my agent. "He hated Irving Thalberg!"

Laraine Day—ACTRESS—

The Locket is my favorite film, but I almost didn't get it.

It came about after an executive from United Artists visited my house one evening. In the course of conversation, he said he'd read an excellent script by Sheridan Gibney called *What Nancy Wanted* and that I should take a look at it. I did, loved it and told my agent about it. He went to RKO to talk to the producer I'd just worked for about my doing it. Suddenly, Bill Dozier, who was running RKO then, got hold of the script and wanted it for his wife, Joan Fontaine. But we all put up such a battle that we finally got it.

The title was changed to *The Locket.*

One of the things "Nancy wanted" was men. I loved working with Brian Aherne, who was also in the earlier *My Son, My Son,* which had helped my career tremendously. I remember when I was just a kid hoping to be an actress, I'd seen Brian playing this flamboyant character in *The Great Garrick* and said to myself, "Someday I'm going to make a picture with him." And I made *two.* Ricardo Cortez was also in *The Locket,* and he was another girlhood idol. Gene Raymond was charming, too, and I already knew Robert Mitchum, who plays a wonderful character in *The Locket,* from the Long Beach Players Guild, where we both acted on stage.

Although the story is a grim one, about a destructive young woman who's a kleptomaniac, the *Locket* set was great fun. We all had a good time because we were happy to be playing roles with a lot of meat on them. My character was the greatest challenge I ever had. The early Nancy is very talkative and vivacious, which I'd never been before on screen, and she goes through many changes and lifestyles. And, of course, she cracks up at the end.

The form of the film—flashbacks within flashbacks within flashbacks—was criticized by some reviewers of the time as too confusing. In those days, people used to walk into a theater in the middle of a picture and then stay to see what they had missed. You couldn't do that with *The Locket*—you'd be totally at sea. Today, though, I'm told its style is highly regarded by film historians.

A lot of its quality is due to our director, John Brahm. He was so strong, had such firm opinions and got the best from his whole company. Years later, I was signed to work with him again on an Alfred Hitchcock TV show. I was really looking forward to repeating our previous work experience. But this time he was very distant, so hurried. There simply was no time to create on TV in those days—maybe there still isn't. It was all so different from *The Locket,* and it kind of soured my memory of working with him on that first project.

I was well received in *The Locket* and got a "Best Performance of the Month" citation from *Photoplay* magazine. This seemed ironic, because a while before, when I was just starting out at Paramount, I wanted so badly to do a small role in Cecil B. DeMille's epic, *The Buccaneer.* But DeMille said I had no talent and couldn't have the part. "Get rid of her," he advised Paramount, and after six months they did just that.

Years passed. I'd been at MGM and had done, among other things, several of the popular Dr. Kildare features playing the sympathetic nurse, Mary Lamont. Although the technical advice we got on these pictures was woefully inferior to what is evident in today's medical movies, Mr. DeMille was now sufficiently impressed by the simple fact that I had played a nurse to hire me to play another in one of his lavish Paramount productions, *The Story of Dr. Wassell,* opposite Gary Cooper.

Around that time I also did *Mr. Lucky,* with Cary Grant—another of my favorite pictures. He was wonderful. He would arrive on the set and everybody's morale immediately lifted. And he kept it that way. The crew was crazy about him, and so was I. I was not the first choice for the role, though. They originally wanted Rita Hayworth but this was RKO, and she was at Columbia, and they couldn't get her. Looking back, it seems I was rarely first choice for any major picture I did. (Except for The Locket, which I fought for right from the start, and won—another reason why it's my favorite.) Frances Dee was already working on *My Son, My Son* when she became ill and I was called in to replace her.

The first thing I had done on my MGM contract was *I Take This Woman,* with Spencer Tracy and Hedy Lamarr. I tested for the part, but Louis B. Mayer, who ran the studio, didn't want me; he wanted Lana Turner for the role. However, Charles MacArthur, who wrote the original story, saw my test and wanted me. For weeks afterward, whenever Mr. Mayer saw rushes in the projection room they would slip in my test; he saw it over and over. Finally, he exclaimed, "Okay, okay, she's got the part!" But he was very angry and held this against me from then on. I did the Kildare films there, but he never really gave me a break. They'd loan me out. Most of the things I did at Metro were program pictures. Finally, they wanted me to do this WAC movie, *Keep Your Powder Dry,* with Lana Turner and Susan Peters. I didn't want to do it, but they said if I did it they would give me *Undercurrent,* with Robert Taylor. So I did the WAC picture. Then they gave *Undercurrent* to Katharine Hepburn, so I left MGM.

Another favorite was *Foreign Correspondent,* for Alfred Hitchcock. He was a character. When he directed, he told you everything—how to look, how to read your lines.

One of my least favorites was

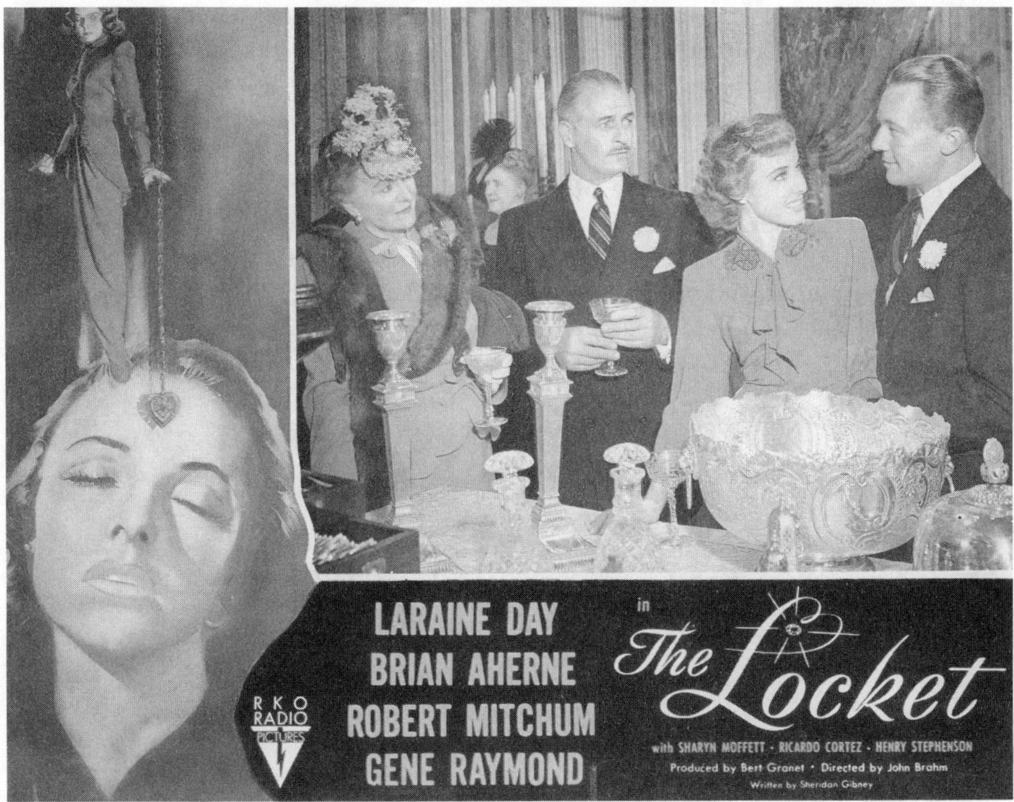

Without Honor, co-starring Dane Clark. Yet it was the best script I ever received. I play a cheating wife, and it was produced by the Hakim brothers, Raymond and Robert. Half-way through, however, they succumbed to censor pressure to whitewash and change my character to give the story a phony, weakly happy ending. I was glad when it proved such a disaster that no one went to see it.

To get back to *Mr. Lucky,* Cary Grant was a very happy fellow on the set, so it came as a bit of a shock to see the not-very-happy Cary away from the picture. Not long before, he had married the very, very rich Barbara Hutton. It was never really a good marriage, though, and Cary was trying to save it. You'd be working with one kind of man, and then go to a dinner party at his house where he'd be very quiet and turn everything over to Barbara completely. Later on, I was told that she had wanted to play my role in *Mr. Lucky* and had tried to persuade Cary to intercede on her behalf with RKO. They were divorced a couple of years later. Cary was very friendly to me during *Mr. Lucky,* but, curiously, I never felt the male-female chemistry that you sometimes experience on a set. I could have been talking to my best girlfriend, or a fine character actor. Maybe this, too, was because he was so involved trying to keep his marriage together—I don't know.

It was very similar to what I felt working with Robert Young, with whom I did pictures like *Dr. Kildare's*

Crisis, The Trial of Mary Dugan, Journey for Margaret and *Those Endearing Young Charms.* Although Bob has always projected this warmth, especially in his TV series *Father Knows Best* and *Marcus Welby, M.D.*, there was a coldness there. He was not unfriendly. We sat on the set and chatted, much as people sitting next to each other at a dinner party would chat. But he was not easy to get close to.

On the other hand, Lew Ayres, with whom I did all the Kildare movies and who projected such earnestness, had a pixiesh charm that he didn't get enough opportunity to show on the screen.

Many movie fans seem to remember me best from the Dr. Kildare series; but, to paraphrase the daughter in *I Remember Mama* (which I wasn't in), first and foremost *I* remember *The Locket.*

Rosemary DeCamp——*ACTRESS*—

I think the director, Michael Curtiz, hired me for *Yankee Doodle Dandy* because of the Kordas—Alexander, Zoltan and Vincent. I had just finished a July-to-November stint in their *Jungle Book,* and those Hungarians were a closely knit (and extraordinarily talented) group.

Anyway, Jimmy Cagney, our star, and Curtiz were fabulous. They matched each other in skill and ferocity. We began filming on the Monday morning after Pearl Harbor with tears and prayers as we heard President Roosevelt's grave voice declaring war on Germany and Japan. I think a lot of the amazing spirit of the picture is owed to that patriotic energy—the news then was *very* bad.

Cagney was a driving force. He came through the Warner Brothers gates every morning at six A.M. in an old Ford with a brown-bag lunch and worked till six P.M. Curtis was also tireless. He saw everything, from the tempo of a scene to a crooked seam in a dancer's tights. Joan Leslie, the leading lady, and Cagney's sister, Jeanne, were charming. We had a lot of fun, though we seemed to be rehearsing the musical numbers forever, as I am tone deaf and have too many feet. Shooting the big "Grand Old Flag" finale took days because it was on a treadmill with wind machines. Cagney was probably the only one who wasn't seasick. My right arm barely recovered from holding Miss Liberty's torch throughout the number.

Yankee Doodle Dandy was a fine picture at a time when our country needed it.

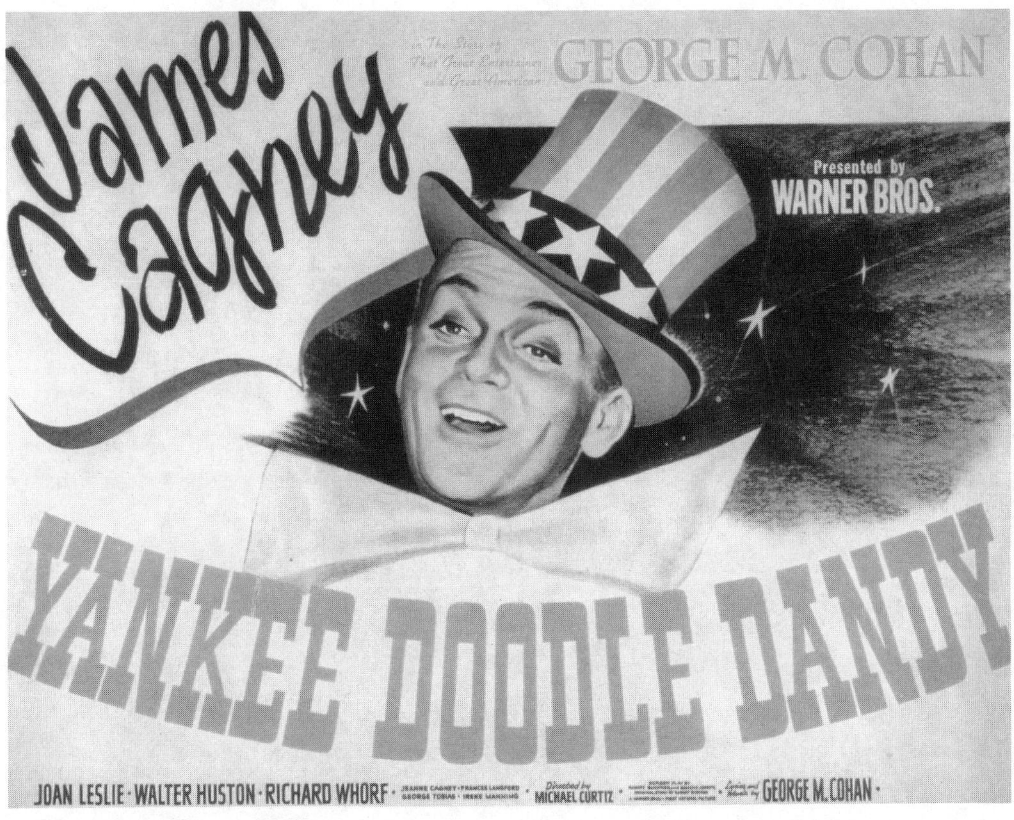

Myrna Dell—ACTRESS—

I know *The Spiral Staircase* was a big hit, but I've never seen it.

At the time I did it, I had been at RKO several months and had been steadily working my way up. I had just made a test for a film to be called *Tomorrow Is Here,* which was supposed to be directed by Ted Tetzlaff (who had been Carole Lombard's cameraman and later directed me in *Fighting Father Dunne*). It was the lead, a great part, a woman who was referred to in the script as "an animal"—which I loved. Everyone was very excited about it, and I was told, "This will make you a star." Suddenly, with no reason given that I can recall, the picture was shelved.

Then I got a call from Robert Siodmak to come about a film he was directing called *The Spiral Staircase.* Dore Schary was producing. I hadn't received the script yet, and I asked Siodmak what my part was. He said, "It's only one scene and the girl has no lines, but it's a wonderful part."

"One scene? No lines?" I said, wondering what was going on.

"No, you have no dialogue," he replied, quickly adding, "but neither does Dorothy McGuire, who goes through the whole movie with nothing to say."

Dorothy, it turned out, was

playing the very showy star role of a mute girl; I was to play a cripple who gets murdered at the beginning of the picture! "God," I said to Siodmak, "couldn't you at least take the limp away?" But no. So I did a bit role in *Spiral Staircase,* which I felt was a comedown after having been up for the lead in a film. And it cost me $15, too. I had just had a manicure and my nails were neatly polished, but they said, "The polish has to go. The story takes place early in the century and the girls didn't paint their nails then." It had to be scraped off. My hands, writhing as I was strangled, had more time on camera than I did!

Critics loved the picture, and business was great, but because of all this I never had any desire to see it.

My associations with Dore Schary, who produced *Spiral Staircase* and soon became head of RKO, were none too pleasant.

A year or so later, I was up for the role of the B-girl in *Crossfire* which won Gloria Grahame (who eventually got the part) an Academy Award nomination. It was done at my studio, RKO, and I knew the producer, Adrian Scott, the writer, John Paxton, and the director, Eddie Dmytryk. I also knew that the picture, the first to deal with anti-Semitism, would be an important one.

No one who had been set for *Crossfire* would test with me. They were aware that Dore Schary, now the boss, wanted Gloria Grahame, whom he knew from his MGM days, and they didn't want to get in bad with him. I asked my good friend Jane Greer to test with me, but she said, "Oh, Myrna, everyone would laugh at us." She was probably right: we were known around the studio for our hijinks. Then Jacqueline White, another contract actress, refused to do the test with me. Finally, Martha Hyer, who was new on the lot, said, "All right," and we shot it. But Dore saw to it that Gloria got the part anyway. You see, if I'd done the film and been good, the previous head of the studio, Charlie Koerner, would have gotten the credit for putting me under contract. With Gloria, all the credit would go to Schary.

I cried when I lost the role. I know John Paxton, the writer, wanted me—he was a friend. As for Eddie Dmytryk, I never talked to him again. I remember that when Kirk Douglas heard I lost out he called to offer encouragement, and I was grateful. (He was kind of nice then, but later he "went Hollywood.")

Then along came a major Western, *Roughshod,* directed by Mark Robson. I was all set for the "saloon girl" lead in this when suddenly—once again—it was tossed to Gloria Grahame! I was so upset I left town. They threatened me with a lawsuit, so I came back and had a meeting with Schary. Now they wanted me to play the second lead, another saloon girl, and to darken my hair so it wouldn't conflict with Gloria, who was a blonde, too. I told Schary I didn't want to change the color of my hair. He said, "Look, Myrna, all the great stars have dark hair—Joan Crawford, Olivia de Havilland, etc." I replied, "What about Betty Grable and Lana Turner, etc.?"

Rather than go on suspension, I agreed to tone down my hair a bit and do *Roughshod.* When I arrived on the set, Gloria told me that she had been afraid of me. But we became friends.

Dore Schary and I did not. He soon left RKO, and so did I.

Two of my better pictures during my RKO years were *Nocturne* and *Fighting Father Dunne.* Joan Harrison, who had been Alfred Hitchcock's associate, was the producer of *Nocturne* and Edwin L. Marin the director. It was Joan who really wanted me in the picture. Marin, I sensed, preferred someone else. Joan was very kind. I had been set for the film but had to do a test for wardrobe. An actor directed the test, and it wasn't very good. For one thing, my hair was pulled back and looked kind of funny. I was playing a maid in the picture, but a sassy and sexy one, and Joan said, "I don't like how she looks in the test." She ordered another, which was better.

After we'd been filming for a while, I was given a couple of weeks off. I was a fanatic then about getting a suntan; still am, really. I like it so much better than heavy make-up. At the time, my roommate was Janet Thomas, who is now married to Fred de Cordova, producer of television's *The Tonight Show.* When we had the time, we were always running off to Palm Springs and chattering about our weight and our tans. Since I wouldn't be filming for a while, we rented a sun lamp and went to work on our tans. We kept comparing to see who was the darker. We had twin beds and we'd see who looked darker against the white sheets. One time Janet put grey sheets on my bed!

One night as we were both preparing to go out, she decided to take her shower first while I tanned myself. So that we'd look especially lush that evening, we both took a few extra minutes with the lamp. I had a nice healthy glow when my escort, whom I was dating for the first time, picked me up. We were sitting at Ciro's when suddenly my eyes swelled up and began to water. Then my lips ballooned and fever blisters formed. Janet had the same reaction. We had stayed under the sun lamp too long in addition to forgetting to wear the goggles! We were so sick we had to have a nurse for three days.

We were still swollen almost beyond recognition when RKO suddenly called me back early to work on *Nocturne.* How to photograph me was the problem. They solved it by re-scheduling to the scene where I am taken to the hospital after nearly being beaten to death. The make-up man took compliments right and left for making me so ugly. But of course that was the way I *really* looked.

As I drove home, people going by would take one look at my grotesque face and pull over to the curb.

During the day on the set, the still photographer took a photograph of me on the telephone, swollen face and all. It was the most frightening thing you ever saw. Not long ago I had some copies of the photo made up and had some fun sending it to friends. On it, I would write, "Dear So-and-So, I tried to call you but I've had a very rough week."

I knew George Raft, the male lead in *Nocturne,* from my early days as an Earl Carroll showgirl. (My first film was *A Night at Earl Carroll's* in 1940.) Not too many showgirls became actresses in those days, so I think George sort of laughed when he discovered that I was going to go for it. I know Jackie Gleason, who was just starting and was going with a girlfriend of mine then, thought it was funny. George seemed surprised when I was cast in *Nocturne.* After working with me in the picture, though, his respect for me seemed to increase. I remember that he did a very sweet thing. He was in New York for the premiere of the picture, and one night he and Toots Shor, who was a great friend of mine, called me from Toots' restaurant to tell me that we'd all gotten good reviews and that *Nocturne* was being selected "Movie of the Week" in *Life.*

George Raft was a very nice, thoughtful gentleman. Everybody liked George. I went out with George a number of times, yet I never really dated him. It was mostly a group thing—we went with a number of other people. The things you remember! Once, when I was about 18, we were sitting around a pool someplace. As I said, I liked to get black from the sun. I didn't shave my legs then and blonde fuzz was beginning to become visible on my darkened legs. George leaned over and said, "When you begin to shave your legs, always shave down, never up against the grain." And he was right: his way, when I touched my legs it didn't feel like a man's beard.

Years later, a group of us went to George's house in Beverly Hills. He was a very meticulous man with excellent taste. When we entered his beautiful den, we noticed a barrel of apples. When I asked why he kept apples there, he explained, "Apples give a home a wonderful scent."

On *Fighting Father Dunne,* they tested about 100 actresses for the main woman's role, the big sister of a wayward boy. Joan Blondell was one of the aspirants, I recall. After I tested, I ran into the screenwriter, Marty Rackin, who said, "I think you'll get it." He was right. Today, when I look at the film, I wonder what all the fuss was about: I don't have that much to do. Of course, some of the footage I shot was cut, apparently to keep the length of the picture down.

Marty and I dated for a while. He was one of the funniest men I've ever known. If you had told me while I was doing *Fighting Father Dunne* that Marty would one day become head of Paramount Pictures, however, I would have laughed even harder than I did at his jokes. During the time we dated, the scripts he turned in to RKO all had leading ladies he had named "Myrna." Finally, he was called into the front office where he was asked, "Don't you think you are going a little too far?" I was never *in* love with Marty, but I loved him.

Pat O'Brien plays Father Dunne. I adored this darling Irishman. We'd laugh constantly on the set. He never used profanity, though. He'd be in his priest's costume and call me over, saying, "I've got a funny story for you." Then he'd turn his collar around and tell me one of his jokes. Pat was a great credit to the industry.

Between takes, I often played football on the lot with all the kids who were cast as Father Dunne's orphans.

People are very nice and sometimes they tell me, "I can't understand why you didn't become a big star." I really feel I was blacklisted.

As the 1950s were starting, I was signed to do a film at 20th Century-Fox called *Love That Brute,* with Paul Douglas, Jean Peters and Cesar Romero. The role was Cesar's girlfriend. It wasn't much of a part, but it was work and would be my first film at 20th. Charles LeMaire was making my costumes and I was running to the gym to lose a pound a day. The first day I was to work, Charles wanted me to try on my costumes before going on the set. My stand-in said, "I'll go down and check the dressing room." In a little while, she came back and said, "Myrna, there's no dressing room for you."

"But I've got all these changes," I replied, confused. "I've never worked without a dressing room."

I was still with Charles LeMaire when a phone call came from Casting. I was told, "You're fired."

Someone had thought I said, "I wouldn't work without a dressing room," and it had gotten back to the powers-that-be. What I said, of course, was, "I've never worked without a dressing room."

All the newspapers immediately reported that temperament caused me to be dismissed from *Love That Brute* and replaced by Marion Marshall. It was so unfair. I'm a very cooperative person. All the crews at RKO liked me. I was never temperamental.

The producer of *Love That Brute* was Freddie Kohlmar. We frequently traveled in the same crowd and we were friendly. When I read all the stories about my firing, I called him to explain my side. I was crying. He said, cold as steel, "When you control youself, call me back."

Every columnist then went to bat for me for weeks. Finally, on the strength of all the stories that pitted big 20th Century-Fox against little Myrna Dell, Lew Schreiber, who was next in power to Darryl Zanuck at the studio, called and said, "We've got to straighten this out. We'll set up an appointment with Kohlmar. All this fuss doesn't look good for you and it doesn't look good for us." I met with Mr. Schreiber and Freddie. Mr. Schreiber said, "I think the best thing to do is to sign you for another picture and release the news as soon as possible."

But Freddie insisted, "I think we should wait a couple of weeks."

"Why?" I asked.

Mr. Schreiber called the head of publicity, Harry Brand, to get his opinion. Brand advised, "Release it now."

So 20th announced that I had been signed for a film. But the damage was done. All anyone remembered was that I was difficult. And no picture at 20th ever materialized for me.

Not long after this, I was doing a little independent picture released by RKO called *Destination Murder.* One freezing morning as I was in Make-up getting ready to begin my bad-girl role, people kept opening the door, allowing gusts of bone-chilling air to come in. Pretty soon someone else entered whom I couldn't see from my chair and I said in (I thought) a humorous way, "Will you close the goddamn door!" Hurd Hatfield, one of the stars, and I became friends during the shooting, and eventually he told me that it was he who had been the recipient of my facetious command that bitter cold day. He confessed that he had thought to himself, "Oh, God, she's starting already!"

Julius J. Epstein—SCREENWRITER—

The 1940s were better than the fifties but not as good as the thirties. It was a miracle that there were any good films during the forties because of censorship. Joe Breen, a Catholic, was the head censor then, and while I certainly don't mean to sound anti-Catholic, it was especially tough to get anything past him because of that. When my twin brother, Philip G. Epstein, and I wrote *My Foolish Heart* in 1949, we had a terrible time with the ending. Our leading character (played by Susan Hayward) was breaking up with her husband—everything in the story leads to this. Breen would have preferred that a woman not be divorced at all on the screen, but since events of the plot made it unavoidable, he said, "Well, she mustn't be happy about it." He actually suggested that we kill Susan off in a car accident "because if you're divorced you'll be punished." We had to fight. We stop short of actually showing the divorce, but it's clearly waiting in the wings.

I was originally a press agent in New York. In 1933 I came out to Hollywood before my brother Phil [now deceased]. He arrived about nine months later. I came as a ghostwriter for two acqaintances who had sold an idea to a studio but couldn't write their own names. I did several films like this. When I sold an original story and one of the fellows I was ghosting for put his name on it, too, I decided to work with my brother Phil—who had been ghosting for the same writer.

Phil and I had already done several films together when *The Strawberry Blonde* came along in 1941. It was based on a play called *One Sunday Afternoon,* by James Hagan, and had been filmed before under that title starring Gary Cooper—the only Gary Cooper movie ever to lose money. When my brother and I wrote the screenplay for Warner Bros., we changed the original setting, a bucolic area, to New York City, and this seemed to make the big difference. Our star, James Cagney, was very hot then, too. And Raoul Walsh, the director, was terrific. He never changed a word of our script, although at one point Walsh, who had worked in silent pictures, did say to us, "Boys, I think you have a little too many titles in this"—meaning dialogue. Cagney, who had a reputation for not getting along with some people, was very nice to us. I know that he didn't get along with the boss, Jack Warner, but neither did Mrs. Warner.

My brother and I never talked too much about *The Man Who Came to Dinner.* We didn't do too much on it. It was from a great Broadway play. I saw it again recently at a film festival in Vancouver, and I must say it holds up pretty well—thanks to George S. Kaufman and Moss Hart [the play's authors]. Ann Sheridan is funny in it. She was a good gal, a no-bullshit dame. All day on the set we would see her sipping from a Coke bottle, but it was filled with gin.

Casablanca, for which my brother and I and Howard Koch won the [1943] Best Screenplay Oscar, started filming without a completed script. David O. Selznick, with whom our feminine star, Ingrid Bergman, was signed, had put a stop date on her contract with Warners to do the picture—I think he had another for her to start right after completing *Casablanca.* So we made it up as we went along. About half-way through, we just ran out of story. One day as we were driving to the studio I said, "Round up the usual suspects." That line of dialogue gave us the key to the end of the picture. We killed off the Nazi Major Strasser, played by Conrad Veidt, and had Claude Rains repeat this line that he had used earlier in the picture. The major's death did not occur in the original unproduced play by Murray Burnett and Joan Alison on which *Casablanca* was based.

As for Howard Koch's co-credit on the screenplay.... He's an old man now and I don't like to minimize

his contribution. But this is what happened. As we were about to start the screenplay, Frank Capra became a major in the Army and was dispatched to Washington to direct the "Why We Fight" documentary films for our servicemen. He wanted us to do some work on them, but Warner Bros. said no. We said, "We're going." We were gone for about four weeks, during which time Howard Koch started writing *Casablanca.* We came back to learn that the studio didn't like what Koch had done, so my brother and I started all over again from the beginning. Despite the enduring success of the film, working on *Casablanca* was not a pleasant experience. There was too much pressure—the stop date for Ingrid, having to write as they filmed.

And my brother and I were never that crazy about the finished picture. It was pure make-believe. There were no uniformed Nazis in the real Casablanca, no such things as letters of transit. A few years ago, a friend said to me, "Do you realize what you guys got away with in *Casablanca?* Ingrid Bergman pulling a gun and saying, 'Give me those letters of transit'." If the script of *Casablanca* were shot today, scene-for-scene, it'd be laughed off the screen. It was the chemistry then of Humphrey Bogart and Ingrid Bergman that made it work.

On *Mr. Skeffington,* which my brother and I produced as well as wrote, we didn't get along at all with the star, Bette Davis. And I think it shows on the screen. I never cared much for the picture. Not long ago, my wife and I went to a showing of it at UCLA. By the time it was over, the only ones left in the theater were my wife, myself and the projectionist.

I recall a scene on which Phil and I wanted Bette to do a retake. She refused and we argued for a while. In desperation, I went up to see Jack Warner. "Who built these sound stages?" he roared. "*We* built them, not Bette Davis! She's not going to tell the Warner Bros. how to run a studio!" When he got down to the set, he cried out, "Bette, darling!" and threw his arms around her. We didn't get the retake.

Bette also improvised too much on *Mr. Skeffington.* It was taking forever. My brother and I left in the middle of the shooting. I just said, "To hell with it." We went to New York to put on a play we had written, *Chicken Every Sunday.* When we returned to the coast, *Mr. Skeffington* was released as a roadshow in New York at three hours and 25 minutes and got murdered by the critics. We finally got it down to two hours and 10 minutes for general release. It may have made a little money.

A while back, there was a memorial service for Hal Wallis, who produced several of the films my brother and I wrote. Bette Davis, now quite enfeebled by illness, arrived accompanied by a nurse. When she got up to speak, she began by saying, "Julie, I know you didn't like me very much during *Mr. Skeffington*. . ." and went on to say some very sweet things. Afterward, I wasn't able to get through the crowd to talk to her, but she wrote me a letter. So I called her, we patched things up and made a date to meet when she came back from Europe. She never came back.

Arsenic and Old Lace was another one from a great play that we didn't have to do a lot of work on. There was one problem, again related to censorship. Cary Grant's character didn't want to continue his recent marriage to Priscilla Lane because he believed he was related to the two sweet but crazy old ladies who have been poisoning people. In the play, when he found out at last that they were not related, he cried out joyfully, "Elaine! I'm a bastard!" It got a big laugh. Well, you couldn't say "bastard" on the screen in those days. And Cary certainly couldn't turn to Priscilla and say, "Elaine! I'm illegitimate!" No laugh there.

My brother Phil came up with the solution. He had the two old aunts reveal to Cary that his mother had been their cook and his father was really a chef on a tramp steamer. Now, Cary could call out for Priscilla, exclaiming, "Elaine! I'm a son of a sea cook!" This got just as big a laugh as the "bastard" line had on the stage.

When we wrote *Romance on the High Seas,* I had just come back from the service. Phil and I wanted to get out of our Warner contract. The word came down: "Do one more picture for us and we'll let you out." It was *Romance on the High Seas.* It had some good songs and introduced Doris Day, which is its big claim to fame.

My Foolish Heart was based on a short story called *Uncle Wiggily in Connecticut,* by the reclusive J.D. Salinger. My brother and I decided we'd

like to buy the story and write the screenplay "on spec." The going price for short stories in 1949 was $1250. He said, "No. The price is $5000." We gave it to him. We wrote the screenplay without any idea of what we were going to do with it. Finally, we took it to Samuel Goldwyn, who bought it and put it into production immediately. He signed Susan Hayward and Dana Andrews for the leads, and Susan subsequently won a Best Actress Academy nomination for it. After that, whenever Salinger did venture out of the house he said we had cheated him.

But, as I've said, the censorship problems concerning the ending of *Foolish Heart* were nightmarish. Eventually, we were able to indicate that the heroine was planning to get a divorce, but Mr. Breen, the censor, insisted that she be miserable about it. Crazy. After all, there are more happy divorces than there are happy marriages!

Joan Evans — ACTRESS

My mother and father, Katherine Albert and Dale Eunson, wrote articles, books, plays, television shows and movies, and Joan Crawford was my godmother. So it was not entirely unexpected that I became an actress.

When I was a little girl, I was up for the role of Gretel in our school play, *Hansel and Gretel.* Many of the other children came from rich, influential families, and my parents said, "No, no, dear, you won't get it." But I did. And when Mom and Dad saw me as Gretel, they said, "Maybe she has talent." Later, when Dad's play *Guest in the House* was in stock, I toured the East Coast in it as the little girl.

I was about 14 when we heard that producer Samuel Goldwyn was looking for a girl to play the title role in *Roseanna McCoy,* a love story set against the legendary Hatfield-McCoy mountain feud. When Goldwyn's casting director, Bill Selwyn, came to New York to look for actresses of 16 or 17 for the role, he asked his friend, actress Catherine Willard, if she knew of any who fit the age requirements. Catherine was also a friend of my family's, and although she didn't know of any actresses in that age group, she said she did know a young girl who expected to be an actress when she grew up: me.

I was asked to come in from the Jersey seashore, where I'd been vacationing, to have pictures taken. So I rushed in, sunburned with seaweed and salt water still in my hair, and did the photo session. The pictures were terrible, but Bill sent them to Sam Goldwyn on the coast. And through some miracle, Goldwyn liked them and brought me out to test for the picture. I did a scene from it with Farley Granger, who was to be my leading man, under the direction of Irving Reis, who was also going to direct the picture. The test was magnificently photographed by Gregg Toland, the great cameraman who had photographed Goldwyn's *Wuthering Heights* and Orson Welles' *Citizen Kane.* I was signed by Goldwyn to a seven-year contract. (I think I was his last contract player.) Unfortunately, Toland died soon after and never got to do the picture, which was shot by Lee Garmes.

Naturally, I was thrilled, especially when Mary Wills, who was the costume designer, found a dress for me to wear that had been worn by Merle Oberon when she played the young Cathy on the moors in *Wuthering Heights.* I was a young, romantic girl whose favorite movie was *Wuthering Heights,* so you can imagine how I felt when I saw the name tag "Merle Oberon" on the dress.

Irving Reis, our director, was something else. I don't think any of us were happy with Irving, especially the younger cast members like myself. Socially, he was quite pleasant, but he was a sadistically driven man, a terrible, terrible person to work for, especially to an inexperienced, insecure kid like myself facing a camera for the first time. I was going to school then and had limited time on the set. To walk onto the stage and immediately be picked on by this man was traumatic. The only ones he didn't pick on were the older, established character players. He didn't dare attack Charles Bickford, Raymond Massey, Aline MacMahon or Hope Emerson. I was always glad when I saw that Charles Bickford was on call. The first day we worked, he turned to Irving and said, "Why do you make Joan act like a zombie?" That was the last time that day that Irving picked on me. So I always prayed for Charlie to be on call.

Near the end of production, Irving had to leave *Roseanna McCoy* to go to 20th Century-Fox and direct *Dancing in the Dark,* with Mark Stevens, who was also known in Hollywood as a very difficult character. We had to return to Sonora, California, to do the final location shooting, which was directed by Nicholas Ray. So we went from one strange director to another.

On *Dancing in the Dark,* Irving Reis and Mark Stevens got into a fistfight right off; Mark won. When the word spread to our set, everyone applauded. Mark was not very well liked either, but we had personal reasons for being glad that Irving got a sock in the nose.

I have a theory about why Mr. Goldwyn put up with Irving Reis, who also had just directed *Enchantment* for him. Goldwyn's favorite film was always *Wuthering Heights,* which was directed by William Wyler, whose working methods were not unlike those of Irving Reis. Wyler would give his actors no instructions, just say "Do it again," and Reis did this, too. When Goldwyn found Irving, and the book *Roseanna McCoy* was brought to him, he thought he had both another *Wuthering Heights* and another Willie Wyler.

He didn't, but I think Goldwyn liked the finished picture, although not quite as much as he had hoped to. I certainly liked it, despite the fact that the original script by John Collier was superior to the altered one we shot. Collier's screenplay had a mystical, poetic quality, but someone apparently said something negative about it to Goldwyn. He then ordered rewrites by Ben Hecht, who (with Charles MacArthur) had written the screenplay of *Wuthering Heights.* Some of the original Collier script was left, but not enough. Hecht's version was more ordinary. I was just a kid, but my parents, Farley Granger and others who knew the original Collier script all liked it better.

Farley was enormously popular with teen-age girls. When *Roseanna McCoy* came out in 1949, I did a big personal appearance tour—37 cities in so many days. Farley joined me for some of the appearances. We did newspaper interviews, theaters, radio shows, television shows. I recall that I did a little television show that a newcomer named Johnny Carson then had in Omaha, Nebraska. Farley joined me in Omaha and we did theater appearances there. But the hundreds of girls had come to see him, not me. They *hated* me for being on stage with him. They literally booed me off!

I'm heartsick at what has happened to the reputation of my godmother, Joan Crawford. My mother was in the publicity department at MGM when Joan was a big star there, and she became Mother's best friend. She named me after her. Many years later, in the early 1950s, when I wanted to get married and my parents didn't want me to, Joan allowed me to marry in her house. My mother and father and Joan never resumed their friendship after that, although, fortunately, my parents and I did reconcile and became very close again.

But after the hatchet job her daughter did in that book [*Mommie Dearest*], Joan's name has become a joke. She always used to be the quintessential movie star, now she's a child-abusing joke. I keep a photo of her in my office at home, and sometimes when workers come in they'll shrink when they see her picutre, muttering, "Oh-oh."

As a little girl and an adult, Joan was always wonderful to me. Joan may have been less than perfect—which one of us *is*—but I never saw any child abuse. I remember once, just before World War II, when I was only about six or seven, I stayed with my grandmother in New York for a while. When I was to join my parents in Los Angeles, I made the trip there with Joan on the 20th Century and the Super Chief. You had to change trains in Chicago then. I'm sure few who were there ever forgot the sight of Joan Crawford descending on Dearborn Street Station with entourage, luggage and tyke in tow. I know I never have.

When my husband and I had our first anniversary, Joan gave us a party. She always called us her son and daughter. My husband is nine years older than I, and when we married he was a very mature 27-year-old who rather resembled the slightly greying actor Jeff Chandler. It was very generous for a still glamorous star like Joan Crawford to call such a mature-looking man her son.

My mother died in 1970, but my father is still active and writing. His 1950s book *The Day They Gave Babies Away,* which is a true story of our family and has been dramatized on radio, TV and in the movies, has just been published for the third time.

Alice Faye—*ACTRESS*

I had some great opportunites in the 1930s (*In Old Chicago, Alexander's Ragtime Band, Rose of Washington Square, Hollywood Cavalcade*), but the forties were good to me, too.

Things got off to a delightful start with *Little Old New York,* which I did with Fred MacMurray for one of my favorite directors, Henry King. I remember it with special affection because it gave me a chance to play comedy, which I loved to do.

The same year, 1940, I did two other good ones: *Lillian Russell* and *Tin Pan Alley.* Playing Lillian Russell was a challenge, but I was helped immeasurably by the director, Irving Cummings, who had been an actor and really made the picture for me. He had known the real Lillian Russell, a great star of the Gay '90s, and was able to advise me on her sense of humor and the way she worked. It's a beautiful film, everything is first-class—the costumes [by Travis Banton], corsets and stockings were all specially made. It was my fifth film with Don Ameche, who was always fun, and I was thrilled to have Henry Fonda as my other leading man. My only complaint was that *Lillian Russell* wasn't in Technicolor, which its exquisite production cried out for.

Tin Pan Alley, with Betty Grable, John Payne and Jack Oakie, was a ball, too. Betty had just become a big star in a film I was originally slated to do, *Down Argentine Way.* I was preparing to start filming when suddenly I had to go to the hospital. It has been written that I had appendicitis, but it wasn't that. And no, it wasn't an abortion. It was just one of those things. Anyway, Betty had just made a hit on Broadway in *DuBarry Was a Lady* and Darryl Zanuck, our boss at 20th Century-Fox, rushed her in as my replacement in *Down Argentine Way.*

Betty was a great dancer. I loved working with her on *Tin Pan Alley.* And we became good friends. I didn't get to see her too much, though, because while I was working on one picture she was usually working on another. Her husband, Harry James, was a very close friend of my husband, Phil Harris. (They were both band leaders.) While we were making the film, Jack Oakie introduced me to Phil at Charlie Foy's, then a popular restaurant at Coldwater and Ventura in the Valley. Jack, always giving out with wisecracks or pulling pranks, brightened every picture he was on.

It was the first of several times I would work with John Payne, whom I loved. More than 30 years later, we co-starred together on Broadway in a revival of *Good News.* That wasn't as much fun, especially for John who sometime before had been badly injured when hit by a car in New York. His leg hurt a great deal, making it very difficult for him to sing and dance and just move around on stage. John was a very well read person and a fine businessman, the least actorish of all the men I worked with.

Walter Lang directed *Tin Pan Alley* as well as *Weekend in Havana,* the latter also starring John Payne plus Carmen Miranda and Cesar Romero, who is so funny in it. Lang, with his great sense of humor, was a pleasure to work with, too. I enjoyed doing *Weekend* because it gave me another comedy role, that of a slightly common Macy's salesgirl. I was born in New York, so I was familiar with the lingo. She refers to her travel "bro-choor" and is constantly using her hands like many of the people I knew from my girlhood in Manhattan. Carmen Miranda was a lovely, lovely lady and a hard worker. And yes, she mangled the English language in person, too. That was not an act she did on the screen. Carmen died much too young. I think she worked *too* hard.

Hello, Frisco, Hello has John Payne and Jack Oakie again, this time under the direction of Bruce Humberstone. It marked my return after having my first child, Alice, Jr. I was beautifully treated by everybody, especially the cameramen [Charles Clarke, Allen Davey] and costume designer [Helen Rose]. And I introduce one of my most popular songs, "You'll Never Know," by Mack Gordon and Harry Warren.

Today, *The Gang's All Here* has quite a cult following, probably because it was directed by Busby Berkeley, that master of outrageous production numbers. Among the biggies in this is Carmen Miranda's spectacular "The Lady in the Tutti-Frutti Hat," replete with waving bananas as big as canoes. I get to sing another one of my best songs, "No Love, No Nothin'," by Leo Robin and Harry Warren. Berkeley had a problem with alcohol, but he was very clever, had a lot on the ball. He had come over from Warner Bros. and MGM for this picture, so I wasn't as close to him as Henry King, Irving Cummings and Walter Lang, who were my pet directors at Fox. (I have no single favorite director, though. I learned something from each one.)

Fallen Angel was my last film for 17 years. It nearly broke my heart. It was produced and directed by Otto Preminger, who had just done *Laura,* and the male star was Dana Andrews, also from *Laura.* So expectations were high. It was a more dramatic film than I was used to, but I was looking for a change of pace. Preminger was very tough to work for. He didn't care what he said or how he hurt you. He got a lot out of me, though; I was proud of the performance I turned in. Zanuck, however, cut most of my best stuff, including the song "Slowly," which had been written by the composer of "Laura," David Raksin. Zanuck did quite a bit of damage to me. Linda Darnell had one of the other leads and Zanuck, who was building her up at the time, wanted more of the focus on her. I wasn't angry at Linda. She was a lovely actress and deserved a build-up. But I felt Zanuck betrayed me. I packed up and left the studio that had been my home for the past decade.

I thought, "I can't fight Pearl Harbor. If that's what Zanuck is going to do to me, I'm not going to stay around and be slaughtered."

That was 1945. I decided to stay home and take care of my family. I kept a hand in, though. I did 10 years of radio with my husband followed by some television. Then, in 1962, I returned to Fox to play the mother in a remake of *State Fair. Fallen Angel* was *Gone with the Wind* compared to *State Fair!*

Geraldine Fitzgerald——ACTRESS——

The Strange Affair of Uncle Harry and *Three Strangers,* two of my better films, were also two of my last films in Hollywood before I moved to New York. Oh, I've always gone back from time to time to work, but I never lived there again.

Uncle Harry, by Thomas Job, had been a famous Broadway play with Joseph Schildkraut and Eva Le Gallienne. In our film, which we did at Universal for producer Joan Harrison (who had been Hitchcock's assistant), George Sanders plays the mild-mannered bachelor who lives a humdrum life with his two unmarried sisters, played by Moyna Macgill (Angela Lansbury's mother) and myself in the Le Gallienne role. In reality, my character, the possessive Letty, is incestuously in love with Sanders and for years has kept him from getting married. Now he falls in love with Ella Raines, and to stop me from interfering he poisons my cocoa. Inadvertently, Moyna drinks it and I am convicted for her murder.

An awfully talented man named Robert Siodmak directed, and everything went smoothly throughout the filming. Afterward, however, the Hays Office decided that we couldn't portray a "perfect murder" and insisted that we make the poisoning and my conviction all a dream. At first, I refused to go back and shoot the new ending, but eventually they got their way. I don't think the film is quite as effective with the dream ending. It seems tacked-on, a cop-out. But what made some people around Hollywood smile at the time was the fact that obliterating the perfect murder restored the brother and sister to the incestuous relationship—another taboo theme on the screen of that day.

At the time, I was renting next door to Marion Davies in one of the two Santa Monica beach homes William Randolph Hearst bought for her. With me were my son Michael, who was about four, and my babysitter, who also took care of me in Ireland when I was small. One day Robert Siodmak came to visit. He was a very unusual-looking individual, rather ferocious-looking in appearance but in actuality a very kind man. On this particular day, he returned from swimming to find my small son in the hall. Michael took one look at Mr. Siodmak and the enormous mass of white hair on his bare chest and cried out to me upstairs, "Mother, come down! He's a witch and a ghost!" Mr. Siodmak had a good laugh.

Three Strangers, at Warner Bros., was directed by Jean Negulesco, who was just starting out and was also very good. It was written by John Huston and Howard Koch. Earlier, Huston had wanted me to be in *The Maltese Falcon,* his first film as a director, but I was fighting with our boss, Jack Warner, at the time and refused. Mary Astor, of course, got the part and the film was a huge success.

Three Strangers did well, too. I play Crystal, the sort of woman who puts a cigarette out on the back of her husband's hand. Alan Napier was the poor man, and as we rehearsed and filmed I kept saying to him, "Am I hurting you?" But he had asbestos covered with make-up on the back of his hand and evidently didn't feel a thing, thank goodness. Not long afterward, I was walking down Fifth Avenue in New York when a woman recognized me and exclaimed, "Oh, how could you do that? Put a cigarette out on a man's hand!" I explained how it was done and that it didn't hurt Mr. Napier, but she replied, in a most accusatory manner, "But you *knew* how to do it!" I've always felt that it should be in all actors to be able to do *anything.*

We had a great cast: besides Mr. Napier, there were Sydney Greenstreet, Peter Lorre, Joan Lorring, Rosalind Ivan. In Europe, Peter had been a doctor of philosophy and also had worked in a circus. For the scene

in which Sydney hits me over the head with the statue, throwing me against a wall and killing me, Mr. Negulesco wanted me to land in a particular spot near the wall. I wondered if I could do it. Peter told me, "I was once in a tumbling act and whenever we wanted to end up in a certain place, we'd always go to that spot first. Go to the wall and touch the place where you want to end and you'll have a good chance of hitting it." He thought the brain could have some control over what happened to our bodies. And it worked.

Once a week during the shooting of *Three Strangers,* Sydney, Peter, Joan and I would have dinner at each other's homes where we'd take turns cooking. We had a lot of fun on the film—and a lot of good meals. I still get mail on the picture, much of it from South America where for some reason it has remained especially popular through the decades.

Rhonda Fleming——————*ACTRESS*—

I had studied voice all my life, but by the time things got going for me in films I had pretty much missed the big era for movie musicals. When

I started, I had just come out of high school and was under contract to David O. Selznick, who did not make musicals. Three months later, he put me up for a dramatic role in *Spellbound,* directed by Alfred Hitchcock.

Well, I had been studying singing. I never studied acting and here I was, poised to play a nymphomaniac and I didn't even know what the word meant! I went home and said, "Mother, I'm going to read for the role of a nymphomaniac!" She didn't know what it meant, either, so we both looked it up in the dictionary. I didn't even know what a cold reading was, and I was nervous while doing it; but they apparently liked what they heard because I got this really wonderful part in the movie with Ingrid Bergman and Gregory Peck. Ingrid was about five-feet-nine, and I'm five-feet-eight, but the first day on the set we appeared approximately the same height. (She wore flat shoes and I wore heels.) She looked at me and said, in her Swedish accent, "Ah, to be able to look eyeball-to-eyeball with someone at last!" Except for Peck, everyone else on the film was so much shorter. She was a delight to work with.

Mr. Hitchcock had great humor, which I was too nervous then to really appreciate. He would say to me, "Rhonda, dear, how is your sex life?," and I would turn green with embarrassment.

Although, as I said, Mr. Selznick did not make musicals, he continued my singing lessons and had me study with a teacher at MGM. And I was the first one to sing for Mr. Selznick and Mr. Hitchcock the words to the "Spellbound" theme. They were to decide whether or not to use them in the film. They wound up not using them, only the incredible instrumental score, with that eerie sound, that Miklos Rozsa composed for the picture.

Finally, I got a musical. On *A Connecticut Yankee in King Arthur's Court,* I replaced Deanna Durbin. She suddenly decided she didn't want to make any more movies, moved to France and never came back. Paramount gave me a $50,000 test in color and black and white—a lot of money in those days. They also tested 250 other women. But Bing Crosby, who was playing the Connecticut Yankee, liked me. Still, it was about two or three months before I knew I had the role. Bing was wonderful. He was like a mother hen. He watched over me and wanted everything just right. And I got co-star billing because Bing never liked his name alone above the title.

Then Bob Hope said, "If Bing's gonna use her, so am I"—we did *The Great Lover* and, later, *Alias Jesse James.*

Nina Foch—ACTRESS

A Song to Remember was my first big picture and only my second feature, Columbia's top production for the year [1945]. Although my role as

composer Frédéric Chopin's patriot sweetheart back in Poland was a supporting one, I was delighted to be in it. When I tell you that my *first* movie was *The Return of the Vampire,* with Bela Lugosi, and that I went on to *Boston Blackie's Rendezvous,* you can understand why.

Song to Remember focused on the relationship between Chopin and novelist George Sand, played by Cornel Wilde and Merle Oberon. In real life, my father was a well known orchestra conductor, and Paul Muni, who got top billing as Chopin's old teacher, was a good friend of my father's. So on the first day I filmed, Muni called me into his trailer and asked, "Do you want to be an actress or a whore?"

I was stunned—this shy young girl who had gone to Miss Hewitt's School in New York, where I grew up. I managed to reply, "I want to be an actress."

"Then you must *work!*" said Muni. Which I already knew.

He was a very serious man, but when you look at his performance today he's doing very old-fashioned acting. We all are, really.

When I got to the set, I was all made up and beautifully groomed for my role. Charles Vidor, our director, suddenly exclaimed, "Ugh! She's been traveling by open carriage. Put some dirt on her!" which they proceeded to do.

A Song to Remember made a star of Cornel Wilde, who was a very nice man. And it changed the buying habits of the American public. The film was tremendously successful, due in large part to its great Chopin music which the public loved. Prior to this, people didn't buy classical records to any extent, but after *Song to Remember*—which many went to see again and again—they did.

It was a lavish Technicolor production, but *My Name Is Julia Ross,* in which I had the lead later the same year, was just the opposite: a black-and-white "B" picture shot in about three and a half minutes. (Actually, it took about two weeks; we worked a six-day week then.) Most of us, except for the director, Joseph H. Lewis, had worked together before and we knew we had a better script than we were used to at Columbia. We broke our asses to make it a good film.

I had a great affection for our cameraman, Burnett Guffey, who 20 years later photographed *Bonnie and Clyde,* and his operator, Gert Anderson, who later became a cameraman, too. They were dear, wonderful, talented men who really loved what they were doing. Still, I recall that Bernie Guffey had an ulcer and drank a lot of milk during the shooting.

I have very little memory of our director, Joe Lewis. When people ask me to name my favorite directors, I just never think of him. I didn't dislike Joe—he simply never comes to mind. I only remember that he took himself extremely seriously—even more so when the good reviews came out for *My Name Is Julia Ross* hailing it as a suspenseful "sleeper." I never particularly cared for the way I looked in it, though. For some reason, I photographed sort of puffy. And the acting, as in *Song to Remember,* seems so old-fashioned now. Nevertheless, the critics liked us all and it was the first time Columbia and our boss, Harry Cohn, paid any attention to me. They said, "Shit, we've got something on our hands here!"

But the studio never did know what to do with me. In the beginning they said, "You can act but you're not pretty." Then in 1947 I played the lead on Broadway in *John Loves Mary,* by Norman Krasna, and became the toast of the town that year. Some of the New York critics said I was (among other nice things) pretty and sexy, so I returned to Columbia and Harry Cohn with a new respect as an actress and got some leads in "A" movies: *The Dark Past,* with William Holden; *Johnny Allegro,* with George Raft; and *Undercover Man,* with Glenn Ford.

The only drawback was that now that my attractiveness had been validated by New York, I got chased around a few desks in Hollywood. Yes, one of them was Harry's. I solved the problem by telling them all that they reminded me of my father!

I was always grateful, though, to those New York writers for helping me through my years at Columbia.

Susanna Foster——ACTRESS—

I was born in Chicago but raised in Minneapolis, where I sang in vaudeville from an early age. Eventually, Carl Johnson, who was conductor of the orchestra there, and Merle Potter, drama editor of *The Minneapolis Star,* had me record a couple of songs I'd learned listening to Jeanette MacDonald in the movie *Naughty Marietta,* "Italian Street Song" and "Ah, Sweet Mystery of Life." They mailed the record to MGM in Hollywood and the studio sent for me.

My mother and I arrived at MGM in 1937, when I was 12 years old. I was at Metro a year, but nothing much happened. The coaching I got was stupid. And MGM wanted me to act, while I wanted to sing. I tested for *Anne of Green Gables,* under the direction of George Sidney. They also wanted me to do *National Velvet,* which made Elizabeth Taylor a star several years later. In the book, Velvet was rather plain, with spaces between her teeth, which certainly described my adolescent stage. But I was very determined and, despite the presence of my mother, very much in charge of my own life. I told them, "I don't want to be in anything in which I don't sing. I want to sing!" I could have been more malleable, but I was just a little girl.

Then my father came out with my two younger sisters. We had no money. Things were very rough. My new singing teacher, Gilda Marchetti, took me under her wing. Days before I had to audition somewhere, she would take me to stay at her home and feed me and get me healthy and ready.

Finally, I auditioned for Paramount where they were doing *The Star Maker,* with Bing Crosby and a new young blonde soprano named Linda Ware. Afterward, LeRoy Prinz, the dance director, followed me out onto the street. "I think you're a great singer," he told me. "You've got to meet Andrew Stone who's going to direct *The Great Victor Herbert* here." Although Linda Ware was expected to do *Great Victor Herbert* as the the daughter of Mary Martin and Allan Jones, after Mr. Stone heard me he insisted that I do the role. Linda Ware stayed on at Paramount for a few months, then left.

Paramount signed me but didn't use me very much. In 1941 I appeared in *There's Magic in Music,* with Allan Jones again, and *Glamour Boy,* with Jackie Cooper. In August 1942, Bill Meiklejohn, the head of talent at Paramount, called me in. "We want to keep you on at your present salary of $450 a week," he told me. I was due a raise. I said, "I don't like the movie business. You just keep me hanging around but don't give me anything to do. I'm leaving." I departed Paramount with the reputation of being more than a little outspoken.

How did I get to Universal? For some reason, I always gravitated to writers and I became friendly with a man who wrote for *The Hollywood*

Reporter. He and his wife had me over once a week for dinner and I would sing on these occasions. One week, Arthur Lubin, who was preparing to direct a big Technicolor production of *Phantom of the Opera* at Universal, was there. Around the same time, I met Nelson Eddy, who was to play the romantic lead in *Phantom,* at the home of W.S. (Woody) Van Dyke, Nelson's favorite director during his preceding MGM years with Jeanette MacDonald.

Arthur Lubin brought me to the attention of George Waggner, who was producing *Phantom of the Opera,* and Eddie Ward, the very talented Italian in charge of the music. I remember that when I went out to Universal to meet Mr. Waggner, I was all dressed in brown—brown dress, brown hat, brown shoes, brown gloves. I was 17—who knows why a young girl does these things? I sang for George Waggner and Eddie Ward, at one point hitting A-flat above high-C. Mr. Ward was thrilled. They both wanted me for *Phantom.*

As a formality, really, they arranged a screen test. In it, a Universal contract actor named David Bruce interviewed me and I sang a couple of songs. I was signed to a seven-year contract.

I did the recordings for *Phantom* in December 1942. In January 1943, the filming commenced. We shot for three months. It was such a happy, classy set. Fritz Feld, a character actor in the picture, would play the piano between scenes and Nelson and I would sing. The crews were great. It was the middle of World War II and soldiers, sailors and Marines often came on the set to visit.

Because so many servicemen already had been maimed or disfigured in the war, the studio was worried about the make-up for the grotesquely scarred Phantom in our story. They were afraid it might prove not merely frightening but, in view of current conditions, offensive to the public. So Jack Pierce, the great Universal make-up man who had created the make-up for Frankenstein, made the Phantom's scars just frightening enough but not really repulsive. Whenever they say that Hollywood had no taste, I always think of this occasion when the studio went out of its way to be sensitive.

Claude Rains, our magnificent Phantom, was a great gentleman. He always had a twinkle in his eyes and was very flirtatious—no wonder he had six wives! Nelson Eddy was a wonderful man, a *harmonious* man. When the picture was finished, he wanted me to go on a concert tour with him. I was scared, though. I hadn't had much training then. If I'd used my bean, I would have realized that Nelson would have protected me, would never have allowed me to get hurt. But I replied, "I can't, not until I've done more. When I'm a little older."

After *Phantom of the Opera* opened, Universal raised my salary to $1,000 a week.

In September of 1943, I recreated for radio my role of the young opera singer who is helped by the Phantom. Recently, someone gave me a recording of the broadcast and I thought I sang better for the radio version than I did for the movie. When I did the recordings for the film, I wasn't feeling too well.

Also, the radio program had a live audience which always spurs a singer on.

The Climax, which I did soon afterward with Boris Karloff and Turhan Bey, was very similar to *Phantom of the Opera*—an opulent Technicolor horror movie with lots of music, again by Eddie Ward. I play another opera singer and loved working with Turhan. We also did *Bowery to Broadway* and *Frisco Sal* together. The studio tried to make us a romantic screen team, and it might have worked. We liked each other very much and dated. He's Viennese and loves music, and I knew all the Viennese songs; he got a kick out of this. We *could* have become a team, if the studio had used more sense. If they had found good personal stories for us, similar to the ones Irene Dunne did, and let the music be injected as part of the plot, we might have made it as a team. But they kept putting us into this spectacular stuff.

Working with Karloff was another matter. Jack Pierce, the makeup man, loved him, but I saw nothing. He was so cold. Except for our dialogue, I never had a conversation with that man. The scene where he has to hypnotize me with this spinning contraption took three days to film, and I would get nauseated watching the thing go around and around time after time. But Karloff never said one word to me.

I also did several films with Donald O'Connor, including *Top Man, Bowery to Broadway* and *This Is the Life.* They wanted to make us a team, too, the Mickey Rooney and Judy Garland of Universal. I adored Donald; he's always been a great talent. We were the same age, but standing next to this kid I looked like a mature woman. My response to the studio was, "Are you crazy?"

Universal had a couple of other young sopranos under contract, too, both of whom were there when I arrived: Gloria Jean and the lot's biggest star of all, Deanna Durbin. I saw very little of Deanna. She was very elusive. Once, I glimpsed her on the set of *Hers to Hold* with Joseph Cotten and some others. Another time, they opened a sound stage door and I caught sight of her. Then, one morning in the make-up department Deanna walked in, looking just as lovely as she had in her films. Jack Pierce introduced us. She had a weird smile on her face and seemed very condescending. When you studied with the old music teachers, as she had, you were told to stay aloof from the hoi polloi; be a Garbo. It was advice that Deanna Durbin took to very easily.

On the other hand, Gloria Jean and I were good friends and had many nice chats on the lot. She has always been very up front in her feelings about Deanna Durbin. She feels that Deanna maneuvered to keep Gloria's career from advancing and recently told me that Deanna stopped my picture, *Frisco Sal,* from being made in color. I'd never heard that. I can tell you one thing: Deanna sang better after I got there.

Speaking of *Frisco Sal,* which was one of my favorites at Universal, I recall that one day I had to re-dub the high notes at the end of the "Beloved" number. I just stood there and hit these three high-Cs. William Tyroler, a wonderful coach there, flipped out. "Where did *those* come from?!" he asked. "I don't know," I shrugged. They had just popped out.

My disagreements with Universal began to heat up about this time. Don't misunderstand me. Universal was very nice to me and my memories of the place are mostly very pleasant. I had a house attached to other houses on the lot and I could come in at night and rehearse. Sometimes, Portia Nelson, a friend from the publicity department who wrote and sang, too, would join me and play the organ while I played the piano.

But when they wanted me to do *Shady Lady,* I refused. I was to be the nightclub singer niece of cardsharp Charles Coburn, a lovely old actor. I didn't want to become a pin-up girl, though. I wanted to sing—seriously. Ginny Simms accepted the part. So Universal gave me $18,500 to go to Europe and study voice for a year. I wasn't so much interested in opera as in the concert stage. In 1945, I left Universal and never returned.

After my year of study, they wanted me back but I didn't like what they offered me. One property was *One Touch of Venus.* I didn't care much for Kurt Weill's music and the show had been changed considerably from stage to screen, so they borrowed Ava Gardner from MGM for it. The final straw was *The Countess of Monte Cristo,* with Sonja Henie. Now Sonja Henie was one of my favorite movie stars, but in this film they wanted me to play her maid! I had no desire to sing while Sonja

Henie skated. Olga San Juan took the part.

By the late 1940s, the whole movie business was changing. Even Bette Davis was having trouble finding the right roles. There was only one picture I can recall that I might have liked doing during this period. Over at Paramount, director Mitchell Leisen made a charming film that I saw later called *Song of Surrender,* with Claude Rains and Wanda Hendrix. She plays his repressed young wife who goes up on a hill and listens to classical gramophone records. If I had done the role, I could have sung instead of just played records. But it wasn't to be.

I married the singer Wilbur Evans, had two sons and dropped out of movies. Rough times were coming. *Very* rough. I hope one day to tell everything in a book.

Farley Granger—ACTOR—

They Live by Night was my first film after coming out of the Navy, and director Nicholas Ray's first film ever.

I had met Nick and the producer, John Houseman, at social gatherings. And when they decided to put this film together at RKO, they thought of me to play the young fugitive. They wanted me to test for it and were very kind: to make me more comfortable, they asked if there was some girl with whom I'd prefer testing. I was under contract to Samuel Goldwyn where I'd been working with Cathy O'Donnell, so I suggested her. They liked the way Cathy came over in the test so much that they also borrowed her to appear opposite me in *They Live by Night.*

Working on it was a wonderful experience. After it was done, I went to New York and when I returned to Hollywood a couple of weeks later, everyone was talking about the picture. Then, Dore Schary, who had been running the studio, left to go to MGM and Howard Hughes bought RKO. Hughes hated our picture. It had no tits and ass, so he put it on the shelf where it remained for a couple of years, unreleased. In the meantime, other directors had seen the picture at screenings and previews and were copying Nick Ray's great work. (It had the first helicopter shots in movies, for instance.) By the time *They Live by Night* finally sneaked out, the bloom was off the rose.

We were all so upset. When the picture was first put together, it was shown at the Museum of Modern Art in New York as one of the most interesting new films. But no one at RKO really understood it. They didn't give it any promotion. It really didn't do my career any harm, but it was Nick Ray's first film and, despite the many fine reviews, he was very depressed about its failure to find an audience.

The story was taken from a

novel called *Thieves Like Us,* but they didn't want to call it that because, they said, "People will think it's *Thieves LIKE Us.*" Then, for a while, it was called *Your Red Wagon.* Finally, it became *They Live by Night,* which people confused with an old Bogart movie, *They Drive by Night.* It was a general Hollywood mess.

Everyone on the Bel-Air circuit had seen it, though, including director Alfred Hitchcock. When he was preparing to film the play *Rope,* which was based on the Loeb-Leopold case, he thought of me for the role of one of the two college boys who commits a thrill murder. I was in New York when I received word from Goldwyn to come back and go to work for Hitchcock on *Rope.*

Unlike *They Live by Night, Rope* got plenty of publicity. It had a provocative plot and Hitchcock always liked a lot of publicity. And he could get it. In an era when few directors were known by the general public, when people went to the movies mainly to see stars like Clark Gable and Lana Turner, Alfred Hitchcock was the rare director who was familiar to audiences. I loved working with him. We got along very well, and a few years later he hired me again for one of his classics, *Strangers on a Train.*

Rope was shot at Warner Bros. and was Hitchcock's first film as a producer, too. It was a very unusual production. Hitch, who worked things out very carefully before shooting began, wanted to make a film with no cuts, but the cameras could only carry 10 minutes of film. Everything was very well rehearsed. Everybody had to be on his toes because of the long takes Hitch wanted. The one-apartment set was all on rollers; everything moved so that the camera could glide in and out of the rooms. The Technicolor camera was as big as a house, literally, and because there had to be so much light when you filmed in color, it was extremely hot. The lighting was very difficult. We had to do several sequences over again because when you'd leave one room and enter another your face might suddenly turn purple.

Jimmy Stewart was a delight to work with, a real pro. *Rope* was the beginning of his very productive association with Hitchcock, who helped him to escape his clichéd MGM image. And the veteran actors Sir Cedric Hardwicke and Constance Collier were as much fun as the young people in the company; maybe more so.

The homosexual aspect of the story wasn't really dealt with. It was just a thing that was assumed; either you got it or you didn't. Homosexuality was totally *verboten* on the screen then. And in the case of *Rope,* I think this was especially wrong. After all, it was part of the original story. Today, *Rope* could be filmed with more freedom.

My next two pictures, *Enchantment* and *Roseanna McCoy,* were done on my home lot, Goldwyn, and started me worrying. My fondest memories of *Enchantment* are of Teresa Wright, who is a lovely actress and woman, and David Niven, a wonderful man and the best raconteur I've ever known. But the director of both *Enchantment* and *Roseanna McCoy* was a man named Irving Reis, who was very neurotic. Up to then, I'd had only marvelous directors: Lewis Milestone on *The North Star* and *The Purple Heart,* Nicholas Ray and Hitchcock. Suddenly, working with Reis, I felt I was floundering. Something inside me said, "This isn't right." And I thought, "I don't trust this person and I'm beginning not to trust my own ability."

I knew then that I had to get out on my own, go to New York and study.

Kathryn Grayson——————*ACTRESS*—

I was never really interested in a motion picture career. I had studied opera from the age of 11—that was what I really wanted.

In my teens, however, MGM began to call me to come out and see them. I had recently signed with RCA Red Seal Records and had just begun recording for them. Eddie Cantor wanted me for his radio show, but RCA said, "No, we don't want another Deanna Durbin." Meanwhile, MGM called me for months. Finally, RCA said, "Go out and see them as a courtesy." I had expected to say, "Thank you very much, but no thanks." My teacher, who took me, and I would pay my respects to Ida Koverman, Louis B. Mayer's influential secretary who had been doing the calling, and leave. Well, I stayed the whole day. The studio even sent a limousine for my parents. I sang all kinds of songs for Mr. Mayer. By the time I left, I had been signed by Metro-Goldwyn-Mayer.

I went to school on the lot. Judy Garland, Mickey Rooney and Lana Turner had finished school that June and I enrolled in September. Our teacher was wonderful Mary MacDonald, who is still going strong at 91. Whenever I work somewhere, she gets herself beautifully turned out and comes to see me. Recently, I did the play *Noises Off* in San Diego and she was there. We had a ball talking over old times.

My first test was directed by George Sidney, who would later direct some of my biggest pictures, *Thousands Cheer, Anchors Aweigh, Show Boat* and *Kiss Me, Kate.* It was a phenomenal test, the most expensive one done up to that date (and probably to this date, too). Tom Conway was in it with me. I sang arias, popular songs, did a comedy scene, a dramatic scene. I recall that Katharine Hepburn, who saw it before I did, came up to me one day in the commissary to tell me that she had liked it. I didn't. A lot of people don't like to see themselves on the screen, and I am one. When the studio saw the test, though, they got the William Morris Agency's Abe Lastfogel and Johnny Hyde to represent me.

There were so many great tests done in those years. Esther Williams did her test with Clark Gable! No one can find any of these tests today. I suspect that Jim Aubrey, when he was running MGM in the late sixties and early seventies, had them all thrown out.

It was two years before I did my first feature, *Andy Hardy's Private Secretary.* Mickey Rooney was Andy, of course, and he was very kind and helpful. I wish I could say that I liked his autobiography, which has just been published. I had no boyfriend in the front office, as he keeps on writing, nor do I recall Mickey ever asking me out, as he claims. I was not one of the nightclub people. The publisher probably pushed Mickey to put in all that lurid material.

Rio Rita, with Bud Abbott and Lou Costello, was an interesting experience. Bud liked to gamble a lot and didn't really pay too much attention to anyone, but Lou was the sweetest, most caring guy. It was my first and only film done on location—Palm Springs. At the time, my new husband, the young MGM actor John Shelton, was in the service and getting ready to go overseas. Before doing so, he came down to Palm Springs to the location to spend a couple of weeks with me. Many years later, long after we were divorced, John was killed during the insurrection in Ceylon. He had been working for the old government, producing a film for them, when the new regime took power, killed John and renamed the country Sri Lanka.

Thousands Cheer was another party: director George Sidney, Gene Kelly in one of his early film roles, an all-star cast, Technicolor. Gene and Tommy Rall, who later appeared with me in *Kiss Me, Kate,* were my two favorite dancers. (Tommy never got the recognition he deserved; he was fabulous in *Kate.*) And as a human being, I adored Fred Astaire. Originally, *Thousands Cheer* was to be called *Private Miss Jones,* after my character; but as more and more big guest stars signed on (Judy Garland, Mickey Rooney, Lucille Ball, etc.), I guess they decided that *Thousands Cheer* had more ballyhoo potential.

When I finished *Thousands Cheer,* MGM sent me on bond, hospital and camp tours. Then they started me on the Loew's theater circuit. They probably felt secure sending me all over because they knew I would behave myself.

I made my in-person debut at the Capitol Theater in New York. I was told that it would probably be four shows a day for two weeks, maybe three, if we were held over. I turned out to be the first person to have a 10-week run there, seven shows a day. After the war, my brother and his roommate, Harry Leek (who would later become Howard Keel and co-star with me in several films), called to tell me that a blond crooner had broken my record at the Capitol. His name was Johnnie Johnston and he eventually became my second and last husband.

George Sidney was my director again on *Anchors Aweigh,* one of my most successful pictures. MGM's advertising slogan was, "How many times have you seen *Anchors Aweigh?*" George and I have been friends for many, many years. We recently did a seminar together in Charlottesville, Virginia. He was absolutely wonderful to work with. He had trained under movie musicals whiz Busby

Berkeley. The studio had the junior directors and the pro's. It was such a great system: everyone had the chance to really learn his or her craft. Gene Kelly and Frank Sinatra are my co-stars—Gene so talented and ambitious, Frank so conscientious and kind to everyone. I think Frank was even kinder to the man who swept up the stages than the top executives. And his dancing in *Anchors Aweigh* was a revelation, I thought. Frank was always a favorite of mine. We worked together again in *Till the Clouds Roll By, It Happened in Brooklyn* and *The Kissing Bandit.*

Till the Clouds Roll By was supposedly the biography of composer Jerome Kern, but it was really an excuse for all the MGM stars to do big, Technicolor numbers. By then, I was going with that blond crooner, Johnnie Johnston, and he had asked me to marry him. We had a Tyrolean number together in *Till the Clouds Roll By* from Kern's show *Music in the Air,* but when a certain Metro executive who had, shall we say, designs on me heard about Johnnie's intentions, our number was cut from the film. Johnnie also appeared with all the other stars in the finale, and now there is a sudden jump in the continuity where he was cut out of that, too, prior to the film's release. Consequently, he is not in the film at all. *I* just about made it.

My first husband, John Shelton, had his career at MGM cut short there because of top level personal interest in me, too. Later on, I also learned that the actors George Montgomery, John Carroll and Van Heflin were all told by my unwanted executive admirer not to ask me out. I think I married young to get away from all that.

Despite the threatening sabotage on *Till the Clouds Roll By,* I married Johnnie Johnston anyway. I was the first real rebel.

That Midnight Kiss was important because it was Mario Lanza's first starring role. Ida Koverman had heard ex-truck driver Mario at the Hollywood Bowl and took Mr. Mayer, Johnnie and me to hear him there, too. We were all overwhelmed by his incredible voice. Over the years, everybody has claimed to have discovered Mario Lanza, but it was really Mrs. Koverman and Mr. Mayer. MGM put him under a minimum contract. Everyone loved his voice, but no one wanted to work with him because he was greatly overweight and lacking in polish. I had just found out that I was pregnant, so Mr. Mayer gave me the nine months on salary to work with Mario and get him into shape to film. We sang, we talked, the masseur rubbed him raw. At the end of the nine months, he looked fine. My daughter, Patricia Kathryn, was born on Oct. 7, 1948, and on Oct. 17, 1948, Mario and I started *That Midnight Kiss.* People at the studio were soon telling me that my voice matched his better than anyone else I've ever sung with, and I like to believe it.

While they were still editing *That Midnight Kiss,* Mr. Mayer came to me and asked, "Would you take Mario on tour with you?" I pleaded, "Johnnie and I have just come back from a record-breaking tour." And Mr. Mayer replied, "Please, this would introduce him to the public."

M·G·M presents
TILL THE CLOUDS ROLL BY
IN TECHNICOLOR
Golden-voiced DINAH SHORE sings "The Last Time I Saw Paris."
Jerry Kern says goodbye to the kind family that had encouraged his start towards fame.
Starring (Alphabetically)
★ JUNE ALLYSON ★ LUCILLE BREMER ★ JUDY GARLAND
★ KATHRYN GRAYSON ★ VAN HEFLIN ★ LENA HORNE
★ VAN JOHNSON ★ ANGELA LANSBURY ★ TONY MARTIN
★ VIRGINIA O'BRIEN ★ DINAH SHORE ★ FRANK SINATRA
★ ROBERT WALKER as Jerome Kern
A METRO-GOLDWYN-MAYER PICTURE

So off we went. Mario's wife, Betty, was pregnant and we became close. The picture came out and was a hit.

Some people can take success, and some can't. Mario couldn't. He was wonderful at first, but it was all downhill after that. Which was too bad, because in the beginning we had fun singing together. I recall that about a year after we'd first heard him at Hollywood Bowl, Mario and I sang there. He'd try to hold a note as long as you, but sometimes he just couldn't and would then try to stop *you.* On one such occasion, he reached over, pulled the stole I was wearing tightly around my throat and, well, choked me to cut off the note.

After we did our next film, *The Toast of New Orleans,* I just threw up my hands. His weight shot up, and so did his temperament. He drank and behaved crudely. When he died, he was still in his thirties and living in Mussolini's apartment in Rome. Betty and the kids came to stay with me for a while. Then, a few months later, Betty died, too. I've lived in this 20-room house for 46 years. People are always staying with me.

The backbone of MGM was always Mr. Mayer. He was a very kind and fatherly man. As for the racy stories that sometimes crop up about him, if you were a lady you were treated like a lady. If you weren't. . .

Louis Mayer was the most brilliant showman of all. He saw the handwriting on the wall. He wanted the studios to run television, not television to run the studios. But no one else saw this, and it was one of the reasons why, in the early fifties, the stockholders had him fired. It was the end of the Hollywood we all knew and loved.

Jane Greer——ACTRESS——

They Won't Believe Me, in 1947, was the film that made me a star.

Up to then at RKO, where I'd been under contract for a couple of years, I'd played mostly heavies and handmaidens. I wanted to get away from that, but I had black hair, white skin and wore red-red lipstick (which Rudy Vallee, to whom I was married for a while, especially liked). This made me seem ideal for those roles.

Joan Harrison, once Alfred Hitchcock's assistant, really saved me from all that. She was now producing at RKO. In 1946, I had tested for one of her pictures, *Nocturne,* which was to star George Raft. I think I did it with Steve Brodie, who was also under contract to the studio—I was always testing with Steve. Anyway, George Raft refused even to look at my test. He wanted a "name" actress to co-star with him, so they got Lynn Bari.

But Joan remembered me and a few months later when she was preparing *They Won't Believe Me,* she thought I might fit in as the sympa-

thetic girlfriend of male lead Robert Young, who was to play one of his rare heavies. She said, "I'm going to test you but I'm going to put a soap cap on your hair"—which is a shampoo with peroxide in it. It didn't make me a blonde but simply put some highlights in my hair, greatly softening my look. I did the test with sweet and helpful Bob Young. That evening a telegram arrived saying, "Dear Jane, Sorry to tell you that your test didn't come off. Maybe another time. Love, Bob Young."

Actually, the telegram had been sent as a joke by Myrna Dell, an actress pal from RKO who has a great sense of humor, and a friend of hers. But I didn't know this then. That evening, I was supposed to meet Myrna and her friend for dinner, but my date and I were an hour late. Meanwhile, I learned later, a very worried Myrna was saying to herself, "Oh, my God, maybe Jane was so upset she killed herself! This is the second time she's been rejected for a big role."

But I knew Bob Young would never have sent such a telegram.

I got the part and everything went well.

After we finished, both Bob and Susan Hayward, who were top-billed, went to the front office and said, "Let's give Jane star billing with us." I was so moved; people in this business just don't do that sort of thing every day.

I was a star.

My next picture is still the one

I'm best remembered for: *Out of the Past,* with Robert Mitchum and Kirk Douglas. How could I fail? It's a real "Alan Ladd part," where people talk about someone in such intriguing terms that when this little five-feet-three guy finally appears, you're too sold to notice that maybe he's not really the biggest, toughest guy in town. That's what happened in *Out of the Past.*

Before it begins, I'd shot and wounded Kirk, stolen $40,000 from him and disappeared. He hires Bob to find me. "I just want her back," Kirk tells him before I finally come on. "When you see her you'll understand better." Others talk me up, too—"quite a gal," etc. And for my first appearance, I walk into the saloon out of the sunlight wearing a big picture hat while soft, romantic music plays on the soundtrack. I was in.

Our director, Jacques Tourneur, was French and didn't speak English very well. I can only recall one piece of direction he gave me. "I'll tell you what I want," he explained. "Eem-pass-seeve. Do you know what eem-pass-seeve means?" I replied, "Yes, I know what impassive means." Then he added, "No big eyes." Well, during the shooting I did throw in a couple of big eyes, but mostly I concentrated on remaining impassive. Which was good direction, in this case, because people could read all sorts of things into my impassive look.

Tourneur knew a lot about what we were eventually to call *film noir.* You can't see half the people in the picture! You have to count the heads at the end to see whom I've killed. Seriously, Nick Musuraca did a great job photographing *Out of the Past,* contributing much to its moody effectiveness. Tourneur knew what he wanted with the camera but pretty much left the actors alone, which I like.

Bob Mitchum was great to work with. The screenplay was very complicated; Bob later said, "You know what happened? They lost a dozen pages in Mimeo and no one knew it."

Bob would walk through anything he didn't like, but if he liked the part and the director, he'd be brilliant. I think he's brilliant in *Out of the Past.*

Recently, I was asked to guest on *Debbie Reynolds' Movie Memories* on the American Movie Classics cable TV channel. Beforehand, I talked to the producer, a knowledgeable man who asked intelligent questions. When Debbie and I got together for the taping, they showed a clip of Bob and me on the beach from *Out of the Past* and suddenly Debbie asked, "How was it working with Bob Mitchum and Kirk Douglas? I understand Bob is known for having affairs with his leading ladies."

I was taken aback but quickly informed her that Bob was like a brother to me, period. He watched over me. Once, he asked the wardrobe lady on *Out of the Past,* "How can you let this girl go into a scene with a dress pinned up in the back?" I had thought, "Oh, well, I'll be facing the camera; they won't see my back." I still expected that they would take care of me. I didn't know yet that I had to do it myself.

Afterward, we thought *Out of the Past* was okay but really just another picture. Years later, when the French coined the term *film noir,* it became a classic. During the 1960s and 1970s, it was playing all the time in France, Italy, England and in New York City. I'm always asked about it, which is fine because it's my favorite picture.

Station West co-starred me with Dick Powell. That was the good news. The director was a dreadful man named Sidney Lanfield who had wanted Marlene Dietrich in my role. At Fox, he had directed some of the early Sonja Henie vehicles and prior to our film had been working at Paramount. One day he told me, "I could pull a better actress than you off any street corner in Hollywood." And he asked the distinguished character actress Agnes Moorehead, who is in the film, too: "Do you ever *think* when you read a line, hatchet-face?" He was a horror, a bully.

Lanfield simply couldn't understand why I wasn't playing as Marlene would have. Finally, Raymond Burr, also in the cast and a fine actor, tried to help me get the kind of sardonic, glamorous Dietrich quality Lanfield sought. Ray coached me: he'd tell me to do things a certain way . . . stand like this or like that . . . look 'em in the eye. Lanfield intimidated me terribly. I *wanted* to be Marlene Dietrich, but that was tough to do.

We locationed in Sedona, Arizona, and the day I got back I married Edward Lasker. Maybe I was saying, "Take me away from all this!" Then I went to Dore Schary, who was running RKO, and told him how Lanfield was behaving. He went to Lanfield and advised him to calm down or else. We finished the film without incident. Lanfield didn't seem to have a problem with Dick Powell, but he really tore the women apart. Finally, he ran out of studios and there was no work for him. The word got around.

The Big Steal came out of left field. Lizabeth Scott had been borrowed from producer Hal Wallis, to whom she was under contract, to play opposite Bob Mitchum in this chase picture to be shot mostly in Mexico. Everyone was ready to go to Mexico when one night Bob went out and smoked some pot. The police arrested him. They had really wanted the actress [Lila Leeds] whose house he was visiting at the time, so they told Bob that they'd look the other way—he could sneak out. But he said no. Everyone expected that he'd just get a slap on the wrist but he got 60 days.

Now Hal Wallis said, "Lizabeth Scott work opposite a felon? No, no. She cannot do *The Big Steal.*" He withdrew her from the film. They asked every actress in town to take over the role. I know Joan Bennett was a strong possibility for a while. But in the end, they all backed off, presumably because of Bob's arrest which was making scandalous headlines around the world.

Eventually, they got around to me. Howard Hughes had recently purchased my studio, RKO. We were friends once, but we had had a falling-out and he had told me, "You'll never work on this lot again." When my name came up for *Big Steal,* he said, "No way." But they were desperate for a leading lady and one of his executives asked him,

"What about the stockholders?" That got to him, I guess, because he phoned me.

"Well," Howard said, first thing, "so you got yourself knocked up." I was stunned. It had been only a few days since I had had the rabbit test, and he knew that I was pregnant before I did! Louella Parsons or Hedda Hopper had called the head nurse at my doctor's office and she had spilled the beans. Somehow, the news had gotten back to Howard. Anyway, he asked me to do *The Big Steal.*

I wasn't crazy about the script. And, finding myself pregnant, I wasn't that anxious to work right then, either—especially for Howard Hughes. But I did want to show that I was behind Bob Mitchum all the way, so I accepted. That was on a Friday; on Tuesday I left for Mexico and the film. The costumes had already been fitted for Liz Scott and I just jumped into them.

The director, Don Siegel, who later became famous for his Clint Eastwood movies, was very nice, but not too well. He had diabetes and while we were in Mexico he had to give himself shots. He had some bad episodes there. It was not my most stress-free film.

When *The Big Steal* was finished, I was four-and-a-half months pregnant.

Fortunately, the fifties were just around the corner with some of my favorite movies, including *Run for the Sun,* with Richard Widmark, and *Man of a Thousand Faces,* with James Cagney.

Signe Hasso—ACTRESS—

The 1940s in Hollywood was truly a golden age. Here is one actress who can say she had no bad experiences as a result of being in pictures then. Well, almost none.

I worked with the most wonderful people. Three of the best directors were Ernst Lubitsch, with whom I did *Heaven Can Wait;* Henry Hathaway, my director on *The House on 92nd Street;* and George Cukor, who hired me for *A Double Life.*

Heaven Can Wait was one of Lubitsch's last films; he died a few years later. I had met him some time prior to the film at, I think, a party where there were a crowd of Europeans like ourselves. Then, one day when I was under contract to MGM, I was having lunch in Romanoff's with a writer from my studio. Lubitsch was also there—with Ann Sheridan, as I recall. He and the writer knew each other, and Mr. Lubitsch asked me to have lunch with him the following week at Fox.

I arrived at his office just as he had to leave for a few minutes. On his desk I noticed that the script for *Heaven Can Wait* was opened, so I started to read. It was at the point where the racy but funny French maid enters. When he came back, he said, "That's the part I want you to

play." He had purposely left so that I would read the part. Naturally I said yes, and he was able to borrow me from Metro to play "Mademoiselle."

Lubitsch was a master. When he directed, he would say, "This is how I think it should be done," and then he would show you exactly how he wanted it. "Showing" is so much better than "telling."

The House on 92nd Street started a trend for crime films shot entirely on actual locations—semi-documentaries they were called then. Our story was based on actual FBI files, and I played the dress shop proprietress who ran a Nazi spy ring in New York. At first, Darryl Zanuck, who ran the studio, 20th Century-Fox, didn't think too much of the project, and gave the producer, Louis de Rochemont, only a small amount of money to make it. When Henry Hathaway said he wanted to direct it, Zanuck increased the budget considerably. Hathaway was great. I've since heard that he was supposed to be difficult, but he wasn't at all; he was like a baby. He just expected people to know their profession.

We filmed in New York, putting on our make-up and changing our clothes in the offices of a plastic surgeon on, I believe, 91st Street. (I can still see all his before-and-after photos.)

All through the movie there are shots of the boss of all the spies, a "Mr. Christopher," going here and there on the streets of New York with his face carefully hidden. In the famous closing scenes, when the FBI has us surrounded, I repair to my room and remove my wig, make-up and dress and am revealed—as I get into a man's suit and hat—as the mysterious Mr. Christopher. It was quite a startling scene for the time [1945]. In the actual case, as I understood it, it was supposed to be a man masquerading as a woman. But the censors then wouldn't allow that; a woman posing as a man (which was how we did it) was all right.

Henry would way to me, "Okay, now you're supposed to be a man," and I'd get up, take off my make-up and become a man. No problem. It helped for me to think back to when my brother and I would play cowboys and Indians in Sweden. Once, when I arrived on the set dressed as Mr. Christopher, someone came up to me and said, "No visitors on this set!" I said, "It's me!" No one had recognized me as a man.

Henry insisted that I wear patent leather shoes as Mr. Christopher. At first, I didn't understand this, because in Europe we only wore patent leather to fancy galas. But Henry used many shots of Mr. Christopher's feet as he went about his nefarious deeds throughout the film, and he wanted patent leather so audiences would know immediately that these feet belonged to Mr. Christopher.

George Cukor helped to make *A Double Life* memorable for me. And he remained the dearest of friends. The story was about an actor who lived his roles, and there were several Shakespearean excerpts; so before we began Universal brought out the distinguished old stage actor, Walter Hampden, to coach Ronald Colman and me. I had played Shakespeare before, but I don't think Mr. Colman had—certainly not in many, many years. And he was a little frightened of it. As it turned out, this performance won him his Academy Award as Best Actor of 1947.

Shelley Winters had her first important part in the film as a waitress. A while ago I ran into her at some event here in Hollywood. I mentioned *A Double Life* to her and she looked confused. "Don't you remember? I played Ronald Colman's wife in it," I said. "Oh, did you?" she answered. She didn't remember that I was in it!

Mr. Colman was a perfect English gentleman. For one scene, he was supposed to choke me and he said in his veddy British manner, "Oh, deah, I'm not going to be able to touch you!" I said, "Oh, *please* touch me!" We tried all afternoon to get it, but Mr. Colman couldn't choke me. Finally, George Cukor said, "We *have* to have that shot!" So Mr. Colman tried again, and this time I watched his eyes change as his hands dug deep into my throat. I was gasping when he let me go. He said, "I say, did I hurt you?" They had to run for a nurse. My throat was black and blue. It had to be covered with make-up for days.

Another time, George said, "I would love you to have the same hairdo for these scenes as Kate Hepburn had in one of her films." So he called Hepburn and asked if she had some pictures of herself with this hairdo that we could borrow. Well, she brought the pictures to the studio herself and stood with the hairdresser to make sure my hair was done the way George wanted, which I thought was awfully sweet.

George Cukor was so special. My son Henry was ill for several years, and George took a genuine interest in him. He had an open line on the set so that Henry could reach us if he wanted anything. He arranged for teachers to go to the hospital and work with him.

After the years of illness, my son was totally cured. Although he had grown very tall and handsoome, he wasn't really interested in acting. But a film came up, so he thought he'd try it, make some money and continue his studies. He was supposed to start filming in three weeks. Then one day when he was out driving with a friend, the car crashed and he was killed. He was 22.

Celeste Holm—ACTRESS

I was having supper at the Brown Derby in Hollywood when *Gentleman's Agreement* was first mentioned to me.

I had just done a benefit for the Lambs Club, and I never eat before I do a benefit, so I was having dinner about 10 o'clock this evening. I noticed that Moss Hart was sitting right across from me, looking just like a writer with his plaid jacket, silk scarf and three-day beard growth. I had known him from New York, and he came over and asked me if I had read the new novel *Gentleman's Agreement,* by Laura Z. Hobson. I told him I'd never even heard of it. He said, "I'm writing the screenplay. Read the book and call me."

So I got a copy, read it and called Moss. As soon as he came on, I said, "Yes. Any part." He said, "Great. I want you for Ann Detrie," the fashion editor. I said, "Wonderful," and we were off.

They made me do the big emotional scene the first day. Darryl Zanuck, the head of 20th Century-Fox, knew me only as a musical comedy performer and didn't think I could handle drama. "Ridiculous," Moss told Zanuck. "She started in Shakespeare." The director, Elia Kazan, had complete confidence in me, too. There was, I guess, the possibility that I might be removed from the film if I couldn't cut this big serious moment. I must have done all right, because everything went smoothly from then on.

Oh, I remember there was one scene that took 25 takes to get. I was serving at a buffet and had to move around and be interrupted by several people, and it took forever. It was worth it, though; it played beautifully on the screen.

Elia Kazan was a wonderful director. A good director is one who considers *you,* and he was very appreciative of me. He worked in subtle ways. He would whisper bits of direction in my ear; he had a kind of private relationship with his actors. When you'd do the scenes, you'd be

trying to figure out what he had told the other actors.

Also, Kazan would have us come in the day before we'd film and rehearse, so we'd be familiar with each other as well as the material.

Our leading man, Gregory Peck, was perfect to work with, and Dorothy McGuire was lovely, too. I remember that she was kind of unhappy, though, because she had just lost a baby. And I had just had one, and was blooming.

Fox was a story studio. They had their stars, but Zanuck saw to it that they were kept under control. *Gentleman's Agreement,* an indictment of anti-Semitism, was just the sort of strong story Zanuck liked. And he must be given credit for having the courage to tackle such a controversial theme. After all, even today, more than 40 years later, people don't want to face their bigotry. Furthermore, there were many Jews in Hollywood, and a large number were trying to pretend there was no such thing as prejudice. Zanuck, incidentally, was one of the few Hollywood moguls of that time who was not Jewish.

Personally, however, I couldn't help thinking he was a jerk. He was all caught up in that macho crap. He used to say, "Tenderness is a sign of weakness." In reality, it is a sign of strength. "Men are meant to lead, women follow." He said junk like that.

My Fox films must have been pretty successful. At a recent summer-long retrospective of 20th pictures at the Museum of Modern Art in New York, I was the only living actress, I believe, to have five films represented. But Zanuck was never really keen on me. Fox had recently had the volatile Broadway star Tallulah Bankhead for two films, *Lifeboat* and *A Royal Scandal,* and she had given the lot plenty of trouble. So when I finally came out to do *Three Little Girls in Blue,* the feeling was, "Oh-oh, here comes another Broadway actress."

I came from great success in the theater, had wended my way through the shoals of Broadway all by myself. But I was certainly no Tallulah Bankhead. I was an entirely different person, quiet and ladylike. I had a mind of my own, though, which Zanuck didn't appreciate. For instance, he wanted me to do *Nightmare Alley,* an ugly story about carnival geeks with Tyrone Power. I told him that if he did this picture it would be a major disaster and I wanted no part of it. It flopped magnificently and Zanuck was furious with me! I accepted *Road House,* but wasn't happy with my role: I mean—a cashier in a bowling alley?

Gentleman's Agreement opened and won three 1947 Academy Awards: Best Picture, Best Director and Best Supporting Actress—me. Anne Revere, who was also in the film, was nominated in the same category as I. Usually, when two people are nominated in one category from the same film, they cancel each other out, but not this time. When the Oscars were announced, I was starring on Broadway in *Affairs of State* and singing in a club.

In the fourth year of my contract at Fox, there was a cutback. Zanuck wrote to my lawyers: "We are so happy with dear little Celeste. She has two pictures unreleased. Would you mind if she didn't get her $500 raise now and got $1,000 in a year?" My lawyers wrote back: "Celeste Holm has fulfilled the terms of her contract. Why can't you?" My lawyers asked me if I wanted out, and I said *yes.*

Several months later, director-screenwriter Joseph L. Mankiewicz insisted I return to Fox to appear for him in *All About Eve.* Zanuck didn't want me and was furious again.

Many years later, I attended a party for the publication of one of Elia Kazan's novels, and, introducing me, he said, "I did *Gentleman's Agreement* with Celeste Holm—one of the greatest actresses I ever worked with." I replied, "Why didn't you ever hire me again?"

I have always been a *blunt* actress, too.

Victoria Horne—ACTRESS—

I always wanted to be the greatest actress in the world, darlin'. Until I met Jack Oakie.

I studied Shakespeare in England and did *Hamlet* on the New York stage with Leslie Howard. I appeared in *Life with Father* on Broadway, too, and toured with it for three years. When we got to Los Angeles, our stars, Louis Calhern and Dorothy Gish, introduced me to Jack Oakie. I took one look at him and stopped breathing and never started again. If there was ever love at first sight, this was it. We were married in 1943. Jackie Gleason always called my Jack "the greatest" (until they began calling Gleason that), and he was, darlin', he *was*.

I was screen-tested at Paramount for a scene in *Going My Way*. I played Risë Stevens' maid. But they decided not to use that scene in the picture, so my agent, George Wallace, took the test over to Universal. They liked it and signed me to a contract. My first picture was *Phantom Lady,* an early [1944] *film noir* with Franchot Tone and Ella Raines, directed by Robert Siodmak.

Then I did *The Scarlet Claw,* a Sherlock Holmes mystery which some have called the best in the series. I dearly loved that series and wish I could have been in more. Basil Rathbone and Nigel Bruce were still playing Holmes and Dr. Watson, of course, and they were a delight. I recall my big scene where the bad guy ties me up and puts me in a closet. Basil Rathbone has to pick me up there and put me in a chair. Bound up like that, I was dead weight, so I asked him, "How can I help? Is there anything I can do to make lifting me easier for you?" He said, "Don't worry," and did it with no trouble. He was so strong! He must have been an athlete. I think he did play a lot of tennis. I know he and my husband were friends long before I ever met Jack.

Jack and I did a couple of pictures together. *That's the Spirit* was the first, and it was such a happy set that I went to the front office and asked to work with him again. So they put us in *She Wrote the Book,* with Jack opposite Joan Davis. I play the small role of a maid. Just before we started it, we were visiting with ex-New York mayor Jimmy Walker in a hotel room when the maid came in, her keys jangling. Jack, that rascal, quipped, "Mommie, you watch what she's doing and research your part."

Over at Paramount, I loved doing *To Each His Own* for director Mitchell Leisen. Olivia de Havilland stars and I play her friend and partner who gets to advise her and tell her off and everything. But Olivia was a lovely person. And then I worked with her again at 20th Century-Fox in *The Snake Pit.* Many years later, after my husband's death in 1978, Olivia came over from her home in Paris and attended a City of Hope benefit where we chatted again. She said, "You have no complaints, Vickie. I can tell you've had a very happy life."

I play Gene Tierney's sister-in-law in *The Ghost and Mrs. Muir,* another plummy assignment. It was directed at Fox by Joseph L. Mankiewicz, who was such a wonderful, creative man. He and Jack were old friends and colleagues—he wrote many of Jack's early pictures. When my husband turned 70, I embarked on the project of getting letter reminiscences from his friends, and Joe's was the most beautiful. It was printed in Jack's posthumously pub-

Proudly
Paramount
Presents
"To Each His Own"
Olivia
DeHavilland
MITCHELL LEISEN
CHARLES BRACKETT
MITCHELL LEISEN

OLIVIA de HAVILLAND
the Snake Pit
20th
MARK STEVENS and LEO GENN
Celeste Holm · Glenn Langan
ANATOLE LITVAK
ROBERT BASSLER
ANATOLE LITVAK

lished book, *Jack Oakie's Double Takes.* Darlin', there was hardly a night on *Ghost and Mrs. Muir* that I didn't carry a note home from Joe Mankiewicz to Jack.

In 1947, Jack and I saw *Harvey,* starring Frank Fay, on Broadway. When the character Myrtle May, the man-hungry niece, came on, Jack turned to me and said, "Mommie, that's your part." In 1950, Universal filmed the play with Jimmy Stewart and I was cast as Myrtle May, one of my best roles. When Jack and I saw the picture, he said, "Mommie dear, you've made enough faces now. Why don't you stay home?"

So I did. Oh, I went back for a few small roles, but essentially it was just Mr. and Mrs. Jack Oakie at home after that. (*Jack Oakie's Oakridge* is the title of a book I recently put together about our lovely Northridge, California, home which Jack bought from Barbara Stanwyck in the '30s.) He was always in demand, but he really wanted to retire, so he had been acting less and less.

Darlin', it has truly been a wonderful life with Jack Oakie. I honestly believe that everything I did B.O. (Before Oakie) was just to lead me up to that introduction to him.

As I said, all my dreams of becoming a great actress went out the window when I met Jack Oakie. I knew that being his wife was the job God really had intended me for.

John Howard—ACTOR

Why they thought of me for *The Philadelphia Story* is still a mystery to me.

I was in New York when a wire came from my agent saying that Paramount, where I was under contract, had made a deal for me to appear at MGM in *Philadelphia Story.* I quickly got a copy of Philip Barry's play from a friend and read it, but I was damned if I could figure out who the hell I would be. When I got back to Hollywood and talked to Paramount, they said, "You're to play George Kittredge, Katharine Hepburn's fiancé." It seemed like a nothing part to me, though, and furthermore I didn't think I was right for it: on the New York stage, it was done by Dick Foran, the big, strapping singing cowboy, whom I in no way resembled. I tried to get Paramount to let me turn it down, but the director, George Cukor, said, "It's an important picture. We want you to do it." Since I was not legally able to turn it down because of my Paramount contract, I went over to MGM and did it.

And I've never been sorry. It was wonderful working with Katharine Hepburn, Cary Grant, Jimmy Stewart and Ruth Hussey. I'd never met Kate before, but I knew both Jimmy and Ruth through mutual friends and Cary was under contract to Paramount when I was there—we'd have lunch together sometimes during those years. Anyway, the film was a breeze to make, although I did get jealous from time to time because all the other actors had better lines than I had. And I wasn't entirely comfortable in the part for another reason: I was hardly ideally cast as a rough-edged, self-made ex-coal miner. I don't know why they didn't use the original guy, big Dick Foran. I loved George Cukor—he was very sensitive—but we did have a few arguments over the reading of some lines. In the long run, though, I did what he wanted.

I thought Cukor was everything a good director ought to be. He'd let the actor work things out himself. He'd hear you off the set, then when you got on, he might say, "The mood should be lighter here." Or something like that. He never told you how to say it, though. The best directors I worked with were like that—Frank Capra, Frank Borzage, Mitchell Leisen. I worked with directors who wanted to run the whole show, and their films were usually not so hot, to my way of thinking.

Hepburn owned the rights to the play and had had a great success in it on Broadway, but she never threw her weight around on the set. She left everything to George. Oh, maybe once in a while she'd go off in a corner with him and put her two cents in, but she was entitled: no one knew the property as well as she did. She was a fun, straight-from-the-shoulder gal. Years later, after the war, Kate and I lived on the same street in New York, and we'd wave to each other.

MGM was very different from Paramount, where I'd been for seven years and done many films, including the Bulldog Drummond series. The only film I did at Metro was *Philadelphia Story,* but I observed that while it was the most efficiently run studio around, and the people there were polite, it could not compare (at least for me) to Paramount. That place was like a big country club where we had members like Bing Crosby, Bob Hope, Carole Lombard, Martha Raye, all of whom were nuts. It was fun to be on the lot. Everyone was whistling when they'd come to work there in the morning. MGM was a much colder place.

When *Philadelphia Story* opened, it was a tremendous hit. Jimmy Stewart won the Academy Award. Kate had a whole new career. It certainly didn't hurt me to be in it, but I don't recall that it did me any great good, either. About a year later, my contract at Paramount came up for renewal, but we argued about terms and I wound up leaving. World War II was coming; I knew I would soon be in the Navy, so I began grabbing any movie that came along. I expected the war to last 10 years, and I wanted to be able to leave my family provided for in my absence.

Luckily, my agent got me a contract with 20th Century-Fox shortly before I left. When I got out three-and-a-half years later, he asked Fox, "What have you got for John?" And they said, "Nothing." Then Leland Hayward, the agent-producer, sent my agent a wire: "I'd like to talk to John Howard about a Broadway play." Leland sent the completed two acts of the eventual three-act play; I read them and felt it was a God-given opportunity. My agent asked Fox for my release; they fell over with glee. The play was called *Portrait in Black.* Geraldine Fitzgerald was our leading lady and it closed out of town. When the third act was finally completed by the writers, it just didn't work as well as the first two. (Years later, it became a successful film with Lana Turner and Anthony Quinn.)

I returned to Hollywood with no plans. There were more films, but none to compare with *The Philadelphia Story.* And to think I wanted to get out of doing it!

Marsha Hunt—*ACTRESS*—

I knew it was the golden age of Hollywood, but I didn't know its days were numbered.

When I did *Pride and Prejudice,* I had just come to Metro-Goldwyn-Mayer and was thrilled to have my first crack at comedy, which I dearly loved to play. I drew Mary, the near-sighted, bookish member of the five unmarried Bennet daughters who sings a little off-key, and I play her for laughs. I had come over from Paramount, where in my first three years in the film industry I had played 12 ingénues—a species, I must add, I have never met in real life. They were really just writers' devices, different only in their changes of wardrobe.

After having done the ingénue bit in four Westerns, it was gratifying at last to have such a literate script as Aldous Huxley and Jane Murfin provided for *Pride and Prejudice.* The whole thing was distinguished, a cultural milestone for MGM. Our stars, of course, were Greer Garson, who had just come over from England, and Laurence Olivier, whom I had discovered a few years earlier in something called *Moscow Nights.* It played the lower half of a double bill, but I stayed around to see it. As Olivier himself noted in his autobiography, his early films were nothing to shout about, but when I saw those hooded eyes, that presence, I went around saying to friends, "Laurence Olivier will be heard from, you'll see." And we all saw!

Although it was hardly a character role, Olivier wore a false nose as Mr. Darcy in *Pride and Prejudice.* He never liked his own face. He was about to play *Romeo and Juliet* with his sweetheart Vivien Leigh on Broadway, and I believe he felt that to portray the classic role of Romeo he had to have a classic nose—you know, a sort of carved appendage to the forehead. And this he did not have normally. I think he used the false nose in our film to see what it would look like in *Romeo and Juliet.* Actually, it was quite subtle.

His mind was really on *Romeo and Juliet* throughout *Pride and Prejudice.* He spent most of his time buried in Shakespeare's text, making notes; then, when he would be called for our picture, he'd do it but it was like a finger exercise.

None of us had any idea the film would be so popular. George Cukor was originally supposed to direct, which was exciting, but at the last minute he was replaced by Robert Z. Leonard, whom everyone called "Pop." We all thought, "Nothing will come of this." Recently, Maureen O'Sullivan, who appears as my sister Jane, told me that when she met with Olivier years later in England they expressed mutual surprise at the picture's success.

Our incredible cast certainly plays its part, starting with Greer Garson, delightful as Elizabeth Bennet. I made three pictures with Greer, including *Blossoms in the Dust,* which came soon afterward. In this, she's cast as Edna Gladney, the real-life woman who started children's homes and had the word "illegitimate" removed from all documents; I am her adored adopted sister who shoots herself when her illegitimacy is made known. I loved the role but during the filming was very cross with our director, Mervyn LeRoy. For the scene in which I quietly go upstairs to commit suicide, he holds the camera relentlessly at the foot of the stairs until the act, revealed only by a gunshot, is accomplished off-camera in an upstairs room. I had seen Andrea Leeds enact a similar scene in an earlier film called *Stage Door,* the camera observing her beautiful, anguished face as she climbs the stairs to her doom. And she won an Academy Award nomination.

I begged Mervyn, "Please shoot it my way, with the camera observing

"I put your father before his murderer — how can I marry you!"

my emotions as I mount the stairs. It will make the episode clearer to audiences. Then we'll try it your way."

"No," he answered. "It will be more effective understated." So, it was done his way. I still think I was right. In view of the fact that the sister's suicide propels Edna Gladney in all her subsequent activities, it should have been underlined.

After *Blossoms in the Dust* came out, I received a beautiful letter from Mrs. Gladney herself saying that I had done a wonderful job evoking her beloved sister. Strangely, I had never seen any pictures of the sister, nor did I really know much about her except that she died tragically. But I must have lucked into something.

A few years later, Greer Garson and I made our last film together, *The Valley of Decision,* another fine but, I think, underrated picture. It doesn't seem to have stayed with people the way it should have. Gregory Peck plays opposite Greer, and Marshall Thompson and I are twins.

One thing happened on this one that is burned into my memory. At the start, Greg returns from abroad and shouts up the stairs. With a squeal of delight, I slide down the bannister into his arms. But it wasn't quite that simple. I had slid down bannisters as a child. I never made a science of it, but I knew that you straddle the bannister and slide down backwards, facing upstairs. However, the director, Tay Garnett, wanted me to come down sidesaddle, face forward—wearing a bustle, yet. I thought, "I'd better practice."

So I'd go up and slide down three steps, then go up and slide down five and so on to work up my courage. After a while, I realized I was hurting where I was doing all the sliding.

Back in my dressing room, I discovered that I had raised a swelling the size of a grapefruit and all the colors of the rainbow! They were just about ready to shoot my "slide for life," as they called it, but when I reported the swelling they put it off till the last day of shooting. That way, the swelling would have time to heal and if, by any chance, I didn't make it down the bannister safely, they could rush in a double—they'd have the rest of my role in the can. This time I was padded. What saw me through it all was the sight of darling Greg Peck standing at the bottom of the stairs to catch me.

Young Marshall Thompson got kind of a crush on Greg as we filmed *Valley of Decision.* You could see he'd found his role model.

He'd follow Greg around and say things like, "What do you think of this?" or "What do you think of that?"

Greer was so lovely in it. I respected her as an actress greatly, but I never got to know her well. She was extremely private, didn't share herself, was very involved in her work. I don't mean that she was cold. She was a very witty and articulate woman; I relished her intelligence. Many years later we met again at a function for the Eleanor Roosevelt Foundation.

Greer, of course, had played Mrs. Roosevelt in *Sunrise at Campobello.*

We met each other as if we were long-lost sisters! That often happens when you run into acquaintances in distant lands. I remember the joy of running into Alfred Hitchcock in Europe once, though I scarcely knew him, ditto meeting David Selznick abroad.

In October 1990, I was invited to the gala opening in Santa Fe, New Mexico, of the new communications facility Greer had donated to the college there.

There aren't too many of us left who have appeared in three films with her! The event was celebrity-studded, with many of Greer's wealthy friends expecting to see her, too. At the last minute, doctors advised her not to attend. The altitude was deemed potentially harmful to her fragile heart. (A while back, she was forced to sell her big ranch there because of the altitude.) She also was just getting over the flu.

Art Linkletter hosted the big banquet on the new sound stage of the Garson Studios in Santa Fe. Over a speaker system, he called her and about 500 of us heard her voice. Later, she sent me a bottle of perfume for attending.

The Human Comedy was another nice one I did. It was a very sentimental picture about a family affected by war that packed Radio City Music Hall in New York for weeks.

I believe it was a favorite of our chief at MGM, Louis B. Mayer. He was a sentimental man who believed in the verities—family and patriotism. He really loved films, more, I think, than the other so-called Hollywood moguls of the time.

Mayer wanted to promote things that made better people, and we don't have that today, sadly. Mickey Rooney was very good in the film—no "Mickey tricks" were discernible on screen. Off-camera, he was the usual Mickey: you never knew what prank he'd be up to.

I play a nice but flighty rich girl who keeps saying, "You do love me, don't you? You know you do." Before we met, my husband, Robert Presnell, Jr., went to see *The Human Comedy* with a young lady who would later be under contract to Metro. When he saw me on the screen, he told his companion, "I am going to marry her!" Which was quite a thing to say to your charming date! It was my line that got to him.

My span of time at MGM was enchantment. They let me do what I most wanted to do: *everything.* I flew in the face of the traditional road to stardom, which was to specialize. Gable was Gable in film after film. That was the foundation on which stardom was built then.

I went in the opposite direction: no two roles that I played were alike.

I was a young girl, but MGM even let me play an old woman a couple of times. One came at the very beginning of my association with the studio in a film called *Joe and Ethel Turp Call on the President.* I was appearing with Walter Brennan, who won three Academy Awards! We were both supposed to age greatly during the film.

On the first day, Walter came to me and said, "I've played so many old codgers. Please help me. When I play the young man, tell me if my tummy is sticking out or if my shoulders are slouching, if I'm doing anything inappropriate." This distinguished actor was asking this much less experienced actress, me, for help. He put me completely at ease and I said to myself, "What a thoughtful man." Later, I learned that politically he was very right-wing. I was more liberal, but I never held it against him.

Smash-Up, the Story of a Woman, done at Universal, was another unique experience. It was probably the first full screen study of a female alcoholic.

Susan Hayward plays the drunk and gives a most telling performance. I am cast as her husband's very sleek, omnipresent secretary. Although my character ultimately breaks down and confesses that she is in love with the husband, she never makes a move toward him. Yet many who see the film consider my role the villain. She is very cool and chic and picks gifts for Susan *at the husband's request,* but I don't think of her as a heavy.

People have come up to me on the street and said, "My, weren't you mean to Susan Hayward in *Smash-Up?*" I reply, "What did I do or say that was so mean?" Audiences view her through Susan's eyes.

When Susan and I had our famed hair-pulling match in the picture, it was the sort of scene you could only shoot once. There was no way to repair the coiffures after we got our hands in them! Susan really gave it to me; she pulled no punches. I learned the wisdom of this the hard way. Years before, I was doing a picture at Metro and Kathryn Grayson

had to slap me. She was a bit timid and just couldn't do it. She'd pull it each time. After a while, I was getting a swollen face from her half-hearted slaps. Finally, she did it but I was nursing a very red and puffy cheek by then. Susan made it real the *first* time!

What was Susan Hayward like? You multiply what I said about Greer Garson 10 times. Susan didn't even acknowledge "good mornings." Whether she was saving herself for the main event, I couldn't say. When you find people on the set are not open to conversation, you respect that.

Professionally, she was on time, knew her lines, gave everything she had. And she had a beautiful speaking voice. But personally, she was a locked-up vault, a fortress.

On the other hand, Eddie Albert, who has one of the other leads, was a delight. Between scenes, he sang folk songs and told me of his war experiences. It seems that he was adrift on a raft or something like that and promised God that if he was ever saved, he would help mankind. And believe me, he kept that promise.

The girl I play in *Smash-Up* was of interest to me because I was born with an extremely expressive face. It shows every emotion.

The screen magnifies everything, so I've had to strip away a lot. Martha, my character in *Smash-Up,* is the distillation of this, the most controlled woman I've ever played.

Ruth Hussey—*ACTRESS*—

The 1940s was a bountiful and beautiful time for Hollywood. And for Hussey.

I was still under contract to MGM in the early '40s and got the decade off to an auspicious start by appearing with Joan Crawford, Fredric March and Rita Hayworth in *Susan and God,* under George Cukor's direction. It was pure joy. Joan was very nice, a hard worker and so dedicated. When she wasn't shooting, she was off somewhere going over her lines. There was no temperament. "If you don't bring me an ice cream cone, I'll scream!"—none of that. All those stories about Hollywood fights and tantrums were just that: stories. I worked with top people who didn't have to be nasty to get attention. They'd get it anyhow.

Fredric March was charming. During *Susan and God,* just before they'd say, "Camera!" he'd wink at me. I finally asked him why he did this, and he replied, "Just to make you feel comfortable." Rita Hayworth was sweet, too, so quiet and shy then.

George Cukor also directed my next film, which happens to be my favorite, *The Philadelphia Story.* I play the *Spy* magazine photographer and received a [1940] Best Supporting Actress Academy Award nomination. George was a perfect director, so patient, imaginative and colorful with actors. He never told you what to do or how to say it, but when he discussed your part with you he *colored* the dialogue so that you knew exactly what approach to take. It was like looking at a sketch: when you put the colors in, it comes to life.

Katharine Hepburn, Cary Grant and Jimmy Stewart were brilliant, witty, sparkling, you-name-it. (Later on, I did *Philadelphia Story* in summer stock—playing the Hepburn socialite role this time, however). Kate also was friendly and most pleasant. People have written that she's eccentric, but I never thought so. She is merely individualistic. So is Jimmy. Once, between scenes, he took one of the artificial roses from a bouquet on a table, twisted the stem in double circles to make it stand and put it on top of his head. "Now what did I want to see Ripley about?" he asked, mincing around as if the flower were growing out of his head.

The Philadelphia Story was an important, popular picture, but I must confess some surprise that it continues to be so widely appreciated today. After all, a couple of generations have come along since then and the film is about flighty rich people from a bygone era. At one point in it, Jimmy Stewart's character says, "The prettiest sight in this fine, pretty world is the privileged class enjoying its privileges." The cast and director, of course, have something to do with its durability, but I think everything starts with the writing. You must have the material. You take a piece of burlap to a London tailor and it still won't turn out so well. Philip Barry wrote the play *The Philadelphia Story,* and Donald Ogden Stewart wrote the screenplay; they knew what they were doing.

Northwest Passage was a big, exciting story, although I didn't have much to do in it. But it was in Technicolor and I was opposite Robert Young, a man I have always admired. Over the years we acted together in many movies, radio programs and television shows. Among the films in which we appeared are *Rich Man, Poor Girl, Honolulu, Maisie, Married Bachelor, H.M. Pulham, Esq.*, and, of course, *Northwest Passage.* He was a pleasure to work with, a very businesslike actor who knew his lines and what he was doing every minute. At the time we made all those movies, I never knew that he suffered from depression and alcoholism; that all came out years later. I recall that when I worked with him on television, he would come down on the set and seemed to be doing just great. Just before filming would begin, he'd insist that we all have a moment of silence so that those who wanted to say a prayer could do so.

I play the wife of Andrew Johnson, our 17th president, in *Tennessee Johnson,* opposite Van Heflin. I enjoyed the experience thoroughly, one reason being that I get to grow old in the part, which every actress likes. However, I had recently married and one day my husband, C. Robert Longenecker, told me that he wanted to come down on the set, which he rarely ever did. I was made up for the elderly Mrs. Johnson and thought, "Oh, I don't want him to see me like this." You know—there were these old-age pencil lines all over my face that don't really show on the screen but look dreadful in person, especially when one is a young bride. Well, he came anyway and was so tactful. He said, "You look lovely. Now I know what you'll look like when you're older."

I still get a lot of mail on *The Uninvited,* which I did over at Paramount with Ray Milland and Gail Russell. Evidently it's shown frequently on television. It's a ghost story and there are many frightening scenes in it. One involves large doors unexpectedly, ominously blowing open. Of course, while we were acting our roles we didn't see the special effects; they were put in later. Consequently, when I went to the preview and those doors up there on the screen suddenly whooshed open, I literally jumped out of my seat.

I was in New York when Paramount called me and asked me to do the picture. I bought the Dorothy Macardle novel on which it was based, got on the train West and settled into my little compartment to read it. I stayed up much of the night reading and at about the half-way point in the book, my blood began to run cold. I broke out in goose pimples! I had never felt like this before. I slept with the light on all night.

One funny thing happened while we were filming *The Uninvited.* Unless you were Greta Garbo, you always had visitors coming onto the set. While we were working one day, the Yale Glee Club showed up to watch. As the crew was getting the next scene ready, I asked the Glee Club, "Oh, couldn't you sing something for us?" The fellows said, "Sure," and broke into a five-minute song. Later, I was scolded by the front office

because that song had kept the company waiting, costing the studio $9,000.

The Great Gatsby was also done at Paramount. Alan Ladd, our Gatsby, was a very serious, quiet man. Once, while they were getting the lighting ready, Alan and I got to talking. He told me, "As far as I'm concerned, all acting is in the expression of the eyes." It was an interesting note on which to conclude my 1940s moviemaking.

Gloria Jean——ACTRESS——

After reading the script of what became *Destiny,* I was overwhelmed: a whole new career seemed to be opening up for me. I'd been doing light musicals, and here I was, going to play the very demanding role of a blind girl. I felt that at last I would be able to prove I wasn't only a sweet, adolescent soprano but an actress, too.

Originally, the story was to be the first segment in a four-part film dealing with the supernatural called *Flesh and Fantasy,* produced by

Charles Boyer and the French director Julien Duvivier, who was also directing. Mr. Boyer was starring in one of the stories, too—not mine, though. I remember I prayed that I would get the part. Universal tested many outside girls for the role, but since I was under contract to the studio and the picture would be made there, I guess they finally decided, "Let's give it to Gloria Jean." One day I was having lunch in the commissary when Mr. Boyer came over to me and said, "Guess who got the part—you!"

The shooting went beautifully. Everyone told me to be careful of Mr. Duvivier—"He's hard, he's a perfectionist." Well, I loved him. He helped me achieve the demure look that was so essential to the role. He saw some of my tests, and felt I was too made up. He wanted me to be more natural-looking, with my hair pinned back, sort of like the French country girls he must have seen back home. I studied with blind people for a while to learn how they looked and moved and behaved. To further insure the effect of blindness, they put a beam of light in each of my eyes; by the end of the film I could hardly see. My vision came back, though.

One day on the set we were visited by the famous columnist Hedda Hopper, who had heard that we were about to shoot the scene where Alan Curtis tries to rape me. "I'm here to see Gloria Jean get attacked!" she bellowed. Everybody roared. Actually, she didn't really get to see it, because with the special effects called for in the scene it took a couple of days to film. Today, it would be like a scene in Sunday school! Hedda was always very kind to me; so was Louella Parsons, her archrival.

It was all shot on the back lot at Universal. Our house was built, but there was nothing inside it. The wind and the rain when I ran through the woods from Alan, the grasping trees and branches, the turbulent river—all these were special effects.

There were lots of big stars in the other segments: Mr. Boyer, Barbara Stanwyck, Edward G. Robinson, Bob Cummings, Betty Field, Robert Benchley. But when *Flesh and Fantasy* was previewed, my segment was the hit of the evening. Still, it was not to be. They took it out of the picture, leaving only three episodes, which is how *Flesh and Fantasy* was released to theaters. It was all very abrupt. Nobody ever gave me an official explanation why my segment had been cut. It was my one chance in a big, dramatic movie. I was devastated.

Sometime afterward, I was told that certain other people on the lot—most particularly another powerful singer there [Deanna Durbin]—were jealous of how well my role in the film had come off and insisted I be cut out. I couldn't believe anyone would do such a thing—but I was certainly out of the movie. (The studio would never loan me out, either. Furthermore, Universal never put me in any Technicolor films, which I dreamed of doing, and when other studios wanted to borrow me for color films my studio said no. There seemed to be concerted efforts to let me go just *so far.*)

My segment from *Flesh and Fantasy* went on the shelf. About six months later, someone took a look at the footage and said, "This is too good to shelve." They decided to make it into a feature film. Of course, as it was, it was too short, so they got Reginald LeBorg to direct additional footage that really only padded it. Now I don't come in till late in the story—too late, I think. Mr. LeBorg was a lovely man, but he was no Duvivier. The core of the film remains Duvivier's, though, which is why *Destiny* (as it was eventually titled) remains my favorite film. But it was only a "B" picture, and while it was liked by many, nobody really paid all that much attention to "B"s in those years. My hopes of a dramatic career never materialized.

Next, the studio put me into *Mister Big,* with Donald O'Connor, which was so upbeat, so full of music and comedy. It was quite a shock for me after being so dramatic in *Destiny!*

Evelyn Keyes—*ACTRESS*

The forties *were* special, weren't they? One of the main reasons, I think, was that Hollywood really cared about the scripts then. They knew the importance of story and had screenwriters under contract to the studios. The camerawork had reached perfection, too. I adored the camera, loved to play to it. Today, they have zoom lenses to pick you up from far away and you don't have the same intimacy with it. Like so many other areas of our lives, the technology has been improved at the expense of the human element.

Although it was only a "B" picture, *The Face Behind the Mask* was very important to my career. It was one of my early films at Columbia and had Peter Lorre in the male lead. He was quite a character, always making fun of everything. I think I was a little young then to appreciate him. I just wanted to get the job done as well as possible. Several years later, when I married John Huston, I got to know Peter better through his pal, Humphrey Bogart, who was also John's good friend. My tolerance for Peter then went up—a bit.

I was so conscientious in those days. For my role as a blind girl in *Face Behind the Mask,* I went to a school for the blind where I talked to the people and watched how they behaved and walked. Franz Planer, our cameraman, was very important to the quality of the film. He had been one of Germany's top cinematographers but had to get away from Hitler. He was also one of the refugees who waited in Mexico to enter the United States that screenwriter Ketti Frings wrote about in *Hold Back the Dawn,* with Charles Boyer. Planer's photography for *Face Behind the Mask* was incredible.

I think the success of this film led to my most important role up to then, the leading lady in *Here Comes Mr. Jordan,* opposite Robert Montgomery. (Decades later, it was remade as *Heaven Can Wait,* with Warren Beatty and Julie Christie.) Montgomery? A cold fish. At the time, I had recently become involved with Charles Vidor, one of Columbia's top directors—he did most of Rita Hayworth's best pictures, among others. Charles was still married then, but separated from his wife who I believe lived in the East. Bob Montgomery heard about our relationship and one day rather sneeringly said to me, "I hear you're running around with a married man."

Full of self-righteousness and probably guilt, I lashed back, "That's none of your business!"

Although we had completed all of our scenes, we still had to pose for photos in the still gallery. We spent the whole day in silence. Bob Montgomery never spoke another word to me. Charles and I were married a few years later, but not for long.

Here Comes Mr. Jordan was a big hit, but *A Thousand and One Nights* was more fun. In the beginning, though, I thought, "What have I gotten myself into?" I was to play a mischievous genie and Adele Jergens was set as the princess. Adele really hadn't done that much in films then, mostly show-girl stuff, but someone—I don't know if it was the producer, the director or Columbia boss Harry Cohn himself—had the hots for her and was seeing to it that she got all the attention as we filmed. I was left almost completely alone, so I had to come up with my own tricks. And I did. All my life I had a habit of snapping my fingers, so instead of saying something like "Hocus-pocus" when my genie wanted things to happen, I'd snap my fingers and a parade of elephants would appear. Another time, when everyone was eating at the banquet, I was left totally out of the action. So I went to the director, Alfred E. Green, and asked, "Can I dance up and down the steps while all this is going on?" He said sure. So—who would *you* look at in such a scene? I had to watch out for myself, and I must have done a pretty good job because when the film came out I got the reviews.

The Jolson Story was a great break for all of us, Columbia's biggest moneymaker up to that time. I campaigned for the role of Jolson's wife. I bombarded Harry Cohn with telegrams and phone calls. The character was, of course, supposed to be dancer Ruby Keeler, but she had had a very bitter divorce from Jolson and wouldn't allow her name to be used. I heard they paid her $25,000 to be able to show her character but the name was changed to "Julie Benson."

Harry Cohn was testing everybody for the part of Julie. I was very friendly with the Cohns and would often attend dinner parties at their home. Once, I remember Harry running tests for "Julie" at his house while I was there. Suddenly, during one of them (I forget who the girl was), I cried out, "No, no, no, *I* want to do it!" At which Joan, Mrs. Cohn, told me, "But Evelyn, you're not as pretty as she is." I replied, "What difference does that make I can act and dance, which she can't!"

I had grown up in Atlanta dancing, but no one in Hollywood ever cared. Not Cecil B. DeMille, to whom I was under contract in the late thirties; not David O. Selznick, who produced *Gone with the Wind,* in which I play Scarlett O'Hara's sister Suellen; not Harry Cohn. Hoping to convince Harry that I was the one for the role, I prepared a number with choreographer Jack Cole's assistant. We sat Harry down in a chair on the set and I swirled and floated and flitted and tapped my little heart out. "Oh, sure, sure," said a seemingly disinterested Harry. But you know something? I think he had me in mind for Julie Benson from the start.

Harry was tough but fair. Oh, he could be a bastard, but no one who rises to his eminence does it by being Mr. Nice Guy.

Eons later, I played Ruby Keeler's original role in the national touring company of the Broadway musical *No, No, Nanette.* I did it for a year with Don Ameche. After I'd left, he returned to it one summer with Ruby. Some of the kids I'd done the show with said, "Let's go and see them." So off we went to this theater-in-the-round where Don and Ruby were doing the show. Afterwards, we went back to see Ruby and I told her how much I'd enjoyed her performance. "Thank you," she replied with considerable coolness.

For 50 years Ruby wouldn't even mention Jolson's name, but people tell me she's now beginning to open up and discuss him a bit. At least that's what I'm told.

The Jolson Story was Larry Parks' great breakthrough role. Al Jolson came to the studio when they were still testing men for the role of Jolson, and I was seated behind Al when they ran Larry's terrific blackface test. Jolie squirmed all through it, leaning one way, then another. He wanted to do the role himself, but by then he was in his sixties and too old.

Larry was a good, honest, dependable, true-blue guy. When he got involved with the Commies, it wasn't because he wanted to overthrow the country, it was because he wanted to help the poor. His intentions were the best. But because of the political climate in the country by the early fifties, his career was destroyed.

We were very serious about what we were doing in *The Jolson Story.* Sidney Buchman, the top producer-writer at the studio, re-wrote the script as we filmed, although he took no credit in the finished product. After we'd work all day, we'd go and rehearse with Sidney. Al Green was our director, but he wasn't getting it on the screen. Before long, Sidney came on the set regularly and really directed *The Jolson Story.* That was how he got to produce and write the sequel three years later, *Jolson Sings Again*—this time with credit. I've never told all this before, but Al Green is dead now and there's something else. . .

When my first memoir, *Scarlett O'Hara's Younger Sister,* was published in 1977, I received a letter from the late Sidney Buchman's brother, Harold, in London. He was a bit angry and wrote, "After all Sidney did, you didn't even mention him in your book." I wrote back and told him that I was writing about *my* life. I couldn't go off on a tangent about Sidney Buchman, then have people see Al Green credited as director of *The Jolson Story,* then have to explain that. When you're telling a story, you have to stay on course, not go traipsing off into territory that is only going to confuse the reader.

But Harold was right about Sidney Buchman deserving credit—the lion's share, in fact for *The Jolson Story.*

Mrs. Mike was another one I liked. I play a Boston girl who marries a Mountie. I did it with Dick Powell, who was such a pro. I've been so lucky in that way. Most of the people I've worked with have been such marvelous pro's.

When Louella parsons saw *Mrs. Mike,* she wrote a Sunday column predicting that I'd win the Academy Award. But United Artists, for which I had done the film on loan-out, released it in January of 1950. By the year's end, blockbusters like *All About Eve, Sunset Boulevard, Born Yesterday* and my then-husband John Huston's *The Asphalt Jungle* had come out, and *Mrs. Mike* was lost in the shuffle. So was I. I didn't even get a nomination. But what could I say? I knew nothing about business then—still don't, really. I couldn't tell Sam Bischoff, the producer, what to do. *Mrs. Mike* could have changed my life if they had handled it smartly.

Speaking of my life, the second volume of my memoirs, entitled *I'll Think About That Tomorrow,* has just come out. And my first book, a novel called *I Am a Billboard,* may become a movie. Not bad for Scarlett O'Hara's kid sister!

Andrea King—ACTRESS—

I had been at Warner Bros. about three months and had done a few pictures when I was given the star role of Lisa Dawn, the treacherous actress, in *Hotel Berlin.* I was thrilled! Then, about three-quarters of the way through the filming, Faye Emerson, who was not really known then and was playing the hotel prostitute, married Elliott Roosevelt, the son of the president of the United States. Suddenly, they switched all the publicity to her, and when the picture was released they put her name first on screen.

I would have been more disposed to wish the couple happiness if they'd waited till Faye's *next* picture to marry!

I couldn't blame the studio, really: how often does a president's son marry a movie actress—one who's playing a prostitute yet?! But it still hurt.

Filming *Hotel Berlin* was a fascinating experience, though—so many distinguished actors were in our company. Peter Lorre, of course, was Peck's Bad Boy, always pulling some gag. I remember a little while later, when we worked together again in *The Beast with Five Fingers,* he was really wild. During a big dinner scene, our director, Robert Florey, would say "Action!" and there would be Peter, stuffing pieces of celery up his nose and in his ear. Victor Francen, the fine, very serious and conservative French actor, was also in the scene with us, and he and Florey stormed off the set and refused to come back for a week.

Peter was no better on *Hotel Berlin.* Like Victor Francen, Raymond Massey was very dignified and also did not appreciate Peter's shenanigans at all. Peter would do something foolish, and Raymond would chastise him: "After all, Peter, you're supposed to be an actor. You *are* an actor, unfortunately. But God didn't give you any talent for this sort of behavior, so stop it, please!"

My leading man, Helmut Dantine, was not fond of him, either. Helmut was a nice guy but didn't have a whole lot of humor. He would occasionally be the butt of Peter's jokes. He would see Helmut, who was German, coming and cry out "Achtung!" [Attention!]. The muscles in Helmut's face would tighten, then he would click his heels and leave the set. I had lunch recently with Kurt Kreuger, who had a major supporting role in the film, and he told me that half-way through *Hotel Berlin* there was talk in the front office of replacing Helmut with Kurt. Maybe Helmut wanted to get away from Peter Lorre!

Lorre didn't only bedevil actors and directors. Whenever he wanted to badger Jack Warner, our boss, into giving him a raise or a role or something, he'd sit outside Warner's office dressed as a peddler with a can of pencils. He seemed to be doing something like this all the time. But Peter had a strong contract; no matter what, he couldn't be fired.

He didn't bother me because he knew I adored his pranks. So it was no fun for him: I was on his side. Oh, I just remembered one time when he got to me. It was on *Beast with Five Fingers.* I'd go into my dressing room and there, hidden in my bathrobe or in my make-up drawer, would be that hideous severed hand prop used in the film. Imagine seeing something like that first thing in the morning. I'd scream!

Henry Daniell was also in *Hotel Berlin*—another fine actor. He had this passion for the sun. Late in the day, when they wanted him for a shot, they'd have to send couriers to some remote corner of the stage where there was still a spot of sun to find him.

We began the film late in 1944 and completed it two months before D-Day, so it was very timely. The advertising reflected that the end of the war was imminent, and that Warner Bros. knew all about it—"It could be tomorrow . . . It could be the day after that. . . ." Everyone wanted to see what it was all about; business was tremendous. There had been many pictures about the Nazis throughout the war, but *Hotel Berlin* gave a rare intimate glimpse into what Hitler's top men were up to during its final days. It remains my favorite film—my most challenging role (I spoke with a German accent).

People seem to remember *The Man I Love,* too, which I also like very much. I'd been playing some not very nice characters and was glad at last to be a decent, good woman. When I originally did my test for

Warners, Jack Warner commented, "She looks a lot like Ida Lupino," whom they also had under contract. Fortunately, this didn't deter him from hiring me. Then *The Man I Love* came along, with Ida Lupino set for top billing and a good role for the actress who would play her sister. They remembered our alleged resemblance and signed me. Ida and I became great friends. We'd go to the rushes and say, "Do you think we really look alike?" and "I don't think so."

At the start, the plan was to have Ida play a thinly disguised Helen Morgan, the singer; but as the shooting progressed, for whatever reasons they weren't always sure what direction they were taking. Several re-writes were done and it became quite a different picture, not really about Helen Morgan anymore. There were many plots and sub-plots which Jack Warner didn't like; he thought we should stick to one story. I think it took longer to shoot than any film I was ever on, maybe five months. One of the delays was inadvertently my fault. During the shooting, my mother was in a car accident in the Adirondacks and I had to go back East to be with her. Fortunately, she recovered but the studio had to shoot around me while I was gone.

The director, Raoul Walsh, didn't usually do this type of romantic film. His specialty had always been Westerns—action films. As our picture went on and on, Raoul would say, "My God, I'm doing an epic here! And I don't even have any horses!" He was so gentle and sweet, though, and handled the picture beautifully. Just the same, when it was finally finished I think he was glad to get back to his horses and ships.

I was at Warners for a year, and only had three days off. I did nine features, several shorts, many tests and loved it all. Then I was dropped. I'd already rejected a couple of parts as unsuitable, and now they wanted me to play a supporting role in *Stallion Road,* with Ronald Reagan and Alexis Smith. I simply felt that after being starred, this was a step backward and decided to go on suspension. Peggy Knudsen took the part. The casting people and Sophie Rosenstein, Warners' drama coach, begged me not to take the suspension. "We have *Johnny Belinda* coming up, and you'll get it," Sophie told me. But the word around the lot was that Jack Warner didn't like the story of *Belinda* and it was looked on as sort of a "B" picture, so I chose then to go on suspension. Well, that one did it; they let me go permanently. And Jane Wyman won the Oscar for *Johnny Belinda.*

If I'd had one more year at Warners, I'd have been given the build-up that would have made me a top name. But it didn't happen and I went on to freelance in many movies and television shows and have a happy, busy, productive life.

Kurt Kreuger—ACTOR—

Unfaithfully Yours is much admired today, but making it was not one of my happiest Hollywood experiences.

It was written, produced and directed by Preston Sturges, who early in the decade had been one of Paramount's golden boys. But he'd had a couple of flops and had now moved over to 20th Century-Fox. He still had plenty of clout, though; he was the only director who ever closed the set to Darryl Zanuck, the head of the studio. No other director had ever been able to do that, not even Otto Preminger.

Still, Sturges was rather intimidated by Rex Harrison, who was top-billed. Rex was the most selfish, unpleasant star I've ever worked with. And as an actor, I admired him very much—his timing was brilliant. During the shooting, as a relative newcomer, I tried to get the benefit of his experience; I wanted to learn how he achieved his lofty status. "My dear boy," he told me, "all I did was act, act, act." I remember that I was in school in London many years before when I had my first viewing of him at work: I saw him in the play *French Without Tears*. But working with him was something else.

In the story, there is the hint that Linda Darnell, who plays Harrison's wife, and I, as his secretary, are having an affair. There were scenes shot that much more strongly suggested this, but Harrison went to Sturges and had them cut out. This was brought back to me later by the cutter and the assistant director. If the scenes had been left in, my character would certainly have been a bit more interesting. But Rex convinced Sturges that if the film was too specific about my relationship with Linda, the public would not buy her coming back to him at the end.

Among the scenes he had cut were an intimate conversation in a restaurant between Linda and me and some dialogue at a nearby table with Barbara Lawrence, Rudy Vallee and Lionel Stander where they gossiped about us. Then we were joined by Rex in the scene. Rex had it cut so that the scene began when he joined it.

Other material that was cut included some by-play between Linda and me in the concert scene. Anything that showed Linda and me together in a favorable light was omitted. Sturges was the boss, but you just don't ruffle the feathers of a star. Certainly not this one.

Rex also used all sorts of upstaging tricks with me. I had quite a few scenes with him. I recall one where the shot was to be profile to profile. That was how we did it in rehearsal. When we began shooting, he turned and moved a little bit away from the camera so you'd now see his full face, while I was maneuvered so that what you saw was mostly my ear. Well, I was very ambitious then and had done a few pictures and I wasn't going to let him get away with it. I worked my face back into the shot. Sturges, however, was at the mercy of his well-established star and said, "Mr. Kreuger, we all know you're a little bit nearsighted, so we'll have to put blocks around your marks to keep you in them."

A few years earlier, I had appeared with the reputedly formidable Humphrey Bogart in *Sahara,* which we shot in the desert, and although he was at least as big a star as Rex Harrison, he couldn't have been nicer or more helpful.

Despite everything, I liked Preston Sturges. He was probably the most intellectual director I ever worked with. He knew that I also spoke French, and sometimes he'd show off a bit and speak to me in French on the set. He owned the Players Restaurant then and when we filmed nearby he would have it cater our lunches. We all had to sit at long tables presided over by Sturges. He used a lot of comic actors and dress extras from his early films and the silent days over and over again in his productions, so he was very loyal that way.

When it came out in 1948, *Unfaithfully Yours* did not do well. That summer, the actress Carole Landis had committed suicide, evidently over Rex Harrison. And our film was released that fall. The studio sneaked it out like a "B" picture. The women's clubs were still very powerful then, and Fox was afraid of a boycott. Remember what they did to Ingrid Bergman when she ran off with Roberto Rossellini? It played for a few days at the Chinese Theater in Hollywood and disappeared. However, it became a great success in Paris, and, of course, today is highly regarded here.

I always looked on Darryl Zanuck as a friend and booster of mine. (Of course, he was much friendlier with the women on the lot.) I was already under contract at Fox when I met Zanuck in Sun Valley, where I liked to ski. He was a ski buff; he didn't do it very well, but he liked it. So we had that in common. When you meet people in the mountains and they don't have their everyday cares with them, they are more susceptible to friendship, I think. He always said he was going to turn me into a Continental leading man and was just waiting for the right property with which to launch me.

"Be patient," Zanuck said. "You'll still look good at 50."

Meanwhile, I played a lot of less-than-earth-shaking roles. I have a German accent (which people tell me is more pronounced today!), and I guess it wasn't easy to fit me into typically American parts.

After *Unfaithfully Yours,* in which I had the second male lead, I was offered a small role in a Fox film to be directed by Henry King. I felt this was a step backwards, and after conferences between my agents and Fox, I gave up my contract, went East to do stock and then sailed for Europe. Anthony Quinn was also on board. He was going to look for better parts, too. He found them; I didn't. I settled in Paris for a while, and ran into Preston Sturges who had moved there. I attended several of his dinner parties. He was the only man I ever knew who owned a Rolls Royce station wagon.

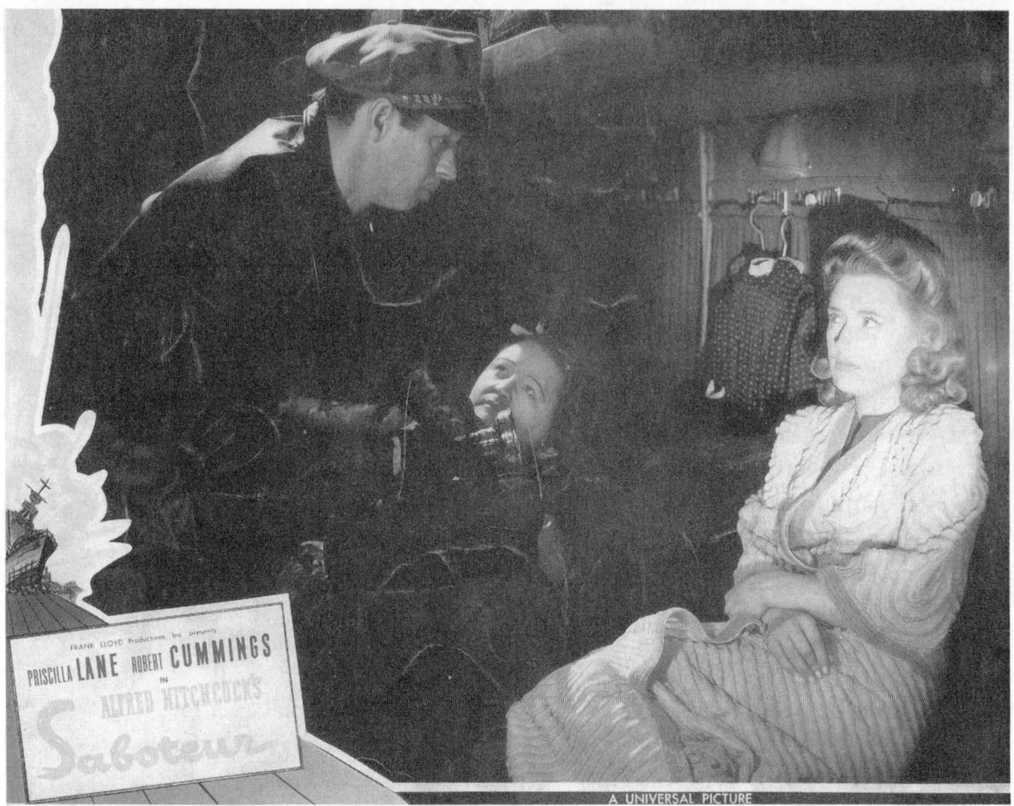

Priscilla Lane—ACTRESS

Saboteur is one of my favorite films. I'd just left Warner Bros., where I'd been since the mid-thirties, and our director, Alfred Hitchcock, heard that I was free and requested me for the role. He was very nice to everyone in the company. All that stuff about him saying, "Actors are cattle"—I'm sure that was just publicity. He was very exacting—unswervable in getting you to do exactly what he wanted. But he was always pulling little gags to keep the set a happy place.

Saboteur took about six to eight weeks to shoot; all the big pictures did then. It was, of course, essentially a cross-country chase, winding up on top of the Statue of Liberty. The funny thing is, it was all shot at Universal Studios in Hollywood. Oh, there may have been a few long shots filmed on the actual locations we were supposed to be passing through, but I don't think any of the principals left the lot. I know I didn't. Different parts of the Statue of Liberty were reconstructed by studio craftsmen for different scenes in which we appeared.

I loved working with Bob Cummings, my leading man—wish we could have done another picture together. Mr. Hitchcock, too. But I married soon after *Saboteur* and, except for a few short engagements, I retired to family life in New England.

Janet Leigh—ACTRESS—

Why were the forties a golden age for Hollywood films?

Our attitudes weren't as diverted as they are now. There was such a focus on the movies—they were *the* entertainment, really. Television hadn't yet made the inroads of today. There were a lot of stars, too, not just a handful. And there were the studio moguls, the Louis B. Mayers, the Harry Cohns, the Darryl Zanucks. The buck stopped there: they made the motion pictures and damn well, too. Today, the entertainment vista is so diluted—there's the sports channel, the movie channel, the comedy channel, videos, the VCR. There's so *much* today. In the forties, movies were special. They were *it.* They were bigger than life.

I came into it all by sheer accident. While I always loved movies, I never planned to be an actress. In 1946, Norma Shearer, who had been the queen of the MGM lot in the 1930s, saw a picture of me at the Sugar Bowl Ski Lodge in Northern California and brought it back to Lew Wasserman at MCA. He gave it to the new talent department there and they took it to MGM. I was signed at $50 a week, hardly a great investment on their part. Very quickly, though, I read for MGM's drama coach, Lillian Burns, who knew that producer Jack Cummings and director Roy Rowland were looking for a girl to play Lissy Anne, the female lead in a picture they were preparing called *The Romance of Rosy Ridge.* Miss Burns had them come down and although another, already established actress on the lot, Beverly Tyler, had practically been set to play Lissy Anne, they tested me, too.

One Saturday night, Louis Mayer, the head of MGM, looked at our two tests at his home. Van Johnson, who was set for the male lead in *Romance of Rosy Ridge,* was there, along with other guests. Afterwards, Mr. Mayer said, "We're going with the new girl. A star is born!" Presto! Jeanette Morrison of Stockton, California, became Janet Leigh of Hollywood. The wonderful thing was that one man could make major decisions like this then.

Later, I heard that Mr. Mayer felt that Beverly was a little too sophisticated for the young farm girl in the story. They wanted a more naïve type, and they sure got her.

Van Johnson became my favorite leading man. Over the years, we did several pictures together and he was always a joy.

If I was thrilled to be in an MGM movie with Van Johnson, I was soon ecstatic to learn I would be playing Dorothy Rodgers, the wife of composer Richard Rodgers, in the

M-G-M
VAN JOHNSON
in
The ROMANCE of ROSY RIDGE

film biography of Rodgers and [Larry] Hart, *Words and Music.* Maybe I didn't sing and dance in it, but I was actually appearing in a big, Technicolor MGM musical! I was so nervous when I met Mr. and Mrs. Rodgers. Just the idea of meeting them and playing a live person made me shake. To prepare, I read about Mrs. Rodgers. I tried to find out the kind of person that she was: what schools she went to, her favorite sports, who her friends were, whether she liked Twinkies or cupcakes. All the things that help you create a real-life character. Usually, when you play a role you manufacture all these things yourself, but Dorothy Rodgers was a living person. And a very elegant and charming one.

One of the most exciting times on *Words and Music* occurred when I worked with the great Judy Garland, who was one of the many guest stars in it. I actually had a scene with her, which gave me goose bumps. Although I didn't know it then, Judy was going through a bad period and she'd often be very late. Mickey Rooney, who was in the scenes with Judy, was the soul of patience with her, no matter what time she'd show up. Arthur Freed, our producer, would finally lead her onto the set like a queen, which she was, really. Once she started, she was sensational.

Act of Violence was a terrific picture, a real stretch for me. I'd been playing a lot of ingénues, but here I'm the plain mother of twins in a violent crime drama. My two leading men, Van Heflin and Robert Ryan, were very supportive, and our director, Fred Zinnemann, was a gem. On the set, however, in my insecurity I had a tendency to keep saying "I'm sorry" whenever something went wrong. Sometimes it was my fault, but not always. The crew finally set up a jar into which I had to put a penny every time I said "I'm sorry." At the end of production, it contributed three dollars to costs for our wrap party.

I was very tired on this picture. I was looping [inserting dialogue] for my previous picture, doing wardrobe for *Little Women* and rehearsing for *The Red Danube.* I was split; my thoughts weren't focused. One day I walked in and Mr. Zinnemann said, "I know the demands on you, Janet, but this is basic, this is your performance and it takes precedence. You must give me a performance!" He could see it in my eyes—I wasn't concentrating. After that, he worked very closely with me and everything went well. I learned a great deal on this one.

I didn't have as challenging a role in *Little Women* as Meg, but the picture has such wonderful warmth. It kind of brings you back to the values we all had as children. June Allyson, Elizabeth Taylor, Margaret O'Brien and myself really did assume the aura of four sisters and had a ball. We cracked up all the time. Once, Mervyn LeRoy, our dear, sensitive director, was ready for a scene and yelled, "Roll 'em!," and we all turned around with our teeth blacked out.

Another time, Peter Lawford flubbed a line and we all broke out laughing. Thereafter, every time he'd try to get the line out we'd break up again. Eventually, we had to quit working for a half-hour until we regained our composure. Mr. LeRoy was great. He put up with us and still managed to turn out one of the most beautiful films I was ever in.

I was still pinching myself when *That Forsyte Woman* came along. I mean, Greer Garson, Errol Flynn, Walter Pidgeon, Robert Young—and me! I was in seventh heaven. Although it was a drama, the set was such fun: Greer and Errol kept playing jokes on each other. For one scene where she was ironing a dress, Greer was then supposed to walk to a closet and open it. Which she did—and there stood Errol in his BVDs. On the last day of filming, she got even. During a carriage scene where Greer and Errol were to kiss, she arranged with one of the electricians for Errol to get an electric shock in his seat when he took her in his arms and kissed her. He shrieked and almost went through the carriage roof. That was *one* kiss Errol Flynn would remember!

The Red Danube has always been a favorite of mine. It was beautifully directed by George Sidney, who was married to Lillian Burns, the drama coach. I play a tragic Russian ballerina—not an easy role. I began studying dancing six months before we began to shoot. When we finally got to it, I didn't do the leaps but I did go on pointe. And this is something you are supposed to start doing at six years of age. It was agony—so painful—just to get on pointe, but I got so I even did a turn.

The story, about the forced repatriation of Russians in Vienna after World War II, was very moving. I felt very involved in what was happening. I was an American, but this was happening to *people.* It became sort of an awakening to put myself into the body of that tragic girl, and to comprehend, at such an early age, what she went through. The picture didn't do as well as it should have, though. The war had been over for a few years, but perhaps people didn't want to see any more movies that reminded them of it.

Although I wasn't thrilled about having to do it, *Holiday Affair* turned out to be another one I loved. I was at Mr. Mayer's house one evening and was introduced to this tall, taciturn, thin man with a mustache. It was Howard Hughes, who had just bought RKO studios. As the evening wore on, I realized that he was being overly attentive, which I really did not appreciate. He was twice my age and besides, I was dating someone else. He made me uncomfortable. Subsequently, I got to know him better, which made me even more nervous about him.

When I got word that RKO wanted to borrow me for three films, at first I said, "No, thank you." But Benny Thau, MGM's executive in charge of talent, convinced me that it would be important to my career to do the pictures Hughes was proposing. One was *Holiday Affair,* opposite Robert Mitchum; another was *Jet Pilot,* to co-star either Cary Grant or John Wayne (it turned out to be the latter); and the third was a big musical called *Two Tickets to Broadway,* with Tony Martin. They would also be very good for me financially. I know that when MGM loaned me out, they made more money than I did on the deal, but I never minded because without them I wouldn't have been there in the first place. I didn't mind paying them back for everything they had done for me.

Holiday Affair proved a delightful film. It's become a Christmas staple on TV. And I enjoyed working with Bob Mitchum and Wendell Corey—I *think.* Bob was such a free soul. Much of the time, I didn't know what to make of him. He was funny and so relaxed he sometimes seemed in danger of falling over. But he was always professional. Both he and Wendell Corey would try to shock me; they knew a patsy when they saw one. Like when Bob was required to kiss me. He kissed me like I'd never been kissed before! During the big Christmas dinner scene, Bob and Wendell each put a hand on my leg. Oh, they never followed through on any of this, they just liked to tease their victim.

As for Howard Hughes, his pursuit continued, but he never caught me. Tony Curtis, a rising young actor at Universal, did.

Joan Leslie—ACTRESS—

High Sierra was my breakthrough role.

I had been doing mostly inconspicuous small parts in films for a few years when, about a month before *High Sierra* was to begin, Warner Bros. signed me. I was 15 years old. For some reason, they decided that I would be groomed and built up and had me study with Sophie Rosenstein, a darling little lady and wonderful coach who had just been signed, too. She came from the University of Washington where she also had taught drama, and helped me to get rid of my midwestern [Detroit, Michigan] accent.

Not long after I arrived, someone came up to me and said, "Be on the set tomorrow to test for the crippled girl in *High Sierra.*" It was a wonderful role. Ida Lupino and Humphrey Bogart had been announced to star, with Raoul Walsh directing. Bogart did the test with me and Mr. Walsh directed. I guess the reason I wasn't overwhelmed by all this was simply that I was such a kid and was used to the school situation where you're given instructions and just go along with them. I thought, "They're going to teach, so I'll simply go along with them and learn."

For the test, the camera was on me alone while Bogart fed me lines off-camera. Bogart was delightful. During the shooting of the picture, he did everything he could to put me at ease. He was a gentleman. This didn't surprise me at the time. But I remember that a little while later, when Bogie and Mayo Methot, then Mrs. Bogart, would get into a public fracas and wind up with black eyes, I would exclaim, "Oh, no, it can't be!" Afterward, I heard that while we were shooting Bogie had made it clear that, because of my tender years, there was to be no swearing on the set. He was backed up by Mr. Walsh. Maybe the edict came down from the front office. They were grooming me as sweet and innocent, and they wanted me to stay that way.

Mr. Walsh had a grand manner and was a perfect gentleman, too. I recall my big emotional scene, where I cry and say I want to live, not marry gangster Bogart. I had never played such a difficult scene before and I was worried. Mr. Walsh came over, patted my hand and said, "Whenever you're ready." There was time then to help a young person get started and grow. It's not like that anymore.

When I was told to test for Gracie Williams, the backwoods bride of World War I hero Alvin C. York in *Sergeant York,* I was working on a film with Eddie Albert. After looking over the York script, Eddie commented, "This doesn't sound like the right thing for you."

I was startled. "Why do you say that?" I asked. "Gary Cooper is playing Sergeant York. Howard Hawks is directing. I'd be the female lead. I think it's a great opportunity!"

What had put Eddie off was the fact that in the first script for *Sergeant York* Gracie was a bit of a sexpot. The studio thought that this would be a shot in the arm to the usual love interest angle; Mr. Hawks, I was told later, initially wanted Jane Russell. But the York family protested the original concept. They said, "We don't want any glamour queen playing Gracie. We want a nice, simple girl who hasn't done any racy roles." To get their permissions, Warners made the character a much sweeter young girl. And this fit my image perfectly.

Nevertheless, they went on testing girls, among them Susan Peters.

On my 16th birthday, it was announced that I would play opposite Gary Cooper in *Sergeant York.* Afterward, one of York's sons, a professor, told me, "We were for you from the beginning."

Howard Hawks was a wonderful director. He permitted me to work on the scenes as much as possible. And he was so smart about camera angles, always trying to find original ways to stage and photograph a scene. We'd break for tea every afternoon. I couldn't attend, though, because I was in school, which was quite disconcerting to the production department and, I think, sometimes Mr. Cooper.

Gary Cooper was a delight, though. We were all trying to sound like we came from the Tennessee Valley and used the lingo all day long to get our accents going. Gary could come up to me and say, "Wal, how ya-all doin', Joanie?" and I'd reply, "Fair-to-middlin', Al-a-vin"—I always called him "Al-a-vin."

Because of my character's poor rural backround, the wardrobe was necessarily very simple. Skirts and blouses and plain dresses. To get them to look old, they were put in barrels and pummeled with stones. They had to fit nice and tight, however, especially at the top—that was the important thing.

The only sour note on *Sergeant York* was the first assistant director, who would bawl me out in front of

people. Maybe he wanted to get me to cry for certain scenes, but I could have done without it.

Subsequently, there were two 1941 Academy Awards for *Sergeant York:* Best Actor, Gary Cooper; and Best Film Editing, William Holmes.

Yankee Doodle Dandy was another very big production, the life of entertainer-composer-dramatist George M. Cohan. How did I get it? Well, I think Warners went about casting the role of Mary, Cohan's wife, in the usual way. The casting director submitted many names, some of them contract players and some of them from outside. I think I had the edge because I sang and danced and knew vaudeville. I had danced professionally from the age of two-and-a-half, and played the accordion, too.

Naturally, I was excited about appearing opposite James Cagney, who, of course, plays Cohan and was a one-of-a-kind superstar. I remember the first day I showed up on the rehearsal stage. Jimmy was already there working out and so was his sister Jeanne, cast as his sister in the film, too. Jimmy was wearing sweat clothes and was drenched in perspiration—a tireless worker. Jeanne was lovely and very talented as well.

When shooting began, one of the first things Jimmy and I had to do was the scene where Cohan and Mary try to sell his song "Harrigan." We put it together right there on the set. Jimmy said, "Joan, I'll take the first line, you take the second." Then, "You do this, and I'll do that. For the second chorus, you take the harmony." Ta-da, it was finished. Our director, Michael Curtiz, then walked onto the set and asked, "How are you going to do it, Jimmy?" We showed him and he said, "Shoot it."

Jimmy put so much of himself into *Yankee Doodle Dandy,* had so much impact on the production. He added creative things to every scene. Mike Curtiz was wonderful, too, though his demeanor changed drastically on the next film we did together, *This Is the Army. Army* had been a stage revue and had no story; a plot had to be contrived for the film version, and this drove Curtiz crazy. On *Yankee Doodle Dandy,* which proceeded like a dream, Curtiz went around hugging everybody, but on *This Is the Army* he was screaming and bawling people out continuously.

George M. Cohan watched the production closely. The only thing he objected to was a song of his I sang called "I Guess I'll Have to Telegraph My Baby." It disturbed him because his first wife had sung it, and she was being completely omitted from his film story. (He was Catholic and I guess he didn't want audiences to know he'd been married twice.) He insisted we cut the song. So with exactly the same staging, I substituted another of his numbers, "The Warmest Baby in the Bunch." Among my treasured stills from this picture is one of me during this number, looking off to the side as Jimmy Cagney throws me a kiss.

Yankee Doodle Dandy won three 1942 Oscar "Bests": Actor, James Cagney; Sound, Nathan Levinson; and Scoring of a Musical, Ray Heindorf and Heinz Roemheld.

It was a joy to work with Ida Lupino again on *The Hard Way.* We had very little to do together in *High Sierra*—most of my scenes were with Humphrey Bogart. But we got to know each other on *Hard Way.* She plays my older sister who pushes me into show business. First, there were rumors that it was really the story of Ginger Rogers and her mother. Then they started saying that it was about my mother and me! Actually, this story is one of the oldest in show biz.

Ida won the New York Film Critics Award as Best Actress of 1943 for *Hard Way.* Dennis Morgan and Jack Carson were also in it, and excellent. And there was a compelling bit by Gladys George as a faded, boozey old star. Ida came to me one day and said, "I can't believe this woman is doing the part with me. She's supreme! She had to cry in her beer all day long until they finally got the scene. I wondered where she got the energy to do it over and over and still be great, so I asked her how she managed to cry those real tears every time. She told me that something very sad had occurred recently in her life and all she had to do was draw on that."

The director of *Hard Way,* a then very young Vincent Sherman, was splendid, very enthusiastic and concerned about the project.

A short time before, when Paramount was preparing to film *Holiday Inn,* with Bing Crosby and Fred Astaire, they were looking for a leading lady who would have to dance with Astaire quite a bit. My agent brought me over from Warners to Paramount, where the picture was going to be made, so they could see me dance. At first, I did some of my old routines. Then Mr. Astaire said, "Let's try it together." We did that twirl where the girl's dress flies around that he had done with Ginger Rogers for years. He seemed pleased and said, "If Joan can't do this picture, we'll do another some time." Marjorie Reynolds got the part.

But Mr. Astaire remembered me and when he went over to RKO to make *The Sky's the Limit,* he suggested my name to the studio for his co-star. I was hired to dance with Fred Astaire, which, as you might imagine, was a great thrill. And I loved my role—a real '90s sort of girl, a photo journalist who is career-oriented, committed, independent, demanding. Mr. Astaire did the choreography himself. He worked out the routines before I came on. We'd work nine-to-five on them. And I'd go home and practice them at night and on weekends. When the first weekend rolled around, we'd gotten half-way through the initial routine. I practiced at home on the weekend and when I got back to the studio on Monday, Mr. Astaire said, "Okay, let's see how much you remember." We went through the number perfectly and he exclaimed, "You practiced!" I was slightly embarrassed, feeling a little like an amateur who'd been caught trying to keep up with the professionals. But Mr. Astaire was absolutely charming and the whole experience was one I wouldn't have missed.

After a while, Warner Bros. began giving me junky roles in things like *Cinderella Jones* and *Two Guys from Milwaukee.* It was a time of economizing; they just weren't spending for the best properties. I decided that I wasn't going to go any farther there and wanted out. I sued Warners for freedom from contract, on the basis that I had now turned 21 and had signed my contract when I was a minor. I felt this gave me the right to reconsider. No one had ever brought this issue up before in California. I won in lower court, so Warners appealed it higher. Naturally, they had the very best lawyers. This time they won, so then I took it to a higher court. Finally, the District Court of Appeals ruled that in most other walks of life, the contract would not stand. But where jockeys, prize-fighters or actors were concerned, it must stand.

But Warners realized that I would never be happy there again, so for a minor financial settlement I was released. Today, with a perspective on what resulted, I think I made a mistake. Other Warner people sat back and waited, but I chose to fight. I could have waited, too—compromised.

It was soon evident that I was being blacklisted at the other studios. Finally, Bryan Foy, who was head of production at Eagle-Lion, was interested in having me play the lead in *Repeat Performance.* But he was worried about the other studios taking retaliation if he hired me. My manager explained that he was legally entitled to do it and that he would profit by publicity that would undoubtedly accrue when he brought me on the picture. So I was signed for *Repeat Performance.*

I think it was a good film, too, alhough I learned that drama is hard on your system. On the first day, I got a headache that lasted throughout

the filming. It was a very demanding role—this woman was haunted and overwrought all the way through. She's got only this one chance to live a year of her life over again and avert tragedy. It was all very taxing.

When I went to New York for the opening and to do publicity, I took a cab from the airport to Eagle-Lion to see what the schedule was. En route, I spied a large billboard ad for *Repeat Performance* showing me holding a gun with a nightie falling off my bare shoulder. When I got to the office, I screamed, "I'm a good Catholic girl! You can't keep that billboard up! I'm almost a mile high with my clothes falling off! It must be taken down!"

But I think it stayed up. Wish I could say the same for that nightie.

Viveca Lindfors—ACTRESS—

Kay Brown, the New York agent who saw Ingrid Bergman in the Swedish film *Intermezzo* and brought her to America, saw me in the Swedish film *Appassionata* several years later and brought me over, too.

I have a theory: by then, Ingrid had left Kay and she said to herself, "I'll find another Ingrid Bergman." Me.

I was a big star at home, the Marilyn Monroe of Sweden, but I realize now that I was a dumb girl then. Kay sold me to Warner Bros. and it was announced that I would make my American debut opposite Gary Cooper in a film called *Cloak and Dagger.* I arrived in the United States early in 1946. The first person I met in New York was Charles Boyer, on whom I had a great crush as a teen-ager back in Stockholm. He kissed my hand and said, "Enchanté, Madame." I thought I was entering paradise. As I said, I was dumb.

In Hollywood, after waiting forever to meet my boss, Jack Warner, I finally accosted him on the grounds near his office. He took me for a stroll around the large cemented lot, which looked more like a concentration camp or a large factory than a place for creativity. He introduced me to Gary Cooper, Bette Davis and Joan Crawford (who gave me my first party in Hollywood). After a while, I told Mr. Warner that my feet hurt. He replied, "My feet hurt, too. I'm a Jew from New York! But I want to introduce you to everyone."

The next thing I heard was that the German actress Lilli Palmer, whom he had *not* introduced me to, had replaced me in *Cloak and Dagger.*

When producer David O. Selznick wanted to borrow me to star in his *The Paradine Case,* to be directed by Alfred Hitchcock, Warner said, "Oh, no, we're going right into production with a big vehicle for Viveca!"

I did as I was told. After many months of studying acting at the studio, going to parties, posing for publicity pictures, doing interviews and having drinks with directors who might want to use me in their picture, I was informed that finally I was to start my first American picture, *Night unto Night.* My leading man was to be Ronald Reagan, in his first post-war film. Reagan had been gaining in popularity when the war interrupted his movie career, but in stature he was certainly no Gary Cooper. Furthermore, I was to play a young widow who hears voices and Reagan was to play an epileptic biochemist. Even to a greenhorn, all this did not sound like an ideal set-up, but I thought, "This is Hollywood—HOLLYWOOD—and they know better than I." I told you I was dumb.

Reagan was very much like he is today, pleasant but hard to get through to; there was a façade. The only time he really let his hair down with me was one day when he got on the subject of sex. He was still married to Jane Wyman then, and he told me, "Sex is best in the afternoon, just after you've come out of the shower." I wonder if Nancy thinks so, too! I hope so.

But I really wasn't paying attention to Ronald Reagan. The director of *Night unto Night* was Don Siegel, who had just done his first feature, *The Verdict,* with Sydney Greenstreet and Peter Lorre. And he was very good. He let the actors do their jobs. A lot of directors interfere too much, don't understand whom they're dealing with. It was beter for actors 100 years ago. We were the bosses. Then came the producers, the directors, the managers, everybody who wanted to

beat us down. But Don was fine and also very attractive. We fell in love immediately and eventually were married.

Unfortunately, *Night unto Night* did not please Jack Warner who refused to release it. (Years later, Don Siegel told a reporter he was so in love with me during the shooting that he didn't pay enough attention to what was happening in our film.) They decided to showcase me on screen first as a Nazi collaborator in a melodrama about post-war France called *To the Victor. Night unto Night* was not released for two years, and although my reviews for it were very good the picture flopped. Not long ago, I saw it again at a festival and thought it much better than I'd remembered. Today, when the unconventional is more readily accepted, the story could be made into a very interesting picture. And Ronald Reagan, I saw to my surprise, is very good in it.

Again, my personal notices for *To the Victor* were excellent, but the picture didn't set the world on fire, either, although the French locations came in for much favorable comment. Dennis Morgan was my co-star; he is good, but Humphrey Bogart, whom they had originally sought for the male lead, would have been better. The character was much tougher than the sort that Dennis, a wonderful, warm fellow, was used to playing.

Next came *The Adventures of Don Juan,* with Errol Flynn in the title role and me co-starring as the Queen of Spain. In Technicolor. I thought Flynn was a brilliant actor, far better than he himself thought, but his drinking had gotten out of hand. By three in the afternoon he'd be out cold. They had to save all my close-ups and those of the other actors till then. Sometimes he'd be rambling and incoherent all day, or just not show up. Shooting dragged on for six months as I grew fat and frustrated, wanting to act more. And all the drinking, and talking about drinking, was embarrassing to me. One day Flynn tried to pressure me into drinking, too. "One is much nicer when one drinks," he said. "All the pettiness flies right out the window."

I wanted to fly right out of Warner Bros.! My last films there were a couple of "B"s. I took my children and moved to New York, where the theater gave me a whole new life, a whole new dimension as an actress and as a woman. In 1954, I starred in *Anastasia,* probably my greatest success, and saw the movie version go to—right—Ingrid Bergman. I revisit Hollywood often to do films and television. I just received an Emmy Award for my guest star performance on the TV series *Life Goes On.* But I haven't lived in California for 40 years. New York is my home. You can't stay dumb forever.

Dorothy McGuire——————ACTRESS——

In 1943, David O. Selznick brought me to Hollywood from the New York stage, where I'd made something of a name as the young wife in *Claudia.* My contract was then split between 20th Century-Fox and RKO. I made my movie debut in the film of *Claudia* for Fox and stayed there to play the tenement mother in *A Tree Grows in Brooklyn.*

As they say today, I was on a roll.

Tree was director Elia Kazan's first picture, and he was wonderful. He was also from the theater, so that was a great bond between us: we were able to tap into that experience together. But the whole company was remarkable. James Dunn plays my husband and won the Supporting Actor Academy Award, I've since been told he drank, but I saw none of that. Maybe it was just the kind of gossip that the envious spread about people who are good. Peggy Ann Garner (another Oscar winner as Outstanding Child Actress), Ted Donaldson, Joan Blondell and Lloyd Nolan are also in it; you couldn't ask for better actors. Our cameraman was the great Leon Shamroy, who really introduced Kazan to some of the intricacies of film-making and had much to do with the success of *A Tree Grows in Brooklyn.* Shamroy used to swear at us all the time, but not in a mean way, more as a character; we all liked him.

My only problem on the film was some apprehension about playing the scene where I have a baby. It was quite a long scene, and I had not yet had a baby in real life and wasn't quite sure how to go about it. Today, you see birth scenes everywhere on television and in movies, but at that time [1945] they were rare. I recall that I had a dressing room on the set with a staircase leading up to it. One day, I was standing on the staircase talking to Kazan about the birth scene. "How should I do it?" I asked him. "I really don't know how to approach it." He let me get all worked up, then turned and called out, "Okay, we're going to shoot the birth scene now!" He used my apprehension about the scene to help make it work.

Then I went to RKO for another of my favorite films, *The Enchanted Cottage,* for John Cromwell, who was also a fine director. I loved my other colleagues on it, too—Robert Young (my leading man in the movie *Claudia*), Herbert Marshall, Mildred Natwick.

But there was a little problem at first. Originally, to play the plain girl transformed by love into a beauty, I was supposed to have elaborate make-up. They made plaster casts of my face and were going to do all sorts of things to make me unbearably ugly, someone you could scarcely look at. I went to Make-up a couple of times, but then I went to John Cromwell and said, "This is wrong. This not a story about make-up. This girl's plainness is something that comes from within." He said, "Do the tests anyway, for the bosses." So I did them and then just walked off. I am not temperamental, but I knew what they were planning was a mistake. My husband and I left for Arizona, where we were living then. Eventually, they re-wrote the script and I came back and did the film without the heavy make-up. Mostly, our terrific cameraman, Ted Tetzlaff, used lighting to help create the girl's drab look.

I remained at RKO for *The Spiral Staircase,* in which I portray a mute girl threatened by an unknown killer. It was beautifully and atmospherically photographed by Nicholas Musuraca and perfectly directed by Robert Siodmak. That's Siodmak's own eye, incidentally, that is shown throughout as the peeping eye of the murderer. And I especially enjoyed working with Ethel Barrymore. Several years before, I had worked on the stage with her brother, John, in the play *My Dear Children.*

At Fox, *Gentleman's Agreement* was an important project dealing with anti-Semitism. It was unusually enjoyable to make because so many of us were friends as well as theater people—myself, Elia Kazan (our director again), Gregory Peck, John Garfield, Celeste Holm, Anne Revere, June Havoc. I play the socialite girlfriend of Greg, who's a writer pretending to be Jewish for a series of magazine articles. I remember that we went East to film a party scene in, I think, a Connecticut house. It wasn't a long scene, and we were able to complete it and return to Hollywood on the same day.

Before we left, though, Greg Peck squeezed in an interview with a local newspaperman. When the man did the story, he wrote that our film was "about real estate." You see, we had been filming in a "restricted" area

and anti-Semitism was still a very sensitive subject there.

Gentleman's Agreement went on to win the Best Picture Oscar for 1947, while Elia Kazan was voted Best Director and Celeste Holm Best Supporting Actress. I was nominated as Best Actress but lost to Loretta Young for *The Farmer's Daughter.*

Whew! I just looked all that up. I never think about awards. I just do my job: acting.

Catherine McLeod—ACTRESS—

Somehow, *I've Always Loved You,* which was my first starring film, seemed preordained to me. My mother died when I was 13, my father when I was 21. We were poor as church mice—I had to go right to work—but my dad encouraged me to be an actress. I just knew something like *I've Always Loved You* would come to me.

I was 24 when I got it. I'd just been fired from MGM, where I'd had small roles in *The Thin Man Goes Home, The Harvey Girls* and *Courage of Lassie,* and was attending the Bliss-Hayden drama school. The noted director Rouben Mamoulian saw me perform and wanted me to go to New York to act in a Tallulah Bankhead play. I enjoyed the stage, but I didn't know if I wanted to travel 3,000 miles at that point. Finally, however, I told my agent, "Maybe I should go." He said, "If you do, I won't get any commission." So I said, "Well, then, get me a great big Technicolor movie!"

He thought a minute and replied, "Republic is ready to go with their first Technicolor picture, and they're having trouble finding a leading lady. Irene Dunne, Maureen O'Hara and Joan Fontaine have all been ruled out for various reasons. The role is a very strong one: a young concert pianist who ages as the story progresses."

I went to Republic and met Frank Borzage, the film's distinguished producer-director. I'd grown up watching all the movies he did with Spencer Tracy, Clark Gable, Joan Crawford and Margaret Sullavan! While he was talking to me, a little man in a checkered suit came in who clearly annoyed Mr. Borzage. I thought he was an agent, but after a while I realized that he was Herbert J. Yates, president of Republic. "You must start shooting in a week," he instructed Borzage. Artur Rubinstein, the great pianist who was going to do the actual playing for my character on the soundtrack, came in next and said to me, "How do you do, my darling." Then he turned to Mr. Borzage and asked, "When are you going to start the film? I'm rehearsing and having a terrible time with Stokowski." (Leopold Stokowski was originally supposed to conduct the music, but when the recording eventually was done Walter Scharf was in charge.)

Mr. Borzage said, "I'd like to test you, Miss McLeod." I replied, "Oh, I can't this week. I'm canning tomatoes and peaches." Mr. Borzage was understandably dumbstruck. My agent quickly spoke up: "Catherine has a contract with the Bell Jar company for an industrial film and has a couple of days left to work." Mr. Borzage said, "Then we'll shoot at night."

So, I canned tomatoes all day and tested at night for the most expensive film Republic Pictures had done up to that point—$2,000,000 in 1946 was a tremendous budget. The following day, I was told I was the leading lady of *I've Always Loved You.*

I wasn't entirely convinced, though. I felt everything could dissolve like a bubble. This was around the time of the *Forever Amber* incident: 20th Century–Fox had brought the young English actress Peggy Cummins over with great fanfare to star as Amber, and after a while fired her and replaced her with Linda Darnell. I was afraid something like that might happen to me. I remembered that when I was at MGM, Angela Lansbury had told me, "Don't count on anything till it's in the movie house."

To make matters worse, I didn't sign a contract until about a month into the filming. I didn't know it, but they were arguing in the front office over who owned me, Mr. Borzage or Mr. Yates. Borzage said he discovered me, but Yates had the clout and wound up with my contract. I would have been better off with Borzage. He would have loaned me out for things—I was up for pictures with Alan Ladd, George Raft and some other stars, but Republic always wanted too much money for me. When I did radio, they took *all* my pay. I finally said, "I don't want to do any more radio."

I had been educated at convents, where, luckily, you had to study piano, so I was able to do all my own fingering at the keyboard for *I've Always Loved You.* The first day on the set I had to "play" Beethoven's "Appassionata" to Mr. Rubinstein's recording. I thought I could still turn out to be another Peggy Cummins, so my right foot was shaking as I put it on the pedal. "That's good," said Mr. Borzage. "Use it." Before long, my arms were very, very sore, because playing a "dead" piano is like playing a table.

Mr. Rubinstein coached me on the movements of a concert pianist. Once he said to me, "Cross your hands during this passage. It doesn't really have anything to do with the playing, but it looks harder. The public always likes things that look hard."

Everything went smoothly with the company, although there was some friction between Mr. Borzage and Mr. Yates. Yates, who had built his studio with low-budget cowboy movies, wanted to become another David Selznick. He wanted to make a classy movie but he didn't want to spend all that money, and he seemed to fuss quite a bit about it.

Working with the great character actress Maria Ouspenskaya was mostly pleasant but a bit ironic. A few years before, when my father died, I decided to become an actress. I didn't know which drama school to attend, so I asked the *Los Angeles Times* for a list of the more reputable ones, which they gave me. The first one was the Pasadena Playhouse, which cost $600 a year and then you didn't get to appear in a play until the third year. I didn't have $600, anyway. The second was the Actors Lab, which had a reputation for being a bit Red. I thought I'd better pass on that. The third was Ouspenskaya's school. I had always admired Madame Ouspenskaya in her films, and she had acted and taught at the Moscow Art Theater under Stanislavsky. So I called her.

"Who are you?" Madame asked. "What have you done?"

When I told her I had done nothing professionally, she said, "I don't train amateurs!" and banged the receiver.

Now, on *I've Always Loved You,* I was the leading lady, with Madame Ouspenskaya supporting me.

Madame was ready to give me lessons at last. When I'd finish a scene, in my exuberance I would jump up and maybe shriek with joy or do an Irish jig. If Madame was nearby, she would scold me, saying, "You shouldn't waste your energy like that. You should save it for your scenes." Maybe she was right.

I've Always Loved You took four months to film. The only real problem I recall during that time was a dreadful strike of studio prop men and "green people" (those who worked outside with greenery and such). I think it kept up for about two years. One day as I was about to drive into the studio, I was stopped by a gang of strikers. "Don't go in there!" they yelled at me. "I have to," I answered. "I have a contract." With that, they picked up my car and began to turn it over—I could touch the sidewalk. I managed to get out and dashed across the street to a café where I phoned Mr. Borzage. He said that his brother, Lew, who was an associate producer, would meet me at the gate and take me in, which he did. But I didn't drive in after that. At least not through that entrance.

Today, people often tell me how much they enjoyed *I've Always Loved You;* the film and I received tremendous publicity. But when released it turned out to be just a medium success. I next co-starred with Don Ameche in *That's My Man,* but Mr. Yates soon had me doing Westerns [*The Fabulous Texan, Old Los Angeles*].

Irene Manning—ACTRESS

Yankee Doodle Dandy was the first of several films I did for Warner Bros., and the best: an enduring classic.

The picture had a six-month schedule, which was very long, even for those years. I did my scenes and songs first as the Gay Nineties star Fay Templeton, then went off and did two other films, *The Big Shot* and *Spy Ship,* while *Yankee Doodle Dandy* was still shooting. James Cagney—who, as everyone must know by now, plays George M. Cohan—rehearsed for two months before he did any dancing. He was a perfectionist—dynamic. While he worked, though, we never dreamed that our movie would be shown regularly for the next 50 years!

I know I had some initial misgivings about the director, Michael Curtiz. He was Hungarian and I thought, "How can a Hungarian direct something as American as *Yankee Doodle Dandy?*" But he soon allayed all fears. He was very sensitive to universal emotions. For one dramatic scene, I asked him how he wished me to do it. "Play it the way you feel most comfortable," he replied, which was smart direction.

Recently, at a Warner Bros. gala in Hollywood where they gathered together 1,001 Warner stars, they were showing quick clips from the studio's films down through the years and I thought to myself, "Oh, I hope they show something of me from *Yankee Doodle Dandy.*" They chose the perfect close-up: a lovely shot of me looking up at Mr. Cagney and Joan Leslie. When we were getting ready to shoot it, I remember again asking Mr. Curtiz what I should do. "Just look at them with love," he said, and that's just what I did. Perfect direction.

At the premiere, everybody was congratulating everybody else on having done their best work. But James Cagney was our leader: he instilled in all of us the *will* to do his or her best. His sister Jeanne was in it, his brother Bill was associate producer—this all helped to give us the real family feeling we all had on this picture. Not many years ago, when the American Film Institute honored Jimmy, I flew down to attend the ceremony. Incidentally, that same evening, I ran into another old Warner Bros. buddy, Ronald Reagan. Later, a friend said to me, "What did you *say* to him?" I told her I said, "Hello, Ronnie, baby!"

Of course, I had made three pictures with Ronnie's then-wife, Jane Wyman: *The Doughgirls, Make Your Own Bed* and *Hollywood Canteen.* I especially loved doing *Doughgirls.* Besides Jane, we had Ann Sheridan, Alexis Smith, Jack Carson, Charlie Ruggles and Eve Arden in it. I tested for the Russian guerrilla eventually played by Eve, but I readily admit she was much better in the film than I would have been. Eve was much better casting. She was more robust; I was too delicate. So I played the heavy who kept coming in and stirring things up.

The Big Shot was important because it cast me as leading lady to Humphrey Bogart, who was just attaining superstardom. However, the director [Lewis Seiler] was not the greatest. Just before we started, he said to me, "Are you going to *sing* your lines?" When I had to be shot to death at the end, I asked how he wanted me to go about it. "I have no idea," he said. So I had to just go and wing being shot in the back and dying in a speeding car.

Bogie? He was basically all business, but not really my kind of guy. He used a lot of four-letter words which shocked me. Still, he was always prepared and professional and he did give me some good advice: "Never mind the camera, never mind the lights. Just get to the set and say the lines."

The Desert Song was another special favorite of mine. I first auditioned for the film five years before Warners actually made it. The original operetta was inspired by the 1920s revolt of the Moorish Riffs against the French protectorate in Morocco. But since Germany's invasion of France seemed immiment, the studio didn't want to do anything that could be construed as critical of the French. They auditioned every soprano in the country for the lead while they tried to solve the "French problem." I sang for them and left immediately to do a play in St. Louis—I always preferred the stage to the screen.

Then, in the early forties, I did a screen test in the part. It was a very expensive test, in Technicolor. I had Bette Davis' favorite cameraman, as well as a top director and Dennis Morgan opposite me. It was done just as if it were to be part of a full production. I helped with the writing of it and even changed some of Oscar Hammerstein's lyrics. (I've been doing that ever since: I am also a lyricist.)

On the strength of this test, Warners signed me, but we didn't do the film of *Desert Song* for about a year. Eventually, the villains were changed to Nazis and filming began.

Again, Dennis Morgan sang and acted the role of the Red Shadow beautifully, and again it was in Technicolor. We spent almost two months on location, with Gallup, New Mexico, standing in for the Sahara desert.

Faye Emerson was Azuri, the native dancing girl. Every night at our hotel she'd live her part and, in her bare feet, dance up a storm. She always tried to get me to join in, but I resisted because I wanted to do my hair and get to bed early so I could look beautiful in the morning. Finally, on the last night of the location shooting she got me to take off my shoes and dance, too.

My boss, Jack Warner? He wasn't one of my favorite people. Let's just say that there was not a lot of class there. Before Hollywood, the Warner brothers were meat packers.

Today, I teach voice, acting, modeling, speach dynamics and personal development in my home in northern California. I have a real United Nations group: black, white, yellow, all the colors of the rainbow. And I love it.

Victor Mature—ACTOR

Kiss of Death and then *Samson and Delilah* were very important to my career. The success of *Death,* I'm sure, helped me to get *Samson and*

Delilah, and *Delilah* led to many good roles in pictures like *The Robe* and *Demetrius and the Gladiators.*

Darryl Zanuck, our boss at 20th Century-Fox, had already okayed me for *Kiss of Death* when I went for my interview with the director, Henry Hathaway.

Henry said, "Nice meeting you, Vic. We've admired your work. Now there's something I want you to know about me when I work. I sometimes get very uptight and excited and every now and then I say something I don't really mean. If I explode with you, just ignore it."

I said, "Henry, here's something you should know about me: when someone around me explodes I react in exactly the same way. Why don't you get Cesar Romero for this part? I don't need the picture." But I was cast in it, and in the end I wasn't sorry, although Henry was true to his word.

Once, when we were filming in someone's house in New Jersey, the dialogue for the scene was changed about 20 minutes before we were to shoot.

Henry became furious, kicking boxes, pounding walls. When I saw this, I left the house and went out and sat in the car. Pretty soon an assistant came out and said, "Henry's waiting for you."

I told him, "You go back in and tell him that that goes for *pantomime,* too!"

In a few minutes Henry came out and put his arm around my shoulder, laughing, "You bastard!" Everything calmed down then—at least for *that* day.

Kiss of Death was Richard Widmark's first picture, and of course he made a sensation in it pushing the old lady down a flight of stairs. But he was a Broadway and radio veteran.

On the first day, I told him, "Don't take any of Henry's shit." The supporting players and extras in the film, which was shot in the East, were all Widmark's peers—theater pros who, in some cases, had even starred on Broadway. And right in front of them all, Henry started eating his ass out. Widmark just gave him the finger, then went and sat down.

When Henry came over, Widmark told him, "I'm a professional and I expect to be treated like a professional." After that, Henry behaved with Widmark.

Cecil B. DeMille, the producer-director of *Samson and Delilah,* always saw all of Hollywood to find the best people for his spectaculars. So when I got the call, I wasn't all that anxious to come in for the interview from Laguna, where I was living then. I thought, "Well, he's seeing everyone and now it's my turn."

Meeting him in his office at Paramount, I found that he had an extensive knowledge of my entire career—that's how thorough he was. When the interview lasted four hours, I knew I was in. While we were talking, he mentioned that he was having difficulty casting another important role, the Saran of Gaza. After he described the character to me I said, "It's got to be George Sanders." And he not only signed me to play Samson, but George Sanders to play the Saran of Gaza. After the picture was finished, I received a wire from

Sanders reading, "Where do I send the 10 percent?"

DeMille hired the best people in town for his films, and since we were all professionals he didn't feel he had to direct us too much. He figured we knew our jobs.

He'd say a few words to us, then shoot the scene. But he didn't miss a trick.

In a scene with 3,000 extras, if one guy in the back was picking his nose, Mr. DeMille would spot it and stop everything to chew him out.

One time he came up to me and said, "Victor, my boy. We're ready to do the scene where you fight the lion. We have a real lion, but he's very tame, a very sweet old lion. His name is Jackie. When you fight him, I'd like you to put your head in his mouth. Now don't worry; nothing can happen—Jackie has no teeth."

I said, "Mr. DeMille, I don't even want to be gummed!"

I did *not* do the stunt. No way! Not if there were six people holding Jackie by the tail!

Hedy Lamarr, who plays Delilah, was gorgeous—George Barnes, who photographed the picture, said to me, "You can shoot her from any angle. She has no bad angles." But I don't think she was well during the picture. Nothing chronic, she was just somehow out of sorts. Let me put it another way: she was not exactly a ball of fire—she just seemed to be loping along. But we got along okay, worked well together, and the camera picked up her beauty and mystique.

When *Samson and Delilah* came out, I received very flattering telegrams from Mr. DeMille and another pioneer filmmaker, Jesse L. Lasky, whose son, Jesse, Jr., had written the screenplay. I still have them.

Recently, I was asked to play Sylvester Stallone's father in a movie, so I gave them my price. It's been a few weeks now and I haven't heard, so it's probably not going to happen. But that's okay, I don't need the work. My father was rich and I took good care of my own money.

Virginia Mayo——— *ACTRESS*

I later heard that at first director William Wyler was reluctant to use me in *The Best Years of Our Lives.* He'd only seen me do the Technicolor comedies with Danny Kaye and Bob Hope and wondered if I could handle the dramatic role of cheating wife to Dana Andrews' war veteran. But I was under contract to Samuel Goldwyn, the producer, who wanted me, so I did a couple of tests for the part. I don't think they were actual scenes from the screenplay, but were similar in tone. They must have turned out all right, because I did the movie.

When I received the script, I brought it to my private drama coach and we worked on it together. She certainly deserves some of the credit for the good reviews I got when the film opened. Willie Wyler was a great director of the day who had impeccable taste. But, although a pleasant enough man, he was hard to figure out. He was so silent. I would come on the set and do what my coach and I had worked out, and Willie would say only, "Okay, let's shoot it." And then, "Print it." He was not very encouraging, would never tell me how I was doing. And sometimes an actress needs some encouragement. It was a very hectic time for me. I was working on two super-productions at once: *Best Years* and *The Secret Life of Walter Mitty,* opposite Danny Kaye. I'd bicycle from the Kaye comedy to the Wyler drama and sometimes wonder, "Who am I now?"

For one very dramatic scene, Willie wanted me to tear off my false eyelashes. I didn't want to be seen on screen without my eyelashes and tried to get out of doing it. "What if you need other takes?" I asked, trying to discourage him. "I won't be able to keep ripping them off." But he replied, "Okay, if it's not right the first time, we won't use it." That's how he got me. We got it on the first take. And people still mention that bit to me. It was the only time Willie told me what to do.

Dana Andrews, with whom I did most of my scenes in *Best Years,* was wonderful to work with, always so helpful. We were old pals on the Goldwyn lot, where we often worked with the coach there on other projects.

The Robert E. Sherwood screen-

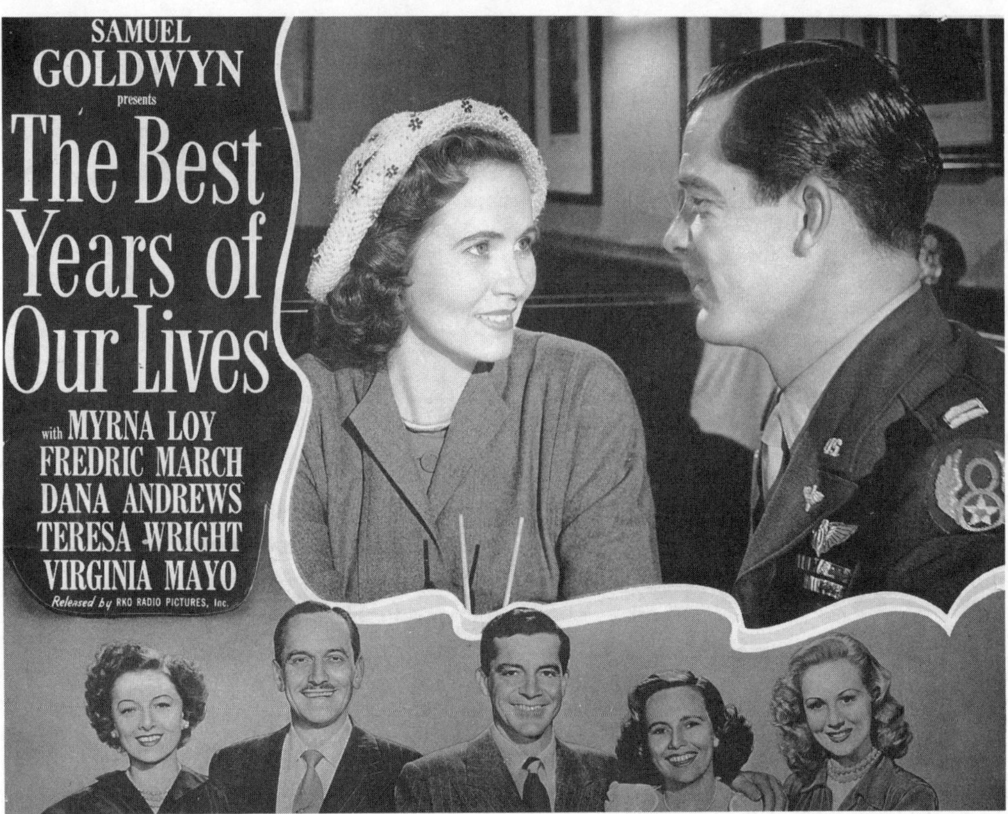

play was perfection. We never had to change an "a" or an "an." Still, maybe because I was harried at the time, I never dreamed it would be such a giant hit and win the Academy Award for Best Picture of 1946.

White Heat came along in 1949, after I'd left Goldwyn and signed with Warner Bros. I hadn't been too thrilled with most of the parts Warners was handing me at first, cheap little things like *Flaxy Martin,* so the role of James Cagney's wife in *White Heat* was a real plum. But I had just done a good picture called *Colorado Territory* for director Raoul Walsh, and he was to direct *White Heat.* He asked our boss Jack Warner for me again and everything was set.

The most exciting aspect was getting to work opposite the great Cagney, who was thrilling to watch. Even then he was a legend. When I arrived on the set I was completely in awe of him. And, no, I can't honestly say that he put me at ease right away. He was very businesslike; we just did the scene required and that was pretty much it. But he was very nice to me. When we came to the scene where he was supposed to knock me off a chair, he came up to me and asked if I minded doing it. I said, "Of course not," and we shot it—no problem. Later, when he wrote his autobiography, I was delighted to find that he had such nice things to say about me.

Cagney brought so much to *White Heat,* and not only in the acting department. He made many fine suggestions to Raoul Walsh that helped

to improve the picture. Like sitting on his mother's lap to suggest his character's mother complex. He gave a tremendous performance, too. I think he should have won the Oscar, but in those days they never gave awards to gangster movies; they thought that they were beneath them. They wanted to give it to pictures like *The Story of Louis Pasteur*—the high-minded stuff.

Raoul Walsh remains my favorite director. Besides *Colorado Territory* and *White Heat,* I also did *Along the Great Divide* and *Captain Horatio Hornblower* for him. He obviously liked me and I loved his brisk direction. Some directors just lag along and don't give any direction, but Raoul was marvelous, he knew how to make a movie *move.* He never got the credit he deserved. And he always kept me laughing. He would say, "Now I want you to run around that building as fast as you can. You just heard that they're serving free beer around the corner."

Despite the lasting popularity of *The Best Years of Our Lives* and *White Heat,* neither is my favorite film. That's one I did called *She's Working Her Way Through College,* which was directed by H. Bruce Humberstone. I made it in the early 1950s with Ronald Reagan. It was a musical and I loved doing the musicals most. I loved to dance.

Constance Moore—ACTRESS—

There are some wonderful memories associated with *I Wanted Wings*—and some not so wonderful.

It was an important film for me, because not only was I the top-billed female in a cast including Ray Milland and William Holden, but I was playing a young woman who was patterned after an idol of mine, the great wartime photo journalist Margaret Bourke-White. And my husband, Johnny Maschio, who was a top Hollywood agent, represented Bill Holden. He never represented me, though. I met him when I went to see him about representing me, but the relationship became too personal very quickly. Johnny and I have been married more than 50 years.

I Wanted Wings got off to a false start. We had been filming for a while at Randolph Field air base in San Antonio, Texas, when our director, J. Theodore ("Ted") Reed, and the Paramount brass began to have differences via long distance. Next thing we knew, Ted was removed. When Paramount called Mitchell Leisen to come down and direct the film, he was already familiar with the story. Mitch was a good friend of ours—he and Johnny had worked for Cecil B. DeMille some years before—and prior to starting *Wings* I had asked him to read the script and tell me what he thought. He said, "Do it!"

Now he was on his way to Texas to do it with us. We met him with flowers that were wilted from the horrendous heat. I'm from Texas, and I can tell you that when it gets hot there, it gets *hot.* Mitch did a great job on the picture. He was talented in so many ways. He designed the bugle-bead evening gown that newcomer Veronica Lake wore in her singing scene. And with her curvaceous figure, she was a sensation in it. He also dreamed up the "peekaboo" hairstyle for Veronica that became her trademark and helped her to become a star. He designed a couple of the outfits I wore in *Wings,* too. Everything was important to him. He'd arrive at the studio, his pockets bulging with his wife's jewelry for us to wear. She'd get angry and tell him, "At least you could give me a credit, 'Jewels by. . . .'"

The filming went on for about four or five months, which was quite long. And this was not just because of the re-shooting when we changed directors. We had to film a lot on the air base, but this was the eve of World War II—things were very tense—and there were many times when we just weren't allowed to use the air base.

I Wanted Wings became one of the top money-makers of 1941. And it made a big star of Veronica Lake, who had previously played only a few bits. She had a supporting role in *Wings,* but when Paramount saw the impact she was making they got behind her with a tremendous publicity campaign.

I kept quiet about Veronica in interviews for years, even defended

her when the occasion arose. But about 20 years ago, she wrote an autobiography that was a pack of lies! Particularly where my mother and I were concerned. Veronica wrote that while we were on location in Texas, I gave noisy parties that kept her awake. Totally false! And worst of all, she attributed some untrue vulgar comments to my mother, who visited us there. My mother was the great lady of all time! I got so angry that I decided not to hold back on Veronica any longer.

This was a girl who was handed stardom on a silver platter. Good roles, more publicity than practically any other actress of the war years, and in a short time she had blown it all. Her lack of professionalism was evident even during *I Wanted Wings,* her big break. She held up production several times. She'd simply disappear, run off here and there. She'd be due on the set on Monday morning, for instance, and on Saturday she'd take off in her car for New Mexico or wherever her husband [MGM art director John Detlie] was working and she'd wind up in a ditch someplace. The studio would learn about it Sunday night and have to reschedule the shooting on Monday.

Veronica Lake was her own worst enemy. She would goof up on personal appearance tours, make enemies. And worst of all, her drinking.

Despite all this, because of Mitch Leisen, Ray Milland, Bill Holden and our good story, which audiences ate up, *I Wanted Wings* remains one of my favorite pictures.

Dick Moore — ACTOR

Out of the Past was the first film I made after World War II.

I was just being released from a veterans' hospital, where I'd spent several months overcoming a rare crippling virus, when the film was offered. I would play Robert Mitchum's deaf-mute buddy in a *film noir* that today has quite a reputation, though frankly I've never been able to figure out what the plot was all about. I'd been a child actor and now that I was grown, I wasn't sure I wanted to act anymore. But the money was good, so I thought, "What the hell."

I was still recuperating at home, and for six weeks before a camera turned RKO sent a tutor to teach me the rudiments of sign language. When I finally got to work (we filmed most of my stuff at Bridgeport, California, near Tahoe), it turned out to be the most fun I ever had on a movie. I think it was the first time I'd felt a total absence of pressure on a movie set—pressure, I must add, that was usually generated from within myself. The people and the lovely location put me at ease.

Jacques Tourneur was one of the best directors I've ever had—kind, sensitive, very laid back. If someone were to ask me to name my five favorite directors among those I worked with, he'd be right up there with Ernst Lubitsch, Howard Hawks and a couple of others.

And Bob Mitchum became quite an influence and a role model for me, as Gary Cooper had been when I appeared with him in *Sergeant York* some years before. At the time, Bob was indulging his talent as a poet, though his subjects weren't always worthy of his gifts for language. I remember one poem he wrote was about a farting horse.

Bob didn't suffer fools too kindly. There was one actor from New York in the picture—and it wasn't Kirk Douglas—who was forever carrying on about how wonderful New York was, how Hollywood was full of hicks, how movies weren't great art and, of course, how much better New York actors were. Having heard enough of this, Bob took the actor aside, told him he was indeed a great talent but that his effectiveness in the current part would be infinitely greater if he would insert certain subtleties into the character that were not in the script. Bob outlined these for him. Consequently, when Mr. Tourneur shot his scenes they came off totally wrong. The whole crew was wise to what Bob had done and was laughing.

Tourneur was confused at first—this wasn't what the New York actor had done in rehearsal—but then he caught on and laughed, too.

Dennis Morgan—ACTOR—

I made an awful lot of movies during the 1940s. *Kitty Foyle,* opposite Ginger Rogers, really put me over in Hollywood.

The Very Thought of You, with Eleanor Parker, was a nice one. The "two guys" pictures with Jack Carson, *Two Guys from Milwaukee* and *Two Guys from Texas,* were popular. And *God Is My Co-Pilot* gave me a strong role.

But I think my favorites are two that the public also seems to like best. At least they have become annual events on television. I'm referring to *Christmas in Connecticut,* which always pops up around December 25, and *My Wild Irish Rose,* a standard on St. Patrick's Day.

Both were commercial successes in their time, too.

Christmas in Connecticut was Warner Bros.' biggest money-maker that year [1945] in proportion to the money spent on it. And *My Wild Irish Rose* was very well received—it made a fortune in 1947.

I didn't see how *Christmas in Connecticut* could miss. My leading lady was Barbara Stanwyck and the supporting cast was full of great, scene-stealing character players liked Sydney Greenstreet, S.Z. Sakall, Reginald Gardiner, Frank Jenks and

BARBARA
STANWYCK
DENNIS
MORGAN
SYDNEY
GREENSTREET
Christmas in Connecticut
PRESENTED BY
Warner Bros.
REGINALD GARDINER · S. Z. SAKALL · ROBERT SHAYNE
DIRECTED BY PETER GODFREY
Screen Play by Lionel Houser & Adele Commandini
From an Original Story by Aileen Hamilton
A Warner Bros.-First National Picture

Una O'Connor. It was a good script and Peter Godfrey was a fine director. Although people today seem to think of Barbara as a dramatic actress, she was also a very good comedienne. We worked well together, but she was quite a taskmaster. She had a bad back and didn't sleep well, so she always got to the studio early with plenty of time to get letter-perfect in her lines. If you weren't on the ball, she'd snap, "Why didn't you study your script?" But she never got me. I knew she did that and was ready for her.

Although the film takes place during a Christmas in Connecticut, we shot it during a summer in Hollywood, and the set was hot as hell. I don't think we worked on location at all—the whole Connecticut home and countryside in the story were constructed on studio stages. The snow that fell on the set was unbleached cornflakes. It looked just like real snow and floated down very believably. We wore winter clothes and sweated so profusely that people had to keep wiping us dry. But we had so much fun we didn't really mind. And it was slightly cooler inside the house set. This house was so beautiful that I hoped to build an exact replica for myself and my family and had the plans for years. I never got around to it, though.

I was generally delighted with the final results of the picture, despite a few things in it I didn't like. Jack Warner, our boss, liked to throw in broad comedy here and there—like the scene where the pancakes fall from the ceiling. He loved this sort of thing; he wasn't the most tasteful man around. But there wasn't enough of this stuff in the movie to spoil it.

Many years later, when *Christmas in Connecticut* had become a staple on television during the holidays, I was visiting Connecticut for a state meeting of the Cancer Society. A fellow stopped me on the street there and said, "Hey, Morgan, why the hell don't you quit ruining Christmas with that picture of yours? They run the damn thing every year!" Thank God he is in the minority!

I played a number of Irish roles on the screen, but the best was in *My Wild Irish Rose:* Chauncey Olcott, a real-life turn-of-the-century singer and songwriter who enjoyed great success in America. It was a joy to sing all the wonderful Irish-American songs in the picture. Did I listen to his recordings prior to filming? Not much. He had a high, squeaky tenor that seemed a bit out of date for our forties audience, so I knew I had to sing in my own style. And it seemed to work.

The filming was generally without incident, except that about 10 days before shooting ended, there was a strike and we had to live at the studio till we finished. At night, a Warner car would take Jack Carson, my late best buddy on the lot (whom I still miss); my beautiful leading lady, Arlene Dahl, who was playing her first real role; and myself out to dinner.

Now, I am not Irish. My real name is Stanley Morner—Morner is a very common Swedish name. My father was Swedish and my mother was Dutch, but because of roles like Chauncey Olcott in *My Wild Irish Rose* everyone thought I was from the auld sod. Not long after *Irish Rose* came out, I had to go to France to film *To the Victor,* with Viveca Lindfors. On the way, I was to land in Shannon, Ireland. As we approached the airfield, our stewardess announced, "We are now landing in Shannon, Ireland. Welcome home, Dennis Morgan." I didn't tell her I wasn't Irish. Later, on the ground, her boyfriend came up to me and said, "I understand you're from here. Whereabouts?" I said, "Just a little north of here" and pointed towards Sweden.

Once, Eamon DeValera, then the president of Ireland, came to Los Angeles for a brief stay. We met, and he told me that he had loved *My Wild Irish Rose.* At a luncheon and then an evening banquet in his honor, I sang some authentic old Irish songs that weren't in the picture. At one point, his big Irish bodyguard whispered to me, "For God's sake, don't tell him you're not Irish!"

After the success of *My Wild Irish Rose,* it seemed a good idea to do another biography. The great Scotch poet and minstrel man Robert Burns had led a very interesting life, so a writer friend and I got together on a treatment for a biographical film about Burns. I told him, "You better make it interesting enough to convince Warner." And he made it *very* interesting. I hoped I would be able to star as Robert Burns.

When Jack Warner read our synopsis, he called me into his office. "We can't make this," he said. "The American public will think we've done a movie about a cigar!"

Recently, someone told me that he'd read that during our Warner years I was making more money than [Humphrey] Bogart, but I don't think that's true. I think we were about even. However, I know that [Errol] Flynn made more than either of us!

Dorothy Morris — *ACTRESS*

I was born in Hollywood. "That's three strikes on you," everybody said. "You can't be discovered here. You've got to go away. No one is discovered here."

I wanted to be an actress since I was three, but I was very introverted and shy and kept it to myself for many years. I attended Hollywood High School, where an agent saw me in the fall play. Next thing I knew, I was acting in an experimental TV drama. This was 1940, and while some people did have television sets in their homes then, there were only about 50 of them altogether and they were only able to transmit programs for a few blocks. Ian MacDonald, who much later played the villain in *High Noon,* did the TV play with me and said, "You ought to study at the Pasadena Playhouse." I didn't have enough money to attend the Playhouse, but I did go to the Sunday readings there. Meanwhile, I studied with the famous character actress Maria Ouspenskaya, who gave me a scholarship. She taught the Stanislavsky Method that was so popular in New York. I learned how to be a mattress and how to be a hot fudge sundae.

One evening at the Pasadena Playhouse they were casting the play *What a Life!* and I went to read for one of the teen-agers in it. Casting people from MGM were there, saw me and asked me to test for a role in *Life Begins for Andy Hardy.* The role was that of a nightclub girl; sexy-looking Patricia Dane also tested for it. Needless to say, she got the part. I was 20 but looked about 14. The test was good for me, though, because I got to dress up and look glamorous, which was so important in films in those days. On the strength of it, MGM signed me to a contract. I was there for four years and did about 40 movies.

One of my early pictures was *When Ladies Meet,* starring Joan Crawford. Whenever I get the chance, I always say nice things about Joan, whom I adored. She plays a novelist in the film and I only had a three-day bit as an autograph-seeker. I was to work Friday, Monday and Tuesday. On Sunday afternoon, my boyfriend and I decided to go to the beach. As we drove out along Sunset Boulevard, I suddenly noticed that Joan Crawford and a companion were sitting in the back of a chauffeur-driven car right alongside us. I clutched my boyfriend. "There's Joan Crawford! I just worked with her!" But I was too inhibited to wave to Joan.

At the studio on Monday morning, Joan asked me, "Wasn't that you I saw on Sunset Boulevard in a car yesterday?" You must understand that this was the day of the star system, when stars were up on pedestals, and Joan Crawford was right up there with the greatest. No one expected them to notice the help, which was pretty much the category I fell into then. I was shocked almost speechless but did manage to whisper, "Yes." Joan continued, "Why didn't you wave? I told my friend, 'That's Dorothy Morris. I'm working with her'." I was thrilled.

If you winked watching *Babes on Broadway,* you could miss me. But the stars were two of Hollywood's most talented, Mickey Rooney and Judy Garland, so it was "run, do not walk" to that set. I had known Judy several years before. We both went to Bancroft Junior High in Hollywood and became good friends. Arthur Miller, the distinguished 20th Century–Fox cameraman who was a good friend of my family's, had photographed Judy in her first picture, *Pigskin Parade,* and introduced her to us. Pretty soon, she was staying overnight with us. She was very lonely. I remember her saying, "Dorothy, you're so lucky. You've got a family."

Judy was terrific, not afraid of anything, including the girl's vice principal at school. She'd call Judy into her office and demand, "Take off that lipstick," which Judy loved to wear. She would come out and put it right back on.

I kept everything to myself, so Judy never knew I wanted to be an actress. Years later, when she first saw me on the set of *Babes on Broad-*

way, she cried out, "Oh, no! You, too!"

Mickey was also fabulous, bursting with talent and creative energy. I worked with him again in *The Human Comedy,* the first really serious thing I ever saw him do. It was Mickey who really directed it—at least the family scenes in which we appear. Clarence Brown, who was supposed to be the director, just let us do what we wanted to do. Mickey worked with us all, bringing out the best we had, but he was especially helpful coaching little Jackie "Butch" Jenkins, who was making his movie debut. Mickey put his heart and soul into that picture because MGM was giving him a chance at last to be someone other than Andy Hardy.

Off-camera, Mickey was a cut-up, as usual. But no matter how outrageous he got, you couldn't get mad at him. Donna Reed was in *Human Comedy,* too. She and I were perfect little ladies, so he knew he couldn't get away with anything with us. He played the piano a lot on the set. He simply had to be creating. The talent would just bubble up like yeast and he'd have to do something. He and Judy were great together. They were so devoted, had such admiration for each other.

I loved my part as the shell-shocked nurse on Bataan in *Cry Havoc.* Maybe I relate to demented people. I never liked wearing a lot of make-up and false eyelashes. At the time, nobody wanted roles like this pathetic nurse. They all wanted to look great on the screen. But I was never a glamour type. I always wanted to be an *actress.* It never occurred to me to be glamorous. People would say, "You don't look like an actress. You don't sound like an actress."

For *Cry Havoc,* I had to have an English accent, so Heather Angel, who plays my sister and was English, coached me. I got to do something really creative in this one; when I go berserk, all attention is on me.

What I liked best about the picture, really, was the rehearsal. Richard Thorpe, our director, said, "Dorothy, I just want to see you do this scene where the girl becomes disturbed. Let's have a full rehearsal." So he just let me go, and I wound up screaming and crying. Everybody there—Margaret Sullavan, Ann Sothern, even Red Skelton, who was visiting from another set—applauded.

"Fantastic!" exclaimed Mr. Thorpe. "But Dorothy, this comes too early in the movie. We can't have that much drama so soon. We'll have nothing to build up to." So I had to give the much quieter interpretation that's in the picture.

It was primarily an all-female cast. We got along fine—Ann Sothern, Joan Blondell, Heather, Ella Raines, Fay Bainter, Frances Gifford, Diana Lewis and Marsha Hunt. Only Margaret Sullavan seemed remote. Not that she was difficult; she wasn't. Just not part of the group. I admired her greatly as an actress. When actors need space, I respect that.

None Shall Escape, done on loan-out to Columbia, is perhaps my favorite picture. I play a tragic 16-year-old who falls in love with a Nazi. Marsha Hunt, cast as my mother, is only five years older than I, so the make-up department had to

get to work on her. Marsha has always been my heroine, as a woman and as an actress. We made five pictures together and she was always an inspiration. Although *None Shall Escape* was a fine movie, I don't think it was a big hit.

30 Seconds Over Tokyo, starring Van Johnson and Spencer Tracy, *was* a big hit, but not with me. I had just married a blimp (or Lighter Than Air) pilot and we were stationed at Laguna and Newport beaches. We were expecting him to go overseas any minute. Suddenly, MGM called me to play a flyer's wife in *30 Seconds Over Tokyo* which was to be shot largely at Eglin Field in Florida.

"Oh, no, please," I implored them. "I was just married. My husband is shipping out."

But they insisted, "You'll be going with Jacqueline White. You two are the only girls under contract that we can trust with all those men down there."

So Jackie and I went, along with only two other girls, Phyllis Thaxter, who was the leading lady, and the hairdresser. I remember saying, "We'll probably come back and shoot all our scenes on Stage 22 at MGM." When we got to Florida, it rained for weeks. They couldn't shoot a thing. So, back we went to Hollywood and did the scenes at MGM. Those scenes of ours on the beach and at the flyers' dance were all done on sound stages.

Our Vines Have Tender Grapes was a charming movie that many remember. At first, I really didn't want to do it. The part was minuscule and another "crazy girl." I had played disturbed characters in *Pilot No. 5,* then *The War Against Mrs. Hadley,* then *Cry Havoc.* And Mr. [Louis B.] Mayer, our boss, had told me, "You're doing the wrong kind of parts. You're never going to be a star if you persist in doing these parts." On top of that, one day as I stepped into a department store elevator, a woman said to her friend, "Oh-oh, there's that crazy girl!" They immediately got out of the elevator.

Then I read the script; the character was a sweet little thing. "It'll only take a few days," they told me. "You're the only girl who can do it." I got into some old clothes and did the test. Mr. Mayer said, "That's her. And I want an extra scene written in for Dorothy." Originally, the part was just one scene with Margaret O'Brien, but they fattened it up a little.

The role turned out to be a breakthrough, of sorts, toward understanding retarded people. Up until then, they had been left pretty much alone in films, or used bizarrely or for levity. This was a sympathetic and lovely girl.

Why did I leave Metro? I wasn't getting anywhere. I wanted to give myself one more year. I never wanted to be a star, just a good featured player. But MGM would put me in bits, then give me leads, then put me in bits again. When I went to MGM, I wanted to be an actress more than anything in the world. But the war had changed my mind. My priorities became having a good marriage and raising a family.

I asked for, and got, my release. They knew I wasn't going to become a star. And if you were not a star who made money for them, they didn't really care about you. Occasionally, they'd loan me out to other studios, but they didn't make a lot on the deals.

It was like going to college at MGM. I learned so much about life there. I learned not to smoke, not to drink, not to do a lot of things I saw others get in trouble doing. I had been so introverted, and MGM brought me out of myself. I always say that I matriculated at Metro-Goldwyn-Mayer.

On my 24th birthday, I was over at Universal shooting *Little Miss Big.* I was pregnant and chose that day to announce that I was retiring. It was the greatest decision I ever made. I eventually had two sons. Ten years after quitting, I came back and, strictly as a hobby, did some TV work. And later, a couple of movies. For some time now, I have been a massage therapist.

Janis Paige — ACTRESS

The Hollywood Canteen played an important role in my life and career.

I was working there when Ida Koverman, who was Louis B. Mayer's executive assistant, saw me and got me a six-month contract at MGM. But all I did during that time was a small part in an Esther Williams film called *Bathing Beauty* in which my one line is something like "They're here!" (To this day, when I run into Esther she always says, "They're here!")

After MGM, I went to Warner Bros. World War II was raging and many civilians couldn't travel. You could be bumped from an airplane to accommodate traveling servicemen, or you just couldn't get a reservation in the first place. This is how I got the film that celebrated the famous Hollywood haven for servicemen—*Hollywood Canteen.* A starlet had been set for the second female lead, that of a studio messenger girl, but she just couldn't get a flight back from New York in time to play the part. I was not doing much except taking dramatic lessons at Warners when Solly Baiano, the head of casting, came to me one day and said, "I'm going to take you down to see Delmer Daves, the writer-director of *Hollywood Canteen.* They're already filming and they don't have a girl to play Angela, Dane Clark's girlfriend in it."

Mr. Daves was shooting on the big sound stage replica of the canteen, where much of the film was done. But he took the time to see me. "She's the one. That's it," he said. Solly took me right down to Wardrobe, where I got my messenger uniform, and I was working the next day.

As we filmed, I walked around with my mouth open. I was just a little girl from Tacoma, Washington, who never dreamed she'd be in the movies. I never dreamed I'd even get to Los Angeles! I grew up at the movies. I was a member of the Saturday afternoon "Popeye Club" and was voted "Miss Olive Oyl." And now I was playing an important role in *Hollywood Canteen,* which had a huge cast of stars who were legends even then [1944]—everyone from the Andrews Sisters to Jane Wyman. One afternoon I was walking back to the set in messenger costume—which was a pale green wool gabardine, beautifully made—when Errol Flynn, dressed in tights for *Adventures of Don Juan* tests, walked right by me. I couldn't *move!* Errol had been one of my idols. You can't imagine what it was like then. Stars were unattainable, on pedestals—they were like people from Mars in those days. This doesn't exist anymore.

Bette Davis plays herself in the picture, one of the founders of the real Hollywood Canteen. She became my life-long friend and advisor. We even did another picture together, *Winter Meeting,* in 1948, although she was fighting then with Warners because she didn't like the story or her leading man, a newcomer named Jim Davis. But there never was a time when I couldn't pick up the phone and call her. She always praised me—she'd say, "You're the talent around here, Janis. I know it when I see it." Years later, around 1960, before I started *Please Don't Eat the Daisies,* I called her for some professional advice. She was just divorcing Gary Merrill, but took the time to give me some pointers on how to protect myself. I remember asking her, "Do I really *need* that?" and she replied, "You bet your life you do!"

A year or two before she became ill, I met her at a tribute she was being given and she said to me, "Well, Janis, it's a *whole* new ballgame, isn't it?" When she got up to speak that evening, she said, "I see a girl here who I thought was one of the most talented people ever at Warner Bros.—Janis Paige." Can you imagine what it meant to me to hear this great woman say that?

Joan Crawford appears as herself in *Hollywood Canteen,* too, and she also became a dear friend. In the '60s, we did another film together, *The Caretakers* (a special favorite of mine). There wasn't a Christmas that went by that I didn't receive a Christmas card. Not long before she died, I received a note from her which began, "Janis dearest, This will be my last note to you. . . ." I had no idea she was ill. She was a friend; she wasn't "Joan Crawford" to me.

Delmer Daves was a marvelous director. He really loved actors—something else you don't see today. They had the time then to get to know them and love them. Now, there's no time, you have to be instantly good. Delmer would sit behind the camera and get involved in the emotion of a scene and cry. Then he'd forget to call "Cut!" He'd say, "Oh, I'm so sorry. I just got so caught up in it." Where would you see that today?

In the 1970s, they razed the actual Hollywood Canteen building. Among other things, it had been a disco for a while, and was painted purple. One day a Los Angeles newspaperman called me and said, "They're tearing down the Hollywood Canteen. Would you come over and walk through it and reminisce?" I did, and a big construction guy asked me, "Is there anything here you'd like to keep?" I told him, "Yes, the 'Exit' sign and a couple of chunks of the patio cement signed by servicemen." So I have the "Exit" sign and some pieces of autographed cement from the Hollywood Canteen.

And many wonderful memories.

David Raksin—COMPOSER—

I came to Hollywood in 1935 and in 1938 began working in the music department of 20th Century-Fox. I specialized in horror films and bits and pieces of musicals. In 1944, however, everything changed when I was assigned to write the musical score for *Laura.*

The picture was in trouble. Rouben Mamoulian had started directing it, with Otto Preminger as producer, but he had a big falling out with both Preminger and Darryl Zanuck, the studio chief. Preminger then took over as director, too. But it was still a film that had the stigma of trouble attached to it. People in Hollywood like to stay away from projects like that: they're afraid it might rub off on them. Preminger

wanted Alfred Newman, the head of Fox's music department, to write the score, but Al backed off, explaining, "It's a detective story, so we ought to get Bernard Herrmann to do it." When he was approached, Bernie said, "If it's not good enough for Al, it's not good enough for me. If it's a detective story, give it to Dave Raksin. He does a lot of detective stories."

Which I did. But I immediately realized, and told them, "This is not a detective story. This is a love story."

And that was how I handled it.

Laura turned out to be a surprise hit, of course, its illustrious reputation continuing to this day. The song "Laura" was not in the picture, however—only the instrumental theme. And it didn't come out with the movie, either. When a picture opens, the composer of its musical score might get five or six fan letters, if he's lucky. After *Laura* was out a while, I stopped counting at 1700 letters. Gene Tierney, Dana Andrews, Clifton Webb, Otto Preminger, Darryl Zanuck, *everybody* received letters asking about the theme, too. So I suggested to the publishers that we bring out a song—sheet music. They disregarded the suggestion. Public clamor continued; dance bands, too, wanted a song.

When they finally agreed to publish a title song from *Laura,* Oscar Hammerstein II put in his bid to write the lyric. He also wanted to publish it, which Fox didn't want. Then a very good and very famous

FOREVER AMBER
Darryl F. Zanuck presents
"FOREVER AMBER"
COLOR BY Technicolor
LINDA DARNELL as Amber
CORNEL WILDE as Bruce Carlton
RICHARD GREENE as Lord Almsbury
GEORGE SANDERS as King Charles II
with GLENN LANGAN · RICHARD HAYDN · JESSICA TANDY · ANNE REVERE
Directed by OTTO PREMINGER
Produced by WILLIAM PERLBERG
From the Novel by KATHLEEN WINSOR
Adaptation by Jerome Cady
Screen Play by Philip Dunne and Ring Lardner, Jr.
20th CENTURY-FOX Triumph!

lyricist did a lyric for "Laura." The head of the publishing company, Robbins Music, called to ask what I thought of it.

"Awful," I told him.

"Who are you to say you don't like this man's lyric?" asked the publisher.

"The composer," I replied.

Finally, we got Johnny Mercer who outdid himself. I remember, though, that there were two phrases in the lyric that caused Johnny some trouble. He couldn't decide which one to choose. He brought them to me and I made the selection. I never heard any complaints.

To date, the song and score have close to 400 recordings. I'm told that it is the second most recorded song ever—Hoagy Carmichael and Mitchell Parish's "Stardust" reputedly is the most recorded song.

The first recording of my score for *Laura?* One day the conductor Werner Janssen came to see me at Fox. He was looking for material for his symphony orchestra, so I played him some of my best music, which was a little more avant-garde than my usual movie music. He said, "Hmmm, fine," but it didn't seem to be what he was looking for. So I took him to hear a small piece for piano and orchestra that Bernard Herrmann had written for the current Fox film *Hangover Square,* with Laird Cregar. "That's great," said Janssen. "But I come to see you and you sell me Bernard Herrmann's music. I was looking for something like the music you did for *Laura.*"

"Oh, that," I replied. So I played it for him. And Janssen made the first recording of the *Laura* score on a 12-inch RCA Victor Red Seal record.

Laura changed my career. I had always been a highly respected member of the profession, but with this picture and score I stepped into another world. A new agent bought out my contract; I got more money. But Fox cut me down to size with my next assignment, a dreadful little "quickie" starring William Bendix called *Don Juan Quilligan.* I didn't feel insulted, though. I thought, "I'm a guy who works in this department and this is the job."

Otto Preminger loved my work in *Laura.* From then on, he became my protector behind the scenes—there are always studio politics to be dealt with. I made five pictures with Otto—a record. After *Laura,* we did *Fallen Angel, Forever Amber, Daisy Kenyon* and *Whirlpool.* Most composers could only manage to get through one movie with Otto. He was not an easy guy. I never knuckled under to him—that was the secret. We had a big fight in the beginning, but things quieted down. He knew my main concern was always for the picture.

A few years later, when *Forever Amber* came up, Preminger, who was directing, asked for me again. This was publicized as the most expensive picture ever made, Zanuck's answer to Selznick's *Gone with the Wind,* with Linda Darnell in the sexy title role. Originally, Al Newman, the Fox music chief, wanted Erich Wolfgang Korngold to do the score, but he was ill at the time and evidently just wasn't up to it. It was an enormous score, 110–12 minutes of music. So Al gave me the job. Afterward, I couldn't help wondering what Korngold thought of the score. I asked his son George if his father had seen *Amber,* and he told me that his father had insisted on doing so. According to George, Korngold *père* said, "It is a very, very fine score by a first-rate young composer."

When *Forever Amber* came out, Darryl Zanuck, who was not a man given to praise, idle or otherwise, sent me a most complimentary letter which he also circulated around the lot. It read, in part, "Dear Dave, You have written a magnificent score for *Forever Amber*. . . ." Some music critics have called it one of the half-dozen best scores of all time. Unfortunately, the film itself didn't do as well as expected, but I liked it. It was handled very adroitly by the screenwriters, Philip Dunne and Ring Lardner, Jr. Later, they often knocked the picture, although I thought they took a rotten job and made the most of it.

Al Newman conducted *Forever Amber* for the screen, but I did the RCA album of the score. At one point they were going to take it away from me when Preminger walked in and said, "Don't. Keep your hands off." So I got the album.

No, *Laura* is not my favorite film score. I really don't have just one. But *Laura* is certainly on my preferred list, as are the scores from *Forever Amber, Force of Evil, Carrie, The Bad and the Beautiful* and a little-seen 1965 religious film I did called *The Redeemer.*

Ann Richards——————*ACTRESS*—

Like the song says, "I'm still here," despite reports to the contrary in several current film encyclopedias. Apparently copying from each other, they have listed me as deceased! How this started I can't imagine.

I came over from Australia on the first ship to leave after Pearl Harbor and the last until the end of the war. The Japanese attack on Pearl Harbor occurred on Dec. 7, 1941, and we left Australia on Dec. 11.

The ship was a beautiful American vessel called the *Mariposa* which President Roosevelt had ordered home. It was white, but just before we sailed they slapped grey paint all over to camouflage it from the Japanese. We were supposed to be taking a lot of gold with us, but at the last minute they decided that this would not be safe, so we stood on deck and watched them remove it all. They thought troops would be all right, though, so we took a batch that was on its way to Canada.

We were blacked out all the way. Once at sea, the captain called for volunteers to be on deck and try to spot Japanese submarines. I immediately volunteered to do my part, but I think they got fed up with me very fast: looking through my telescope, I saw a sub every five minutes. Anything dark against the white waves always looked like a sub to me.

Sometimes we would see a commotion of ships and lights miles away, but the captain felt this might be a ploy of the Japanese to draw us near and would quickly steer our ship in another direction.

Finally, we landed in San Francisco. On the way to the hotel, the taxi driver remarked, "Too bad about the *Mariposa.* The Japanese have been telling everyone that they sank it." I thought of my mother, who would be horrified at this false report, and wired her back in Australia that both the *Mariposa* and her adventuress daughter were safe.

Ken Hall, the noted Australian filmmaker in whose productions I became a star, had put together all my best scenes from Australian films and shipped them ahead to Carl Dudley, a screenwriter who had worked in Australia. Dudley gave the film to a man who had been a nightclub agent but was only just starting in the motion picture field. He didn't know procedure. He didn't know that when you have film on a client, you carry it to an appointed location yourself and arrange for it to be seen personally. He sent it to some movie person and it was lost. I never heard of it again, until many years later, when my daughter Juliet was about 14. One day she came home from school and said that a friend told her that someone he knew had this old film on me from my Australian movie-making years. But her teacher wouldn't give us any information and we let it drop. By then, I was married, the mother of three and basically out of the business.

Through Carl Dudley, I met Roy Myers of the Leland Hayward office. I was fortunate that he wanted to represent me. First off, Roy said, "It's important that we get some film on you to act as a test."

At the time, MGM was preparing to make a short subject called *The Woman in the House* about an English schoolteacher who becomes a recluse, aging 40 years. When a studio didn't have someone under contract who could play a role, they could go off the lot for the right actor or actress. They felt they had no one who could play this role then, and when it was arranged for me to meet Sammy Lee, the director, he said, "You've got it." Of course, by then everyone knew my sad story—how I'd sailed across Japanese-infested waters, lost the film Ken Hall had put together for me. All I had was my scrapbook to prove that I had been an Australian movie star.

The important thing was that I was being *paid.* I was only allowed to take $75 with me from Australia. I had relatives here who I'm sure wouldn't have let me starve, but I didn't want to depend on them.

The minute *Woman in the House* was cut and edited, my agent went to MGM and arranged for it to be shown to all the executives, including studio boss Louis B. Mayer, whom I had met briefly when he came to watch us film. He wanted me under contract and I signed with MGM.

The first feature I did there was the enormously popular love story *Random Harvest,* which starred Ronald Colman and Greer Garson. I play Ronnie's cousin. The producer, Sidney Franklin, told me, "If you had come to the lot earlier, you would have gotten the much more impor-

tant role of Colman's fiancée, which Susan Peters already was signed to play. Colman is an amnesiac, and she is supposed to remind him of his first love, Greer Garson, whom you resemble much more than Susan does."

So I was relegated to playing a family supernumerary during a big breakfast scene, my waist thickened by Wardrobe to make me look older, for some reason. Before the picture was edited down, I did have another moment or two. Recently, someone showed me a still of a going-away scene I had, dressed in furs, with Ronald Colman. There were some others in the scene, but we were embracing. This was cut. Ronnie was extremely charming and made me feel very comfortable. In Australia, I had gone to school with his nieces, the children of his brother Eric, and this formed a little bond between us. Eric was attractive, too, and rather resembled Ronnie, except that he was taller with less delicately defined features.

I loved MGM—except for the waiting. There were long periods when I wasn't being used. I went to Billy Grady, the head of casting, and begged him for work—any work. "I want to be on a set. *Any* set. I don't want to wait for anything big. I want to make this a learning time," I pleaded. Whereupon Mr. Mayer called me to his office. "Be patient," he said. I replied, "I want to do anything that comes up. I don't care if there are no lines. I just want to be on a set. I already have been the star, played the leads, had people crawl over my limousine!" Mayer just shook his head. You never knew if he was going to cry or roar.

Then Billy Grady called and said, "If you're so passionately anxious to play anything at all, learn to play the cello!" So I appeared as a cellist in the film *Three Hearts for Julia,* with Ann Sothern and Melvyn Douglas. I had very little to do, but it was interesting.

I continued to wait for my big chance. Looking back, I don't think I was as pushy as I should have been. I found it very hard to knock on producers' doors and say, "I am perfect for your new picture."

One morning while walking on the lot in front of the Thalberg Building, someone behind me said, "My name is King Vidor. Are you an actress?" I told him I was indeed an actress and gave my name. He said, "I am going to do a picture you might be right for. Can you test?" I told him, "Any time!"

He asked, "Can you come to my office now?" Could I?! He told me about his picture, *America* (as it was then called), a very, very big canvas about a man like Henry Ford who makes cars, then, in wartime, goes into the airplane business. I would be the leading lady, an Irish girl who marries this ambitious Czech immigrant (Brian Donlevy).

My agent soon called to say that Vidor, who was producing and directing in Technicolor from his own original story, wanted me. "But I have to warn you," he added, "when a big part like this in such an expensive film comes up, other actresses on the lot will want to test, too, and no one will be able to turn them down if they've been around for a while." A number of other actresses did test.

Mr. Mayer called me into his office to tell me that I had won the role. "This part will be very good for you," he assured me. "But—dye your hair red!" He loved redheads. Well, I didn't dye my hair red; it looks my own natural slightly reddish blonde in the film. Once, though, I did see a print of the picture where my hair looked quite red. I don't know what they did to the film!

One day while we were filming, Mr. Mayer came down to the set after having seen one of the vivid Technicolor productions 20th Century-Fox was turning out then. He watched us shoot a scene where I'm talking to Brian Donlevy in a bedroom. "All of this looks too pale," interrupted Mayer. "I want it to be as colorful as a Fox picture. After all, we're in California where we have beautiful color all around us every day of the year. Look at the oranges, the flowers, the blue skies. We've got to work in bright colors!" After he left, one of the crew said, "Well, I'd better go see to Belle Watling's bedroom."

Brian Donlevy was extremely thrilled to have such an important part. He was a very serious person, and I have a very English sense of humor. We're inclined to say things that can sound absurd. While we were shooting in a country location, the still photographer said, "I'd like some pretty shots of you and Brian crossing the creek on the stepping stones. Just be careful not to get your skirt wet."

Brian was supposed to help me

over, and as we were doing it he said, "This is such a proper picture. Lift your skirt higher, Ann—it might help the movie if the stills show a little ankle."

With mock, exaggerated seriousness, I replied, "Brian, don't you realize that this is a film about the great American virtues and values, and the noble history of the steel industry? What a wicked suggestion—'show a little ankle'! I'm truly shocked!"

Brian was quiet for the rest of the day. The next morning, Howard Strickling, the head of publicity, called to say he wanted a chat with me. Howard informed me that Brian was very upset because I had told him that his suggestion regarding some still pictures was improper.

I repeated the scene for Howard who laughed and said, "Ann, the English say such things jokingly and kiddingly and they understand each other—but some Americans take everything very literally. Brian did not realize that you were joking—being funny. He felt that you were putting him down."

I immediately apologized to Brian for hurting him without meaning to. I explained, as best I could, the quaintness and absurdness of some types of English humor. I hoped he understood.

Although many Britishers have become American citizens since the 1940s and our expressions and methods of communication have mixed and melded, you will notice that any time an American says something even slightly outrageous, with mock seriousness and humor, he will always follow the remark with "I'm only kidding" or "Just kidding." Whereas a Britisher will always *know* that such remarks are in jest without needing an explanation.

Around then, Brian was going through a very ugly divorce. He had to deal with many shocking things in court, including detectives bursting into rooms to take photographs of his wife. He put everything in his house up for auction. There was an ad in the newspaper that read: "Auction—Brian Donlevy's possessions and furniture all to go," with the date given.

When he joined Mr. Vidor and me on the set for tea he was very upset. "People think I'm auctioning everything because I'm broke. They keep saying, 'Oh, Brian, I didn't know you were poor.'" I said, "Brian, don't be upset. You'd be amazed how many wonderful people are poor. Career-wise, it's certainly nothing to be worried about. No one is going to think less of you." I thought I had made consoling remarks, but he didn't understand at all and became angry again.

As time went on, though, he began to realize what I meant and we became friends. But it was always very hard for him to understand my British humor.

Eventually, our picture was retitled *An American Romance.* And while Mr. Vidor was away someplace, they made a mess of it—cutting out a lot of the personal story and leaving in too much of the steel plant footage. I went to the suburban preview of the picture when it was intact. It was very long but very charming. Mr. Mayer was present, and there were hearty congratulations all around. However, it was released during the

war when everyone was interested in Betty Grable, not a serious epic about immigrants and steel. King Vidor was terribly disheartened by its failure to capture an audience.

MGM kept promising me pictures but gave me nothing. I was told that *Gaslight* was definitely for me. Then David O. Selznick came along and said, "I have this great star, Ingrid Bergman, and no picture for her." She got *Gaslight.* I was promised *The Picture of Dorian Gray,* but Angela Lansbury got it—and was excellent. I went to see Cecil B. DeMille at Paramount for *The Story of Dr. Wassell,* but MGM wouldn't let me work off the lot; Laraine Day was given the role. I had my problems.

I felt that if I could get away from MGM I could do more things. I then had a choice. David Selznick, who had wanted me when I first signed with MGM, asked to put me under contract again. So did independent producer Hal Wallis who had just left Warner Bros. and was now going to make pictures at Paramount. My agent said, "Selznick has so many people under contract, and they're not working. They're having the same trouble you're having. But you'll be the first person to sign with Hal Wallis." I went with Wallis.

Hal Wallis thought I'd be good for the leading part, a girl with amnesia, in *Love Letters,* so Barry Sullivan and I made a lovely test. William Dieterle, a very romantic director who eventually did the movie as well, directed the test with all the European laciness for which he was famous. Once more, along came David Selznick who said, "I have this Academy Award winner, Jennifer Jones, and no picture for her." She got *Love Letters.* And another star from Selznick's stable, Joseph Cotten, was given the male lead. Mr. Wallis called me into his office and said, "Ann, I'm sorry. But I have this wonderful other part in the film for you, Jennifer's friend, Dilly Carson." And it *was* a very good part.

A number of people saw my test with Barry, though. I recall that the columnist Hedda Hopper liked the idea of our doing the leads. After *Love Letters* had come out, she wrote, "If Ann Richards had played the part, she would have broken your heart. It's too bad that the original cast, Ann and Barry Sullivan, weren't used." She must have seen the test.

My next for Mr. Wallis was *The Searching Wind,* a provocative and intelligent political film. I met two extraordinarily interesting women on *Love Letters* and *Searching Wind:* the novelist Ayn Rand, who wrote the screenplay for the former film, and Lillian Hellman, who wrote the play and screenplay of *Wind.* I remember a conversation I had with Miss Rand. I mentioned that my mother in Australia was not well, that I might have to take a sabbatical from my career to go and bring her back to America with me. Miss Rand insisted (and I can still see this little woman's black eyes flashing), "You owe absolutely nothing to anybody! You must not consider doing this thing!" I thought this was rather cruel and said, "But you must help people, especially those dear to you." And she replied, "You must take care of yourself rather than do anything for anybody else!" I did not heed her advice.

Ayn Rand and Lillian Hellman were two completely different women. I found Miss Hellman delightful. We had lunch a couple of times, but I didn't get to know her as well as Miss Rand. Miss Hellman was easier to comprehend, though; she wouldn't throw out edicts. Politically, too, they were at opposite poles: Miss Rand was super-conservative and Miss Hellman was very liberal.

One day during the shooting of *Searching Wind* we were told to be ready to film at 8:10 in the morning—and I say "8:10" but I think it may have been "8:10½!" It was very important that this exact time be adhered to. When we got there, our director, again William Dieterle, said, "First shot. We're all rehearsed. When I give you the sign we must go." The boy scampered for the clapboard. We did it. Afterward, we all wondered why he had insisted that we do the scene exactly at 8:10. I asked him and he explained, "My dear, that time assures us good luck. My astrology told me so." He was absolutely serious.

My last film for Hal Wallis was *Sorry, Wrong Number.* It was a thriller based on the famous radio play by Lucille Fletcher. I wanted to play the very dramatic lead, that of an invalid who overhears her own murder being planned. And there was talk of my doing it. But *An American Romance* had not been out too long and I was still thought of as a newcomer. Burt Lancaster, who was to co-star, had only done a few films at this point and Paramount felt that a big, established name was needed for the starring feminine role. They selected Barbara Stanwyck, which turned out fine, because she was completely professional, always knew her part and the script. I play her friend from school and thoroughly enjoyed the experience.

The director, Anatole Litvak, was good, somewhat more matter-of-fact than William Dieterle but effective. As far as I can recall, we only had a problem with one scene. While telephoning, I was to hear a train whistle and look over my left shoulder. The only trouble was, Mr. Litvak was referring to my left but his right. "Look over your right shoulder," he instructed. I didn't know what to do. Should I look over my right shoulder? The train wasn't coming from that direction. I asked him to explain it. Again, it was "Look over your right shoulder." Now, the train sound wasn't dubbed in at this point but I knew where it was supposed to come from. Mr. Litvak and I were getting nowhere. Finally, I got him aside where no one else could hear and told him, "You know when you say 'your right,' you mean my left."

"Oh, my God, you're absolutely right!" he exclaimed.

I enjoyed working for Hal Wallis very much. He was a marvelous producer. He was very interested. Some people complained that he came down to the set too often, irritating the directors, but I thought he was correct: he wasn't there to criticize but because of his interest.

Lina Romay——*ACTRESS*—

Although I only sang with Xavier Cugat for a couple of years, people always identify me with him. But that's fine with me: it was a wonderful, exciting time. Cugie's was *the* Latin-American big band and I was his "hot" girl singer. He first heard me in Detroit and before long I was singing with the band at the Waldorf-Astoria in New York. He would play the Waldorf for six months, then other hotels and theaters—I never played nightclubs with Cugie.

In 1942, we were hired from the Waldorf to go to Hollywood for our first film, *You Were Never Lovelier,* with Fred Astaire and Rita Hayworth. Naturally, I was thrilled. Mr. Astaire was such a quiet, soft-spoken gentleman, exactly as he appeared on the screen. And Rita was very exciting, but she had no discipline. She was on her own in show business since she was 13 or 14, dancing in Tijuana, Mexico. We were both of Latin-Irish descent, but my father was a Mexican diplomat, I was convent-educated in Brooklyn (where I grew up) and lived at home till I was married. My mother went with me to Hollywood.

Cugie and I did a couple of other films together and then, when I was appearing at the Paramount Theater in New York, producer Joe Pasternak saw me and sent a telegram to my agent offering me a contract at MGM. I started there in 1944 and stayed six years.

My first MGM assignment was *Bathing Beauty,* the picture that made Esther Williams a star. Cugie was also hired for it and they wanted me to sing with him in the picture. But he was angry that I was breaking up the act and wanted one of his girlfriends to sing with the band in the film. He went to Johnny Green, the musical director on the production, but Green told him, "We hired Lina and we like her and we're going to use her in the picture." So Cugie and I did *Bathing Beauty* together, as well as *Two Girls and a Sailor* and *Weekend at the Waldorf.* I was under contract on my own, but no one knew it. Yet.

My first picture away from Cugie was a big one, *Adventure.* It was Clark Gable's first movie after the war. (His wife, Carole Lombard, had been killed in a plane crash in 1942 on my birthday, January 16; I could never forget that.) Greer Garson was his co-star—remember the ad line, "Gable's back and Garson's got him!"? But I was to be sailor Gable's girlfriend at a port in Chile. I was ecstatic: Clark Gable! He was so handsome and all man.

The first day on the set, Clark and I were rehearsing and I noticed that his script was shaking quite a bit in his hands. I thought he was nervous because it was his first picture after coming out of the Army Air Corps. Now, when I acted I not only learned my lines but everybody else's, so I'd know what was coming. So when I saw Clark shaking I said to him, "If there's anything I can do to help in any way, just let me know." I was so naïve. He wasn't nervous. He had a whale of a hangover!

He and Greer Garson hated each other. They were opposites. She'd insist on velvet slats around them when they acted, so no one could see them except the director, Victor Fleming (Gable's favorite). Whereas Gable was a big, open guy who liked to use four-letter words. Of course, she'd go to her dressing room and use four-letter words, too, but when she thought no one was around to overhear her.

For our big parting scene in *Adventure,* Gable and I were embracing on a dock that had been constructed on the back lot lake. He was sailing away but said he'd be back. I said, "I'll be like a statue facing the sea: I won't even move." When he kissed me, his bridgework suddenly popped out of his mouth and into the water! They had to get a diver to go after it. They found it.

Another one I liked was *The Lady Takes a Sailor,* with Jane Wyman. She was so darling to me; she thought I was the cutest thing. She'd invite me up to the home in the hills she shared with her husband, Ronald Reagan, and their two children. They were great fun. When they divorced, Ronnie dated me six or seven times. He was a wonderful president of the Screen Actors Guild and always seemed more suited to political life than to acting.

In 1953, I married Jay Gould III, grandson of the railroad financier, and gave up my career. I would sing at church, but for many years that was it. I had three children and hunted and fished with my family.

I'd see Cugie occasionally over the years. In the late seventies, I was down in San Diego visiting my parents when I heard that Cugie was in town for a showing of his famous caricatures. He was set for a local TV appearance and I decided to sneak on to surprise him. He was saying, "I had so many wonderful girl singers. . ." when I popped out and said, "You didn't forget me, Lina Romay, did you, Cugie?" He was so shocked. He wasn't too well; he had had a stroke not long before.

While in town, he accepted a one-night engagement at a hotel there. I agreed to sing with him and the band that evening. The orchestra, however, was coming from Tijuana and never showed up. Remember the line in the old song, "Manana is soon enough for me"? So I sang my three numbers a cappella, making all kinds of rhythms with my hands and feet. Cugie loved it.

A while back, I put together a show at the Sportsman's Lodge of "famous canaries" featuring Helen O'Connell, Margaret Whiting, Jo Stafford, myself and a number of other well-known former band singers. It took me three months to line them all up. Many of the band leaders were going to attend, so I sent a wire to Cugie: "Please come and represent me. Be here for me." He arrived during the show, leaning on his cane as he walked down the aisle. From the stage I said, "Can you believe he's here and he didn't bring Charo?" It brought the house down.

For several years I have been putting together monthly shows for Pacific Pioneer Broadcasters Association featuring old-time radio personalities. And I was a sports broadcaster at Hollywood Park for 10 years. I am a widow now and try to keep busy.

But my family has always come first. I know I looked like hot stuff in my movies. And I *was* hot stuff! During the war, especially, I was engaged every other week. But we never did anything wrong. They were always overseas!

Elizabeth Russell—ACTRESS—

I had no dialogue or billing in *The Uninvited,* and you could hardly make me out on screen in the few seconds I had, but I made more money from it than I did from some of my large roles.

I play a much-discussed ghost named Mary Meredith. Everyone thought that in life she had been a saint, but at the end she is revealed in all her true malevolence haunting this old house on the English coast. I traveled back and forth between New York and Hollywood in those days. I forget exactly how I got the job. I did a number of films for "horror" producer Val Lewton, some of which were written by my friend DeWitt Bodeen—maybe they recommended me to Paramount and Charles Brackett, the producer of the picture. Anyway, prior to the shooting I had to pose for a large portrait that was important to the story and was to be on display in the film. It was painted by a charming Englishman named Kitchen who had lost most of his stomach in World War I. I went to his studio for about a week and was on payroll all the time.

To say that my part in *The Univited* wasn't much is an overstatement. I was to be seen (barely) floating down the staircase of this isolated seaside house. Although it was just a stint, it took much longer to shoot than they'd expected. They thought it might take a day—two at most. But no. The main problem was getting me to float believably. I was suspended on wires, like Mary Martin in *Peter Pan,* which was not the problem. Unfortunately, they had wrapped me in some kind of gauze for the special effect they wanted and I couldn't bend any of my joints—my knees, my arms, nothing. I was stiff as a board, which would never do. They were finally able to modify the gauze wrapping and get the shot, but it took days to work it out.

People tell me the result on screen was very eerie and believable, though, and worth the trouble.

The portrait Mr. Kitchen did of me was lovely, very much in the style of (I think) Sir Joshua Reynolds, which the studio wanted. Afterward, Paramount said I could have it, but it was so huge that I didn't know how to get it home. And I was living in a hotel then. So I just let it go. Now the portrait is hanging in a Los Angeles museum.

Ellis St. Joseph——*SCREENWRITER*—

I was the fair-haired boy at RKO when they asked me to write *Joan of Paris* as French star Michele Morgan's first American film. Lewis Milestone, who had directed *All Quiet on the Western Front,* was originally supposed to direct it, but for whatever reason he didn't and a very nice man named Robert Stevenson took over.

I worked hard and invented new techniques for the filming. When I wrote a screenplay, I'd describe every action. In Hollywood, you must understand, when things are going good they always hire others to make it better. After I'd finished the screenplay, that is exactly what happened. An English writer I knew named Charles Bennett who had been on several early Hitchcock films was brought onto the project. He said to me, in that way the Hollywood English always spoke then, "I say, old man, I hope you don't mind. They've asked me to polish the screenplay up a bit. It's a masterpiece and I shall do my best not to hurt it."

I went off and Charlie took out a couple of the best scenes and put in some sentimental bits that were damaging. For instance, he had Michele Morgan talking to the statue, saying, "Dear Saint Joan. . . ," something I would never have done. I wrote 90 to 95 percent of *Joan of Paris,* but when I saw the completed film in New York the credit read "by Charles Bennett and Ellis St. Joseph." I was stunned and hurt. I was so young and vain that I thought that if a word of my work was changed it was ruined. But I was so naïve I didn't know how important a screen credit was. I should have protested to the Screenwriters Guild. It should have gone into arbitration.

A few years ago, Charlie said in a book on screenwriters that *Joan of Paris* was his favorite screenplay—and never even mentioned me!

The leading man was Paul Henreid, whom I had met at Lewis Milestone's. He had just done a play in New York. By then, most of the good actors in Hollywood were going off to war, so I thought, "We need a male star and Henreid has this Viennese sour expression. It certainly is better to have a European playing a European." I brought him to David Hempstead, the producer of *Joan of Paris,* who hired him. Before long, he was playing opposite Bette Davis in *Now, Voyager.*

I brought the character actor John Abbott and a new young man named Alan Ladd to the film, too. Ladd's death scene helped him to get *This Gun for Hire,* which made him a big star. I wrote the part of the villain for myself, but when you are replaced in one area you are out everywhere. Much later, Rossellini had a sexually sadistic, gay Gestapo leader running Rome in *Open City,* but we did it first in *Joan of Paris.* If I wasn't going to be permitted to play the role, I thought that Laird Cregar, whom I recently had seen on stage in *Oscar Wilde,* would be wonderful. I knew he could deliver the lines and recommended him. Cregar was just beginning his short but distinguished career, and *Joan of Paris* was definitely a boost to him.

I came from the theater where an entrance line was very important to setting things up, so I devised a strong opening one for Cregar's Nazi deviate. Obese in a white suit, Cregar walked down the aisle of a French church surrounded by people in prayer. "I like to see people on their knees," he mused. The director or someone cut the line out.

At Universal, they already had filmed three episodes for *Flesh and Fantasy* when I came on it. They had the segment with Edward G. Robinson; the one with Charles Boyer and Barbara Stanwyck; and the segment with Gloria Jean and Alan Curtis. France's Julian Duvivier, who was directing and (with Boyer) coproducing, couldn't put it together, though. They needed something to end the film with a bang.

I invented the story of the embittered plain girl at the Mardi Gras who puts on a beautiful mask, falls in love and takes it off to find that she herself has become beautiful. I spoke French, so Duvivier and Boyer and I became great friends. (Off-camera, you know, Boyer's English was none too good.) Later, when I saw Boyer on the stage in New York, I realized that he wasn't simply a romantic idol but a great actor as well. Betty Field and Bob Cummings were hired for the leads in my episode; they were fine. For the role of the mysterious maskmaker, John Huston suddenly appeared to make it known that he wanted his father, Walter, to do it. A few years before, I had written a Broadway play that had starred Walter Huston and on which both Hustons had given me trouble; it closed after three performances. One day Duvivier said, "Ellis, the Hustons are coming over to talk to me about Walter playing the maskmaker. I know how you all feel about each other, so stay in your room till I talk to them." Afterwards, Duvivier told me, "They are still your enemies. They speak well of you."

As an actor, Walter lacked subtlety. He was incapable of an epigram. Nevertheless, he had a name and Duvivier engaged him for the maskmaker. When he saw that Huston wasn't bringing it off, Duvivier fired him. He was replaced by a Universal contract actor named Edgar Barrier. Walter was philosophical about it. He told me, "This is a town where an actor can be hot or cold, and at the moment I'm cold."

Flesh and Fantasy had a mounting quality, but when previewed the film was too long. Duvivier, being smarter than most people, preferred to lose a whole story rather than cut here and there. So the Gloria Jean–Alan Curtis segment was omitted completely. After everyone had left the film, however, the studio inserted a jarring narration of sorts featuring Robert Benchley at his worst. And instead of closing the picture, my episode now opened it—none too sensibly. When the film was released, *Life* magazine devoted four pages to my episode. The other segments weren't even mentioned.

Months later, the Gloria Jean–Alan Curtis story was sent out as "B" film called *Destiny.* The Motion Picture Academy has long wanted to restore *Flesh and Fantasy* to its original four-episode form, much as was done recently with *Lawrence of Arabia.* But a while back there was a fire on the Universal lot where they kept their film, and it appears that the first cut has been lost. And I don't know of any existing original script. But it could be re-assembled, I think, by putting all the sections back in the right order and taking out the dreadful Robert Benchley footage.

Howard Koch had admired me when I was writing for the Federal Theater, which he was running then. He was now a writer at Warner Bros. in Hollywood and recommended me for a film to be produced by Jerry Wald based on a collection of Ernest Hemingway's short stories called *In Our Time.* I was not a particular fan of Mr. Hemingway. I loved his first novel *The Sun Also Rises,* but I thought most of the others stuffed with phoney machismo. I had not read *In Our Time,* but I loved the title. I remember back in the thirties I was sitting in Virginia Woolf's living room when England's Prime Minister Chamberlain came over the wireless proclaiming that there would be peace "in our time." I thought, "What a wonderful line!"

Anyway, Jerry Wald said that our stars would be Ida Lupino and, God help us, Paul Henreid. Aside from the title, there wasn't much that we could use of Hemingway's. I decided to write a modern version of Chekhov's *The Cherry Orchard,* with Poland on the eve of Nazi takeover as the cherry orchard. Alla Nazimova had always been a favorite actress of mine, so we got her and Michael Chekhov for major supporting roles as Polish aristocrats. But I got fired three or four times while we were doing it. It was all too liberal for Jack Warner. There is one scene where Ida Lupino, British bride of Polish nobleman Paul Henreid, gets the serfs, who have never before been in this great big house, to work there as a way of Democratic sharing. Albert Maltz was asked to take over the writing, but he told Warner, "No. I couldn't do it as well as Ellis." Eventually, Howard Koch said he would watch over me so that I could keep the job.

At first, Ida Lupino was delighted with my writing; in the early scenes the focus was on her. She soon changed. Ida belonged to the door-slamming school of acting. These players believed that good actors slammed doors, and great actors slammed them harder. When I would talk to Nazimova, she would say, "I'll be under. Don't write me strong scenes. I'll be under the lines. That'll be my strength." And I complied. She and Michael Chekhov stole the picture. Ida and Paul Henreid felt I was betraying them, and they used their power as stars to thwart me whenever possible. They knew that too much was going to Nazimova and Chekhov. I stayed away from the set because Ida and Paul were saying terrible things about me. Finally, I went down to Henreid's house and told him to stop or he'd be in trouble, because I knew plenty about him. And he did.

When I finished *In Our Time,* I bolted for New York to write the great American novel, as usual.

About a month ago, I ran into Arthur Silver, who was one of Jack Warner's top executives. He told me, "Ellis, I didn't know how the hell to handle that picture of yours. I was baffled by having to sell *The Cherry Orchard.* I had a helluva time!" And he was right.

When *In Our Time* came out, the screenplay credit read "by Howard Koch and Ellis St. Joseph." Here we go again! I was still too naïve to do anything about this, and in a strange way it made me feel good to see my friend's name up there on the screen alongside mine. We were close then. Howard had come out to Hollywood before I. He knew the ropes. I didn't. I remembered his first wife telling me, "I always let Howard cheat at cards. It makes him feel better." A dozen years or so ago, he wrote in his autobiography that I was "possibly the most undervalued writer in Hollywood's history," but he went on to write many other discrediting things about me. He derided my background and personal life, said I was too "highbrow" for Hollywood and that I had long suffered from "writer's block." I know this: after Howard's book came out, I never got another offer to work as a writer or producer.

When a man that you love betrays you, it can really hurt.

Most shocking to me, though, was that Howard Koch, my old

friend, by his own remarks had shown that he never really knew me at all.

His contribution to *Is Our Time?* Zilch! I was grateful that he had gotten me the job, but he did nothing to rate a screenplay credit on it. Howard could adapt but he had no originality or panache.

One of my favorite films is *A Scandal in Paris,* which was directed by the German Douglas Sirk for United Artists release. George Sanders, a wonderful actor, stars as the crook, Vidocq, who becomes head of the French police. I read all five volumes of Vidocq's memoirs and on the screen the credit reads "Script by Ellis St. Joseph. Based on the memoirs of François Eugène Vidocq." It's a solo credit.

A few years ago, Sirk gave an interview in which he said, "I wrote *A Scandal in Paris* together with Ellis St. Joseph, who was a very gifted short story writer"! Moreover, in London someone wrote that *Scandal in Paris* had been written "by Douglas Sirk and Ellis St. Joseph." By now, I had had quite enough of this! I knew why it happened, though. At the time, many cinema enthusiasts had become infatuated with the idea that the director was the most important person on a film—the *auteur.*

Well, I don't want to minimize Douglas Sirk's contribution to *A Scandal in Paris,* but I am the sole author of the screenplay.

Richard Sale—SCREENWRITER/DIRECTOR

Recently, I donated the scripts from all my movies to the Academy of Motion Pictures Art and Sciences Library.

Getting to this point has been a long but interesting trip.

In the thirties I sold a few of my pulpy novelettes to the movies, but in 1940 *Strange Cargo,* starring Joan Crawford and Clark Gable, was my first really important film credit. Although I didn't write the screenplay, it was based on my novel, *Not Too Narrow, Not Too Deep,* which had religious undertones. I used to say, "MGM took God out and put Joan Crawford in."

I was born married. I was married 18 years to my first wife, 24 to my second, Mary Loos (who was Anita Loos' niece and with whom I wrote most of my forties movies) and, thus far, 20 years to my current wife, Irma Foster, a retired fashion designer.

Originally from New York, I was educated at Washington and Lee University in Lexington, Virginia. I'd been dying to go to Hollywood, though, and five years after *Strange Cargo* I finally got here. My wife Mary and I got the idea for a screenplay from an item in Walter Winchell's column. Later, Winchell said we'd been "co-inspired" to write *Rendezvous with Annie,* the story of a GI who goes AWOL to spend a secret weekend with his bride, and nine months later, when their baby mysteriously arrives, has some explaining to do. Initially, Paramount bought it for $10,000, but the censors, the Breen Office, turned it down as being "too suggestive." They were impossible then. Finally, the veteran director Allan Dwan decided he wanted to direct and produce it for Republic. He went to see Joe Breen and said, in his tough, no-nonsense manner, "How dare you? You're trying to take our livelihood away!" Breen okayed the script. The film got great reviews and became a helluva springboard for Mary and me.

I appear in *Rendezvous with Annie,* too. When Eddie Albert and Bill Frawley get off the plane, I'm the MP there. I also act in *Driftwood,* which Mary and I wrote for Dwan. I'm the postman. Natalie Wood, who was then about eight or nine, has the lead; she was adorable. I blew my lines several times playing to her. She was so intense, I found myself just staring at her. She became a close friend. I was at both of her weddings to R. J. [Robert] Wagner.

Allan Dwan was wonderful, so helpful to us. Our association continued with the Republic musicals *Calendar Girl* and *Northwest Outpost.* The former was especially fun for me. My mother was in silent pictures in New York, and I had grown up at the movies. One of my early favorite actresses, Irene Rich, had been cast in *Calendar Girl* with Jane Frazee, who had the title role. I was thrilled to have Miss Rich on a picture I'd written and whenever possible would go down to the set to talk to her. *Calendar Girl* was also memorable because on it Dwan gave me the chance to do something else I dearly wanted to do: direct. He allowed me to be the second unit director.

Nelson Eddy was the male lead in *Northwest Outpost.* Technically, he had a wonderful voice, but there was no real feeling in it. And he was kind of an old auntie. He wasn't gay, but he was sort of fussy and prim. He'd hold one ear and listen to his own voice.

During the time at Republic, our friends George Burns and Gracie Allen were a great help, too. They would come out to the studio with Mary and me and look at whatever picture we'd just done. Sometimes it would be just the four of us in the screening room. Their reactions often helped us to decide what to correct in the picture before it went out to theaters.

Mary and I then signed with 20th Century–Fox, where our first two films were *Mother Is a Freshman* and *Mr. Belvedere Goes to College.* Produced by Walter Morosco (an awfully nice man but an alcoholic), *Mother* is basically much ado about nothing but very tastefully done. Loretta Young is delightful in the title role. Oh, she was very vain but you expected that of actors. Still, her wardrobe tests were longer than the picture. A couple of years later, after I'd really gotten into directing, I worked with her on *Half Angel* at Fox. One day she was sniping at the cameraman, Milton Krasner. At the time she was married to Tom Lewis, and I asked her, "How's Tom? Did you break a chair over his head this morning?" That knocked it out of her. During *Mother Is a Freshman,* Rudy Vallee kept cursing and each time he or anyone else did so, Loretta would charge them. On this one picture, she must have financed a whole wing at the St. Anne Home for Unwed Mothers, one of her favorite charities.

F. Hugh Herbert, the screenwriter of *Sitting Pretty,* one of the big hits of 1948 with Clifton Webb as the "genius" baby-sitter Lynn Belvedere, was supposed to write the 1949 sequel, *Mr. Belvedere Goes to College,* but he ran out of ideas along the way. So Mary and I stepped in to write it. The picture outgrossed everything around then. During its run, there were standees at the Roxy Theater in New York all the time.

Clifton's movies made a fortune for 20th Century–Fox. Understandably, Darryl Zanuck, our boss at Fox, held him in great esteem. One time Zanuck found an old painting in New York of Clifton as "Robin Red-Nose," done by a famous artist when Clifton was about 18 or 19 in Greenwich Village, and presented it to him at a party. Privately, he also said to him, "Clifton, there may come a day when there won't be work for you as an actor. It sometimes happens, even to big stars like yourself. So I want to sign you to a contract that will assure you an income from Fox for the rest of your life." The contract stipulated that Clifton, at the same salary, could be a technician or actor's coach or anything he wanted at the studio. He could not be out of work.

Although Clifton was the leader of the gay community in Hollywood, and I was straight, that did not stop us from becoming the best of friends. We were neighbors, too—our houses were back-to-back. I used to walk him home after parties. We'd have a drink and then he'd walk me home. I remember he always used to say to me in that crisp manner of his, "Richard, you talk too much." He was a wonderful guy, a pleasure to know and to work with.

Father Was a Fullback? Mary and I were just in for repairs on that one. There were several other writers on it. I gave it the title and we fixed it up a bit. Elliott Nugent had started directing the film, which was based on a play, but he was getting kookier by the day—I think he was having a nervous breakdown. He was throwing the schedule off. So they brought in John M. Stahl, a very straight, old-time director, to replace him. The kids, Natalie Wood and Betty Lynn, were fun. Fred MacMurray was nice and Maureen O'Hara was solid, never a fuss, and so beautiful.

In the late forties I had directed a couple of quickies for Republic, *Spoilers of the North* and *Campus Honeymoon.* But it was with 1950's *A Ticket to Tomahawk* for Fox that I really feel I became a full-fledged director as well as a screenwriter. It's my favorite film. Dan Dailey and Anne Baxter star, with Marilyn Monroe, who was just starting out, in a small role. I went on to direct (and frequently write for) such stars as Loretta Young, of course, plus Betty Grable, Macdonald Carey, Claudette Colbert, June Haver, R. J. Wagner, Joseph Cotten, Jeanne Crain, Jane Russell, Maureen O'Hara, Tyrone

Power and, again, Marilyn Monroe.

But Clifton would say I was talking too much.

Ann Savage—*ACTRESS*—

When *Detour* came up, I had just left Columbia Pictures where I'd been for almost two years and had done many pictures, mostly "B"s. (Someone told me that it had been a toss-up whether Marguerite Chapman or I would get the big build-up there, and they decided on Marguerite. I was let go.) I had signed a two-picture contract with Producers Releasing Corporation, and *Detour* was one of the scripts my agent brought me. He took me out to PRC to meet the director, Edgar G. Ulmer, who was shooting another picture then. We talked for about five minutes and I never saw him again until the first day of shooting *Detour* a couple of weeks later.

When I joined the picture, they had already been shooting for about two days. Tom Neal, my co-star, had probably done his narration and some scenes already. My whole role was done in three or three-and-a-half days; *Detour* was a real quickie.

Nevertheless, Edgar Ulmer was the best director I ever worked with, a genius to me. On my first day, we were doing the scene where Tom picks me up on the highway—this evil, sick woman. I did my line and Edgar said, "No, not like that." He gave me a click-click-click tempo that he wanted me to use as the character—much faster than I normally would speak—and I kept that approach throughout the part. He never corrected me again.

Edgar was a stickler for realism. I'd just come from Columbia, where I'd been pampered: never a hair out of place, make-up just right. For the scene when I was out in the desert, Edgar ran cold cream through my hair to make me look a believable wreck. Remember, this was still the period in Hollywood when everyone was looking their best, when your face never got messed up when you cried, when you awoke in the morning with a fresh make-up job.

Tom Neal was a fun guy who liked to cut up on the set. I was very serious about my work, kind of square, I guess. I had a reputation for being very professional. On the other hand, Tom never learned his script all the way through. He didn't know some scenes, and Edgar got very upset with him one day. We were getting ready to do a scene in the motel when Tom said, "Oh-oh, are we going to shoot this now?" Edgar snapped, "Yes, and you better get it!" Despite our minuscule budget, we had to shoot 56 takes on this scene because Tom didn't know it. It was especially hard on me, because I had most of the lines!

Tom and I had worked together several times before, and I learned the hard way never really to trust him. On *Klondike Kate,* which we did at Columbia before *Detour,* he came up to me and did something vulgar, and I hauled off and slapped him—hard. I sort of kept my distance after that.

I never worked with Edgar Ulmer again, and I resented this a little. I know that he was surprised by my performance—I had done mostly light things at Columbia. I know I did an outstanding job in the part: after one of my more dramatic scenes, there was total silence, then the crew broke out in applause and cheers. I hoped Edgar would ask for me again, but he didn't. I think the reason might have been because I didn't get along with Leon Fromkess, who produced *Detour* and was president of PRC. He wanted to sign me to a five-year contract there, but I'd just left a Columbia contract and I wanted to see what was out there. So Mr. Fromkess was a little miffed at me, and since Edgar continued to work at PRC, that may have been why he never used me again.

Detour received some very good reviews at the time [1945]. I got some more work at other studios because of it, but it wasn't until 1983 that I realized what a cult following it had acquired over the years. UCLA was having a retrospective of Edgar Ulmer's films, and Kevin Thomas of the *Los Angeles Times,* in announcing the event, wrote of me, "Ann Savage—never has an actress been better named . . . one of the toughest dames in all of *film noir.*" He called the picture "one of the most relentlessly intense psychological thrillers anyone has ever filmed." A friend called and told me about the article, saying, "You're all over the page!"—a slight exaggeration. The story said that Shirley Ulmer, Edgar's widow, Martin Goldsmith, who wrote it, and some others associated with *Detour* would be among those taking part in a roundtable discussions that evening. They hadn't been able to locate me, and Mr. Thomas wrote that I "reportedly" was living in the San Fernando Valley somewhere.

"You *must* go," said one of the attorneys I was working for then (I've since retired). So my boyfriend and I went to UCLA's Melnitz Theater, sat in the back row and were planning to slip out right after the screening when a student recognized me. So we stayed.

Afterward, when Shirley Ulmer said, "We tried to reach Ann Savage but couldn't," I cried out, "I'm here!" I was greeted very warmly and went down and sat in on the roundtable discussion of *Detour.* That was when I realized that things were happening with this little film I'd made almost four decades ago. Since then, I've done a lot of retrospectives for Edgar G. Ulmer and *Detour,* some with Shirley Ulmer, who has become a good friend.

Risë Stevens——ACTRESS—

The Chocolate Soldier was my first film, and nothing could have been a bigger surprise.

I was on my way to South America to sing opera. Also on the boat were Toscanini and the NBC Symphony Orchestra. When we docked in Brazil, I was posing for pictures with Bidu Sayao (with whom I was going to sing) when my husband, Walter Surovy, took one of me that was published around the world. In Hollywood, from what I heard, Nelson Eddy saw the photograph, evidently liked me in it and asked MGM if I could play his flirtatious operetta star wife in *The Chocolate Soldier.* He was still doing films with Jeanette MacDonald then, but I think they were both increasingly anxious to do things apart, too.

After South America, I went to San Francisco to sing. During intermission one evening, I was told that a delegation from MGM headed by Louis B. Mayer was in the audience and wanted to talk to me in my dressing room afterwards. Mr. Mayer asked me to do a test for *Chocolate Soldier.* I couldn't believe it! My world was the concert stage and opera. I asked the director of the San Francisco Opera if he would release me to do the test, and he said, "Of course." I went up to Los Angeles, tested and returned to complete my engagement in San Francisco. Then, back to the Metropolitan Opera in New York where I received a telegram saying that my screen test was a success: they wanted me for *The Chocolate Soldier.*

Making a movie was very different from what I had presumed. You pre-recorded your musical numbers, of course. And there was no continuity. The way films are made confused me at first. When I sang opera, I began at the beginning and went right through to the end, and I thought that was how it would be in Hollywood. But in films, you shoot scenes first that might come in the middle of the book. We shot the end of *Chocolate Soldier* before we did the beginning! I take my hat off to people who have long careers in pictures!

During the shooting, Nelson Eddy and I had many talks and became friends. I really felt that he could have had an operatic career. He had a big, booming, fine voice. "I trained for opera," he told me, "but then movies came along. Now I want to continue in films." I think that movies made for a much easier life, money-wise, and he liked that. But he really worked at his lieder. He didn't do much of it in his concerts, but I would go to his home and sing Brahms and Schubert with him.

After *Chocolate Soldier* was completed, Mr. Mayer said to me, "You must stay here at MGM and became a movie star. I want you to sign a long-term contract." But then he offered to star me in *The Cat and the Fiddle,* which I didn't think was right for me. It was a bit too Broadway-ish; I wanted something that was more of an operetta. In retrospect, I

suppose this was kind of silly of me, but I wanted to be able to sing more in the manner in which I had established myself. I told Mr. Mayer I would not be joining MGM.

"Where will you go?" he asked.

"Back to the Met," I replied. Opera had been very good to me.

The Chocolate Soldier proved to be a tremendous help to my career. I became a household name to people who might never have gone to hear an opera. It was a lucky break for me.

So was *Going My Way*. Someone else was supposed to do the film, but at the last minute she turned producer-director Leo McCarey and star Bing Crosby down—if you can imagine anyone doing that. At the time, I was singing a concert somewhere in California when Leo called and asked me to lunch. As we sat down, he said, "Bing Crosby and I want you for a movie we're going to do at Paramount called *Going My Way*." I never made a decision like this without consulting my husband who was then in the Army, stationed at Sacramento. I informed Leo, "I have to call Sacramento." He said, "Okay," and a phone was brought right to our table. I called my husband but had to wait quite a while—he was out in the field, or something. Breathless, he finally said, "Hello?" I told him that I was there with Leo McCarey and that he and Bing Crosby wanted me for a picture." He answered, "Take the napkin, sign it and give it to him!"

Leo McCarey filmed with a lot

of improvisation. There would be many takes of a scene, many different ways. Very often, we would get our scripts and Leo would ask, "What would *you* say?" And we'd offer something which might be used. Other times, Leo would shoot the script as written, then say, "I don't know, it doesn't sound natural." Then Bing might offer a suggestion that they'd try, and often it would work and be used. Bing was wonderful at ad-libbing. I loved working with him. When we were doing our backstage scene, Bing was very concerned. He was extremely nervous about playing a priest. It seems safe to say that no crooner had ever attempted this before. He was anxious that our scene indicate that, as written, he and I had been sweethearts before he entered the priesthood, but he didn't want to offend the church; he was a Catholic. We'd be working on it and he'd say, "Hmm, let's try it this way," and I recall that Leo went with his suggestions a number of times. The same was true with Barry Fitzgerald, who plays the old priest and also had his input. Some of his ideas, I remember, were used in the scene where he tells Bing about his mother back in Ireland. I think that's what made *Going My Way* so touching—these personal suggestions that added so much to the story.

Bing was worried, though, about how the Catholic Church would accept him playing a priest. One day, while Bing, Leo, Barry and I were looking at the rushes, Bing said, "I think it's important that the monsignor and the cardinal see this picture before we release it." So, a private showing was arranged for the monsignor and the cardinal which we all attended. Suddenly, right in the middle of the picture, the two church men walked out! Bing called out, "Put up the lights!" Nervous and upset, we just sat there. Some minutes later the monsignor and the cardinal returned, one of them saying, "May we see the rest of the picture now?" At the end, they said things like, "This is the most wonderful picture." "You have all done beautiful jobs." "You have our congratulations!"

A puzzled Bing spoke up. "Why did you leave in the middle?"

Replied the monsignor, "We had to go to the men's room."

Going My Way went on to tremendous popularity and seven [1944] Academy Awards, including Best Picture, Best Actor (Bing), Best Supporting Actor (Barry) and Best Director (Leo).

The movies were a challenge for me: I was able to do lighter things. You know, when I was young I never planned to be an opera singer. I wanted to be on Broadway. When I was 17, I sang with a little opera company in New York, replacing a girl who had fallen ill. A teacher, Anna Schoen-René, heard me and called my mother to ask if she could train me for an operatic career. My mother said she couldn't afford whatever the teacher was charging, so she said, "I'll get her a scholarship." And she did. I left my pursuit of Broadway and was guided by Anna Schoen-René.

One thing led to another, and eventually I was doing 50 to 60 concerts a year, giving performances at opera houses here and abroad. And, of course, doing movies like *The Chocolate Soldier* and *Going My Way.*

James Stewart——ACTOR—

One of the main reasons why the 1940s (along with much of the 1930s) was a golden age in Hollywood was because of the major studios—MGM, Warner Bros., Paramount, Columbia, RKO and Universal. This was the top time for them. They were run beautifully then by "the moguls," a rather pejorative name I've always resented—Louis Mayer, Jack Warner, Harry Cohn, Darryl Zanuck and the others. These men loved the movies—hated sequels. I've always felt that this was the best way to run the studios. We actors who were under contract to a studio got there at eight in the morning, left at six-thirty in the evening and worked six days a week. You learned your craft by working at it. That's why there were more good, individual actors then: they had learned how to do it by working at it, and weren't just actors picked up for a movie here and there.

The Shop Around the Corner, for example, was the kind of experience that helped an actor grow: a dream set-up. First, I was to co-star with Margaret Sullavan, a tremendous and very special actress. And second, the great Ernst Lubitsch was to direct. He was the ideal director. Most directors would have the cast come in and sit around a table, then say, "Now I want the next scene to come out in the following manner. I want you to say it this way and give me these emotions." Lubitsch never did that. Lubitsch had a lot to do with the writing of the script and he just forgot about the way the actors were supposed to speak or emote. That was *their* job. He knew what he wanted to get up there on the screen, was much more concerned with how it was all going to *look.* So were directors like John Ford and Frank Capra.

As for Margaret Sullavan, we sort of started together in the business with the University Players in West Falmouth, Massachusetts, and in the New York theater. She really was responsible for my getting better parts in pictures. I came out to Hollywood in 1935 as a contract player at MGM. Maggie already was a star at Universal. One day a story that she liked came up called *Next Time We Love,* and she told her studio that I would be right for the male lead opposite her. In fact, she talked Universal into borrowing me from MGM. *Next Time We Love,* in 1936, gave me the first real part I'd had since I came to Hollywood.

I never minded taking third billing to Cary Grant and Katharine Hepburn in *The Philadelphia Story.* I'd have taken any billing or any part to be in that picture! There's a cute story behind one scene that Cary and I had. In the script, I'd just come from a late party that was still going on. When I come to Cary's door and call out for him, I've already had quite a few drinks. Our director, George Cukor, said, "You and Cary sit down here and we'll rehearse the scene." We did it once and Cukor instructed, "Okay, let's shoot it." While we were rehearsing it, in the back of my mind I had this idea where, at one point in our scene, I'd hiccup a little. So, when we were shooting it and I had to take another drink, I suddenly hiccupped. And Cary ad-libbed, "Excuse me." Then we both hemmed and hawed a bit, I hiccupped some more and we went on with the scene. Cukor liked what we did and kept our ad-libbing in the picture.

Winning the Best Actor Academy Award for *Philadelphia Story* came as a complete surprise to me. Of course, I knew I had been nominated, but my old friend Henry Fonda also had been nominated that year [1940] for *The Grapes of Wrath.* I thought it was a foregone conclusion that Hank would win. I was working on another picture the day of the awards, was kind of tired and didn't plan to attend. Then a friend called up and told me, "Everybody thinks you should be at the awards." So I went. One of the wonderful things about the Academy Award is that your fellow actors are among those voting. After I won, someone suggested that maybe I had received a sympathy vote, because I had lost the previous year for *Mr. Smith Goes to Washington.*

When it was announced on the radio that I had gotten the Academy Award, my father called me from his hardware store in Indiana, Pennsylvania. It was seven-thirty in the morning his time, but four-thirty our time. "I heard on the radio that they gave you some sort of prize. Was it money?" he asked.

"No," I replied. "It's kind of a statue."

"Well," Dad went on, "you better send it back home and I'll put it in the store."

My Oscar was in the window of my father's hardware store for 20 years.

My last three films till after World War II were *Come Live with Me,* with Hedy Lamarr; *Ziegfeld Girl,* with Lana Turner; and, on loan to United Artists, *Pot o' Gold,* with Paulette Goddard. My stuff in them was shot quickly because I was preparing to go into the service. Although the gals got most of the attention in *Ziegfeld Girl,* and rightly so, I guess I remember it best. This was the kind of lavish musical entertainment at which MGM excelled. And Lana Turner was a perfect example of the young contract actor I was talking about who had been carefully groomed by the studio, learned her craft and was now ready to soar. She was wonderful in *Ziegfeld Girl* and stepped out of it a big star. I was glad to have had a chance to work with her.

Several months before Pearl Harbor, I enlisted in the Air Force and stayed in four-and-a-half years. My MGM contract expired. They wanted me to sign another one, but the contracts then always stipulated that if any "act of God, including war" prevented you from working, the period during which you were unavailable to the studio could be added on to the contract time. My agent, Leland Hayward, advised me not to re-sign.

When I got out of the service in September 1945, I was a full colonel. I was a free agent, but there were no pictures right away. I began to wonder if anyone in Hollywood would

want me again. Hank Fonda had just been mustered out, too, and was in the same boat. So we'd spend days together flying kites or visiting friends. Then, out of the blue, director Frank Capra, for whom I had done *You Can't Take It with You* and *Mr. Smith Goes to Washington* in the thirties, and who had been in the war, too, called and asked me to come over to his house. He said he had a movie he wanted to talk to me about. Although he lived quite a distance, I pulled in his driveway almost before he hung up the phone. He sat me down and began to tell me the story of the picture he wanted me to do with him. It was still mostly in his mind, so he became a little confused in the telling.

"Now, Jimmy," he explained, "it starts in Heaven. It's all about this small-town family man who's in serious financial difficulty and thinks he's a failure. As he's getting ready to jump in the river on Christmas Eve, an angel named Clarence who wants to earn his wings jumps in first. Since Clarence can't swim, our hero has to save him. Then Clarence shows the man what a wonderful life he's had."

Frank scratched his head. "Gee, Jimmy, it doesn't sound so good when I tell it, does it?"

I said, "Frank, if you want me to do a picture that starts in Heaven and play a failure with a guardian angel named Clarence who wants to earn his wings and comes down the chimney on Christmas Eve, I'm your man!"

We made *It's a Wonderful Life,* as

our picture was called, for Liberty Films, which had just been formed by William Wyler, George Stevens, Sam Briskin and Frank Capra who became president. It was released through RKO and while truly a wonderful film, for some reason it did not do too well in 1946. I think that Frank, who had put so much of his heart and soul into its creation, lost some of his enthusiasm for moviemaking because of this. And Liberty Films soon folded. Years later, due to repeated showings on television around Christmastime, our movie became a classic. It has always been my favorite film. Frank's, too.

The Stratton Story did much better and is another of my favorites. I play the real-life big league baseball pitcher Monty Stratton who had a leg amputated at the peak of his career. I was still a free agent, so MGM asked me to return to my old lot and do the part. Monty Stratton himself was hired as an advisor. I told MGM, "I'll do it if, before we start, I can spend at least two hours a day with Monty so that he can coach me playing baseball." This was fine, so Monty and I worked together for over a month before shooting began. He had a special way of throwing which I tried to copy as closely as I could for the film. (There was a fellow there catching for me.) I must have done all right, because after the picture came out instead of fan letters I got baseballs to sign. Monty was wonderful to work with, as was June Allyson, who plays Stratton's wife. It was the beginning of a lovely association with June, with whom I later would make *The Glenn Miller Story* and *Strategic Air Command.*

But those last two pictures were in the 1950s. That was an important decade for me, too, but a whole other book, I guess.

Barry Sullivan—ACTOR

I came out to Hollywood from the New York stage. I'd made a few pictures by the time I did *And Now Tomorrow,* but Alan Ladd, its star, was the first person who ever told me anything about making movies. I fell in love with him! Having come from the theater, I was doing things too big for the intimacy of the camera. I just couldn't look at the rushes. One day, though, Alan forced me to go into the projection room with him and study all the rushes. We'd see what we shot and Alan would point things out, make suggestions. And he'd be right. I was much more comfortable in films after that.

Susan Hayward plays my girlfriend in *And Now Tomorrow;* I adored her, too. Right now, I can't tell you any reasons why—I just did. Although I know she had a reputation for being difficult then, I never saw her that way.

Paramount, which had me under contract, loaned me to Monogram for their most expensive picture to date, *Suspense,* the only ice-skating *film noir,* I'm sure. I loved doing it. By now, I'd learned a little and I was treated like a star. The picture made a lot of money. Belita appears opposite me. I always had a fondness for her because she didn't know what the fuck was happening! She was a great skater, but acting and particularly filmmaking were totally foreign to her.

We did another picture right away for the same producers, the King Brothers. It's called *The Gangster* and is one of my favorites. Frank King, who seemed to be in charge, was a smart apple: aggressive—good—got things done. Gordon Wiles, the director, had been an Academy Award-winning art director, which is undoubtedly why the picture looked rather artsy. He only made a few movies, but he was very capable. Best of all was Daniel Fuchs' screenplay. Fuchs had been a teacher in New York, knew the milieu and really had a handle on the sort of small-time gangster the picture portrayed.

Many movies later, I was at a cocktail party when John Huston came up to me and said, "You once made a picture..." I knew immediately he meant *The Gangster*—that it was a picture he would relate to.

Years after Belita and I did *Suspense* and *The Gangster,* I went backstage to see someone at a London stage production. All of a sudden a blonde lady came up to me, touched my arm and said, "Aren't you going to say hello?" It was Belita! She was in the show. I hadn't recognized her. She must've improved!

The Great Gatsby was another interesting one, mainly because I was with Alan Ladd again. It was certainly better than the version they did in the '70s with Robert Redford. I just don't think that F. Scott Fitzgerald's books translate as well onto film as, say, Hemingway's. But I thought Alan was a marvelous Gatsby. He was a much better actor than people gave him credit for. He had a beautiful voice.

But he did the same part in every goddamn picture, and he wanted to get away from this. *Gatsby* was his chance, but they wouldn't let him escape the mold completely: after the picture was finished, they went back, shot scenes of him with a gun in his hand and inserted them into the continuity. He was an action superstar, and Paramount didn't want to tamper with box office. They worried about Alan first: his close-ups, his clothes, his image. The other actors were looked on as professionals who could go their way, but protecting Alan was always uppermost in the minds of the studio brass.

His films were mostly schlock, yet they always did well. Alan was a smart man who was aware of everything. Sue Carol, his wife, was great for Alan, one of the super dames of all time. She protected him from shit, fought for him all the time. She was one of the great agents, too. Alan adored her.

On the other hand, there was Betty Field, Alan's leading lady in *Great Gatsby.* I don't like to talk about people, even when they're dead, as Betty is, but she was a bit of a pain in the ass. I knew her from New York. On *Gatsby,* she played the part differently from the way she had rehearsed it—something you *don't* do.

Audrey Totter—ACTRESS—

Lady in the Lake was a real stroke of luck for me.

Robert Montgomery had just returned to MGM after being in the war. Some of the stars, like Jimmy Stewart and Lew Ayres, were leaving, and MGM wanted to hold Bob. So, when he brought Raymond Chandler's novel *Lady in the Lake* to them and said he wanted to direct as well as star in it, they said okay. But they had misgivings, because Bob wanted to use a bizarre new technique: everything would be seen in the first person—through the eyes of the hero, private eye Philip Marlowe. Bob enacted the role of Marlowe, but, except for a quick scene at the beginning and at the end, he was only seen in it when he passed mirrors. And when his hands were shown, other actors stood in for him because he was too busy directing. He was really no longer interested in acting, and continued to concentrate on directing for the rest of his career.

Anyway, just about every actress in town—not just the MGM ones—turned Bob down for the leading lady role, the chic crime magazine editor Adrienne Fromsett. No one wanted to stake her career on so chancy and experimental a project.

One day Bob went to the Metro projection room to look at film on other actresses. They were already screening a little "B" called *The Hidden Eye,* in which I had a bit, and he sat down to watch. I had done it mainly as a favor to the director, Dick Whorf, whom I had known when I was an actress in New York. I play a rather elegant salesgirl at a perfume counter. Bob got there in time to see me and cried out, "That's the girl I want! Besides, no one else wants the part."

Billy Grady, the head of casting at MGM, tried to talk him out of it. "Audrey's too new here," he said, "too inexperienced. Remember, the camera will be on her throughout." But Bob prevailed and tested me with the first-person technique he planned to use in his picture. It must have turned out okay, because I got the part.

If I had done more in pictures at that time, maybe *I* would have turned it down, too; I might have been fearful of risking my career. But I had nothing to lose.

I loved working with Bob. He was so sweet and an excellent director. I would rank him with my two other favorites, Michael Curtiz, for whom I did *The Unsuspected,* and Robert Wise, my director on *The Set-Up.* A funny thing: when I was a movie-struck teen-ager, I lived in a house with a fenced-in yard. I could lie on my bed and look down the

A Christmas Eve party is startled by the news of a murder... with a number of suspects at the festivities!

street to a church. One afternoon I fell asleep and in my dream I saw Bob Montgomery coming out of the church in the top hat, white tie and tails he always wore in his films. Then he sat on my fence and beckoned to me. When Bob picked me for *Lady in the Lake,* I told him about my prophetic dream, and he laughed.

The picture was made on a rather tight budget, because the studio was uneasy about its unorthodox filming style. But Bob saw to it that I got grade-A treatment. He told the legendary hair stylist Sydney Guilaroff, "I want something unusual for Audrey." And he got it in a succession of pretzel-twist upsweeps that gave my character the proper smart, taut look. The fabulous Irene did the clothes (she had great problems including alcoholism and eventually committed suicide).

The original ending left it up in the air as to whether Bob and I got together romantically. However, after the picture was "sneaked" the preview cards complained that there was no physical contact between the leading man and leading lady. At one point in the story I kissed the camera, which was standing in for Bob (everything, remember, was supposed to be as his character saw and experienced it), but I never kissed *him.* However, to believe those preview cards, the public wanted to see the old-fashioned boy-girl clinch at the end. Bob was happy with the film the way it was, so was the producer, George Haight. And so was I, though no one asked me. But the studio insisted we go back and film that silly, pasted-on scene at the end where Philip Marlowe and Adrienne Fromsett plan to go to New York and then kiss—"The End." We giggled all through the shooting of it, so it took a long time to do.

The reviews were good, and *Lady in the Lake* definitely helped my career. I was soon doing pictures with Robert Taylor [*The High Wall*], Clark Gable [*Any Number Can Play*] and Ray Milland [*Alias Nick Beal*]. But the first-person technique of *Lady in the Lake* wasn't everybody's cup of tea. I remember my friend, the actor Turhan Bey, telling me, "Audrey! I got a headache watching that picture of yours!" And MGM didn't promote it adequately. They treated it like a "B" movie. Today, though, *Lady in the Lake* is studied by film scholars and is considered a classic.

William Travilla—COSTUME DESIGNER

Various production problems had stalled the making of *The Adventures of Don Juan* for almost three years, but finally it was set to go with a then [1948] whopping budget of $2 million.

The film was set in 17th-century Spain, and Warners had hired a very well-known woman designer to do Errol Flynn's clothes. True to the period, she went ahead and came up with costume sketches of outfits covered with ruffles and lace. Well, Errol took one look at them and wanted none of it. Remembering the things I'd just done for Ann Sheridan in *Silver River,* he laughingly said, "If anyone can make that ugly bitch look good then I want him. I want Billy, Little Billy. Get him in here to do these clothes."

I was on the set for one of the opening scenes when the director, Vincent Sherman, told him, "Now in this first shot, all you have to do is climb up this vine to this young lady who'll be on the balcony above," and Errol said, "You know, Vince, Old Errol is much too old and much too rich to do this. Call my stand-in, I'm going to get laid." And with that he went into his dressing room and the girl waiting inside.

Viveca Lindfors, a Swedish actress Warners had just signed, was playing Queen Margaret in *Don Juan.* She was very elegant and very lovely, but she was also very strait-laced. The scene to be rehearsed was set in Don Juan's apartment where the queen comes to visit unexpectedly only to find him half-dressed, wearing only his boots, tights and belt, only Errol had purposely left off the outer pair of tights and was wearing just the sheer underpair.

Now in comes Queen Viveca in a lavish grey velvet gown, very imperious, and they start rehearsing the scene which begins with Errol's back to her. It's moving along okay, then he turns around and faces her as Viveca keeps on speaking her lines until her eyes wander down his body and she sees Errol in all his silk-covered glory. Her eyes were just riveted on his crotch, and after a few seconds she couldn't remember her lines and Errol couldn't keep a straight face.

Claire Trevor—ACTRESS

Murder, My Sweet was done at RKO, and the shooting went like silk. Except for the first day.

I had a raging headache, which I often got at the beginning of a film before things settled down. And we were getting ready to shoot my opening scene at the mansion and I still didn't have a costume. I suggested white shorts with gardenias in the hair, which would have established the woman's cheapness right off. But they finally decided on a dress, and since everything was rush-rush I had to be sewn into the thing. Then, because it was all last-minute, someone forgot to tell the body make-up woman that I needed her, and I had to make up my legs myself. I thought my head would crack open.

Dick Powell was one of the main reasons why *Murder, My Sweet* was so successful. He was a revelation. Up to this, he was known only as a boy singer but now he was playing Raymond Chandler's tough private eye, Philip Marlowe. And playing it magnificently. People couldn't get over it. I never heard the narration that he does for the picture until I sat down to see the whole thing; I was dumbstruck at how beautifully he handled it. The film revitalized his career. And he was a joy to work with, a most intelligent, adorable man with a wild sense of humor. He used to get two or three of us aside on the set and do imitations of himself when he was starting out as a young tenor. I have to admit that I had sort of a crush on him. As we neared the end, though, he told me that he was going to marry June Allyson, so that was that.

But Dick and June and my husband, Milton Bren, and I became very good friends. Dick loved boats and my husband was a yachtsman, so we often took trips together to Mexico.

Although Edward Dmytryk, our director, did a very good job, I wasn't keen on him personally. He was a young, attractive and talented man, but he was a Commie, as we called them. I remember Eddie and his wife had a two-year-old son and he told me they were going to send him away to school. I exclaimed, "But he's so young!" And he replied, "The experts know better how to raise a child than we do." Later, when he really began to make money, he bought apartment build-

ings and other real estate and became a big capitalist.

When I saw *Murder, My Sweet,* I was elated. I had the same feeling years before when I watched *Stagecoach,* which I did for John Ford, but usually I would slink down in my seat when I watched my films.

Key Largo was one of the good ones.

Humphrey Bogart was another close friend of ours. He loved boats, too; our moorings were right next to each other at Catalina. Like Bogie, my husband had a wicked sense of humor and they'd tease each other all the time. One time Bogie swam over to our boat and Milton kept pushing his hands off the boat. We'd have boat races. Our son Charlie, who was then about four, liked to stand on a stool and steer our boat, with us in close attendance. So one day, when we were racing Bogart and his boat home, Milton said, "We're going to pass Bogie. Everybody go below and we'll put Charlie at the wheel." Bogart's face fell when he saw who was steering the boat. Later, Milton taunted him, "You let a four-year-old beat you!"

So when I told Milton that *Key Largo* was coming up at Warner Bros., that Bogie was going to be one of the stars and that I'd love to play the alcoholic ex-nightclub singer, Milton approached Bogie while they were in a sauna. "Who's going to play Gaye Dawn?" Milton asked. "I don't know," answered Bogie. "Well, Claire would love to do the part," Milton continued. "You're such a great big star, why don't you call Jack Warner and say you want Claire Trevor for the role?" Which Bogart did, and I got it.

Key Largo was like Old Home Week. Lauren Bacall, Mrs. Bogart, was in the cast, as was Edward G. Robinson, a friend and co-star of mine from way back. I had done five years of the radio show *Big Town* with Eddie. What a grind that was. I could do movies while we did the show, but on the day of the broadcast I had to leave the movie set by 12 noon to be able to make it down to CBS where we had to do *two* live broadcasts of a show then, one for the East Coast and one for the West Coast. I remember I was doing *Stagecoach* and they'd spend three or four hours lighting the set for one take. But it would get to be five minutes to 12 and I'd plead, "Listen, boys, I have to go." It was quite a trek down to CBS. "Oh, please, just one take," they'd say, and I'd do it. Then something would go wrong and it would be 12:20 and I'd be late for rehearsal at CBS. It was just hell on both sides, real ulcer-making time.

Big Town, always high in the ratings, was at first a real quality show, and my role was of equal importance to Eddie's. After a while, though, I noticed that more and more Eddie Robinson was inserting his own political beliefs about "the little people" into it. He'd arrive at a location where he'd have a big speech but I'd have to say, "I'll wait for you in the car, Steve." He'd do the big scene, come back to the car and tell me all about it and I'd say, "Really, Steve?" I got tired of this and quit.

Then one day I was at a market asking for lamb chops when the butcher exlaimed, "Lorelai Kilburn!"—the name of my *Big Town* character. Suddenly, I realized the tremendous recognition this role had given me and I was sorry I had quit.

Eddie Robinson loved his art. One time he brought me to his house and showed me a new Picasso he'd just purchased. I hated it. He told me, "I just bought it for $10,000," which in those days was an absolute fortune. And, of course, today a Picasso would be practically priceless.

He was fine on *Key Largo.* It wasn't until many years later when we did *Two Weeks in Another Town* for Vincente Minnelli that I noticed how deaf he had become. It was difficult to converse with him then. I mean, he'd keep saying, "Huh? What did you say? What was that?"

The *Key Largo* company was great—such fun. We'd have lunch at the country club in Toluca Lake and John Huston, the director, would say, "Let's call somebody," and it wouldn't matter where the guy was—China or wherever. Bogart would get on and razz hell out of somebody. John Huston was a joy to work with; you'd wish the experience would never end.

It was all very relaxed. All our dressing rooms were lined up in a row. You could walk along and hear music coming from each one. (We filmed across the street from them.) Then you'd hear Huston's voice over the loudspeaker, "Will Miss Trevor, Mr. Bogart, Miss Bacall, Mr. Robinson and Mr. [Lionel] Barrymore come to the set?" We'd stroll in, and someone would say, "Where's Bogart?" There'd usually be one or two of us missing. Huston didn't care. The shooting went way over schedule—I think it took about three or four months to complete. It could have gone on forever as far as I was concerned.

We rehearsed for about a week before filming; Huston wanted the shots clear in his mind. I'm the rather beat-up, boozey girlfriend of gangster Robinson who at one highly dramatic point promises me a drink if I'll sing. Bogart kept pushing for me to do "Mean to Me," which I guess was his favorite song, but Huston insisted on "Moanin' Low." I wanted to go to the music department and rehearse to a playback, get the gestures of an old nightclub singer down pat. I kept saying, "When can I go to the music department? When can I rehearse?" Then one day Huston said, "I think we'll shoot the song now." I was stunned! Off-stage, a piano hit one note—*boing!* That's how we did it. He did the long shot first right through without stopping, and I thought, "Good, I won't have to do that again." Then he wanted the close-ups, which we shot over and over, in five different keys. It's a good thing I was supposed to be lousy!

Naturally, I was thrilled when it was announced that I had received a [1948] Best Supporting Actress Academy Award nomination for *Key Largo.* A few days before the Oscar show, Bogart was at our house for dinner and I asked him, "What will I say if I win?" He replied, "Just say you did it all yourself and don't thank anyone."

I won but I didn't do as Bogart advised, and neither did he, I might add, when he picked up his Best Actor statuette a few years later for *The African Queen.* When he won, I grabbed him and wanted to kiss him on the mouth, but he turned his cheek to me. Later on, he sent the photo to my husband of him with both hands on the Oscar and me kissing him on the cheek. He wrote on it, "You can see I'm your friend, Miltie."

Ruth Warrick—*ACTRESS*—

I grew up in Missouri and couldn't wait to get to New York City. While attending college, a public relations matter brought me to New York, and although I dearly loved school I just stayed. I was soon making a living doing print modeling and acting on radio.

In those days, we all met at CBS. The woman there took so many messages for us all that she finally decided to get paid for it and went into the telephone answering service business. Hers was the first one I had heard of. I didn't actually know Orson Welles, but I saw him there and I know he saw me. It was the kind of thing where two people don't speak but are very aware of each other. The only thing I had done with him professionally was a *Gang Busters* radio program, but he was the lead and I was in a crowd scene, so that doesn't really count.

Anyway, at the age of 25 he'd made the deal with RKO Pictures in Hollywood to make his first film, *Citizen Kane.* When people like that *New Yorker* critic Pauline Kael write that Herman J. Mankiewicz was really the author of *Citizen Kane,* I get furious. Orson had done a script on it in prep school and acted in it there. A couple of other stories with which he'd hoped to make his movie debut didn't pan out, so he pulled *Kane* out of his trunk. Of course it needed work, and Orson did put Herman Mankiewicz on it to write some dialogue. Orson would look at it, say "Okay," or look at it and throw it in the waste basket. Mankiewicz was a drunk. They locked him up in an old cottage in Victorville to work. They literally kept him a prisoner there so he couldn't get plastered and delay things. But he always managed to find liquor somewhere.

When it came time to cast the wife of Charles Foster Kane, who was supposed to be the niece of the president of the United States, Orson had trouble. Finally, he told a writer that he'd seen this "willowy" (I was always called "willowy") actress in New York who was a possibility. I was in the process of signing a two-year lease on a red barn home I was moving into in Connecticut when the call came to meet Orson. I was so busy that I showed up hours late and Orson was gone. Five minutes later, as I was getting ready to leave, he stormed in saying, "Oh, aren't you wonderful! You waited for me!"

He got right to it. "I'm ready to go on *Citizen Kane* and I don't have a leading lady. She must be a *lady.* I've tested any number of actresses in Hollywood, but there just don't seem to be any ladies in Hollywood. Can you come out and test?" I was on the plane very quickly, did the test and got the part of Emily Norton Kane.

Making *Citizen Kane* was the smoothest thing that ever happened in anyone's life. People always think of Orson Welles as having been this overweight, extravagant, irresponsible egomaniac. Oh, he may have had a weight problem, but he was none of those other things. He produced and directed *Citizen Kane* in eight weeks at a cost of $800,000, which was economical even in 1940. I've never seen anyone so relaxed, so joyous at work. He and Gregg Toland, his cinematographer, were like little boys playing with toys. And as for Orson being a "genius" who, as some claimed, wanted to grab all the credit for himself, at the end of *Kane* he gives Toland equal size billing with himself as director. He considered Toland his collaborator. When Orson had his failures and left Hollywood, Gregg was never the same. He missed Orson terribly.

While we were shooting, Orson said to me, "Work is no chore, it's the most joyous thing in life. Just find what is your heart's desire." And, "Have children, pass on the artistic genes, but don't give up your work." Orson was not a religious man, but he was a very spiritual one. This conversation was especially meaningful to me at that point, because I was married to the actor Erik Rolf and had discovered I was pregnant. When we finished the picture, I went back to Connecticut to have my baby.

You must realize that *Citizen Kane* was never meant to be strictly the William Randolph Hearst story. If it had been, it would never have been passed by the Hayes Office. Orson told me, "It is supposed to be the story of *all* the men who became our heroes and then turned into the despoilers of America."

One day, while I was still in Connecticut, I received a call from RKO's publicity office asking me to give an interview to *PM,* which was an important newspaper then. When I sat down with the writer, he said, "Now what's *Citizen Kane* all about?" (The set had been closed and everything had been pretty hush-hush during production.) I told him what Orson had told me: "It is supposed to be the story of all the men who became our heroes and then turned into the despoilers of America—men like Hearst. . . ." He never let me finish. I was going to mention several others. He suddenly doubled up, as if he'd been poisoned, said, "Excuse me" and hurried away. The next day, everything hit the fan. The article reported that I had said the movie was about Hearst. This was the first that this had been in print. I thought, "This is the end of me." The picture had been booked into Radio City Music Hall, but was now pulled from there. Hearst was a friend of the Rockefellers, who owned Radio City, and he had told them, "I don't want to sue, but I will if you let that picture open at Radio City Music Hall."

Fortunately, Welles, who, as a first-time director, knew that his film could wind up on the shelf, had insisted with a clause in his contract that *Citizen Kane* be premiered in a first-run theater. RKO owned the Palace—so the Palace it was. But Hearst said that any theater that showed *Citizen Kane* would be refused advertising in Hearst papers, so the picture just wasn't shown in many theaters and really didn't do well, despite wonderful reviews. Maybe it was all for the best, though. If it had opened at Radio City, it might have gotten good reviews but then not been understood by most of America. Years later, it was the college kids who really discovered *Kane,* hailing it as a masterpiece of the cinema—and Orson was always very popular in France. I think the revival of interest in *Kane* began in 1956 when I presided over a ceremony in which *Citizen Kane* was put into a time capsule at the Museum of Modern Art.

Actually, the suppression of the film wasn't due to Mr. Hearst entirely. The villain was really Hearst columnist Louella Parsons, who wielded a lot of influence with the boss—some called it blackmail because of a murder she allegedly witnessed years before involving Hearst's mistress, Marion Davies. Anyway, someone tipped Louella about the picture and she demanded a screening. Afterward, when the lights went up she was purple with rage. She insisted that the master negative be burned right then and there in the huge communal ashtray in the screening room. They didn't comply—thank God.

Joseph Cotten, who plays Jedediah in *Kane,* is a friend of Hearst's sons. They told Joe that they didn't think their father ever saw the film, but that if he had he might have liked it. The boycott was mostly Louella's doing. Hearst was a big man. He might have enjoyed the publicity.

Recently, *Citizen Kane* had a major big-screen revival and it was like seeing a new movie. When we came out of the theater, no one said a word. It was almost as if they'd been to a memorial service. We were all in awe. I was in tears. When you see Orson's great performance on a big screen (instead of on TV or the VCR), you see all the nuances of the character's devastating pain and anguish. Pauline Kael (and I hate to keep mentioning her name) wrote that when you see *Citizen Kane* today, "it's really just another picture from that late '30s-early '40s period, no different from the others. The only thing that made it memorable was Orson Welles, who is magical and beautiful." Well, yes, he is, but there's *so* much more to the film! She's like an old maid stooping in an asparagus patch!

Laurence Olivier once told me, "The most beautiful thing I've ever seen is you and Orson at the beginning of the famous breakfast montage, when you're still happy. The love between you two is palpable." I felt it, too. I really did. But I was married, having a child. Joe Cotten, who was one of Orson's closest friends, told me recently, "You were the love of his life." I was a married woman—a *lady*—I had restraints on my life. But I would have made him a better wife than I made my husband. I understand the creative urge—when you work 48 hours straight on a project. Coincidentally, my husband, Erik Rolf, looked like Orson Welles. My daughter looks like Erik, and therefore like Orson, and don't think there weren't some rumors about that, too.

After *Kane,* I did a test for RKO and was signed to a seven-year contract. I was told that Charlie Koerner, who ran the studio, liked my test (in which I looked very alluring) so much that a couple of days a week he used to chase everybody out of the office and watch it all by himself.

A short time later, I worked with Orson again on *Journey into Fear,* as Joe Cotten's wife this time. Norman Foster was the credited director, but as I recall it was a project Orson initiated because he liked the Eric Ambler novel on which it was based. And he wanted to keep his people busy—his Mercury Players whom he had brought to Hollywood for *Kane.* People like Joe Cotten, Agnes Moorehead, Everett Sloane. And me. Everything was fun, laughter. There was never anything unpleasant on a Welles set. Some people considered actors nincompoops, but Orson loved them. He'd always listen to your suggestions, which gave you such confidence. The only thing you couldn't change was the blocking. He treated me like a goddess.

On *Journey into Fear,* Norman Foster, as director, sat behind the camera and yelled "Cut!" But Orson, who wrote the screenplay with Joe Cotten, was always around. He plays Colonel Haki in it but was also there with suggestions and touches that helped everybody.

Another early picture I did was *The Corsican Brothers,* in which Douglas Fairbanks, Jr., plays twins. Done on loan-out to United Artists, it was just the sort of swashbuckler the Hearst papers liked to promote, but anyone connected with *Citizen Kane* remained persona non grata. In the newspaper ads for *Corsican Brothers,* as leading lady I was prominent on a photo, with the Fairbanks "twins" on either side of me. But my name was always taken out of the cast listings. This sort of thing went on for five years, until my publicist arranged a lunch for Louella Parsons and me. We got through it all right and Louella wrote, "Ruth didn't know what she was doing when she did *Citizen Kane.*" After that, there was peace between us. In view of the power of Hearst and Louella, though, it was nothing short of a miracle that I had any career at all.

Song of the South, which I did for Disney, is another one I recall fondly. It's reissued about every 10 years and I'm always there to help. It was then Disney's most ambitious feature-length film combining animation with live action. One day Walt told me, "I'm nervous about this picture. If you don't do it the way I want, I can't rub it out!" My husband Erik also plays my husband in *Song of the South.* I understand that Walt had it put in his will that the film can't be shown anywhere but on a large theater screen, which is why it hasn't been on television or on video.

One afternoon Walt said to me, "I'm so amazed. The most important people in the world want to come on the set." (Disney was on our set all the time.) He went on, "There ought to be a place where the public can go and step into another world. Amusement parks have gotten so dirty and ratty. I want to make a clean and beautiful place where families can go." This was the mid-1940s and Disneyland came along a decade later.

Daisy Kenyon, for 20th Century-Fox, has stood up well, too. Once again, I'm a wife—Dana Andrews'. Joan Crawford has the title role and was very professional, a great star, although one thing annoyed us all: she kept the set so cold we all got pneumonia. They said she was in "the change" and got hot flashes. She'd skip around in shorts while we all shivered in coats. She had the thermostat set at 45 degrees. When she wasn't looking, we'd put it up to 50. But sooner or later she'd feel the change and say, "Oh-oh, getting too warm in here," and put it back to 45. She didn't want to perspire.

As for the charges that she abused her children, we all heard and saw things. In the make-up room, I heard Joan say, "Chris cut his ropes again and ran away last night." People ask me, "Why didn't any of the journalists of the day report this?" Because they would never have been allowed on a studio lot again.

Joan also adopted two little girls whom she called "the twins." They weren't twins, but if Joan Crawford called them twins, they were twins. One afternoon, their nanny brought them on the lot to see Joan. I was in my trailer and saw them coming. They stopped near me and as she was taking off their coats and combing their hair, the nanny said, "When the time comes, you say, 'I love you, mommie dearest, I love you, mommie dearest'." I watched them greet Joan in the center of the stage just that way. It was heartbreaking, embarrassing, obviously staged.

Barbara Whiting—*ACTRESS*

I had always wanted to be in show business. How could it have been otherwise? My father was Richard Whiting, the composer of such popular songs as "My Ideal," "Sleepytime Gal," "Guilty," "Beyond the Blue Horizon" and "Hooray for Hollywood." (He died in 1938.) My sister is the singer Margaret Whiting. Show people were around our house all the time. I wanted to get in on it all.

I finally got my chance in 1945 with *Junior Miss,* my first film. It happened this way.

Our next-door neighbor was Valentine Davies, who wrote many movies including *Miracle on 34th Street.* He lived there with his wife and daughter Judy, who was about my age—13 or 14. At the time, Val was under contract to 20th Century–Fox Studios where they were getting ready to film the Jerome Chodorov-Joseph Fields Broadway hit, *Junior Miss.* Peggy Ann Garner, who had just played her Oscar-winning role in *A Tree Grows in Brooklyn,* had already been set for the lead, but they still needed a little fat slob to play her comic girlfriend, Fuffy. They looked over the garbage cans and said, "There she is!"

Actually, the Davieses gave a 13th birthday party for their daughter Judy, and George Seaton, who was set to write and direct the film of *Junior Miss,* came with his wife Phyllis. I came, too—dateless, a brazen little blimp. I guess the Seatons saw me punching people or throwing someone against the table, because they asked me to test for Fuffy. There was another girl at the party who was up for the role, a professional actress. I think I locked her out the back door. They tested her anyway, but I got the part. They said they were looking for a new face. They sure got it.

I was ecstatic. As I said, I had always wanted to be an actress. I was so jealous of Shirley Temple when Daddy wrote "On the Good Ship Lollipop" for her. My sister Margaret wrote in her autobiography that it was she who was jealous of Shirley, but it was really I who hated that kid with all those silly blonde curls.

Fox put me under contract. But what can you do with someone who's

fat, 14 and funny. There wasn't much for me there.

Peggy Ann Garner and I became fast friends on *Junior Miss* and kept in touch right up until her death a while back. When we made our movies, she spent most of her time at our house. She had a problem with her mother who had several beaus, and she was more comfortable with us. My mother was a straightforward lady whom Peggy Ann knew she could trust.

Peggy Ann and I remained in contact all through her marriages and divorces. Eventually, she became a car salesperson. Then she found out she had liver cancer. A wonderful assistant director from Fox named Artie Jacobson helped her emotionally and financially during her last years. She tried to work, but finally went out to the Motion Picture Country House where she died about six months after her condition had been diagnosed.

Right after *Junior Miss,* we did the comedy-mystery *Home Sweet Homicide* together. The thing was full of kids. Besides Peggy Ann and myself, there was the younger Connie Marshall, whom we kept telling, "Go away, brat." And little Dean Stockwell, the most beautiful child you ever saw. We just knew that he was going to grow up and become a fine, important actor, and he didn't disappoint us.

I didn't have much to do in *Centennial Summer.* They needed a funny kid sister for the family in the story, so they put me in it. My sister

Margaret was dating one of the male leads, William Eythe. It was a period musical, an odd subject for our director, Otto Preminger, who recently had made the very modern murder mystery *Laura.* Mr. Preminger was nice but very strong. Inside, I was frightened of this whole new business of being a movie actress, but to cover up I became a loud-mouthed, big-talking brat. My mother warned me, "Don't get funny around Otto Preminger. Go to your trailer and do your lessons." For once, I listened.

I already knew Jerome Kern, who composed the score for *Centennial Summer* (he died just as the film was to open). He was a friend of my father's. I was a ghastly kid, though, and when I was small Mr. Kern would say to my father, "Get that child away!" He and Daddy played golf not far from where we lived. Sometimes my nurse would take me down to watch them. When Mr. Kern spotted me, he'd say, "Oh-oh, here comes that daughter of yours."

Carnival in Costa Rica was another Technicolor musical. It didn't turn out too well, but I enjoyed doing it. Vera-Ellen was delightful, so sweet and supportive and talented. She could do anything. Dick Haymes was a good friend of my sister's. She recently had had one of her first big recordings for Capitol records singing "It Might as Well Be Spring," which was from his film *State Fair.* He was still married to Joanne Dru and had a passel of kids. He used to take me down to the beach at Ocean Park or Venice—maybe to get away from his kids. Gregory Ratoff, with his thick Russian accent, was the director. One day he said to me, "I give you dime. Come back in five years." Oh, sure.

City Across the River, which I did at Universal, was based on a popular novel about juvenile delinquency called *The Amboy Dukes,* by Irving Shulman. I had been graduated from high school by then but was a couple of months under 18, so I had to have a tutor on the set all the time. Consequently, I couldn't fool around with all the boys, which was tough on me. I did become friendly with Tony Curtis, then just a kid starting out in pictures. We had the same agent. He was out in Hollywood from New York, where his family remained. (They moved West later.) He spent a couple of years at our house. We didn't really date; we were just friends. I remember we once gave him a pair of alligator shoes. Through all his troubles over the years, Tony continued to call or visit my mother to say hello until shortly before she died.

Except for some recent voiceovers, I haven't done anything in show business for ages. I've lived in Detroit for 35 years. Things are very difficult right now. My husband, who is older than I, is very ill and has to have around-the-clock nursing. It's nice to think about the simpler, happier days of *Junior Miss* again.

Robert Wise——*DIRECTOR*——

I spent the first part of my career at RKO, where *The Set-Up* was my favorite film as a director. I say "as a director," because I started as an editor, cutting *Citizen Kane* and other pictures. As a director there, I did, among others, several of the Val Lewton films such as *Mademoiselle Fifi* and *The Body Snatcher.*

But *The Set-Up* was special. When it came up, I had just finished a Western, *Blood on the Moon,* with Bob Mitchum. Dore Schary, who was running the studio then, called me to his office and said that he had a prize-fighting script that was based on a long blank verse poem by Joseph Moncure Marsh. "Read it," Schary said, "and let me know if you want to direct." I did and loved it. He got me together with the producer, Richard Goldstone, who had been working with Art Cohn, the writer of the script. Art had been a sportswriter in Long Beach and San Francisco, and knew the fight game. This was his first screenplay. Several years later, he was killed with Mike Todd when Todd's plane crashed.

Robert Ryan was ideal for the lead. He had been under contract to RKO since the war and was already slated for it when I came aboard. Years before, he had been the intercollegiate heavyweight boxing champion at Dartmouth College, so he not only knew how to handle himself in the ring but was about the right age for this over-the-hill boxer. He was very light on his feet—we had to make him move more slowly, be more lumbering. Bob always said it was his favorite picture.

How Audrey Totter came to be cast as his wife is a longer story. We were already working away on the film but still hadn't cast this co-starring part. Dick Goldstone and I had recently seen *Nightmare Alley,* with Tyrone Power and Joan Blondell as a warm but rather blowsy, mothering wife. We thought she'd be perfect for our female lead, who had to be both wife and mother to Ryan's character.

Around this time, Howard Hughes bought RKO and had a fight with Schary, who left. Hughes (who never came near the studio) put Sid Rogell in charge. Sid was a rough, tough sort of guy, nice enough but not the most sensitive man alive. Goldstone and I went to him to suggest Joan Blondell for *The Set-Up.* "Great idea," he said. "I'll send it up to Howard Hughes." After a while Rogell told us that Hughes, a legendary connoisseur of feminine pulchritude, had shouted, "What's wrong with those two guys? Blondell looks like she's been shot out of the wrong end of a cannon now!"

We came up with some other suggestions—Sylvia Sidney was one of them. Hughes turned them all down, sending back his suggestions of starlets and models. Lists were flying back and forth until finally the name of Audrey Totter appeared on one of them. I wasn't familiar with her work, but Goldstone was and said she was a good actress. So we signed her, and she wasn't just good, she was excellent.

I wanted to make *The Set-Up* as real as possible, and spent as much time researching it as any film I've ever done. I found a fight arena down in Long Beach where I'd go and watch the fighters, the handlers, the managers—how they fought, spoke, behaved and dressed. And I'd watch the audience, making notes all the time.

John Indrisano was a big help to me on the fight scenes. He had been a top middleweight fighter who was robbed of the title years before by some gangsters. Since then, he had carved out a whole career in Hollywood helping to stage fights.

In the film, there is a blind man in thc audience who has the fight described to him by a companion. While this might seem far-fetched at first, Art Cohn, the screenwriter, actually saw this person every week when he was covering the fights in San Francisco.

People ask if it was a problem getting the film to run exactly the amount of time that it takes for the story to unfold continuously on the screen. Not at all. We started and ended it all on the town square clock. For the closing, I did five different takes of the clock till I got the exact time that it had taken for the story to be told.

The Set-Up was very important to my career, prestige-wise. However, it came out head-on with Mark Robson's *Champion,* which made Kirk Douglas a big star and gobbled up most of the box office. But the reviews were very good, especially overseas where, at the 1949 Cannes Film Festival, it won the Critics Award. It was my last picture at RKO. I went over to 20th Century–Fox where one day I ran into Billy Wilder. He told me, "If *The Set-Up* had been made in Italy or France, it would have been a sensation."

The thing I liked about the film was that it wasn't about Madison Square Garden—the winners. It was about tank towns and the lower level of fighting. Afterward, I thought, "Well, now I've done my fight film and can go on to other things." Which I did, but seven years later along came the Rocky Graziano story, *Somebody Up There Likes Me,* which I directed with Paul Newman. This happened again when I did *West Side Story.* I said, "Well, now I've done my musical." Four years later along came *The Sound of Music.*

Alan Young—*ACTOR*—

Margie was a lovely introduction to the movies for me.

I had come from Canada and was doing radio in New York. They asked me to do a screen test there for 20th Century–Fox, and I did one of my monologues—I was also a standup comedian. It was awful: I grimaced and my eyebrows shot off the screen. The man who had arranged the test said he'd do me a favor and not send it to the Coast; I could do another. So this time I wrote a sketch and got Ed Begley, who was acting with me on radio, to do it with me. This one worked, and I was off to Hollywood. Ed went, too. I also took my radio show with me.

I was given a three-picture deal with Fox but nothing happened right away. Still, I was being paid and I'd go out to the studio every day and wander around. I remember saying to Howard Koch, who was the second assistant director on *Margie,* "I feel funny taking all this money and not doing anything for it."

Howard said, "Give it back!"

"Oh, no!" I quickly answered. "I'm Scotch!"

Finally, *Margie* came up. They needed a bumbling young boyfriend for Jeanne Crain, who was playing the high school Cinderella, and I was it. Walter Morosco was the producer; I became one of his "people." At the studios in those days, a producer would spot a guy he wanted to use, and all the other producers would stay away from him. So you had to depend on this one producer for work, which was the downside of the studio system, at least for contract players.

Nineteen forty-six was the last great year of Hollywood studio activity. While we were filming, on other Fox sets I saw Irene Dunne and Rex Harrison shooting *Anna and the King of Siam,* Betty Grable doing one of her musicals and little Peggy Cummins making the much-touted *Forever Amber* [later, she would be replaced by Linda Darnell].

Jeanne Crain, our Margie, had just been married and the next day we all set sail for Reno, Nevada, where most of the town and school scenes were shot. She spent her honeymoon making *Margie!* Her husband, Paul Brinkman, was with us on location, which our director, Henry King, thought was a bit of a distraction, but he stayed around. Jeanne was very much like she was in the picture—wide-eyed but very intelligent, maybe a little sharper than she appeared. And she was so beautiful: you could dip a spoon into her skin like ice cream. Several years later, I played her boyfriend again in *Gentleman Marry Brunettes.* By then she'd had four or five of her eventual seven children and Jane Russell, who was also in it, took one look at Jeanne's svelte figure and said, "I better go on a diet!"

Henry King was a stickler. In *Margie,* I drove an old Ford car and one day the mechanic couldn't get it to go right for the shot—the camera operator couldn't get what he wanted. Mr. King said, "Here, let me drive it." They got the shot.

One evening while we were still in Nevada, there was a production meeting. Mr. King said, "I want snow outside the house." They were going to hire trucks to go up to the mountains and bring back snow. That night it snowed! One of the crew said, "Henry King gets everything he wants!"

Back in California, the studio gave us all lessons for the ice-skating scene. We used Sonja Henie's old rink in Westwood. Conrad Janis, who plays the football hero in *Margie,* couldn't skate at all when we began and he wound up being quite good. When we were filming, I accidentally skated into a pole, but I heard that the cameras were still grinding so I just went on. They kept it in the picture.

The other films I did for Walter Morosco and Fox were *Chicken Every Sunday* and *Mr. Belvedere Goes to College. Margie,* which was set in the 1920s but released in 1946, started a trend for pictures with old songs for titles, and Fox did many of them with Jeanne again, Betty Grable and June Haver. I was supposed to do one with June for Mr. Morosco called *Sweet Sue.* We even did wardrobe tests. But it was never made: Mr. Morosco suddenly became ill and eventually passed away. I might as well have been dead, too. No one at Fox seemed to want to use one of Mr. Morosco's "people."

Later, I did some good films elsewhere like *tom thumb* and *The Time Machine* and a lot of TV, including the series *Mr. Ed.* For a number of years now, I've been doing the voice of Scrooge McDuck for Walt Disney. The first Scrooge McDuck feature, *Duck Tales: The Movie—Treasure of the Lost Lamp,* has just been released.

As for *Margie,* it was said that it made up all the money lost by the costly *Forever Amber.*

Cary GRANT
Katharine HEPBURN
James STEWART
SCREEN PLAY BY DONALD OGDEN STEWART
BASED ON THE PLAY BY PHILIP BARRY
PRODUCED BY THE THEATRE GUILD INC.
GEORGE CUKOR · JOSEPH L. MANKIEWICZ
A Metro-Goldwyn-Mayer PICTURE
in
The Philadelphia Story
RUTH HUSSEY
JOHN HOWARD
ROLAND YOUNG
JOHN HALLIDAY
MARY NASH
VIRGINIA WEIDLER
BROADWAY'S HOWLING YEAR-RUN COMEDY HIT OF THE SNOOTY SOCIETY BEAUTY WHO SLIPPED AND FELL— IN LOVE!

Her first beau . . and her first dance!
Everybody loves LITTLE WOMEN
M·G·M's NEW TECHNICOLOR ROMANCE
JUNE ALLYSON · PETER LAWFORD
MARGARET O'BRIEN · ELIZABETH TAYLOR
JANET LEIGH · ROSSANO BRAZZI · MARY ASTOR
A METRO-GOLDWYN-MAYER PICTURE

CARMEN
MIRANDA
DON
AMECHE
WILLIAM
BENDIX
IN
Greenwich Village
IN
Technicolor
WITH
VIVIAN
BLAINE
THE CHERRY BLONDE
AND FELIX
BRESSART
TONY AND SALLY
DeMARCO
THE REVUERS
DIRECTED BY WALTER LANG · PRODUCED BY WILLIAM LeBARON
20th CENTURY-FOX PICTURE

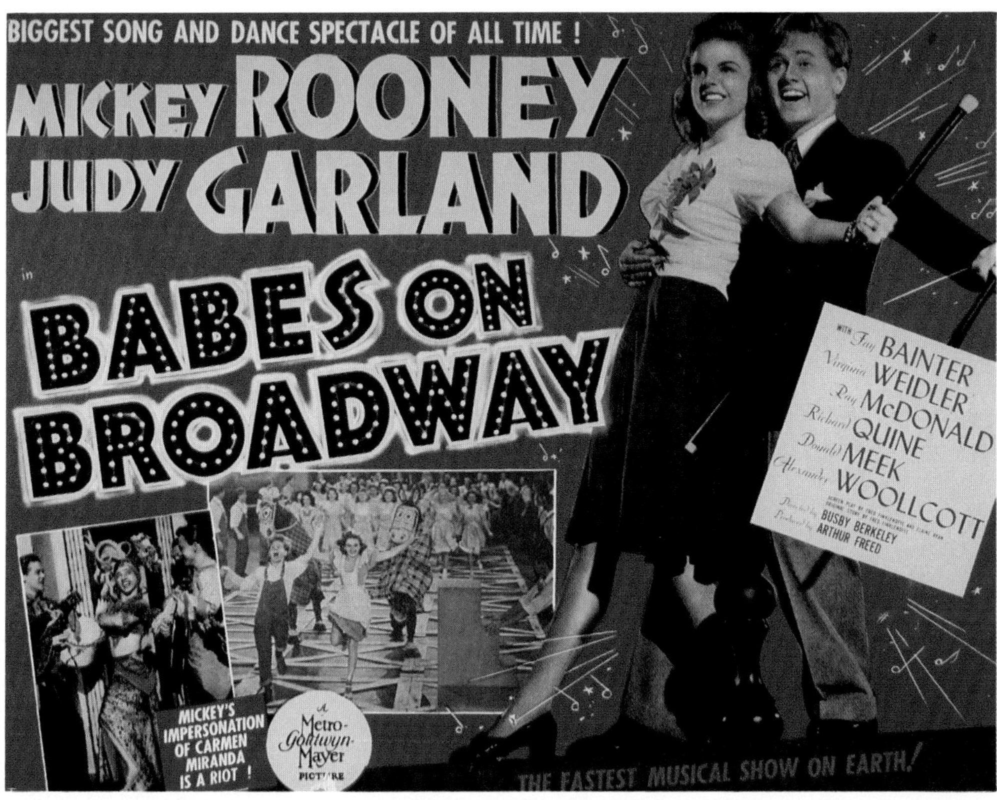
BIGGEST SONG AND DANCE SPECTACLE OF ALL TIME !
MICKEY ROONEY
JUDY GARLAND
in
BABES ON BROADWAY
WITH Fay BAINTER
Virginia WEIDLER
Ray McDONALD
Richard QUINE
Donald MEEK
Alexander WOOLLCOTT
Directed by BUSBY BERKELEY
Produced by ARTHUR FREED
MICKEY'S IMPERSONATION OF CARMEN MIRANDA IS A RIOT !
A Metro-Goldwyn-Mayer PICTURE
THE FASTEST MUSICAL SHOW ON EARTH!

ALICE FAYE CARMEN MIRANDA PHIL BAKER
The King of Swing BENNY GOODMAN
and His Orchestra
THE GANG'S ALL HERE
in Technicolor
A 20th CENTURY-FOX PICTURE
with
EUGENE PALLETTE · CHARLOTTE GREENWOOD · EDWARD EVERETT HORTON · TONY DE MARCO

HUMPHREY BOGART · MARY ASTOR
A
WARNER BROS
FIRST NATIONAL
PICTURE
the Maltese Falcon

Cary GRANT
Ann SHERIDAN
HOWARD HAWKS'
I Was a MALE
WAR BRIDE
20th CENTURY-FOX
MARION MARSHALL · RANDY STUART · WILLIAM NEFF
Directed by
HOWARD HAWKS
Produced by
SOL C. SIEGEL
Screen Play by Charles Lederer, Leonard Spigelgass and Hagar Wilde
From a Story by Henri Rochard

He went searching for love...
but Fate forced a
DETOUR to
Revelry...
Violence...
Mystery!
PRC
DETOUR
TOM NEAL · ANN SAVAGE · CLAUDIA DRAKE
Edmund MacDONALD · Tim RYAN · Esther HOWARD · Roger CLARK
A P.R.C. Production · Associate Producer Martin Mooney
Directed by Edgar G. Ulmer · Screen Play and Original Story Martin Goldsmith

DARRYL F. ZANUCK presents
CAPTAIN from CASTILE
starring
TYRONE POWER
COLOR BY TECHNICOLOR
Captain from Castile
20th CENTURY-FOX
with JEAN PETERS · CESAR ROMERO · JOHN SUTTON · LEE J. COBB
ANTONIO MORENO · THOMAS GOMEZ · ALAN MOWBRAY · BARBARA LAWRENCE · GEORGE ZUCCO · ROY ROBERTS · MARC LAWRENCE
Directed by HENRY KING Produced by LAMAR TROTTI
Screen Play by Lamar Trotti
From the Novel by Samuel Shellabarger

Starring
Paramount's Lady in the Dark In Technicolor

What can a guy do with ten women?

MAUREEN
O'HARA
JOHN
PAYNE
Miracle on 34th Street
with EDMUND GWENN
Gene LOCKHART · Natalie WOOD · Porter HALL · William FRAWLEY · Jerome COWAN · Philip TONGE
Written for the Screen and Directed by GEORGE SEATON
Produced by WILLIAM PERLBERG
20th CENTURY-FOX

IRENE DUNNE ★ CARY GRANT
in
George Stevens'
"PENNY SERENADE"
A COLUMBIA PICTURE
COLUMBIA PICTURES

PART II

Biographies

Robert Alda — ACTOR

I'd never done a movie before, so landing the starring role of George Gershwin in *Rhapsody in Blue* was an incredible break for me. I heard that John Garfield had turned it town, saying, "I don't look good in a tux." We made the picture in 1943, but Warners had an excess of product then so it wasn't released until 1945. Meanwhile, they were showing it to our servicemen overseas who wrote me fan letters saying how much they had enjoyed the movie and me. But it still wasn't shown to the public and I grew more and more anxious. "Am I a star or not?" I kept wondering. It was a trying period for me—but a wonderful one at the same time.

June Allyson — ACTRESS

In *The Stratton Story* we were always laughing at the antics of Frank Morgan, who plays the over-the-hill manager who first discovers the young ballplayer (James Stewart).

The venerable Frank Morgan always called me a brat. One day he came on the set slightly tipsy. The director went over to quiet him down, saying, "Shhh, June Allyson is in the middle of a scene." Frank boomed out, "What for? She can't act anyway."

Anne Baxter — ACTRESS

Grandfather [Frank Lloyd Wright] visited me on *A Royal Scandal* and watched Tallulah Bankhead working. He said quite loudly, "Not bad for an old dame," and Tallulah, who was uneasy about her age, visibly bristled. The next take required her to lightly tap me but she responded with an uppercut that sent me reeling. Then she smiled sweetly and retired to her dressing room.

James Cagney — ACTOR

I don't watch any of my movies except that one, *Yankee Doodle Dandy.*

That was the best. It had everything. I'm still proud to be waving my flag!

The agent never wanted me in that. They offered it to Freddie Astaire and he turned it down. So they went around trying to sell it. I remember George M. Cohan saying, "Sorry, son, you're not what we want." But it was the agent that didn't want me. He was peddling the story around. Sam Goldwyn wanted Freddie Astaire but he said no. And MGM said they didn't want it so the agent went to Warner Bros. and they said fine, we'll get it for Cagney.

Gary Cooper——— ACTOR

Sergeant York and I had quite a few things in common even before I played him on the screen. We were both raised in the mountains—Tennessee for him, Montana for me—and I learned to ride and shoot as a natural part of growing up. *Sergeant York* won me an Academy Award, but that's not why it's my favorite. I liked the role because of the background of the picture, and because I was portraying a good, sound American character.

Michael Curtiz——— DIRECTOR

Yankee Doodle Dandy is the pinochle of my career.

* * *

This man Cole Porter, in *Night and Day*—he sticked to purpose of making good music, come hell or hayride.

Bette Davis——— ACTRESS

Oh, Charles Boyer was so unbelievably attractive in *All This and Heaven, Too.* You didn't want to say, "Good night, Monsieur le Duc," but, "Here I am! Take me!"

William Demarest——— ACTOR

When [producer] Sidney Skolsky offered me the part of Steve Martin in *The Jolson Story,* he said, "I'll bet you a new hat that if you play this role, you'll be nominated for an Academy Award." Sidney was right, although I never paid the bet, because he claimed he didn't wear hats.

Actually, after reading the script, I would have bought him a dozen hats; the part was custom-made for me. It even had me playing the cello, an instrument I have been using in show business since 1905, when I played on the porches of Asbury Park hotels.

I liked the part, too, because it took me away from my usual type of comedy role. I liked the idea that Steve Martin grew more sympathetic as he grew older. The whole picture took me back to my days in vaudeville. I was barnstorming at the same time Jolson was, playing the same towns, and on the set we often swapped memories.

Just as important in making this my favorite role was the fan mail I received. One letter from Canada said, "You are now a member of my farmyard. After seeing you in *The Jolson Story,* I named a pig after you. But don't feel badly; you are in good company. I have two other pigs, named Bing and Bob. But you, I think, are the cutest pig of all."

Irene Dunne — ACTRESS

At first, I turned down *Anna and the King of Siam,* but Darryl Zanuck persisted, and after he enlisted the support of Charles Feldman, my agent, I relented. One can't always be the best judge of what to do professionally. I've always been glad I took Charlie's advice and played Anna.

Henry Ephron — SCREENWRITER

We met with Jack Warner. He was very effusive and full of good cheer. "Congratulations," he said. "*Look for the Silver Lining* is the best musical the studio has made since the Cole Porter story [*Night and Day*]." We hoped the floor would open and swallow up the both of us. *Night and Day* had been the nadir of big musicals!

Henry Fonda — ACTOR

The first film after *The Grapes of Wrath* Darryl F. Fuck-It-All Zanuck had me make was *Lillian Russell* with Alice Faye! Now I've got only good things to say about Alice Faye. But shit! I was only one of ten men in that picture! I swear it. Count 'em. Don Ameche, Nigel Bruce, Eddie Foy, Jr., Weber and Fields, Edward Arnold, Warren William, Leo Carrillo and Ernest Truex.

Barbara Hale — ACTRESS

For *Jolson Sings Again,* I learned my drawl mainly by listening to my parents, who were originally from Kentucky. Mrs. Jolson (my character) was then most recently from Arkansas, but she was born in Kentucky, so it was close enough. After the film came out, Mother added her highest compliment. "You were just like home-folks," she said.

I have one sweet story about Mrs. Jolson. When the film was completed, we had a screening which the Jolsons attended. At the end, I approached Erle and asked, "Mrs. Jolson, did I do all right? Was it okay?" She replied, drawling heavily, "Barbara, Ah thought you did such a good job. But why'd they make y'all talk like that?"

Rex Harrison — ACTOR

I studied a lot about Oriental speech patterns [for *Anna and the King of Siam*], which are very different from ours, and I felt it was very important to get the movements exactly right, especially the hand movements, which are rather controlled in Orientals, so my whole performance had to be rather still and precise. When we started shooting, however, the director, John Cromwell, was horrified to hear the authentic high-pitched laughs and strange gutteral noises I made, and asked me to please speak in my normal, Rex Harrison, voice. After all, that was what they were paying for. I had to enlist the producer [*sic*], Darryl Zanuck, who, amazingly enough, took my part against the director, something unheard of in Hollywood. From then on, I did my part as I wanted to, but John Cromwell never spoke another word to me.

Henry Hathaway — DIRECTOR

The war had come to theaters on newsreels and our backlot efforts looked phony as hell. So when producer Louis de Rochemont came to me with the idea of shooting all of *The House on 92nd Street* on actual locations, I jumped at the chance.

It was not revolutionary—that's the way we shot pictures like Victor Fleming's *Mantrap* in the '20s. We made the Westerns outside the studio. But as the producers' power increased, our mobility decreased. They liked to be in on everything. But films like *Bicycle Thief* had a great influence.

Darryl Zanuck was two ways about the project. He finally okayed it on condition we didn't use big stars, but we didn't want any of those anyway.

Howard Hawks—DIRECTOR

Sergeant York? The producer, Jesse Lasky, gave me my first good job and he was broke at the time and after I talked to him, I called up Gary Cooper and said, "Coop, didn't Lasky give you your first job?" and he said, "Yes," and I said, "Well, he's broke and needs a shave and he's got a story and I think we could do it and I don't think he would hurt us."

So Coop came over and we talked about everything but the story—he talked about a new gun and finally I said, "Let's talk about the story," and he said, "What's the use of talking about it, we're going to do the damn thing, you know that."

And I said, "Let's go over to Warners and make a deal, and if I say 'Isn't that right, Mr. Cooper?' you say yes. So I said, "We'll do it if you let us alone—isn't that right, Mr. Cooper?" "Yes." "If you come in, if you butt in on us, we'll really be hard to handle. Isn't that right, Mr. Cooper?" He'd say, "Yes." So we made the deal and we made the film. And Lasky made two million out of it and we were terribly pleased to have helped somebody.

And the funny thing about it was that it turned out to be a hell of a picture and Cooper got an Academy Award and we had no idea it was going to be anything like that.

* * *

When you make a picture about real people, and their names are used, you have more trouble. Making *Sergeant York* we had to get 20 releases—every member of his squad in the Army, his lieutenant, his captain, his major, anybody that we mentioned we had to get releases. I think the story of getting the releases, where we found the various people and how we paid them off was almost better than *Sergeant York*.

Katharine Hepburn — ACTRESS

When I made that speech against censorship during the McCarthy era, I was severely censured. I had just finished making *Song of Love,* which was enormously hurt by my making that speech.

Betty Hutton — ACTRESS

I've learned from a nervous breakdown how to relax. I'd never been ill in my life when my breakdown came. I was doing *Incendiary Blonde,* the story of Texas Guinan. I wanted to do it terribly, was afraid I

wouldn't be good, so I worked too hard, forgot about rest.

I'd get to the studio at six a.m. to have my hair dressed in period styles. I'd stay until nine or ten p.m. to have fittings for my period clothes. I'd give up lunches to rehearse new songs, and I'd work every single Sunday on dance routines. The picture was shooting four months. I forgot I was only one girl with just my share of strength and endurance. I began to crack and if anyone looked at me, I cried. Before they spoke to me, tears would run down my face. I didn't know what I was crying about, but I couldn't help it.

That taught me you have to take care of your body, treat it right, give it rest, play fair with it, or you can't go on.

George Jessel ——— ***PRODUCER***

Twentieth Century–Fox was considering a film based on the lives of the Dolly Sisters, whom I had known well and worked with many times in vaudeville. Rose and Jenny Dolly had come to America from Hungary when they were kids and had become internationally famous as singers, dancers and actresses, favorites of kings, dukes, earls and millionaires.

I made up my mind that if I could produce anything, it would certainly be a story such as this. I rushed over to Darryl Zanuck's office, ad-libbed a plot and got the assignment, much to the chagrin of many other veteran line producers who had been working for Zanuck for years. I hired Marian Spitzer and John Lar-

The
DOLLY
SISTERS
Technicolor
Together THEY SET A WORLD AFLAME WITH THEIR SONG AND DANCE... AND BROKE A MILLION HEARTS! NOW IT'S ALL MAGNIFICENTLY ON THE SCREEN... ROMANTICALLY... GLORIOUSLY!
Starring
Betty GRABLE
and
John PAYNE
June HAVER
S.Z. SAKALL
REGINALD GARDINER · FRANK LATIMORE
GENE SHELDON · SIG RUMAN
TRUDY MARSHALL
Directed by IRVING CUMMINGS
Produced by GEORGE JESSEL
20th CENTURY-FOX

kin to write the screenplay for my adlibbed plot.

I learned in a very short time that facts have nothing to do with entertainment, and that truth, though often stranger than fiction, is completely unimportant unless it can bring laughter or tears or both. Also, the many gay things about the Dolly Sisters, such as their numerous love affairs, would not suit the requirements of the strict, silly, strangling censorship of the Hays Office of those days.

Nevertheless, we came up with an excellent script, and I started looking around for "The Dolly Sisters." I immediately settled on Betty Grable and Alice Faye. I knew Grable and Faye would make excellent Dolly Sisters in spite of the fact that they were both blonde and their characters were brunette in real life. But Alice, just at the crucial moment, decided to retire. Zanuck suggested I use another of the Fox contract players, but I wanted June Haver—I had made a secret test of her. It took the diplomacy of a latter-day Henry Kissinger to persuade Darryl to let me use this unknown, untried performer. When Darryl saw the test, he agreed I was right. We never argued over my casting after that. *The Dolly Sisters* turned out to be great entertainment and did tremendous business all over the world.

Vivien Leigh ——— ACTRESS

That Hamilton Woman—the war was on and there was no money and we rattled through it in six weeks and it was tremendous fun and in the middle of it, when we had a few days off, Larry [Olivier] and I got married.

Mitchell Leisen ——— DIRECTOR

Bride of Vengeance was a lousy story about a big cannon that went boom. They kept casting these cannons from iron and every time they fired one, it would explode along with the charge. Finally, they hit upon the idea of cooling it in water which tempered the iron. They filled it with shrapnel, fired it and that was it. I said, "Maibaum [producer Richard Maibaum], you're an ass to think anybody would care about this after the atomic bomb," but we had to make it anyway.

Mervyn LeRoy ——— DIRECTOR

"Do I have to dance in *Blossoms in the Dust?*" Walter Pidgeon asked. "You'll have to rewrite it, because I don't know how."

"Why didn't you tell me before?" I asked him. "You've had the script for two months."

The scene was vital, however, so I had to dream up some way for him not to dance while it looked like he was dancing. I had the carpenters build a low platform and we put roller skates underneath it. I put the camera on the platform, with Greer Garson and Walter. There were other couples in the scene, and they danced off the platform, which was revolved on its skate wheels. The result was that it looked as though my principals were dancing skillfully.

* * *

Madame Curie reunited Greer Garson and Walter Pidgeon. By now, they were a solid team, and they knew each other's pace and reactions so well sometimes they had to shake each other up a bit to preserve their freshness. One incident illustrates the way they operated together.

A key scene in *Madame Curie* was the one where the Curies, late at night, go out to the shed where they were conducting their experiments. In the blackness of the night they see the strange glow from the pitchblende, proof that they had discovered a new element—radium. Naturally this was a scene that needed great drama. We rehearsed it and rehearsed it so the audience would have goose bumps when it flashed on the screen.

I called for action, and the cameras were rolling—and then, from out of the darkness, I heard Greer laugh.

"I couldn't help it," she said. "Walter just told me the funniest joke."

The tension that had built up during the long rehearsal period was gone. I waited about 15 minutes, until Greer and Walter stopped their giggling, and then shot the scene. It worked perfectly.

Arthur Lubin——DIRECTOR

On *Night in Paradise,* Merle Oberon took one look at Turhan Bey's bulging biceps. . . ! Fortunately, her husband, Lucien Ballard, was not working on this picture. Merle definitely had a steamy romance with Turhan and was very nervous that it would be too obvious in their scenes. Everyone, me, cameraman Hal Mohr and her old friend Travis Banton, who did her costumes, was sworn to secrecy.

One problem we had was that Lana Turner was herself madly in love with Turhan. She would suddenly appear on the set at odd moments. Since she was Lana Turner, nobody dared refuse her admittance, but she would come from MGM and she would stare at Turhan and Merle in order to unsettle them and make sure that Turhan didn't act out of turn. It became nerve-wracking for everyone as the spying went on. Merle always insisted on a closed set. When she finally did succeed in closing it and Lana was asked to leave, Lana peeped through the scenery! It went on and on.

John Lund——ACTOR

I look best from a great distance and in a bad light. I have a peculiar face, an odd walk and about as much sex appeal as a goat. I was the worst peril Betty Hutton encountered as Pauline [in *The Perils of Pauline*]. Of course I was a success in that one. I portrayed a ham actor. A natural. My finest performance.

Merle Oberon——ACTRESS

Night in Paradise? I have always wanted to be a Persian princess. Since I was a little girl I used to play and go to costume parties as a Persian princess. [Producer] Walter Wanger said, "Would you read this script?" And I opened the page and saw, "The princess is drawn in on a cart with 12 white oxen." So I shut the script and said, "O.K., Walter, I'll play it."

Pat O'Brien ——— *ACTOR*

The first week of shooting *Knute Rockne—All-American,* Bill Howard directing, was mostly exteriors, before we entrained for South Bend. Bill was trying for a comeback—a once fine director come on hard times, given this one more chance.

Bob Fellows, the producer, came to my house on a Sunday morning. He looked like the mother cat who'd just seen her kittens drowned. "They're taking Bill Howard off the picture and replacing him with Lloyd Bacon."

"This will *kill* Bill."

We walked over. It was like going to a wake—the "Dead March" from the opera *Saul.* Bill greeted us enthusiastically, with the script in front of him. "Making changes for the better."

Bob said softly, "I don't know how to tell you this, Bill. They're taking you off the picture."

Bill stared at us in disbelief, rose and walked to the end of the room and beat his fists together. "Boys, this will destroy me. It's a fade-out."

Shortly after, Bill Howard died.

There is no mercy in Hollywood studios.

Larry Parks ——— *ACTOR*

Not long after the filming of *The Jolson Story* got underway, Jolson repaired to his Miami Beach home. But he returned to Hollywood in time to see me play some of the scenes. As I finished one of his songs,

he said, "No, no, that's not it, son. Don't you remember how I used to do that?" I told him I'd never seen him perform, which didn't thrill him. Then he said, "Well, you're doing too much." To show me how to put the number across, he sang it. He almost wrecked the room. He practically hung from the chandelier. When he finished the song, perspiration was dripping from his forehead. "There," he said. "You see? I didn't move a muscle."

William Powell — ACTOR

When I was nominated for the Academy Award for *Life with Father,* Mousie [his wife, Diana Lewis] and I were listening to the awards. In those days it wasn't as mandatory to attend the awards as it is today. When it was announced that Ronald Colman had won the Oscar for *A Double Life,* the Mouse told me she had something to show me. She led me into the dining room. There, hidden under a black silk shroud with two candles on either side, was this golden statue who, as you can see, has been left holding the bag—a man wearing a derby hat like the one I wore in the film and holding a bag. The inscription on the base reads: "For your superb triumph, *Life with Mousie.*"

Claude Rains — ACTOR

I remember clearly the day that [George Bernard] Shaw sent for me, as he had selected me to play Caesar in the movie of *Caesar and Cleopatra.* I found him in his sitting room at Ayot St. Lawrence, wearing knickerbockers, his shoes kicked off and staring at a huge blaze in the fireplace.

His producer was there, and he talked while Shaw sat in almost complete silence. Suddenly, he whirled around to me and demanded, "Do you remember when we first met?" I confessed that I thought this was our first meeting.

Shaw was annoyed. "Don't you remember, in 1905, His Majesty's Theater, London, and a rehearsal of my only verse play, *The Admirable Bashful*? I collapsed in the theater and a young boy—you, sir—went for the doctor.

"The doctor's name was Matthews, and he lived on Suffolk St."

Shaw was proud of his prodigious memory.

Ronald Reagan —— ACTOR

Until I got the part of George Gipp in *Knute Rockne—All-American,* I was the Errol Flynn of the "B"s. I always played a jet-propelled newspaperman who solved more crimes than a lie detector. My one unvarying line which I always snapped into a phone was: "Give me the city desk; I've got a story that will crack this town wide open!"

Naturally, I welcomed the chance to get away from this pattern, especially as it was to play the part of a man I had always admired. Years before, as a sports announcer, I had told the radio audience about George Gipp. How he ran 80 yards through Notre Dame's varsity the first time he put on a football uniform; how he went on from there to become one of the greatest football players of all time; and how, after his early death, he became a legend.

It was the springboard that bounced me into a wider variety of parts in pictures. It's true, I got some unmerited criticism from sports writers. One of them wondered why producers never picked real football players for such parts; as I practically earned my way through college by playing football, that disturbed me. However, this criticism was nicely balanced by some unmerited praise from the same general source. For another sportswriter said I was so accurate in my portrayal of Gipp that I even imitated his slight limp. Actually, I wasn't trying to limp. I just wasn't used to my new football shoes, and my feet hurt.

Walter Reisch —— DIRECTOR/SCREENWRITER

I got catastrophic reviews, and I suffered very much under the effects of it for years and years. If you make a picture called *Song of Scheherazade,* with "Song of India" in it, and the "Caprice Espagnole," and "The Flight of the Bumble Bee," all by Rimsky-Korsakov, and if Yvonne De Carlo is the inspiration for all of this, you are leaving yourself wide open for criticism. Today I accept it with a certain sense of humor. But the studio people just didn't believe in my direction [as a consequence], and I never got a picture to direct in Hollywood again.

Edward G. Robinson —— ACTOR

I've rarely admitted it, but for me one role has loomed up above all the others—Dr. Ehrlich in *Dr. Ehrlich's Magic Bullet.* When Warners came up with the script I thought at first the title was a gimmick to exploit the success of some of the gangster roles they had cast me in, even though this time I was to play a scientist. I had visions of myself in a laboratory with a tommy-gun in my hand knocking off spirochetes. But to my relief I soon found out that "magic bullet" was Dr. Ehrlich's own designation for the amazing cure he had discovered for syphilis.

Richard Rodgers —— COMPOSER

The most terrible lies have been all those Hollywood musicals which purport to be the life story of people like Gershwin, or Porter, or Kern. They give no insight whatsovever into the working patterns of the men they're supposedly about. They did it to Larry Hart and me [in *Words and Music*]. The only good thing about that picture was that they had Janet Leigh play my wife. And I found *that* highly acceptable.

Helen Rose —— COSTUME DESIGNER

Judy Garland, who portrayed Marilyn Miller in *Till the Clouds Roll By,* was pregnant at the time she appeared in the picture. She was in a number with a group of male dancers and she was going from one handsome young man to the other dancing and singing, "Who?" Afterwards, she turned to me and with her usual wit and uproarious laughter said, "What a song to sing in my present condition!"

Rosalind Russell —— ACTRESS

Sister Kenny, which was successful in certain areas of the world and not in others, was made because of my interest in handicapped children. Soon after I came to California I got together with some doctors' wives, and we formed an organization called the League for Crippled Children. Years later Sister Kenny came to the Coast. I became acquainted with her and wanted to do a picture about her remarkable life.

I persuaded the well-known writer, Dudley Nichols, to go to Minneapolis, where that dedicated Australian nurse lived and worked, to prepare a script about her. Then came the tough job of getting it produced. I was under contract to do three pictures for RKO, and had the right to approve the choice of stories. RKO didn't really want to do *Sister Kenny,* and at this point I used what I call gentle blackmail. I hinted that I wouldn't approve *any* scripts if they weren't willing to do the Kenny film.

In the end, the picture did pull out of the red and make a profit for the studio. So I didn't feel too badly about my stubborn attitude. Moreover, it proved to be a boost for Sister Kenny's work, and it helped underscore the fact that something *must* be done to wipe out polio.

Vincent Sherman —— DIRECTOR

Jean Negulesco was scheduled to do *Adventures of Don Juan* and I *Johnny Belinda.* But then Errol Flynn objected to Negulesco because he didn't know him. As it turned out, I got *Don Juan* and Negulesco got *Johnny Belinda.*

I was very unhappy because I had been warned by [directors] Mike Curtiz and Raoul Walsh about Flynn, how difficult he could be. It was an unbelievable experience. It was during a period of his life when he was drinking quite a bit. He showed up on time on the set, but before he was made up and ready it was always 11 or 11:30. I was lucky if I got two shots before lunch. We went well over budget and schedule. In fact, the overall picture took almost nine months.

Errol's health was not really good. I don't know whether it was because of drinking or what. His heart was not good. He was able to duel for like 15 seconds, and then he would be huffing and puffing and almost black in the face, and I would have to use a double.

Alexis Smith ———— ACTRESS

Night and Day had Cary Grant—a marvelous screen actor, and very impressive when you're working with him. But the script on that picture, or rather, the scripts, were unbelievable. If a scene wasn't working to someone's satisfaction they'd dig into a basket and come up with a script typed on a different colored paper. There were about 10 differently colored scripts in that basket.

* * *

Cole Porter came on the set of *Night and Day* [the film about his life] one day, and, of course, we were all very, very excited about that. We were shooting on a great estate that I presume was supposedly his. But there was a band rehearsing on the grounds for some unknown reason, and the drummer was Mel Tormé, who was a baby at the time. And, of course, Cole came in white flannel pants and I think a blazer and a scarf, and looking exactly as Cole Porter should look.

The picture was fantasy; there were certain aspects of his story which at that time they couldn't do.

James Stewart ———— ACTOR

It was the first time I've ever been kicked out of a prison!

It was Joliet State Prison, outside of Chicago. We spent two weeks there shooting scenes for *Call Northside 777.* That picture was the one that really got me started after the war. *It's a Wonderful Life* hadn't done well.

I remember waiting to do a scene and an inmate sidled up to me and said, "Why don't you bastards get out of here? We want to get our privileges back. We have to stay in our cells the whole time you're shooting the damn picture. Why don't you get the hell out of here and leave us alone?"

Lawrence Tierney ———— ACTOR

I said, "I'm going home, back to New York. Hollywood's not for me."

I finally wangled a reservation and was leaving in two days when my agent called. "I've been looking for you for eight months," he said. "RKO wants you back. You'd better sign with them." I signed.

I read somewhere that the King Brothers were looking for someone to play the lead in *Dillinger.* I went over to their office for an interview, and discovered they were in the process of moving. I sat down to wait for one of them to return and saw several scripts in a packing box. One was *Dillinger.* I picked it up. I went across the street to a lunch room and read the script. I knew I could do it. I memorized some of it, returned and asked for the part.

"Nothing doing," I was told. "You haven't a chance. That part is all sewed up."

A couple of weeks later I read where they were still searching for Dillinger. I went back, saw Morris King and read him the script. That's how I got the part.

Jack L. Warner — STUDIO HEAD

George M. Cohan wanted to have the world premiere of *Yankee Doodle Dandy* in New York on the Fourth of July, his birthday. But when the family physician advised us that he could not possibly live that long, we hastily changed our plans. The picture opened on May 29 at Warners' Hollywood Theater at Broadway and 51st Street in New York, and the first-nighters paid $6,000,000 in war bonds for their seats. Cohan, who had already beaten all the quoted odds, clung to life long enough to hear about other openings across the nation, and to have the wonderful reviews read to him.

* * *

Errol Flynn began to open up at the joints when we started filming *The Adventures of Don Juan,* and we performed some difficult welding jobs to keep him in one piece. He was trying to duplicate the script action off the lot, and after four weeks he was so soggy that he ignored the call sheet and stayed home. I assigned some plain-clothes men to keep an eye on him and try to get him out of the bedroom and back on the lot.

One afternoon he called me and said blithely: "Hey, junior chum, why don't you get those coppers off my fanny and I'll come back to work."

I called them in and Errol sobered up for a day. But with five weeks to go, he began folding up in mid-afternoon, and we could only prop him up for short periods before he blacked out. I stopped production, used the same cast and crew to start another film, and when Errol finally recovered from his gargantuan bender weeks later, we finished *The Adventures of Don Juan.*

Cornel Wilde ———— ACTOR

In *A Song to Remember,* they were not by any means making a real biography of Chopin, of course. And since they weren't, I thought they made a warm and dramatic film.

Paul Muni did overact, terribly, which was a big shock to me because he was quite a hero of mine. I thought he was a fabulous actor, and also I assumed that therefore he would have to be a very generous man. He was not. He was very difficult to work with. Far from generous with a new young actor—me. He wouldn't even read the lines with me when we first started. I asked if we could please read some of the scenes together so that I could feel more at home with his characterization. And he said no. He said he didn't want to hear how I did it, he had no interest in how I portrayed it, he had his own conception of Chopin and he told me he had worked on his role in relation to that conception, and he didn't care how I played it.

And that was the approach to teamwork in that film.

Sam Wood — DIRECTOR

Gary Cooper—you're positive he's going to ruin your picture. I froze in my tracks the first time I directed him [in *Pride of the Yankees*]. I thought something was wrong with him, and I saw a million-dollar production go glimmering. I was amazed at the results on the screen. What I thought was underplaying turned out to be just the right approach. On the screen he's perfect, yet on the set you'd swear it's the worst job of acting in the history of motion pictures.

Jane Wyman — ACTRESS

Night and Day gave me another silly showgirl role and I was sick of playing dumb bunnies. We were doing the big production numbers when the roof of the sound stage caved in. They had tried putting blocks of ice up there to stifle the heat and it didn't work. The sets had to be reconstructed, so when I finally reported for *The Yearling* I was both Ma Baxter and Gracie Harris for a few weeks. Racing back and forth between the sets unnerved me.

Philip Yordan — SCREENWRITER

In the '40s the studios, all the majors, had signed a consent agreement not to make gangster pictures. Monogram was not a signatory, so Louis B. Mayer was indignant. He called up [producer] Frank King and said, "Frank, you gotta destroy the negative of *Dillinger* for the good of the industry." Frank said, "Sure, what'll you pay me?" Louis B. Mayer said, "I'll pay you nothing." Hell, the picture cost $65,000 and it made millions. I had a third of it.

Darryl F. Zanuck — PRODUCER

Wilson, which I made during the war, is the picture that I'm proudest of. Unfortunately, even the lousiest Betty Grable movie we did made more money than *Wilson.*

Comedies

Louise Allbritton — ACTRESS

San Diego, I Love You, a charming comedy, was written for me. Before beginning it, I had to leave town, and while away I read in the papers that Susanna Foster was going into it! I raced back to Universal, stormed the front office and, for the one and

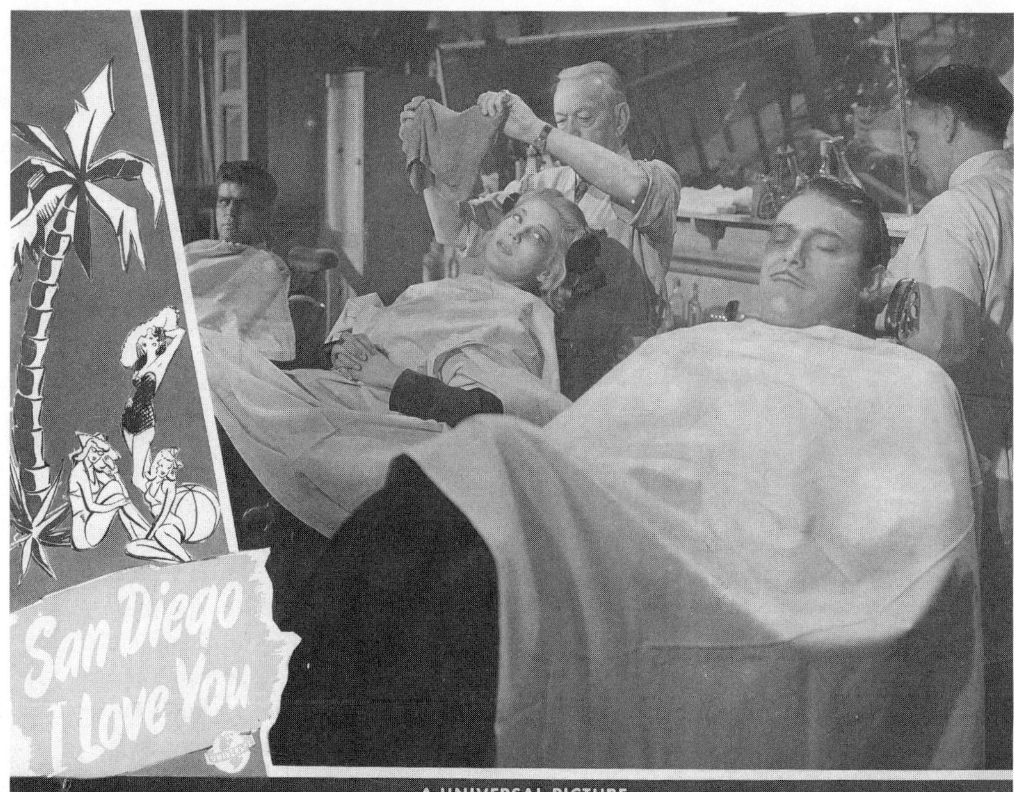

only time during my Hollywood years, I raised hell. *San Diego, I Love You* was *mine!* I did the film. And it was a good thing I spoke up for myself, because it became my favorite of all my pictures.

Fred Allen——————ACTOR

It's in the Bag? I thought it was pretty good until I got a wire from someone in Hollywood saying it was excellent. That's a very weak word for Hollywood where everything is spoken of in superlatives. Since it was only called wonderful, I'm worried.

Don Ameche——————ACTOR

Heaven Can Wait is my favorite of all the pictures I've made, primarily because it was directed by Ernst Lubitsch. He was one of the great directors out there when you kept him where he belonged, and when he was there, why, there was no one anywhere any better, who could touch him in his field. No one came near him in the field of satire.

Ernst had an odd outlook on life, a satirical outlook on life. When he and Samson Raphaelson finished writing the picture, they spent eight months polishing the script before we started shooting. The first day, he assembled the whole cast and told us, "These are the facts and I beg you don't change anything because this is the way I would like it." He was totally persistent in getting exactly what he wanted. He'd go at it and at it and at it. This won't hurt anyone at all, but Gene Tierney couldn't quite come to one scene, and he just kept at her and at her until he broke her completely down. When shortly after she straightened herself around, he rolled the camera and got exactly what he wanted. He knew how to do it. He didn't do it unless he had to, but he was a man totally dedicated to his art.

Evelyn Ankers—ACTRESS

After appearing in several English plays and films, I made my American debut in 1940 in the hit Broadway thriller, *Ladies in Retirement.* Universal Pictures wanted to feature me with Bud Abbott and Lou Costello in *Hold That Ghost,* so I signed a seven-year contract with them on January 8, 1941.

I didn't know, however, that I was to play an American girl, least of all one with a Brooklyn accent—strange, when they had so many American players under contract. That's Hollywood for you, I guess—or *was.* Well, that first American movie was a chore for all concerned. I had to cut down those broad A's I was used to. There were quite a few extra takes when I'd say *new* or *dew* instead of *nu* and *du.* I had trouble, too, saying *recurd* instead of *rec-cord.*

Abbott and Costello thought me stuffy because I was so "English"; they just loved to tease me with their vaudeville tricks, which were too off-color to relate here. Suffice it to say I was always glad to find a wall to stand against, or a chair to sit on, between takes of *Hold That Ghost.*

Eve Arden—ACTRESS

In *Comrade X,* Clark Gable and I worked on the same newspaper in Moscow. I was his girlfriend but lost him to the flawless beauty of Hedy Lamarr. After leaving the studio one evening, I stopped at the gas station across the street from MGM and Clark drove up. He suddenly asked if he could drive me home. Coward that I was, I refused and stepped on the gas while I still had the strength.

Jean-Pierre Aumont—ACTOR

I had been making *Heartbeat* with Ginger Rogers and Adolphe Menjou. Sam Wood, the director, seemed unsure of himself and shot every scene over and over.

From these miles of celluloid the editor somehow managed to piece together an agreeable film. Surrounded by pink floodlights, Ginger gave an effective performance. She was a very courteous co-worker. If my tie was askew she didn't tell me, but called the assistant instead and said: "Would you mind warning Mr. Aumont that his tie isn't straight?" Adolphe Menjou, who had a mustache and eyebrows like commas, had assumed a one-man battle against Communism long before Senator McCarthy. At a time when we had hardly won the battle against fascism, Menjou—also an Adolphe!—was drawing up lists of suspects while putting the finishing touches on his make-up.

Charles T. Barton—DIRECTOR

Bud Abbott and Lou Costello had quite a chip on their shoulders about doing *Abbott and Costello Meet*

Frankenstein, and they'd fight me like hell. But I stood my ground with them, and so did [producer] Bob Arthur. Still, Bud and Lou went home several times during shooting and stayed there for six days or so.

Our budget was very cheap—maybe $1 million, not very much for that time. The only thing that really cost us money was when the boys got on their high horse and wouldn't show up. Another trick they loved to pull was to sit over on the side of the set and play cards for three days. Three days! And for big, big money!

Yet, during all these problems, we never had any trouble with Lon Chaney, Bela Lugosi or Glenn Strange. The "monsters" were as sweet as little babies.

Florence Bates ——— ACTRESS

When James Thurber left a theater where he had seen *The Secret Life of Walter Mitty* [based on his short story], he asked his companion, "What was the name of that picture?"

Anne Baxter ——— ACTRESS

My first picture at 20th Century-Fox was *The Great Profile,* with John Barrymore. He was at the nadir of his life, dissipated but somehow handsome still. I remember he had a male nurse named Karl with him all the time. At one point we had to shoot in a nearby theater location where we shared a kitchen. I noticed that Karl brought him one Coke after another all day long. When I saw that the cooking rum in the kitchen was disappearing, I knew what was happening. Mr. Barrymore was in a fog most of the time—no, make that another world. But when he faced the cameras, he came to life. It was amazing.

Another time, during a scene we had together in a car, he let loose a torrent of profanity. The director apologized to me, but I was very young and naïve and hadn't understood a word Barrymore said.

Jack Benny ——— ACTOR

Making *Charley's Aunt,* there was a scene when I got dressed up as the aunt, and Edmund Gwenn was supposed to fall in love with me, chasing me all around the campus, and finally we were to bump into each other, a real big crash. Naturally, the studio used two stunt men so Edmund and I would not get hurt. All they asked me to do was come in once they were on the ground, turn and get up. That was all I had to do in the scene—get up from the ground. So the stunt men did their chase and crash, and I did my part. Getting up from the ground I sprained my back and couldn't work for three days.

* * *

During his last years, Papa needed a full-time nurse, but even so he went for strolls and his favorite pastime was going to my movies. He saw every one of them at least six times. I always felt sorry for the nurse.

To Be or Not to Be came to Miami Beach. In the first scene in the movie I wore a Nazi uniform and was seated in my office. Another actor entered and my right hand shot up in the Nazi salute, "Heil Hitler!"

My father watched the movie for about one minute and when he saw this scene he grabbed the nurse's arm and stomped out of the theater. The nurse couldn't believe that for once she didn't have to sit through another Jack Benny picture. I imagine she was the happiest nurse in all of Florida.

Vanessa Brown — ACTRESS

Fans? When we were filming *The Late George Apley,* which was about a family, our director, Joseph L. Mankiewicz, had all of us principals take lunch together. This way, he wouldn't have to direct us to portray the family spirit; we would acquire it naturally from our togetherness at lunch. Ronald Colman, who played George Apley, mostly listened during the meals. Edna Best, who played his wife, held court most of the time and was very amusing. Once, she went off on a tirade about fans. "Where are they when you need them?" she said. "When things go wrong, they disappear!" She was quite vehement. Afterward, we noticed a couple of young fans approach her for an autograph. We all thought, "Oh-oh, she'll really give it to them." But she said, "Certainly, dears. Now what are your names?"

Frank Capra — PRODUCER/DIRECTOR

Less than two months after I had broached the idea to [Broadway producer] Howard Lindsay backstage, we were shooting the first scene of *Arsenic and Old Lace* on a Warner stage. And I couldn't have been happier. No great social document "to save the world," no worries about whether John Doe should or should not jump; just good old-fashioned theater—an anything goes, rip-roaring comedy about murder. I let the scene-stealers run wild; for the actors it was a mugger's ball.

The fun had one more week to go, when it was brutally interrupted by—PEARL HARBOR! Next day, Monday morning, December 8, two Signal Corps officers came to the studio stage to swear me in. I was in the Army. I asked for, and was granted, six weeks' leave of absence to finish, edit and preview *Arsenic.* Nights, a tailor fitted me for uniforms.

Jack Carson — ACTOR

One More Tomorrow went pretty well at the preview. In fact, better than we expected. Afterward, Jack Warner said, "This is more than a comedy—it's significant"—now I'm worried.

Claudette Colbert — ACTRESS

My favorite film? *Arise, My Love,* with Ray Milland. It's the kind of picture that rarely happens. Started off as a roaring farce and ended up with the Battle of Britain. Strangely, *The Kansas City Star* accused us of war-mongering . . . of trying to draw America into the war.

* * *

I also wanted to try my hand at directing, and had the chance, but the contract stipulated that I had to *act* in the picture, too, and that would have been too tough. Also, I didn't know if I could see the broad canvas. I guess what it really comes down to is that I didn't have the guts. When I was making *Without Reservations* with John Wayne, he said *he'd* do a picture I directed, and I knew he meant it. I really cherish that remark. I mean, from the he-man of all time.

Hans Conried —— ACTOR

My Friend Irma was a shameful thing in which I only really half-appeared, since the best part of my performance, done in long-shot, was played by Felix Bressart.

I had done *My Friend Irma* for five or six years, when it was a very popular radio show, and I played Professor Kropotkin, an old Russian Jew. They wanted me for this part, which I had established to the delight of millions of radio fans. Well, I was so palpably wrong that happily I had the integrity to say, "You're crazy. I can't play this 80-year-old man." It may have been only courtesy—my pride prompted me to think that they really wanted me. At any rate, very sensibly they employed a fine character actor, Felix Bressart, who died in the middle of production. Then the producer, an old friend of mine, said, "Hans, you've got to fish us out."

So then I played the part; the close-ups are indeed little old me, and very badly performed, I was so obviously made up. The best parts of that performance are the long-shots, in which Felix Bressart still crosses the camera field of vision. My voice was used throughout.

Broderick Crawford —— ACTOR

While we were filming *Seven Sinners,* the producer, Joe Pasternak, kept begging our star, Marlene Dietrich, to go to bed with him. Finally, she told him, "I'll go to bed with you when Hitler is dead." In 1945 he called her and said Hitler was dead. She replied, "Hitler is alive and well and living in Argentina!"

Joan Crawford —— ACTRESS

I begged for Susan in *Susan and God* and got the part only because Norma Shearer didn't want it. Mr. [Louis B.] Mayer called me in New York.

"Joan, will you be willing to play a mother?"

"I'll play Wally Beery's grandmother," I yelled, "if it's a good part!"

George Cukor —— DIRECTOR

I didn't like *Two-Faced Woman* very much. We really had no script and it was just disasterville; the film didn't work at all. Garbo wasn't very happy about it, either. It was the final film she did under her Metro contract, and when it was over she asked to be released. Louis Mayer was lost in admiration over the splendid way she behaved about it.

People often say glibly that the failure of *Two-Faced Woman* finished Garbo's career. That's a grotesque over-simplification. If only life were tied up in such neat packages. It certainly threw her, but I think what really happened was that she just gave up; she didn't want to go on.

Robert Cummings ——— ACTOR

I was in *The Devil and Miss Jones.* Wonderful, wonderful movie. The 1940s one—*not* the recent porno one, *The Devil in Miss Jones.* Nobody got into anybody in our version!

* * *

Too many people told me I couldn't keep up the pace—and that brought out the mule in me. I was so tired most of the time we were making *Princess O'Rourke* I was afraid to look at the camera. Up late every night, on the set early every morning, teaching [flying] all day on Sundays—you've seen the kind of faces that look like they've worn out nine bodies, haven't you? Well, that was the way mine was beginning to feel. What really kept me going was laughs—Jack Carson, Janie Wyman and Olivia de Havilland were good for a howl a minute on the set. Those kids were a shot in the arm to me.

Since it was to be my last picture for the duration [of World War II], I was glad it was a comedy. Leave 'em laughing, Cummings, I kept telling myself—and you can always come back again.

* * *

On *The Bride Wore Boots,* I remember a very long day shooting a steeplechase at a country club. Missy [Barbara Stanwyck] was a fine horsewoman, and I was . . . Well, anyway, 14 times we shot it. The director [Irving Pichel] just wasn't happy. I didn't think I could do it again. Then I saw this tiny figure coming toward us. It was Missy. She said to the director, "If Mr. Cummings rides that race one more time, you and I will never work together again." The director quickly said, "That's a wrap."

Bette Davis ——— ACTRESS

I was the one who got Warners to buy *The Man Who Came to Dinner* for John Barrymore and me. But they wouldn't let him play it because he couldn't remember lines. And I said, "I'll take him just ad-libbing." He should have played it, he *should* have. It would have been the last film he ever made. He was dead shortly after that. As it was, I thought it was a very pedantic film, a very dull director [William Keighley], not much imagination. But it was a great property, and I thought it would make a marvelous movie. If it had had a better cast it might have.

Olivia de Havilland —— ACTRESS

I soon learned that the script first came to the [Warner Bros.] make-up department for a breakdown. The head of the make-up department would have to figure out how many make-up men he needed with wigs or how many make-up artists that knew how to put on beards, all that kind of thing, whether there had to be somebody who was good at making scars. So I would sneak the scripts out of the make-up department and take them home and read them overnight; that's how I got *Strawberry Blonde.*

I went to the producer and said, "I understand that you are making *Strawberry Blonde* and it isn't cast yet and I would like to play the part of

Amy." He said, "You don't want to play the part of Amy." I said, "Yes, I do want to play Amy." He said, "But that's not the title role," and I said, "I don't care if it's not the title role, let anybody else play the title role, the point is that that's a woman I understand and I would like to play her. I just love her and I want to play her." It was very tough getting that part, but I started it, I initiated it and, in a sense, chose it. But it had to be done by these indirect means. That's how it had to be done.

Kirk Douglas ——— ACTOR

I did *A Letter to Three Wives.* Joe Mankiewicz, who had a great sense of humor, was the director. In one scene I had to be sleeping in bed, and Joe said to me, "Kirk, now look. While we're preparing the set-up, I want you to try and fall asleep. Lie in bed, close your eyes and really try to fall asleep. I want that feeling of someone sleeping, not just pretending." So I dutifully obeyed. Finally, I drifted off. I awoke with a start to total silence. I opened one eye, looked around—no one. Joe had gotten me to fall asleep just before lunch, then had everyone tiptoe off the set, leaving me sound asleep in a big, deserted studio.

I played an English professor. Ann Sothern played my wife. We rehearsed the relationship offstage.

Irene Dunne ——— ACTRESS

Life with Father is not one of my favorites. The director, Michael

Curtiz, bombarded me with pleas for weeks before I finally consented to appear in it.

They sent us all down to Westmore's one Sunday morning to get our hair dyed red. When they went to rinse the dye off they discovered that there was no water—the plumbing for the whole block had been turned off because they were repairing the street. We called up the mayor and everybody we could think of, but to no avail. Fortunately, somebody hit upon the idea of diluting the dye with gallons of cold cream; otherwise we would have been bald, hair dyes were so crude in those days.

Allan Dwan ——— *DIRECTOR*

Abroad with Two Yanks was a lot of fun—William Bendix and Dennis O'Keefe dressed up like girls. We used a theater in Hollywood for some of the interiors, right next to the Brown Derby. Now, it was such a hell of a job putting on that make-up and harnessing on those clothes, that they kept them on when we all went out to lunch. And I walked into the Brown Derby with two broads. Well, there was a panic. Can you imagine—two broads like that? The head waiter nearly dropped dead. We finally got stuck in a booth, and people kept looking and weren't sure. Thought maybe they were a couple of pansies out camping. Of course, they were cutting up, playing coy.

Samuel G. Engel——*PRODUCER*

After the first smash reviews of *Sitting Pretty* came in, I approached

our star, Clifton Webb, and said, "Well, now that you're such a success, I suppose you won't talk to us." Clifton replied, "My dear boy, I have *always* been a success. One more hit will not unsettle me."

Ken Englund—SCREENWRITER

It is alleged that James Thurber later communicated with [Samuel] Goldwyn to the effect that he felt the picture *The Secret Life of Walter Mitty* contained far too much violence and gore. Goldwyn immediately wrote Thurber, "I am sorry that you felt it was too blood and thirsty." Whereupon Thurber replied, "Not only did I think so, but I was horror and struck."

Julius J. Epstein—SCREENWRITER

When *Arsenic and Old Lace* was being made, I went to the director, Frank Capra, and said, "Don't you think [Cary] Grant's going a little overboard?" Capra said, "Oh, he's way overboard, but I'll bring it down in the editing." Then, Pearl Harbor happened, and Capra went directly off to war. He never got back to the picture, and it went out as shot.

Joan Fontaine—ACTRESS

You Gotta Stay Happy was made right after *Kiss the Blood Off My Hands,* and I was pregnant with my daughter in both of them. I almost lost her on *You Gotta Stay Happy.* The director, H. C. Potter, made me jump off a hay wagon and in 10 minutes I was in the hospital. James Stewart was a dream to work with. After I went to the hospital, Jimmy came to visit me that very night, which I thought was awfully dear of him. Jean Louis, who did the costumes for the picture, designed some lovely camouflage for me.

Cary Grant ——— ACTOR

My least favorite performance? It was in *Arsenic and Old Lace,* and you know, I *told* the director, Frank Capra. I said, "Frank, I simply cannot do that kind of comedy." And Frank said, "Of course you can, old boy," and I did it, and I overplayed it terribly. *Terribly.* Jimmy Stewart would have been wonderful in that part.

Ethel Griffies ——— ACTRESS

Between Us Girls in 1942 afforded me a good part as an Irish maid. Universal handed the star, Diana Barrymore, one of the greatest roles for a woman I'd ever seen in this. She got to masquerade as a little girl, play Sadie Thompson, Queen Victoria and Joan of Arc, had a crying scene, a laughing scene, got the glamour treatment, everything. They gave Miss Barrymore, who was just starting in pictures, every chance, but she just wasn't up to it. By the time they got to popping her into Joan's armor, the girl's knees were knocking so the clang was deafening. She was a *very* difficult young lady, too.

Rex Harrison ——— ACTOR

I proceeded to do *Unfaithfully Yours,* which has now become something of a classic. Preston Sturges was the most extraordinary man to work with. First of all, he used to direct in a fez, and the reason he wore a fez was he wanted everybody to know where he was all the time. He didn't want people to come on the set and say where's Preston; they would know where Preston was because they'd look for the red fez. And he ran the film set rather like a circus. It wasn't that he didn't want anyone to see what he was doing; on the contrary, he would open the doors of the sound stage and call out: "Come and have a look at this—it's wonderful, come and have a look!" And he used to sit under the camera roaring with laughter, stuffing handkerchiefs into his mouth to stop himself laughing at his own jokes which he'd written.

Howard Hawks ——— PRODUCER/DIRECTOR

I had always thought that the Hecht-MacArthur play *The Front Page* had the best modern dialogue around, so one evening I had some friends in for dinner and we decided to read a bit of it. I read Walter's role, the editor, and had a girl read Hildy's part, the reporter.

Suddenly, I thought, "This could be great with a girl playing Hildy's role, instead of the way it was written—with a man." So I called Ben Hecht and said, "I'd love to do *Front Page* with a girl as Hildy." He liked the idea and we went to work on it as *His Girl Friday.* We hired

Rosalind Russell and Cary Grant, who were great, and the story worked better than it ever had.

———*DIRECTOR*

In *Ball of Fire,* we had a marvelous scene where Gary Cooper had to come in to say something to the girl. She was in bed, you couldn't see her face, just her eyes. I said to [cinematographer] Gregg Toland, "How the hell can I do that? How can I light her eyes without lighting her face?" And he said, "Well, have her do it in blackface." So the next day I saw her and said, "Barbara [Stanwyck], tomorrow don't bother making up. I want you to play in blackface." She said, "What the hell kind of scene is that?" Oh, God, it was a good scene.

* * *

After *I Was a Male War Bride,* Darryl Zanuck said, "I've got a great idea—you and Cary Grant do *Charley's Aunt.*" And I said, "We just did it."

Katharine Hepburn — *ACTRESS*

The Philadelphia Story was the film that saved my career. I did it as a Broadway play in 1937, and then we did the picture in 1940 during a period when I was not doing too well at the box office. In fact, the independent theater owners had labeled me "box office poison."

Sam Goldwyn was trying to buy the movie rights to *Philadelphia Story,* which I owned. I agreed to sell it to him if he could guarantee that Gary Cooper would play C. K. Dexter Haven opposite my Tracy Lord. Well, he couldn't do that. And Jack Warner wanted to buy it for Warner Bros. which was alright with me, if he could guarantee that Errol Flynn would play the part. He couldn't.

And then Louis B. Mayer came to talk with me about it for MGM. He was a very shrewd operator, and he brought along Norma Shearer. You see, I had been playing Tracy a full year before I got any offers to make the picture, because they didn't realize I owned it. So I said to L.B., "Can you get Clark Gable and Spencer Tracy for me?" And he said, "I don't think so, but I will guarantee you Jimmy Stewart and I will give you a certain amount of money to go out and see whom you can persuade to do it."

And so I got Cary Grant.

* * *

I knew, from my first day of working with Spence [Tracy] in *Woman of the Year* that I had met my match—and then some.

The first day I was so nervous that I knocked over a glass of water while filming a restaurant scene. I expected him to stop everything and call a prop man to clean it up, but instead he never batted an eyelash. Looking straight into my eyes and continuing with his lines, he picked a handkerchief out of his breast pocket and handed it to me. I thought, "You old son of a bitch," and began damping up the mess. Then it started dripping through the table, so I just said, "Excuse me," and bent down to mop it off the floor—all the while saying our lines as if nothing unusual had happened! It worked beautifully, and we kept it in the film.

Alfred Hitchcock —— *DIRECTOR*

Mr. and Mrs. Smith I made as a gesture to Carole Lombard. She asked me to do it. The script was already written, and I just came in and did it. She had heard my remark, "Actors are cattle," so when I arrived on the set, I found a little corral with some cattle in it.

Bob Hope —— *ACTOR*

You know, *The Ghost Breakers* in 1940 did $9 million, and Paramount was so happy that they broke out the champagne. And what did I see the other day that *Ghostbusters* had done? $200 million. Can you believe that? Times do change.

* * *

When I got out here in '37, I went down to Del Mar for Bing [Crosby]. He owned a piece of the Turf Club there. I did a Saturday night show there with him, a routine that we'd done at the Capitol in New York in 1932. Everybody who saw it—and it played like gangbusters—said, "Boy, these two guys work together!" So they said, "Let's get a picture for them." There was a pictured called *Flight to Singapore* and they changed it to *Road to Singapore* and that was it [the start of the "Road" films].

* * *

We had a lot of adventures on *Road to Morocco,* some of them in the script.

Like the time Bing and I were washed up on the North African coast. A camel sneaks up behind us and licks us on the cheeks. We begin to think it's love at second sight until we see that it was a camel doing the kissing, not each other.

I don't know if you've ever been kissed by a camel, but I've got to tell you that it's not like being kissed by Raquel Welch. This particular camel may have been listening to my radio show, because after he kissed me, he spat right in my face.

You wouldn't believe what a camel stores up in his chaw. I thought I had been hit by the Casbah Garbage Department. When you see *Road to Morocco* on the late show, you'll notice that I stagger out of the scene when the camel spits at me. Bing broke up, and I was gasping for breath, but director Dave Butler kept the camera rolling.

For years afterward, people asked him, "How did you get that camel to spit at Hope on cue?" Dave replied, "I worked with the beast for weeks until it responded to my direction."

* * *

On *Road to Utopia,* one of the scenes called for Bing Crosby and me to bed down in our Klondike cabin and be joined by a bear. A real bear. They told us it was a very tame bear, but Bing and I had our doubts.

We climbed under a rug and feigned sleep. The bear came sniffing up to us. Then we heard a growl.

Right then I had laundry problems.

"Did you hear what I heard?" Bing asked.

"I sure did," I said. "Lead the way, Dad."

We set an Olympic record for leaping out of bed—Errol Flynn couldn't have done it faster.

"That's it with the bear," Bing announced, and I heartily agreed. The next day, the same bear tore an arm off his trainer.

Ruth Hussey ———— ACTRESS

I've pulled a lot of boners, but I think the worst one happened when I did *Our Wife* on loan-out to Columbia.

The lot was strange to me, and when lunchtime came the first day I meant to follow my fellow workers to the commissary, but was delayed. When I finally started out, there was no one to follow, so I asked directions from the gateman. Unless you've been on a studio lot, you probably can't imagine how confusing the directions can be. Turn left—turn right—turn, turn, turn. That's the way his directions sounded to me and I was very relieved when after trying to follow them, I at last found myself in a room which had a long table and saw several men sitting there busy with menus. So I sat down, too, and gave my order.

I was so engrossed that I didn't notice until after I ordered that absolute silence had fallen on the gathering, and that most of the gentlemen were glaring at me. Mr. Harry Cohn, the boss of the studio, was seated at the head of the table and I smiled at him. I wouldn't describe his answering expression as enthusiastic. I took another look around the room and the truth dawned on me. I was in Mr. Cohn's private dining room—sitting in on his midday conference!

Betty Hutton ———— ACTRESS

I am not a great singer, and I am not a great dancer, but I *am* a great actress and nobody ever let me act except Preston Sturges [in *The Miracle of Morgan's Creek*]. He believed in me.

Gloria Jean ———— ACTRESS

I never saw W. C. Fields eat while working [on *Never Give a Sucker an Even Break*]. I would offer him sandwiches and he would refuse. A man in a white coat would serve him drinks, but he was never allowed to drink in front of me. They warned him if he did, they would close down the set.

One day, they caught him with a "drink" in his hand. He was told: "That is it, Mr. Fields, we're closing down the picture." He replied in his classic way, "Relax, my dear, this is only Listerine." And it was, too!

Garson Kanin ———— DIRECTOR

I knew damn well how the story of *Tom, Dick and Harry* was going to end, and I think all the players suspected. But I wanted each fellow to play it like a potential winner of the hand of Ginger Rogers. I didn't want Burgess Meredith to play it from the beginning like it was all sewed up and I certainly didn't want George Murphy to get that sort of hangdog expression of a loser.

In fact, I not only discussed three endings but I literally *shot* three endings. I shot an ending where she winds up with Burgess, I shot an ending where she winds up with George Murphy and I shot an ending where she winds up with Alan Marshal. George Murphy, a bright fellow who later became a United States Senator from California, said on the day we were shooting the finish where *he* gets the girl, "You're not fooling me, baby." And I said, "George, one never knows. The most important element in all films is the audience. We'll probably preview it all three ways." We didn't, though.

Veronica Lake ——— ACTRESS

It was in the first week of shooting *Sullivan's Travels.* Louise Sturges [wife of the director-screenwriter, Preston Sturges], also pregnant, was sitting on the edge of the set watching the filming. Mary Martin was also there as a spectator. She'd just finished *Birth of the Blues,* was pregnant like the rest of us and jubilant that she could relax until November when her baby was due.

Preston spotted Mary and yelled, "This looks like Paramount's stork club." Everyone laughed. And I saw an opportunity to bring up my inclusion in the club. I leaned over to Louise and whispered, "Don't tell Preston, but I'm pregnant, too."

Louise turned to me and smiled. But her voice had no hint of the smile.

"I certainly will not tell him," she said flatly. "But I'll give you a two-minute running start to tell him yourself."

* * *

I don't believe there is an actor for whom I harbor such deep dislike as Fredric March. He gave me a terrible time during *I Married a Witch.* March considered me a brainless little blonde sexpot, void of any acting ability and not likely to acquire any. He treated me like dirt under his talented feet. Of all actors to end up under the covers with! That happened in one scene and Mr. March is lucky he didn't get my knee in his groin.

* * *

I began working on *The Sainted Sisters,* with Joan Caulfield, a comedy about two confidence dames. I was tipped off early that some devious Paramount brass were waiting for Caulfield and Lake to come to blows—"Let's put Lake in with Caulfield. Caulfield will fix her ass."

I played it so cool. And professionally bitchy. Everyone would come down to see the rushes and walk away shaking their heads at the scenes in which Joan and I appeared together. Every time Joan gave lines, I'd just stand there and stare at her. I was good at that, so good that people in the business began talking about my ability to steal scenes without doing anything. And no one appreciated it more than Joan Caulfield. There were times when she'd leave the screening room in a rage.

Dorothy Lamour——— *ACTRESS*

There have been as many different accounts of how the "Road" films were born as there were people involved. According to one version, the "Roads" were planned for George Burns and Gracie Allen. Another rumor has it that *Road to Singapore* was originally earmarked for Jack Oakie and Fred MacMurray and that only when they were "unavailable" did Hope and Crosby come into the picture. Except that neither Oakie nor MacMurray recalls the story.

I remember I had just finished lunch with Pauline Kessinger in the Paramount commissary, and on the way out stopped at a table where Bob and Bing were carrying on so that I nearly choked from laughing. I was still laughing when I bumped into two writer friends. "What's so funny?" they asked. I told them that I had just been joking with Hope and Crosby, and that if they could only come up with a story involving two crazy guys and a "gal in the middle," I would love to play her.

Those two writers have forgotten our brief conversation, but soon after, the first "Road" story was turned in to the front office and I got my wish—Hope, Crosby and I were set to star in *Road to Singapore.*

Peter Lawford——— *ACTOR*

Fred Zinnemann has directed such distinguished movies as *From Here to Eternity, The Nun's Story* and *A Man for All Seasons.* But back in the forties, when he was a contract director at Metro, he directed me in a little number called *My Brother Talks to Horses,* with Butch Jenkins.

Actually, it was rather cute and got decent notices, but I don't think Zinnemann ever considered it a feather in his cap. A few years ago I ran into him at a Hollywood party. I walked up to him and said, "Fred, it's Peter Lawford. How have you been?" He stared at me. I hastened to explain, "You directed me in *My Brother Talks to Horses.*" An eyebrow arched and he replied, "Enemies. Everywhere, enemies." And moved on.

David Lean——— *DIRECTOR*

Noel Coward came back from entertaining the troops when we ran *Blithe Spirit* in the theater at Denham. Afterward, the lights went up and there was Noel, Noel's back getting bigger and bigger by the second. I couldn't bear the silence any longer and said, "Well, Noel, what do you think of it?"

"My dear, you have fucked up the best thing I ever wrote."

Years later [in 1956], I was in New York and Noel had just done *Blithe Spirit* for television, with himself in the Charles Condomine role that Rex Harrison had played in the film version, and I met Noel afterward. It was really rather terrible, and Noel said, "Well, my dear, what did you think of it?"

I told him, "You have fucked up the best thing you ever wrote."

Mitchell Leisen——— *PRODUCER/DIRECTOR*

Remember the Night is one of my pets. Barbara Stanwyck has a very bad back, and had to wear that wedding dress with corsets. She'd be dressed and on the set at half past eight in the morning. I'd say, "Barbara, for God's sake, come on. I'm not going to use you for an hour; why don't you loosen up those corsets?" She'd say, "No, you might need me." I'd come on the set at quarter to nine, having lined up the sets the night before, and a voice would come out of the fly gallery saying, "Come on, you sonofabitch, let's get this show on the road—where the hell have you been?" It was Barbara. She's a perfectionist if I ever saw one.

———DIRECTOR

We had our problems with censors. If I was afraid something in a scene might not pass, I'd insert another line in the same scene that was absolutely outrageous. Then the censor would start screaming bloody murder that the line had to come out, never noticing the thing I wanted to keep. In *Arise, My Love* when Ray Milland is taking a bath, I had one of his buddies look into the bathtub and say, "I didn't know you were Jewish." Of course they made me cut it out, but they never noticed the line I was trying to keep in.

Arthur Lubin———DIRECTOR

I continued doing "B" pictures at Universal until 1941, when I was assigned to direct the comedy duo Abbott and Costello in *Buck Privates.* They had previously done another film which hadn't made an impact. However, when *Buck Privates* was released, the picture was a sensation. I think it made around $10 million which, in those days, was fantastic. That same year, 1941, I directed them in three more films, *In the Navy, Hold That Ghost* and *Keem 'Em Flying.* In 1942, we did *Ride 'Em Cowboy.*

When we did *Buck Privates* together, they were wonderful. They were always on set on time. They knew their lines. They were so taken aback by what had happened to them it was all they could do to just work hard and behave.

After *Buck Privates* was released, the public reaction was enormous. Suddenly, this short, funny, heavy-set guy and his tall bean-pole straight man partner were the talk of the country. As we progressed from picture to picture, as their popularity continued to grow, pressures came in on them. Their problems became worse. Frankly, they became difficult to direct. They were late getting on the set. Many times, they didn't know their lines. Obviously, it's not easy to go from nowhere to becoming top 10 at the box office, where they remained for years.

Anyway, Abbott and Costello, who were basically great, decent guys, started acting up. But as far as Universal was concerned, their pictures made money and that was what counted, and rightly so.

Ernst Lubitsch ——PRODUCER/ ———DIRECTOR

To Be or Not to Be has caused a lot of controversy and in my opinion has been unjustly attacked. This picture never made fun of Poles, it only satirized actors and the Nazi spirit and the foul Nazi humor. Despite being farcical, it was a truer picture of Naziism than was shown in most novels, magazine stories and pictures which dealt with the same subject. In those stories the Germans were pictured as a people who were beleaguered by the Nazi gang and tried to fight this menace through the underground whenever they could. I never believed in that and it is now definitely proven that this so-called underground spirit among the German people never existed.

* * *

I consider *Heaven Can Wait* one of my major productions, because I tried to break away in several respects from the established moving picture formula. I encountered partly great resistance before I made this picture because it had no message and made no point whatsoever. The hero was a man only interested in good living with no aim of accomplishing anything, or of doing anything noble. Being asked by the studio why I wanted to make such a pointless picture, I answered that I hoped to introduce to a motion picture audience a number of people, and if the audience should find them likable—that would be sufficient for its success. And as it turned out, I was fortunately right. Besides, I showed the happy marriage in a truer light than is usually done in moving pictures where a happy marriage is too often portrayed as a very dull and unexciting by-the-fireplace affair.

Joel McCrea —— ACTOR

Preston Sturges is finally coming into his own. I remember Cecil B. DeMille wanted me for *Reap the Wild Wind* and I said no, because I was going to do *Sullivan's Travels* with Sturges. DeMille said to me, "He's some writer . . . the picture will be forgotten. But a picture with me. . . ." And I said, "Yes, C. B., but I'm not getting a percentage of your picture; I'm just working for a salary. And this fellow has a great script." That's what I based all my opinions on for doing a picture; it wasn't how much money they're going to pay me, it was the script.

* * *

Jean Arthur was always saying how old she looked. She told me when we were doing *The More the Merrier,* "I'm not gonna do any more pictures after this. If I do, I'm gonna do them with Coop and you." She loved Gary Cooper. She said, "Because if they put me with Tyrone Power I'll look like his mother!" And I said, "Gee, you look great, you photograph great." George Stevens and I used to build her up. We would say, "Jean, you look marvelous today." And I'd say, "George, just because you're the director, let me talk to Jean for a while." You know, we pretended like we were a little jealous of one another. She was married to Frank Ross at the time so neither of us were gonna do anything, but we kind of pretended like we were a little over-interested, and it helped her. She needed her ego boosted; it was surprising, because everybody just loved her voice, they loved her, she looked great and she was good. She's one of the actresses I liked working with the most.

Fred MacMurray ——— *ACTOR*

At the end of this shoot [*Remember the Night*], Preston Sturges said, "It's been a pleasure working with you," and I said, "I wish I could say the same about you." I don't like to be that way, but he was terrible, really cruel.

Marjorie Main ——— *ACTRESS*

I would've liked to have gotten away from playing those gravely, scratching old hens. But when I played Ma Kettle in *The Egg and I* and received an Academy nomination, the die was cast. All the roles I got after that were variations of Ma Kettle. I enjoyed 'em, no denying it, but I would've enjoyed 'em more if a queen or two had been slipped in along the way. And I don't mean queen of Tobacco Road.

Joseph L. Mankiewicz ——— *DIRECTOR/WRITER*

A Letter to Three Wives?

A Letter to Four Wives was the script I turned in. I have nothing but praise for [studio chief Darryl] Zanuck, based upon his taste and experience with screenplays the first time he reads them—that's the time you let Darryl tell you. I was having a helluva time getting it to manageable length. He read it and said, "You've got one wife too many." He was right. I cut out a whole story—a former governor's daughter, it was—and everything fell into place.

UNIVERSAL-INTERNATIONAL presents

CLAUDETTE COLBERT

FRED MacMURRAY

"The EGG and I"

with MARJORIE MAIN

LOUISE ALLBRITTON · PERCY KILBRIDE

BILLY HOUSE · RICHARD LONG

a best-seller
becomes
a best picture!

The Egg and I
By Betty MacDonald

From the Best Selling Book by BETTY MacDONALD · Directed by CHESTER ERSKINE

Produced and Written for the Screen by CHESTER ERSKINE and FRED F. FINKLEHOFFE

A UNIVERSAL-INTERNATIONAL PICTURE

Fredric March—ACTOR

Joan Crawford was a nice person, but a real movie star. She even brought her own music to the set [of *Susan and God*]—a whole entourage, a violinist and pianist, to play her favorite songs, to get her into the proper mood for the scene. Director George Cukor never said much about the music—or anything else—to Joan. She was the *star.*

Groucho Marx—ACTOR

We were making a picture called *A Night in Casablanca.* This was the final day of shooting. We were on a very short budget. We had to finish up that night. It was after midnight. And here I was, hanging by my knees, upside down. I said, "What the hell, I'm 62 years old. I've got enough money. What the hell am I doing, hanging by my legs at two o'clock in the morning? I'm through with that kind of stuff."

Virginia Mayo—ACTRESS

The Princess and the Pirate was so successful that I was given a lot of resulting publicity by the Goldwyn Studios that helped forward my career. I got wonderful reviews and would have been the top new star in Hollywood if Lauren Bacall hadn't debuted at the same time in *To Have and Have Not.*

Una Merkel—ACTRESS

I remember the first day I worked with W. C. Fields on *The Bank Dick,* he was two hours late on the set. He was due at nine and came in at 11, and he'd had quite a night the night before, I guess. The first scene was all of us sitting around the table—I was his daughter. I was supposed to say "Good morning, pater," and kiss him. So in the rehearsal he apologized, because you could smell the alcohol, and I said, "Mr. Fields, on you it smells like Chanel No. 5," and he said, "Honey, you're in!" From then on, he was just wonderful to me.

Ray Milland—ACTOR

Director Mitch Leisen, in his perfectionism insisted we use real booze in that scene at the bar where I'm trying to get Claudette Colbert drunk in *Arise, My Love.* Crème de menthe and champagne—what a ghastly mixture.

We did three bad takes, kept drinking through each one, and on the fourth take we got it right. Mitch said, "Just one more to be sure." Claudette looked at me and said, "I don't think I can stand any more." We did it and I managed to stagger away when it was over, but Claudette and Walter Abel turned around and fell flat on their faces, dead drunk. Mitch had to call the studio ambulance to take them home. He was laughing so hard, nobody enjoyed it more than he did, even if he did lose half a day's shooting.

* * *

The Major and the Minor? I was driving home from Paramount after work, exhausted. In the rear window I saw a green car trailing me for miles. Finally it caught up with me at

Melrose and Doheny. I heard somebody yelling at me, "Would you work in a picture I'm going to direct?" It was Billy Wilder. He was grinning. I said, "Sure." I was too tired to go into it with him and thought he wasn't serious anyway. A few weeks later I got the script. I liked the story. It didn't bother me that it was Billy's first picture. Hell, in those days you finished one picture on Friday and started a new one on Monday.

One place where I figured Billy was wrong was in thinking Ginger Rogers would look convincing as a 12-year-old kid. I was wrong. His intuition was right. Like when he put me in *Lost Weekend.* When I saw her in the rushes with her bosom taped down, in bobby sox, no make-up, that white straw sailor hat, sucking a lollipop, she was a delectable little girl.

Marilyn Monroe ——— ACTRESS

Why am I called "the Mmmm Girl"? Well, it seems it started in Detroit where they were having a sneak preview of my picture *Love Happy.* Some people can't whistle so they went "Mmmm."

Dick Moore ——— ACTOR

When I kissed Shirley Temple in *Miss Annie Rooney,* I was 16 and hoped the world didn't know my secret: I had never kissed a girl before. Under any circumstances. And here I was getting paid to kiss Shirley Temple! The director encouraged abandon, urging me, in effect, to renounce the patterns of a lifetime. It was weird. Should I want to kiss her, paid or not? Kissing was something I just *knew* I shouldn't do at all, with any girl, let alone the Princess of the World. What if I got an erection while Hymie Fink and a wall of other cameramen recorded my first sin?

Patricia Neal——ACTRESS

I was quickly introduced to the Hollywood mainstream at a grand New Year's Eve celebration. Early in the evening, a very robust and handsome man took my hand. "I'm Ronnie Reagan," he said. "We're going to do *John Loves Mary* together. I'm very happy to meet you." What a lovely, cheerful man, I thought. The next time I caught sight of him, it was at the stroke of midnight. He was on the terrace with an older woman, weeping into her arms. I later learned that he and his wife, Jane Wyman, were divorcing.

Jack Oakie——ACTOR

Although he didn't realize it at the time he started *The Great Dictator,* Charlie Chaplin, who demanded perfection of himself and took his time achieving it, made a mistake by shooting this picture leisurely.

"Muscles," he said one morning—he nicknamed me Muscles and called me that all through the shooting. "You see what's wrong with this business of ours?" he said, showing me an article in the trade papers which listed the advance schedule of pictures to be made at one of the major studios. "They make 100 pictures in one year, I make one picture in five years."

Although Charlie didn't take five years to make *The Great Dictator,* he still had trouble trying to keep up with the news headlines. By the time the picture was released, Hitler was no longer a funny little clown. By 1940 he had already become a heavy, and was greatly feared. The little man was doing exactly what he said he was going to do: he was going right through all those countries like a dose of salts.

When the picture was released at the end of the year, Chaplin's Hynkel [Hitler] and my Napaloni [Mussolini] found it rough going to get laughs. If Charlie could have made this one in six months instead of what he considered a quick year, the timing would have been better from a comedy point of view.

Merle Oberon——ACTRESS

That Uncertain Feeling was probably the happiest picture I ever made, because director Ernst Lubitsch was such a funny, darling man. He played the piano between every take and there would be laughs. Then I'd always ask him to do the scene for me before I did it only to have a laugh. I remember when Alex [Korda, her husband] came from England and saw the picture, I said, "Alex, how is it, and how am I?" He said, "Oh, fine. You played it beautifully, like a little Jewish girl." Apparently Ernst had been doing the mannerisms, you know, and then *I* did them.

Joe Pasternak — PRODUCER

We were sitting in the commissary when Marlene Dietrich spotted John Wayne. "Mommy wants that for Christmas!" she shouted. She'd never seen him before, she never watched "B" Westerns, and they made a good team. She satirized her Shanghai Lil image in *Seven Sinners* and he blushed furiously when she came on to him. But he'd also put her across his knee and spank her.

Lee Patrick — ACTRESS

Directors I enjoyed working with include Eddie Buzzell [on *Keep Your Powder Dry*]. This starred Lana Turner, Laraine Day and Susan Peters and I had a very good role as a WAC recruit. But this was MGM and I recall Eddie coming to my dressing room and saying, "Lee, you'll be so funny in this if those bitches will just let you."

H. C. Potter — DIRECTOR

I've been able to get along with almost everybody I ever worked with. With Loretta Young in *The Farmer's Daughter,* we ended up doing it my way. She didn't feel very happy about it for several weeks, but after she won the Academy Award, she felt better.

Irving Rapper — DIRECTOR

The Voice of the Turtle had been a big hit on Broadway with Margaret Sullavan, whom they didn't even try to get for the movie. I wanted Olivia de Havilland, but Jack Warner refused to use her because she'd won the seven-year contract dispute with the studio. He said, "I'd rather close the joint down!" I tried unsuccessfully to get June Allyson. Warner suggested I use Eleanor Parker. Eve Arden—who was marvelous—had already been signed. I asked Jack to let me cast the boy. He said, "Okay." I called Dana Andrews. Then I heard that Ronald Reagan had been given the part. I fought it, but lost.

Reagan came into my office, straddled a chair—like a horse—and said: "The story stinks! I don't like it. I'm doing it as a favor to Jack Warner." We went through the motions of filming.

In the middle of the movie, there was a scene at the Plaza Hotel. The soldier (Reagan) and the actress (Parker) have had a fight. He sees her sitting alone and, in pantomime, asks for a dance. While they're dancing, he kisses her. "Cut! What the hell was the kiss for?" He said, "I think it's cute." "Then look for a cute director. If you kiss her now, we might as well throw out the final 60 pages."

He didn't like wearing a sergeant's uniform. I didn't know he had his eye on being Commander-in-Chief.

Martha Raye — ACTRESS

My favorite job in any medium was my role in *Monsieur Verdoux.* Charlie Chaplin called me when I was playing the Latin Quarter in Chicago and asked me to do a role in the film. I thought somebody was kidding and hung up on him. He called back and suggested I have my

agent check him out. It turned out to be on the level.

He wrote the part with me in mind. The screenplay is about the Bluebeard legend, and I played the part of the wife he couldn't kill. I was extremely honored to work with him; I learned a great deal. I was a little nervous when I started, but he was marvelous. He told me he had written it for me and said I should just relax until we had time to rehearse. Then I felt comfortable.

On the set, I called him Chuck and people around were aghast because everyone calls him Charles or Mr. Chaplin. When he was in Hollywood last year [1971], Walter Matthau gave a party for him, and I said, "Hello, Charles." His reply was, "What's the matter with Chuck?"

Ronald Reagan ——— ACTOR

I fussed around trying to get out of *The Voice of the Turtle.* Jack Warner bought the rights to this reigning play by John van Druten a long time before and had earmarked it for me while I was still in the service. I've since learned that he stubbornly hung on even when stars like Cary Grant were offered. Perhaps the fact that I didn't know this at the time points up one of the shortcomings of our business: we just don't talk things over with each other. Here was Jack feeling rebuffed, and all because John Huston had dangled a role in his now classic *The Treasure of the Sierra Madre* under my hammy nose. Both pictures would shoot at the same time, so it was one or the other—there was no way to have both.

I wanted to work with Huston, one of the real geniuses in our world. I'm sure John still believes that if I had stamped my foot firmly before the front office brass, I could have had my choice. What he doesn't know is that I *did* put my foot down. Then the studio put its foot down on top of mine. I was under exclusive contract: if I said no to *Voice of the Turtle,* there would be no part in *Treasure* because it was a Warner picture, too.

So there I was, back in uniform, unhappy but luckier than I deserved to be. If the "uniform" line is confusing, let me recall to your mind that *Voice of the Turtle* concerns a lonely soldier on furlough. The girl the soldier inevitably meets and romances was played by Eleanor Parker, and even here I was a sorehead. A number of new performers had come along while I was flying my Air Force desk and she was one of them. To me she was unknown, and I wanted the studio to borrow June Allyson from MGM.

It only took me one scene with Eleanor for me to realize I'd be lucky if I could stay even. She is one of the truly fine actresses in motion pictures, as three Oscar nominations attest, and by my vote at least a couple of those nominations should have been crowned with victory.

Anne Revere——— ACTRESS

Flame of New Orleans—I'll never forget that one. Director René Clair was a beautiful man, so handsome, but Marlene Dietrich had to have her way, you know. She actually stopped the shooting of one scene because she thought she had discerned that the neckline of my dress was a bit lower than hers. Isn't that funny? Also, during the filming, an assistant director said to me, "You are homely enough to share the same frame with Dietrich."

Debbie Reynolds——— ACTRESS

My first movie was *June Bride,* at Warners. I had a bit as a guest at the wedding. When they were shooting the big love scene between the stars, Bette Davis and Robert Montgomery, I sneaked up on the catwalk about 20 feet above to watch. After a couple of takes, they started to kiss again when suddenly one of my elbows slipped from the railing, causing me to lose my balance slightly and one of my shoes to make a knocking sound on the metal walk. Miss Davis stopped the kiss and screamed, "Who's that? Someone's up there! Someone's watching! This is supposed to be a closed set!" I ran down the stairs and out. I was sure she'd murder me.

Years later, when we co-starred in *The Catered Affair,* we became friends. She always called me "Deborah."

Ginger Rogers——— ACTRESS

My favorite roles? It's like asking a mother which children she loves most. *Primrose Path* was a turning point in my career, and right after that came *Kitty Foyle. Roxie Hart* was another favorite. After hearing just the first 15 minutes of dialogue from a comedy called *The Major and the Minor,* I agreed to do it. The producer said, "We hope you don't mind, but we're going to try out this new director." His name was Billy Wilder.

Gail Russell——————ACTRESS

At first, I wasn't crazy to do *Our Hearts Were Young and Gay.* It was based on the book by Cornelia Otis Skinner and Emily Kimbrough about their teen-age misadventures in Europe during the 1920s. I felt inadequate to portray a distinguished (and still living!) woman like Miss Skinner, even at so early an age.

Also, it was a comedy and things just didn't seem too funny to me at the time. I was still new to pictures and a little frightened of them yet. But my good friend Diana Lynn, who had read the book and was dying to play Emily, thought I'd be right as Cornelia and really pushed me to do it with her. My acting coach, Bill Russell, also said, "Grab it. You'll have fun. But it's a wild and woolly comedy part and you must be prepared to make a damn fool of yourself!"

I gave in. The script had Diana and I doing everything: wearing money bags that dangled between our legs; wrapping ourselves in molting white fur coats; losing our clothes on top of Notre Dame Cathedral; getting measles.

It turned out to be my happiest filmmaking experience and a big success, as well as my favorite movie.

Rosalind Russell———ACTRESS

I'd taken myself off to Fairfield, Connecticut, where the Duchess [her sister] and her husband lived. We were about to sit down to dinner when I got a call from Benny Thau at Metro. "Come back," he said, "get your make-up kit and go over to Columbia. You're gonna do a picture with Cary Grant."

The Duchess told the other dinner guests, "Rosalind's going to work with Cary Grant, isn't it marvelous?" and they were thrilled and agreed. "Mahvelous!"

The next morning, going into New York on the train with my brother-in-law and most of the people who had been at dinner, everyone had his own copy of *The New York Times,* and it said in the *Times* that Rosalind Russell was to play this part in a picture called *His Girl Friday.* Then it said the names of all the women who'd turned the part down. Howard Hawks, who would be directing, had tried to get Ginger Rogers, Irene Dunne, Jean Arthur; he'd asked every leading woman in town before Harry Cohn had stuck him with me. I didn't dare look up from the paper. I kept thinking of all those people saying, "Oh, how mahvelous!"

* * *

His Girl Friday—a marvelous film, a mad memory. We ad-libbed most of that, you know. Made it all up. Sure, we had the Hecht and MacArthur script but we built on it.

There'd be things like the scene where Cary Grant and I were typing away, visible from the waist up. I was trying to stay ahead of Cary—that's hard to do, steal a scene from him. Just as we finished a take, he got up from the table and walked off.

Paramount's
OUR HEARTS WERE YOUNG AND GAY
starring
GAIL RUSSELL
of "The Uninvited"
DIANA LYNN
of "The Miracle of Morgan's Creek"
CHARLIE RUGGLES · DOROTHY GISH · BEULAH BONDI · JAMES BROWN · BILL EDWARDS
Screen Play by Sheridan Gibney
DIRECTED BY LEWIS ALLEN

He was in his undershorts and socks. Perfectly groomed otherwise. With things like that you stay loose.

* * *

The first picture I made after Freddie [Brisson] and I were married was *Take a Letter, Darling* at Paramount. I played an advertising woman who hires Fred MacMurray as her secretary. It was a funny idea—turning the tables, having the lady order the guy around, "Stand up, not bad, go get a fitting for a tuxedo." After that I played a whole gang of career women. If you want to lie down on a table, I can operate on you.

* * *

My Sister Eileen was great; it won me my first Oscar nomination. Janet Blair, who was still new to pictures, played Eileen. Right off, in her insecurity, I guess, she began to upstage me. I took her aside and said, "Listen, honey, Eileen is a sweet but rather selfish little girl and if the audience catches you pulling stunts like that they're going to hate you. Besides, if it's going to be a contest, I've got several more years of experience and can take you." I taught her some legitimate tricks of the trade and she behaved herself after that. We became friends. For years she told this story in interviews until finally I said, "*Please,* Janet, let's get another story, for God's sake!"

Joseph Ruttenberg —— CINEMATOGRAPHER

Garbo always was dressed in tailored clothes. We had a picture, *Two-Faced Woman,* where she did a ballroom scene. And they couldn't fit her dresses. They spent thousands of dollars to fit a dress for Garbo. But her bosoms, you know, they never could pull them up. Finally, the day before we had to shoot, George Cukor went to the wardrobe room, and he saw this dress, and he sent for me and I came up in Adrian's office, and he said, "Joe, how do you like the dress for Garbo?" and I said, "Beautiful dress." And she said, "Oh, Joe, you don't like it, eh?" I said, "You know. . . ." She said, "I know, Joe, what am I going to do? God gave me these."

Allan Scott —— SCREENWRITER

In *Skylark* Claudette Colbert had a tightly blocked comedy routine. She had to prepare a meal aboard a yacht during a storm. It is one of the most hilarious scenes I have ever seen on the screen. As she tried to make a meal, the salad and salad oil fall on the floor and the food she is cooking slides off the stove, spattering. She slips and flounders all over the floor of the galley, trying to rescue some coffee beans she has spilled. She slides the length of the floor, falling against the refrigerator, which opens to a solemn, sad-eyed fish looking at her.

Then, mucky and disheveled, she scoops up some beans, gets back to the sink, grinds the beans into a cup, pours in some cold water and, determined not to spill a drop (and she never did), makes her way gingerly up the stairs. When she triumphantly reaches the top, the boat suddenly lurches and she slides back down the stairs, across the galley floor once again and ends up in a heap, weeping.

Claudette did it in one take, a marvelous piece of funny improvisation. As she passed us on the set, she merely said, "Who the hell said I couldn't clown?" I'll bet Claudette could have repeated it.

Ann Sheridan —— ACTRESS

I did *Good Sam* in '48. We shot 111 pages—more than that. It was a huge, elongated picture and I worked for 11 weeks on it. I think cutting may have had something to do with it [failing]. It was an amusing script and it was a delight to work with director Leo McCarey and Gary Cooper. I'd known them both a long, long time. I think the main thing that was wrong was that Cooper and I did not have that spark together. There was a lot of comedy, but so much was cut out, you cannot believe it.

* * *

I Was a Male War Bride—I loved it. Ten months! I got pneumonia in England, where we went to shoot the film. I was the first one to collapse. And then, just after I had gotten back to working six hours a day, Cary Grant came down with jaundice, hepatitis. Lord! The things we went through.

Walter Slezak —— ACTOR

During the making of *Once Upon a Honeymoon* Cary Grant got married to Barbara Hutton. [Producer-director-author] Leo McCarey admonished us all: "*Please,* no jokes!" So I only gave him a bag of knick-knacks from the five-and-ten and all was dignified. But when he left the studio, a fresh little newsboy stood at the gate, yelling at the top of his voice, "Cary Grant Hits Jackpot!"

Barbara Stanwyck —— ACTRESS

Preston Sturges and I were under contract to Paramount in the early forties, and I met him when I was shooting *Remember the Night,* which he'd written. Mitch Leisen was the director, but Sturges was around a lot, and one day he said to me, "Someday I'm going to write a real screwball comedy for you." *Night* was a delightful light comedy, swell for me and Fred MacMurray, but hardly screwball, and I replied that nobody would ever think of writing anything like that for me—a murderess, sure. But he said, "Just you wait."

He kept his word—and how—but by that time I wasn't under contract and he'd have to borrow me. Which would kill it, I figured. He also wanted to borrow Hank Fonda from Fox—another piece of intriguing casting. Hank had been Zanuck's Abraham Lincoln in so many things, whether his name was Tom Joad or Frank James; how did Sturges know he was a sensational light comedian?

Somehow *The Lady Eve* all came together. It's one of my favorites and certainly one of Sturges' greatest. *Eve* was lucky for me another way. My character, Jean Harrington, is a very glamorous lady and for the first time I got a really sensational wardrobe, designed by Edith Head.

* * *

Christmas in Connecticut—I didn't kill anyone in that picture! In spite of the fact that I've always *loved* to kill on-screen, it was a pleasant change of pace for me. It gave me another chance to do comedy. It was the first of three films I did with director Peter Godfrey. It was fast-paced, which I loved, and we had a delightful cast of pros that included Reginald Gardiner, Sydney Greenstreet, Dennis Morgan and S. Z. Sakall. It was a very relaxed project and I enjoyed participating in it—but never in my wildest dreams did I think it would be resurrected every holiday season! Obviously, from the letters I've received, the public enjoyed it then and still does—*that* pleases me.

Gale Storm —— ACTRESS

One I remember was *Lure of the Islands,* which was shot in the studio [Monogram]. They threw up a few thatched huts and palm tress and we were an island. One of the stars was Margie Hart, a famous stripper in those days. We wore grass skirts and grass bras. Apparently, the weaving on Margie's bras wasn't tight enough, and under the bright lights the real Margie began to show through. The director stopped shooting and hesitantly explained the problem to Margie and told her they'd have to re-work her bra before they could proceed. She said O.K., took off her bra and handed it to him.

Preston Sturges —— DIRECTOR—SCREENWRITER

Paramount released *The Miracle of Morgan's Creek* in January 1944, about a month after I left the studio. It was extremely well received and was shown throughout the world. As a consequence, I received many letters, including bitterly denunciatory ones from analphabets who believed the sextuplets were the result of the heroine having been promiscuous with six different men. Education, though compulsory, seems to be spreading slowly.

Elizabeth Taylor —— ACTRESS

I was terrified before my first screen kiss in *Cynthia,* but my second screen kiss was a breeze. It was with Peter Lawford in *Julia Misbehaves.* Peter to me was the last word in sophistication. He was terribly handsome, and I had a tremendous crush on him. He invited me out twice after shooting, but he never did kiss me in private life. I was so thrilled that he had taken me out, because I was only 16 and felt about 12. The whole company knew I had a crush on him. In the scene where he had to kiss me I was supposed to say, "Oh, Ritchie, what are we going to do?" After the kiss I looked at him, turned a hot scarlet and said, "Oh, Peter, what am I going to do?" And the whole company fell down laughing.

Gene Tierney —— ACTRESS

In 1943 I had a chance to do a costume comedy under Ernst Lubitsch called *Heaven Can Wait.* Lubitsch was a little fellow, with straight dark hair combed to one side with a cigar poking out of the corner of his mouth. He had been one of the great European directors and had cast Greta Garbo in the classic *Ninotchka.* He was regarded as a master of urbane and sophisticated comedy.

But he was a tyrant on the set, the most demanding of directors. After one scene, which took from noon until five to get, I was almost in tears from listening to Lubitsch shout at me. The next day I looked him in the eye and said, "Mr. Lubitsch, I'm willing to do my best but I just can't go on working on this picture if you're going to keep shouting at me."

"I'm paid to shout at you," he bellowed.

"Yes," I said, "and I'm paid to take it—but not enough."

After a tense pause, Lubitsch broke out laughing. From then on we got along famously.

Spencer Tracy —— ACTOR

I thought I'd fix Hedy Lamarr one day. We had a scene in *I Take This Woman* where she had to sit on my lap. The night before we did the scene, I bought a big banana that wasn't ripe yet and was pretty hard. I slipped the banana down the front of my pants, and when Hedy sat down on it, she let out a scream and jumped about 10 fuckin' feet in the air.

Rudy Vallee —— ACTOR

Preston Sturges, the great comedy director, decided to go to the Pantages Theater to see a Ronald Colman picture. It was part of a double feature and Sturges miscalculated his timing. He was therefore subjected to a portion of the other picture, *Time Out for Rhythm,* which starred that great thespian Rudy Vallee. Preston was astounded by the fact that each time I was required to be serious, the audience roared. "My God," he said to himself, "this guy is funny and doesn't know it!"

As luck would have it, he was at that moment planning a picture called *The Palm Beach Story* and needed someone to portray "the richest man in the world, John D. Hackensacker III." In all honesty, I must volunteer the further intelligence that a member of Sturges' staff was related to my agent.

At any rate, I got the part. At the time it was about as off-beat an idea in casting as the industry had ever seen. The front office executives in both Hollywood and New York assumed that Sturges had finally gone completely mad. When Claudette Colbert, who was to co-star with Joel McCrea, was informed of the choice she was stunned. "Oh, *nooo!*" She gasped. Then she thought for a moment. "But, of *course.* Who else could do it?"

Before three days' rushes on the picture had been shown, I had received five more offers.

Salka Viertel—— *SCREENWRITER*

The attacks upon *Two-Faced Woman* were unjustified; it was also not true that it had "degraded" a great actress. I saw it in London 25 years after it was made, when age and events had made me objective and even indifferent. I found the audience amused and appreciative; it had very funny scenes and, thanks to Sam [Behrman], excellent and witty dialogue. But I thought that Garbo was miscast. Unlike *Ninotchka,* in which Lubitsch had humorously exploited her unique personality, *Two-Faced Woman* demanded a flippant comedienne. Nevertheless, Garbo's beauty and charm were prodigiously rewarding even in this unimportant film.

Helen Walker———— *ACTRESS*

I was at a party the other night and a little man I had never met before came up to me and exlaimed, "Betty Hutton! You were in that funny old movie about the whip-cracking hillbilly mother with the half-wit twin sons—where everyone glowed in the dark before they died. What was it called?" Well, I told him *I* wasn't called Betty Hutton—that I *knew.* And with material like that in a picture, wouldn't you think I would be able to remember the title? I simply drew a blank! I finally thought of it this morning: *Murder, He Says*—that was also the name of a song Betty Hutton sang in another Paramount picture. I've been in Hollywood for 15 years, and have done almost 20 pictures, and all they remember me for is *Murder, He Says*—and they don't really even remember *that, or* me!

Joseph Walker ——— *CINEMATOGRAPHER*

On a weekday night, midway of making *They All Kissed the Bride,* I

attended a party with friends at the Mocambo nightclub on Sunset Boulevard. Seldom did we go out while I worked, but this was a special occasion. At the height of the evening's gaiety we passed by a ringside table where Joan Crawford and her party were "living it up." She spotted us at about the same moment we saw her.

"Joe!" she called in a shattering voice. "What the hell are you doing here?!"

I grinned. "I might ask the same of you—what are *you* doing here at this hour? You have close-ups tomorrow!"

"Yeah, but goddamnit," she screeched good-naturedly, "you're photographing me—you gotta have your rest!"

Raoul Walsh ——— DIRECTOR

"Two things I have to tell you." Jack Warner sat back and gave me the executive eye. "Cagney wants you to direct him in *The Strawberry Blonde* and Ann Sheridan thinks I'm Dracula." We had discussed this picture before and I thought the casting was finished. Nobody had told me that Ann was feuding with the studio.

I tried to persuade her to let bygones be bygones. "This can be one hell of a picture, Ann—with you, Cagney, Olivia de Havilland, Alan Hale, Jack Carson; it'll be a natural. And you'll play the title role. Wardrobe, I hear, has done a bang-up job of those Gay Nineties costumes."

I might as well have talked to the wall.

"Who the hell can we get?" Warner grumbled. "That part was made for Sheridan and she knows it. This is a hold-up!"

The name came to me before he finished speaking. I had seen her in a film at Columbia recently. Rita Hayworth became a star overnight as Virginia Brush, the Strawberry Blonde, and started on her way to becoming the love goddess of the 1940s.

Clifton Webb ——— ACTOR

If anyone could have watched us filming *Sitting Pretty,* he would have been convinced I am the fatherly type. The first time I met the child, Roddy McCaskill, I was to give him a bath and he was to struggle with me. But he laughed and had a good time. He liked me.

The director, Walter Lang, had all kinds of trouble with us after that. We got on so famously that Roddy refused to get mad at me. Not even when I dumped the bowl of oatmeal on his head. He smiled, waved his hand and said, "Nice man." I was flabbergasted. So was Lang. We worked for hours to persuade him he should act as if he detested me.

Orson Welles ——— SCREENWRITER

I have written at least five scenarios for comedy and in the theater I have done more comedies than drama. Comedy fills me with enthusiasm but I have never succeeded in getting a film producer to let me make one. One of the best things I did for television was a program in the genre of comedy. For example, I like Howard Hawks' comedies very much. I even wrote about 25 minutes of one of them. It was called *I Was a Male War Bride.* The scenarist fell ill and I wrote almost a third of the film.

Mae West ——— ACTRESS/SCREENWRITER

W. C. Fields was a remarkable, difficult man. A fine comic writer, a miser who had 200 bank accounts under fictitious names all over the world—and a hater of dogs and children and civilization.

Bill's doctors had been after him to taper down to a quart or so a day. Realizing that his system must require some splashing ointment to keep away the shakes, I knew he would have difficulty staying on the wagon [during *My Little Chickadee*].

Eddie Cline, the director, a graduate of the Mack Sennett school of comedy, assigned members of the staff to keep a sharp watch that Bill didn't do any nipping between scenes. But Bill devised various stratagems to have his liquids handy, bringing it in disguised as a Coke, done up in a parcel, wrapped in a napkin—anything that would prevent an accidental gleam of a bottle catching my eye. Once he complained, "Someone has stolen the cork out of my lunch!"

Ready to begin a day's shooting, I saw that Bill was entertaining a crowd of extras, and they were howling. Something told me that he was over-stimulated. The assistant director confirmed my suspicions: "I'm afraid Bill has slipped off the wagon. He's telling the kid actors to go out and play in the traffic."

I asked the director if there were scenes we could shoot without Fields. There were.

"All right," I said, "pour him out of here."

By now *My Little Chickadee* has played for years and has been seen by hundreds of millions in theaters and on TV. Some people have gotten the quaint idea that I made more than one film with W. C. Fields. No way, baby. Once was enough.

Billy Wilder——DIRECTOR/SCREENWRITER

I was once making a picture with Marlene Dietrich and Jean Arthur, *A Foreign Affair.* I had known Marlene when I was a newspaperman in Berlin, and we were very friendly. In the middle of the shooting, one midnight the doorbell rang and there was Jean Arthur, absolutely frenzied, eyes bulging, and in back of her was her husband, Frank Ross.

I said, "What is it, Jean?" She said, "What did you do with my close-up?" I said, "What close-up?" She said, "The close-up where I look so beautiful." I said, "What do you mean, what did I do with it?" She said, "You burned it. Marlene told you to burn that close-up. She does not want me to look good." This is typical. It's a little insane asylum, and they are all inmates.

Shelley Winters——ACTRESS

One glorious day the [Columbia] casting department notified me that I was going to do a part in a film with Rosalind Russell, *What a Woman!* When I got the script, I found I was a secretary with one line: "You can't go in there now, miss." The first words I ever spoke in a film. But I said them to Rosalind Russell herself.

A year or so later, when this so-called comedy was finally released, there was a private showing at the Motion Picture Academy Theater, and my mother went with me to see it. The picture was a good deal less than brilliant. After, I introduced her to Harry Cohn, and my mother's classic remark to him was: "You know, Mr. Cohn, you're very lucky to have Shelley in that picture." His reply: "Yeah, I know. And I see who she takes after."

Loretta Young——ACTRESS

When I got an Academy Award, it was for a silly thing called *The Farmer's Daughter.* And that year I was up against Susan Hayward for *Smash-Up* and Rosalind Russell for *Mourning Becomes Electra.* That's a pretty gutsy role. And I think Joan Crawford was up that year, yes, for *Possessed,* which was also a very gutsy role.

I personally voted for Susan Hayward, because I was absolutely stunned by this performance, and when I saw it, I knew I couldn't do it as well. I knew that woman had done that part magnificently. And I voted for her because I think she deserved it. But I got that award playing a straightforward, honest, factual, good girl.

Robert Young——ACTOR

I thought the script for *Sitting Pretty* was the funniest thing I'd ever read and that the part of the baby

sitter was wonderful. That was the role I assumed I would play. Then, when I was about three-quarters of the way through, there was a section in the screenplay which said the character was a good dancer. There was a footnote which was written in by the writer, F. Hugh Herbert. It read: "And he is—a great dancer." Then, in parenthesis, this was added: "Hi, Clift." It was signed "F. H. H." I couldn't understand this at first and then I realized the part was for Clifton Webb—not me. I had to read the script all over and I decided my part wasn't so bad, either.

Dramas

Dana Andrews — ACTOR

William Wyler didn't want me in *The Best Years of Our Lives.* Since I'd played in his *The Westerner,* Mr. Wyler hadn't seen me in anything but in the meantime I'd done a lot of pictures. *The Best Years of Our Lives* was in 1946 and I had worked for him in 1939. When we worked the first day, we were in the scene where Fredric March, the boy with the paraplegic arms and I were coming into Boon

City. It was up high and I climbed down a ladder and he said, "Dana, come here! What happened to you! You're a very good actor!" I laughed and said, "Willie, thank you very much but I've made 20 pictures since I first saw you. Why, if I hadn't improved somewhat, I'd be a pretty stupid actor." In his mind, it was practically yesterday—he'd been in England all during the war with the Eighth Air Force.

Eve Arden——————ACTRESS

For the first time, censorship was bent [in *My Reputation*]. My screen husband and I were filmed in bed without the obligatory one foot on the floor. A breakthrough, but I refuse to take the blame for where things have gone from there.

Mary Astor——————ACTRESS

I was assigned the role of Marmee in *Little Women.* The schedule was a long one. And there were many sequences in which I didn't appear. Fred Zinnemann was doing a picture called *Act of Violence* at the time and there was a small but interesting part he wanted me for.

So for two weeks I was with the Zinnemann company playing a sleazy, aging whore, with Van Heflin and Robert Ryan. It was such a contrast that it was stimulating—and reviving.

One afternoon when I had some time between shots I walked over to the lovely *Little Women* set just for the hell of it. Director Mervyn LeRoy, who didn't know I was moonlighting in another production, took a startled look at me, came over, shocked, and said, "What the hell have you got that kind of an outfit on for? What's the matter with you, anyway—you look like a two-bit tart!" I was very pleased.

Lucille Ball——————ACTRESS

For *The Big Street,* I was concerned with what I had to do with Mr. [Henry] Fonda. I was very terrified at working with the first big star I'd been associated with. And I was also very concerned with the bitchiness of the character in this Damon Runyon script.

I didn't talk to Mr. Runyon about it, but I did talk to Charles Laughton. And he said, "Well, let me read the script," which was *very* nice of him because he was a very busy man then and a very big star. But I had known him briefly around the studio [RKO].

He called me that night and said, "Could you come over to our house?"

And I said, "Yes, sir!" and found where they lived, out in Brentwood.

And he said, "This is a very fine script, and a very great chance for you. I understand you have never done very much."

And I said, "No sir! I've never done anything comparable to this. I've just done some leads in 'B' pictures."

He said, "This is a fine script!"

And I said, "But it's so bitchy. It's so unrealistically rude, crude, crass."

He said, "You don't set about to soften Damon Runyon. The characters Nicely Nicely Johnson, Racetrack Sam and all those names were characters that he knew."

And he said, "My advice to you is to play the bitchiest bitch that ever was! Whatever the script calls for. And don't try to soften it. Just play it!"

And—the picture *escaped.* It was very strange. It never was—what you call "released," never publicized. The director died, Damon Runyon died, Henry Fonda didn't belong to the studio, I left the studio, the cutter died! And the studio changed hands, and there were just some pictures lying around. *The Big Street* was one of them.

And it went on the second bill at the Pantages Theater—and it's still playing! And that was 20-some years ago, and you can still see it on television, late at night.

* * *

I didn't know Henry Fonda all that well before we began *The Big Street,* and I sure didn't want to know him all that well when we were finished. He hardly talked to me the whole time, and when he did, well...

The director [Irving Reis] and I rehearsed the scene. I started swaying my shoulders, and tried dancing with only my arms. I try to make my legs move, but they won't. I'm dancing, sitting up in bed, looking at my paralyzed legs. Irving was terrific. He said that I had done it perfectly and he wanted to shoot it right away while we still had the mood. I looked over to the door, and Fonda was standing there. He had watched the rehearsal, and as soon as Irving started setting up the shot, he came over to me and said, "You're *not* going to do it like that, are you?" I said, "Well, Irving said it was good." Fonda just shook his head back and forth and walked away. Try to do a scene after that.

Anne Baxter ——— ACTRESS

The Razor's Edge contained my only great performance. When we shot that hospital scene in which Sophie loses her husband, child and everything else, I relived the death of my brother, whom I adored and who died at three. It gives me chills right now to think of it.

Ingrid Bergman ——— ACTRESS

In *Saratoga Trunk,* I played this nasty woman, very egotistical, spoiled, shouting and screaming, and affected in every way. People said before we started filming, "absolutely wrong for you." I couldn't care less because it was exactly what I wanted to do. I was a New Orleans bitch and that was completely new.

* * *

I had been in some very big pictures, but on paper *Arch of Triumph* looked like it could be the biggest yet. Big new studio (Enterprise), big book (by Eric Maria Remarque), big cast (Charles Boyer, Charles Laughton), big director (Lewis Milestone), big budget ($5,000,000). It turned out to be one of the biggest flops in Hollywood history. It helped to close down the studio, and I don't think the careers of Boyer, Milestone or

myself ever fully recovered. As for Charles Laughton, he was soon appearing with Abbott and Costello.

***Curtis Bernhardt*——DIRECTOR**

There were problems at first on *A Stolen Life.* I didn't know Bette Davis when she first summoned me for this task. So I went to a showing of Miss Davis' costumes. The whole staff that she'd assembled was there and I walked in as the new director. The costume designer was a friend of hers. Whenever a new costume would come out, she would rave, "Isn't that wonderful . . . it's glorious. . . ." After the third time of "wonderful, glorious" I asked her very softly, "Excuse me, Miss Davis, don't you think these costumes are a little theatrical?" I thought I was very diplomatic, but my words had the opposite effect.

She burst out in a flood of insults. "Theatrical, theatrical! Let's stop talking that way, Mr. Bern*hardt.*" She went on for ten minutes until I finally said, "Thank you, Miss Davis," and got up and walked out. She asked me where I was going. I said, "You don't need a director, you need a yes-man." She said, "That's not true," ran after me, grabbed me firmly by the hand and led me back. That was my first encounter with Miss Davis. After that, her attitude was a little more demure.

* * *

Compared with Bette Davis, Joan Crawford, whom I subsequently

directed in *Possessed,* was as easy to work with as can be. She was naturally a little subdued because she was the studio's second-ranking star, Bette being Number One. She threw her handbag at me several times when, having just done a picture with Bette, I called Joan "Bette" by mistake.

Joan Blondell———ACTRESS

Thank God censorship has improved since *A Tree Grows in Brooklyn.* They cut the best scene I ever played, and the best piece of acting I have ever done.

Aunt Cissy is quite a woman, and is loved by everybody in the family. She takes the colorful tins the contraceptives are placed in—they have girls' faces on them and names like Agnes or Betsy—and gives them to the children to play with.

One day she accidentally leaves a rubber in a tin. The little boy asks me about it, and in the most beautiful writing the author, Betty Smith, did, Cissy tries to explain to the children what the rubber is, not by talking about the actual thing, but about love and life itself. It was very simply done, and all of us players hugged each other spontaneously at the end of the scene. It was marvelous and the Legion of Decency made us take it out. Wasn't that stupid?

Clarence Brown———DIRECTOR

Mickey Rooney, to me, is the closest thing to a genius I ever

worked with. I still don't know how he did it, either. He never paid attention. Between takes [on *The Human Comedy*], he'd be off somewhere calling his bookmaker, then he'd come back and go straight into a scene as if he'd been working on it for three days. That scene where he reads the telegram announcing his brother's death—we must have shot that thing four or five times and each time he read it as though he had seen the telegram for the first time.

* * *

My favorite picture ever is *The Yearling*. Victor Fleming, one of the greatest directors, originally started the picture. But he had just come off the greatest picture ever made, *Gone with the Wind,* and he just wasn't at home with three people. He went on location to Florida and tried, but it was lousy. They shelved it for a year, and then I took it up. Fleming's problem was the kid. He was lousy. They had publicized in all the papers down South that they were looking for a boy to play in *The Yearling.* All the mothers brought their kids, from two to twenty.

When I shot the picture, I went to seven different cities myself, looking for the right kid. I told everyone, even the teachers, that I was a building inspector. I was in Nashville the day after Valentine's Day, and I saw this boy (in a fifth-grade classroom at Nashville's Eakin Elementary School) taking down the Valentines from the wall, and I knew it was him: Claude

Jarman, Jr. He was only ten years old—almost an alley kid. He had never seen a film, even a camera. When I first talked to him, I told him I was from the University of Tennessee and that I was hunting for football players—and I wanted to start early. He fell for it. His parents didn't want any part of it at first, but finally they agreed. He won an Academy Award on this picture.

——— ***PRODUCER/DIRECTOR***

When I was 16, I spent the summer in Atlanta, Georgia. I went through a whole race riot, saw 16 black men murdered by mobs. So when I read this story, *Intruder in the Dust,* I didn't walk, I *ran* up to the front office at MGM. "I've got to make this picture," I said. "You're nuts," said Louis Mayer, because the hero was a black man. "If you owe me anything, you owe me a chance to make this picture," I said. "Okay, go ahead," he said.

I had trouble, too. I made the picture on location with the people in Oxford, Mississippi. They didn't want me to make it originally. So I went before the city fathers and told them that, if I didn't make it down here, I would make it in Hollywood anyway—the way I wanted to. Finally, they agreed. The first showing was in Oxford, and all those people loved it. It was the greatest night ever in Oxford.

There were four pictures that came out at that time about racial difficulties. I started first, but Metro's wheels grind very slowly. Mine was the last, but by far the best, that came out. I even had a riot in the picture. It was pretty damn good. Well, I got an award from the British Academy, but nothing from the United States. Too hot to handle.

Niven Busch——***STORY EDITOR***

I was story editor on *Little Foxes.* Lillian Hellman had written a big sprawlly script and I said, "Listen, I'd like to cut this." "Well," [producer Samuel Goldwyn] said, "Lillian Hellman says it's all right. [Director William] Wyler loves it." But I cut the shit out of it. And Goldwyn loved the cuts; they saved him a lot of money. When I read the cuts to Wyler he gave me this snarly Hungarian look, but he had to take the cuts.

James Cagney——***ACTOR***

I worked like a dog on *City for Conquest.* There were some excellent passages in Aben Kandel's novel, passages with genuinely poetic flavor, and all of us doing the picture realized that retaining them (as we were doing) would give *City for Conquest* distinction.

Then I saw the final cut, and this was quite a surprise. The studio had edited out the best scenes in the picture, excellent stuff, leaving only the novel's skeleton. What remained was a trite melodrama. When I realized what they had done, I said to hell with it, and that cured me of seeing my pictures. I even wrote a letter of apology to the author. Yet *City for Conquest* did well at the box office, which ought to prove something or other.

M·G·M's Technicolor prize picture
THE YEARLING
THE YEARLING
STARRING
GREGORY PECK · JANE WYMAN
A CLARENCE BROWN PRODUCTION · CLAUDE JARMAN, JR. AS "JODY"
CLEM BEVANS · MARGARET WYCHERLY · FORREST TUCKER · Screen Play by PAUL OSBORN · Based on the Pulitzer Prize Novel by MARJORIE KINNAN RAWLINGS
Directed by CLARENCE BROWN
PRODUCED BY SIDNEY FRANKLIN
A METRO-GOLDWYN-MAYER PICTURE
PHOTOGRAPHED IN TECHNICOLOR

Jack Carson —————— ACTOR

Like all comedians, I wanted to make people cry. Finally, after years of struggle I got a dramatic role in *The Hard Way.* I got the works. I was in love with Joan Leslie, who wasn't in love with me, and lots of other terrible things happened to me. Finally, to escape from my broken heart, I committed suicide. Did people cry? When *I* went to see the picture I used up three handkerchiefs.

Oleg Cassini —————— COSTUME DESIGNER

Was it silly of me to go berserk over the not very credible studio "romance" between Gene [Tierney] and Tyrone Power during the filming of *The Razor's Edge?*

Actually, Tyrone was a good friend throughout our marriage, but there was a period after the war when he angered me greatly. He and Gene were co-starring in *Razor's Edge,* and the studio (to get some publicity) decided to foment a love affair between them in the columns. Now, I knew this was laughably untrue, but our marriage was in a difficult stage and I felt humiliated.

Cyd Charisse —————— ACTRESS

I was in *East Side, West Side,* which Mervyn LeRoy directed. It was only a small part, but it was a good one. I played a model. The star was Barbara Stanwyck. I had only one scene with her, but I'll never forget it. Barbara never even looked at me through the scene. Even when we were off camera, she ignored me. I am convinced her aim was to make things as difficult for me as she could. She succeeded. I was shy and inexperienced, so that was quite a blow.

Dane Clark —————— ACTOR

The Very Thought of You, that's where I had to bark like a dog when I saw a girl. They were always giving me lines like "You woman, you." Remember those pictures? They had me as a teen-age soldier just back from the Pacific or some place.

Well, I've worked in the Hollywood Canteen, and I've seen some movies on those kids. And they do act like that. But that barking! I ask you, how can you be subtle—how can you underplay when you're making sounds like a dog?

Claudette Colbert —————— ACTRESS

Natalie Wood was an astonishing child—adorable. She had to play a little Austrian girl in *Tomorrow Is Forever,* and they bleached her hair and gave her two little pigtails.

She was only about six and couldn't read. So there was a woman who taught her lines each day, which she had to speak with an Austrian accent. And you know, she never missed once.

She was remarkable. In one scene I had to hold her in my arms while she wept. Well, we couldn't make her stop—she was like a fountain.

She was so lovely, everybody wanted to eat her up.

Stanley Cortez —————— CINEMATOGRAPHER

Smash-Up was an interesting experiment: a film about a drunk, with

Susan Hayward. We had a scene in which the heroine is lying in bed and mumbling; she's having a nightmare, and I went to my doctor to ask him what happens in a person's mind when he is drunk. He told me about the flashing of lights across the brain, and I had lights actually *inside* the lens; and I conducted a kind of symphony of light over her. As she reached a pitch of distress I raised the lights to the highest pitch possible. Susan Hayward helped by actually getting drunk to play the part! I didn't want to do the cliché thing and show her distorted impressions, but rather convey her thoughts with abstract play of lights alone. It was fantastic.

Joan Crawford——— ACTRESS

Humoresque will be out soon now. It's a deliberate contrast to *Mildred Pierce.* I'm through being a type. The day of depending on glamour is gone. In my film with John Garfield I don't come on the screen until reel five, another rule I'm breaking. I like it that way for it's unexpected. You'll see me as a dipsomaniac, and I commit suicide. At Metro they always stalled me when I wanted to progress from my "typical Joan Crawford" mold. They insisted only Garbo could get away with a tragic ending. I disagree. Audiences are far superior to Hollywood's frequent concept of their intelligence. *Acting* is what is wanted in movie theaters now, not boring repetition!

* * *

Exhaustion, depression and satisfaction hit me in waves as I made my favorite movie, *Possessed.*

Most of all it was challenge that drove me to complete this role of a nurse who became mentally unbalanced over her love affair with an architect, played by Van Heflin.

Preparation for the movie made in 1947 was nerve-shattering.

Daily at 5:30 A.M. for six weeks, I went to a mental hospital in nurse's uniform to observe patients subjected to straitjackets, shock treatment and truth serums. Those days taught me compassion for people suffering from emotional and mental illnesses. Normally I'm a happy person. But after I finished making that film I was melancholy for two months.

Although I was exhausted I knew I had done a good job—had met the challenge. That was important to me. Give me a challenge any time and I'll come out a better person for it.

I feel the same way about people. If I work with mediocre people, I become mediocre. Give me a Spencer Tracy, a Clark Gable, a Bette Davis—they are real challenges. Being with them has always kept me on my toes.

And meeting the challenge of *Possessed* made it my favorite film.

* * *

Because I'm afraid they might get false ideas about glamour, I seldom permit [the children] to come to the movie sets.

During the filming of *Daisy Kenyon* at 20th Century-Fox, I did make an exception. When Christina finished school, she decided she wanted to go to summer camp. She had only a few days in between and I let her come on the set so that we could be together more.

Because my pictures lately have dealt with adult problems, I haven't permitted Christina and Christopher to see them. Christina amused me the other day when she came to me and said, "Mother, I don't even know what Mildred Pierce did." She still doesn't.

I had a note from her at camp. It said: "Mommie dearest—I got the candy. It was beautiful. I love you." It's little things like that which bring me more joy than all the praise from a role well done.

Marcia Davenport———*AUTHOR*

I was sitting with Carol Brandt in the projection room of the motion picture company that had made the film of *The Valley of Decision,* which was about to open at Radio City Music Hall. We had seen most of the film, and I was just beginning to relax in relief and reassurance over the fine cast and the faithful and gripping representation of the third of the book which had been used, when [MGM publicity chief] Howard Dietz made his way to us across the dark room, leaned over our shoulders and told us that President Roosevelt had just died.

Bette Davis———*ACTRESS*

When one of his money men warned Sam Goldwyn that *The Little Foxes* might be too caustic to appeal to the film public, Sam rejoindered, "I don't care what it costs—I want to make it!"

* * *

Paul Henreid—one of my favorite people. The part of Jerry Durrance in Olive Higgins Prouty's *Now, Voyager* was American. At first I was against the idea of having a man with a foreign accent play him. And when I saw Paul's first test, I was horrified. For some crazy reason that no one remembers today, he was made up with four coats of pancake, his hair was plastered back with brilliantine and they gave him a smoking jacket to wear! It was horrible, and he hated the way he looked. When I saw how attractive he really was in person, I insisted he be tested again.

Well, Paul understood Jerry and was a revelation. Our chemistry was just right. He helped my performance immeasurably and we developed a certain style between us. The public all over the world knew what Charlotte (my character) saw in this man who was caught in an awful marriage. So many times foreign actors leer and posture, but Paul was perfectly natural—plus being so good-looking. When he won Charlotte's heart, he won every woman's heart in the audience.

* * *

Miriam Hopkins was her usual difficult self on *Old Acquaintance*—director Vincent Sherman said he felt like the umpire in a fight ring. The day we shot the scene in which Kit (me) has finally had enough of Millie's tomfoolery and slaps her, the set was jammed with onlookers from other stages. I can, in all honesty, say I never lost my temper with Miriam on the set. I kept it all in until I got home at night. Then I screamed for an hour at least!

* * *

While I was working in *Mr. Skeffington,* someone filled my eyewash with acetone—a corrosive liquid used to dissolve adhesives. Unknowingly, I filled an eyecup with the liquid and pressed it to my eye. It was only the quick thinking of the head of the make-up department, Perc Westmore, that prevented me from losing my sight. He ran for a bottle of castor oil and flushed out the eye. The heavy oil absorbed and carried away the acetone before it could do any damage. I still feel that I owe my sight to Perc.

* * *

I don't often mention Fanny Skeffington. *Mr. Skeffington* wasn't one of my favorite films, no, although Orry-Kelly's costumes are in that. There's never been a more authentic costume job done, those marvelous early 1900s things he did were just beautiful. Then we had to work very hard to make me pretty. *Also,* I was heartbroken that the film was not done in color. It was one of the few pictures that I think should have been in color. But of course I enjoyed playing that part because of my beautiful Claude Rains.

Nancy Davis —— ACTRESS

While we were shooting *East Side, West Side,* Mervyn LeRoy, our director and an old friend, introduced me to an actor over at Warner Bros. whose name was Ronald Reagan.

Rosemary DeCamp —— ACTRESS

From This Day Forward, which was originally titled *All Brides Are Beautiful,* was based on a Clifford Odets story and as first shot was warm, funny and real.

However, Joan Fontaine starred, and she and the head of RKO, William Dozier, would spend lunch hour editing director Jack Berry's beautiful work into a series of close-ups of Joan and leading man Mark Stevens. Joan and Dozier later married for a short spell. She had a beautiful face and a dirty mouth. In the final cut of *From This Day Forward,* there wasn't much left of me or Harry Morgan, who played my husband, and that probably accounts for my malice.

Olivia de Havilland —— ACTRESS

The closest I came to a breakdown was when I made *Hold Back the Dawn.* It was right after my appendectomy. I had gained about 20 pounds and I started to work too soon after my operation. But I wanted very much to do the picture. It was an excellent role—it had depth, humor and character—and I wanted to prove to myself that I could do a good job. It was really a matter of utmost importance to me, so my over-anxiety, on top of my low vitality, may have been responsible for what happened. At any rate, I couldn't sleep at all, my hands shook, I couldn't remember my lines and I used to tremble violently at times. I thought I'd die during the making of that picture.

* * *

I fought to have Mitchell Leisen direct *To Each His Own.* He didn't want to, and Paramount had someone else in mind.

The first couple of weeks on the set Mitch was charming, helpful, a real professional about the whole thing, but his heart wasn't in it. Then suddenly he began to realize he had here one of the best pictures of his whole career, and his whole being just lit up, which was a wonderful relief for me, since I had insisted on him, and it all would have been my fault had it not worked out.

* * *

The whole *Snake Pit* company went up—through arrangements made by Fox—to Camarillo, the state institution near Santa Barbara. We spent three days there in different sessions. The hairdresser went up, the make-up man went up, the sound man went, the cameraman went, the lighting men went, everybody. All the technicians went, all the assistant directors went, the property men, everybody I can think of. Anyway, it was done with such care, such a desire to be precise and exact, that I admire that to this day.

Now, I saw a number of patients and more important than that, I saw every single phase of Virginia's experience. I looked through the doors, the windows—you know, the little windows in the extremely violent and radically disturbed rooms—I saw the patients there. I saw hydrotherapy, I saw electric shock—that was quite disturbing. I saw one patient being given treatment and then I saw her an hour or so later coming out of shock. I saw staff meetings where they interviewed the patients and decided whether they should be allowed to go home for a week or two. I went to a dance. A patient even asked me to dance. One of the male patients came over and asked me and I was terribly flattered. He said I was cute. I didn't dance with him, but I did see that.

So it was out of a combination of all these things, occurring sufficiently in advance of the shooting date, that I was able to prepare.

* * *

Working with Ralph Richardson in *The Heiress* was very, very difficult. I thought he was so brilliantly cast, he's a marvelous performer, but he was also—shall I say this or not?—a wicked, very selfish man. There's a very old-fashioned expletive, which I'll delete—S.O.B. are the initials—but he really is a devil, an unnecessarily selfish artist to work with. I was in a constant stage of outrage over his slick, British tricks. I had to be alert all the time to outwit him and that's no fun. I just wanted to play Catherine and enjoy doing it, just living her life, but I had to be so nimble all the time, outwitting this wicked British actor. Well, I think I succeeded.

He would—oh, those gloves! There was a scene where he would slap his gloves. I had to play some agonizing scenes, and it was impera-

tive that the audience's attention was on Catherine, not on those wretched gloves. That sort of thing, ridiculous kind of upstaging, and then, you know, walking up and down. So I thought, "Okay, you go on and walk up and down." Really wicked things. He wasn't thinking in terms of the scene and the characters and the audience, he was just thinking in terms of ridiculous exhibitionism and he had to be restrained all the time. I think the way he got by on the gloves was because [director] Willie Wyler was afraid to talk to him about them. But he got the cameraman to frame just above the gloves, and it worked.

André de Toth ——— DIRECTOR

On *The Other Love,* we had a scene where Barbara Stanwyck is driving along a road from the sanitarium. The horses gallop briskly when a racing car unexpectedly crosses the intersection—the scene where she meets Richard Conte, the racing driver.

During rehearsals the stunt double was slightly injured. My staff did not want to worry me and I was not told. Before the take Stanwyck came to me saying it was a very difficult stunt, and how much was the stunt girl getting for it. At her insistence I inquired from the production manager and was told the figure. All this happened during the last few days of shooting and Barbara had never asked for anything special till that day. She thought that the girl should have four times as much, as the stunt was dangerous. Naturally

I agreed and gave orders accordingly.

We set up for the take and barrelling along comes the carriage, to my horror driven by Stanwyck. The take is in the picture and of course the stunt girl received her quadruple reward. What else can one say about Stanwyck?

Howard Dietz —— PUBLICITY CHIEF

When Gable was making his first postwar film, *Adventure,* there was widespread speculation as to who would play his leading lady. Greer Garson was picked and to publicize the vital union I wrote the line, "Gable's back and Garson's got him."

Brian Donlevy —— ACTOR

We had just finished the first day of shooting *I Wanted Wings* and that was the first time I had met her. We were riding back to town. She was in the back seat and I was up front next to the driver. Somebody asked me, "What to you think of Veronica Lake?" I said, "Where is it?" She's never like me since then.

Kirk Douglas —— ACTOR

My agents fought with me not to do *Champion.* They wanted me to do a picture with Gregory Peck and Ava Gardner called *The Great Sinner,* an all-star production at MGM, and I wanted to do this little picture that had no money to pay me. They didn't know who the hell Stanley Kramer or Carl Foreman or any of those people were. But this character fascinated me. He was really one of the first anti-heroes, a real bastard.

Irene Dunne —— ACTRESS

Penny Serenade: I don't think I've ever felt as close to any picture. It's very much the scheme of my personal life.

Philip Dunne —— SCREENWRITER

[Director] Jack Ford's idea of a love story is Ward Bond and John Wayne, always. It's always the strong men, and they can be enemies or friends, or brothers, but that's the bond. Almost the only heterosexual love story that Jack Ford ever did really well was in *How Green Was My Valley,* between the girl and the minister. It was a great love story, and Ford caught it, as he never caught another love story in his whole career. Usually he avoided them.

Richard Erdman —— ACTOR

Director Michael Curtiz suggested I play a smaller role prior to *Janie*—I needed "camera experience." So I was assigned the role of a Western Union messenger in *Mr. Skeffington.* I had one line, perhaps the toughest of my career.

The day before we shot my little film debut, a Western Union telegram, a real one, from the War Department, arrived announcing the death of my friend, Charles Wright, killed in action. I was up most of the night with Charles' mother. When morning came, I drove out to the studio, got into my Western Union outfit and walked onto the set. The

first shot was on me. I climbed the steps of an ersatz brownstone, knocked on the door and waited until Bette Davis and Claude Rains opened it. I just stared at them for a moment and then said my line:

"Telegram for Mrs. Fanny Skeffington. From the War Department."

I said it as casually as I could, but something must have crept into it. Then Davis—a tough lady with studio executives but greatly encouraging to young performers—stepped through the door and grasped me by the shoulders.

"That was brilliantly done, young man," she said. "Welcome to Warner Bros."

I just broke into tears. She never knew why, but she went around the studio telling everyone what a fine new actor was under contract.

Virginia Field ——— *ACTRESS*

Miss [Vivien] Leigh was completely upset from start to finish of *Waterloo Bridge.* She was furious at having her Laurence Olivier pulled from the cast to help out *Pride and Prejudice.* Greer Garson wanted him to bolster that film's weak script, and Miss Leigh pouted and knitted unforgivingly to the end of shooting.

Geraldine Fitzgerald —— *ACTRESS*

We had just started shooting *'Til We Meet Again* when I realized I was pregnant with my son Michael. Then Merle Oberon became ill, causing us to shut down for weeks. Meanwhile, I was getting huger and huger. Since I was playing a shipboard honeymooner, this would never do—not in those days, anyway. When we resumed, I had to be filmed with big handbags or in close-up. People watching the movie thought my character was going to turn out to be far more significant because I got one big close-up after another!

Errol Flynn ——— ACTOR

Greer Garson was the first actress I worked with who was fun and helpful. Many of the other ladies were a bit in awe or else hated me.

But in *That Forsyte Woman,* with Miss Garson, I really felt for the first time that I had a character role. I don't know whether I can convey how deep the yearning is of an actor who has been stereotyped, who has that sword and horse wound around him, to prove to himself and to others that he is an actor.

The popular conception of Greer is that she is a kind of Mrs. Miniver: finely bred, the epitome of English cultured womanhood. She is all this, but at the same time a mischievous imp.

Most people on the lot held her in awe, including the high brass at MGM. When I heard I was to do a picture with her, I built up a nervous reaction which I knew would be fatal.

I had to do something about the nerves that were working up in me. When the time came to meet her I primed myself with about three vodkas. When I was introduced, I adopted an air of bravado, the hearty Australian from the outback. I shook hands heartily, then I slapped her on the fanny. "Hi yuh, Red!" I said.

Everybody froze.

There was a brief pause. Then she went into a torrent of laughter. That broke the ice.

Henry Fonda ——— ACTOR

When I did *Daisy Kenyon* with Joan Crawford, she was, well, very attentive. When I failed to respond, she had the wardrobe department make me a rhinestone jockstrap covered with gold sequins and red beads. She wrapped it and presented it to me on the set. When I saw it, my mouth fell open. We then went right into an intimate scene for the picture and she whispered in my ear, "How about modeling it for me later?"

Joan Fontaine ——— ACTRESS

The Russian Anatole Litvak directed Tyrone Power and me in Eric Knight's sensitive novel *This Above All.* It received tremendous word-of-mouth publicity because of an incident that occurred one evening at Ciro's between Paulette Goddard and Litvak. The morning after their rendezvous *The Hollywood Reporter* and *Variety* were being passed from cast to crew and back again on every studio lot. Hollywood was abuzz.

The gossip columns had printed that "Tola" Litvak had disappeared for a suspicious length of time under the table at which Paulette sat serenely. "Litvak" was altered into a crude pun, graphic enough to describe what the onlookers imagined was going on under the white tablecloth. Tola's version was that Paulette had simply dropped her evening bag, and, on his hands and knees, he'd had difficulty retrieving it in the dark. As with most gossip, the readers preferred to believe the lurid version.

* * *

I got *The Constant Nymph,* my favorite film, by a fluke. One day, I ran into the director Edmund Goulding at lunch and he mentioned that he was having trouble with his latest film, *The Constant Nymph,* which was to start in ten days. He'd already signed Charles Boyer and Alexis Smith, but he couldn't find a leading lady. He said, "I need someone underweight, sickly, flat-chested and 14." I said,"How about me?" And he replied, *"Of course!"*

* * *

I never see my movies. I never looked at them when I made them. I did see *The Constant Nymph* not too long ago since it's been out of circulation. When it was over I said, "Get me to the nearest bar and give me a double vodka!"

* * *

With Max Ophuls, who directed *Letter from an Unknown Woman,* I communicated intuitively. After a take, Max would come over to me and start to speak in German, which I scarcely understood. I would nod before he had said six words and he would then resume his position behind the camera. After the next take was completed, he would rush over and say, "How you know egg-zactly vot I vont? Preent dat!"

Clark Gable——————ACTOR

Ava Gardner just has what it takes. The first day we worked on *The Hucksters* I was worried about her. It was at my suggestion that she had accepted such a small role and I wondered if I had done the right thing in urging her. She was in fast acting company with Deborah Kerr, Adophe Menjou, Sydney Greenstreet and Keenan Wynn. Then I took a look at the rushes. "Gable, my boy," I said to myself, "every man for himself. That's girl's good."

Paul Gallico——————AUTHOR

The Clock is a thundering bit of cinematic sleeping potion. At the outset, I wish to absolve Mr. Louis B. Mayer from any blame in connection with this turkeroo. At the time it was being produced, filmed and edited, Mr. Mayer, who is the head of MGM, had the misfortune to fall off a horse and was laid up in a hospital. This was our tough luck. Once he was unavailable, the entire producing unit would have had to fall off horses daily and twice on Sundays to have made any real difference.

My wife, Pauline, and I are ashamed of ourselves, for we could have prevented it. Yes, we could. Because, and I blush to admit it, one of the men who wrote the screenplay from our original story, Mr. Robert Nathan, the poet, was in our house for dinner one evening before departing for Hollywood to keep his assignation to murder our piece, and we

had a chance to kill him then and there. We didn't do it. We knew we should after listening to him talk for ten minutes. Now it's too late. We believe in cool-headed, cold-blooded assassination as a preventive, but not for vulgar revenge. Eventually Mr. Nathan will have to account to his Maker anyway, and there is little to be gained by hastening the day. But it was nothing less than criminal on our part to let the opportunity slip when we had it.

Ava Gardner ——— ACTRESS

They switched roles on me in *East Side, West Side.* I was supposed to play the lead, but then they got Barbara Stanwyck, and she was a much bigger name at the time, so they moved me into the smaller role. It was a much better part. Metro always treated me like that, but that time it worked to my advantage.

John Garfield ——— ACTOR

Tortilla Flat—I tried to steal scenes from Hedy Lamarr, Hedy tried to steal them from Spencer Tracy, Tracy tried to steal from Frank Morgan. Morgan tried to steal from me, and the dogs stole the show.

Lee Garmes ——— CINEMATOGRAPHER

While we were making *Lydia,* director Julien Duvivier was heartsick, depressed almost to tears by the knowledge that France had given up the struggle against Germany so easily, and had allowed itself to collaborate with the enemy in the form of a Vichy government set up under Pétain. Duvivier felt he could no longer be a Frenchman in the circumstances.

One morning we had a late call at ten because Duvivier had driven downtown for an appointment. Merle Oberon hadn't been notified. She had come in at five A.M. for hours of complicated make-up as an old woman. Duvivier wasn't there when she emerged from the make-up room. He came in smiling with news for us all. Suddenly, without warning, Merle, in her old woman's guise, shouted before us all, "What happened? Why are you so late?" Duvivier replied, furious, "Merle, I went down to the Immigration Department to make up my papers as a citizen." And I remember the remark she made in reply, a remark that flabbergasted all of us and turned us against her for a long time. She snarled, "Julien, why would you want to do that?"

Peggy Ann Garner —— ACTRESS

A Tree Grows in Brooklyn was the first picture Gadge [Elia] Kazan ever did. I was supposed to cry in one scene, and after lunch Kazan said, "Do you have a dog, a cat?" I said no, and he said, "Gee, if you did, what if something happened to your pet?" He talked some more about it, and soon I was ready to cry hard.

Kazan had a marvelous quality. In *Tree,* he even knew how to handle Dorothy McGuire, and there was a certain way you had to handle that lady. Then there was sweet, warm buxom Joan Blondell. And Jimmie Dunn, with his hands shaking until someone said, "Knock off the booze or else." Kazan was like a kid with a new toy, doing this film.

Two weeks into shooting, Darryl Zanuck came on the set. He seldom did that. Gadge often printed two takes, something Zanuck didn't like. Gadge said, "If I'm going to do this picture, I'm going to do it my way."

Another day, Mr. Zanuck came on the set and said, "The picture is so great we're going to scrap it and start over in color." Kazan hit the ceiling. At that time, the only type of color used was Betty Grable-Technicolor, and this picture was very low-key—Brooklyn tenements and all. Anyway, Gadge won.

Tay Garnett —— DIRECTOR

I was assigned to another big one: *Mrs. Parkington,* from the novel by Louis Bromfield. Greer Garson, having been awarded an Oscar for *Mrs. Miniver,* was assigned the title role.

During the first scenes it became obvious that Greer had not yet caught onto the "Susie Parkington" character. "Susie" was a bright, spirited, Western mining town girl, bouncy and bubbling with vitality but without artifice. Greer was playing her too Great Lady, too British.

Wise Walter Pidgeon saw the problem, and—grinning wickedly—slapped Greer on the neatest derrière in Hollywood (a stunt he had used in *Mrs. Miniver*) and said, "Relax, honey. It was *last* year that you won the Oscar."

Greer laughed and relaxed. End of problem.

Greer Garson ———— *ACTRESS*

I didn't want to play *Mrs. Miniver* at first. Oh, I don't know. I was still relatively new to Hollywood and maybe I thought that playing the mother of a grown son would type me in mother parts, which would limit my prospects.

Louis Mayer called me into his office and pleaded with me to play the role. I said no. He said, "I brought you to America. Do it for me." Still no. Finally, to prove the opportunities afforded me in the role, he began to read aloud from the script, acting out all the parts. When I couldn't take it any longer, I cried out, "All right! All right! I'll play Mrs. Miniver!"

But I still think Louis Mayer played it better than I did.

* * *

When I went abroad, Paris taxi drivers would say, "Ah, Mother Miniver." [*Mrs. Miniver*] did have a tremendous circulation and popularity.

It is hard today to imagine the impact that the film had in 1941–42. That, of course, was a very emotional time. It's a film that showed home and family life which the Allies were fighting to protect and preserve. In time of war, people really value the basic virtues. They want all their women to be good. They want the family to be secure in their affections and loyalty. They want to see what they are fighting for. Or what they are being asked to defend. The film showed the courage of ordinary people under extraordinary stress.

William Wyler upheld his reputation throughout [as a director who insisted on many takes of a scene]. But he got the end result. About the time the awards rolled around, everybody forgave him and couldn't wait to work with him again.

* * *

My most romantic scene? That was with Ronald Colman in *Random Harvest,* the story of a shell-shocked veteran of World War I and the love he had forgotten. It was just after he recovers from his amnesia. We were meeting at our once beloved little cottage in the country. All the lost years of our love, and all the hopes for the future are crowded into that one scene. It hit the deepest emotional point I've ever experienced in a picture—and it remains a thrilling memory.

Rumer Godden ———— *AUTHOR*

Sam Goldwyn had bought the film rights to *Fugue in Time* the winter before, but I had heard nothing about it until one evening Jimmie Simon and I went, on the spur of the moment, to the cinema where a film called *Enchantment* was being shown. Set in a London house that was vaguely familiar, the names of the characters were mine; there all resemblance to *Fugue in Time* ended. Not even the concept was kept. "Why did Goldwyn bother to buy it?" I wrote to Spencer. "It was like buying a bottle of wine, using only a spoonful and filling it up with sticky lemonade."

"It often happens," Spencer wrote back. "Forget it and think of the beautiful money."

Cary Grant — ACTOR

If it hadn't been for *Mr. Lucky,* I don't know how much longer I'd have held the public's interest.

Ethel Griffies — ACTRESS

There is a remarkable story surrounding my single scene in *Saratoga Trunk* at Warners—where I not only often acted but made myself available for other duties such as conducting private speech classes for foreign actresses. My part was the domineering Saratoga society mother Madame Clarissa Van Steed, implacable enemy of adventuress Ingrid Bergman. The director, Sam Wood, saw me for the part and said no. So they put someone else in, and got the film in the can, as they say. Then they decided they didn't like her in it, so they filmed someone else in the role. Once again they didn't like their Mrs. Van Steed and got still someone else. Didn't like her footage, either! Finally, they said, "Get Griffies!" That's how they did things out there.

Susan Hayward — ACTRESS

Roles in *Beau Geste* and *Our Leading Citizen* served to get me typed as "that sweet Susan Hayward" who couldn't be expected to play anything but doll-faced ingénues. Feeling that I'd never get far with that reputation, and hearing that Gregory Ratoff was going to direct *Adam Had Four Sons,* I asked him for the part of Hester, a remorseless character whose possibilities intrigued me. He laughed off the idea as "absurd!" But Mrs. Ratoff—Eugenie Leontovich, the actress—persuaded him to let me have what turned out to be my favorite role, arguing that such a part would make for drama—casting against type.

Hester fascinated me and, as it was my first really dramatic role, also frightened me. However, Gregory's kidding and clowning soon had me relaxed. He was fun even when he got mad. I liked him so much that even when he would roar in desperation, "Susan, you are the most steenking actress I've ever seen!" I'd collapse in laughter and not be hurt. He wouldn't shrivel you with his criticism, as some directors do. He would challenge and inspire you. Then, when you got things right, he would make you glow with his "Ah, you are marvelous—wonderful!"

In addition, there was the pleasant excitement of working with Ingrid Bergman. Some actors and actresses are like blank walls, so unresponsive you can't do your best. Ingrid is just the opposite—she worked as hard for my close-ups as for her own. Finally, the role particularly appealed to me because of the physical movement which expressed Hester's nature. She was always in action, usually moving forward, constantly revealing her aggressive personality.

After the picture was released, executives stopped assuming I was qualified only for sugary roles. I've had many "bad-woman" parts since then, such as those in *And Now Tomorrow* and *The Hairy Ape,* but none that I enjoyed quite as much as Hester.

* * *

If they don't sober me up in my next movie, I'll have to paraphrase Thomas Wolfe and say, "I can't go home again"—not to Brooklyn, anyway. Ever since I played that oversexed vamp in *Adam Had Four Sons,* my aunts have been uneasy about me.

* * *

One good reason why women drink is men! It's a man's world. It does things to girls who get kicked around in it.

One of the reasons that I jumped at the chance to play the young wife in *Smash-Up* is that the movie deals with a serious social problem. More and more women are seeking careers, and the truth is that they can do almost anything as good as a man. But when these girls marry, some husbands treat them like they were something that came with the apartment. They shut the wives out of their own lives just like Lee Bowman does to me in the movie. Then they get enraged if the wife feels so insecure that she drinks. I've seen it happen to my own friends.

* * *

I've never been difficult. Those stories were highly exaggerated. They said I was temperamental and hard to work with. It made good copy and it got good space. But you can speak to any director I've worked with. He'll tell you the contrary.

One time I must admit I threw a lamp at a guy. I won't mention his name [Martin Gabel, director of *The Lost Moment*]. He'd only done one picture before. He'd done about 15 takes, and I said, "What is it that you want?" He said, "I'll tell you when I get it." I said, "You'd better get it next time." He didn't. I picked up a lamp and threw it. It didn't hurt him much. No, we didn't do another take. I think he went to get Band-Aids.

Edith Head — COSTUME DESIGNER

Director William Wyler is such a perfectionist. *The Heiress,* for example, was set in the 1840s and the 1850s, so we had to deal with two periods. We had crinolines, and we also had hoops, which is a slightly different silhouette. There were scenes in which Olivia de Havilland got dressed. You saw her in petticoats, in little corsets and in corset covers. Wyler even sent me to a fashion institute in New York, which carried a great collection, to be sure that every button and every buttonhole was absolutely accurate. If I had to choose a picture I did that was absolutely perfect down to the tiniest buttonhole, it was *The Heiress.* Wyler insisted on it. In fact, there wasn't a single zipper; everything was done with little buttons.

Van Heflin — ACTOR

When I first came to Hollywood, I was very contemptuous of anyone who was "just a movie star." I first met Joan Crawford when she was married to Franchot Tone. At a party one evening Joan mentioned that she and Franchot would like to do a play together. She was very charming. I was very snooty. I gave out with something about people who had done "only pictures" should leave well enough alone. The net result was—years later, I made a picture, *Possessed,* with Joan—and found in her a tremendous knowledge of acting. She knew everything about the camera. She knew everything about those lights. She knew everything about the psychopathic girl she was playing. She knew everything about the role of a doctor *I* was playing. She knew everything, period. And *I* knew, eating humble pie, that had she wanted to do a play, she would have done a fine job. Had she wanted to do grand opera, ditto.

In *Possessed,* there was a scene in which Joan had to slap me in the face. The scene was shot directly before lunch. I went home for lunch that day, as Joan had known I would. When I arrived, I found a box of flowers waiting for me. The card enclosed read, "Darling, I hated so to slap you before lunch—wanted flowers to arrive a minute after."

It seems a little thing to tell but it gave me an added admiration for the girl.

* * *

Barbara Stanwyck has a sense of humor as lusty as life. A gag-puller, here's one she pulled on me. On the set of *B. F. Daughter* one gray (for Heflin, anyway) morning, Stanwyck spotted, right off the bat, that I'd been out late the night before. In the first scene we shot that morning, a physical action scene—and it couldn't have happened to a sicker boy—I was supposed to pick B. F.'s Daughter up, fur coat and all, and carry her over the threshold of "our" new home. I went into action. I tried to pick her up. *I could not get her off the floor.* The cameras were grinding. The cameraman, crew and cast were grinning. I could not get her off the floor. Guess why? Under the heavy fur coat, the girl had put 300 pounds of chains and weights and window sashes!

Paul Henreid ——— ACTOR

After *Now, Voyager* came out, every comedian would stuff his mouth with cigarettes. In fact it was my idea. The script called for me to light one, give it to Bette [Davis], light another and trade cigarettes with her. Cigarettes would be shuffling all over the place, so I suggested my lighting them both at once.

John Houseman ——— PRODUCER

We couldn't have timed *Letter from an Unknown Woman* worse. It was a disaster—critically and financially. It was released at a period when a very strong reaction was blowing up against so-called "escapism" in favor of a native brand of neo-realism. *Letter* (which was not escapist but romantic) was generally misunderstood on its first American release. Then, little by little and mainly on the rebound from Europe, people began to see the film's qualities, till it finally found its mass audience—on television!

Kim Hunter ———— ACTRESS

No one was ever unaware that Ginger Rogers was the star in *Tender Comrade,* but she was a joy to work with. For her close-ups, they had pink gels put on all the lights. One day, Ruth Hussey came in with a flashlight that had a pink gel on it. "Not to be outdone," she said. Everybody roared.

John Huston ———— DIRECTOR

I never cared for *In This Our Life,* although there were some good things about it. It was the first time, I believe, that a black character was presented as anything other than a good and faithful servant or comic relief. Bette Davis fascinated me. There is something elemental about Bette—a demon within her which threatens to break out and eat everybody, beginning with their ears. The studio was afraid of her.

Elia Kazan ———— DIRECTOR

If we had shot *A Tree Grows in Brooklyn* in New York on the East Side, it would have been truer to life. But much worse than the scenery—the rooms were too clean, too nice, too much the work of the property man—were the hairdressing and costumes. They looked like magazine illustrations.

The only truly correct thing on the visual side of *A Tree* was the face of the little girl, Peggy Ann Garner. Because her father was overseas in the war, because her mother had problems, because she herself was going through a lot of pains and uncertainties, Peggy's face was drawn and pale and worried. It looked exactly right. She was not pretty at all, or cute or picturesque, only true.

* * *

No matter what I think of it today, what I remember most about *Gentleman's Agreement* is that at the time no one said "Jew." When it was being made, all the rich Jews in California were against it. And the Catholic Church was against it, because they didn't want the heroine to be a divorcée. There were a hell of a lot of people who said to Darryl Zanuck, "We're getting along all right. Why bring this up?" And, in that sense, it was a step forward at the time.

On the other hand, it was, as far as it went, essentially a *Cosmopolitan* story, wasn't it? It was all dressed up with these overtones, but essentially it was a very familiar, easily digestible story with conventional figures going through it. There isn't anything unpleasant in that picture. It was kept on a level of respectability. It surprised people, but it didn't shock them.

* * *

Pinky? The story is that [director John] Ford had the shingles. Now I think he didn't have the shingles. What happened was that Ethel Waters hated him, and he hated her. So Ford got the shingles. He just got in bed and said, "I can't get out of here." Zanuck asked me to come out

there and finish it, and I asked, "O.K." I didn't even read the goddamn script until I got off the plane.

Darryl showed me what Ford had shot, and I said I'd like to start from scratch, because actually Ford's stuff was N. G. I think he's a terrific director, maybe the best we ever had. But the stuff he shot in this was no good at all, terrible. I guess he just got into a set-up where he was disgruntled, and he rebelled. So I got things going again. I calmed Miss Waters down, and I calmed Jeanne Crain down, who was sort of terrified by him, too. I shot it in seven weeks. I didn't stay for the editing. I just did a job. I did my best with it, and I guess it has certain values, but it's not one of my favorite films. I also felt there was some essential cop-out in casting a white girl in the lead.

Deborah Kerr ———— *ACTRESS*

My hairdresser stopped in the middle of a brush stroke and sighed.

"Well, Miss Kerr," she said, "what if things don't go right and you don't play the part? It's worth coming 7,000 miles just to kiss Clark Gable, isn't it?"

She was repairing the damage after my screen test for *The Hucksters* in Hollywood. I had met Clark Gable for the first time two days before. We'd just run through a love scene to see how we looked together on the screen. There was no certainty at all, at that time, that we would co-star in the film. And I'm afraid, being a bride myself of only a few months and still honeymooning with my husband, I didn't commit myself on that remark.

I stayed home waiting for a telephone call from the studio. When it came, a familiar voice said excitedly, "Baby, you're in!"

That was how I first knew I'd gotten the part. Clark called and told me himself! I later learned he'd made everyone at MGM promise to tell him first. The minute he knew he'd rushed straight to a telephone to bring the good news.

The only trick Clark Gable played on me all the time we made *The Hucksters* was one inspired by an attempt to give me a pleasant surprise. I'm sure he had no idea it would turn out to be a durable reproach to my vanity.

One day, between scenes, I was in my dressing room when a knock came on the door. It was Clark's stand-in. He was apologetic, but he said he admired my work very much. He wondered—would I give him my autograph?

"Oh, but of course," I answered. I was really quite pleased; it was the first time in America I'd been asked for that favor. In my eagerness to please, I'm afraid I overdid the autograph. I dashed one off in my best Spencerian hand with sweeping lines and flourishes.

"Thanks," he said, and I forgot all about it. I'm not much of a sleuth, I'm afraid. It never dawned on me to suspect that Clark had sent him in to get the autograph. Not until—a week later—he presented me with a lovely leather script cover—with that dreadful, glamour autograph of mine tooled all over the front!

I couldn't wish better luck for an English actress, new to a strange and frightening Hollywood, than to make her first movie with Clark Gable.

***Henry King*——————DIRECTOR**

I had great professional respect for Claudette Colbert. She gave 100 percent to her characterizations. And I resent—positively *resent*—hearing about how she fussed unduly over her looks in front of the camera. George Barnes, who photographed her in *Remember the Day,* would have told you, were he alive, that she went right along with a realistically aged look for her 1940s scenes when, as a middle-aged teacher, she goes to see her now-famous former pupil. Anything the make-up man wanted to do was fine with her. At the time she was best known for her skills as a comedienne, but I always found her wonderfully easy to direct during the shooting, with a dramatic talent so strong that in my opinion she never exploited it as fully as she could and should have.

She was surprisingly poignant and subtle in the role, putting insights into it that even I did not realize were in the part. She was the kind of actress you could leave alone—alone with her own finely tuned instincts, that is—and with a minimum of guidance. And then when you saw the rushes, it would be all up there on film. She was always wonderful with her co-players, had a delightful, warm habit of treating supporting performers whose seasoned talent she respected as equals,

and letting them shine along with her in scenes. I don't think there was an ounce of professional jealousy in her. She was a team player, but then her charisma and talent were so great that in a sense she could afford to be.

She got [child actor Douglas Croft] to glow with confidence and poise, and I saw her do the same thing with her romantic lead, John Payne, who was then a Fox stock player more noted for his good looks than for his acting skills. Payne gave one of his best performances in that picture.

Stanley Kramer —— PRODUCER

I borrowed the fare to fly down to Miami Beach to see this man. His name was Stillman. He was an elderly gentleman. After dinner, Mr. Stillman leaned back in his chair and lighted a cigar four feet long.

"All right, my boy," Mr. Stillman said, "tell me the story. But before you start, I want you to know that I like a lot of fighting and action in a film."

For the next two hours I told Mr. Stillman the story of *Champion.* Carl Foreman had not yet written the script because I had no money to pay him. So I ad-libbed a very liberal interpretation of Ring Lardner's short story. I intruded into it a great many colorful characters and bloody, carnage-laden, action-packed fight scenes. All the fights, of course, were fixed by gangsters who made Dillinger and Clyde Barrow seem like choirboys. There was killing and shooting and mayhem in every frame. Not one bit of what I told Mr. Stillman ever appeared on the screen except the death scene, which was part of my improvisation. That was the scene in the picture when Kirk Douglas smashes his fist against the locker and then collapses and dies. That one piece of business was no great accomplishment on my part. Out of two hours of improvising, I should have come up with *something* I could use in the film.

Mr. Stillman was getting what Mr. Stillman wanted. He went for it hook, line and sinker. He financed the picture for $500,000. *Champion* made Kirk a star and launched me.

David Lean—DIRECTOR

Very rough neighborhood, Rochester [England], but we took the first print of *Brief Encounter* to the manager of the nearby cinema and said, "Look, could you run a new film, call it the premiere and we'll have a first look at it?" He did, and during the first love scene someone down front, a woman with a terrible laugh that I'll never forget, begins to laugh, and one or two others turned and said, "S-h-h," but then some other people in the audience started to laugh with her. And each time a love scene came on, more and more people started to laugh. The whole audience, by the time it was over, was rocking with laughter. I was so ashamed of it. I remember going back to my hotel room that night, thinking was there any way I could break into the lab at Denham and burn the negative?

Janet Leigh—ACTRESS

Early in 1947, Van Johnson and Evie Wynn were married, which caused quite a stir. When I was living in Stockton, I had read about Van's near-fatal motor accident and how he had recuperated in the home of his best friends, Evie and Keenan Wynn. Van had dated many Hollywood glamour queens, but had obviously fallen in love with Evie. Unfortunately, this didn't sit too well with many of his female fans and the press.

The Romance of Rosy Ridge was the first Van Johnson picture released after the marriage, and the box office receipts suffered. It was critically acclaimed, and it did very good business, but it wasn't the expected usual Van Johnson blockbuster.

Vivien Leigh —ACTRESS

People often come up to me and tell me how much they loved me in *Gone with the Wind.* If I'm in a candid mood, I tell them I liked *Waterloo Bridge* (which came right after it) better. *Gone with the Wind* was a grueling ordeal: I was in almost every scene of that *endless* film and Larry [Olivier], whom I was hoping to marry, was 3,000 miles away doing a play on Broadway. When I did *Waterloo Bridge,* I not only liked the story and role better but by then Larry was working in Hollywood, too.

Mitchell Leisen—DIRECTOR

In *Kitty* Paulette Goddard had to be a cockney (in the original book she's a whore, but we made a buckle-thief out of her). I couldn't get anybody who would admit she was a cockney, except Ida Lupino's other, Connie Emerald, so I moved Connie into Paulette's apartment and said, "Talk morning, noon and night. Don't let her speak [posh] English at all." By God, she did it. Ray Milland talked cockney with her, I talked cockney with her on the set. Now she had to become the duchess, so I moved Connie Emerald out and moved Constance Collier in, and we changed the whole pitch of her voice; the first time you heard her speak as the duchess, it was fascinating.

* * *

In *To Each His Own* the girl ages during the picture. Olivia de Havilland had been sick and lost 17 pounds, and I insisted on shooting the picture in continuity. So we started when she was thin, and with as attractive a make-up as we could get on her.

As the picture progressed, I fed her up every day and she gained back the 17 pounds, and she wound up wearing a Frankly Forty foundation garment. They wanted her to have grey hair—I said, "She's only 40, she doesn't have grey hair!" And we used a more unflattering lighting. That's all we did.

Mervyn LeRoy ——— DIRECTOR

The first picture I directed after I went back on the sound stage was *Waterloo Bridge.* There are many who call it my best. My good friend Jack Benny says he considers it his favorite among all my films. Vivien Leigh, who co-starred with Robert Taylor, always said it was the best thing she ever did. Considering the fact that she had just done *Gone with the Wind* when she came to me, I consider that very high praise.

Waterloo Bridge, old as it is today, still plays often on television and still brings tears to the eyes. Bob Taylor, in his later years, when he knew he was dying, grew sentimental. Most actors keep and cherish prints of their pictures, but Taylor never had any. He told friends then that he would like a print of one picture he had made—*Waterloo Bridge.* The people at the Walt Disney Studio, where he was working at the time, got one for him, and he showed it often in his last few months.

* * *

Random Harvest holds the record at Radio City Music Hall for 12 weeks. It could have played longer, but Nick Schenck of MGM in New York, who was head of MGM at the time, wanted to have it played in all of the Loew's theaters, so they took it off after 12 weeks. But the Hall's Russell Downing told me that it could have stayed on for another ten weeks, it was such a big hit there.

Myrna Loy ——— ACTRESS

My only reservations about doing *The Best Years of Our Lives* concerned working with [director] William Wyler, because of stories from Bette Davis and other actors about his endless retakes and bullying. "I hear Wyler's a sadist," I told producer Sam Goldwyn.

"That isn't true," he replied, with

a genuine Goldwynism, "he's just a very mean fellow."

* * *

I knew about Willie Wyler's reputation, and I was apprehensive [about doing *The Best Years of Our Lives*]. I had dinner with Sam and Frances Goldwyn before shooting started, and I warned Sam, "If he tries anything, I'll walk right off the set." They started with the scenes in the plane which I wasn't in, but I went down to the studio one day for my wardrobe tests. I put on the bathrobe for the homecoming scene and went onto the set to show Wyler. He asked me how I was planning to fix my hair. I bent over and shook my head until it was all messed up and then I said, "Like this" and he said "Fine." Then he said, "Are you afraid of me?" I was, but I said, "No" and he said "Fine."

From that moment on, there was the most fantastic rapport between us. Freddy March said, "I can't believe the radar you two have going. You don't even need to talk," and it was true. When the picture was over, Willie told reporters how much Freddy and I had helped him, and I never had any other director do that. It is true that Willie wanted a lot of takes and often we'd go on and on until Sam came down to the set and made Willie start something else. Willie always said, "If we do it again, something special may happen," and sometimes it did.

Sam Goldwyn was a very courageous man to make that picture. Everybody warned him against it, but he had faith in it and in the end proved he was right.

John Lund—ACTOR

When I saw the first day's rushes on *To Each His Own,* I went home and started packing. I had thought I was smiling tenderly at Olivia de Havilland, but on screen I looked as though I were ready to bite her ear off, and I didn't have any eyes at all. After that I refused to look at myself, but I began enjoying the work.

Ida Lupino—ACTRESS

I didn't want to do *The Hard Way.* I was terribly worried. You see, I knew my father was ill but couldn't tell my mother. I was in a terrible state keeping it all to myself, and, as a matter of fact, I had a breakdown right in the middle of the picture when my father passed on. And that was the only award I ever won. I won the [New York] Critics' Award for *The Hard Way,* and I hated myself in it. I went to the preview with my mother and I said, "Connie, excuse me, dear, you stay and see the rest of this. It's making me terribly nervous, my performance." I walked.

—DIRECTOR/SCREENWRITER

I never planned to become a director. The fates and a combination of luck, good and bad, were responsible. For about 18 months in the '40s, I couldn't get an acting job at Warner Bros. because I was under suspension. I was married at the time to Collier Young—a man I loved then and still love—and we founded our own production company to make a series of small, truthful pictures. We co-wrote a script about unwed mothers called *Not Wanted* and put it before the camera. We had just started shooting when our director, Elmer Clifton, had a heart attack. We were much too poor to afford another director, so I stepped in and took over.

Roddy McDowall — ACTOR

I got the role [in *How Green Was My Valley*] when William Wyler was going to direct it. He did my test, then I was brought to Hollywood and the film was canceled. And then John Ford took over. Nobody wanted to make the film because war was looming on the horizon for America, and the stockholders thought it was a very dour subject.

Initially my part was to be very brief, and Tyrone Power was to play my character as an adult. They were going to do the other end of the story. And it's Phil [screenwriter Philip Dunne] who recrafted the whole concept. I'd made some 20 films before that, so I wasn't a novice, but in my memory, even after over a hundred films, it is the most succinct motion picture I was ever on.

Ford was terrific to me, which was very wise, 'cause if he hadn't been, I would have tightened up like a drum. So I think he was a very shrewd psychologist, actually. But there were certain people he was very rough on. I remember his being very tough on Sara Allgood.

* * *

I was so lucky in the people I learned from when I was young. In *The White Cliffs of Dover* I played with Irene Dunne. If I'd had the choice of whom to pick for my mother, it would have been Irene, and there she was, playing my mother in the film. When she started playing the scene where I'm going off to America, tears dancing in her eyes, she made *me* cry. I lost it, I just absolutely lost it.

Richard Maibaum — PRODUCER/SCREENWRITER

Paramount had Alan Ladd pegged as a dubious actor, but I didn't believe them. I was at his house, and he took me up to the second floor, where he had a wardrobe about as long as this room. He opened it up, and there must have been hundreds of suits, sports jackets, slacks and shoes. He looked at me and said, "Not bad for an Okie kid, eh?" I got goose pimples, because I remembered when Gatsby took Daisy to show her his mansion, he also showed her his wardrobe and said, "I have a man who sends me clothes from England every spring and fall." I said to myself, "My God, the Great Gatsby!" And he was, in a way, the Great Gatsby. Success had settled on him as it had on Gatsby. Being a movie star, he had the same kind of aura of success, but he didn't quite know how to handle it. He had the same precise, careful speech, the controlled manner, the carefully modulated voice. So I said to Sue [Carol, his wife] and Alan, "How about we do *The Great Gatsby?*"

Louis B. Mayer — STUDIO HEAD

In my opinion, *The Human Comedy* is the finest motion picture ever made by Metro-Goldwyn-Mayer. So is *Madame Curie.*

Ray Milland——ACTOR

After reading *The Lost Weekend,* I had to pour myself a double Scotch. It was a fine book and a *great* part.

* * *

There was one amusing thing that occurred [on *The Lost Weekend*] while we were shooting the interior of an old Irish bar on Third Avenue called P. J. Clarke's. It had been reborn on Stage Five with absolute exactitude, even to the dusty stuffed cat on top of the telephone booth, and this was the place where I, as Don Birnham, did most of my drinking and rationalizing.

For a full week, at five o'clock every afternoon, the stage door would open and a man would walk in and amble right up to the bar and ask for a straight bourbon. It made no difference to him whether we were shooting or not, and without blinking an eye, Howard da Silva, who was playing the bartender, would pour him out a straight shot from a bottle of the real stuff which he kept beneath the counter. The man would then drink half of it, and with a long exhale of pleasure look around and make some inane remark about the weather. Then he would finish the rest of it, plunk down 50 cents, give a painful little smile to the bartender and leave. While he was there, nobody said a word, and when he left we got on with our work as if nothing had happened.

The man? Robert Benchley. Who else? Like all expatriate New Yorkers, he was homesick. Besides, it would make for a very quotable anecdote.

Vincente Minnelli —— DIRECTOR

The actors delivered 100 percent in *The Clock.* I'd heard that Bob Walker, suffering the heartache of a broken marriage, was looking at life through the bottom of a liquor bottle. But he was always cheerful and on time. I wasn't aware of the toll the picture was taking on his nervous system, but Judy [Garland] knew. Make-up artist Dotty Ponedel recalls one night when Judy was supposed to be having a hen party with the girls, her publicity woman and stand-in included. The two of them actually went through West Side bars looking for Bob. They finally found him and took him to Dotty's to dry him out for the next morning's shooting. Judy never told me of this. Yes, there was much that was noble in her character.

Audie Murphy——ACTOR

In *Beyond Glory* I had eight words to say, seven more than I could handle.

Patricia Neal——ACTRESS

The night we closed production on *The Foundtainhead* was no different except for one thing. Gary Cooper and I were really in love with each other. By now everyone sensed it. No one spoke of it but the energy between us radiated an excitement that brought everyone at the party into its orb. I am sure most were wondering if the affair had begun or not, but at that moment our love was still innocent. Guests finally began to drift away, but Gary and I lingered. His wife was in New York. The moment had come.

Jean Negulesco — DIRECTOR

When J. L. Warner saw *Johnny Belinda,* his first words were "Sorry, boys, I have to take a leak."

When the great man returned—relieved—he spoke memorable words: "It's always in the men's room that I get my best ideas." Then, pointing his accusing finger at us, "We invented talking pictures and you make a picture about a deaf and dumb girl! Only one thing could save it. Narration over her silent close-ups to tell the public what she was thinking."

We fought the decision, and the picture was released as shot.

The next day Warner called me into his office. Though there were still three more years in my contract, I was fired.

I was working at 20th Century-Fox when the year's nominations for the best five productions were announced. Each and every department in *Johnny Belinda* was nominated.

To top all impudence, Jack Warner called me long distance: "Kid, we did it again!"

Merle Oberon — ACTRESS

This Love of Ours was the biggest success they've ever had in Mexico. Bigger than all the Cantinflas pictures. Well, they like that kind of schmaltzy thing, I suppose.

Director William Dieterle used to pick on Charles Korvin at the beginning and say, "This man is such a terrible actor." So I would start taking Charles aside, saying, "Now don't you listen to him at all. You're marvelous and you're going to have the biggest success in this picture, and you're a good actor." In about a week's time he was being a big actor with *me.* I've had that an awful lot, and it's so boring.

Jack Paar — ACTOR

While at RKO I played a small part in *Easy Living* with an attractive comedienne named Lucille Ball. One day she and I and the producer, Bob Sparks, were watching rushes in the projection room. As we sat in the dark, Miss Ball said, "Jack, do you know any young actor who does light comedy like you do who would want to play opposite me in a new TV series?"

I thought for a minute and finally suggested Hal March, a good young light comedian I knew, and Hy Averback, another good young actor I had known in the South Pacific.

When the rushes ended, and she departed, Bob Sparks came over to me and said: "You dumbbell! Don't you get it? She meant you. Why didn't you suggest yourself?"

Lucille finally settled on an unlikely choice to play opposite her—a Cuban band leader who happened to be her husband, Desi Arnaz.

The last time I was in Hollywood I drove wistfully past RKO which was jumping with television activity. It now belongs to Miss Ball and her husband. They bought it with the money they made from a TV series called *I Love Lucy.*

Eleanor Parker — ACTRESS

My favorite role was part constructive, part destructive and all enjoyable. I worked hard to build up a convincing cockney accent for the part of Mildred Rogers in the picture *Of Human Bondage.* Yet the scene I liked best was the one in which I wrecked a room.

"Smash everything," director Edmund Goulding said, handing me a poker. "We can only shoot this once, so let yourself go."

Following instructions, I mowed down furniture and assorted bric-a-brac in a way that would have made a blockbuster envious. That was fun, giving vent to some hidden destructive instinct, I guess. Anyway, it was important to the story because it showed how Mildred reacted to the knowledge that Philip Carey had completely lost his strange infatuation for her.

Building up a cockney accent was much slower and quieter work. I got a book dealing with this dialect as soon as I was assigned the part, and I pretty well wore it out. I studied it so much that I dreamed of the part, and doubtless talked with a cockney accent in my sleep. While the picture was being filmed, an English extra came up to me.

"I made a bet that you were brought up in England," he said. "Do I win?"

He lost; I hadn't even visited England then. But I was so flattered that I'd gladly have paid his bet.

Somerset Maugham made Mildred a wonderfully exasperating person, and the movie tried to keep that tone. Thus the role was essentially a character part, which I enjoyed. Mildred's showy dresses came from what the studio calls the rag bag, and I wore no make-up. I didn't try to look glamorous; I just tried to look Mildredish—a big enough job for anyone.

John Payne ——— *ACTOR*

When Claudette Colbert agreed to have me as her leading man in *Remember the Day,* it was a great boost to my career. And I enjoyed doing the musicals with Alice Faye, Betty Grable, June Haver and Sonja Henie. *The Razor's Edge* was important, and *Miracle on 34th Street* was a surprise hit. But my favorite film of all is a little black and white picture called *Sentimental Journey,* in which I played a grieving widower. When I tell you that the late wife was played by Maureen O'Hara, you'll know why I was grieving.

Gregory Peck ——— *ACTOR*

I worked with some great old-timers: Charles Laughton, Walter Huston, Ethel and Lionel Barrymore. They had fun acting. Lionel would rehearse a scene for hours before they would shoot it. By the time the scene was set, he had spent enough energy for 100 men. The director of *The Valley of Decision* once said to him, "For God's sake, Lionel, stop that. You're going to give yourself a heart attack." Lionel said, "W-e-l-l, who gives a damn!"

* * *

The Yearling was the first script where I could inject a bit of humor here and there. Jane Wyman was maybe the best actress in Hollywood at the time. The boy [Claude Jarman, Jr.] was directed to play the part crying and sniveling. It drove us crazy.

* * *

Dorothy McGuire was and still is a close friend. We felt we were brave pioneers, making a picture [*Gentleman's Agreement*] exploring anti-Semitism in the U.S. John Garfield, director Elia Kazan, producer Darryl F. Zanuck and Moss Hart, who wrote the screenplay—we were all hellbent on making an important picture, and we did. Today it seems a little dated. Maybe because we helped a little to break down those attitudes we felt so strongly about.

Walter Pidgeon ——— *ACTOR*

I began thinking what a break it would be to get the part of the minister [in *How Green Was My Valley*]. At the time my thinking on the matter was objective. We were making the last scenes of *Man Hunt* when the cameraman mentioned casually that he was shooting tests that night for *How Green Was My Valley.*

"Make them all bad," I said to him jokingly. I hadn't been asked to try out. "Want to do it yourself?" he asked. "Sure," I said. And I might have added that I'd enjoy playing Alice in Wonderland, too. It seemed just about as likely.

Then one day a note came from Darryl Zanuck asking me to talk to him and director John Ford about something "that is important to all of us." That was it. They asked me to play the part I'd been dreaming about for more than a year. I've never quite understood how it came about. Perhaps the cameraman did make all the tests bad.

* * *

Everywhere in the world that movie [*Mrs. Miniver*] is rated as my best and people always talk about it. I never told anyone this, but I always like two other films as the best of my career. I thought *Command Decision,* with Clark Gable, and *Madame Curie* were my best.

* * *

The other day my wife said, "There's a picture on TV with you and Greer [Garson]—*Mrs. Parkington.*" I couldn't remember it at all! I must have been out of town or something when it previewed, because I know I've never seen it.

H. C. Potter ——— DIRECTOR

With Cary Grant on *Mr. Lucky,* he would often distrust himself and the scene as written; he wanted to create something. So, very often I would take the scene as written and change some words around, change lines completely all the way through, deliberately. In the morning he would say, "I've been looking at this scene and I don't like it." I would say, "I don't like it much, either." So we would play around. I would gradually re-insert the original lines until we finally had the scene as originally written. But to him, all of a sudden it was brand new, and then we'd photograph it.

Otto Preminger ——— PRODUCER/DIRECTOR

One incident during the filming of *In the Meantime, Darling* involved the actor Eugene Pallette, who was an admirer of Hitler and convinced that Germany would win the war.

The scene took place in a kitchen where Pallette and a black actor were to have a conversation. The black actor was seated at a table and I told Pallette to make his entrance and sit down beside him.

"You're out of your mind," he said. "I won't sit next to a nigger."

I went to Darryl Zanuck and had him fired. Most of his scenes had been shot. We wrote him out of what was left.

Irving Rapper ——— DIRECTOR

Executive producer Hal Wallis asked why I cast Ilka Chase and Bonita Granville in *Now, Voyager,* and I told him, "These are the only people I can find who will needle Bette Davis." Bette Davis on the receiving end for a change, and it had to be very poignant and dramatic. And when she heard that she said, "Oh, Irving, you son-of-a-bitch!"

* * *

Bette Davis and John Dall were playing the very important scene [in *The Corn Is Green*] when she tells him he must go to Oxford. He was sitting down, and I told him to twist his cloth cap in his hands to suggest indecision and tension. He was supposed to stand up and stride manfully out of the room. Suddenly, he rose and began swinging his hips and wiggling his fanny at Bette. She threw up her hands and said to me, "This is impossible! We'll have to get another actor."

I said, "Wait a minute." I went over to John, who was red with embarrassment, and said, "Next time you get up, think of the King of England and imagine the national anthem playing and *march like a soldier.*"

John was a good sport. I called "Action!" and watched his fanny nervously. It didn't swish, and the scene was fine.

Ronald Reagan ——— ACTOR

As an actor, I guess I spent most of my finest moments in bed—the Gipper's death in *Knute Rockne—All American,* then a scene in *Kings Row,* in which I discovered my legs had been amputated by a sadistic and vindictive surgeon who was angry that I had romanced his daughter.

Anne Revere ——— ACTRESS

MGM signed me to a six-month contract at $600 per week. While waiting for them to figure out what to do with me, I became bored with not working. I made the mistake of saying "Use me" to the front office, so they gave me a maid's costume and had me carry a tray in a Robert Young picture, *H. M. Pulham, Esq.* No lines. I did it, then went crying to my agent. He told me, "You asked them to use you."

* * *

The Oscar for *National Velvet* came as a surprise, really. The odds were all against me. I was under contract to Fox, but the picture was MGM's, and MGM wasn't terribly interested in promoting an award for another studio's contract player. Nor was Fox anxious to push a picture made at Metro. Little Ann Blyth was the favorite for her performance in Warners' *Mildred Pierce.* My winning was such an upset, some of the papers the next day were still dazed and wrote things like, "Anne Revere, who played the troublesome teenager in *Mildred Pierce,* won the Best Supporting Actress Academy Award last night. . . ."

Casey Robinson ——— SCREENWRITER

I was leaving with my wife for a vacation to the Philippines and the Orient. This was 1940. Hal Wallis [executive producer at Warner Bros.] sent me a bon voyage present—an advance copy of the book *King's Row.* Well, I encountered nothing that could be used and everything that could not, or so it seemed at the time. There was one case after

another of insanity and of subjects that were forbidden: two love affairs between young people, miscegenation and incest, of all things—Dr. Tower's [Claude Rains] sexual affair with his daughter [Betty Field].

I was pretty horrified and understood why I had heard that this was a book that could not be translated to the screen. I remember well the time I finished the book. We were sailing on a little boat from the Philippines down to Bali—one of the most beautiful evenings you could imagine. I took the book and threw it overboard, saying, "Nobody else is going to see this bunch of trash!" And as it hit the water I got the idea that solved the major censorship problem—to change the subject from incest to an inherited tendency towards insanity. I cabled Wallis immediately: "Buy it."

***Mark Robson*——————EDITOR**

The Magnificent Ambersons. That film was heartbreaking. The great things that happened on that film . . . I guess people didn't care. They just left the theater. I think we must have taken it to dozens of previews. It reached a point when we had to pick up the film at the booth, people were waiting for us as if they were going to beat us up. They were so angered and annoyed.

——————DIRECTOR

On the first day of *Champion,* I was informed by my assigned film editor that a previous engagement precluded him from taking the job. While I was on the stage, an unemployed assistant editor, Harry Gerstad, came by to wish me luck. Harry and I had spent many hours together on the unemployment lines. He still needed a job. I made Harry the editor of *Champion.* Come Academy Award time, I was asked to present the editorial award. In front of the camera, under all those bright lights, dressed in tails—I pulled out the name of Harry Gerstad.

Ginger Rogers—ACTRESS

My first picture was *Kitty Foyle.* It was my mother who made all those pictures with Fred Astaire.

Ruth Roman—ACTRESS

My happiest 26 days in the movies were spent making the picture *Champion.* For, though you hear a great deal about teamwork in Hollywood, you almost never see as much of it as we did while shooting this film.

Whenever there was a question about a scene, we'd hold a group conference, complete with producer, director and cast, to thrash the matter out. Each suggestion was not only considered but also thoroughly discussed. If the suggestion was good, five or six persons would applaud; if not, just as many people would frankly tell you so.

All this was immensely helpful to me in playing the role of Emma, for I was very young in pictures then, and this was a quite different type of role from the few I'd played.

Kirk Douglas surprised me on the second day of shooting by saying, "Do you know that this picture is going to make you?"

I couldn't believe that, but Kirk insisted, and even offered to make a bet on it. If I had taken the bet, I would have lost, for the role of Emma did more for my career than any other role.

The scene I liked best was the one on the beach, and apparently a number of fans agreed with me. About half the letters I received asked for a picture of me in the bathing suit or the suit itself.

But the oddest letter came from a man in Georgia, who wrote that his greatest wish was to spend the last days of his life with me. "Unfortunately," he added, "by the time you read this, I will have been electrocuted. They say I killed a man."

Joseph Ruttenberg—CINEMATOGRAPHER

It was Louis B. Mayer who recommended me to director William Wyler to shoot *Mrs. Miniver.* Greer Garson wasn't too sure about me but after that it was a fight to get her to let anybody else photograph her. When they did the sequel, *The Miniver Story,* in England, she made them release me from another film I was doing and go over and shoot it. It wasn't a very good idea, that sequel, but they had some frozen funds over in England that they wanted to use. And, of course, [director] Hank Potter was no Wyler.

Wyler was another perfectionist. He was so wrapped up in the picture he was shooting that he wouldn't even say "Good morning" when he walked on the set—not being snooty or anything, just intense concentration. And never, ever satisfied. Take after take after take. And if he didn't like the rushes, he'd go back and do it some more. It was tough on the actors and Greer Garson got more and more angry until one Saturday morning she blew her stack, told Wyler what she thought of him and walked off the set. It was quite a scene.

Natalie Schafer——————ACTRESS

In 1948, films didn't dare show women as pregnant. It was talked about but not displayed. I had to fight to have a sandbag strapped around my middle to look pregnant in *The Snake Pit.* The head office had to make a decision as to whether it was all right. Imagine, with what's going on in films today! What a difference!

Martha Scott——————ACTRESS

David O. Selznick brought me from New York to Hollywood to test for Melanie in *Gone with the Wind.* I looked awful in the test, and Mr. Selznick told me to go home. "You're for the theater," he said.

Consequently, when I was asked to test for the film version of *Our Town,* I had no high hopes. Another thing: about 75 girls were tested. Still, I went ahead and did the test with Bill Holden, who was already signed to co-star, and was ready to go home again. I saw the test in a projection room with my agent, whom I kept telling to hold my hand, I was so nervous. I couldn't believe how well it went! There I was up there at the age of 12 with pigtails, and then, with a big bow in the back as a teenager with Bill in the drugstore scene. It was all as good as anything that got in the movie itself.

Bert Glennon, who photographed the test *and* the movie, was a genius. I was 24 but he made me look like a kid!

Ann Sheridan——————ACTRESS

A year before Warners made *King's Row,* Bogie came to me on the set early one morning.

"Sister Annie," he said, "I just read a great book, *Kings Row.* I hear the studio has bought it, and there's a great part in it that you'd be perfect for. Girl named Randy. Better do something about it!"

I did. I read the book. I was excited about the character of Randy. If I could play that role, I'd have a part to "get my teeth into." I learned that I had been suggested for the part, but not definitely cast. I started doing a little campaigning. I offered to do tests. After months of waiting, I got the role. I'll always be grateful to Bogie for that suggestion.

* * *

The Man Who Came to Dinner—I didn't want to do that because I was doing Randy in *Kings Row.* Two pictures at once! And my only love was Randy Monaghan. I didn't care about playing Lorraine Sheldon. I used to work, say, one day on *Kings Row* and the next day on *Man Who Came to Dinner,* or one morning I'd work as Lorraine Sheldon and that afternoon I was Randy Monaghan. It was horrible! And more than that, the make-up, hairdo, everything. Awful thing to have to go through.

I was told later that the New York critics gave *King's Row* bad reviews because they thought it was Communistic—the poor winning over the rich! And don't forget, Warners had just done *Mission to Moscow,* and things were very touchy. If you didn't like bread and butter, it was a Commie thing.

Vincent Sherman——DIRECTOR

When I read the script for *The Hard Way,* I felt it would be the first time there would be an honest picture about backstage, and it would show the theatrical business as it is: a tough, dirty, cut-throat game. I wanted to give it a low-key photography to enhance the realism. Ida Lupino wasn't very happy about it, and we had some problems. But they were later resolved when she won the New York Film Critics Award for her performance in the film.

* * *

Bette Davis made it very difficult for me on *Mr. Skeffington.* The more I resisted, the more impossible she became. She insisted we become lovers. She threatened to have the entire production shut down if I continued to refuse her. I've worked with many actresses, including Joan Crawford, but no one was as destructive as Bette. That sexual suppression you see on the screen, that nervous hysterical energy, was not acting. That's the way she was in real life. The only way I could finish the picture was by having an affair with her.

George Sidney——DIRECTOR

Censorship in the forties? There was a scene in *Cass Timberlane,* with Spencer Tracy and Lana Turner. Tracy and Turner were married, and he was supposed to sit down and talk to her on the edge of her bed where she was lying before going to the hospital. Snow was falling outside and there was a fire in the fireplace. But the censor said, "He can't sit on the bed if there's a lady in it." I said, "That was no lady, that was his *wife.*" But they didn't care. Tracy had to play the scene sitting in a chair by the bed.

Donald Ogden Stewart—SCREEN-—WRITER

It hurt terribly to have done what you thought was a very good scene and you'd find Lana Turner didn't like it and so they'd have you write it the way Lana Turner wanted. The one trouble at first with *Cass Timberlane* was Lana. Spencer Tracy was a terribly professional actor who worked on the script and knew it by heart, and Lana'd come onto the set not having the foggiest idea what the thing was about, not knowing the lines or anything. Spencer was very angry during the first couple of weeks. Then it got better and at the end he said, "That is a good actress." She got his respect eventually and I think *Cass* was quite a good picture.

* * *

It was right after *Edward, My Son* that I got knocked off. That was in 1949, and they were beginning to close in on me. Ma and I came over here to London so I could see the play, and then I wrote the screenplay for Spence [Tracy], with George Cukor directing. There were some people who spread the story around that Metro had sent me over here to get me out of the country, so I couldn't be served with a subpoena by the House Un-American Activities Committee guys. But I did go back to Hollywood and I never did get subpoenaed. Maybe they were looking for some other Don Stewart, but who knows? I'd written a play called *The Kidders,* and an English producer wanted to put it on here, so we came back to London—and we've been here ever since.

Dean Stockwell ———— ACTOR

When I was a kid, working for [director] Elia Kazan in *Gentleman's Agreement,* he had his own particular way of working, and I had this whole emotional thing I had to go through. I found myself forced to just stand there and nod, going uh-huh, uh-huh, and let him say whatever he had to say. Then I'd forget all that stuff and just do it my way.

Mary Stuart ———— ACTRESS

When I had been on the MGM lot about four months, I got a call to go to the wardrobe department for a

"You didn't win, Robie... but you fought like a man — I'm proud of you!"

fitting, and just before she hung up the secretary added, "Mr. Gable will meet you there."

Oh, good grief! It had to be important if Clark Gable cared enough to look at a costume! With fantasies flying, the Ford and I sped out Saint Vincente.

Sure enough, he was there, sitting in a big chair in one of the fitting rooms reserved for stars. He stood up and thanked me for hurrying and explained that it wasn't a big part, but he thought it was important to the picture and that's why he wanted to choose the costume himself. I was to play a model in his new picture, *The Hucksters,* with Deborah Kerr, and the scene would be with him.

Gazing up at a legend, who also happened to be very nice and very handsome, I was too awed and excited to ask questions. I just followed the wardrobe mistress into the little changing room. I couldn't wait to see the costume! I could have waited. The entire little room was lined with bathing suits! Dozens and dozens of bathing suits! For the next three and a half hours I sidled back and forth from the big room to the little one wearing a total, I think, of 83 different bathing suits, while Mr. Gable watched and nodded and smiled.

In the picture, I had to lie on my back, holding up a bottle of suntan lotion, waving my legs in the air, then mutter a line to the photographer as I left, while Clark played a scene with Miss Kerr. I didn't think it was that important at all.

Jessica Tandy——ACTRESS

In *The Green Years,* I was playing [husband Hume Cronyn's] daughter, who was not married, and I was six or seven months pregnant at the time, so I had lots of close-ups. They gave me trays to carry—even gave me a baby to carry at one point—so no one would see I was pregnant.

Elizabeth Taylor——ACTRESS

By the time I left Universal, we'd moved to Beverly Hills and one of Dad's fellow air-raid wardens was a producer named Sam Marx who was doing a film called *Lassie Come Home.* It was almost finished except for perhaps ten scenes. They required a little girl with an English accent. The girl they had cast had grown about a foot since they hired her and now they were in a panic to find a substitute. It was during the war and English accents were hard to come by. Mr. Marx got my father to let me audition. I went down to the studio and pretended to pat an imaginary collie on a bare sound stage. It was a snap for a Walter Mittying dog lover.

* * *

MGM had owned *National Velvet* for a long time and every once in a while they'd sort of dust it off. But they either couldn't find somebody of the right size or somebody who rode or somebody with an English accent. They began casting glances in my direction. Well, it was my favorite book, and I really was a marvelous horsewoman. At three I could jump without a saddle. But when I came down to the producer's office, he saw that though I was 11, I was only as tall as a six-year-old. He measured me on the wall and made a line with a pencil. He said, "I'm sorry, honey, but you're just too short. No one would ever believe that you could get in through the jockey's weighing room. You look like a child." And I said, "Well, I'll grow up."

I was absolutely determined. *National Velvet* was really me. I started riding every morning for an hour and a half before school. And there was this place Tip's, where they had a thing called a Farm Breakfast—two hamburger patties, two fried eggs, a great big mound of hash brown potatoes and after that a whole bunch of dollar pancakes. I used to have two Farm Breakfasts every morning. For lunch I'd have steaks and salads, then swim and do exercises to stretch myself.

In three months I went back to the producer and said, "I did grow." He said, "You do look taller." He still had the little mark by the side of the door, and I had grown three inches. He kept that mark on the wall for years. And I got the part.

I think *Velvet* is still the most exciting film I've ever done.

Shirley Temple——ACTRESS

Although aware of Claudette Colbert's standard prohibition against being photographed from her right side, I was reluctant to cooperate to my own disadvantage [in *Since You Went Away*]. One early occasion found each of us zigzagging backward toward a fireplace to avoid being upstaged by the other. Our

DAVID O. SELZNICK
presents his first production since "Gone With The Wind" and "Rebecca"
"Since You Went Away"
Claudette COLBERT • Jennifer JONES • Joseph COTTEN • Shirley TEMPLE • Monty WOOLLEY • Lionel BARRYMORE • Robert WALKER

respective movements resulted in the necessity for her right side to move into the camera. Suddenly she reached out and grabbed my chin. Firmly holding my head faced away from the camera, she rotated herself to a left exposure, a not-so-gentle hint from mother to daughter that she would not tolerate any tricks.

* * *

A pressing problem [on *I'll Be Seeing You*] was a puzzling antipathy toward me from Ginger Rogers. Someone whom I never recalled meeting before but whom I held in highest esteem, she seemed to have disliked me from a distance . . . I was told she flatly demanded I be taken off the film. . . . From that point Rogers and I regarded each other cautiously. Although several times I attempted to establish some offstage rapport, at every point she seemed to resist intimacy. Usually, she regarded me silently, if at all, with her eyes narrowed, and occasionally she needled me before others.

* * *

Director Peter Godfrey wanted to retake the suicide scene in *That Hagen Girl.* As I edged down a slippery path with wind-driven rain pelting my face, all trace of make-up vanished. The water was murky, but at body temperature and chlorinated, prophylactic measures for both Ronald Reagan's recent infection (pneumonia) and my current condition (pregnancy). Gingerly wading out into the river, I stopped, took a deep breath and ducked under as my hero came flailing through the shallows like a bull elephant. Lifting my sodden, bedraggled form, he removed it to his place rather than mine. In the miracle of movies, I became dried off, clothed in his oversized pajamas and wrapped in a predictable on-camera clinch. As movie kissers go, Reagan was good.

"Just think," I whispered into his off-camera ear, "you've just saved *two* people."

Gene Tierney——— ACTRESS

Ty Power had an impish streak. For a nightclub scene in *The Razor's Edge,* he persuaded the prop man to fill our glasses with champagne, instead of the usual plain or colored water used in such scenes. After a few takes, we felt quite gay and relaxed. This was the silent sequence, with music over it, showing us doing the town in Paris. We had little if any dialogue, while Russian gypsies played enchanting music. The scene had a special glow that came out of our champagne glasses.

Ann Todd——— ACTRESS

We started filming *The Seventh Veil* without a leading man and worked for three weeks while producer Sidney Box tried desperately to find one. I was practically unknown in films, especially in America, and no one wished to play with me.

At last Sidney gathered us all together and said that we couldn't go on unless the money was forthcoming and we had a star. I stood rooted to the ground, unable to speak. Sidney, who had given me this great chance

"Now I know that when you married me... you hated me!"

and so much encouragement, came over to me and said: "This is when you need courage. Many actors before you have had to take these sort of blows, it is how you take it that matters; let's hope for a miracle." That night I prayed and prayed. I must have worn God out.

At the end of the week we had our miracle. James Mason agreed to play the part.

Audrey Totter——ACTRESS

One day while filming *The Saxon Charm* we were in the [Universal] commissary and Bela Lugosi was there, with a young boy. Bob Montgomery said, in a melodramatic voice, "I see that Bela Lugosi is having a small boy for lunch!"

Spencer Tracy——ACTOR

It's rather disconcerting to me to find out how easily I play a heel [in *Edward, My Son*]. I'm a much better actor than I thought. When I was doing Father Flanagan in *Boys Town,* that was acting. This is not acting.

Lana Turner——ACTRESS

We finished most of the shooting on *Green Dolphin Street* and I started my new picture, *Cass Timberlane.* My old champion, Spencer Tracy, was the co-star. Production had just begun when the studio called for retakes on *Green Dolphin Street.* I would have to divide my days between the sets.

For *Green Dolphin Street* I had long dark hair, styled 34 different ways, because I matured in the course of the story. But for *Cass Timberlane* my hair was cut short and dyed back to its usual blonde. How could I do those retakes with short blonde hair? Helen Young came up with the answer. She assembled 34 hairpieces in the appropriate styles. Every afternoon she would spray my hair with vegetable dye and then weave in the false hair. After the retake she'd strip out the dye so I would be blonde the next morning.

Marianne, my character in *Green Dolphin Street,* was British-born, so I'd developed a kind of mid-Atlantic accent. Not quite British, but not quite American, either. But in *Cass Timberlane* I played a thoroughly American girl. I struggled to keep the accents straight, but sometimes my Marianne voice came out. "My, my," Spencer would say, "aren't we British this morning?"

King Vidor — DIRECTOR

Hedy Lamarr at this time was, in the world's eyes, *the* sex-image.

As the New York secretary in *H. M. Pulham, Esq.,* Hedy, in spite of her slight Austrian accent, did a fine job. After the finish of the shooting, we had a party for the entire company, where, traditionally, all participants let down their hair, call each other by first names and generally release the inhibitions and disciplines of shooting a movie. It so happened that the first girl to come up to me at the party in all exuberance was Hedy. She gave me a big kiss.

That evening when I got home Elizabeth [his wife] had some questions about the telltale rouge. "Nothing to get excited about"—I waved it off—"it's only Hedy Lamarr."

Joseph Walker — CINEMATOGRAPHER

Penny Serenade, with Irene Dunne and Cary Grant (and being photographed by another cameraman), had been in production a couple of weeks at Columbia, but things weren't going well. Irene let it be known she wasn't happy with the way she looked in the rushes. I had to rearrange my schedule and take over.

Producer-director George Stevens had the reputation of being an exacting director and difficult on cameramen. I found him exacting all right, and even difficult, but I admired him.

Penny Serenade became an outstanding hit. Some weeks after its release I talked with Harry Cohn about the problems of making it. Cohn mused, "That George Stevens is one son-of-a-bitch to work with. But given the chance, I'd hire him again anytime."

Jack L. Warner — STUDIO HEAD

The way that guy [director Jean Negulesco] fusses over this damned picture [*Johnny Belinda*], you'd think he had another *Gone with the Wind* on his hands. For Christ's sake, it's only about a deaf-mute who gets raped, knocked up and later kills the rapist!

I've heard enough of that "art" shit from Bette Davis. I don't mind if the picture has some class, but I want it to sell, goddamn it!

John Wayne — ACTOR

Long Voyage Home was right after *Stagecoach,* but I was still doing six-day Westerns. I finished one Western at 12 o'clock at night and the next morning I had to start *Long Voyage* where I was a Swedish sailor, presumably with an accent, with no chance for any coaching. I had to play a straight part as a Swede and my accent couldn't ciash with John Qualen's who was playing a comic Swede. I wanna tell you, that was quite a switch from the night before, knocking people around and jumping on a horse.

Clifton Webb — ACTOR

On *The Razor's Edge,* I lost the Supporting Actor Oscar to that man with no hands [Harold Russell in *The Best Years of Our Lives*]. It caused a scandal. Everyone said he should have received just the special award, but he got the Best Supporting Actor award, too.

Orson Welles — PRODUCER/DIRECTOR/SCREENWRITER

I was fired by RKO. They made a great publicity point that I had gone to South America [to film the uncompleted *It's All True*] without a script and thrown all this money away. I never recovered from that attack. They had promised me when I went to South America that they would send a Movieola and cutters to me and that I would finish the cutting of *Magnificent Ambersons* there. They never did. They cut it themselves. So they destroyed *Ambersons* and the picture itself destroyed me. I didn't get another job as a director for years.

Henry Wilcoxon — ACTOR

I played the minister [in *Mrs. Miniver*], and at the end I give this sermon in the blitzed church. We finished the picture and, while they were cutting it, Pearl Harbor came along and suddenly we were at war. I was in the service, and they ran this picture and suddenly realized that the sermon I made was much too pacifistic. They needed something much more Winston Churchillish, so they had to get hold of the Navy Department for permission for me to come back.

The Navy gave me permission for two days' absence; I flew to Los Angeles. [Director] William Wyler and I stayed up all night re-writing that sermon, and finally, with coffee running out of our ears, we opened the curtains; it was broad daylight. It was about seven in the morning, and I had to be on the set at nine. I took a quick shave, got made up and had the thing in the can by noon. Roosevelt liked the speech so much that he had it reprinted and translated, and they had it dropped in leaflets all over Germany, Austria and occupied France.

Billy Wilder — SCREENWRITER

On *Hold Back the Dawn* there was a scene where Charles Boyer is lying in bed. He's a Rumanian gigolo who is stuck in Mexicali in a filthy, dirty hotel, waiting for his luck to change.

He's got no papers, he's got no chance to get into the United States. In this scene a cockroach is crawling up the wall. Boyer's got a little stick and he talks to the cockroach: "Where do you think you're going? Have you got a visa?" And he whacks it.

So co-writer Charles Brackett and I are having lunch at the restaurant across the street from Paramount, and there is Boyer having lunch. And I said, "Well, how's it going. Charlie?" He says, "Beautiful. Love it." And I say, "What are you shooting today?" He says, "Well, we are shooting that scene with the cockroach, but we changed it a little. I do not talk to the cockroach, because that's stupid. How can I talk to a cockroach if a cockroach cannot answer me?"

I was really furious, and on the way out I said to Brackett, "That sonofabitch. If he don't talk to a cockroach, he don't talk to nobody." We went back and finished the third act and we gave everything to Olivia de Havilland.

—— ***DIRECTOR/SCREENWRITER***

In *The Lost Weekend* I again went for a realistic approach. Originally, I wanted José Ferrer to play the part of the drunk: I had seen him as Iago to Paul Robeson's Othello, and he was superb. But Paramount told me to forget it. Buddy DeSylva, the studio boss, said that if the drunk wasn't an extremely attractive man, who apart from being a drunk could have been a hell of a nice guy and wanted to be saved, then audiences wouldn't go for it.

Tennessee Williams —— ***SCREENWRITER***

I once spent several months under contract to MGM in 1943, making $250 a week, and I didn't write a goddamn thing except a thing for Lana Turner called *Marriage Is a Private Affair*. It wasn't bad, but I was writing for a *real* actress and Miss Lana Turner could not say the lines, so they finally told me they couldn't use my script because it was simply beyond her capabilities. When I saw the picture, they only kept two of my lines. Then they asked me to write a movie for Margaret O'Brien and I refused.

Teresa Wright —— ***ACTRESS***

Every one of the roles except mine seemed credible [in *The Best Years of Our Lives*]. I just could not concentrate on the part. I never really liked the girl I played (nor me) in the film. You must be able to understand and believe the character. And I just didn't believe. How could that supposedly sensitive, intelligent girl be capable of turning on her parents in such an adolescent manner with the charge, "You've forgotten what it's like to be in love!"

Outside of that, I loved the picture.

William Wyler —— ***DIRECTOR***

The most satisfaction I can get out of a film, aside from its being successful financially and critically, is if it has been able to contribute something to the thinking of people; socially, politically. In this sense, almost every film should be a propaganda film. Propaganda. That is a dirty word in Hollywood. What they mean is no *obvious* propaganda. *Mrs. Miniver* was pure propaganda. Propaganda against the Germans, and for the English, and for us entering the war. But no one ever accused us of it, because it was entertaining. Many people saw it and, perhaps, it changed the minds of a few. The America First people were violently opposed to it.

* * *

The Best Years of Our Lives contains some of my best work and, oddly enough, it was the easiest to do. It was about returning from the war, as I had just done. I spent four years in research, so to speak. I knew how those boys felt. I was like Freddie March. I was not a young kid anymore; I had no problem getting a job. But I did have a problem getting readjusted to civilian life. I wasn't like Harold Russell, the boy who lost his hands, but I did get hurt a little. I had lost an ear, and it was very bothersome. I knew how it felt to come back in not quite as good shape as when you left. *Best Years* was an attempt to show an important social condition in our country, in all countries that have been at war. In many ways it was successful, it contributed to the life of the people. I got great satisfaction from that.

* * *

Die Besten Jahre unseres Lebens [*The Best Years of Our Lives*]—the dubbed version was very good. You got the impression it was about German soldiers returning home. I wanted to see one reel only, but sat through the whole picture. It was like a different film altogether.

Jane Wyman ——— ACTRESS

I worked on *The Yearling* for nine-and-a-half months. Clarence Brown, our director, had been at it for ages before I joined the company, and Gregory Peck and Claude Jarman, Jr., the little boy who plays Jody, had done a good many scenes. It was my first drab, heavily dramatic part. I was a young-old woman, a plain, hopeless person, full of bitterness and despair. I had played a dramatic role in *The Lost Weekend,* but in that I wasn't doing a character part.

Acting is hard to explain. Some people do it entirely by technique. They work each scene out like a chess problem, and carefully follow the strategy as they planned it beforehand. Some people work at each line, digging into every word, wearing themselves out over a single sentence. I can't do it like that. I have to get a character, understand her, become part of the story. That's all very well if it's a simple character in a light story. "Ma" isn't simple. Playing her matured me.

My father used to say: "Jane, you can't show life until you've *had* life." That's so true. If they had cast me in *The Yearling* ten years ago [1936], I couldn't have done it. I wasn't ready. I believe there's a certain pattern in life. When you are ready for a thing, you can do it, and there's no use getting impatient beforehand. If you got the chance, you couldn't do anything but fail.

* * *

For *Johnny Belinda,* I studied for six months in a school for the deaf and did the whole movie with my ears sealed in wax to blot out every noise except percussion sounds. I still remember the sign language.

That film was almost never released. We filmed up the California coast and Jack Warner hated it because when he saw the footage he yelled, "It's just a simple story and they're up the coast shooting a bunch of damned sea gulls!" After the first preview, he hated it so much he stuck it in cans and nobody knew what happened to it. Everyone was fired at the end of the picture and [director] Jean Negulesco wasn't even allowed to do his own editing. He has never to this day set foot in the Warner Bros. studio again.

One day somebody was rummaging around in a lot of dusty cans of film in the New York office and found some reels of the picture and ran them and it finally got shown and you know the rest. I made Jack Warner take out an ad and apologize to everyone connected with the film, from the grips to the water boy, and he named every person.

Fred Zinnemann — DIRECTOR

The Search was about displaced children in Europe after World War II. Some of the children we used had really been in a concentration camp and others were ordinary Swiss children. For one scene I asked a couple of the latter to look frightened at a woman in uniform because she was supposed to remind them of the female officers in the camp, and they just looked blank. They didn't know the meaning of fear. Then I told the same thing to two of the kids who had been in a concentration camp and the terror that they registered on their faces was incredible. The boy who played the main part [Ivan Jandl] was Czech and he knew German. I tried speaking to him in German but he wouldn't react to anything I said to him in German because it reminded him of the camps. So I had to direct him through a Czech interpreter.

Epics

Charles Bennett — SCREENWRITER

On *Reap the Wild Wind* we hadn't got the climax at all and [Cecil B.] DeMille was getting nervous. We had a conference and DeMille was saying, "Well, what are we going to do with the end of the picture? We've got nothing!" I had been keeping very quiet, but now he turned to me and said, "Charles, haven't you got an idea?"

Well, you don't want to disappoint DeMille, and I said, "Yes . . . I have. I thought it up while I was taking my bath this morning. What if we have John Wayne and Ray Milland down there below the sea, they're about to fight when . . . they are interrupted by *a giant squid!*" And I began to act a whole scene out for him. I played John Wayne's part. I played Ray Milland's part. I played *the giant squid's* part. And by the end I had DeMille sitting there, completely transfixed, seeing the scene before him. And he breathed, *"In Technicolor!"*

It was shot, and I think that squid scene was probably half the reason the picture was such a big hit. And I'd thought of it in my bath.

Ingrid Bergman — ACTRESS

For Whom the Bell Tolls was my first movie in color. We worked 12 weeks in the mountains and later 12 weeks in the studio, Paramount spending $3,000,000 on their biggest film. I enjoyed it all so much, particularly Gary Cooper. What was wrong was that my happiness showed on the screen. I was far too happy to honestly portray Maria's tragic figure.

Linda Christian — ACTRESS

In *Green Dolphin Street,* my role as companion to the female star [Lana Turner] involved many weeks on location for exterior scenes in the majestic pine forests north of San Francisco. The star unexpectedly gave us all an opportunity to explore the beauties of the surrounding scenery when she suddenly went south to Mexico, and shooting was held up for four days until her return. Her holiday had done little to alleviate the cold atmosphere, however, and I found myself being stared at during one of my brief close-ups, when she appeared and demanded sarcastically of the director, "Tell me, what do I have to do to get a close-up like this?" I had been directed simply to react to a sudden earthquake.

Cecil B. DeMille — PRODUCER/DIRECTOR

The part that stumped us was that of Louvette, the fiery, seductive half-breed girl [in *North West Mounted Police*]. We considered a half-dozen or so, without finding the one actress who would be exactly right, until one day Florence Cole came into my private office and said, "Louvette is here to see you." Florence is not given to making practical jokes, and she is extremely careful not to let anyone waste my time. With no idea of what was in the wind, I told her to usher Louvette in.

A dark girl, with eyes that could smoulder or melt, came in, made up as a half-breed and costumed as such a girl would dress on the wild Canadian frontier in the 1880s.

She gave me one insolent look and said, "You teenk you wan beeg director, hah? Me, Louvette, show you!"

That was enough: Paulette Goddard had the part.

Philip Dunne — SCREENWRITER

Forever Amber turned into a conflict between a resistible force (Cornel Wilde) and a moveable object (Linda Darnell).

Douglas Fairbanks, Jr.—ACTOR

I was anxious to go off and win the war single-handed, and just wanted to complete *The Corsican Brothers,* which I thought was going rather badly. I didn't think it was going to be any good; it was black and white instead of color. I thought they were cutting corners, but they weren't listening to me.

So I went off and when I returned, I was astonished to find that it was this huge smash. Today, I can see why it was a popular film, but I can also see how it could have been much better. I don't think I was wrong.

Paulette Goddard—ACTRESS

Unconquered wound up making a lot of money, but, except for working opposite Gary Cooper, I don't have such pleasant memories of making it.

We were always being attacked by Indians, and there was one scene where flaming arrows were supposed to whiz by my head. I told our director, Cecil B. DeMille, that I absolutely, positively would not do anything that dangerous. He cursed me, threatened to kill me, said I was ruining the picture. I packed and ran to New York. He finally shot my scene from afar with my stand-in, who had to wear a wig to match my scenes. Later, I heard that her wig caught fire during the scene. *I* was not wearing a wig in the part!

Mr. DeMille didn't speak to me for years.

Susan Hayward—ACTRESS

On the first day of filming *Reap the Wild Wind,* I said to Mr. [Cecil B.] DeMille, "Excuse me, Mr. DeMille, but do you think that. . . ?" He cut me short and said, "Young lady, I hired you for this film because I want an actress who can think for herself. Do that and you'll take a load of worry off my mind and add years to your own!"

Gene Kelly—ACTOR

I know that by far my favorite movie was [the silent] *The Three Musketeers,* with Douglas Fairbanks. None of the others could touch it. I loved remaking it. I had the image of Douglas Fairbanks, Sr., still fresh in my mind when I made it, and even though ours was a color picture on a greater scale, and the script written at great length, trying to probe the characters more deeply than they were done in silent pictures, I never escaped the influence of Fairbanks.

Hedy Lamarr—ACTRESS

"You know," my producer/director, Cecil B. DeMille, said to me on *Samson and Delilah,* "up to this point in your life every man in the audience wanted to marry you. After this picture every man will want to go to bed with you. I have taken you out of the living room and brought you into the bedroom." Crude but succinct!

When I smiled and told him I preferred being in the living room, he would laugh and say, "How charming you look when you lie."

Angela Lansbury—ACTRESS

Louis B. Mayer never chased me around his desk or tried anything with me. Of course, he never gave me any good parts, either. I'll never forget begging him to let me play Lady de Winter in *Three Musketeers* and watching the part go to Lana Turner while I had to play Queen Anne.

Rouben Mamoulian — DIRECTOR

I made *The Mark of Zorro,* with Tyrone Power . . . took seven days to cut it . . . and we previewed it in a 20th Century-Fox projection room. Darryl Zanuck was there, surrounded by his Greek Chorus. Their reaction was terrific, until the head man ordered me back in the projection room at eight the next evening. "We're going to run the film again—by the time *we* finish, it will be a great picture."

I showed up and sat through a harrowing experience. Zanuck had his film cutter alongside him. Every few seconds he would punch the man in his ribs. Obediently, the cutter wrote down the key words of that scene, so that he could go back and find the places Zanuck wanted to change. I cringed and thought to myself that 20th's boss obviously has a nervous tic. He couldn't possibly have wanted *that* many changes.

Actually, he had decided to cut every lyrical, poetical scene and leave in only the action. I said, "Darryl, you have just ruined a very good picture. Please, take my name off it—and forget about me ever doing another film on this lot."

The Chorus trembled. Zanuck's face was beet red. It was four o'clock in the morning, and he kept yelling at me. Then he said, "You had *your* cut and preview, I want mine."

He took his version of *The Mark of Zorro* out to a theater in suburban Riverside and ran it before a packed house. The audience hated it. Afterward, Zanuck and his group walked out with me. He put his arm around my shoulder and said, "You see, Rouben, you and I *together* are the best cutting team in Hollywood. Now, put every scene back in—and ship it."

Victor Mature — ACTOR

"There's nothing to be afraid of," Cecil B. DeMille assured me when I refused to do a stunt in *Samson and Delilah.* I told him, "I wouldn't walk up a wet step."

Ray Milland — ACTOR

In *Reap the Wild Wind,* the role demanded curly hair, so they gave me women's permanents with the electric curlers and all that. After seven weeks of filming, I found my hair coming out by the handfuls. Ever since, I have used a hairpiece.

Jean Peters — ACTRESS

My mother held no hopes for me in pictures, any more than I did. Her attitude was, "Well, you can have fun for six months and then come back and finish college."

Well, I made the test [for *Captain from Castile*], and shortly after that Mr. [Darryl] Zanuck called me into his office again. When he told me I had won the role, I could do little but stare blankly. I'd never expected any such a thing as this, never in my wildest dreams. As I was leaving his office, he said to me, "If you don't hear from me again, you know all's well, but if you do hear from me, you know it's trouble." I've never seen him again, so I guess there's nothing too wrong.

I didn't have a chance to be nervous at all during the first few days' shooting. For my debut in front of the cameras, I did the scene where Catana has to fight off some dogs that are attacking her. It was a tough, hard scene to do—physically. Henry King, the director, told me later he had purposely made me do that one first so I wouldn't be afraid of anything.

Mr. King was a great help to me, and so was Ty [Power]. I'd envisioned Ty as something like a great god and was afraid he wouldn't be very interested in what I did in the picture. But he did so many things that made my job easier.

There were plenty of problems for me in the picture, too. In one scene, I had to roast chickens on a spit, but every time I turned the handle, the chickens fell off. The smoke from the fire got in my eyes and made me cry. It took quite a while to get that scene right.

Another time, I had to get up on a horse with Ty. The Mexican horse was supposed to be trained to carry two people, but apparently its training had been neglected for it became nervous and made a beeline for the camera. Then when we tried again, I got caught in the sword Ty was wearing and had my legs cut up.

Otto Preminger ——— DIRECTOR

I wanted Lana Turner for *Forever Amber,* and [Darryl] Zanuck had been insisting on Linda Darnell. So, very much in the Hollywood manner, I invited Lana and Zanuck to a dinner party so she could persuade him—and she was practically sitting on his lap. She wanted it. But she was at Metro, and Zanuck wouldn't give it to anybody he didn't have under contract. He said, "If you think Lana Turner is right, then we'll dye Linda Darnell's hair blonde, and she'll be exactly like her." So she played the part, and she wasn't so bad. It wasn't her fault.

The Legion of Decency really emasculated the picture. There was an incredible scene in Spyros Skouras' office. The head of the Legion didn't even want to see the picture. He said to Skouras, "We banned the book. Why did you buy it and make a picture?" And Skouras literally went down on his knees and said, "Father, please, we invested $6,000,000 in this picture. Please. Go and look at it with Mr. Preminger." The man said, "Change the title," because they felt it was very irreverent of 20th Century–Fox to make a film of a book that was banned.

Finally, we had to put on a foreword that spoke about sin and how it is punished ("The wages of sin is death"). Then, whenever two people kissed, we had to dissolve or cut as their lips approached. Anyway, I don't think the film was a masterpiece one way or the other.

Anthony Quinn ——— ACTOR

Jack Warner had a script for me called *Sweet Music.* I read it and it was horrible. I said, "Jack, I want. . . ." And he said, "Just a second, *just* a second! Look, Dick Whorf turned me down, Julie Garfield turned me down, Bogart turned me down, George Raft turned me down. Everybody's turning me down! You, *I'm* turning down. You can quit the studio."

Now quitting at the salary I was getting was rather embarrassing, because it was $750 a week, which was keeping the family very well in those days.

So I went across the street and called up my agent, Charlie Feldman, and said, "Charlie, I haven't got a job." He said, "Yeah, well, I just got you another contract with 20th Century-Fox for $900 a week and you're playing in *Blood and Sand,* with Rita Hayworth and Tyrone Power."

Hal Roach, Sr. —— *PRODUCER/DIRECTOR*

One Million B.C. was a prehistoric picture, a figment of my imagination. D. W. Griffith came over to work for me, and I said, "Dave, I'd like you to cast the picture."

They brought in girls. I wasn't paying any attention. He looked at them. We had already decided on Victor Mature as the man and Lon Chaney as the father. Every time these girls came in, he took them to the back lot. I didn't know what the hell he was doing out in the open spaces. Then one day he said, "I found your girl." It was Carole Landis. "Come out, I want to show you something." He looked at the girl and said, "Take your shoes off. Now run to that post as fast as you can. Then run back to me as fast as you can." She did. I wasn't particularly impressed. That's a hell of a way to pick your leading lady. He said, "I've had 50 girls run to that post and back. She's the only one who knows how to run. You're not going to make believable a girl in a picture of that kind who runs like an average girl. She's got to run like an athlete, a deer."

And she could. Her rhythm was really beautiful. In the picture, you never noticed it. But if she ran like most girls, you would damn well have seen the difference.

Flora Robson —— *ACTRESS*

Errol Flynn and I hit it off from the beginning [of *The Sea Hawk*]. He was naughty about his homework. I told him that because he couldn't remember his lines, it would hold up the picture and I would be delayed going to New York to do a play [*Ladies in Retirement*]. When I told him this, he was very kind and learned his lines to help me. The work went so fast we were finished by four in the afternoon some days. I remember [director] Michael Curtiz saying to him, "What's the matter with you? You know all your words!"

Leon Shamroy —— *CINEMATOGRAPHER*

In *Forever Amber,* I matched the title by using amber-color gelatins. I shot all the exteriors, or many of them, in actual rain. I wanted a dull, monotonous effect, and I used liquid smoke hovering over the bodies when

they painted the doors red to indicate the presence of plague. I showed smoke coming out from the doors to indicate something sinister inside.

There was something strange about that picture: Linda Darnell was burned in the Great Fire of London, and in *Anna and the King of Siam* she was burned to death as a punishment, and then, it's extraordinary, she actually died in a fire. And she only just escaped death in the picture, because during the Great Fire a roof caved in, I pulled the camera back and she just got out with it in time. She was terrified of fire, almost as though she had a premonition.

Lana Turner ——— ACTRESS

Great Dolphin Street just screamed for Technicolor. Why they did it in black and white I will never know. Walter Plunkett gave me 34 really magnificent costumes. So they put all this money in and didn't go all the way and put the cherry on top which would have been Technicolor. That was a great story and instead of remaking *The Postman Always Rings Twice,* which they should have left alone, they could have taken this one and really gone all the way with it.

* * *

When I read the script for *The Three Musketeers,* I found that Lady de Winter was not a starring role. Surprised that my agents had signed me for it, I went straight to Mr. [Louis] Mayer and refused the part. With [fiancé] Bob Topping in my future I felt strong, since I wouldn't have to depend on that weekly paycheck from the studio. We fenced a little. The wily Mr. Mayer said that the studio couldn't *force* me to honor the commitment, but that I would have to cover preproduction costs of several hundred thousand dollars.

"Sorry," I said bravely, "I still won't do that script."

For the first time ever, the studio suspended me. There were meetings and negotiations; they rewrote the script to give me more to do, and finally I agreed to make the picture.

Am I glad I did! I enjoyed the filming enormously. George Sidney flavored the story with humor and comic swordplay. He had Gene Kelly leaping all over the place. It was my first picture in Technicolor and my first chance to play a truly villainous lady. When the reviews appeared, I was singled out. I hadn't wanted to do the picture, but I had made something of it.

King Vidor ——— DIRECTOR

The book *Northwest Passage* was in two parts. One part was the campaign that the man went on, and the second part was his disintegration. Hunt Stromberg, the producer, had been about three years trying to solve the treatment of the second part. I made an attempt, but found him rather adamant about it, and soon the time for shooting came on the first part. There was the question of the water level and weather, so we left and went up to Idaho in two special trains, 95 boats and all this . . . and he said, "I'll have the last part of the script ready for you when you finish."

I finished, and there was no last part, so the studio said, "Come on back." We went back and they dismissed the actors and finally after a month or so they decided to shoot an ending on the first part and release it. I was in New York when they shot the ending, and they never touched the second part of the book.

Richard Widmark ——— ACTOR

Henry Hathaway didn't want me in *Down to the Sea in Ships.* He wanted Van Johnson. But [Darryl] Zanuck pushed me into it, because he wanted to change my image. The first two weeks of the picture, Henry kept needling me. I knew what he was doing, because Van Johnson was standing by—waiting for the explosion. So, I held it in. One scene, we had a little problem and Henry insisted he couldn't work with me. The producer, Louis D. Lighton, called me up and I explained that Henry was just trying to get Johnson in the part.

After that, Henry didn't try anything anymore.

I was his pall bearer some months ago.

Fantasies

Jean-Pierre Aumont—ACTOR

The first day of shooting *Siren of Atlantis,* they hoisted me up onto a pair of shoes with three-inch heels. They explained that Dennis O'Keefe, who played Morhange, was two inches taller than I.

"So?"

"So, you get top billing."

"I don't see the connection."

"It just wouldn't be right for you to look smaller."

"Good. Give me two-inch heels, not three."

"No, you're the star of this film. You should be at least an inch taller than everyone else."

Jack Benny—ACTOR

Soon after *The Horn Blows at Midnight* opened, I bumped into Jack Warner.

"Jack," I inquired, "how's our picture doing?"

"Jack," he answered, "I wouldn't wish that one on Hitler!"

Janet Blair—ACTRESS

Cary Grant was charming [on *Once Upon a Time*], at first. I felt almost faint when I saw him as we started working.

He had fought Harry Cohn over my being cast because I was so much younger. There would be too much contrast. There was a kissing scene between us he insisted be cut out. Sometimes he wouldn't communicate with me at all, just stare into space. He would be cold and distant and then even rude; he would walk past me without saying a word. He was deeply preoccupied with his problems with [wife] Barbara Hutton.

Sometimes he was skittish, jolly, happy and cute, and he would do all sorts of funny things at the piano. He was incredibly limber. Then at the end he gave bottles of brandy to the cast and crew, and I wasn't included. I didn't like brandy, but it was hurtful. He didn't even shake my hand or say goodbye. I thought of barging into his dressing room to talk to him, but finally I just slipped away. It was painful.

Mel Blanc—ACTOR

"What sort of voices do you do, anyway?" Walt Disney's receptionist asked.

I thought for a moment. "I do a great drunk." Which I proceeded to demonstrate in all its hiccuping glory.

"That's really funny," she said. "Okay, okay, I'll see if I can get Mr. Disney." When she returned to her desk, her boss was behind her. Walt enjoyed my characterization so much, he cast me as the voice of Gideon the cat in *Pinocchio,* Walt Disney Productions' second full-length feature.

My *Pinocchio* dialogue was recorded in 16 days, at 50 bucks per. After I collected my $800, I waited like everyone else for the film to open. When it finally did, in 1940, to my great surprise Gideon was mute. Disney, concerned that children might think the cat was a lush, edited out every utterance, except for one hiccup. At $800, it undoubtedly remains the most expensive glottal spasm in the annals of motion pictures.

Richard Brooks —— SCREENWRITER

I worked for eight days and finished the [writing] job. It was a picture with Jon Hall, Maria Montez and Sabu, directed by Arthur Lubin and called, I think, *White Savage.* When I was going back to New York on a train, I read a review of the picture among a number of reviews all lumped together. There was a character in the picture called Tamara. "How are you today, Tamara?" That was the review. I went back to radio.

Frank Capra —— PRODUCER/DIRECTOR/SCREENWRITER

With my accelerator pushed to the firewall, all that I was and all that I knew went into the making of *It's a Wonderful Life.* The pace was that of a four-month non-stop orgasm.

Linda Christian —— ACTRESS

Tarzan and the Mermaids was to be Johnny Weissmuller's final performance as Tarzan, and numerous scenes were shot of his long, powerful arms slicing the water. Unfortunately, part of the picture was made in shallow, snake-filled swamps outside of town, and an extra had to be used to double for Johnny. Since this swimmer's arms were rather short and stubby, the alert moviegoer seeing the film must surely have wondered why Johnny's arms seemed to shrink from one shot to the next, when the film was pieced together.

Charles G. Clarke —— CINEMATOGRAPHER

There was a wonderful scene in *Miracle on 34th Street* in which the love story is developed. It was played between Edmund Gwenn and John Payne on the escalator of Macy's store. In it, Gwenn tells Payne that Maureen O'Hara can be won and suggests an opening gambit. This scene started on the second floor and as the actors stepped on the escalator, the camera and microphone followed them down to the main floor. Such a scene presents quite a lighting problem and it took a bit of doing to get the camera off a flat floor, on to the incline of the escalator and off again while the scene was in progress. I thought it was a necessary and good scene but it was not used in the final version of the picture. After all these years of annual television showings, I am still trying to get them to put it back in the picture!

The studio heads seemed to feel that this was just another run-of-the-mill production and cut it severely. The picture was the sleeper of the year and George Seaton and Valentine Davies, whose original story it was, received Academy Awards for Story, Direction and Original Screenplay. Davies has said that while he was in the Army during World War II, he went into Macy's to buy a present for his wife and there got the germ of the idea which evolved into *Miracle on 34th Street.*

Joseph Cotten — ACTOR

Portrait of Jennie finally had come to an end, if an end it ever had. Joe August, our brilliant, incomparable cameraman, our master of ethereal light, as much our inspiration as anyone (even director William Dieterle vehemently conceded this), walked into producer David O. Selznick's office and said, "I think it's finished now, I'm satisfied." He went over to the sofa, lay down and with a hauntingly beautiful smile on his lips, closed his eyes and never opened them again.

Marlene Dietrich — ACTRESS

For *Kismet,* two make-up artists armed with brushes zealously painted my legs. The whole room reeked of paint, the floor was strewn with golden spots, but the effect was simply fabulous.

I climbed onto the set. The whole crew cried "Ooh!" and "Ah!" Photographers bombarded me with the light of their flashbulbs. The director, William Dieterle, came, nodded approvingly and the music began to play. I danced—the gilding held fast. An hour later, I suddenly became very cold and trembled like a wounded bird. Heaters were brought in to warm me up—in vain. Nevertheless, I worked through the day, good girl that I was. The studio doctor examined me in my dressing room, while I tried to wash the color off my legs with alcohol. He told me that the studio was not covered by insurance for something like "the present case." No one had thought of including an applicable clause in the contract in the event that the paint should permanently close the pores in the lower half of my body. (That's why I was so cold.)

I reassured the doctor I didn't want to give up the paint. We already had one day's work behind us and simply had to go on (since a day in the studio cost a fortune). Meanwhile, my legs had turned green, and I hid behind chairs and curtains until the doctor left.

Irene Dunne — ACTRESS

I suppose the film I thought was most difficult was *A Guy Named Joe.* It was winter, it was dark and raining and the whole set was gloomy. Then Van Johnson had this terrible car accident, so we discontinued shooting. And when we started up again, I had to jump back and forth between that and *The White Cliffs of Dover.* Spencer Tracy didn't like to rehearse, and he was sort of calling the shots on *Joe.* I don't particularly like to rehearse a lot, but I don't like not rehearsing at all.

We had trouble understanding each other. He was my hero. Then, when we started working, he got the idea that I thought he wasn't a hero anymore. Which was not true. But he had this big mental thing, and there was even talk of taking me off the film. That's one thing I'll always say about L. B. Mayer. I knew they were going to be looking at some film, and I made up my mind I was going to be my *best*—my best, my best, my *very* best. So they came out of the projection room and Mayer said, "If we're going to replace anybody, let's replace Tracy." Which they never would have done, of

course. But I'll always remember that. And we ironed everything out, Tracy and I.

***Philip Dunne*——SCREENWRITER**

In 1959, when I was directing *In Love and War,* one of our stars, Hope Lange, came on the set one morning talking about an "old picture" she had seen on television the night before: *The Ghost and Mrs. Muir.* She called it the most moving and utterly delightful picture she had ever seen. When she was told by my assistant that I had written the screenplay, she demanded that I book a projection room and run the picture for her all over again. In a fitting postscript, when a television series later was developed from my script, the part of Mrs. Muir was played, and delightfully, by none other than Hope Lange.

***Samuel Goldwyn*——PRODUCER**

There was criticism because I threw away nearly $900,000 worth of my picture, *The Bishop's Wife,* and started it all over. I can't help it, that's just the way I make pictures. I changed directors in the middle. You might say I had some disagreements on this one. One was with Cary Grant. He said, "You want me to be happy, don't you?" I said, "I don't give a damn if you're happy. You are going to be here for only a few weeks and this picture will be out a long time. I would rather you should be unhappy here, and then we can all be happy later."

Edmund Gwenn ——— ACTOR

I've had many letters addressed to Santa Claus, care of MGM, sent to me. I'd no idea my work in *Miracle on 34th Street* meant so much. Naturally, I'm pleased and a little awed. I'm glad none of the children who write me as Santa Claus ask me to answer their letters, for what could I say to them? One little girl, for instance, asked me to send her a band so she could sing with it. I've also had a lot of requests to play Santa Claus at various department stores and even a flattering offer to ride in a parade opening the Christmas season in Birmingham. I guess I'm typed now!

Rex Harrison ——— ACTOR

In *Anna and the King of Siam* I had to convince audiences that I was in love with Irene Dunne without making love to her, and as the ghost in *The Ghost and Mrs. Muir,* I had to make passes at Gene Tierney without touching her. I'm going back to playing characters who don't have to worry about anything—especially whether they can grab a girl.

Sybil Jason ——— ACTRESS

I had some damn good sequences in *The Blue Bird.* In one scene, Shirley Temple brings the blue bird to me and suddenly I discover I can walk.

About two weeks before the premiere, Walter Lang, the director, called my sister and me to his office and said, "I don't know how to say this. It's the best damned sequence in the whole movie, but Mrs. Temple said if it's not cut out, Shirley and she will walk out of the studio. My hands are tied. It's cut out of the movie. I had to do it."

When the film was shown, the sequence didn't make sense. I'm in the bed and suddenly I'm outside with Shirley.

Van Johnson ——— ACTOR

I always think of The Accident in capital letters. It was April 1, 1943. Prior to that, I had been going great guns in my career. I had made five pictures for Metro-Goldwyn-Mayer and had just been handed the greatest break of my life, a starring part with Spencer Tracy and Irene Dunne in a film called *A Guy Named Joe.*

That balmy April night, Metro was running a movie for me, Tracy's *Keeper of the Flame.* I had invited Evie and Keenan Wynn to go with me, and we all took off in my DeSoto convertible, which I had just bought from June Havoc. I was driving, of course, and had just entered the intersection of Venice Boulevard and Clarington Street, near the studio, when suddenly a small, beaten-up old heap of a car seemed to come charging right into us. The top of my car had been open; but with the impact, it flew up as my head snapped back, and *I* flew up, and the top struck me full force on the forehead. I was catapulted out of the car and into the gutter. Neither Evie nor Keenan was even scratched.

There was a strange zoning law in the area at that time. A Los Angeles policeman couldn't touch you if you were on the Culver City side of the street. I was. A cop came over to me as I lay there in agony, and he said he would have to send for the Culver City police, because I was on the wrong side of the street. I said, "Tell me where the right side is, and I'll crawl there." But instead, I lay in that gutter for 45 hideous minutes until an ambulance came. They tell me I was almost decapitated, but I never once lost consciousness. I spent four months in the Hollywood Presbyterian Hospital after they sewed the top of my head back on. I still have a disc of bone in my forehead five inches long.

I did do that picture, though, because Tracy and Miss Dunne voted to wait for me to recover.

Evelyn Keyes ——— ACTRESS

I was coming along in Rita Hayworth's wake [when I did *Here Comes Mr. Jordan*]. The various departments, believing her image to be the winning one, tried to make me over into a blonde replica. Hairdressing added tons of hairpieces, including one of Otto Kruger's old toupées pasted to my forehead. Wardrobe padded my breasts to match Rita's more generous proportions. My thin frame and small face couldn't take the added weight. I looked absurd and felt worse. It was devastating to my self-confidence.

Ward Kimball ——— ANIMATOR

The reason for the incredible success of the whole Disney operation was Walt's demand for high quality. No half efforts were permitted. He would do things over and over until he was satisfied. *Pinocchio* is a good example. After we'd worked six months on it, Walt thought the story wasn't just right. So he threw out all the animation we'd done and we started over.

Walter Lang ——— DIRECTOR

Sentimental Journey was voted by Harvard the worst picture of all time. It was a weepie, and I loved weepies. I'd cry right along with the actors.

Joseph L. Mankiewicz ——— DIRECTOR

Ordinarily, I hate moppets on the screen. I don't believe they should go to school on a movie lot. They belong in a proper classroom with children who are "civilians." However, Natalie Wood was a notable exception. When I first met her, I asked her if she could read the script [for *The Ghost and Mrs. Muir*] and when she said "Yes" with great authority, I then asked, "Can you spell?" She nodded again. Then I really threw her a curve and I asked her to spell "Mankiewicz." She did and after that we continued this game every morning. I was converted to Natalie on the spot, but I don't remember ever using another five-year-old youngster in a film again!

Maria Montez ——— ACTRESS

When I look at myself in *Arabian Nights,* I am so beautiful I scream with joy!

* * *

Imagine, they are giving me five days only after I finish *Cobra Woman*

before I start *Ali Baba and the Forty Thieves.* And in that five days I must fit all my dresses for the new picture and make tests. How can I marry Jean-Pierre [Aumont] with all that to do and so little time to do it in?

David Niven———*ACTOR*

"The [Samuel] Goldwyn Touch" was legendary, and he spared no expense to perpetuate it. "Good taste" were his watchwords on the screen.

We were rehearsing that subtle fantasy *The Bishop's Wife* (all Goldwyn pictures were carefully rehearsed in their entirety before shooting started). I was playing the bishop, Loretta Young, the wife, and Cary Grant, the angel. Bill Seiter, normally a director of broad comedy, was at the helm.

The day before shooting was to start, Goldwyn decided that the interiors of the bishop's house were not ecclesiastical enough and ordered several sets to be torn down, redesigned and rebuilt. For three weeks, while this was going on, production was halted; then, two days after the cameras finally had a chance to turn, Goldwyn decided that Seiter's hand was a little too heavy on the tiller; he was removed, paid his full salary and after a week Goldwyn hired Henry Koster to start again from scratch—with another two weeks of rehearsal. All this must have cost Goldwyn several hundred thousand dollars, but in the end he got what he wanted.

Maureen O'Hara——— ACTRESS

Sentimental Journey was a tremendous box office hit throughout the world. Very often when I go into different places in the world, people will say, "Oh, you made my favorite movie." And I'm so sure that they are going to say one of the top classics I've been in, but no, they say *Sentimental Journey.*

* * *

I'm very lucky. I've made 55 movies and, out of them, I have two that will *never* die. I'll be long gone but they'll still be running *The Quiet Man* on St. Patrick's Day and *Miracle on 34th Street* at Christmas.

When first paged to go before *Miracle* cameras, however, I wasn't too thrilled. I'd just gone home to Ireland for a visit when I got a message that I had to return to New York for the picture. So there I was, thinking, "But I *just* got here! I don't want to go back!" Little did I realize I was going back to make a classic. Darryl Zanuck was initially reluctant to finance the picture. There was always a rumor on the lot that he wasn't at first enthusiastic about another one of my pictures, *How Green Was My Valley*—and they still list that one when people pick the ten best pictures ever made.

I marvel at the expert casting of the supporting players in *Miracle,* including William Frawley, Porter Hall and Thelma Ritter. Believe me, when *those* people did their scenes, you didn't go and lock yourself in the dressing room. You'd stay around and watch! Thelma Ritter *always* had an audience. John Payne and I had previously co-starred in *To the Shores of Tripoli* and *Sentimental Journey* and would subsequently meet again in *Tripoli.* But I always took that as a compliment, because he didn't say, "God, do I have to work with *that* dame again?"

* * *

Miracle on 34th Street—you'll see it every Christmas. When I'm nailed into the box and long gone, you'll still be seeing it. Just before Christmas I was in New York and coming home from mass, in the middle of the day, and about five young kids came up behind me and pulled on my coat.

"You're the lady that knows Santa Claus, aren't you?" they asked. And I turned around and said, "Yes, I know Santa Claus very, very well."

Donna Reed——— ACTRESS

Working with James Stewart on *It's a Wonderful Life* was the hardest thing I've ever done because he was such a good actor. And Frank Capra was such a fine director, but they were both so intense. They had just returned from the war. It was really my first big role in an important film and everyone was looking for approval but nobody was in a position to give it. I was terrified most of the time.

* * *

I suppose you're wondering why I've decided to come back to work. I have to share something with you. I still get a little fan mail and several weeks ago, I got a letter from a young man somewhere in the South who had, for the very first time, seen *It's a Wonderful Life.*

He really liked it . . . and I have to remind you that film was made in 1946. So he wrote an entire page just about that movie . . . and Jimmy Stewart . . . and me . . . the telephone scene. It was just the best film he had ever seen.

Finally, he closed by saying, "Keep up the good work!"

So here I am.

Gail Russell——————ACTRESS

At that time, I *was* that girl in *The Uninvited,* shy about meeting people. Except for the English accent, all I had to do was be myself. To acquire the accent—five other girls with English accents were competing—Paramount drama coach Bill Russell locked me into a projection room. I saw *Pygmalion* four times, *Rebecca* twice and *Young Mr. Pitt* twice. I finally fell asleep.

When I came out I had a British accent thicker than a London fog. I was told it was too pronounced after executives looked at my test. I made another. That one turned out all right.

Anne Shirley —————— ACTRESS

We were halfway through *All That Money Can Buy* when Thomas Mitchell was injured when thrown from a runaway horse and had to be replaced by Edward Arnold. If you look closely enough at some shots in the dinner sequence, you can still see Mitchell in the background.

Phil Silvers —————— ACTOR

I contributed a few lines and a finale to *A Thousand and One Nights.* Beautiful Evelyn Keyes was the genie. She wanted to do something to reward me at the end of the story. She raised her hand, and there I was in jewels and silks, surrounded by lovely harem girls. The script called for me to say, "I must have had a heart attack!"

I had to tell Harry Cohn it was not a funny line.

"You got something better, Buster?"

I just happened to have a concept for the finale. A wave of the genie's hand, I disappear. The courtyard of the Oriental palace comes into focus. The harem girls are sitting around, entranced, as they hear Frank Sinatra's voice singing "All or Nothing at All." Camera pans to the girls' feet—they're wearing bobby sox. Then up to me on a balcony. I'm wearing a Sinatra wig, and it is *my* voice. The genie sits on the rail of the balcony, enjoying the view of the girls squealing at this sex symbol she has created. I turn to her, singing . . . and she faints dead away.

Frank, as a friendly gesture, spent half a day recording the song and teaching me the lip movements. Cohn liked it. In a few days, my brother Harry, my business manager, received a check from Cohn for $10,000.

Later, Cohn said to me, "You know, that was a goddamn fine thing for that guinea bastard to do."

"Why don't you present him with one of the grand pianos from your studio? For a singer, he has a lousy piano in his living room."

He not only sent nothing to Frank—when he discovered that Frank's wife, Nancy, had her clothes designed by Jean Louis, who was under contract to Columbia, Cohn barred her from visiting him on the lot. There was no explaining Cohn.

***Robert Siodmak*——— DIRECTOR**

Cobra Woman was silly but fun. You know, Maria Montez couldn't act from here to there, but she was a great personality and believed completely in her roles: if she was to play a princess you had to treat her like one all through lunch, but if she was a slave girl you could kick her around any way, and she wouldn't object—Method acting before its time, you might say.

***Natalie Wood*——— ACTRESS**

I still vaguely believed in Santa Claus at that time [*Miracle on 34th Street*], because I was about seven or eight. I guess I had an inkling that *maybe* it wasn't so, but I really did think that Edmund Gwenn was Santa. I had never seen him without his beard, because he used to come in early in the morning and spend several hours putting on this wonderful beard and mustache. And at the end, during the set party, I saw this strange man, without the beard, and I just couldn't get it together.

* * *

Nobody at Fox thought much of the picture or the original title [*It's Only Human*], so they changed it to *Miracle on 34th Street* and dumped it on the market in the middle of the summer, which seemed the worst possible time for a fantasy about Santa Claus. But the public loved it. The studio had everything riding on *Forever Amber,* which failed abominably at the box office, while this little black and white film made millions and became a classic.

Horror Films

***Evelyn Ankers*——— ACTRESS**

For *The Wolf Man,* I was in a scene which called for me to bc chased through a dark and eerie forest. The prop men used the fog machines beforehand to make a low blanket of fog, about a foot from the ground. Something is chasing me. I turn as it gets closer and see it is the Wolf Man. I scream and faint as directed, falling into the layer of fog which covers me completely. He creeps *very* slowly toward me (for suspense) and bends over me. They pan in closer. Then the director shouts "Cut!" and everyone gets to work breaking down the set and getting ready for the close-up—everyone except me. I was out cold after inhaling all the chemical fog I'd been lying in from almost the beginning of the action! Finally, somebody remembered

I had been in the scene, too. It would have been a short career if they hadn't tripped over me at last.

* * *

Weird Woman was my first "heavy" part, and not of my own choosing. This was a new field for me, and I found it very difficult to feel comfortable or convincing. Reggie LeBorg, the director, sensed something was wrong, and on the first day, after each scene, asked, "Evie, what's the problem? It's not believable." I answered, "I know why—I'm miscast. I don't feel a bit mean and I don't want to hurt Anne [Gwynne] because she's my best girlfriend." He answered, "Well, this time forget all that. Think of something mean she must have said or done to you and try it again." He then would say "Action!" and I would sort of squint or narrow my eyes, even attempt to flare my nostrils in desperation—trying to work myself up to appearing evil—then turn my head and look Anne in the eye threateningly. Bang, we would become hysterical with laughter, and so would the whole company watching us.

This happened time and time again, until we were absolutely exhausted. It was not only ridiculous but also costly in time as well as money, not to mention poor Reggie's patience. We felt so sorry for him, even when he tried to get angry with us, which only made it worse. How we ever finished that picture, I'll never know. Universal got the message and never cast me as a villainess again.

Ingrid Bergman ——— ACTRESS

In *Dr. Jekyll and Mr. Hyde* Lana Turner was cast as the little barmaid and I was to play Dr. Jekyll's fiancée. I went to the director [Victor Fleming] and said I was so fed up playing the same part over and over again. I said I'd like to play the barmaid. He said that with my face I couldn't do that. I said, "What do you know about my face? Let's do a little test." He was amazed because I suppose in those days to test meant you weren't sure of yourself. Anyway, the test turned out very well and we switched parts. I'm sure Lana was just as happy as I was because she was always playing barmaids!

DeWitt Bodeen—SCREENWRITER

The preview of *Cat People* was preceded by a Disney cartoon about a little pussycat and [producer] Val Lewton's spirits sank lower and lower as the audience began to catcall and make loud mewing sounds. "Oh, God!" he kept murmuring, as he wiped the perspiration from his forehead. The picture's title was greeted with whoops of derision and louder meows, but when the credits were over and the film began to unreel, the audience quieted, and, as the story progressed, reacted as we had hoped an audience might. The audience accepted and believed our story, and was enchanted.

Lon Chaney, Jr. ——— ACTOR

They cast me as the Frankenstein monster [in *The Ghost of Frankenstein*]. It took four hours to make me up. Then they led me to the set.

They dug a hole in the cliff and put me in. They stuck a straw in my mouth and covered me up with cement. It took till 12 o'clock to get me sealed in. Then everybody went to lunch!

Virginia Christine —— ACTRESS

Evelyn Ankers had played Lon Chaney's leading lady and she was a big girl. So Chaney had asked that they design a strap that went around his neck and around her waist to take some of the weight off his arms when he carried her. One day, on the back lot, we were doing this shot for *The Mummy's Curse* in which the Mummy was to carry me up to the old shrine, the monastery, up these steep, crooked, worn steps.

They were hard enough to navigate if you're sober. And there I was, with this strap inherited from Evelyn Ankers attached to my waist, around Lon Chaney's neck, starting up these steps—and he is absolutely stoned! He was pretty much throughout the picture. We start up the steps, and he's weaving, going side-to-side on these uneven steps. Chaney was a big guy, and if he fell down those stone steps, with me attached to him, I hate to think what would have happened!

Finally, the director, Leslie Goodwins, said, "Cut!" and they took Chaney out of the Mummy suit, and put the stand-in into it. So *he* carried me up, and I was enormously relieved!

Gladys Cooper —— ACTRESS

The film I have done for Universal is called *The Black Cat:* it's what they call a "B" picture though I consider all my work here at the moment to be rather "B." There is a funny little man in *The Black Cat* called Alan Ladd who wears very high heels to make him look taller only I don't understand why he doesn't fall over on them. He had a little part in *Citizen Kane* and they say he will do very well out here, so wonders never cease!

Hurd Hatfield —— ACTOR

The Picture of Dorian Gray? Oscar Wilde's original Dorian is blond and blue-eyed, and here I was, this gloomy-looking creature. I almost didn't go [to the audition], and when I did, all these blond Adonises were to the right and left of me. I looked like one of their agents!

The film didn't make me popular in Hollywood. It was too odd, too avant-garde, too ahead of its time. After all, [director/screenwriter] Albert Lewin always said he had made it for six friends. The decadence, the hints of bisexuality and so on, made me a leper! Nobody knew I had a sense of humor, and people wouldn't even have lunch with me!

* * *

In a manner of speaking, I have been haunted by *The Picture of Dorian Gray.* New York, London, anywhere the picture is showing, anywhere I'm making a personal appearance, people will talk about other things but they always get back to *Dorian Gray.* With Albert Lewin directing, we were five months in the making of the film. For me it was a terrible ordeal in self-control, everything being so cerebral. But not many actors are fortunate enough to have made a classic.

One friend told me it's a good thing I didn't make *Dracula* and have my entire professional life dominated by that!

Reginald LeBorg —— DIRECTOR

Lon Chaney, Jr., had a streak of violence in his personality. In roles that called for it, his rage could become almost uncontrollable. There is a scene in *The Mummy's Ghost* where the Mummy is supposed to kill the professor, played by Frank Reicher. Chaney grasped him and squeezed his neck so forcefully, the poor fellow was almost strangled. Gasping for breath, Reicher sank to his knees. I called out, "Cut!" The scene had played beautifully, but was dangerously realistic. (Every time this scene played in theaters, audiences gasped.) Reicher, a short, slightly built actor, cried out, "He nearly strangled me!" Chaney was most apologetic to the little man. However, at the end of the day, when I talked to Chaney and told him to be gentler in similar scenes, he did not take it too well.

Arthur Lubin —— DIRECTOR

Originally, when Universal decided to make the second [1943] version of *Phantom of the Opera* (the first being the Lon Chaney one), they thought that Deanna Durbin would be ideal for the lead. After reading the script, she turned it down because she thought there weren't enough solo songs in the script that would warrant her being in it. That was because her public wanted her to sing rather than act. I had just finished making *Ali Baba and the Forty Thieves* with Maria Montez; and the studio, not wanting me to be without an assignment which they would have to pay for if I wasn't working, fortunately assigned me *Phantom of the Opera.* It was a lucky break for me.

Vera Ralston —— ACTRESS

Saying goodbye to Hollywood seemed no hardship. In one of my first non-skating movies, *The Lady and the Monster,* I had to act with Eric von Stroheim. Now there was one tough man. I didn't know techniques, and he would [blow] smoke in my face. Just blew it in my face! Each day he would arrive on the set with two young girls and a pair of white gloves. He kept changing the gloves. Here I was just starting in pictures.... Other than von Stroheim, I liked the actors I worked with, all of them.

Elizabeth Russell —— ACTRESS

Producer Val Lewton told a friend, "I wish I could find an actress who looks like a cat [for *Cat People*]." And his friend said, "Well, that's a large order, you know?" But that night the friend and myself, with Maria Montez, went to dinner. He said to me, "I want you to go down and see a friend of mine at RKO by the name of Val Lewton. He's doing a movie, and he's looking for a woman who looks like a cat." I said, "Well, thank you!" and he said, "No, I'm serious."

I had just arrived for the second time in California, and I needed a job if there was going to be one. So the next day, I went down to see him, and he said, "Sure. You're just perfect."

I worked in the picture, and I got a lot of publicity out of that one little part. It wasn't very large, but it was significant to the story. I enjoyed it very much.

Curt Siodmak — SCREENWRITER

Of course I had access to the set of *The Wolf Man,* and I went over, but I didn't like to go there. Lon Chaney, Jr., wanted to kill me! He was angry, because it took five or six hours to put Chaney into the Wolf Man make-up, and an hour to take it off; he couldn't talk in the make-up, and he had to eat through a straw. Chaney said, "If I find the son-of-a-bitch who made up this monster, I'm gonna hit him over the head!"

* * *

Frankenstein Meets the Wolf Man started with a joke. I was sitting in the Universal commissary during the war with a friend of mine who had been drafted and wanted to sell his automobile. I wanted to buy that car, but I didn't have the money.

[Producer] George Waggner was sitting with us, and I made a joke: "Frankenstein Wolfs the Meat Man, I mean, Frankenstein Meets the Wolf Man." He didn't laugh. He came back to my office a couple of days later and asked, "Did you buy the automobile?" I said, "For that I need another job." He said, "You have a job. *Frankenstein Meets the Wolf Man.*"

* * *

I wrote *The Beast with Five Fingers,* not for Peter Lorre, but for Paul Henreid. Paul said, "You want me to play against a goddamned hand? I'm not crazy." I would love to have shot it with him, because I thought a man looking so debonair was a much more interesting murderer than that freakish Lorre.

Spencer Tracy — ACTOR

Freddie March, who'd won an Oscar for the 1931 version, called me up to congratulate me when my *Dr. Jekyll and Mr. Hyde* came out. I told him, "Cut the crap, man. I just did you the greatest goddamn favor of your life!"

Melodramas

Joan Alison — PLAYWRIGHT

I had wanted Clark Gable and Carole Lombard in *Casablanca.* I was never an admirer of Ingrid Bergman—I thought she had an unpretty face—and I thought Bogart was vulgar, a drunk and not a nice person. At one point, even Ronald

Reagan had been a contender [for the male lead]. Then they would have had *no* picture at all.

Leon Ames——————*ACTOR*

Song of the Thin Man? Bill Powell was bored with the role, but that was nothing. Here was America's happiest couple [Powell and Myrna Loy]. For years, the public had believed that. And they never talked. Except when they were in front of the camera. I'm surprised that they talked even then. Some of the time, they talked to the camera alone and the film was edited together later.

Judith Anderson———*ACTRESS*

There was a crying scene Joan Fontaine had to do in *Rebecca.* It involved shedding real tears; glycerine tears wouldn't do. Suddenly, without warning, she said, "Slap my face!" I was shocked. I said, "What do you mean, slap your face?" I told her I wouldn't do it, and to my amazement she went over to [director Alfred] Hitchcock, who wasn't too pleased with her trying to make such an arrangement, and she said to him, "Slap my face!" And he lit out and gave her a great big smack and she sat down and humped her little shoulders and out came the tears.

Dana Andrews————*ACTOR*

Darryl Zanuck was a Francophile and he had seen *La Grande Illusion,* so he made a contract with Jean Renoir to come over to 20th Century–Fox and make pictures. And Renoir picked *Swamp Water* out of all the scripts they had. Zanuck was quite put out that he picked a simple little story and Renoir's answer was "Mr. Zanuck, if I make pictures in France, I make pictures about France. If I make pictures in America, I make pictures about America—and this is the only typically American picture that I can find." Mr. Zanuck took his name off the picture. It turned out to be very successful—so successful that they made it again with Jeff Hunter—and Mr. Zanuck, I'm pretty sure, was sorry he'd taken his name off it.

* * *

I gave much better performances in *The Ox-Bow Incident, Swamp Water* and even *Wing and a Prayer* than I did in *Laura.* They weren't as flashy. That's why I was so determined to get the part in *Laura.* It would have made a star of anyone who played it.

Mary Astor—————*ACTRESS*

We didn't want people around watching us [while making *The Maltese Falcon*]. We had an odd childlike territorial imperative on our set. It was hard work, and we didn't want anyone looking over our shoulder, so to speak. Also, we had a sneaky feeling that we were doing something different and exciting, and we didn't want to show it to anyone until it was finished.

One afternoon we were lined up on a shot where I sit down and cross my knees elaborately—I think it was in Sam Spade's office. I looked down and said, "Hold it a minute, I've got a goddamn run in my stocking." I looked up and a little to the side of the camera was the publicity man with a half-dozen gentlemen of the cloth. They were ushered out politely by the publicity man who looked a little pale.

When the big doors closed, everybody whooped and hollered and said, "That's our girl! That's the way to get 'em off the set!"

Lauren Bacall ——— ACTRESS

You know, considering how crazy I am about this guy called Bogie, it's really funny the reaction I had when I first heard I was to work in a picture with him [*To Have and Have Not*]. I had always believed everything I saw on the screen. I fell for that "dese, dem and dose" routine he always gave out with in his characterizations. When Warner Bros. offered me a contract I was walking on stars. I had visions of playing opposite Charles Boyer or Ty Power. When they said "Bogart," I screamed.

"Gosh!" I wailed. "How awful to have to be in a picture with *that* mug; that illiterate! He mustn't have a brain in his head. He won't be able to think or talk about anything!" We had a fast meeting, and then he went overseas. It wasn't till he came back, and we started to work together, that I began to realize what a wonderful guy he was—well-informed, considerate, interested in everything.

Tallulah Bankhead——ACTRESS

Hitchcock offered me $75,000 to play the leading role in *Lifeboat* and off I dashed to Hollywood. It had been 11 years since I faced a camera.

Hitchcock confined the entire action of the picture to a 40-foot lifeboat adrift at sea. The plight of the passengers was the result of a U-boat torpedo. Although the derelict craft was supposed to wallow for days in the Atlantic, beset by hurricane, death and destruction, the picture was made in the studio with the drifters photographed against a bogus ocean. In the trade these are called process shots. In the picture the players were shivering from cold, but in its making I sweltered for 15 weeks. I had to wear a mink coat. Blazing lights were focused on my every move. In a bow to authenticity, tons of water were sloshed over us at intervals.

I was black and blue from the downpours and the lurchings. Thanks to the heat, the singeing lights, the fake fog, submersions followed by rapid dryings-out, I came up with pneumonia early in November. Temperature 104 degrees and rising.

A Dr. Fox dosed me with sulpha drugs. After three days I tottered back to the boat, rubber-legged and dizzy. Three more days amid the ice and brine and the bluster of the Nazi agent (Walter Slezak) who hoped to do us all in, and my temperature shot up to 104 again. Guess what this time? Another case of pneumonia!

William Bendix——ACTOR

All of us in the cast of *Lifeboat* were supposed to be survivors from a torpedoed ship, you remember, and we were fished out of the sea all dripping with oil—all except Tallulah Bankhead, who stepped into the lifeboat at the beginning and didn't even get her feet wet. Anyway, every day for three weeks I was dunked in crankcase oil. At the end of each day's work I'd take three showers, one on the set, another in my dressing room and still another when I got home.

The showers didn't do any good. Crankcase oil kept oozing out of my pores. When my wife and I went to a restaurant for dinner, people would ask if they could change tables, to get as far away from Bendix as possible. It was six months before I got that stuff out of my system.

Ingrid Bergman ——— ACTRESS

I liked Michael Curtiz. He was a good director but *Casablanca* started off disastrously and it was not his fault at all. From the very start Hal Wallis, the producer, was arguing with the scriptwriters, the Epstein brothers, and every lunchtime Curtiz argued with Wallis. There had to be all sorts of changes in the script. So every day we were shooting off the cuff: every day they were handing out the dialogue and we were trying to make some sense of it. No one knew where the picture was going and no one knew how it was going to end, which didn't help any of us with our characterizations. Every morning we said, "Well, who are we? What are we doing here?" And Curtiz would say, "We're not quite sure, but let's get through this scene today and we'll let you know tomorrow."

And all the time I wanted to know who I was supposed to be in love with, Paul Henreid or Humphrey Bogart?

"We don't know yet—just play it . . . in between."

* * *

We didn't know how we were going to end *Casablanca.* We were going to shoot two endings and then choose the best one. One would have me leaving Bogart and flying off with Paul Henreid. The other would have me staying behind with Bogart. We shot the one where I leave with Henreid first, and when we saw it, the producer and director said, "That's it. That's the ending. We don't have to shoot the other one."

* * *

I realize *Casablanca* is a very good movie and it captures people's fancy and they like to see it. But I think it's a pity it's the one they run so often because some of my other movies I like very much, but it's always *Casablanca* that comes back and back and back. Still, there were films like *Saratoga Trunk, Notorious, Dr. Jekyll and Mr. Hyde* and *For Whom the Bell Tolls.*

* * *

Our opening shot in *Gaslight,* out of sequence as always, was when I arrived at a railway station in Italy. I leapt out of the carriage and raced across to where Charles Boyer was standing in the middle of the platform waiting to catch me in his arms, passionately embrace me and kiss me. No woman in her right mind would object to being kissed by Charles Boyer, but I had to do all the running because there he was, all alone in the middle of the platform perched up on a ridiculous little box since I was quite a few inches taller than he. So I had to rush up and be careful not to kick the box, and go into my act. It was easier for us to die of laughter than to look like lovers.

* * *

I met Alfred Hitchcock one evening and happened to tell him that I received so many awful scripts that I just threw them across the room. Then one day he sent me the script of *Spellbound* with a note that read: "Please remove your husband and child before you throw this across the room."

Curtis Bernhardt — *DIRECTOR*

The character in *Conflict* has no primary contact with anything, even his job. I think that was Humphrey Bogart's problem when I knew him in those days. In fact, on the first day of shooting, I treated him like I treated every other actor. I was speaking to him. I turned away for a second, and when I turned back he was gone.

I asked the assistant where Mr. Bogart was. "Oh," he said, "you've said something to him that infuriated him and he's quit the picture." I couldn't imagine. I wasn't conscious of having done anything.

I went to his dressing room, and there he was—very high on alcohol, with bloodshot eyes. He came very close and said something to the effect of "Who do you think you are?" I said, "Mr. Bogart"—later I called him by his first name—"I'm not aware of having done anything which could hurt you." He slurred, "You said something . . . who do you think you are?"

I said, "This is not a very nice way to start a relationship." Somehow, this worked and he came back on the picture. He tried to intimidate me, which he couldn't.

Henry Blanke — *PRODUCER*

Robert Rossen wrote the script for *The Sea Wolf* in 29 weeks. Barry Fitzgerald, Alexander Knox and Ida Lupino were in it, with John Garfield. I produced the picture. Jack Warner stormed into our office and screamed, "Here's an article about Jack London. He wrote the original book in eight days!" A movie studio can be very colorful.

Ann Blyth — *ACTRESS*

I remember Joan Crawford as being most helpful [on *Mildred Pierce*], as if I were indeed one of her children. She was very supportive. And she had a great dedication to the life she had chosen.

Humphrey Bogart — *ACTOR*

When I was suggested for the romantic lead in *Casablanca,* Jack Warner cracked, "What woman would want to kiss that puss?" When Ingrid Bergman said, "*I* would," I got the part.

* * *

I didn't do anything I've never done before in *Casablanca.* But when the camera moves in on that [Ingrid] Bergman face, and she's saying she loves you, it would make anybody look romantic.

Leigh Brackett—SCREENWRITER

The Big Sleep is a confusing book if you sit down and tear it apart. When you read it from page to page it moves so beautifully that you don't care, but if you start tearing it apart to see what makes it tick it comes unglued. Owen Taylor, I believe, was the name of the chauffeur. I was down on the set one day and Bogart came up and said, "Who killed Owen Taylor?" I said, "I don't know." We got hold of William Faulkner and he said he didn't know, so they sent a wire to Raymond Chandler, the book's author. He sent another wire back and said: "I don't know." In the book it is never explained who killed Owen Taylor, so there we were.

Geraldine Brooks—ACTRESS

Barbara Stanwyck was cold as ice [on *Cry Wolf*]. Throughout the whole film, she treated me as though I were a piece of furniture. Because I had nothing to offer her. I was unsure of the technique of filmmaking and I was scared. Her attitude was not helpful.

Errol Flynn worked beautifully in the morning, but in the afternoon he was pretty drunk and stumbling over his lines. God, it was sad. He really didn't want to live up to that image. It sounds corny, but he once told me, "I have to—they expect me to."

Richard Brooks—SCREENWRITER

I'll tell you about [the studio moguls]. They were monsters and pirates and bastards right down to the bottom of their feet, but they *loved* movies. When we previewed *Key Largo* back in 1948, Jack Warner stood in the lobby talking to everybody who came out and said, "Great picture!" and "How did you like it, little lady, it's a powerful picture, don't you think?" before they even got their preview cards filled out. These guys today should be running gas stations.

James Cagney—ACTOR

I went back to Warner Bros. to do *White Heat,* and although it turned out to be a good picture in a number of ways, it was another cheapjack job. There was a limited shooting time, and the studio put everybody in it they could for six bits.

The original script was very formula. The old knock-down-drag 'em-out again, without a touch of imagination or originality. The leading character, Cody Jarrett, was just another murderous thug. For some kind of variant, I said to the writers, "Let's fashion this after Ma Barker and her boys, and make Cody a psychotic to account for his actions." The writers did this, and it was a natural prelude to the great last scene in the picture where I commit suicide by pumping bullets into the blazing gas tank I'm standing on.

James M. Cain—AUTHOR

I had to see *Double Indemnity* probably half a dozen times in various connections, and I was never bored. I must say Billy Wilder did a terrific job. It's the only picture I ever saw made from my books that had things in it I wish I had thought of. Wilder's ending was much better than my ending, and his device for letting the guy tell the story by taking out the office dictating machine—I would have done it if I had thought of it.

——— *SCREENWRITER*

I was supposed to write for an actress named Maria Montez. Universal showed me a film so I would know what kind of creature I was writing for. Well, when she came on the screen, I suddenly realized that I knew this girl personally. Her voice and every gesture were completely familiar to me. I think she must have checked hats someplace in Hollywood.

The script they handed me [*Gypsy Wildcat*] was simply weird. It was a horrible pipe dream—a director's script. It was full of "Interior—Stage Coach—Medium Shot—Night." Christ, there was more cinematic gobbledygook—eight different sequences intercutting each other at the same time. I took this script and worked on it day and night. I turned it in and thought, "I've done something that makes sense."

My last day I walked over to the producer's office to thank George Waggner and say goodbye. I saw him in there, *rewriting* my script! I told him I was sorry he didn't like it. "Jim," he said, "I'm delighted with what you've done. But *she* couldn't play your dialogue. It has to be translated into the kind of baby talk she can handle." He told me, "I'm pinching myself for the wonderful thing you've done with this bad dream I threw at you. Now I can put this thing in front of the camera."

——— *AUTHOR*

One of my friends took me to see *The Postman Always Rings Twice* the other night. I was surprised that it was no worse than it was. It was a passably viewable picture, the first time I ever actually saw the release form. After the "sneak" in Glendale in 1946, I went up the aisle on my hands and knees for fear I would run into Carey Wilson, the producer. The rough-cut they showed at this preview was just so utterly ghastly. But when I saw it the other night, the stuff that made my blood curdle out in Glendale had been cut out.

There's a place in the book where he runs off with a girl who had a cat act, and he takes her somewhere in Mexico. Well, in the first version I saw, they had this girl's cat act in the picture—leopards and pumas and lions and everything rolling around with each other—and it had no more relationship with the story than the man in the moon.

Shortly after the picture was released, I was having dinner alone in Murphy's, a corned beef and cabbage kind of place, and I looked up and saw Harry Ruskin in front of me, the guy who did the script. He was standing with his hands on his hips in a very belligerent way, and he said, "Well, why don't you say it? It *stinks.*"

I told him I didn't think it stunk any worse than most of them do.

Corinne Calvet ——— ACTRESS

William Dieterle was an autocrat. He ran the movie set more like the führer's headquarters. He had always been known for wearing white gloves, and was never seen without them. Some said he had a contagious skin disease, others that he had a phobia about germs, still others that he was just a complete snob. Since no one had ever seen him eat lunch, nobody knew whether he ate with his gloves on or off. As a director, he was uncommunicative. I confided in Burt Lancaster that I could not understand Dieterle's heavily accented English. Whenever I asked him to repeat he would scream at me.

"You heard him, Mr. Lancaster," I said to my co-star. "When he says 'vye dit dey gif me such a stupit actress to verk vit?' at the top of his lungs, you've got to help me. What should I do?"

"The first thing is to call me Burt."

"Burt," I smiled, "would you be kind enough to direct me?"

The success that came to me in *Rope of Sand* can be attributed to Burt Lancaster's guidance. He gave me confidence. I was good and I knew it. There was nothing but smiles around me on the set when I finished a scene.

Raymond Chandler ——— AUTHOR

When and if you see *The Big Sleep* (the first half of it, anyhow), you will realize what can be done with this sort of story by a director with the gift of atmosphere and the requisite touch of hidden sadism. Bogart, of course, is also so much better than any other tough-guy actor that he makes bums of the Ladds and the Powells.

The Big Sleep has had an unfortunate history. The girl who played the nymphy sister [Martha Vickers] was so good she shattered Miss [Lauren] Bacall completely. So they cut the picture in such a way that all her best scenes were left out except one. The result made nonsense and [director] Howard Hawks threatened to sue to restrain Warners from releasing the picture. After long argument, as I hear it, he went back and did a lot of re-shooting.

But if Hawks got his way, the picture will be the best of its kind. Since I have nothing to do with it, I say this with some faint regret. Well, that's not exactly true because Hawks time after time got dissatisfied with his script and would go back to the book and shoot scenes straight out of it.

Harry Cohn ——— STUDIO HEAD

The Lady from Shanghai—I'll give a thousand dollars to anyone who can explain the story to me!

Claudette Colbert ——— ACTRESS

Hollywood feuds? I never did see much of that sort of thing. There wasn't the jealousy around you might imagine. The closest thing I saw of that was on *Boom Town* with [Clark] Gable and [Spencer] Tracy. There was not much love lost between them but they were always polite.

"Now they all know what I am..."
COLUMBIA PICTURES presents
RITA HAYWORTH
as
Gilda
with
GLENN FORD
GEORGE MACREADY · JOSEPH CALLEIA
Screenplay by Marion Parsonnet
Produced by
VIRGINIA VAN UPP
Directed by
CHARLES VIDOR

Jack Cole——CHOREOGRAPHER

There was no completed script on *Gilda.* It was made up as we went along, and if you really look closely at the story you'll see that it doesn't make a whole lot of sense. But audiences didn't care, because Rita Hayworth and Glenn Ford look throughout like they want to fuck each other's brains out.

Ronald Colman——ACTOR

My Oscar gives me new faith in trying unorthodox roles. It confirms what I have long believed: that the public is weary of Hollywood formula stories and is ready to patronize more mature films. Of course any innovation must be entertaining and first class, but the public is receptive. As a result of this, I am now no longer reluctant from a professional standpoint in accepting such roles in such pictures. There was a great deal of doubt in my mind about playing the murderer in *A Double Life.* But with such gifted artists as Bill Goetz, Michael Kanin, Garson and Ruth Kanin and George Cukor all willing to take a chance, we tried it. Now I've not only won an Oscar out of it, but feel a new maturity of craftsmanship in myself.

Elisha Cook, Jr.——ACTOR

I love to play tricks. *The Maltese Falcon,* analyze it—everybody was a shitheel in it. There wasn't one decent person in the whole picture, and look at what a film it was. Everyone was a bum. And people, I don't know what it is, they love to watch bums.

* * *

The Big Sleep had the greatest line I've ever had—thanks to director Howard Hawks. These bums are beating the crap out of Bogey in the alley and I'm standing there watching them and I don't do anything. I take him upstairs, he's washing up and he says, "What the hell kind of man are you?" And Hawks just came up with this line—I said, "Listen, when a guy's doing a job, I don't kibitz."

Gladys Cooper——ACTRESS

People who have seen *Rebecca* say they can't understand how I was once known as a famous English beauty unless there weren't many other beauties around at the time, and I must say I can't blame them.

Joseph Cotten——ACTOR/—SCREENWRITER

Orson Welles invited me to join him in adapting *Journey into Fear* from Eric Ambler's novel into a screenplay. When Eric saw the movie, he was delighted with it and said it bore so little resemblance to his book that he'd be able to sell it again.

——ACTOR

I made three [sic] pictures with Alfred Hitchcock, and the collaboration went swimmingly until one day on the set of *Under Capricorn* when I called it "Under Corny Crap." I never worked with Hitch again.

Joan Crawford ——— ACTRESS

Poor Mr. [Louis B.] Mayer. He had borne with me as the bitch in *The Women,* the bleak-looking woman in *Strange Cargo,* the mother of a subdeb in *Susan and God,* now he balked at my playing a scarred woman who hated the world. Luckily, director George Cukor took up the cudgels for me, and *A Woman's Face* scored my high point at MGM. I was extolled as the first lady Lon Chaney, for as Anna Holm, I wore from eye to mouth on the right side of my face a hideous mass of seared tissue created by Jack Dawn. The studio released no publicity art. They were concerned that my mutilated face would keep people away from the theater. The scar didn't deter me; there are too many beautiful women in pictures anyway.

What worried George Cukor was my emotionalism. He anticipated that wearing a scar could affect me as wearing a cape has been known to affect some actors. To offset the possibility, he rehearsed the very life out of me. Hours of drilling, with camera and lights lined up for the opening sequence in the courtroom, *then* Mr. Cukor had me recite the multiplication table by twos until all emotion was drained and I was totally exhausted, my voice dwindled to a tired monotone.

"*Now,*" Mr. Cukor said. "Now, Anna . . . tell us the story of your life."

I say a prayer for Mr. Cukor every time I think of what *A Woman's Face* did for my career. It fortified me with a measure of self-confidence I'd never had . . . the greatest rave notices I'd ever had . . . the *succès d'estime* I'd longed for . . . what critics called "The best picture to emerge from Hollywood in a long, long time."

* * *

Warner Bros. put me under contract two days after I left Metro for two pictures a year at one-third the salary I'd received at MGM. But the scripts submitted were not suitable, in my opinion, and I wasn't going to start off at a new studio in the familiar rut of stereotyped stories. All I did in two years was a guest appearance in *Hollywood Canteen,* in which all Warner stars appeared, including Trigger the horse.

One producer at Warners who didn't think I was box office poison was Jerry Wald who found *Mildred Pierce* for me. *Mildred* was a meaty James M. Cain story. Warner star Bette Davis had turned it down. Director Michael Curtiz wanted Barbara Stanwyck. Jerry fought for me.

For my early scenes, the studio designed some cotton frocks. Mr. Curtiz said *no,* they looked too smart. So I went down to Sears Roebuck on my own and bought the kind of housedresses I thought Mildred would wear. When I arrived on the set for wardrobe tests, Mr. Curtiz walked over to me, shouting, "You and your Adrian shoulder pads! This stinks!" And he ripped the dress from neck to hem.

"Mr. Curtiz," I sobbed, "I bought this dress this morning for two dollars and 98 cents. There are no shoulder pads!" and I rushed to my dressing room.

Mildred Pierce grossed the studio

$5,000,000 and I got the Oscar. Happy ending to a big gamble.

* * *

In *Mildred Pierce,* I loved every scene with Ann Blyth as my daughter except where I had to slap her and she had to slap me back. I have a phobia about slapping, dating back to my childhood, when my father once slapped me for telling a lie at the dinner table. After I slapped Ann, I burst into tears and found myself apologizing frantically. Later, it wasn't quite so hard to have Ann slap me, but my head was shaking as the scene faded out, and then it was Ann who was remorsefully apologizing.

* * *

The first time I heard the words *film noir* was in New York. I was being interviewed by a critic of the "cinema," which, as you might know, has nothing to do with the "movies." He kept talking about this *film noir* style [in *Mildred Pierce*] and I didn't know what the hell he was talking about. When it came up again sometime later, I called [producer] Jerry Wald and said, "Darling, what is this *film noir* they're all talking about?" He explained it to me, which made me appreciate the film even more. I already knew what a terrific bunch of guys we had on that picture. They weren't just artists, they were geniuses.

Hume Cronyn ——— ACTOR

The controversy over *The Postman Always Rings Twice* was due to the way the film seemed to give some seal of acceptance to the adulterous relationship between Lana Turner and John Garfield. I don't think either of them was particularly concerned about the film hurting their careers, though the producers softened the obvious by dressing Lana in white in virtually every shot, since white is generally associated with virginity. I seem to recall that the white wardrobe was the joint idea of Lana and the costume designer.

George Cukor ——— DIRECTOR

With a successful picture, you're good news. When you're not, people become rather offhand and casual. After I was taken off *Desire Me,* three colleagues came to visit me, and I said, "Now I know who'll come to my funeral."

Michael Curtiz ——— DIRECTOR

When I started the tests for *Mildred Pierce,* I heard my star was very deefeecult. So I say okay, [Joan] Crawford, Curtiz will be *more* deefeecult. She took it. Like a trouper. We have now finished the picture and I see she is one swell actress. We get along fine on the picture. I luff her.

Laraine Day ——— ACTRESS

In one particularly scary scene for *Foreign Correspondent* I had to sneak down a dark corridor. When I got to the end, there was Mr. [Alfred] Hitchcock, sticking out his tongue and flapping his hands in back of his ears. I didn't dare laugh, because the cameras were turning. But he certainly eliminated any tension I felt in playing the scene.

Bette Davis — ACTRESS

I was pregnant during *The Letter,* and Tony Gaudio, the cameraman, kept looking at me sideways. Obviously, I couldn't have the baby and I was upset as hell. I had already had two abortions. I was only 32 and thought to myself that, if I married again and wanted to have a baby, my insides might be in such a mess that I couldn't. I cried and cried, but I knew what I had to do. Where was that damn pill when I needed it?

I went to the doctor on a Saturday and showed up for scenes on Monday morning wearing a form-fitting white eyelet evening dress for a scene, and that damn Tony said, "Jesus, Bette, it looks like you've lost five pounds over the weekend!"

* * *

"What a dump!"—my saying that is the only thing about *Beyond the Forest* anybody remembers. I had to address a group of young people last year in San Francisco. I didn't know how to start, so I came in and said, "What a dump!" about the beautiful auditorium. They laughed their heads off for 15 minutes.

Olivia de Havilland — ACTRESS

The Dark Mirror was a tremendously hard film to do. The technical problems involved in playing a dual role were extremely difficult to solve, and that horrible Terry I had to play in that picture haunts me to this day.

Richard Denning — ACTOR

I was at Fox in a picture with George Sanders, *Quiet Please, Murder.* Evelyn Ankers and I just took Labor Day weekend off [to elope to Las Vegas], and we didn't get any sleep. And the next morning, on the set, I had a scene with Lynne Roberts where she's supposed to go to the door to run away from Sanders; she faints, and I'm supposed to pick her up and pull my gun out of the holster, then shoot the door open so we could escape. Of course, I was very tired. We went through the scene, shot it once, and I tried to get her through the door and thought, "Oh, brother, I better give this everything I've got, because I haven't got very much left!" I got her through the door, and the director said, "Aw. Dick, you did that like an old man! Now come on, let's do it again!"

I thought, "Oh, no!"

Well, we kept on doing it—five takes! And finally at the end of the fifth take, I said, "Look! This is it! I cannot pick this gal up again!" And the director said, "That's OK. The first take was perfect. We just wanted to see if you could do it!"

Buddy DeSylva — PRODUCTION HEAD

Ugh—that lousy blonde wig! We hired Barbara Stanwyck for *Double*

Indemnity and got George Washington.

Edward Dmytryk——DIRECTOR

Farewell, My Lovely was a success with the front office and the critics, but when it was first released somewhere in New England, it did miserably at the box office. We quickly discovered that the public thought a film called *Farewell, My Lovely,* starring Dick Powell, had to be a musical, and they wanted no part of it. The studio recalled the film, changed the title to *Murder, My Sweet* and rushed it out again. It was one of the very few instances where a change of title had a positive effect. *Murder, My Sweet* was an unqualified success. Dick Powell never had to sing another note again.

Kirk Douglas——ACTOR

The Strange Love of Martha Ivers—I was young, scared, trying to look older than I was. I didn't know what it was all about, this new world of movie-making. Everyone had told me how nice Barbara Stanwyck was, so I was looking forward to working with her in this hostile environment. The crew adored her. They called her "Missy," and when she came on the set she went around hugging them, asking about their wives and children by name. She was a professional, she was there, always prepared, an excellent actress. But she was indifferent to me. Crew members need and want affection, but who needs help more than somebody working on his first picture?

Several weeks later she noticed me. I could see it happening, like the lens of a camera turning into focus. She looked at me, made eye contact for the first time: "Hey, you're pretty good." I said, "Too late, Miss Stanwyck."

* * *

Out of the Past was a picture I did on loan-out for RKO with Robert Mitchum. I don't remember much about him, except that his stories about being a hobo kept changing every time he told them. What I do remember was devastatingly beautiful Jane Greer. Whenever I could, I spent time with her. Beautiful Jane could also be very funny. I loved hearing her stories of her brief marriage to Rudy Vallee at the age of 17, and how he insisted that she wear black panties, black net stockings and black shoes with heels so high she teetered.

Dan Duryea——ACTOR

Whenever I knock the gals around, as I did Joan Bennett in *Scarlet Street,* my fan mail goes up.

Frances Farmer——ACTRESS

I was rude, critical and demanding toward the motion picture industry. I appeared to belittle everything about it.

A picture taken of me on the set of *Flowing Gold,* a mediocre film made after my return from the stage, showed me drenched with mud, and

the story was that Hollywood had, at last, gotten even with me when the director [Alfred E. Green] insisted on 14 retakes of a scene that called for me to fall facedown in a mud puddle. It was now the industry's turn to throw it, and the trade seemed delighted in the get-even method used.

Joan Fontaine ——— *ACTRESS*

I made about seven tests for *Rebecca. Everybody* tested for it. Loretta Young, Margaret Sullavan, Vivien Leigh, Susan Hayward, Anne Baxter, you name her. Supposedly, Hitchcock saw one of my tests and said, "This is the only one." I think the word he used to describe what set me apart was "vulnerability." Also, I was not very well-known and producer David O. Selznick probably saw the chance for star-building. And may I say he also saw the chance to put me under contract for serf's wages? David's brother, Myron, was a top agent and got 10 percent of clients, but David, who loaned me here and there and never used me again in one of his own productions, took 300 percent, and I was always expected to be grateful to him.

If my sister, Olivia de Havilland, hadn't freed the contract slaves later on by winning a precedent-setting suit against Warner Bros. forbidding suspension time to be added onto player's contracts, I'd still be under contract to Mr. Selznick!

* * *

The very first week of shooting *Rebecca,* director Alfred Hitchcock confided to me that Laurence Olivier wanted his fiancée, Vivien Leigh, in my role.

One morning Larry used a 14-letter word when he blew a take, and Hitch said, "Larry, old boy, Joan is a new bride." Larry turned to me and said, "Who's the chap you married?" I proudly boasted, "Brian Aherne." Mr. Olivier strode off, hurling over his shoulder, "Couldn't you do better than that?" It just destroyed me.

But the worst thing was my 22nd birthday party. Hitch had arranged it. The whole crew had presents for me. But only Hitch and Reginald Denny were there. Judith Anderson, George Sanders and Laurence Olivier were all in Gladys Cooper's dressing room and they refused to come!

They wanted to break me. They all wanted me off the film. But remember, the war had broken out, and Olivier wanted to go home desperately. He didn't like America and he didn't like films. He thought it was a minor art, if an art at all. And I think Vivien was nagging him. He wasn't getting divorced from his first wife. When he got to England and became an aviator, he crashed so many planes that they finally had him do something else!

* * *

It took me six months to make *Suspicion,* which seems a long time for such an intimate story, but I just unearthed some old letters to prove it. It was originally filmed with Cary Grant, as my husband, murdering me at the end. Then we went back in and shot the happy ending, the one finally used. Cary was a superb professional, with impeccable timing. He knew where every single light should be. I do believe he thought it was his picture, though, and then half-way through he found out it wasn't. He reacted *coolly.* He came to my house several times after and he was . . . constrained.

* * *

Orson Welles was a huge man in 1943. Everything about him was oversized, including his ego. *Jane Eyre* was simply a medium to show off his talents.

The first day on the 20th Century–Fox lot, the director, slight, timid, gentlemanly Robert Stevenson, the cameraman, the script girl and the cast assembled at one p.m. for rehearsal, an hour continuously changed by Orson but finally settled upon. We sat in a circle hour after hour, waiting for the arrival of the leading man, whose empty chair loomed large on the half-lighted set. At four that afternoon the stage door burst open. Orson whirled in, accompanied by his doctor, his manager, his secretary and his valet, "Shorty." (Shorty was rightly named, being less than four feet tall.)

Orson strode up to a lectern, which we had not noticed before. Placing his script upon it and standing before our astonished group, he announced, "Now we'll begin on page four."

Glenn Ford — ACTOR

When I went into *Gilda,* Rita [Hayworth] was finished with Orson Welles, and we gave Harry Cohn a few grey hairs. We were told by the sound department that Harry had had a microphone planted in my dressing room. That was kind of interesting. He was worried about my carrying on with Rita, so we gave him some marvelous things to listen to.

Ava Gardner — ACTRESS

Director Robert Siodmak was helpful [on *The Killers*]. A German director who was giving Alfred Hitchcock a run for his money with suspenseful films like *Phantom Lady* and *The Spiral Staircase,* he was an expert at this kind of dark drama, filling the screen with deep, troubling shadows and knowing just how he wanted me to look.

One day early in the filming, I saw him and his cameraman looking at me very carefully. "What is that stuff all over your face, please?" he said in his typically fractured English.

"Regulation MGM make-up."

"This not MGM. Will you please go away and wash it all off?"

I did as I was told, and quite happily, in fact. My regulation face was gone for good.

* * *

People are always expecting to see a girl like Kitty from *The Killers* and Jean Ogilvie from *The Hucksters* instead of me.

John Garfield — ACTOR

I've usually had to learn something for any movie I made—how to fish in *Tortilla Flat,* how to man a machine gun in *Air Force.* But in *The Postman Always Rings Twice* my task was making love, and that's something I didn't have to learn.

Tay Garnett — DIRECTOR

On *Postman Always Rings Twice,* there was great chemistry in the combination of Lana Turner and John Garfield. We almost didn't get Garfield. He went into the Army, and we tested Cameron Mitchell. He did a great test, then Garfield was invalidated out of the service—he had a bad ticker even then.

It was a real chore to do *The Postman* under the Breen Office, but I think I managed to get the sex across. I think I like doing it better that way. I'm not a voyeur, and I don't like all the body display that you get in pictures nowadays. I think that's just a crutch for untalented directors and writers.

* * *

There was some rather raw kidding going on during *Postman Always Rings Twice.* When we finished the picture, Lana Turner gave me a fur-lined jockstrap. She'd bought a regular jockstrap and had it fur-lined, and she said, "Don't let anyone say you don't go first class."

Samuel Goldwyn — STUDIO HEAD

When I decided to star David Niven in *Raffles,* I was afraid that stardom had come so suddenly and so easily that he might take it a little too lightly. I decided to worry him a little. I gave instructions to a young player to come to the studio every morning and dress in a *Raffles* costume, and just hang around all day during rehearsals. Everywhere David went, there was another actor, ready and made up to take his part if he fell down. When the picture began, David put his heart into it, and did a wonderful job.

The name of the unknown young actor? Dana Andrews.

Cary Grant ——————— ACTOR

Alfred Hitchcock is so patient. I'll never forget when we were shooting *Notorious* with Ingrid Bergman. In the morning we started a scene that was quite difficult because, you see, Ingrid had to say some of her lines a certain way so that I could imitate her readings. Well, anyway, we started and Ingrid just couldn't get it. We went over and over the scene and she was in some sort of daze. You know, she just wasn't *there.* But Hitch, he didn't say anything. He just sat there next to the camera, pulling on his cigar. Finally around 11 o'clock, I began to see in Ingrid's eyes that she was starting to come around. And for the first time all morning, the lines were coming out right. And just then Hitch said, "Cut." And I thought, "What on earth is he stopping for *now?*" Hitch just sat and looked up at Ingrid and said, quietly, "*Good* morning, Ingrid."

Jane Greer ——————— ACTRESS

I can remember being completely astounded when I watched the rushes on *Out of the Past,* which I did with Robert Mitchum a while back. I felt I not only had turned in a more honest performance in that film than I had ever done before, but I even looked different. And the reason for it was Mitchum.

On the set, he pretends an enormous disinterest in the scene, the role, even the picture. He'll come in in the morning, glance once at the script, raise an eyebrow—and then sit down to chat for hours with the crew. He'll say something like, "It would be nice if I knew this stuff," or "You can teach me the writer's immortal words when we get to them." And that's all.

The first place I saw him do this I became frantic. *Out of the Past* was the first big picture I had done and I was so nervous I hardly knew my own name. And the thought that Bob might blow his lines or not even have learned them at all nearly finished me!

But then we'd go into a scene. And "Mitch" would be so sure of himself and of every tiny detail of action and mood that I'd stand openmouthed in amazement. Furthermore, he was so calm about the whole business that it was catching. Instead of being terrified, I began to quiet down. The butterflies left my stomach.

Henry Hathaway ——— DIRECTOR

My first assignment from Darryl Zanuck was to turn Tyrone Power into a he-man. Zanuck reckoned Ty had done too many juvenile comedies with Loretta Young and needed toughening up. The pretty boy image was hurting him emotionally, too—the critical jibes. I thought we did a pretty fair job with *Johnny Apollo* and, in fact, you actually watch him strengthening as the film progresses.

* * *

Lucille Ball in *The Dark Corner:* I thought she could be just right as the sympathetic secretary who has a few years on her boss. But Lucy wouldn't work hard at first. One day she came on the set not knowing her lines and I told her off in front of the crew and sent her to her dressing room like a naughty child. She said it was an invaluable lesson and she finally caught the character's wisecracking wistfulness. I thought, "Sometimes a director has to be cruel to be kind."

Howard Hawks —— PRODUCER/DIRECTOR

When we were preparing *To Have and Have Not,* we discovered that Lauren Bacall was a little girl who, when she became insolent, became rather attractive. That was the only way you noticed her, because she could do it with a grin. So I said to Bogey, "We are going to try an interesting thing. You are about the most insolent man on the screen and I'm going to make this girl a little more insolent than you are." "Well," he said, "you're going to have a fat time doing that." And I said, "No, I've got a great advantage because I'm the director. I'll tell you one thing: she's going to walk out on you in every scene." It was sex antagonism, that's what it was, and it made the scenes easy.

* * *

We made a picture that worked pretty well called *The Big Sleep,* and I never figured out what was going on, but I thought that the basic thing had great scenes in it, and it was good entertainment. After that got by, I said, "I'm never going to worry about being logical again."

Rita Hayworth —— ACTRESS

That strip I did in *Gilda*—"Put the Blame on Mame, Boys." Remember it? Just with those long white [sic] gloves, but I took 'em off—wow! And there were great scenes with Glenn Ford, slappin' each other, kissin' each other. It was a marvelous big mess!

* * *

When Orson [Welles] and I made *The Lady from Shanghai,* we were separated but we were still friends. See, Orson was trying something new with me, but Harry Cohn wanted The Image—The Image he was gonna make me till I was 90! *The Lady from Shanghai* was a very good picture. So what does Harry Cohn say when he sees it? "He's *ruined* you—he cut your hair off!"

Ben Hecht —— SCREENWRITER

"I won't do this movie," said Ingrid Bergman of *Spellbound,* "because I don't believe the love story. The heroine is an intellectual woman, and an intellectual woman simply can't fall in love so deeply." She played the part very convincingly.

***Mark Hellinger*———PRODUCER**

Everything about *The Killers* was important to me. It was to be my first independent production. If it turned out a hit, I would probably be a hero for a couple of months, which is about as long as any hero lasts in Hollywood. But if I failed, I might have to go to Jack Warner and ask him to give me back my old job of producing for him. This latter thought caused me to take a sleeping pill every other night.

I had a hunch that, if I could only find the right "Swede," I might bat *The Killers* for a home run. Originally, I had tried to get Wayne Morris for the part. But Warner Bros. had his contract and, while everyone knows that the Warner organization is amazingly generous and big-hearted and friendly to anyone who makes a request for anything, I was unable to make a deal.

I tested potential "Swedes" until I thought I was going slightly smorgasbord. If someone had suggested Garbo, I would have tested her, too. It was all pretty discouraging.

The starting date of *The Killers* was drawing uncomfortably close, but I'm a guy who hates to take woe for an answer. Somehow, somewhere, I was going to find the right man to play "Swede."

Came the day, then, that I was lunching with Marty Jurow, an extremely able young citizen who was at that time an assistant to Hal Wallis. Marty told me of an actor that Hal had just signed; a big, brawny bird whom they had brought out from New York. His real name was Burt Lancaster, and they were planning to call him Stuart Chase.

A few days later, after going through the motions of a test, I signed a contract with Burt. And for films beyond *The Killers,* too.

***Paul Henreid*———ACTOR**

I started here in *Joan of Paris,* the first "A" picture for a new young actor, Alan Ladd. He played a member of a squad of Free French fliers shot down near Paris. I was the captain, and we try to hide out from the Nazis in the city. Michele Morgan and Thomas Mitchell, who played a priest, are in the underground and help us escape. Ladd is shot, and he has a death scene in the sewers of Paris.

It was an unfortunate scene. Ladd simply couldn't die properly, and director Robert Stevenson shot and reshot the episode. Ladd's eyes showed no expression. They were like glass balls, no matter how much Stevenson worked on him. Later, watching another scene being shot, Stevenson asked me, "Those three young actors who play the airmen—which of them, if any, do you think will make it?"

I shrugged. "Certainly not Ladd. Maybe Dick Fraser." Stevenson agreed.

How wrong we both were! Fraser never got a break, but in his next picture, *This Gun for Hire,* Ladd was cast as a glassy-eyed gangster who showed no emotion. He was an instant success.

* * *

Director Mike Curtiz, befitting the reputation of most Hungarians, was a practiced womanizer known to hire pretty young extras to whom he promised all sorts of things, including stardom, just to have them around at odd hours when there was a break in the shooting [of *Casablanca*]. He would choose any private place on the set, usually behind some flat in a secluded area. He'd have the grips move a piece of furniture there, a couch or even a mattress—almost anything to soften his lovemaking.

He thought none of us knew, but Peter Lorre, an inveterate practical joker, found out and went to the sound department, where he coaxed them into wiring up a hidden microphone and loudspeaker at Mike's favorite love rendezvous. We were all resting between takes one afternoon when suddenly, over the loudspeaker, we heard Mike moaning, "Oh God! Oh no, no, no. . . ."

Alfred Hitchcock —— DIRECTOR

Saboteur was not successful to my mind because I don't think Robert Cummings was right. He was too undramatic, he had what I call a "comedy face," and half the time you don't believe the situations. Think of the difference between that and Robert Donat in *The Thirty-Nine Steps*.

From an audience point-of-view, I should have reversed the positions of Cummings and Norman Lloyd on the Statue of Liberty at the end of the picture. The audience would have been much more anxious if the hero had been in danger, not the villain.

The picture was overloaded with too many ideas. But what annoyed me most was the casting of the heavy, Otto Kruger. I had a concept: fascists in those days were middle-westerners, America-Firsters, and I wanted Harry Carey, western style, as the rich rancher. His wife came to see me and said, "I couldn't let my husband play a role like that, when all the youth in America look up to him." So I couldn't get him, and Kruger was all wrong. I also tried to get Barbara Stanwyck, but I had to take Priscilla Lane. I wanted Barbara Stanwyck and Gary Cooper to lift the picture up.

* * *

Shadow of a Doubt is one of my favorite pictures. The opening scenes of Uncle Charlie on the run from his hotel room were shot in Newark, New Jersey, before Joseph Cotten had been cast. I shot them three times—there were only about four setups—using three different men: tall, medium and short. So when Cotten was cast I used the shots with the tall man.

James Wong Howe —— CINEMATOGRAPHER

I made a fight picture, *Body and Soul,* starring John Garfield, that required a lot of close shots of the fighting. It was difficult to follow the action with a big camera on a dolly, so I put on a pair of roller skates and used a hand-held camera while the man who was my grip pushed me around the ring. The resulting effect was very exciting. It brought the audience right into the ring. In movie theaters, the audiences would stand up and yell and root for the fighters! Well, I thought that was a first I had discovered, until just a few months ago I looked in an old magazine and saw a picture of Sidney Franklin doing a shot for a silent film and he was on roller skates with a hand-held camera!

John Huston — DIRECTOR/ SCREENWRITER

Working on *The Maltese Falcon,* Bogart once arrived at 9:15—15 minutes late. He was completely chagrined, embarrassed, ashamed. It really bothered him even though that was the morning that his wife, not Betty Bacall, but the older one [Mayo Methot], had stabbed him in the stomach with a knife.

— SCREENWRITER

I wrote a Hemingway story into a picture once, with a collaborator. It was during the time I was in the Army and I didn't want there to be any semblance of moonlighting, so my name didn't appear on the screen. One time Ernest/"Papa" was saying that they'd never done any good pictures of his books and stories. He said that there was only one he liked—*The Killers.* And I didn't tell him that I'd written it. He found out later and called me a dirty name.

Anne Jeffreys — ACTRESS

About three years ago, a woman came up to me in London and said, "You're Tess Trueheart from the Dick Tracy pictures!"—and I did not know *what* she was talking about. I told her: "You must be mistaken—I *never* appeared in one of those!" But about three days later, I realized she was right! I had forgotten all about them [*Dick Tracy, Dick Tracy Versus Cueball*]—which is what happens when you make eight pictures a year for RKO. But it was horribly embarrassing and that poor woman must think I'm a raving lunatic!

Louis Jourdan — ACTOR

Alfred Hitchcock is a great director because he never directs an actor, simply supervises him. I used to get all wound up in a problem about a scene in *The Paradine Case.* I'd go to Hitch with it, he'd look at me and say very quietly, "Don't worry, Louis. It's only a movie."

Garson Kanin — SCREENWRITER

I was in the Army for five and a half years and overseas for two, and we [Ruth Gordon] had just been married. When I came back to the United States, it just seemed that if I went to work in the normal way, say, writing and directing movies in California, and she went to work in her normal way, being an actress in the theater in New York, we'd be separated again. I was going to write something, an idea I had in the Army, a theater subject—a Ronald Colman picture called *A Double Life*—and I said to Ruth, "Why don't we write it together?" I meant that we could be around each other all the time.

We intended just to write that

one together, and then she was going on with her own stuff and I with mine. But it turned out to be a big hit. Ronald Colman won the Academy Award and we were nominated ourselves. Pretty soon we were asked to do another picture together, and we did *Adam's Rib* with Tracy and Hepburn—and that was an even bigger hit. We were sort of hooked into writing as a team for a couple of years.

Leonid Kinskey ———— *ACTOR*

Once, during the rehearsal of a freshly rewritten scene for *Casablanca,* director Michael Curtiz sent one of the second assistants for some new pages on the rewrite he had left in his portable office on the other end of our big stage. The short few minutes that the young assistant was absent seemed hours to the impatient Curtiz, anxious to rehearse a new scene. Suddenly he exclaimed, "The next time I have to send a silly fool, I'll go myself!"

Veronica Lake ———— *ACTRESS*

Filming *I Wanted Wings* was an exciting challenge to me. Especially the big café scene where we performed on a set with lots of extras, many of them kids I'd worked with before. Here I was, a new star with a pretentious name, sexy costumes cut down to here, careful make-up by the best and a lot at stake. I can remember their faces as clearly as if it were happening today. They sat there, faces set in a semi-sneer, eyes squinting against success or failure. They seemed to be saying, "Come on, you cocky little punk from Brooklyn. We knew you when. Come on and show us what you can do. We dare you!"

I mentioned this to the assistant director. And he gave me the best advice I'd had to that point: "Fuck 'em!"

* * *

Alan Ladd died in *This Gun for Hire* with his head resting in my lap. *Variety* commented, "Better men have died with their heads in less pleasant places." I always meant to ask Alan about his feelings on the subject but never got around to it. He probably wouldn't have answered me.

Hedy Lamarr ———— *ACTRESS*

This was the screen version of the sex-ridden stage play, *White Cargo.* As Tondelayo (that name kills me) I was a half-caste jungle temptress. John [Loder, her husband] thought from the start I was ridiculous to play it, but there was so much sex in it I couldn't resist the temptation to kill the "marble goddess image" for good!

John was right. It was like the debonair Cary Grant playing a beach bum in *Father Goose* or for that matter this little girl Carroll Baker playing the voluptuous Jean Harlow.

I thought with some interesting make-up, a sarong and some hip-swinging I would be a memorable nymphomaniac. Walter Pidgeon and Frank Morgan maybe didn't fire me or maybe director Dick Thorpe couldn't give me what I lacked or maybe screenwriter John Gordon's words weren't right—anyway, it was all hopeless. My costume of ringed earrings, bra, spangles and anklets helped little.

I know, though, that in my cocoa-butter-smeared nudity I contributed to the war effort. Soldiers all over the world sent fan letters to "Tondelayo." The fault with remakes is that what appeals to one generation doesn't appeal to others. The 1930 stage version of *White Cargo* had disrupted London, but Victor Saville's production in 1942 just looked like a sex satire. Critic George Jean Nathan listening to "Me Tondelayo. Me stay," got up and said, "Me George Jean Nathan. Me go."

Dorothy Lamour —— ACTRESS

Once, right after a tender love scene with Tyrone Power in *Johnny Apollo,* where we were standing near a sofa, he pulled me right down on the sofa. As he sat me down, there was a loud raspberry sound. It came from a special device that Ty had placed on the sofa. He wanted to see the expression on my face as that device gave me a raspberry. My facial expression must have been pretty funny, for the next day studio chief Darryl F. Zanuck ran the rushes for his own amusement, and people came from all over Hollywood to see them!

Burt Lancaster —— ACTOR

In *The Killers* I was a big, dumb Swede. I could be very simple in the part; there was no need to be highly ostentatious or theatrical. For a new actor this is much easier than something histrionic. There's no question about the good fortune of being ushered into films in that kind of role.

I had always been a Hemingway aficionado. I'd read everything he'd ever written. I remember [producer] Mark Hellinger asking me what I thought about the script, and I said, "Well, the first 16 pages is Hemingway verbatim, and after that you have a rather interesting whodunnit film, but nothing comparable to Hemingway." He said, "Well, you're not really a dumb Swede after all."

Fritz Lang —— DIRECTOR

I do not look at the oldest profession with a wagging finger. And this part Joan Bennett played in *Man Hunt,* of the little streetwalker who falls in love with Walter Pidgeon—a love that is doomed from the beginning—I must admit had all my heart. I think I understood her and I think Joan understood her very well. This love affair—in those days you could still say love without being laughed at—the tenderness of it . . . This girl cries like a child because the man whom she wants so very much doesn't sleep with her. There is so much in it: shame—"maybe I'm not good enough for him?" Desire—"why can't it be fulfilled?" And I think it was beautifully written.

But, naturally, the Hays Office insisted that we couldn't show or glamorize a prostitute. You know how we overcame it? We had to prominently show a sewing machine in her apartment: thus she was not a whore, she was a "seamstress"!

Angela Lansbury ——— ACTRESS

"The money's running low," Mother said one day, and that climaxed it. Discouraged about the cinema, I went to work at Bullock's-Wilshire, a fashionable Los Angeles department store. One evening, after I had been working there for quite some time, I heard that *Gaslight* was being cast. I asked for a leave of absence from the store and fortunately was able to contact director George Cukor, who arranged a test.

The test was a great disappointment. I was not the type he had in mind for the role of the cockney maid. Bitterly discouraged, I was about to start back to work at the store when Mr. Cukor phoned me.

"The role is yours. It has been tailored to fit your talents."

My amazement was nothing compared to my surprise at the success of my portrayal. Getting the Academy nomination for it, of course, was about the most thrilling moment of my life. This role turned the key of my future, and the chance to prove my versatility in many roles.

Norman Lloyd ——— ACTOR

Saboteur starred Robert Cummings, Priscilla Lane and some very good character actors like Otto Kruger, Egon Brecher, Alma Kruger, Alan Baxter and Ian Wolfe. Hitch [Alfred Hitchcock] was shooting when I arrived. I came on the set and he greeted me most charmingly. I waited. The shooting day was almost over and he invited me for a drink. This was my first experience drinking with Hitchcock; from then on, I was on my guard.

We went across the street from the lovely old Universal lot to a bar and restaurant run by one of the prop men, Eddie Keyes. Hitch ordered a martini, and I said I would have the same. When Hitch's "usual" arrived, it was in a goblet the size of those used to serve grapefruit, when the grapefruit is surrounded by ice. Mine, of course, was the same. I looked at it with fear. At no time in my life have I been much of a drinker; I was also not accustomed to driving, having learned when I was in Hollywood in 1939 with Orson [Welles], and not having driven in New York since. The drink made me fear for my safety; on the other hand, I was afraid that if I didn't drink it, I might lose the part. I just sipped while Hitch drank one, then another. He never got drunk; it was his normal appetite.

The Statue of Liberty sequence has become one of the most famous Hitchcock ever made. [It] is probably my claim to fame, for people always say, "Oh, yes—you fell off the Statue of Liberty."

Jean Louis ——— COSTUME DESIGNER

The most famous dress I ever make was the little black satin one I design for Rita Hayworth in *Gilda.* Everybody wonder how that dress can stay on her while she sings and dances "Put the Blame on Mame." Well, inside there was a harness like you put on a horse. We put grosgrain under the bust with darts and three stays, one in the center, two on the sides. Then we mold plastic around the top of the dress. Poor Rita. She was rehearsing so hard, her feet were bloody, but the dress does not fall down.

Ida Lupino ——————— ACTRESS

I find it very hard to cry in front of a whole crew, especially when they'd say, "Quiet! Everybody quiet!" I'd freeze up. I couldn't do anything. On *High Sierra,* Bogey sensed this—this was the side of this man, this tough guy, that his friends knew but I didn't know. So he took me to one side, he looked at our director, Raoul Walsh, and gave him a sign. And he said, "Listen, doll. If you can't cry, just remember one thing: I'm going to take the picture away from you."

Well, I started to laugh and I said, "Now, listen, Bogey. I can't cry. Don't break me up." He said, "All right, you're relaxed." I said, "Yes, I am, but now I can't cry." He said, "All right, next step. Come on." He walked me further away and he said, "Just try and think of one thing. If you can't relate it to me or my character right now, go back to your childhood. Can you remember when you had to say goodbye to somebody, somebody you loved and you thought you weren't going to see again?" And I said yes. And he said, "Well, think of that, baby, think of it." And there were tears in my eyes. And before I knew it, I was crying!

* * *

There is only one performance I ever gave I'm proud of: Ellen in *Ladies in Retirement,* a role played with great success on Broadway by Flora Robson. I never saw her performance, or I probably would have run screaming into the night with fear that I just couldn't play the part.

On Broadway Flora Robson played the oldest sister, a woman about 60; her mad sisters were supposed to be 45 and 50.

A man called Lester Cowan—a production executive—took a chance on a 21-year-old girl—myself—to play the Robson role. He and director Charles Vidor decided to have Ellen be the youngest sister—45—and to have Elsa Lanchester and Edith Barrett play two older women. One was supposed to be 50, the other about 60. Actually Elsa wasn't in her fifties yet, neither was Edith, but the age jump wasn't as great for them as for me.

At the time Harry Cohn—God rest his soul—was the head of Columbia Pictures, which would release the film. When Mr. Cowan told him, "I am sure this girl can play the part," Mr. Cohn said, "You are out of your mind—choosing this child to play that role!"

Cowan explained that I would be playing a woman of 45, not 60, but Cohn still thought he was mad to take a chance on me.

Joel McCrea ——————— ACTOR

On *Foreign Correspondent,* director Alfred Hitchcock had a habit of drinking a pint of champagne at lunch, I remember. After lunch one day, there was a long boring scene with me just standing there and talking. When the scene was over, I expected to hear "Cut!" and I looked over and there was Hitchcock snoring with his lips sticking out. He had fallen asleep. So I said "Cut!" and he woke up and asked, "Was it any good?" I said, "The best in the picture!" And he said, "Print!"

Fred MacMurray —— ACTOR

I enjoy doing comedy more than anything, I guess. But, honestly, I have to come back to *Double Indemnity* and say that was my best role. Although it was a dramatic role, and it was certainly different from what I had done before, Billy Wilder wanted me to do it, and I read the script and I thought, gee, it's a great story!

But I held off saying I would do it, because, in the first place, I wasn't sure that I was *able* to, never having done anything of that type before. And then, also, I thought, well, people aren't going to like me if I kill somebody's husband. So I had second thoughts about doing the picture, but I'm very happy that I did it, because it turned out so well.

Daniel Mainwaring —— SCREENWRITER

Robert Mitchum smoked marijuana all the time on the set [of *Out of the Past*]. He had a vicious sense of humor. The executive producer on the film was a guy named Robert Sparks, a very nice guy, dignified and sweet. Sheilah Graham, the commentator, came on the set to see Mitchum, and she was talking to him when a drunken dress extra came up and started pestering Mitchum. Finally Mitchum had to tell him to get the hell out of there. Graham said, "Who was that?" Mitchum replied off-handedly, "That's a very sad story. That's our executive producer, Robert Sparks. He's an alcoholic." Sheilah was busily taking notes the whole time, but luckily the publicity man overheard and took her aside and said Mitchum was kidding. Well, she wouldn't believe him and finally had to be taken up in Sparks' office to meet him.

Joseph L. Mankiewicz —— DIRECTOR

I wrote the script for *House of Strangers* without signing it. I was very satisfied with the result, but if it has been very popular in Europe, it was unhappily not the same in the United States. [Cinematographer] Gianni Di Venanzo said to me the other day that *House of Strangers* was the only portrait of Italy that an American has brought off successfully (the Sicilian family in America). Only, the shooting coincided with a personal tragedy that happened in the private life of one of the big Hollywood directors, whose family drama the film recreated almost exactly. It was for that reason somewhat sacrificed. I have always regretted that it did not do well in the United States, while everywhere I go abroad it is, with *People Will Talk,* the one film of mine that has been the best received.

George Marshall —— DIRECTOR

Susan Hayward's courage turned up on *The Forest Rangers* which I directed early in her eareer. If you saw it, you may remember the part where she and Paulette Goddard had to run through some fire. Paulette was frightened, and in spite of our

showing her all the safety factors and how impossible it was for her to be injured or burned, she still backed off and started to cry. I really think she had a date and wanted to get off early.

Susan came up to me and whispered, "Get the cameras going." Then she went over to Paulette, as though to comfort her. When I gave her the signal, she grabbed Paulette by the hand and said, "For God's sake, stop being such a baby!" and pulled her through the scene. Ironically, in the story it was Susan who was supposed to become frightened.

Mike Mazurki ———— ACTOR

In *Nightmare Alley,* I was supposed to take care of this girl [Coleen Gray] and Tyrone Power abuses her. I'm waiting for him when he comes into this tavern, and I tell him, "You gotta marry her." He refuses. I grab him by the collar—he breaks away—which is not in the script. He does this three or four times. Finally, the director, Edmund Goulding, says, "Mazurki, you big stoop, you're a wrestler and you can't hold Tyrone Power?!" I'm embarrassed as hell. So the next time I grab him—I grab hair, skin and all. This time he stays put. Well, Ty shrieked like a wounded bear. "Let me go, you big S.O.B.—let me go!" When I did he ran to his dressing room and locked himself in for two solid hours.

Now George Jessel, the producer, approaches me and says, "Mazurki, what are you trying to do to my star?" I didn't want to tell him Ty refused to cooperate—that I didn't want to hurt him. "I'm sorry," I said. So Ty comes out and finally tells them, "Actually, it was my fault. I tried to show this big bastard up. I tried to show him I could break his hold." Ty apologized to me. "Mike, I'm sorry. I didn't know how strong you really are." I said, "Well, Ty, I didn't want to hurt you, that's why I grabbed you so easy." After that, we became the best of friends. Ty was an individual, and there will never be another man to take his place.

Lewis Milestone —— DIRECTOR

During rehearsals for *The Strange Love of Martha Ivers,* we were faced with the problem of how to establish that Van Heflin had become a professional gambler. Then I recalled a piece of business I had noticed at the casinos in Las Vegas. Some of the dealers, superlatively skillful with their hands, could take a coin, a dollar or half-dollar, insert it in the space between two knuckles and deftly manipulate it to twist it end over end, over and over, to and fro across their knuckles. I decided that this would be the perfect piece of business to help Van establish a believable character as a gambler.

When I suggested this to him, I told him it wouldn't be effective unless he practiced it a long time so he would be able to do it mechanically. Van practiced for hours, and he could deliver pages of dialogue while his hand performed the coin trick automatically.

Barbara Stanwyck watched this during rehearsal, then said, "Van, that's a wonderful piece of business, but if you do that during my important lines, I have a bit of business that will draw attention away from yours." She pulled her skirt way up over her knees.

Robert Mitchum —— ACTOR

I felt like I was always working during this period. *Desire Me, The Locket* and *Undercurrent* were being made simultaneously. I did one in the morning, one in the afternoon and the third at night. I was a very busy boy.

Robert Montgomery —— ACTOR/DIRECTOR

I had a little trouble making this picture [*Lady in the Lake*]. That is, if you can call eight years of arguing trouble. Nobody seems to want an actor to become a director. And the idea for this film wasn't exactly a pushover to sell.

Alan Napier —— ACTOR

Ministry of Fear was my first encounter with the Germanic type of direction. In my first scene, I remember, I had to go down a corridor, turn and go into an elevator. In order to show director Fritz Lang that I was sincerely interested in the proceedings, I said, "What am I feeling at this moment?" He said, "It does not matter what you feel. You just walk into the lift! That is all I ask!"

* * *

I'm the only "Holy Friar" who has ever appeared in Shakespeare's *Macbeth.* [Producer/director/screenwriter] Orson Welles wrote the part. He didn't write the lines, he culled them very skillfully from other characters' speeches here and there in the play. Oddly enough, the English critics resented his imposition of the part far less than the Americans.

He tried out the production first as a play in Salt Lake City, and I had to refuse the part because I was doing something else. Jeanette Nolan's husband, John McIntire, played the Holy Friar then, so I was a little flattered that Orson came back to me to play the film. He would have two scenes going on at once on this huge stage. One scene was rehearsing here, another there, and he'd shout at the top of his voice, "Run, don't walk. This is a 'B' picture!"

I told my wife what fun we were having. "The only thing," I said, "Orson wants me to play in a slightly higher tone than my normal voice." When we saw the picture she said, "You silly fool. He didn't want your voice to conflict with his!"

Jean Negulesco ——— DIRECTOR

Darryl Zanuck spoke: "I saw your last picture, *Deep Valley.* A good job. I asked my people in the studio to see it—the way pictures should be made on location."

He picked up a script and handed it to me. "Here is a script that four directors refused—good directors. Only they couldn't see what this property offers." His voice suddenly got loud as he stood up. "I know its potential, and I'm sure you will, too." He started to walk the length of his office.

"We made this kind of picture at Warners for years—James Cagney, Ann Sheridan and Pat O'Brien. Focus on the girl's tits, and if somebody drops a hat, start a fight."

That first picture [at 20th Century-Fox] was *Road House,* with Richard Widmark, Ida Lupino, Cornel Wilde and Celeste Holm—a solid success. It featured two outstanding songs: "Again" and "One More for the Road." No-voice Ida Lupino sang them and placed them first on the *Hit Parade.*

Lloyd Nolan ——— ACTOR

Lady in the Lake—I almost lost an eye on that picture. In the final scene, I'm supposed to be shot by a gun fired from outside the window on the fire escape. They had to physically shoot a gun pellet through the glass to get the splintering effect. The pellet ricocheted at a 90-degree angle.

One piece flew into my eye, actually curving around the cornea. They rushed me to a hospital where a female doctor carefully removed it.

Lee Patrick ——— ACTRESS

Mike Curtiz was another scrupulous director I enjoyed working with, though I only did a small part for him in *Mildred Pierce.* But he was just as careful and thoughtful about my contribution as he was with Joan Crawford, whose first [starring] film it was away from MGM. She used to come on the set beautifully turned out and he kept mussing up her hair and changing her make-up. "I don't

IDA LUPINO · DANE CLARK · WAYNE MORRIS
Warner Bros. Present
DEEP VALLEY

IDA
LUPINO · CORNEL
WILDE
CELESTE
HOLM · RICHARD
WIDMARK
ROAD HOUSE
JEAN NEGULESCO
EDWARD CHODOROV
20th
2

want you to look like an actress," he kept saying.

Gregory Peck ——— *ACTOR*

Ingrid Bergman was wonderful in *Spellbound.* Neither of us could ski. The snow is cornflakes painted white. The mountain is on a back projection screen. Director Alfred Hitchcock, weighing in at 300, kept up a running patter of suggestive remarks directed at Ingrid. English schoolboy stuff, from the master of suspense.

Dick Powell ——— *ACTOR*

Paramount had a dramatic story that I was dying to do, *Double Indemnity,* but instead they assigned me to another nothing musical called *Bring on the Girls.* I went to see Frank Freeman, head of the Paramount lot, and told him, "Frank, I can't do this kind of picture anymore. They're ruining what's left of my career. Let me go." He did, and I went over to RKO, where they offered me *Murder, My Sweet,* as Raymond Chandler's tough detective, Philip Marlowe. I grabbed it, and it not only changed my career but my life.

Otto Preminger ——— *PRODUCER/DIRECTOR*

I went to Darryl Zanuck about getting Clifton Webb for *Laura,* and we called in the casting director, Rufus LeMaire. He was against it. What happened in these studios was that these people always guessed what the executives wanted. They knew. They were trained to know who Zanuck favored. And LeMaire felt immediately that Zanuck would not like Clifton Webb. So he said: "You can't have Clifton Webb play this part. He flies!" I said: "What do you mean?" I didn't even understand what he meant. I already knew Clifton was a little effeminate, but that didn't bother me at all. I said I would like to make a test with him.

* * *

Director Rouben Mamoulian knew that I wasn't on the best of terms with Darryl Zanuck. So, he ignored my function as producer [of *Laura*] by making foolish changes in the sets and costumes without consulting me. He began to shoot the picture and asked me not to come to the set.

He claimed I made him nervous. When he began making changes in the script, I fought him. Zanuck liked the script, so Mamoulian gave in.

I was satisfied with none of the acting. I thought the performances of Dana Andrews, Gene Tierney and Clifton Webb were very amateurish. So I airmailed the rushes to Zanuck, who was in New York on business. Zanuck looked at them and agreed with me. Mamoulian re-shot everything, but when Zanuck returned, he was again dissatisfied.

Then, he invited me to a luncheon meeting, where the top brass at Fox were present. Zanuck asked me, "Should I take Mamoulian off the picture?" Without any hesitation I said, "Yes!" Later, as we were leaving the dining room, he said, "You can start directing *Laura* right away."

* * *

Laura became a classic only later on, which is a great satisfaction for me. It got very mixed reviews at first. Some really bad ones, in fact. I met one of the reviewers after he retired, and he told me, "I saw *Laura* on television the other day, and it is one of the greatest pictures I've ever seen." I didn't have the heart to remind him that he wrote an absolutely devastating review when it opened.

Vincent Price ——— ACTOR

Laura is the best movie I ever made. It's one of those few pictures that are perfect. Not pretentious, very simple, a really brilliant picture. Otto Preminger had taken over the direction from Rouben Mamoulian. We re-shot every single scene that Rouben had done. Rouben was a very nice man and a very good director, but he had no concept about these kind of upper scum people. They are not his cup of tea, but *were* Otto's. Otto succeeded in giving all of us an underlying evil that is there all the time. Nobody in that picture is normal—not a soul. Even Gene Tierney is pretty kinky.

I loved her. I was very, very close to her. We got along marvelously well, and we worked together well. I think she's the reason *Laura* has not dated.

* * *

Darryl F. Zanuck was away at the war when *Laura* was made. When he came back, he saw it and he didn't like it. I don't know why he didn't like it. I suspect because he didn't have a hand in it, but maybe it's better because he didn't have a hand in it.

* * *

When I went to see Joseph L. Mankiewicz about playing the coveted male lead opposite Gene Tierney in *Dragonwyck,* Joe, who was making his directorial debut on the film, told me I was a big, fat slob. I lost 35 pounds and got the part. It was my first Gothic picture in a long line of Gothic pictures.

George Raft ——— ACTOR

I made a picture with Bogart called *Invisible Stripes,* and there was a very peculiar thing. We were in the shower together. I think that I was a little taller than Bogart in reality, but when we came out of the shower and were walking out of the penitentiary together he was a little taller than me. So I looked down and noticed that he had little lifts on his shoes. I had a young man with me at the time by the name of Mack Grey, and I yelled, "Stop the camera! Mack, get those shoes I wore with Gary Cooper in *Souls at Sea.*"

* * *

I could drive a car blindfolded. I learned how when I was helping to move booze, and the associate producer of the movie and my old pal, Mark Hellinger, must have known that when he assigned me to *They Drive by Night.* Some people say I got nothing from Owney Madden but a bad reputation—but the driving skill I acquired when I worked for him in

New York years before undoubtedly saved my life and those of the people in the picture with me.

In this scene, Humphrey Bogart, Ann Sheridan and I are highballing down a long hill in an old beat-up truck. Halfway down, the brakes really went out—a situation that wasn't in the script. Bogart saw me press the pedal and when nothing happened, he began to curse. "We're going to get killed!" he yelled. Ann screamed and turned her eyes away from the road as I fought the wheel. I couldn't have been more scared myself. The speedometer hit 80 when I saw a break on the right where a bulldozer had started a new road. I pulled hard on the wheel and the truck went bouncing up the embankment. Thank God—it finally stopped.

Ann was too upset to talk, but Bogart said, "Thanks, pal."

"Don't thank me," I thought to myself, because I didn't have the breath to answer. "Write a letter to Owney Madden or Feets Edson."

* * *

In *Background to Danger,* the director had me tied up. Peter Lorre was sitting on a table in front of me. He was a mean little guy. Lorre blew cigarette smoke in my face. I didn't like it. Lorre grinned. We had retake after retake. Lorre kept blowing smoke in my face. He kept getting closer and closer to my eyes with that cigarette. "Untie me," I said, before the next retake. I grabbed Lorre. "You keep that cigarette out of my face," I said. Lorre ran away and locked himself in his dressing room. When they had me tied up again, he comes prancing out. He sits on the table. He blows smoke in my face. And he flicks the cigarette around, real close to my eyes. When I got untied, I slugged him. I told him he was a German spy. That upset him. But he didn't blow smoke at me again.

Claude Rains——— ACTOR

We were doing the scene in *Casablanca* where I enter Rick's place to arrest Paul Henreid. I did nine takes and still our director, Michael Curtiz, wasn't satisfied. Finally, I implored him, "Mike, *please,* what is it exactly that you want?" He replied, "I want you should come in faster." After a bit I said I was ready to give him what he wanted. When the door opened for the take, I peddled in furiously on a bicycle.

* * *

In *Notorious,* I, standing five-foot-seven-and-a-half inches, performed upon a carpet-covered elevated platform in order to be within eye level of five-foot-eight Ingrid Bergman. This bit of contriving, Alfred Hitchcock, who directed *Notorious,* called "The Shame of Rains."

Irving Rapper——— DIRECTOR

The definition of good acting has always been *reacting.* Paul Henreid can't even spell it! I didn't want him in *Deception.* I wanted Charles Boyer, but Bette Davis begged me, "Don't break up a team."

We'd do an eighth take, a ninth—and no reaction. He told me,

"You worry about the camera, I'll worry about my acting." "Your *acting?*" I asked. "I told you on *Now, Voyager* that that was the only time you'd be good—and I was right!"

Deception didn't come off. I warned Bette that it wouldn't be a tour-de-force—especially after *Now, Voyager* and *The Corn Is Green.* I couldn't tell her that Claude Rains would run away with it.

Rains was a gracious man, a prize actor. By whispering, he could undercut anybody!

Allen Rivkin —— SCREENWRITER

John Huston and I collaborated on *The Maltese Falcon.* And that was some collaboration. We were office mates, and we had a secretary between us. He came in one day and says, "Jack Warner wants us to take another shot at *The Maltese Falcon.*" They had made it before and it was a bomb. He says, "Have you read the book?" And I said, "No." He says, "Read it." So I read it.

And he says, "Let's give the book to the secretary to break it down into scenes and dialogue." Now, in every studio, whatever a secretary types goes into the pool for copies. How it got to Jack Warner, I don't know, but John came in one day all elated. He says, "What do you know! Jack says I can direct *Maltese Falcon.*" I said, "Well, good. So we've got to write the script." And he said, "No. The *secretary* did the script, and that's what he wants me to shoot!" And he took credit on it, naturally, because he was the director.

Edward G. Robinson —— ACTOR

A lot of *Manpower* was inane, yet [Marlene] Dietrich and I (I say this in no immodesty but rather as a fact) were a stunning combination, and our joint presence was tough box office. Add George Raft and you had showmanship casting. Bad—but showmanship. Raft was touchy, difficult and thoroughly impossible to play with. He threw a punch at me, and I was ready to walk; Hal Wallis had to act as peacemaker.

Ruth Roman —— ACTRESS

Bette Davis in *Beyond the Forest?* She was great. I kept blowing my lines in one scene with her because they were so awful to try to say. I finally told the director that and Bette immediately came to my rescue. "She's right," Bette shouted, "this girl is absolutely right." Later she told me, "Ruth, never forget what you did today . . . never be afraid to fight for what you know is right." And I never did forget.

Miklos Rozsa —— COMPOSER

The Paramount musical director described my title music to *Double Indemnity* as more appropriate to *The Battle of Russia.* He was convinced that when the artistic director of the studio, Buddy DeSylva, heard the score it would be thrown out and all of us would suffer.

The film was previewed in Long Beach and DeSylva called the man over as he tried to make a hasty exit. He walked over like Louis XVI going to the guillotine, expecting heads to roll. DeSylva, however, began praising the music to the skies, saying that it was exactly the sort of dissonant, hard-hitting score the film needed. The only criticism he had to make was that there wasn't enough of it. By this time the musical director was grinning from ear to ear and put his arm around DeSylva, saying, "I always find you the right guy for the job, don't I?"

Dore Schary — *EXECUTIVE PRODUCER*

Joe Smith, American, starring Robert Young, directed by Richard Thorpe, picked up wonderful reviews, big business and a stack of awards. It was at the preview of *Joe Smith* that [producer] Harry Rapf grabbed my shoulder and whispered in triumph, "Believe me, this is going to be a feather in your eye."

— *PRODUCER*

The success of *I'll Be Seeing You* was followed by *The Spiral Staircase,* which had been designed for Ingrid Bergman, who rejected it. Dorothy McGuire jumped at the script and the cast included Ethel Barrymore, George Brent and Kent Smith. The script was based on the book *Some Must Watch,* a good thriller. However, the heroine was not a girl muted by shock.

Her disability came about during a story conference with Mel Dinelli, the screenplay writer, Paul Stewart, then employed as an assistant, and Laura Kerr, who was my story editor.

We had reached a cul-de-sac. The girl was trapped in a series of logical moves, but now the question I asked—"Why the hell doesn't she yell for help?"—had no appropriate answer. Finally, Paul, as we reached the dead end, laughed and said, "She don't yell because she's a dope—a dumb dame." Then came the pause that usually follows a forced joke and my eyes must have lit up like a pinball machine—"That's it—she can't talk!"

Everything slipped into place. We had a better motive for the crimes—more suspense and terror and an emotional ending. Dinelli's script was a lesson in screenwriting. The script itself reads like a good mystery novel. Our cameraman was Nick Musuraca, a brilliant cinematographer who gave us sharp black and white contrasts, and director Robert Siodmak caught the mood and style of the script accurately. The picture was a success, critically and commercially.

Vincent Sherman — *DIRECTOR*

The Unfaithful was one of the first pictures in which a woman [Ann Sheridan] commits adultery and the marriage didn't break up. According to the censors, the woman had to be killed accidentally. Or, something terrible had to happen to her.

Anne Shirley — *ACTRESS*

I read the script [of *Murder, My Sweet*] and even though it wasn't a large role, I fell in love with the Claire Trevor part. I was dying to play a heavy. Then Claire told me she was sick of doing heavies and would love to do the role assigned to me. Claire and I put our heads together and conspired to reverse the femme casting. We even ganged up on the producer and director, probably giving better performances for their benefit than we did in the film. But it all did us no good. Claire went back to being bad and fascinating and I went back to being good and dull.

Sylvia Sidney—————ACTRESS

I knew about this script, *Blood on the Sun.* A friend of mine said, "James Cagney wants Merle Oberon, but Merle won't play it. She doesn't want to play half-caste type stuff. You've got to get Cagney to know you're alive again." I'd been out of films for a long time, so my friend said, "Get Russell Birdwell." Now, Russell Birdwell at that time was *the* P. R. man in the world; he did P. R. for the Queen of Romania, everybody. So I went to see him and said, "I want one ting: to get Cagney's attention."

Well, I picked up the *Los Angeles Times* one morning, and there had been a meeting of I-don't-know-how-many artists at some institute in Chicago, and they had named the ten most beautiful women in the world. The first was Lana Turner; the second was Sylvia Sidney. But *Sylvia Sidney* had the photograph. I'll never forget the photo. And it was all over the country. And in those days I paid him not *that* much money. Honey, to be named the second most beautiful woman in the world . . . and the first most beautiful woman in the world doesn't get her picture in, but the second *does*—isn't that wonderful P. R. work? In a couple of days I got a call from Cagney.

Gale Sondergaard————ACTRESS

I played a Eurasian in *The Letter.* I went to Wardrobe at Warners to be fitted before we were to begin, and they brought out all these cheap, horrible things of a second class whore. I said, "Why should she look like that?" If you remember the story, the Bette Davis role, the white woman, had had an adulterous affair with a man; the man had married the Eurasian woman, and the white woman had shot the man dead.

"Did that make her cheap and out of the gutter?" I asked. "This doesn't make any sense to me; I don't understand—is it because she's yellow? Because she's half Chinese and not all Caucasian?"

So William Wyler, who is a marvelous director, and a marvelous man in every way, said, "Well, let's think about it a little. Come back tomorrow and we'll look at clothes again." I came back next day, and he said he hadn't slept all night; he thought about it and he realized I was right. Why would we make her a lesser woman than the white woman who had lived this way? So then we began to design some gorgeous fashions which gave her dignity—which made the picture so much more interesting.

Barbara Stanwyck———ACTRESS

Phyllis Dietrichson in *Double Indemnity* was the most hard-boiled dame I ever played. I had never played an out-and-out killer. When Billy Wilder sent me the script—the most perfect script, bar none, I ever read—I was a little frightened of it.

Back in his office, I said, "I love

the script, and I love you, but I'm a little afraid after all these years of playing heroines to go into an out-and-out cold-blooded killer." And Mr. Wilder—and rightly so—looked at me and said, "Are you a mouse or an actress?" And I said, "I *hope* I'm an actress." He said, "Then do the part." And I did and I'm very grateful to him.

* * *

The very best screenplay I was ever sent was *Double Indemnity.* It's brilliant, of course, but what's amazing is that not one word was changed while we were shooting. Billy Wilder had it all there, and I mean *all*—everything you see on the screen was in the script. The moves, the business, the atmosphere—all written.

When I mention "atmosphere" in *Double Indemnity*—that gloomy, horrible house the Dietrichsons lived in, the slit of sunlight slicing through those heavy drapes—you could smell that death was in the air, you understood why she wanted to get out of there, away, no matter how. Can you imagine the picture being "colorized"? My God! And for an actress, let me say that the way those sets were lit, the house, Walter's apartment, those dark shadows, those slices of harsh light at strange angles—all that helped my performance. The way Billy staged it and John Seitz lit it, it was all one sensational mood. Color? How dare they?

* * *

People say terrible things about Errol Flynn. I never worked with anybody nicer. He was on time, he knew his lines, he was a perfect gentleman. Now there's that terrible book that says he was a Nazi spy. I don't believe that for a minute. I was with him ten weeks on *Cry Wolf* and he didn't have time to make a phone call, much less be a spy.

* * *

I had 12 days of terror in bed [in *Sorry, Wrong Number*]. Anatole Litvak was the director and he very kindly asked me if I wanted to do those 12 days all at once or spread them out. I thought it would be better to do it all at once, so that I myself might have continuity. Of course, I worried every night that I went home, because at six o'clock, if I had hit a high emotional peak, I had to come back the next morning and *start* up there. Now I don't know whether that had something to do with my hair turning gray, but it did start then.

Donald Ogden Stewart—SCREEN-WRITER

On *A Woman's Face* they got Albert Basserman who was one of the big German stars and it was an important part yet a small one, so I took care to get just the right words to say; I didn't know he didn't speak any English at all. So I went down to the set to see how it was coming—they pointed over in the corner and he had with him another German and he was learning my lines by heart—he didn't have the least idea what they meant, he just learned them. When he played the part he almost stole the picture—somehow it worked to have him sing these speeches which I thought should have John Barrymore to bring the right emphasis on the verb and the noun.

James Stewart—ACTOR

Malaya was a constantly edgy situation. Spence [Tracy] was more cantankerous than usual because the film was a real potboiler. We knew that was a dangerous situation: he could pull one of his famous disappearances at any time. So I decided on a strategy to keep him interested in something other than the picture: a trip to Europe and Asia.

Every day, we'd talk about what countries we were going to visit, and I kept collecting brochures to show him. He'd pore over the brochures and talk with great excitement about Greece and Rome and the Taj Mahal. Wal, anyway, the strategy seemed to work and Spence showed up every day and did his usual fine job. When it was over, I said to him, "Wal, have you gotten your passport yet?"

He said, "What passport?"

"For our trip to Europe and Asia."

"Europe and Asia?" he said. "Why, I wouldn't go across the *street* with you, you son-of-a-bitch!"

Jean Sullivan—ACTRESS

Escape in the Desert was an updated remake of *The Petrified Forest* in which I had the Bette Davis role.

Coincidentally, on the first day of shooting *Desert,* I was assigned the dressing room next door to one being used by Bette. It was 7:30 in the morning and I heard her bellowing, "Who left these dead flowers in here? Take them away! I couldn't work seeing these dead flowers!" It was an omen.

I never thought the picture would end. The story was now about Nazis, and although set in the desert it was shot entirely on a studio sound stage. There were tons of sand in which they wanted me to romp about in high heels. This looked ridiculous, so I fought them—and lost again. We filmed with Zachary Scott opposite me for months, then it was decided he was miscast and Philip Dorn replaced him. We had three directors, including Robert Florey. The script wasn't right, either, so the two producers, ex-gag writers from radio, began working on it. That didn't pan out, so they brought in William Faulkner, no less, to work on it.

One day my make-up man, who had a horse ranch in the Valley, told me that Faulkner went riding there and since I liked to ride, why not come out. I did, and Faulkner and I became good friends. We rode together two or three times a week when we weren't working. He'd say, "What am I doing in Hollywood? I have to get away. They've messed up the script so badly. The only time I feel free is when I'm riding." Years later he invited me to his daughter's wedding in Mississippi.

Escape in the Desert was in production for about seven months. Finally, director Byron Haskin was hired. He made a beautiful storyboard, knew exactly what he wanted and brought the film in at last. It did not do well at the box office.

Robert Taylor — ACTOR

Lana Turner wasn't very career-minded, and preferred men and jewelry over anything else. Lana wasn't as "busty" as her pin-up pictures, but her face was delicate and beautiful. I have never seen lips like hers, and though I was never known to run after blondes, Lana was the exception. I couldn't take my eyes off her, and there were times during *Johnny Eager* that I thought I'd explode. Her voice was like a breathless child. I don't think she knew how to talk without being sexy. When she said, "Good morning," I melted. She was the type of woman for whom a guy would risk five years in jail for rape.

Gene Tierney — ACTRESS

I was worried about doing *Laura* at first. Even after it was in production, I didn't feel it was going well. But Marie [Walters, her hairdresser] continued to assure me it would be a hit. I am glad now that I listened to her and didn't follow my first instinct to get out of the picture. I'm glad that I've always listened to her.

* * *

I never felt my own performance in *Laura* was much more than adequate. I am pleased that audiences still identify me with Laura, as opposed to not being identified at all. Their tributes, I believe, are for the *character*—the dreamlike Laura—rather than any gifts I brought to the role. I do not mean to sound modest. I doubt that any of us connected with the movie thought it had a chance of becoming a kind of mystery classic, or enduring beyond its generation.

* * *

I was at a cocktail party one evening in Romanoff's when Darryl Zanuck told me he was thinking of giving me the part of Ellen in *Leave Her to Heaven.* I had read the novel by Ben Ames Williams, coveted the part and knew Fox had bought the film rights. The role was a plum, the kind of character Bette Davis might have played, a bitchy woman.

I quickly told Zanuck that he would never regret it if he gave me the part. In a few days he called and said, "You're Ellen."

That performance brought my only nomination for an Academy Award.

Yet I suppose the most sincere compliment of all came from a gentle black lady who cooked for friends of mine in Cape Cod. When I went to visit, they asked in some embarrassment if I would speak to the cook. "She has seen your new film," the wife said, "and when she heard you were coming she threatened to leave."

I went to the kitchen and said hello. We chatted and, after a few minutes, the cook smiled and said, "Oh, ma'am. You sure were mean in that picture. Now that I've seen you, you are real nice."

Ann Todd — ACTRESS

I will never forget the first film I made in Hollywood: *The Paradine Case.* The first day in the studio was a nightmare. They were filming the dinner scene and I was terribly

nervous. Alfred Hitchcock, the director, had arranged for the camera to film the whole dinner table showing everyone present in close-up, all in one shot without cutting. It started on Charles Laughton, then moved along to Gregory Peck, Ethel Barrymore, Alida Valli, Charles Coburn, etc., and finally me. "Cut" said the cameraman. "What's the matter?" asked Hitchcock rather crossly. "She," he answered, pointing at me, "has a rash and bumps coming up on her neck and chest. I can't film her." The great David Selznick, the producer, looked at his watch, everyone else looked at me. "This pause is costing money," they seemed to be saying. "Take her outside for some fresh air," ordered Hitch.

They walked me up and down to cool my nerves. Back I came and apologized. We started again. It was no good. Again I was banished, this time underground somewhere and a nurse gave me an injection. When I returned they shot the scene, rash or no rash. The last thing I heard as, with head bowed, I returned to my dressing room, was someone saying very loudly, "I hope we are not going to have her like that all through the film—good God!"

Audrey Totter—ACTRESS

I did the voice of Phyllis Thaxter's wicked other self in *Bewitched,* with no billing. It was similar to what Mercedes McCambridge did much later as the voice of the Devil in *The Exorcist,* though I understand that

after a while they changed a number of prints to include Mercedes' name. I wasn't so lucky.

Anyway, Phyllis wasn't too happy that I was hired to do her evil voice. Later, she told me, "I could have done it, and wanted to, but they said no." Maybe she could have, but she was very young at the time, and as a former radio actress I naturally had a lot of experience with different voices. So I guess that's why MGM, where I'd just been put under contract, got me to do it.

Lana Turner———— *ACTRESS*

The public never knew that we almost couldn't finish *The Postman Always Rings Twice.* Director Tay Garnett once had a drinking problem. He'd been on the wagon for three years when we went down to Laguna for the beach footage. A fog rolled in and we had to stop shooting.

Hoping the weather night be better at a new location, we packed up and moved to San Clemente. But we found ourselves socked in there, too. Back we went to the starting point, but the fog still hung over the beach for days. The studio's budget people were frantic. That's when Tay fell off the wagon. Nobody could control him. He was a roaring, mean, furniture-smashing drunk. The studio sent nurses, but even they couldn't help. Rumors flew—Tay would be replaced, or the production shut down.

Since Tay had been drawing

good performances from us, John Garfield and I both hoped that he wouldn't be replaced. So we decided to go and see him. John went first. He said, "It's terrible, Lana. He didn't know who I was. . . . He came at me with a cane!"

The nurses had managed to take his cane away, and what I found was a besotted man who regretted what he'd done. I did my best to comfort him, and he sniffled and begged my forgiveness. Now he was rational enough to be sent back to Los Angeles for treatment. By the time he returned a week later the fog had obligingly lifted and we were able to complete the film.

Edgar G. Ulmer — DIRECTOR

The brother-in-law of Tony Quinn wrote a very bad book called *Detour.* Martin Goldsmith was his name. I took the thing to [associate producer] Martin Mooney and rewrote the script. I was always in love with the idea and with the main character, a boy who plays piano in Greenwich Village and really wants to be a decent pianist. He's so down on his luck that the girl who goes to the Coast is the only person he can exist with, sex-wise—the "Blue Angel" thing. And then the idea to get involved on that long road into Fate, where he's an absolute loser, fascinated me. The same thing, of course, happened with the boy who played the leading character, Tom Neal. He wound up in jail after he killed his own wife. He did practically the same thing he did in the picture!

Charles Vidor — DIRECTOR

It's my peculiar fortune to make my pictures with Rita Hayworth at a time of some personal crises in her life. When we began *The Lady in Question,* she was getting her divorce from Ed Judson. When we started *Cover Girl,* she was just about to marry Orson Welles. During the shooting of *Gilda* she separated from him.

King Vidor — DIRECTOR

I had some trouble with Bette Davis on *Beyond the Forest.* I suppose I exerted my will over hers. I told her to throw a bottle a certain way in a quarrel scene and she wouldn't. She stormed off the set and said to Jack Warner, "Either he goes or I do." Her career had been on a downgrade. He told her who would go. A couple of days later they cleared out her bungalow. She came to me and said, "After 16 years, they can do *this* to me?"

I'll never forget, years later, going to see *Who's Afraid of Virginia Woolf?* When Elizabeth Taylor said, just like Bette in *Beyond the Forest,* "What a dumppp," with all those p's, I was stunned. It brought an overpowering sense of total recall.

Jerry Wald — SCREENWRITER

When Bogart and George Raft were playing truckdrivers in *They Drive by Night,* Bogey developed a bit of business in which he kept a match in his mouth. Raft objected to the director, Raoul Walsh. Raft also wanted a match in his mouth. Finally, Bogey took the match out of his mouth and put a cigarette behind his ear. That was also distracting to Raft. Bogey has lots of little pieces of business like that. But it always comes out Bogart. He acts Bogart better than anybody else in town.

———— ***PRODUCER***

My boss, Jack Warner, agreed to get Joan Crawford for *Mildred Pierce.* Then our troubles began. Many writers wouldn't tackle the picture because Crawford was in it. They said she was washed up.

Top directors didn't want to get involved in a Crawford picture. One director liked the script but refused to do the thing with Crawford. Finally, Michael Curtiz agreed to direct *Mildred Pierce.* He was reluctant at first, but after a talk with Joan, he developed the enthusiasm I felt.

Then the battle of the shoulder pads began. And lipstick. And hair. Crawford was used to the MGM way of doing things. Mike and I wanted to deglamorize Joan, make her look like a woman who lived in a suburb and bought the cheapest dresses.

At first Joan wouldn't go along with her. But after several lengthy meetings—filled with blood, sweat and tears—we all agreed to make the picture realistic in every aspect.

The first week of filming was terrible. Full of fights between Curtiz and Crawford. I was the referee. Then everybody settled down and things went smoothly.

But the wise Joes and Janes in the business were predicting: "The picture won't be made, another star will replace Crawford."

Raoul Walsh ———— ***DIRECTOR***

In *The Roaring Twenties* when [James] Cagney finally caught up with Bogart and killed him, he left the house and ran down the street—one of Bogart's henchmen shot him and it was a great death scene Jimmy played, running down the street. He fell and knocked over a trash can, picked himself up and crossed the street, ran to the church steps, up the church steps, staggered, fell, rolled down—and died in the gutter. One of the festivals I was at, somebody said, "Why did it take so long for Cagney to die?" I said, "It's always hard to kill an actor."

* * *

Bogart had yet to hit it big and was playing supporting roles. Already he was becoming known as "Bogey the Beefer." While we were on location making *They Drive by Night,* Bogart found something else to beef about. The partitions in the hotel where the cast was staying were too thin. Bogey's room was next to the one occupied by the actor who played the part of the sheriff. He launched his peeve at breakfast: "I can't knock any man for gettin' his ashes hauled, but there's a time and place for everything. I don't know who that sheriff had in his bed last night, but it was like listenin' to a goddamn earthquake!"

George Raft and Bogart gave fine performances, but pretty, talented Ida Lupino walked off with the picture. Her scene in the courtroom, where she went berserk, made her a star overnight. It got her a seven-year contract at Warners.

* * *

George Raft was slated for *High Sierra,* but Raft wouldn't die in the picture. Since the character had committed six killings, the censors demanded that he die. So Bogart got the role instead. It was the first picture where he got big billing.

Jack L. Warner — STUDIO HEAD

When we were first discussing *Casablanca,* which won the Academy Award in 1943, director Mike Curtiz and I were going over the script. "Vell, Jock," he said, "the scenario isn't the exact truth, but ve haff the facts to prove it."

Clifton Webb — ACTOR

I made my film debut [sic] in *Laura* in a bathtub because my clothes were lost en route. We did that scene first until they showed up. I arrived in Hollywood on a Monday and was in a bathtub on the set Tuesday morning.

Orson Welles — DIRECTOR/SCREENWRITER

Edward G. Robinson got into a big sulk the first week of *The Stranger.* I couldn't understand what it was about. Finally, he said, "You keep shooting me on my bad side." Now can you imagine Eddie Robinson having a bad side? I was shooting him that way because Loretta Young's side was the other one! I told her about it and she said, "All right, shoot me on my bad side and keep him happy."

When you work with actors you have to make love to them; that's the business of the director, to carry on a continual courtship of the people he sticks in front of the lens. And when you deal with stars—real stars—you have to *really* make love, and it had seemed to me natural to direct my attentions to Miss Young. There was a little jealousy there between Eddie and Loretta.

— PRODUCER/DIRECTOR/SCREENWRITER

We had this enormous cast, a show [*Around the World in Eighty Days*] with 23 scenes and our costumes were being held at the railway station until we could put up $50,000. So I was standing in the box office, thinking, "Who can send me $50,000 within an hour? Who has the courage and power to?" And I thought of a fellow with whom I'd been battling for years, Harry Cohn, president of Columbia Pictures. I called him and, fortunately, he answered. There was a ticket girl sitting near me in the box office, and I glanced at what she was reading, a paperback book. I said to Harry, "There's the greatest story I've found in my life. It's called"—I leaned over to read the title—"*The Man I Killed* and I want you to buy it and I'll make the picture for you for $50,000, if you'll send it to me in an hour."

I got the $50,000 within the hour, so I had to go and make this paperback novel, which didn't make much sense, into a movie. So we wrote a new story and called it *The Lady from Shanghai.* I'd intended to make a "B" picture and then run out of town, but Harry Cohn persuaded me to do it with Rita Hayworth, who was then my wife, and it turned into an "A" picture, as well as an interesting picture, because it's still being shown.

Richard Widmark —— ACTOR

I almost didn't get the part [of the maniacal killer] in *Kiss of Death.* The director, Henry Hathaway, didn't want me. I have a high forehead, and he thought I looked too intellectual. But Darryl Zanuck wanted me to test. For the test, I wore a wig that brought my hairline way down like an ape. But Henry sat on the test. Finally, the production manager sent it to Zanuck. My getting the part didn't make Henry too happy. He gave me kind of a bad time.

Billy Wilder —— DIRECTOR/ —— SCREENWRITER

I had great difficulty finding a leading man for *Double Indemnity.* In those days none of the big ones dared to play a murderer. When I told the story to George Raft, he told me he would play it if the lead turned out to be an FBI man at the end, trying to pin down Barbara Stanwyck as the murderess.

Shelley Winters —— ACTRESS

I wanted the job of understudy to Judy Holliday in *Born Yesterday* on the stage and I called Garson Kanin and he said the job was taken by "an actress named Jan Sterling," but that he would call George Cukor and have me screen test for *A Double Life.*

Abner Biberman played Ronald Colman's role in the test—I didn't meet Colman till the first day on the set. Biberman and I did the first scene of the waitress, where he still has the chicken cacciatore in front of him and I say, "Well, it's your stomach." And George Cukor had a way of locking the camera and the sound so that you didn't know it; he would signal them by hand. I said, "O.K., I'm ready to shoot," and Cukor said, "You just did it." He had shot the rehearsal!

Cukor directed the test, then went on to direct the picture itself. The first day I went 96 takes on that same scene, a record for Hollywood!

Teresa Wright —— ACTRESS

I was terrified of Hitch [director Alfred Hitchcock], of course. There was that myth about him not liking actors. It was a pose, I think, and it made good copy. Hitch was a really remarkable storyteller. He could see the whole film in his mind's eye, frame by frame. The first time I met him, he told me the whole story of *Shadow of a Doubt.* Eight months later, I went to see the movie. I thought, "I've already seen it!" It was exactly as he told it that day in his office. Hitch was very articulate.

William Wyler —— DIRECTOR

When they show *The Letter* on television, I wish they would cut off the ending, where Gale Sondergaard is arrested for murdering Bette Davis. I had to tag that on as a concession to the Production Code. You could not, in those days, have a murderer go free. So we had to put in two cops to apprehend her; it is very bad.

Darryl F. Zanuck — *STUDIO HEAD*

The woman in *Leave Her to Heaven* deliberately kills her own unborn child, drowns the crippled brother of her husband and endeavors to send her adopted sister to the electric chair. And yet, despite all this, there are certain things about her that you rather like.

Fred Zinnemann — *DIRECTOR*

Kid Glove Killer? I just remember that, during the sneak preview, all the executives from MGM got up and walked out in a body. The news had come that Carole Lombard had crashed in a plane.

Musicals

Larry Adler — *ACTOR*

In *Music for Millions,* I was to enter a café that had a string orchestra playing and be recognized by June Allyson and Margaret O'Brien. June—I don't think you're going to believe this—was a pregnant double-bass player in the film, Margaret her niece—June's husband was in the Pacific. She calls me over, tells me that "their" song was "Clair de Lune," it was their wedding anniversary and would I play it for her? You can only do these things in the movies; not only would I play it, not only did I have a mouth-organ in my pocket, not only did the orchestra leader agree to accompany me, he even knew my *arrangement.* While I played it, June cried, Margaret cried and, from the reactions I got around the world, a lot of other people cried.

June was an easy weeper, she would cry over seed catalogues, but Margaret O'Brien could match her tear for tear. In fact, Margaret said to director Henry Koster, "When Uncle Larry plays and I cry, shall I let the tears run all the way down my face or shall I stop them half-way down?"

June Allyson — *ACTRESS*

It happened in a scene with Jimmy Durante in *Two Girls and a Sailor.* We were in an empty warehouse and Jimmy was hiding there and supposed to frighten me and Gloria De Haven. He certainly did. He let out such a blood-curdling sound that Gloria screamed for real and the caps she was wearing over her teeth to make them look perfect flew out and went sailing right to me before landing on the floor. The horrified look on my face as I watched the teeth sail by stayed in the movie.

* * *

In *Good News,* Peter Lawford plays an American football hero who

is about to flunk out if he can't pass his French test. It was my job to teach him enough French to get by.

Everything about the movie was unbelievable. No one made any effort to change Peter's British accent to American. For that matter, my French accent was atrocious, his superb—he spent hours teaching me how to teach him French. Peter said, "This is the most ridiculous part I've ever had or hope to have."

Dana Andrews ——— ACTOR

I let them hire another singer to dub me in *State Fair.* They paid him $150 for it. I could have saved the studio some money and sung the tune a lot better. But I kept my mouth shut. I don't like what happens to singers in Hollywood—nobody will accept you as an actor.

Patty Andrews ——— ACTRESS

The Andrews Sisters' first film was *Argentine Nights.* We went to the premiere at the Fordham Theater in the Bronx, and we looked like the Ritz Brothers in drag. Our make-up was done by the man at Universal [Jack Pierce] who did the make-up for *Frankenstein.* We were so ugly that Maxene walked all the way back to Manhattan from the Bronx in tears.

Eve Arden ——— ACTRESS

Ziegfeld Girl—just the thought that Metro believed I could pass for a Ziegfeld girl, particularly next to

Lana Turner and Hedy Lamarr, was the most flattering thing that ever happened to me.

Fred Astaire ——————— ACTOR

Marjorie Reynolds and I did a comedy jitterbug in a New Year's Eve nightclub sequence for *Holiday Inn* which emphasized my inebriated condition. I had to look plenty drunk in that bit and figured there was only one way to do it.

I took two stiff hookers of bourbon before the first take and one before each succeeding take. I had to fall down on my face and be carried out for the finish. It was hot on that stage, too! All in all, we did it seven times. The last one was the best.

* * *

The Columbia lot was heavily occupied with production at the time [of *You Were Never Lovelier*] and it was difficult to find a place to rehearse. For a while Rita Hayworth and I had to work out in Hollywood at a civic auditorium. The rest of the time, until the picture started actual shooting, the only available place near the studio was a room in a funeral parlor of the Hollywood Cemetery.

Every time a funeral came through the gates we could see it from the windows and naturally we'd have to stop until it moved well on past. One of the men from the office downstairs would come running up half whispering, "Hold it a minute, folks, they're bringing one in."

One day he was particularly excited as he stopped us and looked out the window counting the cars in the procession, "One—two—three—ten—twelve—etc." Afterward, he said, "Mmm, this is really one of the biggest we've had."

* * *

When it came time to start *Barkleys of Broadway* at MGM, I was disappointed to find that Judy Garland could not make it on account of illness. Luck was with us, however, and Ginger Rogers happened to be available. Gin and I had often discussed the possibility of getting together for a rematch and here it was out of a clear sky. It was hard for Gin and me to realize that nearly ten years had passed since our last show together.

When we finally got around to shooting our first dance, I thought Ginger for some reason seemed taller than usual. I asked Hermes Pan, "Am I crazy or is Ginger on stilts?" He said, "I know—something is different." I went to Ginger.

"Hey—have you grown or have I shrunk?" She laughed and confessed that she had snuck some higher heels over on me.

Mary Astor ——————— ACTRESS

On *Meet Me in St. Louis,* Judy Garland was no longer a rotund little giggler, but her growing up was not maturing. The fun was still there and she seemed to have great energy. But it was intense, driven, tremulous. Anxious. She was working way over the capacities of any human being. She was recording at night and playing in the picture during the day, and people got annoyed when she was late on the set, and when she got jittery and weepy with fatigue. Including myself. I often felt that her behavior was due to bigshotitis and very unprofessional.

I walked into Judy's portable dressing room one tense morning, and she greeted me with her usual cheery, "Hi, Mom!" I sat down on the couch while she went on primping, and said, "Judy, what the hell's happened to you? You were a trooper—once. You have kept the entire company out there waiting for two hours. Waiting for you to favor us with your presence. You know we're stuck—there's nothing we can do without you at the moment."

She giggled and said, "Yeah, that's what everybody's been telling me."

That bugged me and I said, "Well, then, either get the hell on that set or *I'm* going home!"

She grabbed me by the hand, and her face had crumpled up, "I don't *sleep,* Mom!"

Lucille Ball —————— ACTRESS

Desi [Arnaz] and I met on a set at RKO in the summer of 1940. He had been brought in for a picture, *Too Many Girls*—he had done the play in New York. I was given the ingénue lead. I had never played an ingénue before, nor did I want to. But I did it. We met that day, dated that night. Six months later, I was in New York giving an interview about why I was a bachelor girl and would *remain* one. Desi was playing the Roxy. That night, Desi made up his mind we'd elope. I said, "I've spent the whole day telling everybody why I won't get married!"

However, we got married the next morning in Connecticut and hightailed it back to the Roxy for his third show. In the meantime, the entire audience had been given rice by the management. I think I had rice in my ears, my hair, my teeth, my clothes.

Binnie Barnes ———— ACTRESS

Jeanette MacDonald and Nelson Eddy in *I Married an Angel?* Both of them were convinced it would be this big hit. But the story was terribly bad and the sight of them spitting at each other up close as they sang—it was very funny. I tried to lighten it but it was no use.

Busby Berkeley ——— DIRECTOR

Gene Kelly did a wonderful job in this, his first film. I taught him a great many things, because he had never been before a motion picture camera prior to the making of *For Me and My Gal.* I had to teach him the tricks of using his eyes to give expression and animation to his facial projections. This is very important in pictures. I have to see a person's eyes and what they reflect, because the eyes can tell more than words.

I consider *For Me and My Gal* one of the best pictures I have ever made, because it was a musical drama. It had music in it, but it had a great love story also. And it was a big money-maker for Metro-Goldwyn-Mayer. I think that of all the films I have directed, this is my top favorite.

THREE LITTLE GIRLS IN BLUE
IN Technicolor
20th CENTURY-FOX
with
JUNE HAVER · GEORGE MONTGOMERY
VIVIAN BLAINE · CELESTE HOLM · VERA-ELLEN · FRANK LATIMORE
Directed by BRUCE HUMBERSTONE Produced by MACK GORDON
Screen Play by Valentine Davies · Adapted by Brown Holmes, Lynn Starling and Robert Ellis and Helen Logan
From a Play by Stephen Powys · Lyrics by Mack Gordon · Music by Josef Myrow "This Is Always" Music by Harry Warren · Dances Staged by Seymour Felix · Ballets by Babe Pearce

Vivian Blaine———ACTRESS

I was to be the "new" Alice Faye. In another picture, *Something for the Boys,* which had been bought for Betty Grable (who didn't make it because she was, I think, having her first baby), I was, by implication, "another Betty Grable."

Twentieth Century-Fox didn't develop *my* personality. My own real self was, in time, completely lost. I never made a definite attack in motion pictures because I never had a definite personality with which to make an attack.

Other factors, or cards, were stacked against me. *Nob Hill,* for instance, was a big success for me, personally, and if Fox had followed it up with something as big for me, they might have had a big star on their hands. But they didn't. A couple of black and whites [*Doll Face, If I'm Lucky*], both mediocre, were the follow-ups. When the vehicles were strong—well, take *State Fair,* a very good and successful picture—Jeanne Crain was the star and I went through the entire film virtually, you might say, off-scene.

When the break with Fox came, an agent got Harry Cohn of Columbia Pictures very excited about me—and an appointment was made for me to see Mr. Cohn. "I must see some film on you," said Mr. Cohn. Since I was leaving on a P. A. there was no time to make a test, but out of the ten or more pictures I'd made at Fox, some acceptable film, surely, could be found. *I* thought. But when we ran the ten films there was not one foot in the lot of 'em I'd want anyone to see. Finally, however, we weeded out some footage from *Nob Hill, State Fair* and *Three Little Girls in Blue,* sent it to Mr. Cohn and the answer was just, "*No.*" Flat, firm and final. Then there was, I must confess, a deadness in me. The deadness that is the loss of faith in yourself.

Eddie Bracken———ACTOR

One of my favorite stories is a touching story that happened to a man by the name of Victor Schertzinger, who was a wonderful songwriter. He was directing Betty Hutton and me in a scene from *The Fleet's In,* a movie that was quite successful in the forties. The scene was Betty Hutton making love to me in a song, and I was a sailor who was hungry, and I was eating bananas, paying no attention to Betty. So she's all over me, pulling my hair and biting my ear, and I'm still eating the banana. Well, Mr. Schertzinger wanted this scene to be just right, I guess, because he took this scene 22 times and I ate 22 bananas. That night when I went home, for the first time in our married life my wife had made banana cream pie!

Also, that night Victor Schertzinger died, which meant that during the day he was slowing up, the reason he took the scene so many times. When he was buried, Bing Crosby sang the last song he had written for *Fleet's In* called "I Remember You," and rather than tell you the lyric, go look it up and just picture what it did to Mr. Schertzinger's wife as Bing sang it. The lyrics were so poignant and so *right.* I look upon it as being one of *the* moments in Hollywood.

Joan Caulfield —— ACTRESS

Buddy DeSylva, the production head of Paramount, came to see me on Broadway and afterward exclaimed, "You have great legs! We'll put you in musicals!" No one cared if I could sing or dance. I had "great legs," so I was to do musicals. I was brought to Hollywood and starred with Bing Crosby and Fred Astaire in *Blue Skies.*

* * *

Generally speaking, I can't say that I've ever been short on self-confidence. When the late producer Mark Sandrich, who was to direct *Blue Skies,* first approached me about doing the lead and asked, "Do you think you can dance and sing well enough to carry it?" I didn't have a qualm, and answered sincerely, "Sure, I can." He gave me the part.

It was a great break, starring opposite Bing Crosby. It would automatically make any newcomer a star.

Then came the sudden tragic death of Mr. Sandrich, and another producer took over *Blue Skies.* The new movie maestro, together with the dancer who was set for a starring role [Paul Draper], decided between them that I wasn't right for the part. But they neglected to inform me. Other girls were tested for the role, and finally just before the picture was ready to go I was told that other arrangements were being made and I was out.

I wouldn't have minded if they'd just told me at the beginning that they felt I wasn't suitable for the role. But I can't stand evasion in any form. Ironically enough, when the picture finally got under way, the producer and the dancer were out, and I got my big chance anyway. But I'll never forget those few days between.

Cyd Charisse —— ACTRESS

It was my first really major part. There was one funny aspect to *The Unfinished Dance.* I was playing one of two ballerinas, Karin Booth the other. Karin wasn't a dancer at all; I think she got the part because she was going with an important MGM executive.

My friend, David Lichine, did the choreography, and he and the director, Henry Koster, had to figure out ways to make it look like Karin was a skillful dancer. And she had trouble even moving her feet. They wound up placing her on a machine that whirled her around, so it looked like she was dancing.

Jackie Cooper —— ACTOR

I went back to Metro as part of an all-star cast assembled for *Ziegfeld Girl.* I played Lana Turner's brother —Judy Garland's boyfriend. Among the others in that biggie were Jimmy Stewart, Hedy Lamarr, Tony Martin and Charles Winninger.

I went there figuring it would be a lot of fun, working opposite Judy. It wasn't. Maybe it was because of our past relationship, but she was acting differently. She was cold and distant and an entirely new, and unlovely, person. It could have been pills, as I think back on it, but that never occurred to me then. I just knew that the five weeks of pleasure I had anticipated had turned into many weeks of unpleasantness.

Five weeks had been the deal, at $5,000 a week. But it turned out to be longer than that. The ladies, bless their temperaments, caused problems. First it was Lana; she decided she couldn't work when she had her period. So, of course, neither would Hedy or Judy. Then there were script changes, production problems. Delays, delays. My five weeks, at $5,000 a week, stretched out, longer and longer.

In the tenth week [L. B.] Mayer called my agent, Charlie Feldman, and said he wanted to cut my salary. I had worked twice as long as I had been originally contracted to work. Since all the others in the cast were MGM contract players, it turned out that I would be making more on the film than any of them—more than Stewart or Lamarr or Turner or anybody. Feldman said no, a deal is a deal. I kept on getting my $5,000 a week.

Sam Coslow—PRODUCER/SONGWRITER

On *Copacabana,* everyone told me Groucho Marx would be a big temperamental headache with his continual demands. Actually, he was very little trouble. He did insist on a clause in his contract stating that he wouldn't be called on to kiss Carmen Miranda at any time. He never explained why. I think the fiery Carmen would have smacked him in the kisser had she known about the clause.

Jeanne Crain—ACTRESS

If I played the farm girl in *State Fair* today, they'd probably want me to do it in the nude.

* * *

My most romantic scene? In *Centennial Summer,* Cornel Wilde and I are in love but haven't yet admitted it. We're sitting at a table in a café with Linda Darnell and William Eythe. I stand up, saying, "I must go now." Distressed, Cornel begs, "Oh, please don't leave so soon." But I insist, saying, "I must go, I have something awfully important to do." The scene was shot and I immediately left the studio—and that very afternoon Paul Brinkman and I were married. So you see why this scene of implied romance and its apropos dialogue takes on so much added importance to me.

Joan Crawford—ACTRESS

Hollywood Canteen was a very pleasant pile of shit for wartime audiences.

Bing Crosby—ACTOR

Irving Berlin wrote "White Christmas" for me for a movie I did called *Holiday Inn.* It was during the early part of World War II. "White Christmas" was done at a piano, alone. My girl in the film had just broken off with me. I was sitting there ruminating. And I sang "White Christmas," with a little violin accompaniment which was put in later. Nobody had any idea it was going to become a big standard song. I thought it was very pretty. I didn't realize where it was going.

But I guess the big thing was nostalgia. And it was during the war. It was so poignant. Everybody was away from home. And everybody could relate to it one way or another. They still do. I remember singing it overseas, in hospitals or rest and recreation centers up around the front, and I hated to sing it. But they'd holler for it, and I'd sing it, and they'd all start crying. I'd start crying. Everybody would be sobbing. Because these guys are 3,000 miles away, and they don't know where they're goin' the next day. Into action, probably. Guys who'd had half a leg shot off would thank me for singing that song. Whoo—thanks for what?!

* * *

I remember *Holiday Inn* because in it Fred Astaire danced himself so thin that I could almost spit through him. He did one number 38 times before he was satisfied. He started the picture weighing 140 pounds. When he finished it he weighed 126.

Gary Crosby—ACTOR

In 1944, when I was 11, my father Bing told Louella Parsons about how he found himself with a minor insurrection on his hands when he sent the four of us [brothers Gary, Dennis, Philip and Lindsay] over to Paramount for two days to do a scene in *Duffy's Tavern.*

"The night after they finished the first day's shooting," Louella wrote, "the twins said, 'We're not going back unless we get more lines to say.' 'Remember you have a contract, and you're going back!' their father told them. It was then Dixie said, 'We'll have no more of this nonsense.' 'I guess,' Bing grinned, 'she thought one ham in the family is enough.'"

The anecdote was pure fantasy. We were much too afraid of him to consider getting up the nerve to proclaim what we would or would not do.

Xavier Cugat—ACTOR

The chihuahua was an accident. The first time they engaged me to make a picture for Columbia, *You Were Never Lovelier,* with Rita Hayworth and Fred Astaire, I told the producer, "I am a musician, not an actor. I don't know what to do with my hands."

So he said, "I'll tell you what: to hold in one hand, we'll give you a little doggie." When the picture came out, the chihuahua got more fan mail than Hayworth.

Louise Currie—ACTRESS

When I made *Sensations of 1945* with W. C. Fields, he used a blackboard because he then truly could not remember his lines. That being an "A" picture, we took much time with every take. He would look at the blackboard and get his lines but then he'd forget to look at me. By the time Fields would finally get the line correct and look at me at the right moment, I couldn't remember a thing because it took days to do a tiny vignette and I was so used to doing it fast that the length of time really threw me. By the time he got it right, I had forgotten where I was!

Dan Dailey—ACTOR

On the first day of *Mother Wore Tights,* which was my big break, I was very nervous and I think it showed. My leading lady, Betty Grable—only the biggest female star in the business then—came over to me and said, "I've had mine, now go get yours. I'll help in any way I can."

* * *

Betty Grable? She'd murder you. I remember once I got her angry on *Mother Wore Tights.* She stormed over and said, "You know why I'm doing this picture? I thought they said Dan *Duryea!*"

* * *

When My Baby Smiles at Me was one of my favorites. It was actually from the play *Burlesque.* In those days, the title *Burlesque* was considered too risqué for the movies.

Betty Grable and I had a lot of fun making it. We were great pals and got along very well. In the 12 years we worked together we had a marvelous time. We used to kid each other a lot; Betty's sense of humor fit mine. One day at the commissary I was having a luncheon interview with a very important columnist and the waiter brought a silver tureen with a big cover to our table. He told me, "Betty Grable sent this over." I opened it up and in it was a live lobster which came crawling toward me. Betty used to do things like that for laughs.

I used to play pranks on her, too. One time when she said, "Could I have a little extra mayonnaise?" I pushed it right in her face. She had to go back to Make-Up for two hours! We did lots of terrible things. Once someone at our table had a hangover, and I borrowed two big cymbals—each about four feet in diameter—from the music department and suddenly hit them together. The noise was deafening.

Doris Day——————ACTRESS

I was in terrible shape [after two divorces] when I ran into two songwriter friends, Sammy Cahn and Jule Styne. They were doing the music for *Romance on the High Seas.* What's more, they said, Michael Curtiz, the director, was looking for a feminine lead and they were certain that I would fill the bill very nicely.

Mr. Curtiz decided that he would like to hear me sing, anyway, so I got together with my song-pals to decide on a number. They picked "Embraceable You." The sentimental lyrics, naturally, threw me for a loop and I ended the song in a big burst of tears.

Of course it would so happen that Mr. Curtiz had slipped into the rehearsal and took in the sobbing. He was very sympathetic and understanding.

Sobs or no sobs, he somehow saw talent in the crying songstress and ordered a test for me. I'd been working before people much too long to be bothered by anything as easy as a screen test and I slept as I was being made up. The girl was amazed, said most everyone was all keyed up before a test. *I* was worn out with all my heartaches.

Gloria De Haven————ACTRESS

Two Girls and a Sailor was the breakthrough for all of us—not only myself but June Allyson and Van Johnson and Jimmy Durante, who at that time had more or less retired. Jimmy hadn't done too much, and they brought him back in a character role which meant a whole new career for him. The movie was made for a very small budget, because none of us were known, and all the names that were later in it—Lena Horne, Gracie Allen, Xavier Cugat—were brought in after the movie was made and previewed. They found that they had a very successful movie on their hands that only ran about an hour and a half, so they proceeded to bring the movie back in, and in order to sell it, since they couldn't sell it on any of *our* names, they added all of those cameo appearances. And it ended up *Two Girls and a Sailor* with Lena Horne, Harry James—everything you can imagine to get them into the theaters to see us. And that was the start for all of us.

* * *

Late one afternoon, while Mick [Rooney] and I were filming *Summer Holiday,* I ordered some tea from the commissary to be sent to my dressing room on the set. To my amazement it was delivered not by the usual waiter but my Mickey himself. Balancing an unnecessarily large tray on which were only one tea pot, a water jug, cup and saucer, he stepped into my room, tripped, fell and the tray-load scattered all over the floor.

I yelped, quite naturally, and fussed a little until I realized that the pots and dishes were empty, that Mick's fall had been a planned rib and no damage had been done. A minute later director Rouben Mamoulian called Mick on the set for one of the most emotional scenes in the picture, and Mick did it perfectly on the first take.

Mick is like that. He seems to have two completely different personalities. One is the high-spirited boy, with his Andy Hardy bounce and devil-may-care exterior; the other is a serious young man, a hard worker, an amazingly gifted actor.

Stanley Donen—CHOREOGRAPHY ASSISTANT

In *Anchors Aweigh,* I worked for a year on one sequence which is eight minutes long. One solid year. I didn't even direct the picture, but I did that one sequence which took a year out of my life.

Tom Drake—ACTOR

In one scene for *Meet Me in St. Louis,* Judy Garland had to wear a costume which probably never could have been duplicated had anything happened to it. That was the scene in which I had to carry her across a plank over some mud. I was scared I'd drop her and she knew it. "Don't be nervous," she said, giggling. "If you slip and we fall in the mud we'll do the scene in blackface!"

Douglas Fairbanks, Jr.—ACTOR

I was making *That Lady in Ermine* for Ernst Lubitsch and Otto Preminger. In the film, there was a big dance number I did with Betty Grable. I had to jump up on tables, swing on chandeliers, pick Betty up and put her down again, all in time to a waltz. The sequence took a lot of rehearsal, because I wasn't a natural dancer like Betty.

When the day came to film the scene, Darryl F. Zanuck, the head of

20th Century-Fox, had invited a group of people on the set to watch this production number. The music had been pre-recorded and it was the first time I was going to do the number in costume. Up to then, I had practiced the dance in work clothes. The costume, however, was a Hungarian uniform with very tight britches. The music started. When I made my first step up on the table, I split my pants!

Everybody laughed, but the studio had to stop production on the film for two days while they made me another pair of britches.

Alice Faye———*ACTRESS*

I was well endowed. To some girls that is a source of pride, but to me it was always a source of embarrassment. When Betty Grable and I did our famous "Sheik of Araby" number in the movie *Tin Pan Alley*—it had boys and men all over the world drooling—we had to wear very revealing outfits. I was so busty and so embarrassed about it that I wore a shawl over my costume until the last possible second.

Betty, on the other hand, was just the opposite. Her figure had to be given an assist; the costume department supplied what Mother Nature had neglected to. She envied me, Betty said, and I know I envied her. And we laughed about it. She could wear dresses I never could, and vice versa. So we never borrowed each other's clothes. (By the way, all that stuff about a feud between us was just something the Fox publicity department dreamed up to draw attention to our films. The truth was that we liked each other very much and became good friends, and stayed good friends until the day she died.)

I was then so terribly embarrassed about the fullness of my figure that I begged the Fox executives to let me wear costumes that would hide God's (and nature's) generosity. But, of course, Darryl Zanuck and the rest of the 20th Century-Fox brass tried to show as much of me as the standards of those days would permit.

Jane Frazee———*ACTRESS*

I rarely had a day off in the 1940s, but I was never in any big movies like *Rebecca* or *Meet Me in St. Louis.* I did many "B"s at Universal, Columbia and Republic. They usually had a few songs, a few laughs, maybe a few thrills—you might have a good time while you were in the theater, but there was nothing much to remember afterwards.

To my surprise, all these years later, I am still recognized on the street. Even more surprising is the picture that people almost always mention to me: *Rosie, the Riveter.* It was just a six-day wonder thrown together almost overnight at Republic to capitalize on the wartime novelty song, "Rosie, the Riveter." What puzzles me is that in 1944, when *Rosie* came out, there were certainly no stampedes at box offices to see it, and it's rarely shown on TV. Where did all the people who say they loved me in it see it?!

Arthur Freed———*PRODUCER*

When I first signed Gene Kelly, nobody in the studio liked him. They said, "You're not going to put him

opposite Judy Garland in *For Me and My Gal?*" I said, "He's perfect for it; he's an Irishman." Eddie Mannix said, "But he's the wrong kind of Irishman." I had lunch one day with Louis B. Mayer and I said, "I want to tell you something: I'm starting the picture next week, and everybody thinks I'm doing the wrong thing by putting Gene Kelly opposite Judy." He says, "How do you feel?" I says, "I love him." He says, "Well, then, don't listen to all those schmucks."

* * *

I was in New York to find beautiful girls for *Ziegfeld Follies.* The moment I saw Lucille Bremer [at the Versailles nightclub] I realized she had the elegance of a Marilyn Miller. I watched her work in the chorus, then do a number alone. I sent for her. I just figured that she'd make a wonderful showgirl for my picture.

But when I spoke to her, I was impressed. She was completely at ease, yet intense, as we talked. I had her brought to the Coast and she went through a scene from *Dark Victory* for her test. I took Mr. [Louis B.] Mayer to see it. They had run off only 150 feet—that takes about a minute and a half on the screen—when Mr. Mayer said, "Who is this girl? Don't let her do little things, Arthur. She's going to be big, very big."

Then I sent her to our dramatic coach, Lillian Burns. Two days later, Lillian called me up. "This is the greatest girl," she told me, "who has ever been sent down here to me."

Remember, this was a girl, a

dancer, whom I had found in a nightclub. I put her in *Meet Me in St. Louis,* with Judy Garland. She was swell in that. But I wasn't surprised. From the beginning, I'd never been so enthusiastic about any newcomer—not since we discovered Judy Garland.

You see, Lucille is a woman, a girl who can do things—the sort of things Irene Dunne does, that Bette Davis does. And what a dancer! When we wanted a new partner for Fred Astaire for *Ziegfeld Follies,* we looked at everyone in Hollywood. Finally, I had Lucille dance for him. Remember, Fred is a worrier, a perfectionist. Everything has to be just right or he won't go ahead. But he watched Lucille Bremer dance for only a couple of minutes, then he leaned over and said to me, "There's my new partner! That's the girl I dance with!"

* * *

There was no rivalry at all [between Fred Astaire and Gene Kelly on *Ziegfeld Follies*]. Each is a genuine admirer of the other. My only problem was their deference to each other. Each was willing to do whichever dance the other wanted. I had suggested "The Babbitt and the Bromide" to Fred and he liked the idea, but after the first rehearsal Gene privately told me he didn't think too much of the material. I mentioned this to Fred, who then said we should drop it and do whatever Gene wanted, which was an Indian dance and song written for him by Ralph Blane and Hugh Martin. But when Gene heard this he said no, we should do the number that Fred liked. It was a real Alphonse and Gaston routine.

Ava Gardner ——— *ACTRESS*

Robert Walker, poor baby, who tried so hard to stay off the drink, just couldn't make it. He actually lived at Universal Studios, in his dressing room, a sort of bungalow, with a man who did exercises with him and was supposed to make sure he didn't drink. He was a fine actor, but he simply couldn't handle alcohol. I made *One Touch of Venus* with him.

Judy Garland ——— *ACTRESS*

They called me back to work at the studio. It was still 1947, and I guess they thought I was all rested up. They put me in a picture called *Easter Parade.* They were very unhappy at the studio because I had gained a few pounds, and that caused a delay. After another crash diet, I started rehearsals for the picture. I had no idea how I was going to get through it, but I started. Also, they decided that I had to do some retakes at the same time on *The Pirate.*

I don't know how I ever got through *Easter Parade.* I did, somehow. They kept promising me six months off after I finished. When shooting was over, they sent me to another sanitarium, institution, rest home or whatever you want to call it. This one was more expensive than the others. By now, they were all getting to look alike to me. I moved in and was just getting acquainted with a new assortment of "inmates" when MGM called me back again.

The Happiest Musical Ever Made is

IRVING BERLIN'S

EASTER PARADE

from M·G·M

JUDY GARLAND · FRED ASTAIRE

PETER LAWFORD · ANN MILLER

Color by Technicolor

IRVING BERLIN · ROBERT ALTON

CHARLES WALTERS · ARTHUR FREED

Tay Garnett —— DIRECTOR

Bing Crosby was not much of an actor but at the time [1949] he was one of the biggest stars in the world, and hot as firecracker as a singer. He was very conscious of that and perhaps a little inclined to throw his weight around. Not that he caused me any particular trouble, but there were times on *A Connecticut Yankee in King Arthur's Court* when it was a little embarrassing. For instance, when he was working with the kids he was very impatient with them if one of 'em would blow a line. If Bing blew a line it was one thing, but if the kids blew one, God help 'em. So I didn't emerge from the picture as an ardent fan of Bing's from that standpoint, although I think in later years he mellowed out a great deal.

Betty Garrett —— ACTRESS

I remember the first day of shooting *On the Town.* I came up behind Frank Sinatra and patted him on the fanny to wish him luck. We'd been doing that for six weeks in rehearsals, but this time he turned on me and snarled, "Don't you ever do that again!" I couldn't figure out what was wrong with him until Gene Kelly told me that when they put the sailor pants on him, he didn't have any behind. In fact, he was actually concave. They had to call Wardrobe and make symmetricals for him, which are like padded cheeks for the fanny. He was humiliated that he had to be built up like that, and didn't want any of us to find out.

* * *

Lots of *On the Town* was done right here in New York. I don't think that had ever been done before, but the girls—Ann Miller, Vera-Ellen, me—weren't going to go to New York until Ann cried crocodile tears to producer Arthur Freed. So Arthur sent us.

But the only shot we girls did here was at the Brooklyn Navy Yard, where we're saying goodbye to the boys. Something went wrong. They had to do it over again with extras, a long shot from far away. All I can say is, whoever did my part had the broadest behind I've ever seen.

Paulette Goddard —— ACTRESS

After *Second Chorus,* I'll never try dancing on the screen again. I was determined that the dance would be good. Imagine me dancing with Fred Astaire. And I guess it was all right. We did it just once, one Saturday morning for the cameras. Just one take. I'm glad it was all right, for I couldn't have done it again. I couldn't possibly ever have done it once again.

Betty Grable —— ACTRESS

Twentieth Century-Fox signed me to a long-term contract, the best I had ever had. And a few days later, I received an offer from Broadway to play the dancing-singing ingénue in *DuBarry Was a Lady.* It was agreed that my film contract would begin upon my return. There was no guarantee that *DuBarry* would be a solid hit or that I would get good notices in it—but both things happened. Then the question was: Would all this lead to my getting a real chance at screen stardom?

The answer came in an unexpected way. Alice Faye, a grand girl and a great star at 20th, suddenly fell ill as she was about to start *Down Argentine Way.* Alice's misfortune was my good luck, for Darryl F. Zanuck, production head at the studio, gave me a chance to play her role.

Down Argentine Way put me over the top. A superb production, it gave me a once-in-a-lifetime opportunity. Without that chance, I might still be alternating between the stage and screen with indifferent success.

* * *

I wish someday a magazine would promise to print a complete list of all the people I know who have helped me. The trouble is it would take about ten pages in small type. I do hope, though, to get one in right now. That's Frank Powolny, the head portrait cameraman at 20th Century–Fox. He'll tell you it was nothing. That I just happened to stand in front of the camera. But it wasn't easy, even if it was an accident.

We were making a picture called *Sweet Rosie O'Grady* at the time, and in one scene an artist was to draw me for a cover on *Police Gazette.* He wanted the measurements and the figure just right, so I climbed into the tight bathing suit and posed for a bunch of pictures. Frank, as usual, wasn't quite satisfied. Then he got the idea for the pose with me looking back over my shoulder. It never was really intended for publication, but when the boys in the publicity department saw it they had a few thousand prints made. Thanks to the servicemen overseas it turned out to be a pin-up sensation and it did a lot for me. But back of the picture was Mr. Powolny and his camera genius.

Kathryn Grayson——ACTRESS

I thought the song "There's Beauty Everywhere" was foolish and I didn't want to do it [in *Ziegfeld Follies*]. Benny Thau, who was head of talent at MGM, asked me to come to his office. I took the music, marched in there and threw it down on his desk. I said, "Benny, this song is terrible and I won't sing it!" A voice from behind said, "Oh, dear, I wrote it!" The voice was that of Arthur Freed, who was also producer of the picture. I stood there like a zombie, very embarrassed. I ended up doing the song but was still unhappy with it.

Howard Hawks——DIRECTOR

A Song Is Born? Danny Kaye had always done his wife's material. He'd separated from her and was a basket case, stopping work to see a psychiatrist twice a day. Now you can imagine working with that. He was about as funny as a crutch. It was an altogether horrible experience. I've never seen the picture.

Rita Hayworth——ACTRESS

I guess the only jewels of my life were the pictures I made with Fred Astaire [*You'll Never Get Rich, You Were Never Lovelier*]. You know, in his book Fred said I was his best partner.

I can tell you one thing—they're the only pictures of mine that I can watch today, Fred and me dancing, without laughing hysterically. And *Cover Girl,* too.

Edith Head ——— COSTUME DESIGNER

The Emperor Waltz was a musical about, among other things, the love affair between two dogs. Bing Crosby was the owner of one, and Joan Fontaine the owner of the other. When Joan signed for the film, she said to me, "Oh, Edith, please give me plenty of décolletage so I can compete with those two damn dogs!"

Lena Horne ——— ACTRESS

I finally made my movie debut in *Panama Hattie.* The picture starred Red Skelton, Ann Sothern and Marsha Hunt. But I never worked with them. I did a musical number that was not integrated into the script. The idea was that it could be cut out of the film, without spoiling it, by local distributors if they thought their audiences would object to seeing a Negro.

George Jessel ——— PRODUCER

I was dating Carole Landis, with whom I had a long affair until she met Rex Harrison and died so tragically. While Carole never did make a picture for me, I did want her to star in *Dancing in the Dark.* I was stymied because of studio politics. Zanuck wanted to sign Cary Grant for two pictures, but Cary wouldn't agree unless we guaranteed to star his wife, Betsy Drake, in a film or two. Instead of starring Carole, who had the experience, the name, the voice and the camera know-how for a tight schedule, I was forced to use Betsy.

The role called for a well-built young lady to star with Bill Powell in a backstage show business story. After seeing Betsy in the first few days' rushes, I was aghast. She had no bosom or cleavage whatsoever. When I mentioned this to the wardrobe department, they said she refused to wear any, shall I say, padding in the vital spots. I went upstairs to see Darryl. He always liked full-bodied women.

"Darryl," I moaned, "this is the first time in the history of motion pictures that I have an electrician on the set with bigger tits than the leading lady!"

Even though he laughed uproariously, he insisted I stick with Betsy and use her in the film. "I need Grant for two pictures, George; that's all there is to it. You know how these things are."

Van Johnson ——— ACTOR

Judy Garland [leading lady in *In the Good Old Summertime*] was a most natural, underrated talent. She was what I call a loose performer and actress. I think she was underrated as an actress. Talent, we know—music hall singing and concerts—but an underrated actress. I never saw her study a script. She did her homework, I'm sure. She could read it, go through it once, rehearse it once. She didn't like to rehearse too much. I'm a rehearser, but I always conformed to her.

I learned an awful lot from Judy Garland. She's one of the unsung ladies in my life. That first comic business with the hat [in *In the Good Old Summertime*] took three days. That was our first day's work. I was so thrilled to be working with Judy Garland at last, I made it stretch.

We were pals. I made her laugh. She was a joy to work with. When the picture was over, Mr. [Louis B.] Mayer called me into his office and said, "What did you do?" I said, "What do you mean, Mr. Mayer?" He said, "We came in on schedule!" Poor Judy had a reputation for holding up production sometimes. Well, she never did it when I was with her. I just made her laugh. I gave her love. She needed to be patted on the head every once in a while and told she was beautiful. She never thought she was beautiful. I thought she was beautiful. We came in on schedule because I made her giggle. She was happy.

Johnnie Johnston — ACTOR

I want one thing specifically clear. I introduced "That Old Black Magic" in 1943 in a picture called *Star Spangled Rhythm.* (Bing Crosby had turned the song down.) Billy Daniels started singing "Black Magic" in 1948 and made a career, such as it was, on the song. I don't care about that. But what made me mad is this. He was performing at the Latin Casino in Philadelphia and I was sitting ringside. He never acknowledged that I was in the room and never mentioned that I was the guy who introduced it. That steamed me. I've never gotten over that.

Gene Kelly — ACTOR

Stanley Donen was the man who really understood everything I was trying to do. He's a famous director now, but when I brought him out to assist me on *Anchors Aweigh,* Louis B. Mayer fought us all the way. We thought up the idea of dancing with cartoon figures, and everybody thought we were crazy. I'd dance through a scene and we'd count—"1, 2, 3, pan"—and nobody knew what we were doing. But later, after we worked the drawings of Tom and Jerry in, Mayer said, "Those kids weren't so stupid after all."

* * *

Marie McDonald [leading lady in *Living in a Big Way*] is a triple threat: she can't sing, dance or act.

* * *

I loved doing *The Pirate* with Vincente Minnelli because it was a picture we had fun on. Vincente and I felt that we had the world licked on that. We had me playing it like John Barrymore; it was an inside joke, but we thought the public would grab it. Nowadays with all the kids that know so much about cinema lore, this might have worked, but then it didn't. We couldn't even give dishes away to sell the picture, except in a few cities, like New York, Chicago, maybe L. A. The critics jumped on it. They said, "Who is this second-class Barrymore?"—whatever Minnelli and I did, we somehow missed the boat on that. Now when *The Pirate* plays, it is a cult picture. The kids all get it, and it plays colleges and does well.

* * *

The picture I'm fondest of? *On the Town.* It was my first directorial chore. It was a film that broke new ground. It was a film the studio wasn't crazy about and felt would never really do anything. L. B. Mayer never wanted that picture to be made. And we never realized that. We never realized it until after we had made the picture and he came to me and said, "I was wrong about that picture. You fellows did a good job." I was passing him in the barbershop. That's the only discussion I ever had with him about that picture.

Dorothy Kingsley ——— SCREEN-WRITER

While I was working on *Girl Crazy,* I met [producer] Jack Cummings, who was having a lot of trouble with a picture called *Bathing Beauty.* I had some ideas about it, so he asked [MGM executive] Sam Katz if he could have me to work on it. There'd been a million writers on it but the script was just *bleh,* lying there. They couldn't shoot it, even though they had commitments with Esther Williams and Red Skelton, with Harry James, the trumpet player, and with Xavier Cugat, the cha-cha-cha man. They had shot the musical numbers and they had no story! They had shot a great number with Cugat, only nobody in the script had any reason to be there to see this number!

I had to think up something and then send a page down to the set for them to shoot. It was really wild. That's not the way you should make a picture, on the whole. I had a real baptism of fire. But the picture worked out, it was a big hit, Esther's first big picture.

During the war, people liked escapism. I was told that *Bathing Beauty* was the biggest hit in Russia! Because it was gay and light and had so many pretty girls in it.

Walter Lang ——— DIRECTOR

During *Greenwich Village,* Carmen Miranda's fiancé died in Rio, I think, and she went all to pieces—went into shock and couldn't work. So we put her into the hospital for several days with doctors in constant attendance, and when she came back she remembered her lines but she couldn't hear what other people were saying. So we had to shoot the rest of that picture cutting her off above the hips, and when it came time for her to speak—she had read it, she knew what was going on but she couldn't hear—we would have to poke her with a stick out of camera range to give her the cue to speak her lines. About two or three months after that, her hearing returned. But it was very difficult, and we were very tender with her because we loved her. I'd never seen a person disintegrate as she did over that.

* * *

Our contract stipulated that when we finished certain of the big numbers in *State Fair* we had to send them to Rodgers and Hammerstein to see how they liked them. "It Might as Well Be Spring" I did with the girl (Jeanne Crain) sitting by a window and the camera almost imperceptibly creeping up on her till it came to a big close-up. We did it simply because I thought it was a mood song, and so did Al Newman. We sent it to Rodgers and Hammerstein for their opinion and got back a letter saying they were very disappointed. They thought it should have had a big production behind it because it was one of the big numbers in the score. So we put a big production behind it costing $100,000 and sent it to them to see if it fitted in with the way they'd suggested it be done. They sent it back saying, "Put it back the way you had it first."

Mitchell Leisen ——— *DIRECTOR*

One day we were doing the scenes on the couch for *Lady in the Dark* and Ginger Rogers blew take after take until I thought I'd go out of my mind. Finally she said, "I'm sorry. I just can't keep my mind on this because I'm getting married tomorrow." Buddy DeSylva let her go off and get married in the middle of the picture and the entire company just sat there for two weeks. He said, "You can shoot around her." I said, "No, we can't. She's been late every day and we've shot up every scene she's not in." She came back and gave us two weeks at the end of the picture free. She would have been sued if she hadn't.

Joan Leslie ——— *ACTRESS*

Bette Davis was a guest star in two wartime pictures I did, *Thank Your Lucky Stars* and *Hollywood Canteen,* but we only worked together in *Canteen.* Of course I had seen her around the lot, visited her sets and was proud just to be in the same movie with her. We had one scene together in *Hollywood Canteen.* She was a founder of the canteen and, I think, the person who talked Jack Warner into giving the film's proceeds to the canteen and the USO. In the plot, the canteen decides to give the one millionth serviceman to enter there anything he wanted.

Well, in our scene, Bette, as herself, calls me and tells me about the winner (Robert Hutton) and that what he wants is a date with me—Joan Leslie, movie star. She was required to do most of the talking, leaving me mainly with, "Oh, of course. I'll do it." Now, at the same time, Bette was working on another film, one of her big starring vehicles in which she was, as always, totally absorbed, and she had quite a bit of dialogue in our little scene. So here she was, suddenly thrust onto this strange set, with a totally new crew. She blew her lines a few times. Finally, she exclaimed, "Oh, I don't think I can do this. I can't play myself! If you give me a gun, a cigarette, a wig, I can play any old bag, but I can't play myself!"

Everyone laughed. This broke the tension on the set and allowed the scene to proceed smoothly, as this super, sophisticated lady probably knew it would.

Oscar Levant ——— *ACTOR*

A picture I did at Warners, *Romance on the High Seas,* was directed by

Michael Curtiz. It launched Doris Day. And drydocked me.

Jeanette MacDonald — ACTRESS

When Nelson [Eddy] and I went into *I Married an Angel,* which was based on a Broadway success by Rodgers and Hart, we hoped it would be our crowning glory. When it came out, the critics crowned us, all right—but good!

Rouben Mamoulian — DIRECTOR

We had Charles Schoenbaum as cameraman on *Summer Holiday.* We had shot half of the picture, and we hit a scene in a bar in which Mickey Rooney as the young boy sees a floozy (Marilyn Maxwell) get bigger and bigger and redder and redder; he's drunk, and she's overpowering to him, she's his first woman. We had to change gelatins, and I said to Schoenbaum, "I don't like that red shadow on the wall." And he said, "I can't see a red shadow at all. It's green." It turned out this top color cameraman was color blind! And the sound man at the studio [MGM], Douglas Shearer, brother of Norma, was deaf!

Mary Martin — ACTRESS

I almost lost her [daughter Heller Halliday] every month because of my blood type. Rh-negative. We didn't know much about it then. At the end I had to stay in bed with my feet up for three months. The most dangerous moment was earlier, when Bing Crosby and I were doing *Birth of the Blues.* We were racing to finish because of my pregnancy, and there was a scene in which we were on a beer truck going down the street, dubbing a song. I always loathed dubbing because I could never sing the same song the same way twice.

We were bouncing along, singing like crazy, when all of a sudden I fell off the truck. Bang, right into the street. Bing looked horrified but he never missed a beat. Instead of singing "That's the birth of the blues" he sang "That's the birth of Heller." I laughed so hard at him that I didn't even feel the bump much. It didn't hurt me, and it didn't dislodge Heller. Finally, she arrived, safely.

Ann Miller — ACTRESS

I came in at the tail end of the Metro-Goldwyn-Mayer "golden era" when Louis Mayer was still there. While it *was* golden, there were also a couple of disasters. *The Kissing Bandit,* starring Kathryn Grayson and Frank Sinatra, was considered so bad that after a horrendous preview they had me insert a Flamenco-tap number to help jazz it up. I think it turned out to be the worst movie ever made.

* * *

I was still in and out of the traction bed and steel brace for my injured back when my agent, Vic Orsatti, told me that Cyd Charisse had fallen and torn a tendon in her leg and was out of MGM's *Easter Parade* opposite Fred Astaire. The role was up for grabs and producer Arthur Freed was testing girls. Was I ready to try for it? Was I ready! To be in a picture with Fred Astaire was every dancing girl's dream.

I don't know how many girls auditioned for that role—but I got it! And I won it strictly on my own and not through my erstwhile friendship with Mr. [Louis B.] Mayer, as some of the gossip columnists implied. It was Freed and Astaire who made the decision, though for a while it was touch and go whether I was going to get the part, even after winning the auditions.

Fred Astaire was very hesitant about working with me, and it had nothing to do with my test. I was five-feet-seven-inches tall, really too tall for Astaire and there for a moment or two I was afraid he wasn't going to let me have the part. But he liked my test and finally agreed that I should do the picture—if I would wear ballet shoes in my dancing scenes with him. It was decided that the scene could be shot so that my feet wouldn't show. I also had to wear my hair flatter than usual, with a low chignon, to make me appear shorter.

Liza Minnelli———ACTRESS

My first movie was *In the Good Old Summertime,* with Mama [Judy Garland] and Van Johnson. They brought me on at the end in a quick park scene. I was about two and a half. When you see the film, I look very uncomfortable. And no wonder. I had insisted on dressing myself and I didn't put on any panties. When Van lifted me up, his hands were very cold!

Vincente Minnelli —— DIRECTOR

When *I Dood It* was released, I received a letter from an outraged fan. He'd taken exception to the scene where Red Skelton, very confused about his [romantic] predicament, is sitting on a park bench. Butterfly McQueen, Eleanor Powell's maid, joins him. Her little black dog (played by Baba, my pet poodle) sits on the other side. Red, in bewilderment, first talks to Butterfly, then turns to talk to the dog. I thought it was a mildly amusing bit. "How dare you make fun of black people by equating them to a dog?" the moviegoer wrote. I was surprised by such an interpretation. Like my general attitude to the picture, this was the farthest thing from my mind. My thoughts were too filled with the carrot producer Arthur Freed was dangling before me in the form of our next project: *Meet Me in St. Louis.*

* * *

At first, Arthur Freed asked George Cukor to direct *Meet Me in St. Louis,* but he went into the Army at that time. Chuck Walters did the choreography for the superbly harmonious musical numbers. The cost of building the street was about $100,000. The studio said, "Why should we spend all this money on a street? There's no story here. A man wants to take his family to New York, and they don't want to go!"

From the first, I wanted Judy [Garland]. At that time, she was riding very high at MGM and was against doing it. Everybody was telling her that it would kill her career. She came to me full of objections. She had already been to see Freed and hadn't got anywhere with him, but she thought she could make short shrift of me. When I finished explaining what I had in mind and how right she would be for the film, she left my office bewildered, having agreed to do it.

* * *

The Pirate was the first picture that we [Judy Garland] did when we came back from our honeymoon in New York (we were there for three months and sublet an apartment). She was pregnant with Liza, so I had to shoot about three numbers that she did long before the picture was done. They had to fit them in later, but that was necessary because she was getting bigger every day.

George Montgomery———ACTOR

When I was due for a discharge [from the Signal Corps], Victor Mature was doing *Three Little Girls in Blue.* It had already been in production three weeks when Darryl Zanuck heard I was coming out and decided to take Mature out of the fim and put me in. He had already fired Mature from the part by the time I got home. My agent, Ben Melford, said, "Now we've got Zanuck over a barrel. I'll get you a lot of money. He'll have to pay it." I sat in a car and waited while Medford was up in Zanuck's office arguing with him. He finally got me $2750 a week—but Zanuck was furious. He said, "I'm going to see that he's killed in this business." He did a pretty good job of it.

George Murphy———ACTOR

There was supposed to be a finale dance in *For Me and My Gal* with Judy Garland, Gene Kelly and me. They had a sneak preview of the picture and there was a flaw in the story. Remember when Kelly slammed the trunk down on his fingers so he wouldn't have to go to war? I told them they couldn't make a hero out of a fellow like that. The audience just wouldn't accept it and the preview proved that. All the cards came back that *I* should get the girl—not Gene.

Well, they went back and shot 20 days of retakes. They wrote in a whole sequence where Gene saves the ambulance over enemy lines, making him a hero. They re-shot the whole finale without me. That was a real heartbreaker for me.

* * *

I'll never forget one embarrassing scene during *This Is the Army* in 1943. The episode occurred during the filming of the finale—a huge scene involving hundreds of people singing Irving Berlin's classic "This Is the Army, Mr. Jones." The director was the late Michael Curtiz, a wild Hungarian about whom there were as many stories as there are about Samuel Goldwyn.

"Bring on the white soldiers!" Curtiz bellowed. (The Army, like all military services, was still segregated in World War II.) The white troops entered in full formation. Then Curtiz said: "Bring on the nigger troops!"

"Hold everything!" I demanded.

"Mike," I explained, "you just don't use that word. It's offensive to Negroes and it's offensive to me. Call them 'colored troops.'"

Curtiz looked genuinely astonished. "I didn't mean anything by it," he apologized. "I just didn't understand."

Once again Curtiz bellowed his instructions. The cameras began to roll. "Bring on the white soldiers," he ordered. Then he shouted, "Bring on the colored niggers!"

Anna Neagle ——— ACTRESS

We had to sit through Orson Welles' rushes of *Citizen Kane* at the studio every morning waiting to see our own rushes of *Irene.* No one at the studio seemed interested and I believe it had been mentally written off as unshowable. Herbert [Wilcox, her husband] and I alone enthused and Orson has always remembered.

Elliott Nugent ——— DIRECTOR

We had a little set-to before we even started to shoot *Up in Arms.* Danny Kaye's wife didn't like the girl Sam Goldwyn wanted to put in the lead and I didn't like her, either. We made a test and she was beautiful, but she couldn't act. Goldwyn had gotten her out of a nightclub show where she worked with a horse. He signed her because she was beautiful and he had her taking acting lessons from some big shot from New York who was out there charging $100 an hour.

Since both Mrs. Kaye and I were opposed to this girl, he got mad one day and said, "I'm tired of this. I may just have to put my foot down and say, 'That's your leading lady,' and you'll have to take her." And I said, "Then I might say, 'Get another boy'." And he said, "Well, maybe I would." I said, "Look, have we really reached such a point of hostility so early in the game? Why can't we talk this over and arrive at some agreement?"

So finally we didn't have to take her; we got another girl (Constance Dowling) who was a little better but didn't go anywhere. The one I didn't like was Virginia Mayo, who later became a star. She *was* very beautiful—maybe I was wrong—but I felt that since it was Danny's first picture, he needed a girl with more acting experience to feed him and play up to him.

Margaret O'Brien ——— ACTRESS

On *Meet Me in St. Louis,* director Vincente Minnelli was *such* a stickler for detail. Everything was authentic—the St. Louis street that was constructed on the back lot, the Victorian house we lived in, even every ornament on the Christmas tree. I'd just stare at that tree in awe! Being a kid, Christmas was *the* big time of the year and I had no trouble getting into the spirit, even though we shot in the spring.

The story has always been that Minnelli got me to cry by telling me that my dog had died, and I'd love to set the record straight! At the time, June Allyson was also known as a big crier—in fact, the two of us were known at MGM as the "town criers"—and so we were sort of in competition. When the tears weren't coming for the scene in which I destroy my family of snowmen, my mother said, "You know, dear, June's getting ahead of you and people think she's the better actress. Maybe we should have the make-up man put on the false tears?" And that worked like a charm! I *burst* into tears whenever that make-up man came anywhere near me!

Virginia O'Brien —— ACTRESS

They had written my part of Alma throughout the whole movie [*The Harvey Girls*]. The song that Marjorie Main does, "Round and Round and Round We Go"—I had rehearsed that song, but I was expecting my first child. Judy Garland, our star, wasn't showing up at work like she should every day, so I got bigger and bigger, as you might see in the movie. I have pillows on my lap when I'm on the train sitting next to Marjorie. After six months on the movie, I just had to quit. They had to re-write the script. I wish I could have finished it. I still love the movie. It's my favorite.

Hermes Pan — CHOREOGRAPHER

I did the numbers in *Sun Valley Serenade,* with Sonja Henie. The big one was the "Black Ice Ballet," but Henie wanted another one. Darryl Zanuck said no, he was limiting the money spent on her pictures because she was giving everyone such a rough time.

I created the "Black Ice Ballet," with the help of the set man who said, "We'll fill her rink with nicozine dye." But Henie wouldn't listen to you; she only wanted to do what *she* wanted to do. She would get into a beautiful sit-spin on the ice and wouldn't get out of it if her life depended on it. I warned her, "There are 16 boys coming down on you and they'll run into you if you don't leave the spin when I count eight." She wouldn't come out of it, though, and the boys hit her, knocking her down into the nicozine dye. When she got up, she was black.

She stormed off to her dressing room, refusing to work for the rest of the day. She and her mother spent the time cursing in Norwegian.

Joe Pasternak —— PRODUCER

There was trouble on the set of *Presenting Lily Mars.* Judy Garland didn't feel the material was special enough and she felt it should be in color. Some of her so-called studio friends watched a rough cut and told her it stank and she went to Louis B. Mayer. He called me in and ordered me to shoot a lavish new finale. I obeyed but it threw my little film out of whack. Afterwards, I would curtly nod to Judy when we passed on the lot, no more.

Walter Plunkett —— COSTUME DESIGNER

A lot of *Can't Help Singing* was shot in June/July, and during one very hot period we used to arrive on the location in the morning and find it covered by fog. Sitting around waiting for it to clear, Deanna Durbin asked us into her dressing room, where she had cartons of champagne and baskets of food. Later, when the fog lifted, her dress was too tight from all the food and champagne, so she said, "Let's go home for a rest, we can shoot it tomorrow." So the shooting was called off for the day, and there was this beautiful sunshine.

Well, the next day, the same thing happened. We arrived and there would be this heavy fog, so into her dressing room we went for champagne and food, and by the time it had cleared for shooting to begin her dress was bulging again, and we went home for a rest. This went on for quite some time; I don't know how we ever finished, but we did.

She was a great big beautiful baby doll with a pretty voice, and I think that at this stage she no longer cared very much about her career.

Eleanor Powell———ACTRESS

During the three weeks of rehearsal on *Broadway Melody of 1940,* it was always "Mr. Astaire" and "Miss Powell." You would think we were two scientists in a laboratory, we were so serious!

It was Fred's first picture after Ginger [Rogers], and people expected so much from us. Well, there really wasn't much time for laughter, but we both liked to work hard and our respect for each other was tremendous. Do you know that on "Begin the Beguine" we rehearsed for two solid weeks on just arm movements? And I can remember one day when we did a step in counter-rhythm—same rhythm, different steps—and he was so pleased, he rushed over, lifted me in the air and said, "Oh, Ellie!" And then he put me down and said, "I *do* beg your pardon!" And I said, "Look, we can't go on like this. I'm Ellie, you're Fred. We're just two hoofers!" And the ice was broken.

Of course, the reason you work so hard is to make it look easy. And both of us would always say, "Could we do it just one more time?" We would still be there now [1981] if somebody hadn't been there to say, "Look, it's just fine. Print it!"

But Mr. Astaire, I still wish we could do it just one more time!

Jane Powell———ACTRESS

I'd never heard of W. C. Fields until *Song of the Open Road.* It was toward the end of his career and he had yet to become a legend. When I appeared in the picture with him, he was boozing it up all the time at a bar he kept in the back of his station wagon. Nobody could ever find him after lunch.

* * *

If Louis Calhern was my favorite movie dad, my *least* favorite was Wallace Beery. Beery played my father in *A Date with Judy.* I thought he was a fine actor, and a big cuddly teddy bear—but no. He ignored everybody and everything. He never said hello. He never said goodbye. He never smiled.

When Dick Moore was doing his book on child actors, he asked Margaret O'Brien how they got her to cry in films and she answered, "All they had to do was tell me that Wallace Beery was going to steal the scene."

Beery used to steal more than scenes—everything he could get his hands on he would rent back to the studio; and he got away with it. He was stingy. If filming on a picture was coming to an end and he suspected there might be some retakes, he'd take home his entire wardrobe. One time he took a canoe that said "Property of MGM" on the bottom and rented it to the studio for retakes!

Otto Preminger — PRODUCER/DIRECTOR

Centennial Summer? Everybody makes mistakes. I worked on the script with Michael and Fay Kanin for a very long time, a year. It was a very unusual script. Then I took the script to Darryl Zanuck, and he said that it would never make a motion picture. So he wrote a memorandum which straightened it out so that every character became a cliché, because he felt that only chiché characters could be in a musical comedy.

Ronald Reagan — ACTOR

The first week of shooting *This Is the Army* I was introduced to Irving Berlin five times, and each time he was glad to meet me. Then one day he sought me out. The night before he had seen the film we had shot those first few days. He said, "Young fellow, I just saw some of your work. You've got a few things to correct—for example, a huskiness of the voice—but you really should give this business some serious consideration when the war is over. It's very possible that you could have a career in show business." I thanked him very much and began to wonder if he just hadn't seen any movies, or if the war had been going on so long I'd been forgotten.

Marjorie Reynolds — ACTRESS

Luck played a big part in my great break. Danny Dare, who was directing the dances in *Holiday Inn,* remembered me from the days I danced in college musicals. Mark Sandrich, the producer/director, said he wanted someone who could act as well as dance and sing. Danny told him I must be able to act if I could do the lead in Boris Karloff thrillers.

Mr. Sandrich said he'd look at a print of a Karloff horror film that I'd worked in. That's where the lucky break came in. Everything happened on a holiday Friday. The film exchanges were closed that day and the next. Mr. Sandrich couldn't get a print of a Karloff picture.

I'd never have been given the part if Mr. Sandrich had ever seen me in one of those Karloff quickies. Instead, I got a chance to read for him. Incidentally, the reading stage at Paramount is something to make any young actress nervous. There's a glass screen between you and the people who are auditioning you. They can see you but you can't see or hear them. It's supposed to put you at ease, but it did just the opposite to me.

In a way, I'm sorry that the chance to dance with Fred Astaire came so early in my career. That was the peak, the greatest thrill of my professional life.

Leo Robin — LYRICIST

I was completely in awe of Jerome Kern from the minute we got together, and it cramped my style a little bit. He was a very nervous, impatient man, very erudite—I remember once I used the word "encyclopediac" in referring to a man we knew, and Kern said, "Encyclope*dic.*" He was that kind of person.

A very cultured musician, too; he knew music and he knew orchestration. What can you say about Kern? When we did the picture *Centennial Summer* he said to me, "Look, we're going to do this picture with straight actors—there's not one singer in the picture. I've never done that before." So he took a big gamble on the project. After we got started, he used to call me up every day, bugging me—"You got anything yet?" I wanted so much to please him and to measure up to his high standards that I don't think I did my best work in that picture. But I had one song that Kern liked very much—"In Love in Vain." He used to play it at parties.

Richard Rodgers —— COMPOSER

One unusual aspect of *State Fair* was that after we had completed the score [in New York], we were told that Darryl F. Zanuck, the head of 20th Century-Fox, wanted to see us in Hollywood. Since the company had been extremely cooperative in letting us do the job the way we wanted, it would have been ungracious to refuse—particularly as we were to be guests of the studio and they were even thoughtful enough to invite our wives. Obviously there must be important things that Zanuck wanted to discuss with us that required a face-to-face meeting.

So the [Oscar] Hammersteins and the Rodgerses got on the cross-country train and spent a week in Hollywood. The accommodations were elegant, we met friends, attended some parties and saw a few screen tests of actors being considered for the film. It wasn't until the day before we were to return home that Oscar and I were at last summoned by Zanuck. We were ushered into his pale-green office and there he was, riding crop across his lap, sitting behind a huge desk chewing on a huge cigar. And what did we talk about? Actually, I can't recall that Oscar or I said much. For 20 minutes Zanuck held center stage as he reminisced about his recent wartime experiences. Then, when our allotted time was over, we were ushered out. We never saw him again.

Why was Zanuck so anxious to have us travel 3,000 miles to see him after we had completed our work? Largely, I think, it was a matter of pride and muscle. He had paid us a lot of money and had acceded to our working conditions, but he wanted the satisfaction of being able to make us do as he wished. It was one more example of the kind of ego-satisfying extravagance that eventually contributed to the downfall of the Hollywood studio system.

Ginger Rogers —— ACTRESS

The most challenging scene I ever worked on was in *Lady in the Dark,* when Don Loper and I dance in smoke. They closed the doors and filled the place with dry ice. I rehearsed it and rehearsed it, and by the time we filmed, I was exhausted from the fumes. None of the scenes with Fred Astaire were that difficult.

*   *   *

On the first day of *The Barkleys of Broadway,* I went down to the rehearsal hall to see Fred [Astaire]. He was sweet and friendly, but I could see he was slightly disappointed. I had learned that Judy Garland had originally been signed as his co-star. They'd just worked together on *Easter Parade* and I knew Fred had a slight crush on her. When Judy was taken off *The Barkleys,* I was pressed into service.

Mickey Rooney———ACTOR

The first time I saw Ava Gardner was on the set of *Babes on Broadway* in 1941. Ava was dressed like a princess and I was dressed like Carmen Miranda. I walked over in my samba skirt, my wedgee shoes, my bodice blouse and my fruity hat and asked her for a date.

*   *   *

Judy Garland and I were going to do *Girl Crazy,* the movie adaptation of a Broadway hit written in 1930 by none other than George and Ira Gershwin. It was hard work, but I thrive on it. I wish I could say the same for Judy. A month into the picture, Judy was down to 94 pounds and completely exhausted. I didn't have to ask her what the matter was. I knew: married life with David Rose was not so rosy. At the end of January 1943, her physician told the studio Judy couldn't dance for six to eight weeks.

In fact, Judy was back at work in *two* weeks—only to collapse again. She was on the lot, and off, all through February and March and April, then managed to work for a solid month from April 19 until May 19, when we finished shooting—two months over schedule. Some people say the studio doped her up at this time, giving her downers at bedtime and uppers so she could get up and go to work in the morning. This was simply not true. MGM would never do this. Judy had taken to drinking and sleeping pills.

Later on, Judy would blame the studio or her mother or some nameless "theys" for getting her started on the road to self-destruction. Who ever wants to blame themselves? She was only human, but the most human woman I've ever known, and she didn't want to take the blame—the blame for killing Judy Garland, the Judy Garland that I (and the whole world) loved.

Gail Russell———ACTRESS

When I was a child in Chicago, there would be weeks when I'd go every single afternoon to the movies. I'd walk blocks to my favorite picture house and sit there often right through dinner, seeing a film two and three times. My father would have to come and find me. Once—I'd just seen a Ginger Rogers picture—my father met me dancing through the streets, singing, speaking lines. Ginger was my idol and I'd sat through the picture three times and had memorized the dialogue and lyrics of the songs. It may seem odd that anyone so shy could dance and sing in the street, make a spectacle of herself. But when I felt I was not me, you see, I wasn't afraid. I suppose that really explains why I am in pictures, for on sound stages I don't have to be me.

It's strange, isn't it, that I should have been cast in *Lady in the Dark,* my second picture, with Ginger Rogers? When I first saw her on the set, I stood there with my mouth open. The first day of actual shooting when I came on the set, I was told I would have to learn the Charleston in 15 minutes, flat. I had a broken toe. And my best friend, Bill Russell, dramatic coach at Paramount who had literally held my hand in every scene I'd made, was away with the flu. I was frantic. I thought, I am going to faint; I thought, I will run away and hide. Then Ginger Rogers came over to me, put her arm around me, took me into her dressing room, gave me tea and went over the script with me. Best of all, she told me how scared she had been when she first got into pictures. That was the warmingest thing she could have done for me. And she taught me the Charleston!

After that, we used to talk about art, Ginger and I, between scenes on the set. And about music. And books. I drew cartoons of Ginger and she put them in the mirror in her dressing room. Ginger was, so to speak, the turning point in relaxing me.

Peggy Ryan —— ACTRESS

In 1942, I was signed by Universal and did *What's Cookin'?* Of course, Donald O'Connor was in it along with the rest of the Jivin' Jacks and Jills group. But then the original male lead, David Holt, suddenly couldn't do the part, so they promoted Donald to the lead. I was still in the background and happy that Donald had gotten his break. Every one of the "kid" dancers—that was actually the name of a specific category, kid dancers—was pushing and shoving trying to attract attention and "become a star." Fortunately for me, Donald and I were paired off on a couple of numbers.

Since Donald and I were old buddies, he was very cooperative. When a particular scene ended, we'd head for the camera and say nutty things. Like Donald would look at me and ask, "Have you taken a bath lately?" And I would reply, "No, is one missing?" It was really corny stuff, but we kept doing it every chance we had.

Anyway, comes the night of the preview in Santa Barbara, or one of those outlying towns where they used to take films to get a "typical response." At the end the audience filled out reaction cards. A majority of them said, "Who was that cute dark-haired couple that was so funny together?" When I came to the studio the next day, I found out that now both Donald's name and mine were to receive top billing.

Arthur Schwartz —— PRODUCER

As far as I was concerned, there was only one man in Hollywood who could do it [the male lead in *Cover Girl*], and that was Gene Kelly. But each time I mentioned this to Harry Cohn, he would explode. "That tough Irishman with his tough Irish mug?! You couldn't put him in the same

frame as Rita Hayworth!" he growled. "Nonsense. Forget it. Nothing doing. Besides, he's too short. I saw him in *Pal Joey* and he's too goddamn short."

***George Sidney*——DIRECTOR**

Bathing Beauty with Esther Williams was a challenge. We shot under water for weeks. It was necessary to devise equipment capable of playing music under water for the bathing beauties to swim to. We developed cameras and lighting equipment that had mobility on top or underneath water, plus make-up, hairdress and choreography. The rhythmic cueing had to be kept to a low volume, because water acts as a conductor and the sound could easily have shattered the swimmers' eardrums.

The water had to be an exact temperature at all times, not too hot, not too cold. One morning we were shooting at Lakeside Pool on a bitterly cold January day. The boys and girls refused to go in the water, it was too cold. I took off my overcoat, two sweaters, long underwear. I stripped naked and dived in myself. I swam up and down—and I broke every Olympic record. When I hit that cold water—*wow!* I came out purple! But I shamed them into action.

* * *

Gene Kelly was due to report to the real Navy, and I wanted the dance with him and Mickey Mouse [in *Anchors Aweigh*]. Walt Disney had agreed his studio could do it, but his brother Roy phoned and said Walt was so far behind on his own projects that he could never deliver the footage. So we cut a mouse from cardboard, and put it on a long stick and lined up our shots that way. We photographed Gene, said goodbye to him, then MGM animators added their own Jerry to the scene. It didn't look right at the end, so I had to go to [producer] Joe Pasternak for more money. The animators had forgotten to add shadows where Jerry dances to match Gene's. That meant another 10,000 drawings of mouse shadows.

* * *

For the "Atchison, Topeka and Santa Fe" number in *The Harvey Girls,* I did the rehearsals for several days on a scene that was going to run at least nine minutes. Judy Garland saw a "dance-in" go through it only once and then floored me by saying she was ready. I had hundreds of dancers and extras poised and all doing bits—spinning lariats, running in and out of frame. Judy got it right on the first take with all the beats correct but with added nuances and feelings.

This widespread notion that the studio somehow destroyed her is nonsense. Her personal life got too much for her. I prefer to think of her as she is in *The Harvey Girls,* near the peak of her talent.

Phil Silvers —————— ACTOR

The nominal producer of *Cover Girl* was Arthur Schwartz, the director Charles Vidor, but the genius on the film was Gene Kelly. Naturally there was friction, and "sonovabitch" was like saying "good morning." Vidor, a skilled director, was Hungarian, and in Hollywood Hungarians had the reputation of entering a revolving door behind you and coming out ahead. Gene would slap his cap to the floor and Vidor would stalk off. [Studio President] Harry Cohn immediately came barreling onto the set and knocked heads together. Cohn had spies everywhere; he even knew which horses I bet.

Rita Hayworth had become involved with Orson Welles. Passionately. They had to see each other; like Romeo and Juliet, nothing would stop them. *Citizen Kane* had closed a lot of doors to Welles because William Randolph Hearst felt that Orson had shafted him by using him as a model for Kane. Harry Cohn barred Orson from the lot, but Gene and I would let Orson in through a back door to see Rita. Rita and Orson married in 1943 and divorced four years later.

Frank Sinatra —————— ACTOR

When I arrived at MGM to do *Anchors Aweigh,* I was a nobody in movies. And because I didn't think I was as talented as some of the people I was working with, I used to go through periods of depression and get terribly embarrassed at myself. After all, what was I then? A crooner who'd been singing for a big band for seven years and whose only claim to fame was that girls swooned whenever I opened my mouth.

But after working with Gene Kelly, who always saw me through my depressions and encouraged me to do a little better than I thought I was capable of doing, I felt I actually had some talent. I was born with a couple of left feet, and it was Gene and only Gene who got me to dance. Apart from being a great artist, he's a born teacher. I felt really comfortable working for him and enjoyed his company, in spite of his insane insistence on hard work. Gene somehow tricked and cajoled me into working harder than I had ever done in my life before, and I found myself locked into a room rehearsing some of the routines for as long as eight weeks. Eight weeks! You can shoot a whole picture in that time!

* * *

I was under contract to MGM between 1944 and 1950. Here's what happened. We made *Anchors Aweigh* which grossed a whole lot of money, and that was the start of the "Formula." You may remember that in *Anchors* I was cast as a friendly little sailor with nothing much to say for himself. Then came *It Happened in Brooklyn,* where I played the part of a friendly little GI with nothing much to say for himself.

By the time we reach *On the Town,* they'd made me a sailor again, as inarticulate as ever, though in all fairness let me add that this latter one was a very good movie in other respects. But you see the rut I was in. Even the story was mostly the same. Gene Kelly and Sinatra meet girl. Kelly hates girl, Sinatra loves girl, girl likes Sinatra but loves Kelly, girl rejects Sinatra, Sinatra finds that he loved another girl all the time, Kelly finds out that he loved the first girl all the time—fade out. Sometimes it was someone else instead of Gene, but any other variations were strictly superficial.

The quickies I made for RKO [*Higher and Higher, Step Lively*] before signing with MGM were never meant to be anything much, and *Miracle of the Bells,* in which I had my first non-musical acting part, turned out less well than we had hoped.

The first role I could really get my teeth into was when Universal made *Meet Danny Wilson* in 1952. It was an unsympathetic character that some people took to be partly biographical, it seems. To that I can only reply that if anyone believes everything he sees in the movies, he must be awfully mixed up, mentally.

Milton Sperling —— PRODUCER

For *Sun Valley Serenade,* we went on location for the ski scenes in Sun Valley, Idaho. The place was overrun with handsome young blond ski instructors from Austria and Germany. I'm sure that Sonja Henie knew all of them—*intimately.* I think she ran through the whole bunch, one at a time. They all spoke highly of her. I'm sure she was very good in the sack, she had such enormous enthusiasm. She was always hungry for sex.

Sonja was frolicking with these guys every night, and they all looked it the following morning, and still her country [Norway] had been invaded by Germany. Although we weren't in the war yet, I thought it very strange that she seemed to find nothing wrong with the Nazi ski instructors who were, by the way, picked up shortly thereafter and interned until after the war.

Jule Styne—*COMPOSER*

We were set to start with Betty Hutton in *Romance on the High Seas* when she rejected the script, and a replacement was needed desperately. There was a girl [Doris Day] I'd heard at a little bistro in New York, she'd been with Les Brown's band but was now on her own, so we brought her out—not knowing that she'd already been turned down by Warners on a screen test. Her singing was beautiful but she couldn't walk while she was singing, she'd never appeared before a camera before and when they tried to make her move she'd burst out crying.

This time we got Henry Blanke, a great producer, to supervise her test, and when we ran it he told our director, Michael Curtiz, "If you don't use her in this picture, I'm using her in mine." Well, the rest is history. From *nothing,* living in a trailer, not even having the price of milk for her baby—we bought milk for it—we gave her three big songs, "It's Magic," "It's You or No One" and "Put 'Em in a Box." Went on to make $20,000,000 for herself, never give you a tie. . . .

Elizabeth Taylor—*ACTRESS*

A Date with Judy was the first time I put on make-up for the screen, dressed like a young woman and had a leading man who wasn't four-legged.

Lana Turner—*ACTRESS*

When we started shooting *Ziegfeld Girl* I had a small part. But as we went along I kept getting more rewrites. The director was Robert Z. Leonard, but everyone called him "Pops." He was a lovable teddy bear of a man. He had some smarts and he went to Louis B. Mayer and said, "I think we have something in this little lady. Let's build up her part."

Suddenly it was my film. All the dramatic parts were put in for me. I was thrilled. Somebody finally noticed I was not just a pretty face, with legs and boobs, but I could act.

Charles Walters—*DANCE DIRECTOR*

On *Meet Me in St. Louis,* I staged all the numbers—"The Boy Next Door," "Skip to My Lou" and "The Trolley Song." I even had a mock-up trolley in the rehearsal hall along with the principals, Judy Garland and Tom Drake, plus the dancers and piano player. I worked very closely with Vincente Minnelli, the director—in fact, the only number I didn't stage was "Have Yourself a Merry Little Christmas" which was really a story-point. There was also a number I did, a beautiful song by Rodgers and Hammerstein called "Boys and Girls Like You and Me," which Judy sang on the site of the fairground. It was a gorgeous song and after cutting it from *St. Louis* the studio tried it in two other movies; but, somehow, it never was used, somehow the mood was too slender and fragile.

—*DIRECTOR*

Easter Parade, at twice the budget of *Good News,* came about because

MGM was so pleased with my handling of the earlier picture. Gene Kelly was to have starred, and Vincente Minnelli was to have directed. Judy Garland was always set—and Bob Alton had been signed for the dances. The reason why Vince backed out was that he and Judy were going to the same psychiatrist who advised them against making the picture—they shouldn't be together both day *and* night! (By this time, they were very much married, of course.) Then, while we were in rehearsal, Kelly broke his ankle playing football in his back garden. Producer Arthur Freed then persuaded Fred Astaire to come out of retirement. But if you look closely, you'll see that the numbers didn't really fit Fred.

I never had any problems with Judy. We were very close—in fact, we almost got married once! But Judy loved to growl, loved to *pretend,* and when she heard I was assigned to *Easter Parade* she said, "Look, sweetie, I'm no June Allyson, you know. Don't get cute with me. None of that batting-the-eyelids bit, or the fluffing-the-hair routine for me, buddy. I'm Judy Garland and you just watch it!"

With Fred you always have to settle a little short. He's so self-conscious—can't stand the sound of his own voice, did you know that? Worry, worry, worry about everything. A real old maid. A charmer but a worrier. How good he was with Judy in "A Couple of Swells." Garland and Astaire as a couple of deadbeats, for God's sake! All I had to do was stand back and let it happen. Judy always adored that number. You know who did it with her on opening night at the Palace? Me!

Harry Warren ——— COMPOSER

For *Weekend in Havana,* they asked me to have all the music written in four weeks, because Carmen Miranda was leaving for another engagement. I worked nights as well as days and turned out a lot of music, some of which was dropped from the picture. I fell ill at this time and was taken to a hospital, where they found I had pneumonia. It got worse, and I was on the critical list for some time.

It was about three months before I returned to the studio. I found they had taken me off salary for the period of the illness but they had kept [lyricist] Mack Gordon on all the time. I stormed into Darryl Zanuck's office, waving my walking stick and cursing, but they wouldn't let me see him. Maybe he didn't know anything about it, but his lieutenant did. They were horrible people. I demanded that my contract be terminated but they wouldn't do it, and my lawyer couldn't do anything about it, either. I had to stay. But Fox didn't seem the same to me after that, and I was always looking for ways to get out.

* * *

I never saw *The Gang's All Here.* It was bad enough having to work on it.

Ethel Waters ——— ACTRESS

I objected violently to the way religion was being treated in the screenplay. All through the picture there was so much snarling and scrapping that I didn't know how in the world *Cabin in the Sky* ever stayed up there!

"I'll tell you what I'll do... I'll match you for him!"

Esther Williams ——— ACTRESS

MGM took a chance starring me in *Bathing Beauty.* I'd only done a couple of small roles before that. Luckily, *Bathing Beauty*—which was helped immeasurably by the box office draw of Red Skelton—was a big hit. Nevertheless, if my second starring film, *Thrill of a Romance,* with Van Johnson, hadn't been successful, MGM probably would have taken my pool and filled it up with bones for Lassie. After all, Lassie worked for less and gave the studio good, dependable grosses with all her pictures. As it turned out, *Thrill of a Romance* was an even bigger hit than *Bathing Beauty,* one of MGM's top money-makers for 1945.

Darryl F. Zanuck—STUDIO HEAD

There was a big scandal when Carmen Miranda danced [in *Weekend in Havana*] and didn't have any pants on under her skirt. I don't think she ever wore pants when she danced. She was not a tart by any means. A real lady. A real professional. It was a matter of her freedom of body movement. But one time a freelance still photographer had a camera set at a low angle as she danced. It revealed *everything.* Millions of the pictures were suddenly being sold. We had the FBI trying to trace who was behind it. It was the finish of her. It was one of those Hollywood periods when the women's organizations ganged up on us, those pressure groups. Those super-puritanical pressure groups.

Political Films

Lauren Bacall ——— ACTRESS

November 1945, brought the release of *Confidential Agent.* It was a disaster. The critics said they'd made a mistake—I was not Garbo, Dietrich, Hepburn, Mae West all rolled into one, as they had thought, I was just terrible me and should be sent back where I came from. As brilliant, exciting and glorious as I had been just a few months ago [in *To Have and Have Not*], that's how amateurish, tedious and just plain bad I was now.

Frank Capra ——— PRODUCER/DIRECTOR

Originally, I had Spencer Tracy and Claudette Colbert for *State of the Union.* One day, with everyone already on salary, Claudette came to me and said, "You know, Frank, I don't work a minute past five o'clock. My agent puts this in all my contracts now. My doctor says I get too tired." Her agent was her brother and she was married to her doctor. I told her that I couldn't tie my hands to a seven-hour shooting day. She left. I no longer had Claudette Colbert.

When I told Spence, he said, "Kate [Hepburn] isn't hamming it up right now. Ask her." Kate said yes immediately—no clock-watching, no temperament.

John Carradine ——— ACTOR

For *Grapes of Wrath,* we filmed a scene down in Needles, California. It was supposed to be a hot day and we went into the river to cool off. It was the coldest water I was ever in in my life. My bones ached instantly. We were standing there shivering during the whole scene. Afterwards, they gave us a bottle of brandy to warm us up. Old Russell Simpson had false teeth and dialogue. They had to redub it in the studio because his teeth were chattering so you could not understand one word.

Broderick Crawford ——— ACTOR

All the King's Men was shot off the cuff. Nobody in the cast had a script and only [producer/director] Robert Rossen really knew what he was doing. He let us read the script only once and then he took it away from us. We really had to stay on our toes.

Henry Fonda ——— ACTOR

I'd worked with [Darryl] Zanuck before, several times. I did *Young Mr. Lincoln, Drums Along the Mohawk* and *Jesse James* and he was always after a contract, but I wasn't interested. Until *Grapes of Wrath.* That was the bait.

He said, "I'm not going to let you play Tom Joad if I can't control you." Well, bullshit, I did *Grapes of Wrath* and I followed it with some of the worst shit that I've had to do in films, so I'll never forgive Zanuck.

John Ford ——— DIRECTOR

I finished *Grapes of Wrath* under budget and turned it in. With Darryl

Zanuck I didn't have to worry about how it would be cut because he was a great cutter. The night I finished I got on my boat and started to sail to Honolulu. Before I left, I had a meeting with Darryl and I said, "I think it's a good picture. It's meaty and down-to-earth. But I think it needs a happier ending. I hate to see the picture end with Henry Fonda walking across the dance hall and disappearing into the darkness. I think it should end with the mother."

He said, "That's a good idea. Let's think it over."

I sailed on the midnight tide. I was three days out and had a good forwarding breeze. I was at the wheel when a phone call came from Darryl.

He said, "Listen to this scene I've written. I've looked at the picture twice since you left, and I agreed with you that it needs a happier ending. It needs an ending of hope for the future. Listen to this carefully."

He read me the scene and asked if I wanted it re-written.

I told him no, it was great.

Then he said, "Who's going to direct it?"

I said, "Darryl, it's only a two-shot. I'd appreciate it if you went out and directed it yourself."

So he did it himself in one take. And they put it in as the end of the picture.

Howard Koch — SCREENWRITER

Fashions change in politics as they do in manners and morals; *Mission to Moscow* is a prime example. The film, patriotic in the forties, became subversive in the fifties, which caused the embarrassed Warners to bury it deep in their studio vaults. During this same postwar period, the picture was shown all over the Soviet Union. Then, when Stalin fell into disrepute, the Soviets stopped showing the film, since he appeared in one of the scenes. And recently, in celebration of détente between the two countries, *Mission* was dug out of its vaults and given a gala reopening in Washington under the auspices of the American Film Society!

Angela Lansbury — ACTRESS

On *State of the Union,* I slithered up to Spencer Tracy in a slinky robe and tried to seduce him while Katharine Hepburn watched us from the sidelines. Somehow I got through it, but under that robe my knees were literally knocking together.

Paul Lukas — ACTOR

When I did *Watch on the Rhine* on Broadway, I killed a man in the play. So when I got to Warner Bros. in Hollywood to do the film, the censor insisted a new scene be written at the end where I died. I hated this idea, so when the time came to shoot it I just disappeared. They had to rewrite it again.

Agnes Moorehead — ACTRESS

I think Orson [Welles] is determined to make me the ugliest girl in pictures. I was one of his Mercury Players on Broadway and when he asked me if I wanted to come to Hollywood and appear in his pictures, I thought, "Ah, now I'll get the

Hollywood glamour buildup." But in my first picture, *Citizen Kane,* I wasn't allowed a smitch of make-up and I played the role with gray lips. Then in *Magnificent Ambersons* Orson ordered all the irregularities of my face brought out with certain lighting. And in *Journey into Fear* Orson gives me big hips and puts warts on my face.

Robert Parrish—EDITOR

All the King's Men was three hours long and had been disastrously previewed when I was brought on the film by the producer/director, Robert Rossen. There were thousands of feet of film, and although it was all formless—senseless—much of the footage had real impact. We spent months working on the picture and there were many more previews—all disasters, too.

Columbia boss Harry Cohn was raising hell.

Finally, at our lowest point, Bob Rossen suddenly said to me, "Remember *The Roaring Twenties,* which I wrote at Warners? I want us to look at it." We ran it, then Rossen said, "The reason *Roaring Twenties* works is because it gallops from one scene to another, like one long montage. Before the audience can realize the story is full of holes, they're into the next scene. That's what we're going to do with *All the King's Men.* We'll chop off the beginning and end of all the scenes. But we've got to hurry. Harry is threatening to take the picture away from me."

We did as Bob suggested. We got the picture down to under two hours and it made exciting sense at last. It won the [1949] Best Picture Oscar, Broderick Crawford was named Best Actor and Mercedes McCambridge Best Supporting Actress.

Robert Stack—ACTOR

The Mortal Storm was Hollywood's first involvement with powers outside the realm of show business. Phyllis Bottome's best-seller, along with *Confessions of a Nazi Spy,* did not go unnoticed by the Third Reich. About two weeks into filming, an official-looking gent arrived on the set and was seen talking to the producer, Victor Saville. By the expression on Victor's face, I knew the news wasn't good. Then I saw Robert Young pacing back and forth, mumbling, "My children, what about my children?"

The Swiss consulate had received word from Germany that everyone connected with *Confessions of a Nazi Spy* and my *Mortal Storm* would be "taken care of" when Hitler won the war. Since Hitler's war machine had pierced the "impregnable" Maginot Line in a few days, and now stood on the edge of the English Channel, the threat seemed more than mere hyperbole. The German-American Bund began making ugly noises. The atmosphere on the set was tense. Fights broke out, and the book-burning sequence almost got out of hand.

Donald Ogden Stewart—SCREEN-WRITER

Keeper of the Flame is the picture I'm proudest of—in terms of saying the most about fascism that it was possible to say in Hollywood. It was a very good novel about the possibility of fascism in America—a dictator taking over—and I didn't change it much. We had to keep it concealed from Mr. [Louis B.] Mayer—it wasn't what you'd call a Republican picture. There is a story that the first time he saw it in Radio City in New York he was so angry at the message of the picture that he got up and walked out. I'd be very happy if it were true.

Orson Welles ——— ***PRODUCER/DIRECTOR/SCREENWRITER***

It was the opening night of *Citizen Kane* in San Francisco, and I found myself going to the Top O' the Mark in the elevator with Mr. [William Randolph] Hearst. I introduced myself to this strange dinosaur—he had ice cold blue eyes and a very high, unformed voice. And I said, "Mr. Hearst, I had some good tickets for the opening of *Citizen Kane.* Would you like to come?" He didn't answer, and I got off the elevator thinking, as I still do, that if he *had* been Charles Foster Kane, he would have gone.

* * *

Make me one promise. Keep Ted Turner and his goddamned Crayolas away from my movie [*Citizen Kane*].

Robert Wise ——— ***EDITOR***

Orson Welles was, I think, as close to a genius as anyone I ever met. Dynamic, creative, full of life, loved stories, loved food, loved ladies. It's kind of sad, but looking back on it, *Citizen Kane* is kind of autobiographical—Kane, big talent, big career, downhill, downhill, losing it all in the end.

Religious Films

Ingrid Bergman ——— ***ACTRESS***

From the minute I played in *The Bells of St. Mary's* everybody knew what I should do forever afterwards. I should be a nun—oh sure, a very funny nun, but a nun just the same. The only really good thing I found about being a nun was that all I showed was my face. The rest of me was shrouded in large black drapes. I could eat ice cream forever. No one worried about my weight.

* * *

I'd wanted to do *Joan* since 1940. But no one would listen. They said it had too much war and religion—and no love story. Later, when I did *Joan of Lorraine* on the stage, they changed their minds. Victor Fleming, the great director, saw me do *Joan* on the stage, and he sat in the audience and cried. He said, "I've got to do *Joan of Arc.*" He used to sit all day and only read and read and read about Joan of

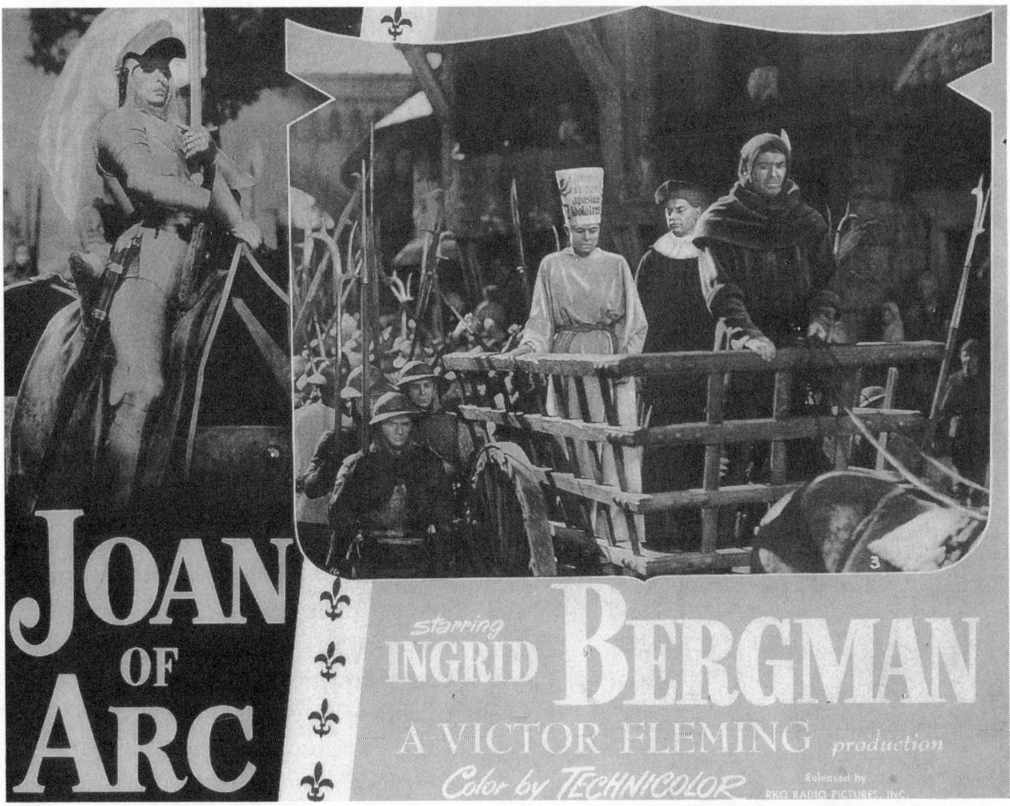

Arc. Then he'd go to museums and study her. And I also studied endlessly, because we wanted to prove to the French people that we could do their heroine. When we got ready to start the picture, I was so inspired and kept asking, "Where is the church? Where is the church? Where is the church?" There it was—one wall! Not even two. To cut down expenses. And the solyers [soldiers]! The English solyers would change their helmets and become French solyers. I said to them, "Good heavens, you're French today!" I told them, "You shouldn't come so close to the cameras, you'll be recognized!"

Bing Crosby ——— ACTOR

The story [producer/director/author] Leo McCarey told the studio heads for *Going My Way* bore no resemblance whatever to the story he finally shot. But he made the tale so absorbing that they had to go for it. I think probably 75 percent of each day's shooting was made up on the set by Leo. The production department always demanded 20 or 30 written pages in advance of shooting. So Leo would dictate reams of stuff which he had no intention of using and then he would write what he intended to use when he came on the set in the morning. He would go immediately to the piano and play some ragtime for an hour or two, while he thought up a few scenes. This was especially tough on the actors who had already learned the lines he had sent to the story department, but it didn't bother me because I never learned by heart until I came to work.

* * *

You know, when *Going My Way* was first released, it couldn't play any Latin American countries for several years because the priest wore a sweatshirt and a baseball cap. To them, that was absolutely sacrilegious. But as for my own impact on the priest being [recognized as a] human being, well, I think it was coming anyhow. I was just kind of part of that movement.

* * *

My memory of the award-giving at Grauman's Chinese Theater is not too clear. I'd heard there was a chance I'd get an Oscar [for *Going My Way*], but I was sure that it would go to someone who was recognized as an able actor rather than a crooner. So I didn't take it too seriously until shortly before the ceremony, when it began to look as if I had a chance. After that I took it seriously enough to put on a dinner jacket, which is unusual for me. I'm not a great lad for getting into a dinner jacket.

Gary Cooper was chosen to hand me the award. I don't remember what he said, but when he managed to put the idea over to me that I had won the award, a great warm feeling came over me. I stumbled up on the stage like a zombie. Neither Cooper nor I said much.

I asked, "Are you talking about me?"

And he said, "Yup."

* * *

At the end of *The Bells of St. Mary's* there's a farewell scene between Ingrid Bergman and me and throughout the film there'd been a note of something more than just a priest-nun relationship. Father Devlin [the film's religious adviser] was watching us rehearse this scene the way it was going to be, then [producer/director/author] Leo McCarey said, "Now we'll take it." We got to the line where I had to say goodbye and I reached for Ingrid, took her in my arms, bent her over and gave her a real big soul kiss. I really hung in there!

There was shocked silence and when I pulled away Father Devlin was ashen. He was shaking and his eyes were sticking out a foot. Then, of course, everybody laughed and he saw it was a gag. He was so relieved, but for a moment it was really something.

José Ferrer——————ACTOR

Working with Ingrid Bergman in *Joan of Arc?* It was an experience. She was very professional on the set. A very serious, no-nonsense actress. She was always on the set on time, and she was cheerful, pleasant, warm—perhaps a bit aloof, but very gracious. She looked upon me as a newcomer, as well I was in Hollywood; I felt I was in a strange place. In fact, I still think Hollywood is a strange place. In later years, Ingrid and I got to be good and loyal friends.

Despite its cost and the popularity of our star, *Joan of Arc* did not do well in movie houses, perhaps because it seemed to me a little glamourized. Joan's armor was always spotless. The whole thing didn't seem quite real. And even in those days, audiences wanted some semblance of reality.

Y. Frank Freeman———STUDIO HEAD

Nobody will go to see this picture [*Going My Way*], except Catholics in church basements.

Rumer Godden ——— AUTHOR

There is not an atom of truth in the film of *Black Narcissus*—famous as it has become. I have taken a vow never to allow a book of mine to be made into a film again.

Jennifer Jones———ACTRESS

Winning the Academy Award a year ago for *The Song of Bernadette* was a wonderful thrill I'll always remember. And the role of Bernadette was the chance of a lifetime. But it has had its drawbacks, too. Mr. [David] Selznick pointed them out to me. "You're through with Bernadette," he said. "You've got to become Jennifer Jones again." It's amazing how people have become so conscious of Bernadette that they see me on the street and say, "There's Bernadette!" not, "There's Jennifer Jones!" Of course, it's a terrific compliment, except that if the feeling persists, people won't accept me in any other type of role. People who remember *Bernadette* expect me to be wan and spiritual. Not only on the screen, but in my private life. And Jennifer Jones is a very human person. She'll never have wings!

Not that I'm not grateful for the award. I think Franz Werfel wrote a book that was needed when the world was in upheaval. I think that's why the picture went right to people's hearts. It gave them something to believe in; it refreshed their memories of undying faith. In fact, it was almost mandatory to do a good job in portraying Bernadette, because it was such a terrific responsibility. People would either believe or not. It was necessary not to fail those who wanted that story to come to life in all its truth and beauty.

But, professionally, *Bernadette* has been almost like something to live down. Because I never want to be a type—either spiritual or otherwise. I want to do exciting parts, *right* parts. And here is where I am more than glad my future is in Mr. Selznick's hands. I am sure he will never let me do any pictures except those that will help round out Jennifer Jones as a whole. When he cast me in *Since You Went Away,* I stepped away from the saintly to just the average young American girl. In my new picture for Hal Wallis, *Love Letters,* I play the dramatic part of a girl who has lost her memory. And I know I need this picture, too. My next for Mr. Selznick will be the exciting *Duel in the Sun.*

You see, eight other pictures were offered to Mr. Selznick for me. The pictures as a whole had a terrific range, every type role from risqué to biography. He picked *Love Letters* because it is a very human story, and he felt such a picture now would combat the public opinion that Ber-

nadette and Jennifer Jones are one and the same. Like I said, I'll never have a halo!

Henry King —————— *DIRECTOR*

There's a scene in *The Song of Bernadette* where Bernadette sees the Blessed Virgin. Well, before I tested Jennifer Jones, 12 other actresses had been tested for the part. All of them *looked* at the Blessed Virgin, but Jennifer *saw* Her.

Leo McCarey ——— *PRODUCER/DIRECTOR/AUTHOR*

In 1945, I was feuding with David Selznick, who had Ingrid Bergman under an ironclad contract. I wanted her desperately for my picture *The Bells of St. Mary's.* She was in Minnesota appearing in bond drives at the time, so I got a friend of mine to run an item in the Minnesota papers saying, "Wait till Ingrid Bergman hears the idea Leo McCarey has for her." She took the bait, and when she came back to Hollywood I was able to tell her about the nun's part. She then began to work on Selznick with such tenacity that she eventually wore him down. She kept saying, "If you don't let me do this, I'll go back to the old country." He finally gave in.

Oscar Millard — *SCREENWRITER*

I once wrote a film whose title, *Come to the Stable,* sounded like an invitation for a roll in the hay, but which, in fact, was purer than a bar of Ivory soap. It was about a couple of Benedictine nuns, but sure enough the Hays Office memo sternly warned against allowing them to expose their breasts, although even if they'd been so inclined, they'd have had a helluva time locating them under those starched breastplates.

Arthur Miller——CINEMATOGRAPHER

I very much enjoyed making *The Song of Bernadette.* At the beginning of the picture, in Bernadette's home, when she first comes in, and stands there for a minute, you see a little glow on the wall, hardly noticeable, just like you would use to make the head stand away from an object behind it, but more intensified. I had this spotlight glow to the very end of the picture. And here is a perfect example of how little directors control things like this. When we looked at three cut reels Henry King said, "Do you notice something?" And I said, "What?" And he said, "Every time she appears there's something glowing at the back of her head." Maybe he thought this was something spiritual that had crept into the picture from heaven!

Anne Revere——ACTRESS

While we were filming *Song of Bernadette,* in which Jennifer Jones played the French saint, Jennifer announced her separation from Bob Walker one morning. That afternoon a very long sable coat was delivered to her at the studio—a gift from producer David Selznick.

Loretta Young——ACTRESS

Come to the Stable was a film I was crazy to do. It was a nun story but not at all sticky sweet. These nuns were battlers. Darryl Zanuck had bought the story for Irene Dunne, then shelved it because he thought it was uncommercial. He offered me *Mother Is a Freshman* and I said I'd do it plus *Come to the Stable.* Well, *Mother Is a Freshman* came and went and probably made a few cents. But *Come to the Stable* won me an Oscar nomination and very definitely made a lot of money. It's revived on television every Christmas. So I knew what suited me better and Darryl still did not.

War Films

Donald Barry——ACTOR

One of my favorite films has always been *The Purple Heart,* done on loan-out to 20th Century-Fox. I liked it not only because it was a good role in a big, successful picture, but because I wasn't playing a cowboy in it. I'd been typed in "B" Westerns, mostly at Republic Pictures, where I was under contract. Darryl Zanuck, head of Fox, tried to buy my contract from Herbert Yates, president of

Republic, but Yates said, "No, we've got big plans for Don. We're going to build him into another James Cagney"—whom people said I resembled. Those "big plans" included little numbers like *Slippy McGee.*

Anne Baxter ———— ACTRESS

Billy Wilder was the director on *Five Graves to Cairo* and highly competent in his own right. But he did not count on the incessant advice he got from Erich von Stroheim. Erich would take me aside to coach me and I appreciated it, until I realized he wanted the scenes to go his way. One sequence had him in bed and he was very conscious of his belly and double chin so he'd call to his mistress on the sidelines, "How are my little babies?"

Nancy Coleman———— ACTRESS

Errol Flynn got me drunk on the set of *Dangerous Journey* one day. I was having a little trouble with lines. I guess it made me nervous. Flynn said, "Have one of these." It was a "milk punch." I never had had one and thought it was pretty good. This was in his dressing room. He said, "Now go out there and you'll be fine." I went out and couldn't remember a line. They had to close the set down for the day.

Laraine Day ———— ACTRESS

In my last picture, *The Story of Dr. Wassell,* I played opposite Gary Cooper. In the kissing department Gary turned out to be the surprise of my young life. He is so convincing with his stammering, stuttering, awkward little boy manners that I thought kissing him would be just like kissing a shy little boy who has just brought you a bunch of dejected daisies. When the action called for "Dr. Gary Wassell" to kiss me, I got all set for a bashful boy kiss. Gary fumbled and faltered, as if there were 50,000,000 obstacles in his path, and at last made contract. Well! It was like holding a hand grenade and not being able to get rid of it! I was left breathless. Gary kisses the way Charles Boyer *looks* like he kisses!

Edward Dmytryk———— DIRECTOR

The budget for *Hitler's Children* was a straight $100,000. We got a bit more when the bosses saw how well it was going. It grossed over $3.2 million in the United States alone and was one of RKO's biggest hits in years. We made it all on the back lot. The subject matter was shocking to wartime audiences: sterilization, illegitimate babies to forge a master race. I can't say Bonita Granville and Tim Holt were very German, but that was their appeal. We were really showing how American kids would behave under the same circumstances.

Allan Dwan ———— DIRECTOR

The only trouble on *Sands of Iwo Jima* was John Wayne used to like to stay up at the bar quite late, and he could put away a lot—he had a terrific capacity. But some of these young actors in the cast—fellows like John Agar—used to try and stay along with him and they'd be a pathetic sight in the morning. At least, they were the *first* morning.

I didn't lecture them. I just asked General Erskine, the commandant down at Fort Pendleton, to give me the toughest drill sergeant there, and he sent me a big, husky guy—six-foot-eight—who could have lifted any two men in my company. I said, "I want you to make Marines out of these actors—full packs and rifles—and I want you to drill them. Give them the full routine including double-time. I want them to get into physical shape."

He eyed the hangovers doubtfully. Well, he worked them for two solid hours until they fell on their faces. Then he let them sleep a little while and got them up and worked them some more. After the third day, they were pleading for mercy, but they were Marines. And not one of them ever stayed up late again—they crawled into that hay at 10 o'clock and they avoided Wayne like the plague.

Tay Garnett——————DIRECTOR

The *Cross of Lorraine* set was being honored by a galaxy of star-grade Army brass with Our Boss [Louis B. Mayer] in full charge. We happened to be filming the grim simulation of a Nazi prisoner-of-war camp. Peter Lorre, as a black-clad SS sergeant, was doing his diabolical damnedest from the depths of his Jewish heart.

Between scenes, the Great White Father summoned Lorre, introduced him, patted his shoulder patronizingly and observed, "Well, Peter, you look fit—almost as if being a storm trooper agreed with you."

Peter, accustomed to, but unappreciative of, Mayer's ten-ton "little jokes," laid those enormous, guileless eyes on Louis B. and said in the tone of the top sergeant, "Oh, yes, sir, it does. I eat a Jew every morning for breakfast."

Frances Gifford——————ACTRESS

My first film at MGM was *Cry Havoc,* under a seven-year contract. I remember the cast with affection, and considering it was an all-girl one, there was little or no friction which is, perhaps, amazing. When we first started it, the whole lot said, "Oh, boy, 13 women, that will really be a cat fight," but we never had a bit of trouble the entire shooting.

Margaret Sullavan was always taking pills both on and off screen and seemed nervous throughout the shooting. At the film's conclusion she presented each member of the cast with a bottle of pills (phenobarbitol). We were all glad to have them as we had our problems with "camera nerves," too.

Signe Hasso——————ACTRESS

The first time I met Cecil B. DeMille, he had riding boots on. The funny part is I didn't know who he was. I had two agents coming with me, and they were so nervous. I wasn't nervous at all, just meeting another director. I didn't even know of his fame at the time. I lived next door to something called the West Side Tennis Club. He had a brother and I had met this Mr. DeMille at the Tennis Club. When I came to the studio to meet Mr. DeMille, I said,

"I think we have met before." He said, "Where?" I said at the West Side Tennis Club. He said, "That was my brother." The agents almost died. They thought I wouldn't get the film [*The Story of Dr. Wassell*] because of what I had said. While the agents were explaining that I was very new, Mr. DeMille said, "Listen, Miss Hasso speaks very well for herself." We became the best of friends.

Hurd Hatfield——ACTOR

Dragon Seed was some experience! They sent me to the back lot, where I met a retired actress from *The Good Earth*—a Chinese water buffalo! One of the most difficult actresses I've ever worked with! I had to learn to ride her, and her back wasn't made for the human crotch. I couldn't stay on! A nightmare! Walter Huston was my father, Katharine Hepburn, my sister, Aline MacMahon from New York, my mother, Turkish Turhan Bey, my brother, Russian Akim Tamiroff, my uncle—it was a *very* odd Chinese family!

Robert Hutton——ACTOR

It was my first day in *Destination Tokyo.* It was also my first role, and I was very anxious to please. Jerry Wald, the producer, came over and took me aside. He explained that insofar as Cary Grant was the star of the picture and was married to Barbara Hutton, it wouldn't look good for me to use my name. It might seem as though I were trading on her name. That was a new one on me, but I couldn't talk back to the boss, so I nodded. Then he suggested that I change it and said he thought the name Oscar Shimmelhock, or something like that, would be a good name. I thought he meant it and, being very green, I said I'd do it. I couldn't sleep all night worrying about it. It wasn't until the next morning that I learned it was a gag.

Nunnally Johnson——PRODUCER/SCREENWRITER

A director who shall remain nameless was assigned to my screenplay of *The Pied Piper.* Just before shooting was to start, he spoke to me for the very first time to suggest that our star, Monty Woolley, after spending the night in a barn, accidentally light up his pipe with manure. I went to Darryl Zanuck and said, "This is the only suggestion the man can make? I want it clear that if there's any shit in this picture, I'm going to put it in!" The director was replaced.

Arthur Kennedy——ACTOR

There was a lot of drinking done on Saturdays during *Desperate Journey.* Actors felt the whole country—except us—had the day off. We'd gather in Errol Flynn's dressing room. All the drinkers were there: Errol, director Raoul Walsh, Alan Hale, Yours Truly and Ronnie Reagan.

Every so often on one Saturday, Ronnie would dump his whiskey into a cuspidor. He didn't know it, but everyone saw him. The assistant director, Race Horse (Russell) Saunders, finally came in and asked, "When are you bastards going to get a shot?" Out we went; Flynn was staring into nothing and Ronnie had the first line, which he delivered flawlessly. Flynn just looked at him and finally said, "Why don't you go—yourself!" Raoul said, "Print it!"

Peter Lorre ——————— ACTOR

Mike Curtiz does not have a sense of humor. When he was directing *Passage to Marseilles,* in our drunken stupor we decided to blackmail Curtiz into a sense of humor. Curtiz has no sense of humor when shooting. He eats pictures and excretes pictures. Bogey and I are one-take people. In addition to that, we were not supposed to waste any film during the war.

We came in from a horrible night. Bogey apologized to Warner. Then we went on the deck of a big boat set. Bogey was in the first shot. Curtiz says to Bogey, "You do this," and Bogey says, "I heard the most wonderful story," and tells some stupid, square joke—endless. Bogey gets through and Mike says, "Now we shoot." He made 19 takes and didn't get it. He almost went out of his mind. Then I started to tell a long story. It took Curtiz about two days to find whenever he laughed he got the scene in one take and whenever he didn't laugh he didn't get a take. Two mornings later, Bogey and I, two staggering little figures, arrived on the big set. Mike saw us a block away and started laughing like crazy.

Raymond Massey ——————— ACTOR

On *Action in the North Atlantic,* the scene called for our doubles to jump from the bridge of a burning tanker into the water below, which was aflame with oil. Bogey turned to me and said, "My double is braver than yours." I said that wasn't so, that *my* double was the braver man. Then Bogey looked at me and said, "The fact is I'm braver than you are." I said that was nonsense. And the next thing I knew we did the damn stunt ourselves. I burned my pants off and Bogey singed his eyebrows.

Gary Merrill ——————— ACTOR

Winged Victory was to become a motion picture. Moss Hart had promised that we'd each play his own part in the picture. There was a great flurry of dental appointments prior to leaving New York. Dental plates were made, and teeth were capped with permanent or temporary crowns. During the trip some of the temporary caps were lost; and there was much comparing of plates and prices.

One of the more serious actors had a major amount of dental work done. Later on, in his big scene out on the desert, the entire production was brought to a halt as the cameraman tried to find the cause of a very bright reflection. The source was the sun bounding off his beautiful new teeth. The make-up man was summoned to dirty up the lovely choppers, much to the chagrin of their owner. When he discovered later that this episode was a put-up job to embarrass him, he went berserk, screaming that we had wasted money and had held up production, all for a lousy joke. But escapades such as these helped us keep our sanity.

Robert Mitchum —— ACTOR

The Story of G.I. Joe? That part would have made anybody, it didn't require acting. All I had to do was to look dead and trust that the mules didn't steal the top scenes from me while I had my eyes closed.

Robert Montgomery —— ACTOR/DIRECTOR

I got my chance to direct by accident. That's usually the way such things happen. Two weeks before John Ford was to finish *They Were Expendable,* he broke his leg. The studio asked him if he wanted to wait until he was well enough to go on the set or get another director to wind it up, there being nothing but effects stuff left to shoot. "Let Montgomery do it," he said. That's how I got my opportunity.

Ford did 99 percent of the good work on that picture, I only one percent, but the relationship between us, as director and actor, had been so perfect I knew just what he wanted. He's as good a director as there is in the business. He always talks the picture over with his players. That makes you want to do what he wants you to do.

George Murphy —— ACTOR

Battleground introduced Denise Darcel in a bit part which mainly consisted of wiggling her derrière. When Denise was introduced to director William Wellman, he said, "She looks just great. She looks like a good, husky, big-busted French gal—one that could really withstand the bombardments of war."

The casting director took her away for about two hours. When Wellman sent for her, she returned wearing a fancy hairdo that couldn't possibly have been on a woman's head in a war-ravaged area.

Wellman was really angry. He picked up a bucket of water and, after drenching Denise with it, threw some dirt on her. Then he took a long look at her and announced, "Okay, gentlemen. Miss Darcel is ready for her scene."

Pat O'Brien —— ACTOR

There was a young Cuban in *The Navy Comes Through,* an avid, fanatical cardplayer; so were many of the cast and crew with the exception of myself. We were shooting on location out on the old back lot at Pathé. They had erected a few tents. The Cuban played cards whenever there was an idle moment. He had quite a chili-and-rum accent, and a lot of the boys used to heckle him about it. A game was at its height, and some loser upset the tent and it tumbled down on all of the participants in the game. The Cuban rushed out of the fallen tent and in boiling words interspersed with a few foreign exclamations, shouted, "All right, all right, smart guys! You all be sorry! Some day I buy this studio and show you!" He was sure a prophet in his own land. His name was Desi Arnaz, and eventually he and his wife, Lucille Ball, did buy RKO with their TV loot.

Maureen O'Hara —— ACTRESS

John Payne was a particular favorite of mine. I made four films with him. He was married to Anne Shirley when we made *To the Shores of Tripoli* in 1942. He came into my dressing room one day and sobbed like I've never seen a man sob. Without any knowledge that anything was wrong, he woke up to find that Anne had left and was getting a divorce. He was totally heartbroken. He kept saying, "Why didn't she ever tell me she was unhappy?"

Lee Patrick ——— ACTRESS

[Director] Wesley Ruggles was a perfect gentleman throughout a most difficult assignment, *Somewhere I'll Find You.* It was scheduled to be made the week Carole Lombard was killed, and it was touch-and-go for at least a month as to whether Clark Gable would do it. He wanted no part of it, but was finally persuaded to do it. I played a Greenwich Village type of kook and friend of Lana Turner. Clark won the admiration of the entire company for his cooperating spirit and dedication. As far as I was concerned, he was a prince in every sense of the word . . . and right after it was finished, he enlisted in the Air Force.

Gregory Peck ——— ACTOR

Superlatives scare me. I'm just an average adjective guy. Probably because of my first picture, *Days of Glory,* when the bosses called my rushes sensational, terrific and colossal, and the New York reviewers called me—well, a lot of other things. I couldn't understand why I could stink in New York and be sensational in Hollywood. Until one of the crew said that after years of thought he decided that between Hollywood and New York something strange happens to the film. It fades or something on the train.

Allan Scott ——— SCREENWRITER

My favorite screenplay? *So Proudly We Hail.* Originally, we were asked to make a two-reel film for the Red Cross, because at that time they were in charge of getting nurses for the Army. I happened to be in Washington (I was one of a group of speech writers) when I heard that the nurses rescued from Corregidor were at Walter Reed Hospital. They were being kept from the press; but through Harry Hopkins I had met Eleanor Roosevelt, and she arranged a meeting with five or six nurses who could reasonably be questioned—the remainder were still in terrible shock. I heard the story from these girls—the atrocities and rapes committed on their comrades in the Bataan peninsula. To this day the Army has not revealed that particular catastrophe. The "long march" left no survivors among the girls other than . . . well, no point in going into it. I wrote a first script. It was censored by the Army only because it told the truth. However, I did get an excellent script eventually, and it was one of the most distinguished pictures of the year.

Walter Slezak ——— ACTOR

We were shooting the film *Lifeboat.* I played the captain of the rammed German submarine who is picked up by the survivors of the steamer he has torpedoed. To give my appearance an extra coat of deceptive harmlessness, Alfred Hitchcock thought it would be a nice idea if I had curly hair, and I was given a permanent wave. But somehow it didn't take and I looked like a sick caracal lamb. So every morning at seven I had to report to the hairdressing department to be manhandled by a curling iron. There the glamorous ladies of the cinema sat in their styling chairs in one long row and were being made alluring for the day's shooting. Like them I was covered with a shampoo cape and somehow they forgot that an outsider was sitting in their midst. My vocabulary of the unprintable grew with every session. The most intimate incidents, the habits and the practices of their most private lives were most indiscreetly confided and discussed. I doubt if there exists a man's locker room that could match their colorful conversation. It was always a letdown to have to leave this happy little group, go on the sound stage and just listen to Tallulah Bankhead.

***Robert Stack*——————ACTOR**

Walter Wanger had been responsible for bringing such stars as Jeanne Eagles, Claudette Colbert, Ginger Rogers and the Marx Brothers to the screen. So when word came that the love interest in *Eagle Squadron* would be a renowned stage actress, I expected someone really extraordinary. The someone turned out to be a sad and thoroughly mixed-up lady with a famous name: Diana Barrymore.

Diana had a special way of playing a love scene. She would lean forward and, out of the upstage corner of her mouth, the side invisible to the stage audience before which she was used to performing, she editorialized. "An an actor, you really stink," she might coo.

Once, we went to see the rushes. Diana was endearing. "I don't understand it," she said. "How anybody who is as lousy as you are looks so much better on film?" I just smiled and said, "Maybe I'm not as lousy as you think I am, and maybe you're not as good as you think you are."

***John Wayne*——————ACTOR**

Bob Montgomery was [director] John Ford's pet on *They Were Expendable.* He could do no wrong. I guess it was because he had been in the Navy. Jack picked on me all the way through it. He kept calling me a "clumsy bastard" and a "big oaf" and kept telling me that I "moved like an ox." Now if I couldn't do anything else, at least I *moved* well.

We almost got into a fistfight at one point. It was while we were shooting a process scene where my boat is strafed by an airplane. A special effects guy was shooting ball bearings at my boat, and he had forgotten to replace the windwhield with a nonbreakable plexiglass one. Real glass went flying into my face. In a rage I grabbed a hammer and went after the guy. But Jack stepped in front of me and said, "No you don't. They're my crew." "Your crew, goddammit, they're my eyes!" I said.

—ACTOR/PRODUCER

The Fighting Kentuckian was a damn good story in which we combined sophisticated French men and women with simple frontier people. I was producing and starring. I wanted to have some say in who was going to play the French girl. She's the daughter of a French general. I wanted a girl who was French. Simone Simon or Danielle Darrieux, Corinne Calvet. Many were available to us.

But no. Herbert J. Yates [president of Republic Pictures] made me use Vera Hruba Ralston. I don't want to malign her. She didn't have the experience. She talked with this heavy Czech accent. I was looking for a light Parisian type of speech, which my rough pioneer dialogue would play against. Yates made me cast her. It hurt the picture, because we now had to hire other Czech and Austrian actors to play French characters so her accent would be matched. Hugo Haas played her father. Can you picture him as a general of Napoleon's? He was always playing her father. He played her father in *Dakota.*

I've always been mad at Yates about this because we lost a chance to make one damn fine movie. Yates was one of the smartest businessmen I ever met. But when it came to the woman he loved, his business brains just went flyin' out the window.

Billy Wilder —— DIRECTOR/ SCREENWRITER

Erich von Stroheim influenced me greatly as a director. I always think of my style as a curious cross between Lubitsch and Stroheim. When I first saw him at wardrobe tests for his role as Rommel in *Five Graves to Cairo,* I clicked my heels and said, "Isn't it ridiculous, little me directing you? You were always ten years ahead of your time." And he replied, "Twenty, Mr. Wilder, twenty."

Westerns

Dana Andrews —— ACTOR

Probably my biggest "sheer chance" thing happened right down there on 44th Street [in New York City]. I had just made my first movie, *The Westerner,* starring Gary Cooper. Down there, they put up a huge sign . . . "*The Westerner,*" it said, "starring Gary Cooper and Dana Andrews." I had exactly four lines in the picture. Nobody had ever heard of me. But the publicity department had done that for all the billboards. They thought Dana was a girl's name, and was the girl in the picture, and that it looked more exciting to have Cooper and a girl. If I'd used my real first name, Carver, maybe I'd never have made it.

Gene Autry —— ACTOR

The success of our radio show led, inevitably, to a picture called *Melody Ranch.* I don't believe any Republic film in 1940 carried a bigger budget—close to $400,000—with the likely exception of *Dark Command,* starring John Wayne and Claire Trevor. *Melody Ranch* was what the studio in those days modestly referred to as a blockbuster. The cast included Jimmy Durante, Ann Miller, Horace MacMahon, Gabby Hayes, Bob Wills and his Texas Playboys and special music by Jule Styne.

I even had a kissing scene with Ann Miller, but when that tidbit appeared in the papers during the filming, the mail from angry and disillusioned little boys was so heavy it was cut from the movie. The mail was along the lines of the question asked by a young baseball fan of Shoeless Joe Jackson when he was implicated in a World Series fix: "Say it isn't so, Joe."

Humphrey Bogart——ACTOR

I got my part in *Treasure of the Sierra Madre* through my friendship with John Huston. We were shooting on location in Mexico. In one sequence that kept shooting for four days, I was looking for water. Jack Warner looked at the four days of rushes at the studio and said, "If that son-of-a-bitch doesn't find water soon, I'll go broke!"

Edgar Buchanan——ACTOR

When I was in Portland, Oregon, working with Duffy's Stock Company, Jane Darwell was our character woman. I had a grandmother who was dying of cancer, and it was about five miles over to this hospital. We'd rehearse in the morning, knock off about 11:30 and come back at 2:00 for a matinée. So she'd always give me a five-dollar-bill, say, "Go get a taxi and see your grandma, son." I'd go and see my grandma, wait for a taxi and then come back. Where I waited was an old, empty brick building, and it used to be a Metro-Goldwyn-Mayer film exchange. There was a huge picture of Wally Beery in the window. I'd be standing around there looking at that, and I said out loud to myself, "Some day I'm going to work for that outfit."

You won't believe this, but Metro-Goldwyn-Mayer was the last studio I worked at; I'd worked in all of them but MGM. I finally went over to do *Sea of Grass.* I was trying on some mustaches one day, and I'm looking in there and thinking, "Well, here I am. I said I'm going to work for you, and here I am." Wally Beery came over, put his hand on my shoulder and said, "Hi, Edgar," and walked on out. You just can't believe those things, but they happen. I had an old prof in physiology, who woke me out of a sound sleep one day saying, "You boys can be or have anything you want in the world, if you want it badly enough." And I never forgot that. I love to tell it now to little kids, because it's the truth. If you really want something bad enough, you can do it.

Niven Busch——SCREENWRITER

How did Robert Mitchum come to be in *Pursued?* Well, he'd been in *Till the End of Time.* He was not a star at the time, but they thought he could be made one. Now we're looking for a leading man. You wouldn't believe the people we tried out. Montgomery Clift had never been in a film. He comes out from New York, completely green. He just goes on raw nerve and talent. This little skinny guy, they throw some Western clothes on him and they give him two great big guns. When he comes in he looks like he's got two broken hips. A very bad test.

Then Kirk Douglas. I liked him; he was very good-looking. Manly and everything. So we got some film, and Jack Warner said, "I don't like that dimple in his chin. Let's see it again." So we ran it, and I said, "Jesus, what a performance he's giving." Jack said, "I know, but that dimple in his chin." Of course Mitchum, he's got one, too. I loved his performance.

Raoul Walsh and Jimmy Howe didn't get along at all. He knew what a great cameraman Jimmy was, but he didn't give a shit about camera art. He would say, "Goddamn Chink is going to put us behind schedule." But he was so modest. He said to me, "You know, Niven, I don't think I understand all the scenes. Would you mind being on the set to tell me if I'm getting off the track?" Now how many directors would say this to you?

Joseph Cotten ——— ACTOR

The whole essence of our present film, *Duel in the Sun,* was sweat, dust, intense heat. It is so hot we can hardly bear it. It's this heat that does dreadful things to us—so we went on location to Arizona and it snowed! Everyone sneezed and shivered, no one could get warm. We should have called the thing *Duel Without Sun*. In our story, Jennifer Jones is a half-breed Indian, and I come in driving a team of horses. Someone suggested that we change Jennifer to a half-breed Eskimo and bring me in with a dogsled.

* * *

There are fewer feet of original film in *Duel in the Sun* than there are of retakes.

There was one particular scene that simply refused to fall into any dramatic order of interest, but producer David O. Selznick thought the scene necessary and was determined to make it fall into its place—wherever that was. Jennifer Jones and I were the only actors involved.

We had originally shot it in the dining room. No good. Then we shot it in the parlor, then in the pool room. David gave Jennifer a scanty costume, and we tried it in the bedroom. Still no good. We were now shooting in the stable. Six o'clock came and we called it quits for the day. The assistant announced, "We'll continue here in the morning at 9 a.m."

I turned to the boss. "We're slipping, David," I said. "We always wrap this scene in one day."

He looked puzzled for a moment, then brightened. "Ah, but we never had a horse in it before."

Laraine Day ——— ACTRESS

Ronald Reagan and I suffered through *The Bad Man* (with Wally Beery) together. The company went to New Mexico on location and the weather was so bad that we sat there for a solid month without taking a single shot.

I can highly recommend Ronnie as a good man to be shipwrecked with on a desert island. I would have gone crazy if it hadn't been for him. I had never cared much about games before, but Ronnie, a great one for games, had me playing everything from tiddley winks to indications. But even more than playing games Ronnie likes to talk. He can talk a blue streak about anything. Jack Warner, Errol Flynn, Will Hays, the Screen Actors Guild, the New Deal, what's wrong with pictures, what's wrong period. It used to be my ambition to get Ronnie and Bob Cummings in a room together by themselves and see who could out-talk the other. No wonder it took so long to finish *Kings Row*—with both of them in it.

Yvonne De Carlo———ACTRESS

On the morning of Sept. 18, 1944, I got up early to take a walk before reporting to the studio. As I started out the door I stumbled over a stack of newspapers. I had no idea where they had come from. The paper on top was the *Los Angeles Daily News.* I picked it up and read the headline: "ALLIES CROSS THE RHINE." I glanced further down and saw the caption: "CONTEST WINNER." Then I saw the subhead: "MOST BEAUTIFUL GIRL IN THE WORLD SAYS WALTER WANGER OF UNIVERSAL." I didn't dare breathe with the suspense.

I finally came to the small article and the words that said, "SHE'LL STAR IN 'SALOME, WHERE SHE DANCED.' THE NAME'S YVONNE DE CARLO, INCIDENTALLY."

With my heart pounding, I sat on the stoop and scanned the other newspapers; although the wording differed, the message was the same. I, the little girl from Vancouver, had won the part. I, if you can believe it, was then and there "The Most Beautiful Girl in the World"! It had been the idea of the Universal publicity department to plant the newspapers on my stoop. They thought it would be a nice surprise—and indeed it was.

Olivia de Havilland——ACTRESS

I expected better things after *Gone with the Wind.* I got *Santa Fe Trail.* That was doubly terrible because the star of that picture [Errol Flynn] had taken a passionate dislike for me. I don't know why. He refused to look at me during any of our scenes together. He stared at my forehead instead or pulled any number of tricks to upstage me. It was infuriating.

John Ford————DIRECTOR

I knew Wyatt Earp. In the very early silent days, a couple of times a year, he would come up to visit pals, cowboys he knew in Tombstone; a lot of them were in my company. I think I was an assistant prop boy then and I used to give him a chair and a cup of coffee, and he told me about the fight at the O.K. Corral. So in *My Darling Clementine,* we did it exactly the way it had been. They didn't just walk up the street and start banging away at each other; it was a clever military maneuver.

Lee Garmes——*CINEMATOGRAPHER*

I went back to [David] Selznick again for *Duel in the Sun:* he had fired two cameramen—he was up to his old tricks and had argued with them over the physical presentation—and I did about 60–70 percent of the picture. All of the interiors were mine. I did the scene of the galloping ranch hands and the clash with the railway when the wires were cut. I did the scene of the meeting of the carriages on the skyline bathed in red on the stage, with everything in red gelatins. We were retaking the barbecue picnic scene with the lanterns under the trees on the last day of shooting and just as we got two kids up in the tree watching, we got word that the Japanese had surrendered; the war was over.

Selznick came on the set and gave us the news. He said, "Please stay with us and get a good take, then everyone can go home." At 11:30 we finished, and the picture was over the same day as the war. It was a great moment.

Howard Hawks——*PRODUCER/DIRECTOR*

John Wayne read the script for *Red River* and said, "I don't know whether I want to play an old man." I said, "You're going to *be* an old man pretty soon, and you ought to get used to it. And you better start playing characters instead of that junk you've been playing." So he said, "How do I show that I'm old?" and I said, "Did you ever see me get up? Just do it that way." So he did it, and when he saw the film he said, "Lord, I'm old." He didn't have to do a lot of damn silly things to get that impression across.

* * *

On *Red River,* I called Walter Brennan and said, "I'll tell you the story." He said, "Where's the contract?" I said, "It isn't ready yet." He said, "After I sign the contract, then you can tell me the story." So he came in the next day and signed. He said, "Now tell me the story." I said, "Go read it, you son-of-a-bitch. I'm not going to tell you. You're signed now."

And he read it. There was one line in the story that said the cook's name was Drood. He said, "Gee, that's a good story. Am I going to play that guy?" I said, "Yeah." "How'm I going to play it?" I said, "You're going to lose your teeth in a poker game to an Indian, and every time you eat, you're going to have to borrow your teeth back." He said, "Oh, no, we're not going to do that." I said, "Yes, we are"—and we did it. He got another Academy Award nomination.

* * *

When I made *Red River,* with thousands of cows, I had enough of them. I no longer wanted to work with anything but human beings.

John Huston——*DIRECTOR/SCREENWRITER*

I thought *The Treasure of the Sierra Madre* was very good, and I told Bogart, "This might be a great picture." Bogey said, "You're out of your mind. It's a good Western."

Nunnally Johnson —— *SCREEN-WRITER*

Well into the writing of my screenplay for *Along Came Jones,* I ran into our star, Gary Cooper. I asked him if he'd like to read the novel on which I was basing the screenplay. He said, "Yup."

A couple of weeks later, I ran into him in the commissary and asked him how he liked the book. "Oh, fine," said Coop. "I'm half-way through it. I'm reading it word by word."

Jennifer Jones —— *ACTRESS*

Playing love scenes with Gregory Peck in *Duel in the Sun* wasn't exactly the hardest job I've ever had to do.

Elia Kazan —— *DIRECTOR*

There's one story about *The Sea of Grass* that tells it all. I wanted to make a picture about the West, because I feel something glorious died there. And I love country—I live in the country now. I had a great feeling for that subject.

I went to see Pandro Berman, the producer, and the first thing he said was, "I've got 10,000 feet of the most beautiful background footage you've ever seen in your life!" I should have got up, said, "Thank you very much, Pandro," and walked out. But I was too dumb to quit. I was in a mechanism called Metro-Goldwyn-Mayer, which was run not by Pandro Berman and not, oddly, by L. B. Mayer, but by the head of the art department, Cedric Gibbons. He ran that damn studio. There was a rigid plan about how every film was going to be made, and this film was going to be made in front of a rear projection screen.

So it ended up, to my vast humiliation, that I never saw a blade of grass through that picture! Or there'd be two or three live horses, and behind them a rear-projection screen with other horses standing there. I was ashamed of myself all through it.

Arthur Kennedy —— *ACTOR*

On *They Died with Their Boots On,* they had a group of Oglala Sioux, magnificent horsemen, who were always in the front line. Now, they had seen guys take saddle falls—which were done deliberately—and say, "Adjustment." One of the Sioux asked, "Why those men do that?" I explained, "Each time it happens, a guy gets 35 bucks." Well, the Indian found that *very* interesting. The next scene called for only three of us left. I was dying and Errol Flynn had his sword out. The Sioux came tear-assing up the hill and we fired *three* shots. A *dozen* Indians fell off their horses and shouted, "Adjustment!"

Stephen Longstreet —— *SCREEN-WRITER*

Raoul Walsh, directing *Silver River,* came to me and said, "Kid, write it fast. They [Errol Flynn and Ann Sheridan] are not drinking, they promised Jack Warner that, but you never know."

At first the shooting of the picture went well. Work was good, as Walsh, experienced at handling actors, kept matters in control. But one morning I found Walsh tearing pages out of the script. I asked why and he said, "Removing the chicken shit. The dialogue. Too much yak-yak."

I knew then the picture was in trouble. Yet, the morning shooting was satisfactory as the stars sipped ice water. But by noon the lines were blurred, the action a bit wobbly.

I went over and tasted the ice water. It was pure 90-proof vodka. No wonder the picture was running behind.

The stars' behavior resulted in delays, which led to cost overruns, which forced the studio heads to declare *Silver River* finished. It is the only major studio film I know of for which there is no ending; the picture ends in midair, but no one, as far as I know, ever bothered to ask why.

Robert Mitchum —— ACTOR

I started out playing a villain in a Hopalong Cassidy movie, *Hoppy Serves a Writ.* They paid $100 a week and all the horse manure I could drag home.

Margaret O'Brien —— ACTRESS

While we were on location for *Bad Bascomb,* we'd go into town and play the slot machines. Then at night Marjorie Main would come in with toilet paper wrapped around her arms to keep germs away. And she had a place set at the table in the log cabin for her dead husband and she'd talk to him during dinner.

Gregory Peck —— ACTOR

One day out in Arizona director King Vidor walked off *Duel in the Sun* and told producer David Selznick what he could do with it in no uncertain terms. David was directing over his shoulder and no real director will stand for that for very long. King is a patient man and he'd accepted it for a while but the day came when David began to direct the actors. King simply walked up to David and said, "Take this picture and *shove* it."

He left and never came back. The picture was only about half-finished. David stood there for a long time, watching King. I'll never forget how King walked down that long, scrubby hill to the road where his car—a black Cadillac—was parked. It was a long, long walk and his driver was waiting beside the car. He got in and the car drove off slowly across the desert and eventually disappeared.

David finally said, "Did I say something wrong?"

Ronald Reagan —— ACTOR

We finally reached the end of *Santa Fe Trail* and the hanging of John Brown. Director Mike Curtiz was furious when he discovered he couldn't actually hang Raymond Massey but would have to use a dummy. When he was shooting a picture, Mike—who was normally a kind, good-natured soul—became a ruthless tyrant, as hard on himself as anyone else. In that hanging scene he was setting up his shot, looking through the viewfinder and motioning to a very elderly actor who played the minister to move first to

the left, then to the right; finally he kept motioning him to move back. The poor old fellow moved back one step too far and fell 12 feet from the scaffold, breaking his leg. Mike walked across, looked down where he lay on the ground, turned to his assistant and said, "Get me another minister."

Jane Russell ——— ACTRESS

I thought *The Outlaw* was ghastly and that I looked like a wooden dummy. I don't know how I ever got another part. All that fuss over my, well, physicality was very embarrassing.

David O. Selznick ——— PRODUCER/SCREENWRITER

Duel in the Sun was simply—from my standpoint almost more than any other film I've made—an exercise in production. Seeing how successful Westerns were, I decided to create one that would just contain more spectacle than they'd ever had in a Western and combine a violent love story with it. I felt that if the two elements could be combined there was no reason why I shouldn't have great success. It was rather fun doing it tongue-in-cheek. Instead of having one gun duel, I had, I don't know, maybe five or six. Instead of having a hundred horses, I had thousands of horses. Just multiplied everything. It turned out to be an enormous success, despite the fact that it received the worst notices of any picture I've ever made.

***Dimitri Tiomkin*—COMPOSER**

On *Duel in the Sun,* David Selznick told me, "Dimi, this [love theme] is still not right. It hasn't the unbridled, throbbing urge." So I had to write it again, this time giving it plenty of throb, with violent palpitations in the orchestra. (This was my third try.)

When the summons came, I went to his office. "What is wrong now?" I restrained myself with difficulty.

"Dimi, that is not the way I make love."

With that, my Russian inflections thickened in a shout of rage: "But that is the way *I* make love!" He burst out laughing. That was the end of it. He agreed I should make musical love in my own way.

***Claire Trevor*—ACTRESS**

They cut so much out of *Honky Tonk.* I was so heartbroken when I went to see it that I started to cry. I don't cry easily. I started to cry and couldn't stop. I thought, "I hate this business. I hate it. I'm through with it. I don't want to do it anymore." They cut some of my best scenes out, the scenes that I built up to a certain point; they'd left the point in, but they didn't leave the "build" in, you know? When you write, if you're writing up to a certain climax and then this is all destroyed, it looks horrible, doesn't it?

***Lana Turner*—ACTRESS**

Clark Gable and I rehearsed our first love scene for *Honky Tonk*—ours was a wonderful chemical rapport which came over on film—and suddenly I turned around and froze. There was beloved Carole Lombard. Mrs. Gable! She seldom came on the set but I guess she wanted to see who the new kid was. Well, it's one thing to work with a King but quite another to have his Lady there. I retreated to my dressing room and when director Jack Conway came to say we were ready to shoot, I wailed, "I can't!" Whether Jack told Clark, I don't know. I just know that while I sat in my dressing room suffering, beautiful Carole disappeared.

***William A. Wellman*—DIRECTOR**

I went to all the producers for whom I had worked and got turned down [to make *The Ox-Bow Incident*]. Darryl Zanuck was the only one with guts to do an out-of-the-ordinary story for the prestige rather than the dough.

Zanuck was in the Army, stationed in London. The studio head was Bill Goetz. The production head, Bill Koenig, and Lew Schreiber did the dirty work.

I had the green light on *Ox-Bow* and was working hard and fast to get it rolling before some of the principals might be called into service. The budget had been completed and the estimated cost determined. That was it. When the unholy three heard the amount, they decided that it was a bad deal at the time and prepared to cable Zanuck, informing him in no uncertain terms their opinions on the project. All emphatic no's. Goetz, being a fair and decent executive and an unusual one, called me in to his office and let me read the verdict and asked if I wished to add my point of view. I wrote, "This is to remind you of our handshake; regards, Bill Wellman." Next day they got word back, "Let Wellman go ahead."

* * *

One of my favorite actors is in that [*Yellow Sky*]—Greg Peck. I say that sarcastically. We made a good picture with him, *despite* him.

BIBLIOGRAPHY

Books

Adler, Larry. *It Ain't Necessarily So.* New York: Grove, 1987.

Allyson, June, with Frances Spatz Leighton. *June Allyson.* New York: Putnam, 1982.

Astaire, Fred. *Steps in Time.* New York: Harper Brothers, 1959.

Astor, Mary. *A Life on Film.* New York: Delacorte, 1971.

Aumont, Jean-Pierre. *Sun and Shadow.* New York: Norton, 1977.

Autry, Gene, with Mickey Herskowitz. *Back in the Saddle Again.* Garden City, N.Y.: Doubleday, 1978.

Bacall, Lauren. *By Myself.* New York: Knopf, 1979.

Bankhead, Tallulah. *Tallulah.* New York: Harper Brothers, 1952.

Benny, Jack, and Joan Benny. *Sunday Nights at Seven.* New York: Warner, 1990.

Bergman, Ingrid, and Alan Burgess. *My Story.* New York: Delacorte, 1980.

Black, Shirley Temple. *Child Star.* New York: McGraw-Hill, 1988.

Blanc, Mel, with Philip Basche. *That's Not All, Folks!* New York: Warner, 1988.

Bogdanovich, Peter. *Allan Dwan: The Last Pioneer.* New York: Praeger, 1971.

________. *The Cinema of Howard Hawks.* New York: Museum of Modern Art, 1962.

________. *Fritz Lang in America.* New York: Praeger, 1969.

________. *John Ford.* Berkeley, Calif.: University of California Press, 1968.

Bowers, Ronald. *The Selznick Players.* Cranbury, N.J.: Barnes, 1976.

Brochu, Jim. *Lucy in the Afternoon.* New York: Morrow, 1990.

Cagney, James. *Cagney by Cagney.* Garden City, N.Y.: Doubleday, 1976.

Calvet, Corinne. *Has Corinne Been a Good Girl?* New York: St. Martin's, 1983.

Capra, Frank. *The Name Above the Title.* New York: Macmillan, 1971.

Carpozi, George, Jr. *Marilyn Monroe.* New York: Belmont, 1961.

Cassini, Oleg. *In My Own Fashion.* New York: Simon and Schuster, 1987.

Chierichetti, David. *Hollywood Director.* New York: Curtis, 1973.

Christian, Linda. *Linda.* New York: Dell, 1962.

Clarke, Charles G. *Highlights and Shadows.* Metuchen, N.J.: Scarecrow, 1989.

Considine, Shaun. *Bette & Joan: The Divine Feud.* New York: Dutton, 1989.

Cooper, Jackie, with Dick Kleiner. *Please Don't Shoot My Dog.* New York: Berkley, 1982.

Coslow, Sam. *Cocktails for Two.* New Rochelle, N.Y.: Arlington House, 1977.

Cotten, Joseph. *Vanity Will Get You Somewhere.* San Francisco, Calif.: Mercury, 1987.

Crist, Judith. *Take 22.* New York: Viking, 1984.

Crosby, Bing, with Pete Martin. *Call Me Lucky.* New York: Pocket, 1954.

Crosby, Gary, with Ross Firestone. *Going My Own Way.* Garden City, N.Y.: Doubleday, 1983.

Davenport, Marcia. *Too Strong for Fantasy.* New York: Scribner's, 1967.

Davidson, Bill. *The Real and the Unreal.* New York: Lancer, 1962.

________. *Spencer Tracy: Tragic Idol.* New York: Dutton, 1987.

De Carlo, Yvonne, with Doug Warren. *Yvonne.* New York: St. Martin's, 1987.

DeMille, Cecil B. *Autobiography.* Englewood Cliffs, N.J.: Prentice-Hall, 1959.

Dialogue on Film: Olivia de Havilland. American Film Institute, 1974.

Dickens, Homer. *The Films of Gary Cooper.* New York: Citadel, 1970.

Dietrich, Marlene. *Marlene.* New York: Grove, 1989.

Dietz, Howard. *Dancing in the Dark.* New York: Quadrangle, 1974.

Dixon, Wheeler. *Producers Releasing Corporation.* Jefferson, N.C.: McFarland, 1986.

Dmytryk, Edward. *It's a Hell of a Life But Not a Bad Living.* New York: Times, 1978.

Douglas, Kirk. *The Ragman's Son.* New York: Simon and Schuster, 1988.

Dunne, Philip. *Take Two.* New York: McGraw-Hill, 1980.

Ephron, Henry. *We Thought We Could Do Anything.* New York: Norton, 1977.

Farmer, Frances. *Will There Really Be a Morning?* New York: Putnam, 1971.

Faye, Alice, with Dick Kleiner. *Growing Older, Staying Young.* New York: Dutton, 1990.

Flynn, Errol. *My Wicked, Wicked Ways.* New York: Dell, 1961.

Fonda, Henry, with Howard Teichmann. *Fonda: My Life.* New York: New American Library, 1981.

Fontaine, Joan. *No Bed of Roses.* New York: Morrow, 1978.

Ford, Dan. *Pappy: The Life of John Ford.* Englewood Cliffs, N.J.: Prentice-Hall, 1979.

Fordin, Hugh. *The Word of Entertainment.* Garden City, N.Y.: Doubleday, 1975.

Gardner, Ava. *Ava: My Story.* New York: Bantam, 1990.

Garnett, Tay, with Fredda Dudley Balling. *Light Your Torches and Pull Up Your Tights.* New Rochelle, N.Y.: Arlington House, 1973.

Godden, Rumer. *A House with Four Rooms.* New York: Morrow, 1989.

Goodman, Ezra. *Bogey: The Good-Bad Guy.* New York: Lyle Stuart, 1965.

Graham, Don. *No Name on the Bullet.* New York: Viking, 1989.

Gregory, James. *The Lucille Ball Story.* New York: Viking, 1989.

Griffin, Merv, with Peter Barsochini. *From Where I Sit.* New York: Arbor House, 1982.

Gussow, Mel. *Don't Say Yes Until I Finish Talking.* Garden City, N.Y.: Doubleday, 1971.

Harris, Warren G. *Natalie & R.J.* New York: Doubleday, 1988.

Harrison, Rex. *A Damned Serious Business.* New York: Bantam, 1991.

Haver, Ronald. *David O. Selznick's Hollywood.* New York: Knopf, 1980.

Henreid, Paul, with Julius Fast. *Ladies' Man.* New York: St. Martin's, 1984.

Higham, Charles. *Bette: The Life of Bette Davis.* New York: Macmillan, 1981.

________. *Errol Flynn: The Untold Story.* New York: Doubleday, 1980.

________. *Hollywood Cameramen.* Bloomington: Indiana University Press, 1970.

________, and Joel Greenberg. *The Celluloid Muse.* London: Angus & Robertson, 1969.

________, and Roy Moseley. *Cary Grant: The Lonely Heart.* San Diego, Calif.: Harcourt Brace Jovanovich, 1989.

________, and ________. *Princess Merle.* New York: Coward-McCann, 1983.

Hope, Bob, and Bob Thomas. *The Road to Hollywood.* Garden City, N.Y.: Doubleday, 1977.

Horne, Lena, and Richard Schickel.

Lena. Garden City, N.Y.: Doubleday, 1965.
Jessel, George, with John Austin. *The World I Lived In.* Chicago, Ill.: Regnery, 1975.
Kelley, Kitty. *His Way.* New York: Bantam, 1986.
Keyes, Evelyn. *Scarlett O'Hara's Younger Sister.* Secaucus, N.J.: Lyle Stuart, 1977.
Kiersch, Mary. *Curtis Bernhardt.* Metuchen, N.J.: Scarecrow, 1986.
Knox, Donald. *The Magic Factory.* New York: Praeger, 1973.
Kobal, John. *Gotta Sing Gotta Dance.* London: Hamlyn, 1970.
________. *People Will Talk.* New York: Knopf, 1985.
________. *Rita Hayworth: The Time, the Place and the Woman.* London: W. H. Allen, 1977.
Koch, Howard. *As Time Goes By.* New York: Harcourt Brace Jovanovich, 1979.
Kotsilibas-Davis, James, and Myrna Loy. *Myrna Loy: Being and Becoming.* New York: Knopf, 1987.
Lake, Veronica, with Donald Bain. *Veronica.* London: W. H. Allen, 1969.
Lamarr, Hedy. *Ecstasy and Me.* New York: Bartholomew House, 1966.
Lamour, Dorothy, with Dick McInnes. *My Side of the Road.* Englewood Cliffs, N.J.: Prentice-Hall, 1980.
Leamer, Laurence. *As Time Goes By.* New York: Harper & Row, 1986.
Leigh, Janet. *There Really Was a Hollywood.* Garden City, N.Y.: Doubleday, 1984.
LeRoy, Mervyn, with Dick Kleiner. *Mervyn LeRoy: Take One.* New York: Hawthorn, 1974.
Levant, Oscar. *The Unimportance of Being Oscar.* New York: Putnam, 1968.
McBride, Joseph. *Hawks on Hawks.* Berkeley: University of California Press, 1982.
________. *Orson Welles.* New York: Viking, 1972.
McClelland, Doug. *Blackface to Blacklist.* Metuchen, N.J.: Scarecrow, 1987.
________. *Susan Hayward: The Divine Bitch.* New York: Pinnacle, 1973.
Mcgilligan, Pat. *Backstory.* Berkeley: University of California Press, 1986.
________. *Backstory 2.* Berkeley: University of California Press, 1991.
Madsen, Axel. *William Wyler.* New York: Crowell, 1973.
Maltin, Leonard, ed. *The Real Stars.* New York: Curtis, 1973.
________, ed. *The Real Stars.* New York: Popular Library, 1979.
Mank, Gregory William. *The Hollywood Hissables.* Metuchen, N.J.: Scarecrow, 1989.
Marill, Alvin H. *Samuel Goldwyn Presents.* South Brunswick, N.J.: Barnes, 1976.
Marshall, J. D. *Blueprint on Babylon.* Tempe, Ariz.: Phoenix House, 1978.
Martin, Mary. *My Heart Belongs.* New York: Morrow, 1976.
Martin, Pete. *Hollywood Without Makeup.* New York: Bantam, 1949.
Martin, Tony, and Cyd Charisse. *The Two of Us.* New York: Mason/Charter, 1976.
Merrill, Gary. *Bette, Rita and the Rest of My Life.* Augusta, Maine: Tapley, 1988.
Milland, Ray. *Wide-Eyed in Babylon.* New York: Morrow, 1974.
Miller, Ann, with Norma Lee Browning. *Miller's High Life.* Garden City, N.Y.: Doubleday, 1972.
Minnelli, Vincente, with Hector Arce. *I Remember It Well.* Garden City, N.Y.: Doubleday, 1974.
Moore, Dick. *Twinkle, Twinkle, Little Star.* New York: Harper & Row, 1984.
Morella, Joe, and Edward Z. Epstein. *Lana: The Public and Private Lives of Miss Turner.* New York: Citadel, 1971.
Morley, Sheridan. *Gladys Cooper.* New York: McGraw-Hill, 1979.
Murphy, George, with Victor Lasky. "Say . . . Didn't You Used to Be George Murphy?" New York: Bartholomew House, 1970.
Neagle, Anna. *There's Always Tomorrow.* London: W. H. Allen, 1974.
Neal, Patricia, with Richard DeNeut. *As I Am.* New York: Simon and Schuster, 1988.

Negulesco, Jean. *Things I Did . . . And Things I Think I Did.* New York: Linden, 1984.

Niven, David. *Bring on the Empty Horses.* New York: Putnam, 1975.

Oakie, Jack. *Jack Oakie's Double Takes.* San Francisco, Calif.: Strawberry Hill, 1980.

O'Brien, Pat. *The Wind at My Back.* Garden City, N.Y.: Doubleday, 1964.

Osborne, Robert. *Academy Awards Illustrated.* Hollywood, Calif.: Marvin Miller, 1965.

Paar, Jack. *I Kid You Not.* Boston, Mass.: Little, Brown, 1959.

Parish, James Robert. *The RKO Gals.* New Rochelle, N.Y.: Arlington House, 1974.

________. *The Tough Guys.* New Rochelle, N.Y.: Arlington House, 1976.

________, with Gregory W. Mank. *The Hollywood Reliables.* Westport, Conn.: Arlington House, 1980.

________, and Michael R. Pitts. *Hollywood Songsters.* New York: Garland, 1991.

________, and Don Stanke. *The Glamour Girls.* New Rochelle, N.Y.: Arlington House, 1975.

Parker, Francine. *Stages: Norman Lloyd.* Metuchen, N.J.: Scarecrow, 1990.

Peary, Danny, ed. *Close-Ups.* New York: Workman, 1978.

Pero, Taylor, and Jeff Rovin. *Always, Lana.* New York: Bantam, 1982.

Peters, Richard. *The Frank Sinatra Scrapbook.* New York: St. Martin's, 1982.

Pike, Bob, and Dave Martin. *The Genius of Busby Berkeley.* New York: CFS Books, 1973.

Powell, Jane. *The Girl Next Door . . . And How She Grew.* New York: Morrow, 1988.

Pratley, Gerald. *The Cinema of Otto Preminger.* New York: Barnes, 1971.

Preminger, Otto. *Preminger.* Garden City, N.Y.: Doubleday, 1977.

Quirk, Lawrence J. *Claudette Colbert.* New York: Crown, 1985.

________. *Fasten Your Seat Belts.* New York: Morrow, 1990.

________. *Jane Wyman: The Actress and the Woman.* New York: Dembner, 1986.

Reagan, Nancy, with William Novak. *My Turn.* New York: Random House, 1989.

Reagan, Ronald. *An American Life.* New York: Simon and Schuster, 1990.

________, with Richard G. Hubler. *Where's the Rest of Me?* New York: Duell, Sloan and Pearce, 1965.

Reed, Rex. *Do You Sleep in the Nude?* New York: New American Library, 1968.

________. *People Are Crazy Here.* New York: Dell, 1974.

Robinson, Edward G., with Leonard Spigelgass. *All My Yesterdays.* New York: Hawthorn, 1973.

Rodgers, Richard. *Musical Stages.* New York: Random House, 1975.

Rooney, Mickey. *Life Is Too Short.* New York: Villard, 1991.

Rose, Helen. *Just Make Them Beautiful.* Santa Monica, Calif.: Dennis-Landman, 1976.

Rosenberg, Bernard, and Barry Silverstein. *The Real Tinsel.* New York: Macmillan, 1970.

Rozsa, Miklos. *Double Life.* New York: Hippocrene, 1982.

Russell, Rosalind, and Chris Chase. *Life Is a Banquet.* New York: Random House, 1977.

Schary, Dore. *Heyday.* New York: Berkley, 1981.

Schickel, Richard. *The Man Who Made the Movies.* New York: Antheneum, 1975.

Server, Lee. *Screenwriter: Words Become Pictures.* Pittstown, N.J.: Main Street, 1987.

Shipman, David. *Movie Talk.* London: Bloomsbury, 1988.

Siegel, Joel E. *Val Lewton: The Reality of Terror.* New York: Viking, 1973.

Silke, James B. *Here's Looking at You, Kid.* Boston, Mass.: Little, Brown, 1976.

Silverman, Stephen M. *David Lean.* New York: Abrams, 1989.

Silvers, Phil, with Robert Saffron. *This Laugh Is on Me.* Englewood Cliffs, N.J.: Prentice-Hall, 1973.

Slezak, Walter. *What Time's the Next Swan?* Garden City, N.Y.: Doubleday, 1962.

Smith, Ella. *Starring Miss Barbara Stanwyck.* New York: Crown, 1974.

Stack, Robert, with Mark Evans. *Straight Shooting.* New York: Macmillan, 1980.
Steen, Mike. *Hollywood Speaks.* New York: Putnam, 1974.
Stine, Whitney. *I'd Love to Kiss You....* New York: Pocket, 1990.
Storm, Gale, with Bill Libby. *I Ain't Down Yet.* New York: Bobbs-Merrill, 1981.
Strait, Raymond, and Leif Henie. *Queen of Ice, Queen of Shadows.* New York: Stein and Day, 1985.
Stuart, Mary. *Both of Me.* Garden City, N.Y.: Doubleday, 1980.
Sturges, Preston. *Preston Sturges.* New York: Simon and Schuster, 1990.
Talbot, Daniel, ed. *Film: An Anthology.* Berkeley: University of California Press, 1966.
Taylor, Elizabeth. *Elizabeth Taylor.* New York: Harper & Row, 1964.
________. *Elizabeth Taylor Takes Off.* New York: Berkley, 1988.
________. *The Films of Gene Kelly.* Secaucus, N.J.: Citadel, 1974.
________. *Harry Warren and the Hollywood Musical.* Secaucus, N.J.: Citadel, 1975.
Thompson, Charles. *Bing.* New York: David McKay, 1975.
Tierney, Gene, with Mickey Herskowitz. *Self-Portrait.* New York: Wyden, 1979.
Todd, Ann. *The Eighth Veil.* London: Kimber, 1980.
Turner, Lana. *Lana: The Lady, the Legend, the Truth.* New York: Dutton, 1982.
Tuska, Jon, ed. *Close-Up: The Contract Director.* Metuchen, N.J.: Scarecrow, 1976,
________. *The Detective in Hollywood.* Garden City, N.Y.: Doubleday, 1978.
Vallee, Rudy, and Gil McKean. *My Time Is Your Time.* New York: Obolensky, 1962.
Vidor, King. *A Tree Is a Tree.* New York: Harcourt, Brace, 1953.
Viertel, Salka. *The Kindness of Strangers.* New York: Holt, Rinehart & Winston, 1969.
Wagner, Walter. *You Must Remember This.* New York: Putnam, 1975.
Walsh, Raoul. *Each Man in His Time.* New York: Farrar, Straus and Giroux, 1974.
Warner, Jack L., with Dean Jennings. *My First Hundred Years in Hollywood.* New York: Random House, 1964.
Watters, James. *Return Engagement.* New York: Potter, 1984.
Wayne, Jane Ellen. *Gable's Women.* New York: Prentice-Hall, 1987.
Weinberg, Herman G. *The Lubitsch Touch.* New York: Dutton, 1968.
Wellman, William A. *A Short Time for Insanity.* New York: Hawthorn, 1974.
West, Mae. *Goodness Had Nothing to Do with It.* New York: Macfadden-Bartell, 1970.
Wilk, Max. *They're Playing Our Song.* New York: Atheneum, 1973.
Winters, Shelley. *Shelley Also Known as Shirley.* New York: Morrow, 1980.
Yablonsky, Lewis. *George Raft.* New York: McGraw-Hill, 1974.
Young, Jordan R. *Reel Characters.* Beverly Hills, Calif.: Moonstone, 1986.
Zolotow, Maurice. *Billy Wilder in Hollywood.* New York: Putnam, 1977.
________. *Shooting Star.* New York: Simon and Schuster, 1974.

Periodicals

Action
After Dark
American Classic Screen
American Film
American Movie Classics
Aquarian
The Asbury Park Press
Boston Post
Cahiers de Cinéma
The Chicago Tribune
Cinefantastique
Cinema
Classic Images
Courier-Journal and Times [Louisville, Ky.]

Detroit Free Press
Drama-Logue
Esquire
Film Comment
Film Fan Monthly
Film History
Filmfax
Filmograph
Films and Filming
Films in Review
Focus on Film
Globe
Good Housekeeping
Hollywood
The Hollywood Reporter
Hollywood Then & Now
Interview
Ladies' Home Journal
Life
Los Angeles Herald Examiner
Los Angeles Times
McCall's
Memories
The Miami Herald
The Milwaukee Journal
Mirabella
Modern Screen
Motion Picture
Movie
Movie Collector's World
Movie Digest
Movie Show
Movie Stars Parade
Movieland
Movieline
National Enquirer
New York Daily News
New York Herald Tribune
New York Journal-American
New York Post
The New York Sun
The New York Times
Neward Evening News
Newark Star-Ledger
On Film
Parade
People
Photoplay
Playboy
Premiere
The Press
Quirk's Reviews
Salute
San Francisco Chronicle
Saturday Evening Post
Screen Facts
Screen Stars
Screen Stories
Screenland
Serial World
Sight and Sound
Silver Screen
Soap Opera Digest
Starlog
The Sunday Star-Ledger [Newark, N.J.]
This Week
TV Guide
TV Radio Mirror
Us
The Velvet Light Trap
Woman's Home Companion

Television

American Masters: "You're the Top"
Biography: Starring Natalie Wood
Debbie Reynolds' Movie Memories
The Joe Franklin Show
John Huston
60 Minutes
The Tonight Show Starring Johnny Carson
With Orson Welles: Stories from a Life in Film

INDEX